CHRISTIANITY AND RABBINIC JUDAISM

A Parallel History of Their
Origins and Early Development

On the Cover: Madaba map of Jerusalem. This sixth-century Byzantine mosaic map found in a church in Madaba, Jordan, shows prominent features of Byzantine Jerusalem including the Cardo, the Church of the Holy Sepulchre and the Nea church. *Photo by David Harris*

CHRISTIANITY AND RABBINIC JUDAISM

A Parallel History of Their Origins and Early Development

Edited by
Hershel Shanks

BIBLICAL ARCHAEOLOGY SOCIETY

WASHINGTON, D.C.

CONTENTS

List of Illustrations

List of Color Plates

The Authors

LOUIS H. FELDMAN is professor of classics at Yeshiva University in New York and adjunct professor of classics, Jewish studies and history at the New School for Social Research. He is an authority on Josephus and Josephus scholarship and has written or edited eight books and numerous articles. Most recently he co-edited *Josephus, the Bible and History* (Wayne State Univ. Press, 1989).

E. P. SANDERS is professor of religion at Duke University; from 1984 to 1990 he was Dean Ireland's Professor of Exegesis at the University of Oxford and a fellow of Queen's College, Oxford. His award-winning books reflect his interest in Judaism and Christianity in the Greco-Roman world. His latest book is *Judaism: Practice and Belief, 63 B.C.E.-66 C.E.* (Trinity Press International, 1991). Professor Sanders is a fellow of the British Academy; he has received honorary degrees from Oxford and the University of Helsinki.

HOWARD CLARK KEE was William Goodwin Aurelio Professor of Biblical Studies at the School of Theology at Boston University until 1989 and has been a member of archaeological teams in Jordan and Israel. He received his Ph.D. from Yale University. Currently, he is a senior research fellow at the University of Pennsylvania and a consultant for translations for the American Bible Society. Of his many books, the latest are *What Can We Know About Jesus?* (Cambridge Univ. Press, 1990), *Good News to the Ends of the Earth* (Trinity Press International, 1990), and *Christianity: A Social and Cultural History* (Macmillan, 1990).

LEE I. A. LEVINE is professor of Jewish history and archaeology at the Hebrew University of Jerusalem and also serves as head of the Seminary of Judaic Studies in Jerusalem. He received his Ph.D. from Columbia University after having been ordained at the Jewish Theological Seminary of America. He led the excavation of the synagogue at Horvat 'Ammudim and was co-director of excavations at Caesarea. His latest books are *The Rabbinic Class of Roman Palestine* (1989) and *The Galilee in Late Antiquity* (Scholars Press, 1992).

HAROLD W. ATTRIDGE is professor of theology and dean of the College of Arts and Letters at the University of Notre Dame. He received his Ph.D. from Harvard University. An editor of the Society of Biblical Literature's Early Christian Literature series, he is also book review editor for *The Second Century*. He is the editor of *Nag Hammadi Codex I (The Jung Codex)* (Brill, 1985) and co-edited *Of Scribes and Scrolls: Studies on the Hebrew Bible, Intertestamental Judaism and Christian Origins* (University Press of America, 1990); his latest book is *Hebrews: A Commentary on the Epistle to the Hebrews* (Fortress, 1989).

SHAYE J. D. COHEN is the Ungerleider Professor of Judaic Studies at Brown University. Before assuming this position in 1991, he was the Shenkman Professor of Jewish History and dean of the Graduate School at the Jewish Theological Seminary in New York. He received his Ph.D.

from Columbia University. He is the author of books and many articles on Judaism and antiquity, including *From the Maccabees to the Mishnah* (Westminster, 1987).

ISAIAH M. GAFNI is associate professor of Jewish history at the Hebrew University in Jerusalem; he served as visiting professor of Jewish studies at Harvard and Yale universities in the 1991-1992 academic year. He has published extensively in both Hebrew and English. An English translation of his 1990 book, *The Jews of Babylonia in the Talmudic Era: A Social and Cultural History*, is being prepared for publication by Yale University Press. He is currently at work on a study of the relationships between the Jews of Israel and the Diaspora in late antiquity.

DENNIS E. GROH is professor of the history of Christianity at Garrett-Evangelical Theological Seminary. He is co-director of the Tel Nessana Excavation Project of Ben-Gurion University and associate director of the Sepphoris Excavations of the University of South Florida and has participated in excavations at Caesarea and Meiron. He received his Ph.D. from Northwestern University. The author of books and numerous articles on patristics and early Christianity and the archaeology of Israel, his most recent book is *Augustine: Religion of the Heart.*

JAMES H. CHARLESWORTH was named George L. Collord Professor of New Testament Language and Literature at Princeton Theological Seminary in 1984. He also serves as director of the Princeton Seminary Dead Sea Scrolls project. He received his Ph.D. from Duke University and did postgraduate work at the Ecole Biblique in Jerusalem. He is a member of the editorial advisory board of the Biblical Archaeology Society's *Bible Review.* Among his many books are *The New Testament Apocrypha and Pseudepigrapha* and *Jesus Within Judaism.* He also served as editor of *Old Testament Pseudepigrapha*, 2 vols. (Doubleday, 1983-1985).

GEZA VERMES is director of the Oxford Forum for Qumran Research at the Oxford Centre of Postgraduate Hebrew Studies. He is also professor emeritus of Jewish studies at Oxford University, where he taught from 1965 to 1991. He is the editor of *Journal of Jewish Studies.* He is senior editor of the revised edition of Emil Schürer's *The History of the Jewish People in the Age of Jesus Christ* (T & T Clarke, 1973-1987). His *Dead Sea Scrolls in English* is now in its third edition. Professor Vermes is a fellow of the British Academy.

HERSHEL SHANKS is founder and editor of *Biblical Archaeology Review* and *Bible Review.* He is the author of *The City of David,* a guide to biblical Jerusalem, and *Judaism in Stone,* tracing the development of ancient synagogues. He has edited numerous books on biblical and archaeological subjects, most recently *Ancient Israel: From Abraham to the Roman Destruction of the Temple* (BAS/Prentice-Hall, 1988) and *Understanding the Dead Sea Scrolls* (Random House, 1992). A graduate of Harvard Law School, he has also published widely on legal topics.

Timeline

Roman	Jewish	Christian
Augustus (Octavian) 31 BCE-14 CE*	Herod, 37-4 BCE	Jesus, c.6/4 BCE-30/33 CE
Tiberius, 14-37 CE	Philo c.15 BCE-c.50 CE	Paul, d. c. 62/64 CE Vision of Jesus, c.34 CE Mission to Gentiles, c.50 CE
Caligula, 37-41 CE	Agrippa I, 37-44 CE King of Judea, 41-44 CE	
Claudius, 41-54 CE	Agrippa II, 53-mid-90s CE	
Nero, 54-68 CE	First Jewish Revolt Against Rome 66-70 CE Destruction of Temple, 70 CE Fall of Masada, 73/74 CE	Pauline epistles, 50-58 CE Gospel of Mark, c.68 CE
Vespasian, 69-79 CE	Yohanan b. Zakkai Academy at Yavneh c.70 CE Beginnings of Rabbinic Judaism	
Titus, 79-81 CE	Josephus, 37-c.100 CE *Jewish War*, 75-81 CE	Gospels of Matthew, Luke and John c.70-100 CE
Domitian, 81-96 CE	Gamaliel II Emergence of patriarchate c.90 CE	
Trajan, 98-117 CE	Diaspora revolt, 115-117 CE	
Hadrian, 117-138 CE	Second Jewish Revolt against Rome, 132-135 CE Simon Bar-Kokhba, d. 135 CE R. Akiva, c.50-135 CE Jerusalem rebuilt as Aelia Capitolina, c.135 CE Judea became Syria Palaestina	*Didache*, c.2nd century CE
	Academy moved to Galilee c.140 CE	Justin Martyr, c.140-170 CE
	Judah ha-Nasi, fl.** 175-220 CE Growth of patriarchate	Irenaeus, fl. 175-c.195 CE
Severan Dynasty, 193-235 CE	Completion of Mishnah 200-220 CE	Origen, c.185-253 CE
Decius, 249-251 CE	Emergence of rabbinic academies in Babylonia Rav and Samuel, c.220-250 CE	

Roman	Jewish	Christian
	Monumental Galilean synagogues late 3rd/4th centuries CE	
Diocletian, 284-305 CE		Beginning of monastic movement late 3rd century CE
Empire divided into East and West		Empirewide persecution of Christians, 305-311 CE
Constantine, 306-337 CE		
Battle at Milvian bridge, 312 CE		Eusebius of Caesarea, 260-340 CE *Ecclesiastical History,* 303-324 CE
		"Edict of Milan," 313 CE Religious freedom for Christians
		Christianity declared official religion 324 CE
		Council of Nicaea, 325 CE Nicene Creed
Constantius, 337-361 CE	Gallus revolt, 351 CE	Arian controversy, 318-381 CE
Julian the Apostate, 361-363 CE		Council of Constantinople, 381 CE Doctrine of Trinity
	Establishment of permanent Jewish calendar—Patriarch Hillel II (c.359 CE)	John Chrysostom, 354-407 CE
	Julian's abortive attempt to rebuild the Temple, 363 CE	St. Augustine, 354-430 CE *The City of God*
Theodosius I, 379-395 CE		Christianity became official religion
	Jerusalem Talmud, c.400 CE	of empire, 392 CE
		Sack of Rome by Visigoths, 410 CE
	Disappearance of patriarchate c.425	Council of Carthage, 419 CE Adopted New Testament canon
Justinian, 527-565 CE		Council of Chalcedon, 451 CE
	Babylonian Talmud, c.500/600 CE	Nicene Creed acknowledged *Definition of Faith*

MUSLIM CONQUEST 634–640 CE

* Dates given for political figures are for years of their reign, others cover lifetime, unless otherwise specified.

** Flourished, dates of major activity.

Abbreviations

AJA	American Journal of Archaeology		JAAR	Journal of the American Academy of Religion
Antiquities	Josephus, Antiquities of the Jews		JBL	Journal of Biblical Literature
Apion	Josephus, Against Apion		JJS	Journal of Jewish Studies
ANRW	H. Temporini and W. Haase, eds., Aufstieg und Niedergang de römischen Welt (Berlin: de Gruyter, 1972-)		JJML	Journal of Jewish Music and Liturgy
			JPS	Jewish Publication Society
			JQR	Jewish Quarterly Review
ATR	Anglican Theological Review		JSJ	Journal for the Study of Judaism
ASOR	American Schools of Oriental Research		JSP	Journal for the Study of the Pseudepigrapha
b.	ben, bar: son of		JSS	Jewish Social Studies
BA	Biblical Archaeologist		JT	Jerusalem Talmud, or Yerushalmi (Palestinian Talmud)
BAR	Biblical Archaeology Review			
BASOR	Bulletin of the American Schools of Oriental Research		JTS	Journal of Theological Studies
BHT	Beitrage zur historischen Theologie		JTSem	Jewish Theological Seminary
			Life	Josephus
BR	Bible Review		Loeb	Loeb Classical Library (Cambridge, MA: Harvard Univ. Press; London: Heinemann, ongoing)
BS	Byzantine Studies			
BT	Babylonian Talmud, or Bavli			
BZNW	Beihefte zur Zeitschrift für die neutestamentliche Wissenschaft (Berlin: de Gruyter)		LPNF	P. Schaff and H. Wace, eds. and transl., A Select Library of the Nicene and Post-Nicene Fathers
CBA	Catholic Biblical Association		n.s.	new series
CBQ	Catholic Biblical Quarterly		o.s.	old series
CSCO	Corpus Scriptorum Christianorum Orientalium		PAAJR	Proceedings of the American Academy of Jewish Research
EAEHL	M. Avi-Yonah and E. Stern, eds., Encyclopedia of Archaeological Excavations in the Holy Land		PG	J. Migne, ed., Patrologia Graeca
			PL	J. Migne, ed., Patrologia Latina
			R.	Rabbi
Eccles. Hist.	Eusebius, Ecclesiastical History		REJ	Revue des Etudes Juives
EJ	Encyclopaedia Judaica		SBL	Society of Biblical Literature
HDR	Harvard Dissertations in Religion		SC	The Second Century
			Suetonius	Lives of the [Twelve] Caesars
HTR	Harvard Theological Review		TAPA	Transactions of the American Philological Association
HUCA	Hebrew Union College Annual		War	Josephus, The Jewish War
IEJ	Israel Exploration Journal		ZNW	Zeitschrift für die neutestamentliche Wissenschaft
IES	Israel Exploration Society			

Acknowledgments

Our appreciation goes to all the contributors to this book. Each is an expert who willingly made his expert knowledge accessible to the general reader. Carol Andrews assiduously copy-edited the manuscripts, edited the endnotes and communicated with the scholars to assure a consistent text. Nita Sue Kent wrote the captions to the pictures. Cheryl McGowan handled the challenging picture search. Proofing and correcting was carefully done by Laurie Andrews and Robin Cather. Robert Sugar and Sharri Harris Wolfgang of AURAS Design Studio designed the book. Our thanks also to Susan Laden, publisher, Suzanne Singer, managing editor, and Judy Wohlberg, who coordinated the project.

FOREWORD

WHAT IS HERE PRESENTED TO THE PUBLIC IS AN INVITATION TO ruminate on the larger themes of history. It is an ongoing task.

No single scholar could have written this book. No single scholar controls the vast and often arcane sources that comprise its subjects. Typically, Jewish history and Christian history are taught by different teachers; they are even considered different disciplines. As Oxford don Geza Vermes points out in his introduction, this book is unique; it is a parallel history of early Christianity and Rabbinic Judaism, an attempt to trace their stories side by side. This is what beckons us to ruminate on larger questions.

Paradoxically, these two histories have a common source; they grew out of the same soil—Second Temple Judaism. Yet their stories are very different. No figure in Rabbinic Judaism is as central to it as Jesus is to Christianity. A chapter in this book is devoted to the life of Jesus. There is no comparable chapter on a figure in Rabbinic Judaism.

Judaism started out as a nation in this story; it twice rebelled against its Roman overlords; twice it was defeated. Early Christians sometimes suffered persecution, but there is no comparable strand of Christian history.

Christianity started out as a little off-beat Jewish sect—and conquered the West. Judaism, from being a nation, became a tiny minority in larger, often hostile cultures.

For Christianity, the questions were of doctrine and institutionalization; for Judaism, of adapting for survival as a people without a place. No wonder their histories—their stories—are so very different. No wonder they took such divergent paths.

Even the sources are very different. Rabbinic Judaism can point to nothing parallel to the Gospels or Paul's letters. The Mishnah and the Talmudim are not only very different from the earliest Christian documents, but they were compiled much later. And they are methodologically so arcane that it takes years of study to penetrate them competently—something few scholars of Christian history have done. The patristic literature of Christianity is also unique. Few scholars of Jewish history control this vast literature which, simply in its quantity, threatens to overwhelm us.

All this cannot help but make us stop and puzzle over how to achieve an understanding of the critical early centuries of Rabbinic Judaism and Christianity. This book—parallel histories—is not simply a compendium of summaries and generalizations. Here the reader will find the details too, the basic evidence (and, for the student who wishes to pursue any particular subject, the references and citations).

I confess this has not been an easy project. That it took six times as long as I expected may be a reflection of my essential optimism, rather than any particular difficulty with the project. But the truth is that there are vast differences in how such a history as this might be written. Scholars differ on what the basic questions should be and on how to assess the evidence. They often differ in their conclusions too. It is far too early for a definitive history of this kind to be written. Indeed, because of the limitations of our sources, it is not possible, even theoretically, to write a definitive history of this period. Each of the authors of the chapters in this book is a leading scholar and expert in the material covered by his chapter, and their assessments are in the mainstream of modern critical scholarship. Even so, these scholars sometimes have divergent viewpoints. I have not tried to suppress them—only to clarify them and make them explicit. Still, there will be plenty of room for disagreement. And there is enough detail so readers can make their own assessment.

We have worked very hard to make these sometimes recondite stories as understandable and readable as possible. For this I must express my gratitude to the authors for their long and sometimes lonely labors—and for their patience and understanding when I continued to request clarification and, sometimes, simplification. I hope they—and, more importantly, the reader—will agree that the result has been worth the effort.

Hershel Shanks

August 1992, Washington, D.C.

INTRODUCTION

Parallel History Preview

GEZA VERMES

THIS COLLECTIVE ENTERPRISE, A PARALLEL HISTORY OF JUDAISM AND Christianity that covers a period of over six centuries crucial to the development of both, is unprecedented in the annals of scholarship. Histories of the Jews and of early Christianity abound at every level, from the rudimentary to the highly sophisticated, but so far no one has attempted to set out, side by side, two autonomous accounts, written by leading experts for the benefit of all, the learned and the learner alike. It is my great privilege to offer here a preview and a foretaste of the eight chapters that follow. Being myself a student of Judaism, I will be judging matters primarily from a *Jewish* historical vantage point; the balance will be provided by a *Christian* overview at the end of the volume.

It should be observed that during the opening decades of the period surveyed, say until the middle of the first century C.E., no *parallel* history is conceivable because it was only then that Christianity began to appear as distinct from Judaism, especially because of the larger number of Gentiles among its ranks. This was well after the death of Jesus, who was crucified about 30 C.E. Indeed, even the Judaism—or as it is nowadays fashionable to say, the Judaisms—of the first 70 years of the Common Era (outlined by Professor Louis H. Feldman in chapter 1) was (or were) different from that based on the Mishnah and the Talmud because of the then-prevailing *multiparty* religious system. First-century Pharisees, Sadducees, Essenes, etc., seem to have coexisted in a spirit of tolerant hostility in clear contrast to the progressively standardized "orthodoxy" of later ages. Also, if the often asserted claim that before its destruction in 70 C.E. the Temple of Jerusalem was the "central focus of the Jewish religion" is accepted as true (in fact, for most Jews living beyond easy reach of the Holy City the Temple was more an idea than a tangible reality), the sanctuaryless Judaism of the post-destruction, rabbinic age must be seen in practice as a fresh departure.

Jesus of Nazareth belonged to pre-Orthodox Judaism, not to "Christianity." I find Professor E. P. Sanders' chapter 2, outlining Jesus' life and message, to be both judicious and informative, but I do not expect conservative Christians to agree with the definition of Jesus as a Jewish charismatic prophet, healer and teacher, though this description is very close to that of the first-century Jewish historian Flavius Josephus, who described Jesus as a "wise man" and a "performer of paradoxical deeds" (*Antiquities* 18.63). Unlike many of his fellow New Testament scholars, Sanders believes that a great deal can be discovered in the Gospels about the historical Jesus "if we are content with a broad outline"–e.g., that he was associated with John the Baptist, was accompanied by disciples, expected the "kingdom," went from Galilee to Jerusalem, threatened the Temple and soon thereafter was tried and crucified. Professor Sanders interprets the episode of Jesus' overturning the money-changers and merchants' tables as an actual attack on the Temple, but it could just as well have been the instinctive reaction of a hot-blooded rural Galilean holy man at the sight and sound–in sacred precincts–of what must have resembled a Levantine bazaar. In other words, if Jesus was responsible for an affray in the Temple court, it was probably inspired, not by hostility, but by reverence for the "house of God."

The emergence of Christianity between the crucifixion and the First Jewish Revolt against Rome (66-70 C.E.), attested by Paul's letters, the Acts of the Apostles and the Gospels, is neatly outlined in chapter 3 by Professor Howard C. Kee in conformity with contemporary academic conventions. In his view, one which many Jewish historians are likely to query, primitive Christianity was "distinctively different" from "official Judaism" (by which he understands the religious system represented by the priesthood and the Temple) and consequently from the outset was not a Jewish movement. Kee's strange denial of the existence in the first century of a "distinctively Jewish Christian group" is consonant with this opinion, as is his description of the Ebionites–who flourished between the second and the fifth centuries C.E.–not as the original Palestinian followers of Jesus but as a Christian splinter group. If his premises are accepted, Professor Kee's exposition of Christianity on a Pauline basis appears coherent. He further asserts that the teaching preserved in the collection of Gospel sayings (the so-called Q document, from the German *Quelle,* or "source") is "compatible" with the epistles of Paul and that there is a convergence between the Jesus portrait in the earliest Gospel of Mark and that arising from Q. The statement that Mark ends on an "expectant note," when in fact it speaks of shaking, trembling and terror-stricken women in the "empty tomb" (Mark 16:8), and the use of the phrase "baby-sitter" in connection with Paul's metaphor concerning the Law as a "pedagogue" (Galatians 3:24) may strike some as rather eccentric.

Jewish history from the destruction of Jerusalem to the defeat of the Bar-Kokhba revolt (70-135 C.E.) is discussed in chapter 4 by Professor Lee I. A. Levine. He correctly observes that the lost war against Rome hurt but did not break Judaism and analyzes the non-rabbinic writings dating to the late first or early second century C.E.—the Apocalypse of Baruch, 4 Ezra and Pseudo-Philo's *Book of Biblical Antiquities*—before turning to the work of Yoḥanan ben Zakkai and the assembly of the sages at Yavneh which resulted in the swift and successful restructuring of Jewish religious life in conformity with the new circumstances created by the sack of the Temple by the Romans. Such a smooth reorganization would be hard to understand if the cultic worship in Jerusalem had genuinely played as important a part in real Jewish life as many scholars presume.

The history of the Church from the fall of Jerusalem in 70 C.E. to the conversion of Constantine to Christianity (312 C.E.) is the subject of a well-documented presentation by Professor Harold W. Attridge in chapter 5. Starting with the non-Pauline New Testament documents and continuing with second-century polemical authors (pseudo-Barnabas, Justin Martyr and Bishop Melito of Sardis), Attridge explains that one of the paramount aims of Christianity was to define itself against Judaism. It was claimed not only that the Church inherited all the divine promises and privileges formerly granted to Israel, but also that Jewish rejection was foreseen and predicted by the biblical prophets. In the course of the second century, the heresy of Gnosticism was confronted and overcome, and subsequently, during the late second and the early third centuries, the great Alexandrian Church Fathers—Clement and Origen—set out to lay the teaching of the Gospels on philosophical foundations that eventually gave birth to a thoroughly Hellenized Christian theology. Prior to triumphing over pagan Rome, Christians shared the experience of religious persecution and martyrdom, as did the Jews in the age of the Maccabees in the 160s

B.C.E. and under Hadrian during and after the Bar-Kokhba revolt in the 130s. But the suffering inflicted on the Church by the last Roman imperial persecutors—Decius, Diocletian and Galerius, in the second half of the third and at the beginning of the fourth centuries—was soon overshadowed by the power and glory of the Christian empire inaugurated by Constantine the Great.

The period between the defeat of Bar-Kokhba (135 C.E.) and the death of Rabbi Judah the Patriarch (c. 220 C.E.) saw the reorganization of Jewish life in Galilee. The presence of Jews was no longer welcome in Judea, renamed Syro-Palaestina, and Jerusalem was transformed by the victorious emperor Hadrian into a pagan city called Aelia Capitolina. This period saw not only the strengthening of the patriarchate to head the communal rabbis and represent Jewry before the imperial authorities, but also the compilation of the Mishnah in six orders, or divisions, and 63 tractates. This complex of topics is succinctly but powerfully sketched by Professor Shaye J. D. Cohen in chapter 6. He seeks to navigate a middle course among the conflicting theories regarding the nature of the Mishnah. Discarding the traditional but superficial definition of it as a law code, and the recent theory that it is essentially the expression of a philosophical worldview, Cohen sees in the Mishnah a radically new venture, a book of laws containing conflicting opinions attributed to named sages without, as a rule, any reference to the Bible, and apparently bestowing complete autonomy on human reason. The main problem with such a thesis, as Professor Cohen himself realizes, is that the same Mishnaic rabbis, when they comment on the Torah, or are quoted in the Talmud, do not seem to agree with it.

The development of a literary formulation of Jewish law and lore which began with the Mishnah around 200 C.E. was further pursued during the subsequent four centuries in Palestine and Babylonia and resulted in the Jerusalem, or Palestinian, Talmud (c. 400 C.E.), the Babylonian Talmud (c. sixth century) and the early Bible commentaries dating to approximately the same period. These are outlined in chapter 7 by Professor Isaiah M. Gafni, together with what is known of the history of the Jewish people during the talmudic age. By that time Christians had become demographically significant, so much so that in the sixth century they formed the majority of the population of the Land of Israel. Jewish sources sporadically include polemics thought to be directed against Christian teachings. Rabbi Abbahu of Caesarea in particular is seen as inserting anti-Christian twists into his interpretation of the Bible. But the main topic of the chapter is the study of anti-Jewish legislation in the Christian Roman empire prohibiting mixed marriages, Christian participation in synagogue worship, the building and restoring of synagogues and pressure by Jewish authorities on would-be converts to Christianity. With the political upheavals in the Roman-Byzantine world, Jewish messianic expectation was reborn, whereas the Jews in Mesopotamia remained satisfied with Persia and accepted the secular "law of the kingdom." Apparently they even occasionally managed to persuade Christians to embrace Judaism, and there was little concern about conversion in the opposite direction.

The age from Constantine to the Arab conquest (312-640 C.E.), expertly portrayed by Professor Dennis E. Groh in chapter 8, saw within the Christian Church a series of major doctrinal conflicts relating to fine theological distinctions concerning the nature of the divine Christ. Propounders of heresies, Arius and Nestorius, were fought by ecclesiastical dignitaries, Athanasius and Cyril of Alexandria, in councils of bishops at Nicaea (325 C.E.) and Chalcedon (451 C.E.). Christian monasticism flourished, and great theologians, among them Augustine of Hippo in North Africa and Jerome, translator of the Bible into Latin—after learning Hebrew from a rabbi in Lydda (Lod)—and outstanding Greek Church Fathers, erected the monumental edifice of theology. John Chrysostom was fulminating against the Jews in Antioch and Constantinople; but in Palestine, despite hostile imperial legislation and the anti-Jewish preaching of bishops, splendid synagogues with beautiful mosaic floors continued to be constructed. In the West Roman power gave way before a barbarian onslaught; and in the East the armies of Islam curtailed the power of Byzantium.

By the time this parallel history ends, Christianity and Judaism are definitely two distinct and distant religions.

A BIRD'S-EYE VIEW OF THESE 600 YEARS OF JEWISH AND CHRISTIAN HISTORY, concerned first and foremost with mutual contacts and attitudes, cannot fail to note some curious but significant phenomena.

First, the relationship between Judaism and Christianity is not fully reciprocal. This is of course easy to understand; Judaism is fully comprehensible in itself, whereas Christianity, originally a Jewish religious subgroup, by necessity had to define itself *against*, and distance itself from, Judaism.

Second, this basic inequality is manifest throughout the various periods surveyed in this volume. The earlier layers of rabbinic literature, now that the myth of the specifically anti-Christian intent of the late first-century C.E. curse of the heretics (*minim*) in the synagogal prayer (*Amidah*) is revealed for what it is, contain no statement against, indeed hardly any allusion to, Christianity.

Christianity, definitely in its Gentile form, seems to touch Jewish consciousness only from the third, and especially the fourth, century onward, by which time it was fast becoming the official religion of the Roman empire. Open and deliberate doctrinal conflict on the Jewish side had to wait until the Middle Ages, whether in the form of the crude and popular caricature of the Gospel story in the various versions of the *Toledot Yeshu* (Life of Jesus) or in theological and philosophical polemics of a higher order.

Third, apart from such theologically nonsensitive matters as the identity of the plant (gourd or ivy) under which Jonah sat (Jonah 4:6)—on which an early fifth-century bishop of Oca in Libya was happy to consult the Jews according to a letter of Jerome to Augustine—a civilized and peaceful dialogue is a post-Holocaust phenomenon. A collaborative venture such as this parallel history would have been inconceivable even half a century ago. It is a remarkable achievement.

To finish on a lighter note, an anecdote recorded in the Babylonian Talmud (*Menahot* 29b) portrays Moses as seeking permission from God to attend in spirit a lecture given by Rabbi Akiva. He is allowed to slip into the classroom and sit inconspicuously in the back row. There he listens attentively to the exposition and the lively questions and answers, but Moses has absolutely no idea what the teachers and pupils are talking about until Akiva discloses that he is expounding a *halakhah* (legal teaching) brought down by Moses from Mt. Sinai.

One may well wonder whether Jesus of Nazareth would have been equally dumbfounded had he been given a similar chance to eavesdrop incognito on the sessions of the Council of Nicaea where his nature was the subject of much heated debate.

ONE

Palestinian and Diaspora Judaism in the First Century

LOUIS H. FELDMAN

ERHAPS NO CENTURY IN THE ENTIRE HISTORY OF JUDAISM SAW more revolutionary changes than the first century of the Common Era. In this relatively short period of time two great religions developed—Rabbinic Judaism and Christianity. During this period the man Christians consider the son of God lived and was crucified. During this period his greatest apostle wrote the canonical epistles to struggling new churches. During this period the Jewish Temple was destroyed. With the destruction, major changes occurred in the role of the high priests. Apocalypticism, proselytism and sectarianism, all of which had flourished before the destruction of the Temple, drastically declined. This period also produced the two most outstanding Hellenistic Jewish writers—the philosopher Philo and the historian Josephus. Finally, this period laid the foundations for the Jewish academies that debated the Law and ultimately led to its codification in the greatest Jewish work since the Bible—the Talmud.

In this chapter, we shall examine the political, economic, social, religious and cultural factors that lie behind these developments, as well as the events that presaged them, both in Palestine and in the Diaspora.

I. The Palestinian World

The political background: The Augustan age
After a century of almost continuous civil strife, Rome finally achieved what historians call the *Pax Augusta*, or *Pax Romana*. Under the emperor Augustus (he called himself *Princeps*, that is, "First Citizen"), who ruled from 31 B.C.E. to 14 C.E., the empire (except for the Jews) enjoyed a measure of tranquillity that lasted for two centuries. Augustus was a kind of preview of Napoleon after the French Revolution. His contemporaries looked upon him as a benefactor, deliverer, savior, almost messiah.[1]

At the time, Judea was considerably smaller than the present state of Israel. Herod (his father Antipater was Idumean,* his mother may have been Nabatean), whose long reign lasted from 37 to 4 B.C.E., had brought relative peace and prosperity to the tiny principality. Visitors to present-day Israel will see ample evidence of Herod's building activities—at Jericho, Masada, Caesarea and, above all, Jerusalem, where he solved the problem of unemployment by establishing a kind of WPA, giving employment to thousands of workers who completely rebuilt the Temple. Ironically, it was a king of non-Jewish descent who rebuilt the Temple. According to the fourth-century Church Father Epiphanius, Herod himself was believed by some to be the messiah. His popularity was doubtless due in part to the strong-arm measures he instituted to deal with muggers who roamed the city streets as well as the countryside—evidence of considerable social unrest. Herod made it safe for senior citizens to walk the streets at night.[2]

To be sure, Herod's personal problems would have required a team of psychiatrists. In the end, he ordered his wife Mariamne, her brother Aristobulus, her mother, Alexandra, and his two sons by Mariamne, Alexander and Aristobulus, to be killed. He also resisted the advances of the notorious Cleopatra.[3] Yet he managed to win the confidence of such excellent and diverse judges of responsible administration as Julius Caesar, Marc Antony, the Roman general Agrippa and Augustus himself. Indeed, considering the uprisings that broke out in Palestine after his death, we may well conclude that his repressive policies actually saved thousands of lives and preserved the Jewish state from extinction for a century.

When Herod died, his kingdom was divided among three of his sons. The major part, consisting of Judea, Samaria and Idumea, was bequeathed to Archelaus, his son by a Samaritan woman.[4] Archelaus so antagonized both his Jewish and Samaritan subjects

---

* Scurrilous legend makes Antipater the son of a temple slave of Apollo at Ashkelon in Philistia.

that they complained to the Roman emperor. As a result, he was deposed and Judea was organized as a Roman province (6 C.E.) under a Roman procurator, who, in turn, was under the jurisdiction of the governor of Syria.[5]

Syria was a key Roman province in the East, responsible for protecting the border with Rome's greatest and most persistent rival throughout the next centuries, Parthia (Persia). The governor of Syria was often the most distinguished of the Roman emperor's administrators. The inhabitants of his province could expect careful and fair consideration of their complaints by a man who had considerable clout even in the halls of the emperor in Rome.

The procurators of Judea, however, were neither so fair, nor so talented. One of them, Tiberius Julius Alexander (born 14/16 C.E.), was even an apostate Jew, a fact that hardly ingratiated him with his Jewish subjects. Between 6 C.E., when Judea became a Roman province, and 66, when the First Jewish Revolt against Rome broke out, there were 14 Roman procurators, who served for an average of only four years. Obviously they often suffered from lack of experience, but if this were not bad enough, they also sought to make money during their brief incumbency by accepting bribes.

The most notorious of these procurators, Pontius Pilate, remained in office for ten years (26-36 C.E.), a tribute either to his efficiency or to Tiberius' deliberate policy not to replace administrators lest the new ones sap the economic strength of the province. The last of the procurators, Gessius Florus (64-66 C.E.), was friendlier to the more Hellenized urban non-Jews than to those Jews who were concentrated in the farming areas and the small towns of Judea. The Roman historian Tacitus, who was no friend of the Jews, tells us that the Jews' patience lasted until Gessius Florus became procurator.[6] After Gessius Florus, the revolt broke out.

The rule of the procurators was interrupted briefly–between 41 and 44 C.E.–when the kingship of Judea was given to Herod's grandson, Agrippa I, who had helped Claudius to become emperor.[7] Because of his connections in Rome, Agrippa was apparently regarded as the leading vassal king in the East. When he attempted to convene a number of other petty rulers in Tiberias, however, the Roman governor of Syria, Marsus, was quick to break up the conference,[8] presumably because he suspected they might revolt or might join the great national enemy of the Romans to the east, the Parthians. Shortly thereafter Agrippa died.[9] Some suspect that the Romans poisoned him–with arsenic, the standard poison of the time. The Romans were presumably uneasy about his great popularity with both the rabbis[10] and the masses. Agrippa was not only generous to the people, he also scrupulously observed the tenets of Judaism.[11]

ZEV RADOVAN

COIN OF THE FIRST JEWISH REVOLT. Minted by Jews who revolted against Roman rule in 66 C.E., it bears a chalice and the value—a half-shekel. Above the chalice are the letters *shin* and *bet*. *Shin* stands for *shenat*, or year (in the construct form); *bet*, the second letter of the Hebrew alphabet, has the numerical value two. They date the coin to the second year of the insurrection, or 68 C.E. The other side of the coin shows a stem with three pomegranates surrounded by "Jerusalem the Holy" in archaic Hebrew characters.

One source of tension between the Jews and the Romans stemmed from a frequent request by the Jews for a limited autonomy equal to that of non-Jews. This issue arose both in Caesarea on the Mediterranean coast of Palestine and in Alexandria in Egypt. Non-Jews regularly opposed this request; indeed, it was clashes between the Jews and non-Jews in Caesarea over this issue that sparked the great Jewish Revolt against Rome in 66 C.E.

An additional factor that fueled the Jewish revolutionaries was the gradual assumption of political power in Rome by anti-Jewish freedmen of Greek origin. They gave aid and comfort to the non-Jewish elements in their strife with Jews in cities such as Caesarea.[12]

The economic background of the Jewish Revolt against Rome

Since the time of Julius Caesar (100-44 B.C.E.), the Jews had been granted special privileges—exemption from quartering troops, exemption from military service, exemption from worshipping the emperor, permission to assemble and reduction of taxes. One may well wonder why the Jews of Palestine should have revolted against the Romans. Josephus places the chief blame on the Fourth Philosophy,[13] a movement that started in 6 C.E. in opposition to a tax on property in Judea instituted by Quirinius, the Roman governor of Syria. The followers of the Fourth Philosophy proclaimed that they could accept the overlordship of no one except God Himself.

Other economic factors also played a role.[14] The Temple collected vast sums of money each year from Jews throughout the world and was a veritable bank, supporting large projects and giving employment to thousands. When the Temple rebuilding project (instituted much earlier by Herod the Great) was completed in 64 C.E., all the people who worked on it were thrown out of work. Unrest soon followed.

Moreover, the high priests, usually lackeys of the Romans, sent slaves to collect tithes and even beat people with staves when they failed to pay.[15]

Other economic factors were also significant in triggering the revolt. The heavy burden of taxation became even greater as a result of the extravagance of Agrippa I (41-44 C.E.). Strife developed between the owners of large estates and the landless. Poorer Jews hated wealthier Jews who had befriended the Romans, especially absentee landlords who exploited lowly Galilean peasants.[16] One of the first acts of the revolutionaries when the revolt broke out was to burn the records of debts.[17] Pervasive poverty was aggravated by restriction of the average Jewish peasant's holding, resulting from the vast increase in population. The struggle for cultivatable land became intense. Josephus tells us that there were 204 cities and villages in the Galilee,[18] the smallest of which had 15,000 inhabitants,[19] indicating a total of at least three million people. He also tells us that 1,100,000 Jews were killed in the revolt.[20] Though these figures may be vastly exaggerated, they nevertheless give some indication of a great growth in population from the time when the Jews returned from the Babylonian captivity in the sixth century B.C.E.

But the dissatisfaction with Roman rule was not restricted to the lower classes. This is reflected in the fact that the aristocratic Jewish leaders refused to identify the culprits who had insulted the procurator Gessius Florus by passing around a basket as if they were begging on his behalf,[21] and in the fact that Florus loosed his soldiers against the upper classes with particular severity.[22]

Strangely enough, there is reason to believe that the economic situation in Judea actually improved during the first century, certainly for the inhabitants of Jerusalem. If nothing else, the fact that so many Jews—according to Josephus, at the outbreak of the revolt there were 2,556,000 Jews in Jerusalem[23]—came to Jerusalem and stayed for considerable periods of time indicates a tremendous tourist trade. Moreover, the outstanding success of Jewish proselytism meant that vast sums of money continued to pour into the Temple for all kinds of capital improvements.

We know of at least two instances in the first century when the Romans offended Jewish religious sensibilities by attempting to bring into Jerusalem busts of the emperor attached to military

The religious background of the revolt

standards, once during the procuratorship of Pontius Pilate (c. 26 C.E.)[24] and again during the governorship of Vitellius (37 C.E.).[25] On another occasion (40 C.E.) the Roman authorities tried to place a statue of the emperor Caligula in the Temple.[26] In each case, the vigorous protests of the Jews forced the authorities to rescind the orders. But the insult lingered.

The Jews were also in constant conflict with the Samaritans.[27] The Samaritans not only had a different text of the Torah, but they did not accept the books of the Prophets nor the third segment of the Hebrew Bible, known as the Writings. The Samaritans also refused to recognize the Oral Torah (the rules that ultimately became codified in writing in the Talmud) and they had a different calendar. Finally, the sacred mountain the Samaritans recognized was Mt. Gerizim, not the Temple Mount in Jerusalem. The bitterness between Jews and Samaritans was exacerbated when the Roman procurator Cumanus (48-52 C.E.), having been bribed by the Samaritans, failed to take action when some Jews on their way to Jerusalem for a religious festival were attacked by Samaritans. Similar incidents between the two groups could be multiplied.

Moreover, the high priests provided the Jews with no real religious leadership.[28] Since the Persian control of Palestine in the sixth century B.C.E., the high priesthood had become simply a political plum. In the Roman period, it was dominated by a few families, closely supervised by the Romans. Moreover, there was little continuity, as high priests were constantly being replaced. Tension existed even between the high priests and ordinary priests. Significantly, one of the first acts of the revolutionary Zealots when they occupied the Temple during the First Jewish Revolt against Rome was to choose by lot a high priest.[29]

The rise of messianism also contributed to Roman uneasiness during this period.[30] The first messianic claimant of whom we hear is the infamous Herod, as already noted. Suetonius[31] and Tacitus,[32] as well as Josephus,[33] mention a widespread messianic-like belief that a man, or men, coming from Judea would rule the world. The Romans were particularly wary of charismatic, messianic-like leaders who managed to attract large crowds. The fact that huge crowds came to Jerusalem for the three pilgrimage festivals* provided ample opportunity for charismatic leaders to cause trouble for the Romans (according to Josephus, as we have noted, there were more than 2.5 million people in Jerusalem at Passover when the revolt broke out).[34] According to Josephus, in about 44 C.E., a certain Theudas professed to be a prophet and persuaded masses of people to take up their possessions and follow him to the Jordan River,[35] which, he asserted, would part at his com-

---

* Passover, Pentecost and Tabernacles.

mand. The Roman procurator Fadus slew Theudas and many of his followers.

The events surrounding Jesus' death would seem to be somewhat similar. The first question put to Jesus after his resurrection, according to Acts 1:6, was whether he would restore the kingdom to Israel, that is, whether he would create a state independent of the Romans.

The vast expansion of Judaism through proselytism may also have made the Romans nervous that their ancestral religion would be overwhelmed. According to Baron, who bases his estimate on biblical and archaeological data, Judea in 586 B.C.E., prior to the destruction of the First Temple, had no more than 150,000 Jews. By the middle of the first century C.E., he estimates, the world Jewish population had risen to about eight million, with approximately two to three million living in Palestine.[36] Even if these figures are inflated, it is clear that the increase in Jews throughout the empire could not have been achieved by natural birthrate alone.

Before the Roman destruction of Jerusalem in 70 C.E., the central focus of the Jewish religion was the Temple.[37] It was much more than a religious symbol; it was also a powerful economic force, as we know from the fact that it was plundered of its riches from time to time. Jews throughout the world annually contributed vast sums to the Temple. Not surprisingly, the various revolutionary groups contended for control of it during the revolt against Rome.

Religious developments in Palestine

The high priest, as the person in charge of the Temple, had great power. From a social and economic point of view, Josephus is quite justified in calling the government of Judea a theocracy,[38] a term which, incidentally, he apparently invented. After the reigns of Herod and Archelaus, Josephus tells us, "the high priests were entrusted with the leadership of the nation."[39] Nonetheless, in 59 C.E., bitter enmity between the high priests, on the one hand, and the ordinary priests and the populace of Jerusalem, on the other hand, erupted in ugly violence.[40]

The supreme political, religious and judicial body of the Jews in Palestine was the Sanhedrin (from the Greek *synedrion*, "a sitting together," or "session").[41] According to the Mishnah, a collection of debates on Jewish religious law assembled in about 200 C.E., the Sanhedrin* had jurisdiction in trials of tribes, false prophets and false priests, as well as a number of other matters;[42] it could declare that a scholar was rebellious and it could choose a king or a high priest.[43] Whether this is a description of an ideal Sanhedrin or whether the Sanhedrin actually exercised all these functions is a matter of scholarly debate.[44]

* For more on Sanhedrin, see footnote on page 122.

Another scholarly dispute concerns the composition of the Sanhedrin. According to rabbinic sources,[45] the Sanhedrin was composed of Pharisaic scholars headed by the two foremost among them, the *nasi* (administrative or legislative head) and the *av beth din* (judicial head). In the Gospels (Matthew 26:57ff.; Mark 14:53ff.; Luke 22:54), the Sanhedrin is said to be headed by the high priest. Numerous other discrepancies exist between the description of the Sanhedrin in the Gospels and in rabbinic sources: In the Gospels (Mark 14:53; Matthew 26:57-58; Luke 22:54; John 18:13,24), the Sanhedrin met in the home of the high priest; the rabbinic sources (Mishnah *Sanhedrin* 11:2) indicate that it met in the Chamber of Hewn Stone. In the Gospels (Mark 14:53-54; Matthew 26:57ff., 27:1-2), it tried Jesus at night; in the rabbinic sources (Mishnah *Sanhedrin* 4:1), the Sanhedrin was not allowed to try criminal cases at night. According to Mark (14:64), Jesus was convicted on the same day he was tried; according to the Mishnah (*Sanhedrin* 4:1), in capital cases it was not permissible for a verdict of guilty to be reached on the same day. According to the Gospels (Matthew 26:64-65; Mark 14:62-63; Luke 22:70-71), Jesus was convicted on his own testimony; according to rabbinic law (Tosefta *Sanhedrin* 11:1), a person may not be convicted by his own testimony.

One solution to these discrepancies is to deny the historicity of the Gospel accounts; indeed, the Gospel of John says nothing about an assembly of the Sanhedrin and declares that the Sanhedrin lacked jurisdiction to put anyone to death (John 18:31). According to Josephus, however, in the year 62 the Sanhedrin did order the execution of James, the brother of Jesus.[46]

Another solution is to stress that the Mishnah, which is our earliest rabbinic source, is a Pharisaic work dating to the end of the second century. Some of the high priests in the first century, it is argued, were Sadducean,[47] and the membership of the Sanhedrin (at least according to Acts 23:6) was composed in part of Pharisees and in part of Sadducees. According to this view, the trial of Jesus was conducted in conformity with Sadducean law, rather than Pharisaic law. Still another solution suggests that the Sanhedrin mentioned in the Gospels justified its violation of the rules of procedure by appealing to the principle that this was permitted in cases of emergency. Still another solution postulates two Sanhedrins, one political and one religious.[48] Or the Sanhedrin before which Jesus appeared may have acted simply in an advisory capacity to Roman authority.[49]

It is sometimes forgotten that long before the destruction of the Temple, the synagogue was an important religious institution. The earliest references to synagogues in Palestine are in the New Testa-

THEODOTUS SYNAGOGUE INSCRIPTION. Written in Greek and dating from the reign of King Herod (37-4 B.C.E.), the Theodotus synagogue inscription indicates that synagogues had been established in Jerusalem for some time. The text reads:

"Theodotus Vettanos [or son of Vettanos], priest and synagogue leader [*archisynagogus*], son of a synagogue leader, and grandson of a synagogue leader, built [restored?] this synagogue for the purpose of the reading of the Law and for the instruction of the commandments of the Law, the hostel and guest rooms, and the baths [ritual baths?] for foreigners who need them. This synagogue was established by his forefathers, the elders and Simonides."

ment (Matthew 13:54, in Nazareth; Mark 1:21, in Capernaum; Acts 6:9, in Jerusalem) and in Josephus–he mentions synagogues in Caesarea, Dora and Tiberias.[50] The Jerusalem Talmud notes that there were 480 synagogues in Jerusalem at the time of the destruction of the Temple;[51] the Babylonian Talmud gives the number as 394.[52] These need not be exaggerations; many of the ancient synagogues that have been excavated were quite small, and many others probably operated out of private homes, leaving no archaeological trace. Even the Temple had a synagogue.[53] The earliest synagogues unearthed by archaeologists–at Masada, Herodium and Gamla–date from the first century and possibly earlier. An inscription from Jerusalem refers to a synagogue that had been built before the turn of the era.[54] Hence, when the Second Temple was destroyed in 70 C.E., the spiritual vacuum was hardly as great as it had been after the destruction of the First Temple by the Babylonians in 586 B.C.E.

The synagogue served not only as a house of prayer but also as a house of study, as a meeting house and as a guest house.[55] The synagogue inscription already referred to, known as the Theodotus inscription,[56] speaks–in Greek–of a synagogue built for the reading of the Torah, for the teaching of the commandments and as an

ARCH OF TITUS. Standing in Rome near the Colosseum, the Arch of Titus celebrates the emperor's destruction of Jerusalem in 70 C.E.

The relief of a triumphal procession in which soldiers carry the looted Temple treasure shows a detailed, but perhaps not totally reliable, representation of the Temple menorah.

inn for those who come from abroad, presumably for the pilgrimage festivals. That this synagogue was built by a single individual suggests that it, like many synagogues, was really nothing more than, in effect, a private club, often operating out of a private house. There were no rabbis for these synagogues, and they were not joined in any kind of umbrella organization.

In a remarkable statement, Elias Bickerman declares that the Roman general Titus, by destroying the Temple and, in effect, putting an end to the sacrificial system, was the greatest religious reformer in history.[57] Most historians look upon the rabbinic period as beginning in 70 and regard the shift from Second Temple Judaism (prior to the destruction of the Temple) to Rabbinic Judaism as a monumental change. The fact is that Judaism could never have survived such a traumatic experience had not alternative and supplementary institutions, such as prayer, the synagogue and the academy, already been in existence. Unfortunately, the earliest extant rabbinic work of note, the Mishnah, dates from more than a century after the destruction of the Temple. Josephus, whose life is almost evenly divided between the period before and the period after the destruction of the Temple, has almost nothing to say about the impact of this destruction on the rabbis and on their method of study or, indeed, about the impact of the loss of the Temple on Judaism generally. This may be because Josephus is interested primarily in political and military, rather than religious and cultural, history; but the fact remains that he says almost nothing about the affects of this allegedly traumatic event. Surely if the affect on the rabbis and their academies was so traumatic, we would expect that Josephus would give us at least a clue that this was the case.

By the first century B.C.E., the great sages Hillel and Shammai had established what were, in effect, rabbinic academies. Hillel is said to have held the office of patriarch (*nasi*) for 40 years[58] until approximately the year 10 C.E. He was not merely a great scholar and model of virtue, but he was also the founder of a school of legal religious thought (Beth Hillel). In addition, he was the founder of a dynasty that led Jewish life in Palestine for the next four centuries. His liberal attitude toward the admission of proselytes[59] had a profound influence upon the attitude of the later rabbis. According to talmudic tradition, Yoḥanan ben Zakkai, who is usually regarded as the key figure in the metamorphosis of Judaism after the destruction of the Temple, was one of Hillel's disciples.[60] Hillel's grandson, Rabban Gamaliel the Elder, who lived in the first half of the first century, is said to have been a teacher of Paul (Acts 22:3).

We should say something about the position of women in Jewish life in Palestine. Unfortunately, the evidence is scanty. Josephus, at any rate, had a derogatory view of them, if we may judge from his comment about the woman at Masada whom he describes as superior in sagacity and training to most women, as if women can be praised only when compared with other women.[61] In an addition to the Bible, he says that the testimony of women is inadmissible in Jewish law because of their levity and boldness.[62] However, Pseudo-Philo, Josephus' presumed contemporary, has considerably greater respect for them.[63]

Jewish sects   The Jerusalem Talmud tells us that there were 24 sects of heretics[64] at the time of the destruction of the Temple.[65] Josephus tells us about three schools of thought (the Greek word he uses, *hairesis*, has given rise to our "heresy," although it had no such connotation in the original).[66] These three schools are represented by the Pharisees, the Sadducees and the Essenes. In a subsequent discussion, Josephus adds another school of thought, the Fourth Philosophy,[67] which sought to establish an independent theocratic Jewish state. Philo describes still another, the ascetic Therapeutae,[68] who flourished near Alexandria. The Herodians are mentioned in the Gospels (Mark 3:6, 12:13; Matthew 22:16) as a political party which, after the death of Herod, may have regarded him as the messiah.[69] In any event, they sought to reestablish the rule of Herod's descendants over an independent Palestine. The Samaritans constituted still another faction, and, of course, the Christians (if they may be grouped together) another. Perhaps we should add the *haverim*,[70] who, through their meticulous observance of the laws of purity and of tithes, separated themselves from the unlearned rural masses known as the *'am ha-'aretz* (people of the land) and would not eat with them.[71]

The views of the Pharisees have survived in the rabbinic literature. Unfortunately, we have no writings of the Sadducees or of the Essenes (unless we identify the Dead Sea sect with the latter, as most scholars do). Accordingly, we must rely on Josephus for much of our information about these movements. We also have some writings of the Samaritans, but they come from a later period.

The movements that were active in first-century Palestine may perhaps be divided into two groups: those that attempted to make a mass, egalitarian appeal (the Samaritans, Pharisees, Sadducees and the Fourth Philosophy) and those that were separatist, monastic, utopian, ascetic, esoteric and preoccupied with ethics (the Essenes and/or the Dead Sea sect and the Therapeutae). The *haverim* have some but not all of these latter qualities. Christianity would seem to have elements of both.

A major common denominator of the Samaritans and the

Sadducees was their rejection of the Oral Torah, which greatly expanded and interpreted the written Law. While a rejection of the Oral Torah made it easier for Samaritans and Sadducees to understand their religious tenets, since the Oral Torah was much more complicated than the written Torah, it also deprived them of the flexibility that the Pharisees gained through their liberal interpretation of the written Torah.

Though many of these movements originated before the first century, they seem to have flourished particularly in the period just before the destruction of Temple. All of these groups, with the exception of the Pharisees and the Christians,* apparently disappeared with the destruction of the Temple.[72] This, then, is a clue that much of the controversy centered around the Temple, its ritual and its purity laws.

The Sadducees,[73] though few in number,[74] seem to have had considerable influence because their power base was the Temple[75] and because they included men of the highest standing.[76] Sadducean support of Jewish nationalism was undoubtedly a major attraction for the many influential Jews who joined the party, including the important Hasmonean ruler of Judea, John Hyrcanus, who switched his allegiance from the Pharisees to the Sadducees in the second century B.C.E.

So long as the Temple stood, its vast treasury enabled those who controlled it to exercise considerable political, economic and religious power. We may guess that one reason the high priests of the Temple had such short terms of office was that the Romans would not tolerate the nationalism that was so integral a part of their Sadducean orientation. The Pharisees, on the other hand, recognized the value of the *Pax Romana*. The first-century Pharisaic sage Ḥanina Segan ha-Kohanim enjoined Jews to "pray for the peace of the ruling power, since but for fear of it men would have swallowed each other up alive."[77] Indeed in the year 62 C.E., the Pharisees brought a formal accusation before the Roman procurator against the Sadducean high priest Ananus, accusing him of arbitrary action in convening the Sanhedrin to condemn James, the brother of Jesus, to death;[78] the Sadducean high priest was removed from office. Eventually, it was the Pharisees' acceptance of Roman rule that caused a split in their ranks and gave birth to the Fourth Philosophy; as Josephus observes, the Fourth Philosophy agreed in all things with the Pharisees, except that they would not accept foreign rule.[79]

If the relationship between the Pharisees and the Sadducees was as bitter as would seem to be the case from Josephus and from later rabbinic writings, one wonders why we never hear of

---

* A few hundred Samaritans still live near Tel Aviv and in Nablus.

The Rabbinic Sources

There are no written rabbinic sources dating from the first century. The oldest extant code of Jewish law is the Mishnah, edited about 200 C.E. by Rabbi Judah the Prince. It is a legal code of 63 tractates, dealing with agricultural matters, with the law of persons and property, with legal procedure and with ritual. Accordingly, we should not expect and, indeed, do not find, except very incidentally, references to contemporary or historical events. The same is true of the Tosefta, a supplementary collection of interpretations of the Oral Torah (of which the Mishnah is the core). The Tosefta was edited, according to tradition, by Rabbi Ḥiyya bar Abba, a pupil of Judah the Prince, but it never achieved the status of the Mishnah. Of the rabbis who are most frequently quoted in both the Mishnah and the Tosefta, the overwhelming majority date from the second century.[1]

The traditional Jewish view of the Mishnah is that it is part of a divinely revealed Oral Law which is to be interpreted as part of a chain of tradition culminating in rabbinic discussions called the Gemara. Jacob Neusner has challenged the usefulness of the Mishnah as a historical source for any period prior to its completion in about 200 C.E.[2] He has argued vigorously that the Mishnah is to be viewed as an independent work by a small group of men, reflecting the age in which it was composed, and that the views ascribed to various rabbis are to be viewed not as those of the rabbis but rather as those of the redactors (editors).

The rabbinic discussions based on the Mishnah and known as the Gemara originated in both Palestine and Babylonia. The Palestinian Gemara was eventually edited about 400 C.E.; it constitutes, together with the Mishnah itself, the Jerusalem Talmud. The Palestinian Gemara on most but not all of the 63 tractates of the Mishnah has been preserved. The same is true of the Babylonian Gemara, which was edited about 500 C.E. and which, together with the Mishnah, constitutes the Babylonian Talmud.[3] The Gemara in the Babylonian Talmud is fuller than that in the Jerusalem Talmud, and there are

the excommunication of the Sadducees, especially in view of the fact that they refused to accept the Oral Torah, so central in Pharisaic thinking.[80] On the contrary, the Pharisees and the Sadducees seem to have managed to serve together in the Temple and in the Sanhedrin. The fact that the Sadducees are not even mentioned in the voluminous works of Philo* or in the Apocrypha** or Pseudepigrapha† would appear to indicate that the division between them and the Pharisees was not as sharp as one would gather from Josephus. Indeed, Josephus himself hints that the division was perhaps not so great when he reports that the Sadducees "submit to the formulas of the Pharisees, since otherwise the masses would not tolerate them."[81]

even more digressions, but there is little pertaining to historical or contemporary events.

Rabbinic tradition of a homiletic type known as *midrash* (plural, *midrashim*) consists of exegesis of biblical passages. Forerunners of *midrash* are found in the commentaries discovered among the Dead Sea Scrolls. The golden age of *midrashim* begins with *Genesis Rabbah*, which was not edited until perhaps the fifth century.[4] Many midrashic elements are, however, embodied in the Septuagint[5] and in Josephus' *Antiquities of the Jews*.[6] Some otherwise lost *midrashim* have been preserved by the Church Fathers, notably Origen and Jerome.[7] Only one rabbinic work of midrashic nature even purportedly contains historical data, the *Seder Olam Rabbah*, ascribed to the second-century sage Yose ben Ḥalafta; but it contains many late additions, and in any case is more of a chronology than a history.

As to the reliability of rabbinic sources for the history of the period before they were compiled, Shaye Cohen has argued that Josephus' traditions are older and more original than those of the rabbis, that in not a single case is there a compelling reason to assume the contrary and hence that Josephus provides a "control" for the study of rabbinic texts.[8] However, the rabbis have at least one great advantage over Josephus, in that they represent many different points of view and present their comments only in passing, and hence with no particular historiographical mission in mind.

Two small details indicate that the rabbis in the centuries that followed the Roman destruction of the Temple at least tried to be historically accurate: (1) A talmudic saying tells us that "Whoever reports a saying in the name of its originator brings deliverance to the world."[9] (2) A recently discovered manuscript of one of the tractates of the Talmud (*Avodah Zarah* 8b) clearly indicates that an *early* second-century sage wrote down the laws pertaining to fines;[10] hence, these laws, at least, are considerably earlier than the time of the compilation of the Talmud in which they were included.

As to the Fourth Philosophy, there was apparently some connection between their ideology and that of the militant Maccabees in the second century B.C.E. Both fought against a great power (the Maccabees fought against the then-ruling power, the Syrians)

* See box, pages 30-31, concerning Philo.

** These books are considered deuterocanonical by the Roman Catholic Church and are included as part of the Catholic Bible. They are designated as apocryphal in Protestant Bibles, but are not included in Hebrew Scriptures.

† A body of Jewish religious texts written between 200 B.C.E. and 200 C.E., incorrectly attributed to people mentioned in the Bible or to authors of biblical books, similar in nature to biblical books but not recognized as part of the canon of the Bible or the Apocrypha.

in order to establish an independent state.[82] Indeed, Josephus ascribes to the Fourth Philosophy all the troubles that eventually befell the Jews of Palestine. Those who subscribed to the Fourth Philosophy refused to pay tribute to the Romans; they advocated rebellion on the ground that they could acknowledge only God as their master. Unfortunately, Josephus provides us with hardly any history of the movement (and he is our only source), except that it began in 6 C.E. in opposition to the census of Quirinius, the Roman governor of Syria. When Josephus gives us a catalogue of the five revolutionary groups he does not even mention the Fourth Philosophy;[83] perhaps he regarded it as an umbrella group for all the revolutionaries, or perhaps he identified the Fourth Philosophy with the Sicarii, another militant group.[84] Until relatively late in the revolt, there appear to be no traces of intraparty conflict among the revolutionaries, although this may indicate only that the early incidents were largely spontaneous and not managed by any organized party.[85]

Messianism undoubtedly played an important element in the revolt, judging from the fact that Menahem, the leader of the Sicarii, appeared in Jerusalem at the beginning of the revolt "like a veritable king"[86]–that is, like a messianic leader. He was murdered while wearing royal robes.[87] Another revolutionary leader, Simon bar Giora, was captured, after the destruction of the Temple, in a white tunic with a purple (that is, royal) mantle;[88] he was said to have arisen out of the ground at the very spot where the Temple formerly stood. But Josephus appears to suppress the messianic ideals of the revolutionaries, perhaps to avoid the wrath of the Romans, who regarded a belief in a messianic ruler as treason. In the last books of his *Antiquities of the Jews*, however, Josephus mentions at least ten leaders who probably were regarded as messiahs by their adherents, though Josephus himself (except in the case of Jesus, in a passage[89] which is probably interpolated by a later editor[90]) avoids calling them messiahs.

The meaning of the term "messiah" was apparently flexible enough to accommodate these various careers. Indeed, though Josephus presents Eleazer ben Dinai as a mere revolutionary,[91] the rabbis call our attention to his messianic pretensions.[92] We may also note that two later Jewish revolts against Rome, that of 115-117, led by Lukuas-Andreas in Cyrene on the North African coast* and that of 132-135, led by Bar-Kokhba in Palestine, were both definitely headed by messianic claimants.

Of the minor sects, the Essenes were of the greatest interest to Josephus. Whether the Essenes were the Dead Sea sect whose library was discovered in our own day in the cliffs of the Wadi

* See page 146 and footnote on page 195.

TEMPLE SCROLL. The longest of the Dead Sea Scrolls from the caves of Qumran, the Temple Scroll contains detailed instructions for building the Temple not found in the Pentateuch, the first five books of the Bible. It is written in the first person with God himself giving the commands as part of his original revelation to Moses. The Dead Sea Scroll sect probably regarded it as sacred scripture on a par with the Torah itself.

QUMRAN. The first Dead Sea Scrolls were found in caves in this arid wilderness by Bedouin shepherds in 1947. Excavated ruins of the community that hid the scrolls are on the plateau on the left, overlooking the dry wadi to the right. The Dead Sea is in the distance. Of the more than 800 scrolls discovered thus far, only about a dozen are intact; the rest are mere fragments. The scrolls include biblical commentaries, prophecy, rules for the community and parts of every book of the Hebrew Bible except Esther.

Qumran on the northwestern shore of the Dead Sea is still a matter of debate among scholars. But whether the Essenes and the Dead Sea sect are the same or just similar in some respects, one or both reached their height in the first century.[93]

The Temple Scroll, the longest of the Dead Sea Scrolls, was (according to its modern editor, Yigael Yadin) regarded by the sect as a veritable Torah of the Lord. In it God Himself gives commands as part of his original revelation to Moses. The quotations from the Bible in the Temple Scroll differ somewhat from the Masoretic text (the standard Hebrew text), from the Septuagint (an early Greek translation) and from the Samaritan Pentateuch. Apparently, the author of the Temple Scroll had a different version of the Hebrew Bible.

In another text, known as MMT (for *Miqsat Ma'aseh ha-Torah*, "Some Legal Rulings Pertaining to the Torah"),[94] the sect appears to agree with the Sadducees in a number of controversies it had with the Pharisees. With many of the documents still to be published,[95] it appears more and more likely that the Dead Sea Scrolls, as they are collectively called, reflect the thinking of more than one sect or splinter group. Several of the scrolls, such as the Testaments of Levi, Judah and Naphtali, belong to the Pseudepigrapha. Some scrolls contain apocalyptic sections, as well as messianic references. Indeed, with the cessation of prophecy, according to tradition, at the time of the destruction of the First Temple in 586 B.C.E.,[96] apocalyptic visions of the mysteries of creation and of the secrets of the end of days, in effect, replace prophetic visions. Books containing such visions have a close connection with the biblical Book of Daniel; like Daniel, they stress the impossibility of a rational solution to the problem of theodicy (explaining undeserved evil in light of a beneficent God) and the imminence of the day of salvation, to be preceded by terrible hardships, presumably reflecting the then-current historical setting. Such works had particular influence on early Christianity.

The question arises as to whether the Gnostic systems, some of which go back to the first and second centuries, are related to the collapse of the apocalyptic strains in Judaism when the Temple was destroyed in 70 C.E.* It is highly doubtful that there is any direct Jewish source for this Gnosticism (from the Greek, *gnosis*, "secret knowledge"); but some characteristic Gnostic doctrines are found in certain groups of apocalyptic first-century Jews, particularly the Essenes (or the Dead Sea sect). Gnostic-like doctrines are also found, to some degree, in such works as the first-century *Biblical Antiquities* of pseudo-Philo:[97] the dichotomy of body and soul and a disdain for the material world, a notion of esoteric

* On Gnosticism, see pages 173-179.

knowledge and an intense interest in angels and in problems of creation.

Cultural developments in Palestine

The effect of Hellenism on Palestinian Judaism cannot be denied. Whether it was as intense as in the Diaspora is a matter of scholarly controversy. Some scholars have gone so far as to suggest that we should stop differentiating Palestinian Judaism from Diaspora Judaism in this respect.[98] Admittedly, both show Greek influence, an influence that is said to be manifest at a much earlier point than has been previously thought—in fact, at least a century before the beginning of the Maccabean revolt in 168 B.C.E. Still, I believe there are differences between Palestine and the Diaspora in this respect. Let's look at some of the evidence.

The coins of the Hasmonean rulers of Palestine in the second and first centuries B.C.E. bear legends in Greek and Hebrew; those of the Herodians in the first century B.C.E. and the first century C.E. are in Greek alone—presumably because at least for commercial purposes Greek was the *lingua franca* of Palestine. Undoubtedly, the tremendous number of Greek-speaking Jews from the Diaspora who came to Jerusalem for the three annual pilgrimage festivals—Pesach (Passover), Shavuoth (Weeks) and Sukkoth (Tabernacles)—brought with them not only the Greek language but also some elements of Greek culture. In addition, the tremendous success of the Jewish proselytizing movement must have brought to Palestine many converts whose native language was Greek. Yet Greek travelers, on the whole, seem to have ignored Judea, possibly because they feared being robbed by highwaymen; they visited the coast primarily, where Jews were not concentrated.[99] Moreover, though Greek is often found in tombstone inscriptions, perhaps to deter non-Jewish passersby from molesting the graves, the level of Greek in these inscriptions is very elementary.[100]

The fact that in the year 64, Josephus, a mere youngster of 26, was chosen for an extremely important and delicate mission to the Roman emperor, presumably because he knew Greek (and perhaps because he had connections at the imperial court), is evidence that the general knowledge of Greek was not deep. Josephus himself, never one to refrain from self-praise, admits that though he labored strenuously, he was unable to acquire a thorough knowledge of Greek because of his habitual use of his native language, Aramaic. To be proficient in other languages, principally Greek, was a skill common to freedmen and even slaves, Josephus remarks, the implication being that it was not common among freeborn people.[101]

Indeed, it is clear from many sources—letters, contracts, documents, ossuary inscriptions, pseudepigrapha, Dead Sea Scrolls,

DAVID HARRIS

OSSUARIES. An ossuary—literally, a bone box—is a rectangular box, usually carved from limestone and measuring about 20 by 10 by 12 inches, in which bones were reinterred a year or so after an individual's death. The person's name was often scratched into the soft stone, frequently in Aramaic, indicating the widespread use of that language from the time of the Babylonian captivity in 586 B.C.E. until well after the Arab conquest of Palestine in about 640 C.E.

the New Testament and rabbinic works—that the predominant language of the Jews from the time of the Babylonian captivity in 586 B.C.E. until well after the Arab conquest of Palestine in 640 C.E. was not Greek, but Aramaic. Thus when Titus sought to get the Jews to surrender Jerusalem, he sent Josephus to speak with them in their "ancestral language," presumably Aramaic.[102] Again, when Paul addresses the Jews in Jerusalem he speaks not in Greek, but in Hebrew (or in Aramaic) (Acts 21:40, 22:2).

It has been suggested that Greek was the language only of the upper classes, such as the Herodian princes who were educated in Rome or Josephus; Aramaic, so the argument runs, was spoken by the uneducated, especially in rural areas. But the poor quality of the Greek on expensive ossuaries (bone depositories) from Jerusalem (presumably used by the wealthy), as well as the continued use of Aramaic by Josephus in the first century, indicates that such a distinction is not defensible.

Moreover, the archaeological evidence indicates that before the destruction of the Temple in 70 C.E., virtually all Jews refrained from any attempt at painting or sculpture, presumably in deference to a literal interpretation of the biblical prohibition against graven images (Exodus 20:4). Indeed, so great was the opposition to such art that at the outbreak of the Jewish Revolt in 66 C.E. the Jewish forces in Galilee were ordered by the Jerusalem assembly to press for the destruction of the palace of Herod Antipas in Tiberias simply because it contained representations of animals.[103] So this aspect of Hellenism does not appear to have taken hold in Judea.

Erwin R. Goodenough in his magisterial 13-volume work concluded that Christianity spread so rapidly because Judaism had already been thoroughly Hellenized.[104] But we now know that it did not spread so rapidly, certainly not at first, as compared with, for example, the later spread of Mithraism or even of Judaism itself before the destruction of the Temple.

Within Palestine were 30 Greek cities[105] where Hellenization was far advanced, as suggested by the archaeological evidence. But, remarkably, not a single Greek urban community was founded in Judea. Nor did Hellenism become deeply rooted in Samaria or Idumea. Moreover, unlike modern Jews, who live primarily in cities, only a small percentage of the Jews during the first century lived in cities such as Jerusalem (with probably fewer than 100,000 inhabitants)[106] or Caesarea on the coast (where contacts with non-Jews in commercial and governmental matters, and hence with the Greek language and culture, were more frequent). The great majority of Jews, as is clear from Josephus and rabbinic literature, were farmers, most of whom tilled very small tracts of land.

The Jews were apparently particularly numerous in Galilee, where, as we have noted, there were 204 cities and villages,[107] the smallest of which had 15,000 inhabitants[108]—giving Galilee, if Josephus is to be believed, approximately three times as many inhabitants as it has today. Not until the second century do we find Greek inscriptions in Galilean synagogues. Moreover, we must draw a distinction in degree of Hellenization between Upper and Lower Galilee. Upper Galilee is almost devoid of Greek epigraphic remains from the first and second century; the iconography is limited to menorahs, eagles and simple decorative elements. Lower Galilee, on the other hand, had several sizable urban centers that

Who Was Josephus?

Flavius Josephus (37-c. 100 C.E.)[1] is our chief source of historical information about the Jews from the period of the Maccabees (168 B.C.E.) to the
Roman destruction of the Temple (70 C.E.).

Josephus was born in Jerusalem of a distinguished priestly family. On his
mother's side, he was descended from the royal Hasmonean house.[2]

According to his own account, he showed such precocity that at the age of
14 the chief priests and the leading men of the city constantly consulted him
for information about Jewish law.[3] The years from 16 to 19, he spent gaining
personal experience, living successively as a Pharisee, a Sadducee and an
Essene, after which he became a disciple of a hermit named Bannus.[4] Finally,
he began to engage in public life, following the school of the Pharisees. When
he was only 26, by gaining the ear of the emperor Nero, Josephus succeeded
in freeing some priests who had been imprisoned in Rome.[5]

When the First Jewish Revolt against Rome began in 66 C.E., the 29-year-
old Josephus, who apparently had no previous military experience, was entrusted by the Jewish leaders with the generalship of Galilee, the most important theater of the war at that time.[6] His military career is clouded by the fact
that after a few months Josephus surrendered to the Romans[7] after all but
one of his companions had killed each other rather than be captured. Brought
before the Roman general Vespasian, Josephus, like Rabbi Yoḥanan ben Zakkai
after him,[8] predicted that Vespasian would become emperor. After the war,

were linked to the more cosmopolitan and Greek-speaking West.

It is in Lower Galilee, significantly, that Jesus spent most of his
career. The snide remarks of the later talmudic sages about first-
century Galilee and some of the clichés in the New Testament are
comments on the degree of accommodation to Hellenism in Lower
Galilee.[109] Yet, real contact with non-Jews must have been slight;
we know of only one occasion when Jesus refers to non-Jewish
practices: Gentiles, when praying, he remarks, heap up empty
phrases (Matthew 6:7).

What about literature in Greek by Jews in the first century?
Josephus' rival, Justus of Tiberias, wrote *A Chronicle of the Jewish
Kings* and *A History of the Jewish War*, neither of which has sur-
vived. Josephus grudgingly admits that Justus was not unversed in
Greek culture.[110]

Of course, the supreme example of Hellenization in literature
of a Jew from Palestine is Josephus.[111] However, he concedes that
he needed assistants to help him with the Greek of the *Jewish
War*,[112] which he originally wrote in his native Aramaic.[113] When
he did not have these assistants, as apparently was the case in

Vespasian gave Josephus lodging in his former home in Rome, as well as a pension and Roman citizenship.[9]

It was in Rome that Josephus composed his four works, the *Jewish War* (79-81 C.E.)[10]–originally written in Aramaic,[11] then translated into Greek with the help of assistants[12]–covering the period from Antiochus Epiphanes' intervention in Judea in 170 B.C.E. to the capture of Masada in 74 C.E.; the *Jewish Antiquities* (93-94 C.E.), covering the period from the creation of the world to the outbreak of the revolt against Rome; the *Life* (c. 100), the first extant autobiography from antiquity, largely a defense of his generalship in Galilee; and the treatise *Against Apion* (c. 100), a defense of Judaism against the attacks of a number of critics of the Jews.[13]

As to the reliability of Josephus, modern scholarship gives Josephus mixed grades.[14] He is generally reliable in the topography and geography of the Land of Israel, but he is far from infallible, as on-the-spot observation and archaeology have shown. As a political and military historian, especially when he is not involved personally, he is generally reliable in the instances where we can check him against other sources. But he can be a propagandist, especially in his defense of Judaism, in his appeal to pagan intellectuals and in his stance against Jewish revolutionaries. Inasmuch as almost all of classical literature is lost and inasmuch as scientific archaeology is still a new discipline, it is seldom that we are able to verify or refute Josephus in the mass of his details.

Antiquities, his style suffered considerably. Moreover, Josephus addressed his *magnum opus*, *Antiquities*, primarily to non-Jews; he believed that the entire Greek world would find it worthy of attention.[114]

In summary, Hellenization in Palestine, particularly in Upper Galilee, could hardly have been profound. The rabbis, in the talmudic tractate *Avodah Zarah* (Idol Worship), did not regard idolatry as an immediate problem. We hear of few apostates; on the contrary, there were apparently far more non-Jews who were attracted to Judaism either as proselytes or "sympathizers." Contacts with Greek culture were frequent only in the larger cities, where relatively few Jews lived. As for the alleged Greek influence on the rabbis, unlike the case in the medieval period, we know of none who distinguished himself in philosophy or who wrote any treatise in Greek; nor are there any Greek philosophical terms in the talmudic corpus. Indeed, one wonders about the Greek philosophical influence upon people who regard the obscure Oenomaus of Gadara (c. 120 C.E.) as the greatest Gentile philosopher of all time.[115]

II. The Diaspora World

The political background In the first century, the chief centers of Jewish population outside of Palestine were in Babylonia (under the Parthians), and in Syria, Asia Minor and Egypt, each of which, according to Baron's estimate, had at least a million Jews.[116] That these Jews had sunk deep roots in their environment is clear from the fact that, except for a contingent from Adiabene (in Mesopotamia), we hear of no Jews from the Diaspora joining the revolt against the Romans in 66 C.E.

In Babylonia, in the early part of the first century, we hear of two Jewish brothers, Asineus and Anileus, of very ordinary background, who established an independent robber-state[117] and even, for a time, routed the Parthians. The brothers were defeated in the year 35, however, and the Babylonians then vented their long-standing hatred on the Jews. The Jews sought refuge in Seleucia on the Tigris River, but the Syrian and Greek inhabitants there slaughtered more than 50,000 of them.[118]

In Syria, the largest Jewish community lived in Antioch, the capital of the province. There, King Seleucus Nicator had granted civic rights to the Jews in the third century B.C.E.;[119] in all probability, this meant only that they were given the privilege of organizing themselves as a community. Josephus makes a special point, however, of their numbers and wealth.[120] In particular, he notes that they had been successful in winning proselytes and "sympathizers."[121] This success undoubtedly alarmed the non-Jewish inhabitants. That the Jews in Syria were hated is clear from the fact that at the outbreak of the revolt against Rome in 66, a general uprising against the Jews occurred.[122] Only in Antioch, Sidon and Apamea were the Jews spared.[123] After the fall of Jerusalem in 70 C.E., when Titus passed through Syria on his way home, the inhabitants of Antioch entreated him to expel the Jews from their city.[124] When this petition was denied, they requested him, though unsuccessfully, to revoke the privileges of the Jews.

Already in the first century B.C.E., Cicero indicates the large number of wealthy Jews in Asia Minor by noting the huge amount of money that had been collected from them for the Temple.[125] In city after city in Asia Minor, decrees were issued during the first century B.C.E. and the first century C.E.[126] permitting the Jews to send money to the Temple, exempting them from military service, excusing them from appearing in court on the Sabbath or in the late afternoon on Friday[127] and allowing them to form corporate groups. These concessions often aroused jealousy and hatred. Although the Romans were particularly sensitive to the charge that money sent to the Temple by the Jews was draining the state of

PLATE 1. HEELBONE OF A CRUCIFIED MAN. A nail still pierces the heel of a man crucified in Jerusalem within decades of Jesus' death. The bone was found in an ossuary in a tomb. The point of the nail is curled, probably from hitting a knot in the wood when it was driven into the cross.

© ERICH LESSING

GARO NALBANDIAN

PLATE 2. OSSUARY INSCRIBED "JOSEPH BAR CAIAPHA." The inscription on this limestone ossuary, or bone box, may refer to Caiaphas, the high priest who presided at the trial of Jesus and was present when Peter and John, arrested for preaching in Solomon's Portico of the Temple, spoke before the Sanhedrin (Acts 4:6). The name is scratched in Aramaic, the common language of the time.

PLATE 3. HADRIAN. The Roman emperor Hadrian (ruled 117-138 C.E.) may have triggered the Second Jewish Revolt against Rome (132-135 C.E.), sometimes called the Bar-Kokhba revolt, when he announced his intention to build a new Roman city to be called Aelia Capitolina on the ruins of Jerusalem. When the revolt was crushed, Judea was renamed Syria-Palaestina, thousands of inhabitants were sold into slavery, the practice of Judaism was restricted and Jews were forbidden even to enter Jerusalem. This statue of the emperor was discovered by an American tourist in 1976 near Tell Shalem in Israel, perhaps the location of the headquarters for the Roman Sixth Legion.

PLATE 4. BAR-KOKHBA CAVES. When Simeon bar Kosba, known as Bar-Kokhba, led a rebellion against the Romans (132-135 C.E.), his followers fortified caves in the Judean desert as hiding places and supply depots. These were the last strongholds to fall to the besieging Romans.

PLATE 5. HILARION. This 13th-century mosaic of the hermit Hilarion, the fourth-century founder of Palestinian monasticism, is located in the Church of San Marco in Venice. A monastic life, whether lived in solitude or as part of a community, is usually based on vows of celibacy, poverty and obedience to a spiritual leader.

PLATE 6. SYNAGOGUE AT DURA-EUROPOS. Located on the Euphrates, Dura-Europos was destroyed in 256 C.E. Completed five or ten years before that, the highly decorated synagogue reflects a sea change from the Hellenistic period when paintings were rare. Above the Torah niche are a menorah, *etrog*, *lulav*, the Temple in Jerusalem and the binding of Isaac. Above a ram and a tree, Abraham holds a knife, Isaac lies on the altar and Sarah stands in a tent. All face the hand of God to the left of the tent.

PLATE 7. PILGRIM SHIP GRAFFITO. Painted some time before 335 C.E., when the area was covered by construction, this ship came to light in 1971 in the Church of the Holy Sepulchre. Typical of a small boat of the third to fourth centuries, the ship is above a Latin inscription DOMINE IVIMUS, which means, "Lord, we went." It may allude to Psalm 122 which begins, in its Latin translation, "*In domum Domini ibimus,*" or "Let us go to the house of the Lord."

PLATE 9. ARIAN BAPTISTERY AT RAVENNA. Theodoric (c. 475-526 C.E.), king of the Ostrogoths and of Italy, attempted to reestablish Arianism, an understanding of the nature of Christ and Christ's relation to God the Father, which had been declared a heresy by the Council of Nicaea in 325 C.E. Maintaining a policy of religious tolerance, Theodoric built this octagonal Arian baptistery around 500 C.E. When orthodox Christianity reestablished its dominance, a new baptistery was built and the Arian baptistery was turned into a chapel. This mosaic of the baptism of Jesus shows John the Baptist on the right, the Holy Spirit descending like a dove (Matthew 3:16; Mark 1:10; Luke 3:22; John 1:32) over a beardless Jesus and a figure on the left that may represent the spirit of the river.

PLATE 8 (left). THE HOLY WOMEN AT THE SEPULCHER. This mosaic in St. Apollinare Nuovo, a church built in Ravenna by Theodoric (c. 475-526 C.E.), shows the mother of Jesus and Mary Magdalene by the open tomb. Mosaics, the art of creating pictures or patterns from small pieces (tesserae) of stone, tile or glass, reached new heights in the Italian city of Ravenna during the fifth and sixth centuries C.E.

GARO NALBANDIAN

PLATE 10. BASILICA AT KURSI. This late fifth- or early sixth-century basilica and monastery overlooking the Sea of Galilee was built on the traditional site of the swine miracle. The story of Jesus casting demons from a man into a herd of pigs is mentioned with variations in the three Synoptic Gospels (Mark 5:1-20; Luke 8:26-39; Matthew 8:28-34). Covering four acres, the monastery complex was constructed as a hospice for pilgrims as well as a community for monks.

HERSHEL SHANKS

PLATE 11. MAR SABA. For 1,500 years monks have lived at Mar Saba in the Judean desert east of Jerusalem. One of the oldest occupied monasteries in the world, Mar Saba is still home to a small number of Greek Orthodox monks. The first monastery was built in 482 C.E. by the hermit St. Sabas (439-532 C.E.) as a place of worship for the many other anchorites who lived in caves in the surrounding cliffs. St. Sabas' mummified body is housed in the domed church. Destroyed and rebuilt over the centuries, Mar Saba's current structure was built in 1840.

money, the Roman authorities nevertheless pressured at least eight cities in Asia Minor to stop harassing their Jewish population.

The most important Jewish settlement in the Diaspora was in Egypt. Josephus tells us that Julius Caesar set up a bronze tablet in Alexandria declaring that the Jews were citizens;[128] Philo likewise speaks of Jewish citizens.[129] Nevertheless, in light of the so-called London Papyrus 1912, in which the emperor Claudius in the middle of the first century clearly contrasts the Alexandrians and the Jews and speaks of the Jews as living "in a city not their own," most scholars have concluded that the Jews possessed not citizenship but equal status as a community.[130]

The special privileges granted to the Jews, as well as the Jews' political and economic influence, aroused resentment among the Greek residents. When the Jews refused to participate in the state cults (having been granted a special privilege not to do so), they were accused of being unpatriotic.

In the year 38, the tetrarch Agrippa, who was later appointed by Caligula to be the king of Judea, visited Alexandria. The ostentatious display of his bodyguard of spearmen, decked in armor overlaid with silver and gold, aroused the envy of the Greek residents, who dressed up a lunatic with mock-royal apparel and saluted him as *Marin*, the Aramaic word for lord. This was quite clearly intended to imply that the Jews were guilty of dual loyalty and constituted themselves as a state within a state. Even though Agrippa had considerable influence with the mad Roman emperor Caligula, Flaccus, the Roman governor of Egypt, thereafter deprived the Jews of their civic rights, denounced them as foreigners and herded them into a very small area—the first ghetto in history. The mob in its fury at the Jewish status as a state within a state burned Jews alive and did not spare even their dead bodies. The Jews were accused of storing arms, presumably plotting a revolution—perhaps in conjunction with Palestinian revolutionaries. That Flaccus was recalled in disgrace and eventually executed is evidence that the Jews' influence with the powers-that-be in Rome was still strong, but not strong enough to have prevented the massacre at the outset.[131]

Shortly after this incident, the Alexandrian Jews sent a delegation, headed by Philo, to the emperor Caligula in Rome to ask him to reassert the traditional Jewish rights granted by the Ptolemies and confirmed by Julius Caesar and Augustus.[132] The opponents of the Jews also sent a delegation to Rome, headed by the grammarian and intellectual Apion. Here, as Victor Tcherikover has aptly remarked, the "Jewish question," for the first time in history, was discussed before a high tribunal.[133] Apion's argument was that the Jews were unpatriotic, since they did not pay the honors due the emperor. Philo, in his treatise, *Legatio ad Gaium*, describes the ridicule which the emperor poured upon the Jewish delegation. Shortly thereafter, however, Caligula was assassinated; and when factional war was renewed between the Jews and their opponents, the new emperor, Claudius, issued an edict reaffirming the civic rights of the Jews.[134]

When the Jewish Revolt against Rome broke out in Palestine in the year 66, a second major eruption of violence against Jews occurred in Alexandria.[135] When a mob of Greeks seized three Jews with the intention of burning them alive, the whole Jewish community rose to their rescue. In the resulting riot, ruthlessly put down by the Roman governor, Tiberius Julius Alexander—a nephew of Philo and an apostate Jew—50,000 Jews were said to have been massacred.[136] The fact that the Romans were not without casualties would seem to indicate that at least some Jews were armed; and the fury of the Roman assault, which knew no pity even for infants, would seem to indicate that the Jews fought tenaciously. As for the Greek mob, so intense was its hatred that considerable effort was required to tear them from the corpses. The date of the massacre may be significant; it coincided with the outbreak of the revolt against Rome in Palestine. One of the reasons for the viciousness with which the Romans crushed the Jews may have been to assure that they would not assist the Jews of Palestine.

Rome too was a major center of Jewish population, although it was not so large as Alexandria. As early as 59 B.C.E., Cicero remarks—to be sure with the exaggeration of a lawyer defending his client—how numerous the Jews in Rome are, how they stick together and how influential they are in informal assemblies.[137] Julius Caesar, in return for the aid the Jews of Palestine and Egypt had given him during the civil war against Pompey, conferred many special privileges on the Jews, as we have already noted. According to Suetonius, it was the Jews above all who in 44 B.C.E. mourned Caesar's death, flocking to his funeral pyre for several successive nights.[138] Augustus not only renewed his granduncle's edicts, but he added the additional privilege that if the monthly distribution of money or grain to the populace happened to fall on a Sabbath, the distributors were to reserve the Jews' portion for the following day.[139]

Especially in the reign of Tiberius (14-37 C.E.), do we find Jewish influence in high places. The Jewish king Agrippa—later to be the key figure in arranging the accession of Claudius—and his mother Berenice were unusually influential with the Roman royal family.[140] Agrippa's son (Agrippa II) was actually brought up in Claudius' household. Agrippa II's sister, also named Berenice, later lived in Rome as the mistress of the emperor Titus; it was even said that he promised to marry her (she was 12 years older than he, had been married three times, was the mother of two children and was reputed to have had an incestuous relationship with her brother).[141] Eventually, however, apparently bowing to popular pressure, Titus sent her from Rome, "against her will and his own."[142]

During the reign of Claudius' successor, Nero (54-68 C.E.), a Jewish actor, Aliturus, was a special favorite at court.[143] Nero's wife, Poppea Sabina, was a "God-fearer."[144]

The economic background

Egypt was by far the most important Roman province because it functioned as a granary, the chief source of food for the Roman army as well as for the masses of Rome itself. Naturally, Alexandria was the chief outlet for the Egyptian grain export. Within two generations of its founding by Alexander the Great in 332 B.C.E., Alexandria displaced Athens as the leading commercial and cultural center of the Mediterranean. As noted above, Alexandria in the first century was also the largest Jewish community in the world, with an estimated Jewish population of 180,000.[145] It was, in effect, the New York City of its day, with Jews constituting 30 to 40 percent of the population; they lived in all five sections of the city, although they were concentrated particularly in two of them.

In his description of the devastation wrought by the pogrom of 38 C.E., Philo gives us a valuable picture of the economic life of the Jews: "The tradespeople had lost their stocks; and no one, husbandman, shipman, merchant, artisan, was allowed to practice his usual business."[146] Under the Ptolemies, the economy had been, in effect, a kind of state socialism very closely controlled by the ruler; after 31 B.C.E., when the Romans won control of Egypt, the path was opened for individual initiative. Apparently the Jews took full advantage of this opportunity.

The reference to the craftsmen in the passage quoted above is further elaborated by a famous passage in the Talmud,[147] which states that the seating in the great synagogue in Alexandria was by occupation—specifically goldsmiths, silversmiths, blacksmiths, metalworkers and weavers. Thus, when a poor man entered the synagogue he recognized the members of his craft and on applying for employment obtained a livelihood for himself and his family.

Alexandrian Jewish artisans had a reputation for great skill; the rabbinic sages sent to Alexandria for specialists in baking, as well as in preparing incense.[148] In addition, the doors for one of the gates of the Temple court were prepared by Alexandrian craftsmen.[149] Craftsmen from Alexandria were even imported to repair a cymbal and a bronze mortar in the sanctuary of the Temple.[150]

The great majority of Jews who came to Egypt from Palestine

had been farmers; it is not surprising therefore that many continued that occupation in Egypt as well.

Under the Ptolemies, many Jews served in the army. In four cases,[151] they reached the rank of commander-in-chief. Under the Romans, however, we hear of no Jewish soldiers, nor were there Jewish tax collectors, policemen or bureaucrats, as there had been under the Ptolemies. We hear of only one Jew who attained high rank, a governor of Egypt; and he was an apostate.[152] Perhaps Jews were not trusted with such positions because of the revolutionary movements that surfaced in Palestine early in the first century.

The religious background   Within two generations of the founding of the city of Alexandria in 332 B.C.E., Greek displaced Hebrew and Aramaic as the language of the city Jews. This is clear from inscriptions and from their readiness to adopt the translation of the Pentateuch from Hebrew into Greek (the Septuagint). Even the overwhelming majority of names of Jews preserved in papyri are Greek.

Nevertheless, the masses of the Jews remained true to their Jewish religious practices. Philo affirms this when he states that although all people are tenacious of their own customs, the Jewish nation is particularly so.[153]

Philo records the generosity with which the Alexandrian Jews, presumably of all classes, contributed to the Temple in Jerusalem.[154] Josephus also confirms the loyalty with which Jews throughout the world contributed to the Temple.[155] The Mishnah tells us that Egyptian Jews gave relief funds to the poor of Judea during the sabbatical year through the poorman's tithe.[156]

The Jews of Rome also had a reputation for piety. At the end of the first century B.C.E., Horace pokes fun at their readiness to accept everything on faith as if it were proverbial: "Let the Jew Apella believe it!"[157] He likewise alludes to the strictness with which the Jews observe the Sabbath: "Today is the thirtieth, a Sabbath. Would you affront the circumcised Jews?"[158] Horace's contemporaries, the poets Tibullus[159] and Ovid,[160] likewise refer to Sabbath observance by Jews. The notion that the Jews fasted on the Sabbath, found in several pagan writers,[161] may have arisen from a statement of Strabo that confused the Jewish abstinence from work on that day with abstinence from food.[162]

On the other hand, a number of sources indicate that Egyptian Jews may not have been so intensely religious.[163] We have no reference to any academies in Egypt for the study of the written or Oral Torah parallel to those in Palestine. In contrast to Palestine, where we hear that Rabbi Joshua ben Gamla established a system of universal elementary education,[164] we hear nothing of such education in Egypt. Philo speaks only of Sabbath schools intended for adults, where the four cardinal virtues, so prominent in Greek culture, were taught.[165]

Despite the proximity of Egypt to Palestine, we hear of few rabbis going to Egypt and few Egyptian Jews going to Palestine. Even Philo, wealthy as he was, made a pilgrimage to Jerusalem only once, so far as we know.[166]

In apparent violation of the Torah (Deuteronomy 12:13-14), the high priest Onias, after fleeing from Palestine, erected in Leontopolis in Egypt a replica of the Jerusalem Temple at which sacrifices were offered.[167] This temple was closed down on orders from Vespasian in the year 73 C.E., because of suspicions that it was a center of Jewish revolutionary activity.[168] Philo speaks of "Yom Kippur Jews," that is, "those who never act religiously in the rest of their life," but who are zealously pious on that day.[169] He also attacks intermarriage as leading to the abandonment of the worship of God.[170]

There are still other indications of assimilation in Egypt. For example, a Jewish inscription dating from the first century[171] speaks of the shadowy region of Lethe and the house of Hades; such terms are not merely poetic terms for death—they had significance in contemporaneous Greek religion. And, despite the clear prohibition in the Bible against interest on loans to Jews (Exodus 22:25; Deuteronomy 23:20), several papyri recording loans between Jews, including two dated to 10 B.C.E., specify interest.[172] Another papyrus, dating to 13 B.C.E., is a deed of divorce dissolving the marriage of a Jewish couple;[173] it is drawn up in the usual form of Greco-Egyptian divorces as known from other papyri and gives full equality to the wife in language at complete variance with both the Bible and the Talmud, where the husband alone is permitted to initiate a divorce.

According to the Talmud, Alexandria had a *Beth Din* (a Jewish religious court).[174] Various papyri, however, indicate the Jews relied instead on Gentile courts; this was true in rural as well as urban Egypt. Here we have a clear violation of the talmudic declaration by Rabbi Tarfon, in the generation after the destruction of the Temple, forbidding one Jew to summon another before a Gentile court, even when its law is the same as Jewish law.[175]

Philo himself is at variance with Jewish law, as set forth by the Palestinian rabbis, when he declares, for example, that unmarried daughters who have no fixed dowries share equally in the inheritance with the sons.[176]

We must say something about the position of women in the Diaspora. Again, our evidence is meager. Philo, who was the head of the Alexandrian Jewish community, has an extremely deroga-

Who Was Philo?

Philo was a Jewish philosopher and theologian who lived in Alexandria during the first century C.E. His extant works provide considerable information regarding Jewish life during this time.

Little is known of his life. Even the date of his birth is uncertain, though we may guess that he was born sometime between 15 and 10 B.C.E.[1] To judge from his frequent citations of many classical Greek authors, he must have had an excellent education in the liberal arts and was particularly well versed in music.[2] As we can see from his frequent allusions, he often attended the theater, was a keen observer of boxing contests, attended chariot races and participated in costly suppers with their lavish entertainment.

He tells us nothing of his Jewish education, which must have been weak, since he apparently knew little or no Hebrew.[3] Moreover, the only Jewish schools of which he speaks met on the Sabbath for lectures on ethics.[4] That Philo was personally observant, at least as he understood the law, seems clear from his vigorous denunciation of the extreme allegorists who deviated from the traditional observance on the ground that the ceremonial laws are only a parable.[5]

After the popular outbreak against the Jews in Alexandria in 38 C.E., Philo led an embassy of Jews to the Roman emperor Gaius Caligula, in opposition to a delegation headed by the anti-Jewish Apion, who charged the Jews with being unpatriotic because they did not worship the emperor.[6] This embassy, the subject of an essay by Philo (*Legatio ad Gaium* [*Embassy to Gaius*]), ended in failure, but soon thereafter Caligula was assassinated.

Philo's works may be classified into three groups:

1. Twenty-five scriptural essays and homilies based on specific verses and

tory view of women, if we may judge from his comment that the reason Moses commanded the Israelites to take a perfect male sheep rather than a female is that the female is nothing more than an imperfect male.[177] Again, we may take note of contempt for women in his comment on Genesis 25:5-6: "The sons of the women and those of inferior descent are certain to be called female and unvirile, for which reason they are little admired as great ones."[178] Furthermore, we may note his sharp attack on women's wiles in his explanation of why the Essenes do not marry, namely that "a wife is a selfish creature, excessively jealous and an adept at beguiling the morals of her husband and seducing him by her continued impostures."[179]

The success of Jewish proselytism And yet, a kind of spiritual transfusion was taking place in this period. Side by side with defections, there were apparently numerous additions to the Jewish fold.[180] Philo's remark that Jews com-

topics of the Pentateuch, especially the Book of Genesis. The most important of these essays is *Legum Allegoriae* (*Allegories of the Laws*), an allegorical exposition of chapters 2 and 3 of Genesis, and *De Specialibus Legibus* (*On the Special Laws*), which is his exposition of various laws in the Pentateuch, especially the Ten Commandments.

2. General philosophical and religious essays. The most important of these are *Quod Omnis Probus Liber Sit* (*That Every Good Man Is Free*), in which he proves the Stoic paradox that only the wise man is free; *De Aeternitate Mundi* (*On the Eternity of the World*), in which he proves that the world is uncreated and indestructible; and *De Providentia* (*On Providence*), in which he argues that God is providential in his concern for the world.

3. Essays on contemporary subjects. These include *De Vita Contemplativa* (*On the Contemplative Life*), in which he praises the ascetic Jewish sect of the Therapeutae; *Hypothetica* (*Apology for the Jews*), a fragmentary work that has a number of parallels with Josephus' essay *Against Apion* (here Philo answers the charges of critics of Judaism through a defense of the Torah); *In Flaccum* (*Against Flaccus*), in which he describes the maladministration of Egypt by the Roman governor Flaccus; and *Legatio ad Gaium*, which, as we have noted above, deals with Philo's unsuccessful embassy to the Roman emperor Gaius Caligula.

As to Philo's reliability as a historian, E. Mary Smallwood has recently argued that Philo has greater reliability than Josephus when they discuss the same events, despite the fact that Philo is primarily a philosopher and a theologian rather than a historian.[7] This is particularly true where Philo is closer in time to the events, as, for example, when he discusses the procuratorship of Pontius Pilate.

prise half of the human race,[181] even though an exaggeration, must allude to their extraordinary success in proselytism. Indeed, he condemns those who do not convert as "enemies of the Jewish nation and of every place."[182] He significantly ascribes to a non-Jew, Petronius, the view that the Jews gladly receive proselytes of other races no less than they welcome their own countrymen.[183]

Josephus also remarks on the gracious welcome extended by Jews to all who wish to adopt their laws.[184] He states that many Greeks (speaking of Greeks throughout the Mediterranean world) agreed to adopt the laws of Judaism; some remained faithful, while others reverted to their previous way of life.[185] In particular, he refutes the charge of the renowned first-century B.C.E. rhetorician Apollonius Molon that the Jews refused admission to "persons with preconceived ideas about God."[186] In a sweeping comment on the success of the proselytizing movement, Josephus declares that "the masses have long since shown a keen desire to adopt our religious observances; and there is not one city, Greek or barbarian, . . . to which our customs have not spread."[187]

The zeal with which the Jews sought proselytes in the first century and the enthusiasm, in turn, with which the proselytes practiced their newly acquired Judaism, had apparently become proverbial, as we may discern from Jesus' pronouncement (Matthew 23:15): "Woe to you, Scribes and Pharisees, hypocrites, for you traverse sea and land to make a single proselyte, and when he becomes a proselyte, you make him twice as much a child of Gehenna as yourselves."[188] Though the verse may be an exaggeration, it must have some element of truth in order to be credible. If Matthew was living in Antioch[189] where, as Josephus tells us, the Jews had been constantly attracting multitudes of Greeks to their religious ceremonies,[190] the verse reflects a real situation.

Moreover, a number of Greek and Latin writers allude to the eagerness of the Jews to receive proselytes. At the end of the first century B.C.E., Horace refers to the zeal of Jewish missionary activity as if it were well known: "We are much more numerous, and like the Jews we shall force you to join our throng."[191] Horace is, of course, a satirist; but his satire would fall flat if there were no basis for his obvious exaggeration.

In the middle of the first century, the philosopher Seneca, one of the emperor Nero's chief advisers, writes caustically: "The customs of this accursed race [the Jews] have gained such influence that they are now received throughout the world. The vanquished have given laws to their victors."[192]

At the beginning of the second century, Tacitus bitterly remarks that "the worst ones among other peoples, renouncing their ancestral religions, always kept sending (*congerebant*) tribute and contributing to Jerusalem, thereby increasing the wealth of the Jews."[193] The use of the imperfect tense, *congerebant*, indicates that the contributions were continuous and repeated.

A similar hostility is seen in Juvenal, Tacitus' contemporary, who, after deriding those who sympathize with Judaism by observing the Sabbath and avoiding pork, denounces their children who worship clouds and a heavenly divinity, undergo circumcision and observe all the laws of the Pentateuch. Like Tacitus, Juvenal denounces such converts as renegades from the Roman tradition.[194]

One somewhat speculative theory to explain the widespread success of Jewish proselytism suggests that the Jews absorbed the far-flung Phoenician settlements, which seem to have disappeared in the first century. When the Phoenician mother-cities of Tyre and Sidon on the Syrian coast and the chief daughter-city Carthage in North Africa lost their independence, the Phoenician settlements throughout the world were, in effect, an orphaned diaspora. Their people may have been attracted to Judaism because of the parallel with the kindred Jewish Diaspora. Scholars have long been puzzled by the disappearance of the Phoenicians in the first century; Nahum Slouschz has suggested that Phoenician owners of Jewish slaves may have been exposed to Jewish customs and ideas and may easily have passed over into Jewry, since they had practiced circumcision for ages.[195] Consistent with this theory is the statement of Rav in the third century that "From Tyre to Carthage they know Israel and their Father in Heaven."[196]

The inhabitants of Syria, speaking a kindred language (Aramaic), were similarly attracted to Judaism. Thus, on the eve of the Jewish revolt against Rome, the inhabitants of Damascus, according to Josephus, were fired with a determination to kill the Jews but were afraid of their own wives, "who, with few exceptions, had all become converts to the Jewish religion; and so their efforts were mainly directed to keeping the secret from them [their wives]."[197] That women, in particular, were attracted to Judaism may be due largely to the fact that they did not have to undergo circumcision, a major operation for an adult male; but it may also be due to the relatively more elevated and respected position of women in the Jewish community.

The most remarkable success of the proselytizing movement during this period took place in Adiabene in Mesopotamia in the early part of the first century.[198] According to Josephus, whose lengthy account is confirmed, in large part, in rabbinic sources,[199] a certain Jewish merchant named Ananias visited the Adiabenian king's wives and taught them to worship God after the manner of the Jews. Significantly, it is the women upon whom the emissary had his greatest impact. Through these women, Ananias was brought to the attention of the heir to the throne, Izates; Izates too was won over to Jewish practices, though without actually converting.[200] After becoming king, Izates was determined to become a proselyte, but his mother, Helena, who in the meantime had converted to Judaism, and the Jewish merchant Ananias urged him not to, as his subjects would not tolerate the rule of a Jew. Another Jew, named Eleazar, however, urged him to undergo circumcision. Izates, together with his older brother Monobazus and his kinsmen, were circumcised.[201] The piety of the Adiabenian converts is stressed by both Josephus[202] and the Talmud.[203] Josephus also notes that kinsmen of Monobazus, who succeeded his brother, distinguished themselves for valor on behalf of the Jews in their great war against Rome.[204]

Apparently proselytism was very much in evidence in Rome also. The most important rhetorician and literary critic of the Augustan Age next to Dionysius of Halicarnassus was a convert to Judaism, Caecilius of Calacte.[205] As early as 139 B.C.E., the *praetor peregrinus* (the Roman magistrate in charge of administering justice to foreigners) banished the Jews from Rome "because they attempted to transmit their sacred rites to the Romans."[206] In the year 19 C.E. we are told that, because of the deception practiced by some Jewish embezzlers on a noble Roman lady who had become a proselyte, the emperor Tiberius ordered the entire Jewish community to leave.[207] (It is hard to believe that Tiberius, who was so careful to adhere to the letter of the law, would have expelled all the Jews without due process; apparently the expulsion order was the work of his adviser, Sejanus.[208] In any case, the expulsion, if it occurred at all, must have been brief, since we find the Jews back again within a short time after Sejanus was dismissed.) In the reign of Domitian (95 C.E.), Flavius Clemens (a cousin of the emperor) and his wife (the emperor's niece) were charged, together with many others, with having "drifted" into the practices of the Jews.

All this is strong evidence of the success of Jewish missionary activity in Rome.

One of the great puzzles of the massive proselytizing movement is how to explain its existence when we do not know the name of a single Jewish missionary (except Paul).[209]

Perhaps the Septuagint, the earliest translation of the Pentateuch—from Hebrew to Greek—played an important role. The first-century pseudo-Longinus, the most celebrated literary critic after Aristotle, not only paraphrases parts of the first chapter of Genesis (specifically 1:3 and 1:9-10), but cites it as an example of the most sublime style.[210] The fact that this passage refers to the "lawgiver of the Jews" without bothering to identify him by name would seem to indicate that the author expected his readers to know that the reference is to Moses.

In addition to proselytes, we hear of some people who adopted some Jewish practices without actually converting to Judaism.[211] Philo refers to the widespread observance of the Sabbath and of the Day of Atonement (Yom Kippur) among non-Jews.[212] Eleven passages in Acts (10:2,22,35, 13:16,26,43,50, 16:14, 17:4,17, 18:7) referring to "fearers of God" and "reverencers of God" are usually regarded as alluding to this group. Josephus probably refers to them when he remarks that many Jewish customs have found their way to the cities; he declares that the masses have been greatly attracted to Jewish observances, and that there is no city where the Jewish Sabbath—as well as the fasts, the lighting of lamps and the dietary laws—is not observed.[213] The fact that Josephus singles out specific observances shows that he is referring not to proselytes but to "sympathizers."

Additional evidence includes the name "Sambathion," apparently given to children born on the Sabbath, which appears in a number of Egyptian papyri[214]–five of them dating from the first century. The name apparently was popular among adherents of a sect of Sabbath-observers, since their kinsmen seem to be non-Jewish and the papyri were found in villages that, so far as we know, were not Jewish. It is striking that no other Hebrew name was ever borrowed by non-Jews. The most likely explanation for the choice of name is that the parents were Sabbath-observers.

Suetonius tells of a Sabbath-observer, the grammarian Diogenes, who, in the first century, used to lecture every Sabbath in Rhodes.[215] The Roman satirist Petronius, in the middle of the first century, distinguishes between those who worship the "pig-god [presumably those who observe the dietary laws] and clamor in the ears of high heaven,"[216] on the one hand, and those who are circumcised and who observe the Sabbath according to the law, on the other. The distinction is between sympathizers and full Jews. Epictetus, the Greek Stoic philosopher of the latter part of the first century, asks "Why do you act the part of a Jew when you are a Greek?" He then adds: "Whenever we see a man halting between two faiths we are in the habit of saying, 'He is not a Jew, he is only acting the part.' But when he adopts the attitude of mind of the man who has been baptized and has made his choice, then he both is a Jew in fact and is called one."[217] The fact that Epictetus uses the word "whenever" and that he cites this as an example to illustrate a point in a popular exposition of philosophy would seem to indicate that he is describing a frequent occurrence, one which is actually proverbial. He is clearly pointing to a distinction between the part-Jew and the full Jew.

Recent archaeological discoveries provide the final bit of evidence. In 1976 two Greek inscriptions were found at Aphrodisias in Asia Minor, dating apparently from the third century.[218] One lists donors with clearly Jewish names; at the end is the phrase, "and those who are God-fearers (*theosebeis*)"; this is followed by a list of clearly Greek or Greco-Roman names. A second inscription lists a number of donors who are Jews (as we can tell from their names), followed by the names of two proselytes and two "God-fearers." One of the inscriptions mentions a *patella*, which may refer to a soup kitchen or to some kind of dish for distributing food, to which the donors on the list may have contributed. Indeed, for those who were poverty-stricken, the food may have been one of the attractions to Judaism, or at any rate to the synagogue.

Some scholars argue that these God-fearers are merely Gentiles who befriended the Jews.[219] The existence of a distinct class of sympathizers in the third century seems, however, to be confirmed by a passage in the Jerusalem Talmud,[220] which quotes a third-century Palestinian rabbi as saying that in the time of the Messiah only Gentiles who had nothing to do with the Jews during their bitter past would *not* be permitted to convert to Judaism, but that those "Heaven-fearers" (*yirei shamayim*) who shared the tribulations of Israel would be accepted as full proselytes, with the emperor Antoninus at their head.[221]

This evidence of course relates to the third century, not the first century. But since we find a similar term, "God-fearer," in Acts, it seems most reasonable to conclude that a class of God-fearers existed in the first century also. This seems confirmed by a passage in Juvenal (c.55-c. 140) where he differentiates true proselytes from sympathizers (he uses the term *metuentem*, "fearer") who observe the Sabbath; the latter are not yet full-fledged Jews.[222]

The cultural background   As we have noted, within two generations after the founding of Alexandria, Hebrew and Aramaic virtually disappear from the papyri and are replaced by Greek. We may guess that the translation of the Pentateuch from Hebrew into Greek, generally dated about 270 B.C.E., was undertaken at least as much for the sake of the Jewish community as for the sake of Ptolemy II Philadelphus' request to have it in his library (the reason given in the Letter of Aristeas).[223] The Jews of Alexandria annually celebrated the date of the completion of this translation (the Septuagint) as a holiday and regarded it as perfect.[224]

The greatest representative of Alexandrian Jewry, Philo, possessed little or no knowledge of Hebrew, which he regarded as a "barbarian" (that is, foreign) language.[225] If he had known Hebrew he would surely not have claimed that the Greek of the Septuagint corresponded verbatim with the original.[226] If he had known Hebrew he would surely not have commented on the significance of the addition of the Greek letter *rho* to Sarai's name (*Sara* in the Septuagint) to form Sarah (*Sarra*);[227] instead we would expect him to comment on the substitution of the Hebrew letter *heh* for the Hebrew letter *yod* (*Sarai* to *Sarah*).

Philo mentions a wide range of Greek writers, especially the epic and dramatic poets; he shows an intimate acquaintance with the techniques of the Greek rhetorical schools;[228] and he exhibits an extraordinary knowledge of the theory and practice of music.[229] On the other hand, he says nothing about his Jewish education, nor does he mention any rabbis by name, though the great Hillel and Shammai were his contemporaries in Palestine. When he describes Moses' education, he tells us that Moses learned arithmetic, geometry and music from Egyptian teachers, while he studied the rest of the seven liberal arts with teachers imported from Greece[230]– but he tells us nothing about Moses' Jewish education. Clearly, for Philo, the liberal arts, rather than the Torah, are the stepping stones to the highest study, which he declares to be philosophy,[231] since it is through philosophy that man, mortal though he may be, is rendered immortal.[232]

Jews, or at least those of the upper classes who could afford it, were apparently eager to enter their children in Greek *gymnasia*, which were dedicated to various pagan deities whose busts adorned them. The athletic contests in which the students participated took place at pagan religious festivals. Philo himself avidly watched boxing,[233] wrestling[234] and racing;[235] indeed, much of the imagery in his works is taken from athletics. For alumni, the *gymnasium* was a social center, the equivalent of a modern country club. It must have been a tremendous blow for these wealthy and ambitious Jews when the emperor Claudius in his rescript of 41 C.E. expelled the Jews from the games presided over by the *gymnasiarchs*, which, in effect, meant exclusion from the *gymnasia*.[236]

The Palestinian rabbis forbade attendance at theaters because of their association with idol worship[237]–the plays were performed only at festivals of the gods. And yet Philo remarks that he has often been to the theater.[238]

We know of one Jewish playwright, named Ezekiel, who apparently lived in the first century B.C.E. and who wrote a tragedy called *The Exodus*, dealing with Moses and the Exodus from Egypt, with the intention of showing that Jews also had heroic subjects for tragedy and that they could present them in the best style of Euripides, the favorite playwright of the era. Unfortunately, only fragments of Ezekiel's tragedy survive.

Undoubtedly, the most important and most influential cultural achievement of the Hellenistic Jews was the philosophy of Philo, who, largely through the efforts of the late Harry Wolfson,[239] is now regarded as a major philosopher in the Western tradition. Philo was the first in a long series of thinkers–Jewish, Christian and Muslim–who attempted to synthesize faith and reason. Thus, the history of Christian philosophy begins not with a Christian but with a Jew, Philo, an older contemporary of Paul. The Church itself preserved the numerous treatises of Philo still extant; on the other hand, Philo is not cited by a single Jewish writer (except briefly by Josephus) until the 16th century.

Scholars have long debated whether Philo is a Greek in Jewish clothing or a Jew in Greek clothing. Using a kind of literary psychoanalysis, Wolfson concludes that Philonic Judaism is really a derivative of Pharisaic Judaism.[240] However, the very fact that Philo asks how the Greek philosophers could have arrived at the truth without direct revelation[241] implies that the Greeks did have the truth. Philo's twofold answer is that either the Greeks borrowed from the Bible or that philosophy itself was a divine gift to the Greeks to enable them to discover by reason and by the senses what the Jews had learned through revelation.

Because Socrates and Plato were his ideals, Philo converts Moses into an anti-Sophist Socrates-like figure whose speech impediment is transformed into a disdain for sophistic rhetoric.[242] Philo's cosmological proof for the existence of God is derived from Plato's *Timaeus*. With the help of Plato, Philo resolves the seeming discrepancy between the first two chapters of Genesis in their accounts of creation.[243] The first chapter, Philo tells us, describes the creation of Platonic universals, forms or ideas; the second chapter describes the creation of particulars. (In the Greek—the only version of the Bible Philo knew—Genesis 1:2 says that the earth was "unseen"; from this, Philo deduced, in accordance with Plato, that prior to the visible world there existed an invisible world.) Platonic philosophy can also be seen in Philo's explanation of why God did not give the Torah to Abraham: because Abraham actually observed a higher form of law, of which the *Nomos* (the Septuagint's translation of the word Torah) was only a copy.[244] Here Philo paves the way for the Christian view (cf. Galatians 3:19) that the Torah is inferior to the higher law built into nature, which, according to most Christian theologians, was reaffirmed by Christianity when it abrogated the inferior law.

Philo was obviously disturbed by the thought that God, who is perfect form, should have created lowly matter. To explain this, Philo postulates the intervention of a mediator, the Logos, a term he inherited from the pre-Socratic philosophers. He terms this Logos "the idea of ideas,"[245] "the first-begotten son of the uncreated Father" and a "second God,"[246] "the man of God."[247] Concepts like these paved the way for the notion of the God-man, as well as the intermediary between God and man reflected in Christian theology.

Philo is original, however, in enunciating the doctrine that God is unknowable in his essence, as well as unnameable and ineffable, and in his insistence on an individual Providence who can suspend the laws of nature, rather than, as with the Stoics, a universal Providence who is himself subject to the unchanging laws of nature. He is likewise original in postulating a great chain of being held together by the Logos.[248]

Although Philo speaks disparagingly of the Greek mysteries as humbug and buffoonery[249] (perhaps, we may guess, because they were attracting Jews in sizable numbers in Alexandria), he clearly sees in Judaism elements of a superior mystery cult. He was obviously influenced by non-Jewish ideas (Wolfson to the contrary notwithstanding).

In a rare autobiographical comment, Philo tells us he himself was initiated into the Greater Mysteries of Judaism.[250] He distinguishes between the Greater and Lesser Mysteries; he refers to Moses as one who had been instructed in all the mysteries of his priestly duties;[251] plainly, Philo is adopting terminology from the Eleusinian Mysteries of Demeter and Persephone. When he talks of a "corybantic frenzy," he evokes the image of the Corybantes, the companions of the earth goddess Cybele, who followed her with wild dances and music.[252] His casual use of the mystic oxymoron "sober intoxication"[253] betokens a borrowing from the spirit of the mystery cults, as does his repeated use of the mystic *enthousiasmos* (having God within one).[254]

In his attitude toward marriage, Philo adopted an ascetic stance hardly consistent with the mainstream of Judaism. In a passage recalling Paul's "better to marry than to burn" (1 Corinthians 7:9), he says that the institution of marriage was merely a means for perpetuating the human race.[255] Elsewhere he remarks that Moses participated in it merely for the lawful begetting of children.[256] Many passages show how much he prized everlasting virginity.[257] His high praise for such ascetic groups as the Essenes[258] and the Therapeutae (a Jewish sect in Egypt with many similarities to the Essenes)[259] confirms this attitude.

In the first century, Judaism was at a high point both in numbers and in influence, in Palestine as well as in the Diaspora. Were it not for the disastrous results of the revolts against Roman rule—between 66-70 C.E. in Judea, between 115-117 C.E. in Cyrene and elsewhere, and between 132-135 C.E. in Palestine—and for the rise of one of its versions called Christianity, Judaism might well have conquered the world. On the other hand, there were many "Judaisms" during this period. Who could have predicted which would have prevailed?

The "what-if's" of history

T W O

The Life of
Jesus

E . P . S A N D E R S

W HAT CAME TO BE KNOWN AS CHRISTIANITY, A NEW RELIGION
that would spread throughout the world, began in a
very modest way, among the followers of Jesus of
Nazareth, a Jewish prophet, teacher and healer. Jesus lived from
approximately 4 B.C.E. to 30 C.E. He came to be regarded as the
Messiah by his followers—the anointed one whom many Jews expected to come and to restore Israel. "Anointed" is *meshiaḥ* in
Hebrew and *christos* in Greek, whence the English words "messiah," "Christ" and "Christianity." At an early date, within about
15 years of Jesus' death, some Greek-speaking Christians began to
use the title "anointed" as if it were a proper name, and thus Jesus
became "Jesus Christ" or "Christ Jesus." Christians have regarded
him as the inaugurator of a new era. By the sixth century after his
birth, they had begun to date events either B.C. (Before Christ) or
A.D., *Anno Domini* (in the year of our Lord). It is now customary
in many circles to use the abbreviations B.C.E. and C.E., "Before
the Common Era" and "Common Era," since these allow non-Christians to employ the dates of the Christian division of time. Thus 4
B.C.E. is the same year as 4 B.C., but put in terms acceptable to all.

That Jesus was born before the beginning of the era that starts
with his birth is one of the minor curiosities of history. In the sixth
century a Scythian monk who was resident in Rome, Dionysius

Exiguus, introduced a calendar based on the division before Christ and after Christ, but he miscalculated the year of the death of Herod the Great, putting it four years too late. Since Jesus was born near the time of Herod's death, his birth was also misdated by four years. When subsequent research established the correct year of Herod's death, the calendar was not revised: year 1 was kept where Dionysius had placed it, and both Herod's death and Jesus' birth were dated to 4 B.C.E.

The story of Jesus is found in the four canonical Gospels in the New Testament. These books were written anonymously, but in the second century Christians began to attribute them to four men: Matthew and John (Jesus' followers) and Mark and Luke (early Christians, but not direct disciples of Jesus).[1] Early Christians wrote many other accounts of Jesus, some of which survive as the apocryphal gospels ("hidden," or "secret," noncanonical gospels). Historians have repeatedly studied these in the hope of finding solid information about Jesus, but without much success. The Gospel of Thomas, which is known from a manuscript found at Nag Hammadi in Upper Egypt, has interesting versions of some of the sayings of Jesus that are also in the canonical Gospels, and it is possible that in a few cases its version is earlier than the one in the New Testament. In general, however, our knowledge of Jesus is limited to the information in the New Testament.[2]

A few non-Christian authors who wrote in the first or second century mention Jesus, but only as the originator of a movement that came to their attention. They add no new information to that given in the Gospels.[3]

Although the canonical Gospels contain almost the only worthwhile information about Jesus, they are by no means straightforward histories or biographies in the modern sense. The material in them was passed on orally for some years, being modified in the process. Further, the authors of the Gospels were more interested in theological truth than in bare historical accuracy, and their theological concerns sometimes shaped the material.

Even if the Gospels were academic histories, full of well-researched information, we would still be faced with problems in describing the life of Jesus. They do not provide us with a simple, consistent portrait of him. Moreover, there are large gaps—things we would like to know about which the Gospels say little or nothing. They tell us virtually nothing, for example, about Jesus' appearance and upbringing, only the name of his village and the names of his parents.

On the other hand, if we are content with a broad outline, we do know a lot about his life and teaching. Let us begin by considering the kind of man he was.

The Jesus who exercises the greatest hold on the public imagination is the Jesus of the Sermon on the Mount (Matthew 5-7). This is the Jesus who blessed the poor in spirit and the meek, who told his followers to "turn the other cheek" and to pray for their persecutors. This portrait of Jesus has served to bolster social and ecclesiastical reform. It supports criticism of those who are preoccupied by worldly concerns, and it helps shape the conscience of countless individuals who are moved by Jesus' example to examine themselves and moderate their behavior.

But we can also find numerous other miniportraits in the Gospels. Around the turn of the present century, Christianity was surprised and shocked by the discovery of the eschatological Jesus, the wild-eyed proclaimer that the end (in Greek, *eschaton*) was near, who predicted that

> "The sun will be darkened, and the moon will not give its light, and the stars will be falling from heaven, and the powers in the heavens will be shaken. And then they will see the Son of man coming in clouds with great power and glory. And then he will send out the angels, and gather his elect from the four winds . . ." (Mark 13:24-27 and parallels: Matthew 24:29-31; Luke 21:25-28).

This Jesus also promised that some of his hearers would not die before the kingdom of God arrived (Mark 9:1).

We can also find a portrait of Jesus as a kind of revolutionary: "Do not think that I have come to bring peace on earth; I have not come to bring peace, but a sword" (Matthew 10:34). Perhaps this is the Jesus who was executed by Rome for claiming to be "king of the Jews" (Matthew 27:11,29,37).

There is, of course, more than one side to anyone's character. We should not be surprised that this is true of Jesus. Nevertheless, competition among these and other portraits does leave the reader wondering: What was the essence of the man? Where was the center?

Scholars have been writing answers to that question for 200 years. Only toward the end of the 18th century did scholars begin to apply the critical method of historical research to the Gospels. Even today, there is some reluctance among many Christian scholars to use this methodology as vigorously when studying the Gospels as they do when studying other material. Most scholars who deal with the Gospels have a *belief about* Jesus that is not subject to historical scrutiny. One of the consequences is that Jesus usually gets a very good press. Put crudely, people tend to project their own ideals—whatever they happen to be—onto him.

In the end, Jesus remains a more shadowy figure than his greatest apostle, Paul. In Paul's case, we have some of his own letters.

There is no mistaking the driving force, the cut and thrust of his mind. We would like to get as close to Jesus as to Paul. It is a disappointment that it cannot be done, since we do not have equally good sources.

The problem Naturally, in reconstructing the life of Jesus, in searching for his
of the sources essence, scholars look for the most reliable material. For several decades they have progressively reduced the range of the literature in which he is sought. The earliest source to be excluded was the Gospel of John. This was done partly because the other three Gospels—Matthew, Mark and Luke—line up against John, and the scholar is frequently forced to choose one or the other. This is especially the case in studying the teaching of Jesus, as we shall see below.

Matthew, Mark and Luke are called the Synoptic Gospels because they can be studied in a synopsis. This does not refer to a précis (although that is the common meaning of the word now), but to a book in which similar accounts can be viewed together (*synoptō* in Greek means "see together"). This is done by arranging Matthew, Mark and Luke in parallel columns.[4] Here is one example, Jesus' prediction of his arrest. Although the texts are parallel, there are numerous variations in detail.

Matthew 17:22-23	Mark 9:30-31	Luke 9:43b-44
As they were gathering in Galilee,	They went on from there and passed through Galilee.	But while they were all marveling at everything he did,
Jesus said to them, "The Son of man is to be delivered into the hands of	And he would not have any one know it; for he was teaching his disciples, saying to them, "The Son of man will be delivered into the hands of	he said to his disciples, "Let these words sink into your ears; for the Son of man is to be delivered into the hands of men."
men, and they will kill him, and he will be raised on the third day."	men, and they will kill him; and when he is killed, after three days he will rise."	

A study of all the Gospel parallels makes it obvious that these three Gospels, the synoptics, relate very closely to one another. They tell basically the same story, according to the same outline, placing the same events at the same point in the outline, often using identical wording. There are exceptions to these rules, but the most striking single feature of the synoptics is their similarity. They are especially close together when they give the same teaching material. As in the example above, the synoptics vary more in describing the setting of Jesus' teaching than in giving the teaching itself.

John's Gospel, on the other hand, cannot be fitted into the synoptic scheme in any way. The outline of events is different, and there is little agreement between John and the synoptics with regard to content.

Moreover, the differences between John and the synoptics are not such that the accounts are complementary; rather, the accounts are contradictory to a very great degree. We may consider some examples: According to the synoptics, during Jesus' public career he went to Jerusalem for Passover once; according to John, twice. In the synoptics Jesus "cleanses" the Temple at the end of his ministry; in John at the beginning. The synoptic Jesus is an exorcist (for example, Mark 3:22-27); the Johannine Jesus performs no exorcisms.

There are even more striking differences between John and the synoptics. In the synoptics, Jesus declines to say who he is; he even refuses to give "a sign," and he rebukes those who seek one (Mark 8:11-12 and parallels; cf. Mark 8:29f.). In John, on the other hand, Jesus talks almost exclusively about himself, and he provides several specific signs. (Note the prominence of the "I am" sayings in John, e.g., 6:35-51, 8:12, 10:7. For "signs," see John 2:11, 4:54, for example.) The Jesus of the synoptics preaches the kingdom of God, while the Johannine Jesus discourses about himself.

Moreover, the style and manner of speech are entirely different. In the synoptics, Jesus speaks in short, pithy sentences, parables, similes and metaphors. In John, Jesus offers long allegorical monologues. For example, we may compare the synoptic parable on sheep (Matthew 18:12-13) with the Johannine allegorical discourse on sheep (John 10:1-18). Matthew's parable is short, only two verses:

> "If a man has a hundred sheep, and one of them has gone astray, does he not leave the ninety-nine on the hills and go in search of the one that went astray? And if he finds it, truly, I say to you, he rejoices over it more than over the ninety-nine that never went astray."

Thus, in Matthew Jesus uses the story to describe an aspect of God and his kingdom: the inclusion of the lost; a single point is made by telling a short, illustrative story. John, on the other hand, places in Jesus' mouth a long, allegorical monologue; on the surface it is about sheep, but beneath the surface it is about the person and work of Christ, including his death and resurrection (John 10:18). In John's long monologue, we are intended to understand Jesus as being both the shepherd and the door to [God's] fold—which does not make sense, even in the allegorical terms of the parable.

These and other factors resulted in a still-held scholarly consensus: The historical Jesus is to be sought in the synoptics, not in John. The Johannine Jesus is the Christ of faith. That is not to say that John is "fiction"; somewhere behind John's Gospel there are traditions. The author probably knew one or more of the synoptics; he may have had independent access to other information about Jesus. Some parts of John's narrative (as distinct from the discourses) are intrinsically more probable than the synoptic account. Since Jesus was a law-abiding Jew, and since the Bible commands attendance at the pilgrimage festivals (Passover, Shavuoth, Sukkoth), Jesus probably did go to Jerusalem for more than one festival. (In John, Jesus goes four times, twice for Passover [John 2:13, 12:1] and twice for other festivals [John 5:1, 7:10]. In the synoptics, he makes only one pilgrimage [Mark 11:11 and parallels].) John's view of Jesus' trial before two of the chief priests is also intrinsically more probable than the synoptic trial scene (see below). Despite these and similar points in favor of John, the overall portrait of the synoptics must be preferred.

As we shall see, the synoptics' description of Jesus makes sense in context, while it would be impossible to explain early Christian eschatology if the historical Jesus was like the Johannine Christ. John is better read as a series of meditations on the theological significance of Jesus' coming that the author chose to write in the first person, as if Jesus had said them.

Since the middle of the 19th century, John has been mostly ignored in the search for the historical Jesus. But even the Synoptic Gospels pose difficulties for historical research. As we noted above, they are not biographies or histories in the modern sense. The most important point to consider is the nature of the material they contain.

The problems
of context   The Synoptic Gospels are composed of independent compositional units with very little context. We probably owe such context as there is to the Evangelists. We may think of each unit as a snapshot, with the individual snapshots arranged and introduced by the Evangelists (or Christian preachers and teachers before them).

If we want to explain what someone was like—not to give a few random facts about him or her, but to get to the heart of the matter—we aim for *intention, cause and effect* and an *understanding of the circumstances.* "Abraham Lincoln *wanted* all along to free the slaves; he waited until relatively late in the war *because of* tactical considerations." Such a statement requires that we know the sequence of events and that we have enough knowledge of what Mr. Lincoln *thought*—in addition to what he *did*—to allow us to weave desire, external action and the force of circumstances into a coherent whole. How can we do this with Jesus, since we have (1) snapshots that (2) have been transmitted for a generation or so in a language other than Jesus' own and in a variety of contexts? (Jesus spoke Aramaic, the Gospels are in Greek.) Unfortunately, we cannot know as much about Jesus as about Paul (or Lincoln or Churchill). On the other hand, we do not remain entirely in the dark, as we shall see.

That what we have are isolated incidents, quite probably rearranged and reset in unoriginal contexts, is easily shown: The settings of individual passages sometimes vary from Gospel to Gospel. We must assume that, during the period of oral transmission, Christian teachers exercised this kind of freedom. That is, the material was used, not embalmed; when used, it had to meet a current issue, and thus the context changed. If this were not so, the material would not have sustained the early Christian communities.

The Evangelists not only arranged the material, they added new introductions and conclusions. We may consider a few examples. Both Matthew and Luke include Jesus' lament over Jerusalem, and they have virtually identical wording in a passage that in Greek is just over 50 words long. Thus they used the same tradition, not a generally remembered Aramaic saying of Jesus that was passed down and translated in various ways. The lament contains this prediction: "You will not see me again until you say, 'Blessed is he who comes in the name of the Lord.' " Luke places this passage early (Luke 13:34-35), and it is fulfilled in Luke 19:38, when the crowd cries out, as Jesus enters Jerusalem, "Blessed is he who comes in the name of the Lord." In Matthew, however, the prediction that people will not see Jesus again until they make the appropriate proclamation comes *after* his entry into Jerusalem: the entry into Jerusalem is in Matthew 21:9, the prediction in Matthew 23:37-39. This means that, when the Gospel of Matthew closes, the prediction is still unfulfilled, and the saying, "You will not see me until . . . ," points forward to the post-resurrection return of the Lord. Thus we must ask: Did Jesus predict his triumphal entry into Jerusalem (Luke) or his own return after his death (Matthew)?

The setting or immediate context of an individual unit is also frequently different from Gospel to Gospel. An example is the parable of the lost sheep quoted above. A shepherd leaves 99 safe sheep to search for the one that is lost. In Matthew's setting, Jesus tells the parable to the disciples; the meaning is that they should act accordingly (Matthew 18:12-14) and seek the lost. In Luke, the parable is directed against the Pharisees; it defends Jesus' own action in mingling with "tax collectors and sinners" (Luke 15:3-6).

Sometimes scholars reach a consensus in favor of one arrangement or setting, but sometimes there is no consensus. In the two examples I have given, most scholars now would favor Matthew's setting for the saying "You will not see me again." Jesus probably had in mind the future kingdom rather than his next trip to Jerusalem. On the other hand, most scholars accept Luke's setting for the parable of the lost sheep and take it to be a rebuke to the Pharisees for not seeking the lost. Occasionally someone is bold enough to doubt both settings. The correct decision is not self-evident. The answer depends on an overall view of Jesus, and it requires a reconstruction of the larger context of his life and work. Yet since the larger context is provided by other passages that were transmitted by the very same sources, it is difficult to avoid circular argument.

The problem is even more difficult. Not all the material goes back to the historical Jesus. Besides being arranged and set in new contexts, much of it was revised and some was even created. To illustrate how this occurred, we may consider a passage in one of Paul's letters. Paul wrote that he besought the Lord in prayer that his "thorn in the flesh" be removed. The Lord replied, "My grace is sufficient for you, for my power is made perfect in weakness" (2 Corinthians 12:8-9). From Paul's letter, we know that the Lord who spoke this saying was not the historical Jesus, but either the risen Lord or God himself, speaking through the Spirit. If Paul had used the saying in a sermon, however, and it was then quoted and used in different contexts, it would be unlikely that everyone would maintain the nice distinction between the historical Jesus and the Lord who answers prayer.

Christians believed that the Lord still spoke to them, and that sometimes the Holy Spirit spoke through Christian prophets. Paul and other Christians held that they knew the mind of God and that they spoke "in words not taught by human wisdom but taught by the Spirit" (1 Corinthians 2:9-13). Since "the Lord is the Spirit" (2 Corinthians 3:17), words that were "taught by the Spirit" were often attributed to Jesus (whom the Christians called "Lord") when the Gospels were composed. From the point of view of the first Christians, why not? The same Lord spoke. Yet the result was that they created sayings that were then placed in the mouth of the historical Jesus.

A second source of newly created material was the Jewish Scriptures, which the Christians accepted as their own. Christians believed that Jesus had fulfilled the biblical prophecies, and this view led them sometimes to draw on those prophecies for information about him. An example is Matthew's statement that, when Jesus entered Jerusalem shortly before his death, he sat on both an ass and a colt. Matthew derived this "information" from the Scripture that he thought Jesus fulfilled:

> "Rejoice greatly, O daughter of Zion!
>   Shout aloud, O daughter of Jerusalem!
> Lo, your king comes to you;
>   triumphant and victorious is he,
> humble and riding on an ass,
>   on a colt the foal of an ass."
>
> Zechariah 9:9, cited in Matthew 21:5

Hebrew poetry makes extensive use of parallelism, and in this case "a colt the foal of an ass" is a parallel that defines "an ass" in the previous line. Matthew, studying the Scripture, decided that Jesus had fulfilled this prophecy in a very literal way, by riding on both an ass and a colt.

So there are two problems: unknown context and uncertain contents. If we knew enough about the overall thrust of Jesus' life and work—the context of his own life—we could better control the contents, since some things would fit in the context and some would not. Or if we had a completely reliable list of things Jesus said and did, we could search them to try to determine what context they fit best.

Scholars have addressed both problems, context and content. Drawing partly on general knowledge of the period and partly on more particular knowledge of what happened before and after Jesus' life, they have studied the context in which he worked. To a fair degree these efforts have been successful. Recent studies of religious, social and political currents in Palestine have clarified the general context of Jesus' life. Judaism is now much better understood than it was before World War II. The discovery of the Dead Sea Scrolls—which are still being published, ever so slowly—has provided new information. Rabbinic literature—in its present form compiled 200 years or more after Jesus' death—was once considered to represent "first-century Judaism." Jewish society is no longer viewed as having been dominated by the rabbis, and this permits a more realistic assessment of the role of charismatic teachers and healers. Good progress has also been made in the chronological stratification of rabbinic literature, with the result that we can now confidently assign some of it to the period before 70 C.E.[5] This material is useful for our purposes.

The criteria of content   The contents of the synoptic material itself remain difficult. A lot of careful academic effort has gone into establishing criteria of authenticity to test the sayings.[6] Paradoxically, the more the criteria have been refined the less certain we are about which sayings are authentic. In the early days of sifting the sayings, scholars tended to apply the criteria of authenticity mechanically: If saying *x* is contrary to later Christian opinion, Jesus really said it, since a Christian author would not have invented something with which he disagreed. We do not always know what a later Christian author would or would not have invented, and consequently the criteria themselves are subject to doubt. The result of three decades of study is that we know less than we used to think we knew.

Nevertheless, some things are securely known. No one doubts most of the "framework" of the story of Jesus:[7]

He was born about 4 B.C.E., near the end of Herod's reign.

He grew into manhood in Nazareth, a Galilean village.

He was baptized by John the Baptist.

He called disciples.

He taught in the towns, villages and open areas (apparently not cities) of Galilee.

He preached "the kingdom of God."

About the year 30 he went to Jerusalem for Passover.

He created a disturbance in the Temple area.

He had a final meal with his disciples.

He was arrested and interrogated by Jewish authorities, specifically the high priest.

He was executed on the orders of the Roman procurator, Pontius Pilate.

His disciples at first fled; they saw him (in what sense is not certain) after his death; as a consequence, they came to believe that he would return to found the kingdom. They formed a community to await his return and sought to win others to believe in him as God's Messiah.

The context of Jesus' career and the framework of his ministry   Jesus' public ministry was bracketed by the preaching of John the Baptist, at its beginning, and the missionary activity of the early Church, after his death and resurrection.

We may be confident that Jesus was baptized by John because of the way the Gospels handle the subject. They all have the Baptist predict that he will be succeeded by one who is greater than he (Matthew 3:11; Mark 1:7; Luke 3:16; John 1:26-27), and Matthew and John both have him explicitly acknowledge Jesus (Matthew 3:14; John 1:29-31,36). The Baptist was widely regarded as a prophet—probably more widely than Jesus.[8] The early Christians were no doubt embarrassed that Jesus began his work by accepting John's baptism. The Christian insistence that Jesus' baptism did not imply his subordination to John shows that he was in fact baptized by him. The authors of the Gospels would not have invented a story which they found embarrassing. John's explicit acknowledgement that Jesus was his greater successor is probably a bit of early Christian apologetics. More likely to be authentic is John's question to Jesus from prison, "Are you he who is to come?" (Matthew 11:3).

From this we learn that Jesus began his mission by accepting baptism at the hands of a man who expected God to establish his kingdom in the immediate future.

Paul, whose letters are our best evidence for early Christian preaching, expected the same thing. He had told his Gentile converts in Thessalonica that they would still be alive when the Lord returned. When some of them died, the survivors wondered about the fate of those who were gone. In answer, Paul promised that the dead converts would not lose out. Quoting a "word of the Lord," Paul predicted that when the Lord returned the "dead in Christ" would rise and that both the dead and the living Christians would be caught up "in the clouds to meet the Lord in the air" (1 Thessalonians 4:13-18). Later, when Paul was in prison, he began to think that he might not live to see the day (Philippians 1:22f.), but he still expected the imminent return of the Lord and the establishment of his "commonwealth" (Philippians 3:20f.; Romans 13:11-14). This was not a point of contention between Paul and the Jerusalem apostles: Early Christians in general thought that the day was at hand.

Jesus, too, no doubt had this expectation. Since John the Baptist had it before him and Paul, his apostle, had it after him, it would be very difficult to leapfrog over Jesus' own conviction, especially since sayings very much like 1 Thessalonians 4:13-18 are attributed to him: "Truly, I say to you, there are some standing here who will not taste death before they see that the kingdom of God has come with power" (Mark 9:1; see further Matthew 16:27-28, 24:31). Precisely what Jesus thought about the kingdom is less certain. This depends on close exegesis of sayings in the Gospels, which may have been modified or even invented. That Jesus held some sort of expectation about the arrival of "the kingdom" is secure. Nuance and precision, however, can be postulated with less certainty.

This is one of the points that proves that the synoptic Jesus is closer to the historical Jesus than is the Johannine Christ. The synoptic sayings just cited are very close to what Paul thought that Jesus had said, and there are no comparable sayings in John.

The role of the disciples The next part of the secure framework of Jesus' life is that he called disciples. Both the Gospels and Paul (quoting an earlier tradition) specify that there were 12 special followers (1 Corinthians 15:5; Matthew 10:1-4; Mark 3:13-19; Luke 6:12-16; John 6:67-71). The synoptics, however, name a total of 13, 11 of them in common (Luke disagrees with Matthew and Mark about the name of the 12th, thus providing a 13th name). John's Gospel names another disciple, Nathanael (John 1:45-51), who is not mentioned in the synoptics. The early Christians seem to have had 12 as a firm number, but they were not certain who should be included. It is probable that Jesus himself spoke of "the twelve," though he was not necessarily followed all the time by precisely 12, nor by precisely the same people. If this is right, the value of the number was symbolic: "the twelve" represented the 12 tribes of Israel. Jesus promised the disciples that "in the new world, when the Son of man shall sit on his glorious throne, you who have followed me will also sit on 12 thrones, judging the 12 tribes of Israel" (Matthew 19:28). This has the effect of "enthroning" Judas, who was one of the 12 on everyone's reckoning, despite the fact that Judas betrayed Jesus. The early Church, knowing of Judas' betrayal, would not have invented a promise from Jesus that would give Judas a place in the new age, and thus we may accept the saying as authentic.

The use of 12 as a symbolic number and the explicit reference to the 12 tribes points to a very concrete expectation: that the 12 tribes of Israel would be restored. Centuries earlier the Assyrians had scattered ten of the tribes. Obviously it would take an act of God to get them all back together. Numerous Jewish authors hoped that this would happen. Ben Sira (c. 200 B.C.E.) looked to God to "gather all the tribes of Jacob" and "to give them their inheritance, as at the beginning."[9] The sect associated with the Dead Sea Scrolls (probably a branch of the Essene party) expected the reassembly of the 12 tribes.[10] This same expectation appears in the pseudepigraphical Psalms of Solomon 11, 17:28-31,50 and elsewhere. The tradition was continued in early Christianity (Revelation 21:12).

Jesus himself was a Bible-believing Jew, and like many others he thought that God would honor his promises to the patriarchs and restore the 12 tribes in the last days—just as God had previously wrought miracles on behalf of Israel.

Apparently the disciples thought that they would play an important role in the kingdom that God would establish. In the passage quoted above (Matthew 19:28), Jesus promised to enthrone them in the role of judges. In another passage the disciples debate among themselves about who is greatest. Jesus rebukes them by saying that those who wish to be first should be last (Mark 9:33-35). More significantly, James and John (who, with Peter, were leading disciples) asked if they could sit at Jesus' right and left in his "glory" (Mark 10:35-45). It seems that there was some dispute among disciples about who would have the leading places in the kingdom.

The other concrete expectation we can attribute to Jesus is the hope for a renewed Temple. This is reflected in an act and in two sayings. Jesus went to the Temple, where he overturned the tables of the money changers and the stalls of those who sold pigeons (Mark 11:15). When challenged, he justified his action by saying that the Temple, which should be "a house of prayer for all the nations [Gentiles]" (quoting Isaiah 56:7), had been turned into "a den of robbers" (Mark 11:17; quoting Jeremiah 7:11).

The destruction of the Temple

Later, Jesus predicted that "there will not be left here [in the Temple] one stone upon another, that will not be thrown down" (Matthew 24:1-2; Mark 13:1-2; Luke 21:5-6). According to Mark, this prediction was made privately, to one disciple, while according to Matthew the disciples in general heard it.

After Jesus was arrested, witnesses at his trial before the high priest accused him of making a different statement about the fate of the Temple: "We heard him say, 'I will destroy this Temple that is made with hands, and in three days I will build another, not made with hands' " (Mark 14:58; Matthew 26:61 lacks the phrases "made with hands" and "not made with hands"). The Gospels maintain that this testimony was false (Matthew 26:59-60; Mark 14:56-59). Nevertheless, when Jesus was on the cross, passers-by taunted him by saying "Aha! You who would destroy the Temple and build it in three days, save yourself . . . " (Matthew 27:40; Mark 15:29-30).

Thus we have an action at the Temple accompanied by a saying in favor of Gentiles; a prediction that not one stone would be left on another; and "false testimony" that Jesus threatened to destroy the Temple. It is difficult to see how these traditions fit together—if they do fit together. Why would Jesus both prepare the Temple for Gentile use and predict its destruction? Did he both *threaten* to destroy the Temple and *predict* that it would be destroyed? We begin with the prediction and the threat and consider first the probable early Christian view of them.

By the time the Gospels were written, Christianity had spent several decades making its way in the Roman world. The dominant thrust of the movement was toward acceptance of Roman rule. The Christians' kingdom, they said reassuringly, was not of this world (John 18:36); they posed no threat to Rome, civilization and good order (all of which were more-or-less synonymous). In fact, Christianity was potentially revolutionary, both politically and socially. In some parts of Christianity there was fierce hatred for Rome. In the following passage, "Babylon" is a code word for Rome:

> "Fallen, fallen is Babylon the Great! It has become a dwelling place of demons, a haunt of every foul spirit" (Revelation 18:2).

Christian leaders and spokesmen spent considerable effort trying to convince the rest of society that they posed no threat. On the whole, they were successful. The author of Luke and Acts (both were written by the same man) was especially concerned with this problem. Acts is filled with stories designed to show that Jews made trouble, but the early Christian apostles were completely law-abiding and were always found to be so when tried by a Roman official (e.g., Acts 18:12-17). Not surprisingly, then, the Gospel of Luke does not contain either of the two passages in which Jesus is accused of threatening the Temple. The accusation was known to the author of Luke from his source, or sources (Mark and Matthew), but he simply deleted it.

One way to test the Gospel material for reliability is to ask whether or not it is "against the grain" of the authors or of early Christianity. If it is, it is probably reliable, since an author would not invent a passage that was "against the grain." With regard to the Temple, all three synoptics want the reader to believe that Jesus *predicted* the destruction of the Temple but did not *threaten* it. We should suspect that in reality it was the other way around: Whatever he did and said with regard to the Temple, it could easily have been taken as a threat of its destruction. We may put this another way: If originally the traditions about Jesus contained a mere prediction of destruction, why would the Christian Church convert the prediction into a threat and then attribute it to false witnesses? The answer is that it would not have done so. The passages in Mark and Matthew about a threat to destroy the Temple are probably there because the accusation was actually made, either at Jesus' trial or when he was on the cross, or both. The Gospels defend him: that was false testimony; Jesus merely predicted, he did not threaten. By the time the Gospels were written, the prediction had been fulfilled: The Temple was destroyed in 70 C.E. A prediction that was fulfilled increased the stature of the prophet.

We can understand why the tradition would have moved from some sort of threatening word or deed to the accusation of making a threat, and then to the Christian reply that the accusers were false witnesses and that Jesus merely predicted. It is difficult, however, to understand the reverse development: A simple prediction, made privately to one or more of his disciples, that had no public consequences would not have resulted in the presence of the threat theme in the Gospels. The authors would have preferred that the threat disappeared entirely. In Luke it does disappear, while in Matthew and Mark it is called "false testimony." It is probable that Jesus really was accused of threatening to destroy the Temple, and Christianity had to answer the accusation.

We may conclude that the accusation that Jesus threatened the Temple is earlier than the claim that he only predicted its destruction. Two reservations must be lodged. First, we cannot hope to know "what Jesus really said." It is possible that he merely predicted and that his words were taken to constitute a threat.

The second reservation is that Jesus did not think, nor could his accusers have thought, that he and his followers could pull down the stones of the Temple or do any serious damage to it. Herod's Temple was enormous, and the stones were monumental. Many of these stones still stand where Herod's workmen laid them. When the high priest and his council heard that Jesus threatened the Temple, they would not have taken it to be a boast of military and engineering skill. However he worded his threat, he would have meant that God would destroy the Temple. The leaders of Jerusalem were not physically afraid of Jesus and his few followers, nor would they have believed that he knew what God would do. They were probably anxious lest his prediction of coming upheaval and the intervention of God should touch off riots.

We now turn from what he said about the Temple's destruction to what he did: overthrowing the tables of money changers and the seats of dove sellers. Biblical law required that sacrifices be offered for numerous reasons and that they be unblemished. This necessitated an inspection of the animal or bird to be sacrificed, an inspection that was carried out by high-ranking priests. At the time of pilgrimage festivals—Jesus was there at Passover—the Temple was full of people wishing to offer sacrifices, and the problem of inspecting the large number of sacrificial victims on the spot would have been considerable. Most offerings were of birds; the solution to the problem was to inspect a lot of doves or pigeons in advance and offer them for sale. Presumably the Temple and its dealers turned a profit on this, but there is no reason for thinking that it was exorbitant.

Overthrowing the tables of the money changers

The Bible also required that adult males give to the Temple each year the Temple tax of one-half shekel, or two drachmas. The Temple demanded that this tax be paid in a standard and reliable coinage, and so pilgrims would need to change their money. Again, there are no accusations of unreasonable charges. In this case, the evidence is against it. Although the Temple tax could be paid at the Temple, it could also be paid in one's own community. If pilgrims found the fees of the money changers too high, news would spread, money would be changed elsewhere and the Temple money changers would be out of business.

What was Jesus doing when he upset the tables and stalls of these worthy citizens who were helping pilgrims to fulfill their biblical obligations? The action of turning over tables and seats was symbolic. The space in which people exchanged money and bought sacrificial birds was large, and just before Passover it would have been crowded. Jesus' action did not seriously disrupt the Temple's business. What did he intend to symbolize? According to the Gospels, he was "cleansing" the Temple for suitable worship. The quotation from Jeremiah in Mark 11:17 (the Temple had become a "den of robbers") gives the tone to the whole: either the charges were unfair, or the entirety of the trade was wrong and should be removed. A supplementary explanation is based on the quotation from Isaiah, "a house of prayer for all peoples [i.e., Gentiles]." This leads to the view that Jesus wanted to break down the barriers built into Temple practice that separated Jew from Gentile. Jesus' attack on money changers and dove sellers was really an attack on the cult itself, or on the Temple's separation of people into a hierarchy of purity—priests, Levites, laymen, women and Gentiles, in descending order.

Although these views are readily derived from the Gospels, we must look on them with doubt. It is most unlikely that Jesus attacked sacrificial practice or purity distinctions, and very improbable that he sought Gentile equality in the Temple. After his death and resurrection, the disciples worshiped in the Temple. They knew nothing of Gentile equality. Paul's letters indicate that full commonality between Jews and Gentiles developed in Christian circles outside of Palestine (although Acts assigns this dramatic innovation to a series of visions seen by Peter [Acts 10]). In any case, the earliest Church did not attribute to Jesus the idea that there was to be no separation of Jew from Gentile. The quotation from Isaiah in Mark 11:17 probably reflects a desire on the part of second-generation Gentile churches to ground their own practice in a statement by Jesus himself.

What about the authenticity of the phrase from Jeremiah, "den of robbers" (also Mark 11:17)? This does not suggest that Jesus wanted to overturn the cult, only to purify it of dishonesty. Many scholars, however, delete it from the earliest tradition, and I am inclined to do so as well. The phrase could have been lifted from Jeremiah by anyone. Putting it on Jesus' lips allowed the Christians to depict him as a moral reformer against abuse in high places.

It is probable, then, that we owe both of the quotations in Mark 11:17 (house of prayer for Gentiles; den of robbers) to the later Church. If we delete this verse entirely, Jesus' action in the Temple takes on a different coloration. The symbolic action of overturning seats and tables, in and of itself, points at least as readily to destruction as to cleansing. Had Jesus wished to announce symbolically a coming destruction, there is little else that he could have done. A hammer and a carpenter's chisel could have taken out a small hunk of wall, but turning over some tables would have been more public and obvious. This interpretation has the advantage of making sense of both the action and the saying about the Temple's destruction. It is reasonable to think that what he did and what he said ("not one stone left on another") go together. The most likely explanation of this complex of material is that Jesus expected the kingdom to come in the immediate future, at which time the Temple would be destroyed and then rebuilt or transformed. It remains possible, however, that he thought only that the current Temple practice should be reformed for the new age.

To sum up thus far, we have placed Jesus and his message securely in a context of eschatological expectation. He, no less than John the Baptist, Peter and Paul, looked for the arrival of the kingdom in some decisive or final sense. The evidence that has been examined points not to the end of the world, but to a new world, one with leaders (himself and the 12) and a restored or rebuilt Temple.

We should pause to clarify the important term "eschatology." Many people today think that when ancient Jews thought about the end-time (*eschaton* in Greek) they had in mind the last moment before the physical dissolution of the universe. Jewish eschatology, however, usually looked forward to a new world in the sense of a new order. Peace and justice will prevail, the lion will lie down with the lamb, life will be easy and food abundant. Jesus and his followers probably shared this general view. Paul thought that Christ, when he returned, would reign for a while before turning the kingdom over to God (1 Corinthians 15:23-28).

The best evidence for Jesus' expectation consists of (1) the saying that the disciples will judge the 12 tribes, (2) the disciples' debates about who will be greatest, (3) Jesus' promise to drink wine with his followers in the kingdom (Mark 14:25) and (4) the material that shows that he expected a renewed or new Temple. All this material is at least basically authentic, and it converges on the same point: the future establishment of the kingdom of God as a new order on earth. "Eschatological expectation" in some sense or other is certain; "new order" is less certain but still highly probable.

Sayings about   The word "kingdom" has a diversity of meaning in the Gospels, a
the kingdom   diversity that probably goes back to Jesus himself. We may distinguish five sometimes overlapping meanings.

1. The kingdom is a transcendent reality that people enter one by one. Here the kingdom is a sovereignty, or reign, that individuals may accept; acceptance guarantees admission:

> "Unless you turn and become as children, you shall not enter into the kingdom of heaven" (Mark 10:15).

> "It is hard for the rich to enter the kingdom of heaven" (Mark 10:23).

> "Not everyone who says to me, 'Lord, Lord,' will enter into the kingdom of heaven, but the one who does the will of my father in heaven" (Matthew 7:21).

2. The kingdom is a future reality that will come, but how it will come and what it will be like are not specified:

> "Thy kingdom come!" (Matthew 6:10, in the Lord's prayer).

3. The kingdom will be established by God's angels, or by the Son of Man, and its arrival will be accompanied by cosmic signs.

Many of the passages that reflect this view do not actually contain the word "kingdom," but the establishment of God's rule is the subject. How the end-time figure came to be called the Son of Man is not clear. Even murkier is Jesus' own view of the relationship between himself and the Son of Man—assuming that he actually predicted the coming of the Son of Man. These are two of the principal passages:

> "Whoever is ashamed of me and my words in this adulterous and sinful generation, also the Son of man will be ashamed of him when he comes in the glory of his Father with the holy angels . . . . There are some standing here who will not taste death before they see that the kingdom of God has come with power" (Mark 8:38-9:1 and parallels).

> "But in those days, after that tribulation, the sun will be darkened, and the moon will not give its light, and the stars will be falling from heaven, and the powers in the heavens will be shaken. And then they will see the Son of man coming in clouds with great power and glory. And then he will send out the angels, and gather his elect from the four winds, from the ends of the earth to the ends of heaven" (Mark 13:24-27 and parallels).

4. The kingdom will be a new order on earth.
Several passages already discussed belong in this category: Mat-

thew 19:28 (the disciples judge the tribes of Israel); Mark 9:33-35 (who is greatest?); Mark 10:35-45 (who will sit at Jesus' right hand?). There is one further passage that is difficult to assess. According to Matthew 16:18-19, Jesus told Peter that he was "Rock," and that on this rock he would build his Church. The saying continues, promising that what Peter binds or looses on earth is bound or loosed in heaven, a promise that is made to the disciples in general in Matthew 18:18.

All scholars agree that Jesus did not foresee an institutional Church with a professional priesthood that would have authority to absolve sins. If that is what the saying means, it is so anachronistic that it cannot be authentic. On the other hand, the nickname "Rock" shows that something authentic lies behind the passage. The name of the disciple whom we call Peter was actually Simon son of Jonas (Matthew 16:17). Paul, however, called him not Simon, but either Cephas (1 Corinthians 1:12, 3:22, 9:5, 15:5; Galatians 1:18, 2:9,11,14) or Peter (Galatians 2:7-8). "Cephas" is the Aramaic word for "rock," while "Peter" is the corresponding Greek word. In other words, Simon son of Jonas went by the nickname "Rock" in both languages. The Gospels were written in Greek for readers of Greek in the second and third generations after Jesus. The synoptic authors felt no need to refer to Simon's Aramaic nickname: he was "Simon" (Mark 1:16 and elsewhere), "Simon called Peter" (Matthew 4:18, 10:2) or simply "Peter" (Mark 5:37 and elsewhere). Paul, however, had met the man in Jerusalem and knew by what name he actually went: Cephas, which Paul turned into Greek (Peter) in only one passage.

The importance of this is that the meaning of Simon's Aramaic nickname was preserved in Greek. It is as if the popular Munich beer were called "Lion's Brew" in the English-speaking world, except by people who had been to Munich and who knew some German, who called it "Löwenbräu." If the brewer wanted to emphasize the "lion-ness" of the beer, he would change its name from country to country: in English it would be "Lion's Brew," in French "Bière de lion," in Hebrew "bîrah shel 'arî" and so forth. In fact, this is not what the brewer has done. What matters to the brewer and the advertising agencies is that it be identified as *German*: its lion-ness is not important. The case of Simon's name, however, fits the hypothetical situation in which Löwenbräu becomes "Lion's Brew." What mattered was the *meaning* of Simon's nickname, "Rock."

From this we should infer that Jesus really did give Simon the name "Rock" or "Rocky" and that the meaning of the nickname was significant. Presumably it did not refer to craggy features, and probably not to strong nerves and emotional stability. Jesus made use of symbols, as we saw in discussing "the twelve." It is a reasonable hypothesis that "rock" was symbolic. If so, "foundation stone," or "cornerstone," as suggested by Matthew 16:18, is a reasonable translation.[11]

Foundation or cornerstone of what? Matthew proposes "Church," certainly meaning thereby the Christian Church that he knew (cf. Matthew 18:17). This is the anachronistic part of the saying, which we cannot attribute to Jesus. Jesus could well have thought of Peter as the symbolic cornerstone of the eschatological people of God, including both the reassembled 12 tribes and the Gentiles (for Gentiles, see Matthew 8:11).

I have spent this many lines on a difficult passage for a reason. This is one of the numerous sayings in the synoptics that will never yield secure results. We first establish the Aramaic word that Jesus said, and this can be done with certainty. But what did it mean? Did Jesus actually name Simon "Rock" after a messianic confession (so the setting in Matthew)? Was the name symbolic? If so, of what? We may infer here, suggest there, sometimes guess.

Although certainty eludes us, I suspect that the name "Rock" fits some way or other into Jesus' expectation that there would be a new order in which he and his disciples would have the major roles. Beyond this we cannot reasonably go.

5. The kingdom is present in Jesus' words and deeds.

> "Being asked by the Pharisees when the kingdom of God was coming, he answered them, 'The kingdom of God is not coming with signs to be observed; nor will they say, "Lo, here it is!" or "There!" for behold, the kingdom of God is in the midst of you'" (Luke 17:20-21).

> "Now when John [the Baptist] heard in prison about the deeds of the Christ, he sent word by his disciples and said to him [Jesus], 'Are you he who is to come, or shall we look for another?' And Jesus answered them, 'Go and tell John what you hear and see: the blind receive their sight and the lame walk, lepers are cleansed and the deaf hear, and the dead are raised up, and the poor have good news preached to them. And blessed is he who takes no offense at me'" (Matthew 11:2-6).

Some said that Jesus "casts out demons by Beelzebul, the prince of demons." In his reply Jesus said, among other things,

> "if I cast out demons by Beelzebul, by whom do your sons cast them out? Therefore they shall be your judges. But if it is by the finger of God that I cast out demons, then the kingdom of God has come upon you" (Luke 11:15-20 || Matthew 12:24-28).

These passages have convinced a majority of New Testament

scholars during the past few decades that Jesus taught that the kingdom was "somehow" present in his teaching and healing. Although this view is passionately held by many, the evidence for it is not very good. The first passage, "the kingdom . . . is in the midst of you" (Luke 17:21), may also be translated "the kingdom . . . is within you." Apart from the question of authenticity, the passage does not attribute the presence of the kingdom to Jesus' words and deeds. It is, rather, a denial that the kingdom will be seen in any one place, so that one can point to it. In other words, the kingdom is omnipresent, not a penumbra around Jesus.

Nor does the second passage (Matthew 11:2-6) claim that "the kingdom" is present in Jesus' words and deeds. It is an answer to the question, "Are you the one who is to come?" not "Is the kingdom present wherever you are?" Jesus certainly thought that he was "the one": if his disciples would be the judges of Israel, he presumably would have a higher rank. He may very well have offered his healings and teaching as "signs" to John the Baptist (though to others he said that he would give no signs [Mark 8:11-12]). We noted above that the question of the Baptist is more likely to be authentic than his explicit acknowledgement of Jesus (p. 51-52). It does not, however, show that Jesus thought that the kingdom was present, but rather that in his own view *something crucial* was happening in his ministry.

The third passage (Luke 11:20 || Matthew 12:28) states that the kingdom has come upon "you" if Jesus' claim is true, namely that he casts out demons by the power of God, rather than by black magic. Luke does not identify "you," but according to Matthew Jesus' saying is addressed to Pharisees; in any case, it is directed to people who doubted that he acted by the power of God. What does it mean that the kingdom has "come upon" his opponents? Perhaps that they have run into its power and condemned themselves by not accepting Jesus? In this case, the saying would recall Mark 8:38: "For whoever is ashamed of me and of my words in this adulterous and sinful generation, of him will the Son of man also be ashamed, when he comes in the glory of his Father with the holy angels." This saying makes crucial one's response to Jesus in the present, but puts the kingdom (the glory of his Father) in the future.

The proponents of the view that these passages show that Jesus thought that the kingdom was present are pushed into saying "present in some sense." But in what sense? It was not present in the sense that God's enemies were defeated. Tiberius, Pilate, Antipas and Caiaphas still ruled. God's will was not yet done "on earth as it is in heaven" (Matthew 6:10).

Admittedly, there is nothing inherently impossible about Jesus' having thought that the kingdom was in some way present, while in another way future. Paul could say that the kingdom of God is found where there is "righteousness and peace and joy in the Holy Spirit" (Romans 14:17). The Lord, however, did not yet reign as king; his enemies were not yet defeated. Only after he defeated them would he hand over the kingdom to God the Father (1 Corinthians 15:24-28). By analogy, Jesus could have said that the kingdom of God exists wherever people accept it and live accordingly, but that it would fully come only in the future. He could have thought that the kingdom of God was proleptically (that is, anticipating a future state as though it already existed) and selectively present whenever people encountered him, or that it was omnipresent but unseen. The problem is that the passages about the kingdom do not prove that he thought this. We may accept that he thought that his own work was crucial, and that response to him would determine what happened to the individual when the kingdom arrived; yet it appears that he did not use "kingdom" to refer to the present situation of confrontation and acceptance or rejection. This remains only an intriguing possibility.

What conclusions may we draw about the meaning of the "kingdom of God" as Jesus understood it? The material we have examined neither excludes nor proves any particular meaning beyond doubt. They are all harmonizable: Jesus could have thought that in his own work the kingdom was present by anticipation; that it would come in the future; that it would be marked with cosmic signs and the appearance of the Son of Man with angels; that he and his disciples would have the most prominent places in it; that individual commitment would determine who would enter it when it arrived; *and* that people could enter it in the present time, in the sense of accepting God's reign in their lives and living in accord with his Spirit.

If, however, we ask what is certain, we must answer only that he believed that the moment of decisive change was near and that God was about to establish a new order on earth. This view of the kingdom has sayings in its favor, as do other views. What moves the expectation of a new order from being a mere possibility to a higher status, a meaning that we may confidently attribute to Jesus, is that this is what John the Baptist thought and this is what Jesus' followers thought after his death. Jesus must fit his context; his followers could not have misunderstood him entirely.

Jesus' distinct   This is not to say, however, that Jesus thought only what is com-
teaching   mon to John the Baptist and Paul. One can make distinctions. The
about the   descriptions of John the Baptist, both in the Gospels and in
kingdom   Josephus,[12] indicate that he called all Israel to repent and to live

righteously. By contrast, Jesus seems not to have been primarily a preacher of repentance, and the Gospels do not attribute to him a call for *national* repentance. John issued a general appeal for repentance, but Jesus conducted a more personal ministry. John sounds like Billy Graham, but Jesus does not. Many of Jesus' most striking sayings are directed not to crowds, but to a few interlocutors or followers.

It was very much "with the grain" of the Christian movement for Jesus to preach repentance. Both Matthew and Mark summarize Jesus' message as being similar to John's: "The time is fulfilled, and the kingdom of God is at hand; repent, and believe in the gospel" (Mark 1:15; cf. Matthew 4:17), but they give no particular occasion on which he called on "the crowds" to repent. The absence of particular events is especially striking in view of the preference of both authors. Presumably they would have included more passages about repentance if they had them. Luke has several passages on repentance, but the majority of these are best viewed as Luke's own creations. In none of the Gospels do we hear anything of a mass response in which people renounced their sins (as in the case of John the Baptist), craved God's forgiveness and turned over a new leaf. I am not arguing that Jesus was opposed to general repentance, but rather that his particular message was not that of the mass revivalist.

The thrust of Jesus' ministry—its distinctive character—was that the kingdom would include even sinners if they accepted *him*—not if they reformed. Accepting him may have implied reform, but his message was more the promise of inclusion, especially of sinners, than the requirement of general repentance.

The Gospels several times mention Jesus' association with "toll collectors and sinners" (e.g., Matthew 11:19). We may consider the meaning of each term. In Galilee, toll collectors worked for Herod's son, Antipas. He paid tribute to Rome, but his toll collectors did not directly serve a foreign power. Nevertheless, people assumed that, as a class, the collectors abused their positions by overcharging. In Jesus' view, even they were to be included in the kingdom.

"Sinners" was not a term for ordinary people who, in the normal course of life, sometimes transgressed. The word, rather, represents the Aramaic or Hebrew word that would better be translated as "the wicked"—those who were generally regarded as being beyond God's mercy. People who transgressed and made atonement were not wicked. In the Psalms and subsequent Jewish literature the term is reserved for those who did not attempt to live in accord with God's law. It is these with whom Jesus associated and whom he included in the coming kingdom of God.

Jesus' critics, rather than Jesus himself, used the term "wicked" of some of his followers. Jesus called them by more revealing terms, such as "the lost" (Matthew 10:6, 15:24) and "the poor" (Matthew 11:5 || Luke 4:18).[13] It is intrinsically likely that Jesus' followers were on the whole from the lower socioeconomic orders. Those who were well placed in the present kingdom were less likely to look for another than were the poor. In the ancient world large numbers of people had little stake in the social order, and it was they who could be mobilized by charismatic leaders. The crowds who followed Jesus, hoping for healings, probably consisted largely of such people.

On the other hand, some of the leading disciples seem to have been fishermen who owned their own boats (Mark 1:16-20) and toll collectors, who were not financially impoverished. Luke indicates that some of Jesus' supporters were women of means (Luke 8:2-3).

Thus "poor," and probably other terms such as "meek" (Matthew 5:5) and "lowly of heart" (Matthew 11:29), may be partially accurate and partially misleading if taken as a socioeconomic description of those whom Jesus especially sought. On the one hand, he did not seek out the prosperous burghers and the aristocratic priests. The major cities of the Galilee (Tiberias, Sepphoris and Scythopolis) are not mentioned in the Gospels, and Jesus may never have gone to one of them. In the towns and villages where he did go he would not have met the elite. The crowds he attracted consisted mostly of the economically poor. Yet on the other hand at least some of his followers were economically above the level of day laborers, and the one group of "sinners" that is identified, the toll collectors, was not financially poor.

Perhaps it is a mistake to try to identify too closely the people to whom he directed his message. We certainly cannot correlate his offer of the kingdom to the sinners with a socioeconomic group. The overwhelming impression of the teaching attributed to him is that it was *inclusive*. He proclaimed the kingdom, and he included even sinners in it. We can now say that he did not go to the cities; this may not have been policy on his part, a rejection of urbanism. Perhaps he simply spoke to those who were at hand, the villagers of his native Galilee.*

The inclusive character of his teaching comes out best in the parables that describe the kingdom as standing the expected order

* The Gospels attribute a few miracles to Jesus while he is en route to or near Gentile cities (Mark 5:1, 7:24,31), but they depict no activities *in* these cities. The authors of the Gospels all believed fervently in a mission to Gentiles, and they work in references to Gentile territory, but they cannot actually describe Jesus as working within Gentile cities. More likely to be authentic is Jesus' limitation of his mission, and that of his disciples during his lifetime, to "the lost sheep of the house of Israel" (Matthew 10:6-7, 15:24).

of things on its head. Laborers who work a short period of time are rewarded as much as those who work all day (Matthew 20:1-16); the lost sheep that is found causes *more* rejoicing than the ninety-nine that did not stray (Matthew 18:12-13 || Luke 15:4-7); the prodigal who returns is feasted, not the obedient and faithful son (Luke 15:25-32). In a word, "many that are first will be last, and the last first" (Mark 10:31, cf. 9:35; Luke 22:26).

What did Jesus expect his followers to do? The usual problems of authenticity are especially severe in the area of ethics, but there are two even greater difficulties. One is the audience: Did he give ethical admonitions to the populace in general (that is, to all those who would listen), or only to the relatively few who actually *followed* him? The second problem is the relationship of ethical instruction to his expectation that the kingdom would soon come: Did he envisage a very short period during which exceptional moral standards should be maintained? **Behavior of Jesus' followers**

We turn first to the Sermon on the Mount (Matthew 5-7), the most famous collection of teachings attributed to Jesus. The admonitions of this sermon have three characteristics: they are pacifist, they are perfectionist and they are interiorized. "Interiorization" is seen most clearly in two of the so-called antitheses: murder and adultery can be committed in the heart (Matthew 5:22,27-30).

Perfection is a main theme. The disciples are to observe every commandment in the Law and Prophets and to leave none out (Matthew 5:17-19); to be more righteous than the scribes and Pharisees (Matthew 5:20); to be perfect as God is perfect, loving enemies as well as friends (Matthew 5:44,48). Perfection is implied in many of the individual commands, such as not to take oaths (the perfectly upright do not need to back up their statements); to fast without appearing do so (avoiding calling attention to oneself); not to pile up wealth (Matthew 5:34-37, 6:16-18, 6:19-21).

Pacifism is one of the hallmarks of the perfect: they pray for their persecutors and are blessed when they are persecuted (Matthew 5:11,44); they "turn the other cheek," give to their legal adversaries more than their suit demands and, if coerced into labor, do more than is required (Matthew 5:39-42).

The admonitions of the Sermon on the Mount are hothouse ethics: They require a special environment and do not do well in the everyday world. The hothouse could be a small sect that partially withdraws from the world, to which members make long-term commitments. They are to grit their teeth, take any manner of abuse and do without all but the bare necessities, knowing that at the end of this life they will gain the eternal kingdom. Or the sect could be eschatological, made up of people living from hand to mouth while they wait for the end of the age. This requires less organization and discipline than the previous possibility and is inherently less stable.

Albert Schweitzer proposed that Jesus taught "interim ethics," that is, ethics valid only for the short period before the arrival of the kingdom, which Jesus expected (according to Schweitzer) within a very few months.[14] Schweitzer's view has generally been rejected, usually because it seems to make Jesus' teaching irrelevant to the ongoing world. There is another objection. Apart from the petition in the Lord's Prayer, "Thy kingdom come" (Matthew 6:10), there is not a whiff of eschatology in the Sermon on the Mount. There is a threat of individual destruction at the end (Matthew 7:24-27), but nothing about the *arrival* of the kingdom or about a looming decisive change.

The perfection required by the Sermon on the Mount is not short-term, buoyed by the expectation of the end, nor is it pneumatological, based on participation in the Spirit of God. Pharisaic daily practice is the model (Matthew 5:20). The differences between Pharisaism and the sermon are interiorization and perfection. One grinds it out, hoping for reward from God (Matthew 6:4,6,18).

Is this the teaching of Jesus? Certain details suggest that it is not. The legal perfection required in Matthew 5:17-20 is counter to the theme that Jesus was not overly strict with regard to the Law, as we shall see below. The sermon's requirement to fast is curious in view of the complaint against Jesus that his disciples did not fast (Mark 2:18-22). The ascetic tone is quite different from Jesus' reputation as one who ate and drank, and who associated with toll gatherers and sinners (Matthew 11:19). Toll gatherers, heroes of other passages, are outsiders according to the sermon (Matthew 5:46).

The conflict of individual passages does not, however, constitute irreconcilable contradiction. We must remember the occasional character of Jesus' teaching and also the fact that we can never know whether or not we have the original context—even if we do not doubt the saying itself. He could have said one thing on one occasion but another in different circumstances.

The problem of the Sermon on the Mount
There is a more fundamental problem with the Sermon on the Mount. Considered as a unit, it does not seem to catch the spirit of Jesus' teaching. He expected the kingdom to come in a climactic sense in the near future. If this is correct, the Sermon on the Mount must be seen as striking the wrong note. Expectation of the end of the present order is such a strong factor that it would color everything. Jesus probably taught a perfectionist ethic, but we should view it in the context of eschatological expectation rather than

strict intracommunity discipline and practice.

The best evidence for perfectionism is the prohibition of divorce or remarriage. Paul attributes a saying on divorce to Jesus (1 Corinthians 7:10f.), as do four passages in the Gospels. A short form of the prohibition appears in Matthew 5:31-32 (|| Luke 16:18) and a long form in Mark 10:2-12 (|| Matthew 19:3-9). Paul's version and the short form in the synoptics basically prohibit remarriage after divorce, though Matthew's version assumes that divorce makes the woman commit adultery because she will have no means of support unless she remarries. Thus Matthew's short form is tantamount to a prohibition of divorce. The long form, on the other hand, forbids divorce on the basis of biblical interpretation: God originally "made them male and female"; and the Bible states that, when he marries, a man leaves father and mother and becomes "one flesh" with his wife. "So they are no longer two but one flesh. What therefore God has joined together, let not man put asunder" (Mark 10:6-9 || Matthew 19:6).

This, the best attested of all Jesus' teachings, perfectly illustrates how uncertain we are of precisely what he said. Was it "no remarriage after divorce" (Luke and Paul)? "no divorce because it requires remarriage, which is adultery" (Matthew's short form)? or "no divorce because it is contrary to God's intention when he created humans" (the long form)? All the versions are stricter than biblical and common Jewish law, which allowed a man to divorce his wife and permitted both parties to remarry. While we cannot know which of these strict views was Jesus' own, we should nevertheless point out that the long form is probably eschatological. Many people who expected a new order thought that it would be a reestablishment of the original order of creation. The two biblical passages quoted in the long form, "male and female he created them" and "the two become one flesh," are from Genesis (1:27, 2:24), and thus they were read as referring to the paradisal state. The long form of the passage on divorce, by referring back to the time of creation, implicitly points forward to the new age and requires Jesus' followers to start living as if the new age has arrived.

Once we accept one perfectionist teaching, shall we accept them all? Or should we doubt that the "winebibber and glutton, the friend of toll collectors and sinners" required a superhuman perfection of his followers? What counts against the perfectionism of the Sermon on the Mount is its hothouse and noneschatological character. The impression of a small group, striving heroically to be more righteous than the Pharisees, is too communitarian to correspond to the historical circumstances of Jesus and his movement. Perfectionism requires either intense eschatological expectation or a small, disciplined community, or both (as in the sect associated with the Dead Sea Scrolls). The Sermon on the Mount offers us instead the perfectionism of a disciplined community without eschatology. It is unlikely that this kind of perfectionism corresponds to Jesus' movement during his own lifetime, which had the reverse characteristics: eschatology, not a stable, closed society.

Authenticity of individual sayings   This judgment does not decide which individual sayings within the sermon are authentic. These have to be studied one by one. We shall consider a few examples.

The numerous admonitions not to be self-seeking fit well into Jesus' own lifetime. The long passage in Matthew (6:25-34) on not being anxious about material possessions is a case in point. For example:

> "Look at the birds of the air: they neither sow nor reap nor gather into barns . . . . Consider the lilies of the field, how they grow; they neither toil nor spin . . . . If God so clothes the grass of the field, which today is alive and tomorrow is thrown into the oven, will he not much more clothe you, O men of little faith?" (Matthew 6:26-30).

Jesus and his closest followers did leave their homes, families and possessions, at least for a short period (according to 1 Corinthians 9:5, Peter traveled with his wife), and these verses fit that context. But Jesus was not a 1960s hippie, he was a first-century proclaimer of the kingdom of God. What fueled this passage (assuming that it is his) and the action based on it was eschatological expectation, not childish irresponsibility.

In early Christian literature we can see the Church struggling with this aspect of Jesus' eschatological ethic. Paul urged his converts to "deal with the world as though they had no dealings with it"; the basis for this was the belief that it was "passing away" (1 Corinthians 7:31). Yet this did not mean that they should quit their jobs and beg on the street. Paul had to admonish the Thessalonian Christians to live quietly, mind their own affairs and work with their hands, so that they would be "dependent on nobody" (1 Thessalonians 4:11-12). According to Acts, the members of the early Christian community in Jerusalem sold their possessions and lived in common (Acts 4:32-37). Using capital for daily expenses had the result that we should expect: the funds were soon exhausted. Paul spent a considerable portion of his career taking up a collection for Jerusalem from his hard-working Gentile converts. (On the collection, see Galatians 2:10; 2 Corinthians 8-9; Romans 15:25-27.)

From these difficulties over money and work in the early Church, we may infer that the admonition to give up one's possessions and family does go back to Jesus' own teaching, especially his call to follow him (see Mark 8:34-37, 10:29-30; Matthew 10:37-39). It is probable that Jesus did not expect, or even want, many to "follow" him in this way. He proclaimed the good news of the coming kingdom to more people than he directly called into discipleship.[15] He almost certainly thought of surrender of home, property and family as being for a short period only, until the kingdom arrived. In the Sermon on the Mount the admonition to "give to the one who begs from you" (Matthew 5:42) and the implied admonition to live like the lilies of the field are probably authentic sayings, but they have been separated from their original eschatological context. We do not see, on the basis of these chapters, how the Christian community could give practical effect to these sayings. From Acts and Paul we learn more: Share until the money and food run out, then appeal for aid.

Thus in the Sermon on the Mount we have sayings which, individually judged, may be deemed authentic (as well as some that are unauthentic), but which have been transferred from their original context. Originally, they probably applied to a small number of followers for what Jesus thought would be a short period of time.

If we generalize on the basis of this analysis, we shall conclude that Jesus probably did expect "perfection" of his immediate followers: They gave up everything for his sake and the sake of the kingdom. It is, however, doubtful that this was his message to the crowds. Even Matthew 5:1 depicts the Sermon on the Mount as being directed to the disciples, not the multitude. In Luke's parallel (the Sermon on the Plain), Jesus heals many in the crowd, but he delivers the sermon to his disciples (Luke 6:19f.). We further note that in many of the other crowd scenes there is little or no teaching, and no perfectionist teaching at all (Mark 2:4, 3:9,20, 4:1-9 et al.).

In short, Jesus proclaimed the kingdom to all who would hear; he called only a few to a special life of discipleship. To oversimplify only slightly: Parables of the kingdom were directed to the crowds, perfectionist ethics to the disciples.

Jesus told the crowds that God loves the lost and that they would be in the kingdom. What did he expect *them* to do? Presumably to act accordingly. If God treated them with mercy and tolerance, they should treat others in the same way. If Jesus gave them detailed instructions, we do not have them. He seems to have worked on the basis of a principle that was formulated some decades later:

"In this is love, not that we loved God but that he loved us . . . .

Beloved, if God so loved us, we also ought to love one another"
(1 John 4:10-11).

"Love" is the central word in the "two greatest" commandments
that Jesus selected from the Hebrew Bible: Love God, love your
neighbor (Mark 12:28-34, quoting Deuteronomy 6:4f.; Leviticus
19:18). He could summarize the entire Scripture using only the
second of these commandments:

> "So whatever you wish that others would do to you, do so to
> them; for this is the Law and the Prophets" (Matthew 7:12).

This is not, however, ethical instruction, since it is not sufficiently detailed to determine individual decisions, especially when
there are competing claims on one's love. But the main element of
Jesus' teaching was the all-encompassing love of God that moti-
vates and inspires those who receive it. We may, after all, find the
heart of his ethical teaching in the Sermon on the Mount: "Love
your enemies . . . , so that you may be children of your Father who
is in heaven" (Matthew 5:44-45). Human perfection is based on
God's love of all, both the good and the evil.

The Law Several stories in the Gospels concern Jesus' relationship to the
Jewish Law.[16] These passages create the impression that Jesus was
lax about observance of the Law, but on closer examination we
shall see that there are no clear instances of actual transgression.
Most of the legal debates concern the Sabbath. In some cases, he
was questioned for healing on the Sabbath (Mark 3:1-6; Luke 13:10-
17, 14:1-6). According to one passage, he defended his disciples
for plucking grain on the Sabbath (Mark 2:23-28). He is depicted
as debating handwashing and vows of gifts to the Temple (Mark
7:1-13). One saying seems to be directed against the food laws:
"There is nothing outside a person which by going in can defile;
but the things that come out are what defile" (Mark 7:14-19). He
discussed which are the greatest commandments (Mark 12:28-34).
In a section of the Sermon on the Mount called the antitheses, he
appears to set his own teaching over against the Law (Matthew
5:21-47). We shall begin with the last section.

The format of the antitheses is this: an opening statement, "you
have heard that it was said . . . " (or "it was said"); a biblical quotation; the response "but I say to you . . . ." Many scholars have
understood "but I say to you" as antithetical to the biblical passage
and thus as showing that Jesus opposed the Mosaic Law. We saw
above that one of these passages, the saying on divorce, is doubtless authentic, at least with regard to general contents:

> "It was also said [in the law], 'Whoever divorces his wife, let

him give her a certificate of divorce.' But I say to you that every one who divorces his wife . . . makes her an adulteress . . . " (Matthew 5:31-32).

Many scholars think that here Jesus sets his own authority directly against the Law. This is, however, incorrect. The antitheses are not actually antithetical to the Law;[17] they are rather interpretations of the law, as the terminology indicates. In traditional Jewish legal debate, the verb "say" means "interpret." "Concerning this we say" in the Dead Sea Scrolls means "this is our interpretation." In rabbinic literature, "Rabbi X says" is used in the same way. The terminology in the antitheses does not imply that Jesus directly opposed the Law of Moses.

In the prohibition of divorce, Jesus' view is stricter than that of the Law, but it is not against the Law. If one never divorces, one will not transgress the Mosaic stipulations (Deuteronomy 24:1-4).

A second example is the saying on murder and anger:

"You have heard that it was said to the men of old, 'You shall not kill . . . .' But I say to you that every one who is angry with his brother shall be liable to judgment . . . " (Matthew 5:21f.).

Here "You shall not be angry" is "the revelation of a fuller meaning [of the commandment] for a new age. The second statement unfolds rather than sweeps away the first."[18] Jesus is the interpreter of the Law, not its opponent. This was certainly the understanding of the earliest known student of these sayings, the person who put together the Sermon on the Mount, where the antitheses are not against the law, but rather exemplify the preceding passage: "I have not come to abolish [the Law and the Prophets] but to fulfill them" (Matthew 5:17)–fulfill them by going beyond them in some instances.

Going beyond the law may imply a kind of criticism of it: it is not rigorous enough, or it is not adequate for the new age. We have already noted this point in discussing the pericope on divorce, and it may be accepted as true of Jesus' teaching to his close followers.

Did he at any point actually oppose the Law? The only passage that says this is Mark 7:19, "He declared all foods clean." This is Mark's interpretation of the saying that it is not what goes in that defiles, but what comes out. The Mosaic Law explicitly forbids the consumption of some foods (Leviticus 11; Deuteronomy 14). If Jesus said, and literally meant, "what goes in does not defile," he opposed the Law. It is, however, more likely that this is an example of hyperbolic antithesis, a well-known device for making a rhetorical point, frequently used in the Bible and subsequent Jewish literature. Hyperbolic antithesis uses "not . . . but" in an exaggerated way to mean "less . . . more." When Moses told the Israelites that their murmurings were *not* against Aaron and himself *but* against the Lord, they had just been complaining to *him* (Exodus 16:2-8). The sentence means, "Your murmurings directed against us are in reality, and more importantly, against the Lord, since we do his will." When the author of the Letter of Aristeas wrote that Jews "honor God" "*not* with gifts or sacrifices *but* with purity of heart and of devout disposition,"[19] he did not mean that sacrifices were not brought, nor that he was against them (he approved of sacrifices[20]), but rather that what matters most is what they symbolize. Similarly Mark 9:37, "Whoever receives me, receives *not* me *but* the one who sent me," means "receiving me is tantamount to receiving God."[21] "*Not* what goes in *but* what comes out" in Mark 7:15, then, could well mean, "What comes out—the wickedness of a person's heart—is what really matters," leaving the food laws as such untouched. If this interpretation is correct, there is no conflict with the law.

There is a very good reason for doubting that Mark's comment ("he declared all foods clean") correctly describes Jesus' view. The first generation of Christians did not know that Jesus had "canceled" the food laws. According to Acts 10, Peter was first told in a repeated vision that all foods are clean. He found this so hard to accept that, after seeing the vision three times, he was still "inwardly perplexed" (Acts 10:17). In view of this ignorance, we must conclude that Jesus did not command his disciples to ignore the food laws. The saying is either unauthentic or hyperbolic. In either case, Mark's interpretation does not give Jesus' own view.

The other passages on the Law do not even represent Jesus as opposing it. In Mark 2:23-28 he justifies a minor transgression on the part of his disciples by arguing that the Sabbath was made for humans, not humans for the Sabbath; therefore, since they had no food, they were justified in plucking grain. In Luke 13:10-17 he justifies healing a woman on the Sabbath by laying his hands on her, again arguing that human need overrides the Sabbath law. Most Jews agreed with this principle, though there were disagreements about when to apply it, some holding that life must be at risk. In any case, the justification of minor transgressions by means of legal argument shows basic respect for the Law. A person who defends minor transgression does not oppose the Law itself.

The controversies over handwashing and the use of the word *korban* (given to God) in vowing goods to the Temple do not touch the written Law, but are (as Mark 7:3 correctly notes) only against the traditions of the scribes and Pharisees.

We must also note that the settings of many of these passages are contrived and appear unreal. Pharisees did not really post themselves around Galilean cornfields on the Sabbath hoping to catch a transgressor (Mark 2:23-24), nor did scribes and Pharisees make special trips from Jerusalem to Galilee to check on the state of people's hands when they ate (Mark 7:1). Further, in both cases it is the *disciples* who were criticized, not Jesus himself; he only springs to the defence. The likeliest explanation of these passages, as Rudolf Bultmann proposed long ago, is that the settings derive from the post-resurrection Christian Church, sections of which had stopped observing the Sabbath and food laws.[22] They utilized sayings in new contexts to defend their own departure from the Law. Jesus may have said "the Sabbath is made for humans, not humans for the Sabbath," but only the Marcan context makes it a justification for transgressing the Law.

Finally, while in some few instances Jesus is represented as a kind of legal expert—most notably in the antitheses—this was by no means his primary role. Jesus was a charismatic teacher and healer, not a legal teacher.[23] The contrast between a charismatic, individualistic and populist teacher and a legal expert should be emphasized. Jesus is sometimes called "rabbi" in the Gospels (Mark 9:5, 14:45) or "teacher" (Matthew 8:19, 12:38), and often he is said to "teach" (Mark 1:21, 2:13). Consequently modern scholars sometimes write about Jesus the Rabbi. In such books he is thought of as sitting down with his listeners, opening the Bible (or recalling a passage from memory), laying out competing interpretations and offering his own. Jewish "parties" or "schools" disagreed about interpretation of the Law, and Jesus is often seen in this context: he studied the Law, adopted distinctive legal positions and schooled disciples.

Following this model, one would expect the primary topic of his teaching to be the Law. But the whole model is, I think, wrong. If Jesus' teaching had been of this sort, we should have more material like the antitheses, where he is depicted as taking up a biblical passage and offering his interpretation of it.

The great bulk of his teaching, however, is about the kingdom, and the characteristic style is the parable or brief saying. The focus is on what God is like (he includes the lost and is surprisingly merciful) and on what the kingdom *will be* like (values will be reversed; those who are last will be first). Outside the antitheses, there is virtually no *legal* exegesis.

We misconceive Jesus if we think of him primarily as a teacher of the law—a rabbi in that sense. Rather, he preached the kingdom and God's love of the lost; he expected the end to come soon; he urged some to give up everything and follow him; he taught love of the neighbor. His message did not have primarily to do with how the law should be obeyed.

Miracles   We can better understand the kind of man Jesus was, and how he attracted crowds and followers, if we focus on his miracles. People flocked to him seeking to be healed (see, for example, the summary in Mark 1:32-34).

Neither he nor others thought that his miracles showed that he was a supernatural being. They were evidence, rather, that he had the Spirit of God. Some doubted even that. His opponents charged that he cast out demons with the help of the Prince of Demons (Mark 3:22). He replied, in effect, that it was the Spirit of God that empowered him (Matthew 12:28)

The miracles attributed to Jesus are not significantly different from those attributed to pagan deities, especially the Greek god Asclepius, and to other miracle workers. We glimpse this even within the Gospels. When the Pharisees accused him of casting out demons by the Prince of Demons, Jesus asked, "By whom do your sons cast them out?" (Matthew 12:27), thus acknowledging that the "sons" of the Pharisees—that is, members of the Pharisaic party—could also exorcise. In another instance, someone who was not a follower of Jesus was nevertheless casting out demons in his name (Mark 9:38-41). This probably shows the consciousness of the early Christians that they had competition.

Jesus and his followers, like most other ancients, believed in spiritual powers, some demonic, and they attributed many illnesses, as well as antisocial behavior, to them (see, for example, Mark 5:1-13, where Jesus sent the evil spirits that inhabited a demoniac into 2,000 swine, which rushed into the Sea of Galilee and drowned). They also believed that God sent sickness and death as punishment for sins; this is reflected in the story of Jesus healing a man by telling him that his sins were forgiven (Mark 2:1-12 || Matthew 9:1-8).

Jesus' followers, and possibly Jesus himself, besides seeing the miracles as proof that he had the Spirit of God, saw in them the fulfillment of prophecy. When John the Baptist sent a message to Jesus, asking, "Are you he who is to come?" Jesus appealed to the miracles:

> "Go and tell John what you hear and see: the blind receive their sight and the lame walk, lepers are cleansed and the deaf hear, and the dead are raised up, and the poor have good news preached to them" (Matthew 11:4-5).

This answer draws on both Isaiah 35:5f. and 61:1. There is a very good possibility that this reply is authentic. We noted above that the later Christian Church, which held that from the outset John had recognized Jesus as "the one who is to come," would probably not have invented a question by John on that point. If the question is authentic, the answer may well be also. Jesus responds that his miracles fulfill prophecy and show that he is "the one who is to come." The precise definition of "the one," however, is left open.

During his ministry, at least according to the account in the synoptics, Jesus made only one trip from Galilee to Jerusalem; within a week of entering the city he was dead. The trip moved him not only from one geographical region to another, but also from one political sphere to another. Galilee was ruled by Antipas, one of Herod's sons. Although he reigned at Rome's pleasure, he was Jewish. He had his own troops and his own system of justice. When Jesus entered Judea, he moved into a Roman province, in which a Roman held full military and legal authority. *Conflict and death*

In Jesus' day the Roman prefect was Pontius Pilate. Pilate, like other Roman administrators, used local leaders to handle day-to-day affairs. In Jerusalem, the high priest, surrounded by a council of other aristocrats, governed.[24] He had at his disposal a very large armed police force. The high priest was the man in the middle. If he failed to control the local population and Roman troops had to be used, more blood would be shed than if he maintained order. The Roman troops hardly loved the Jewish population, and we may be sure that the Jews were not fond of them. It was the high priest and his guards who kept the two sides apart, by maintaining order and suppressing unrest.

Jesus came to Jerusalem at Passover time—one of the three pilgrimage festivals of the Jewish year, and the most popular. Jews came from far and near to worship and to eat the Paschal lamb in or near the holy city. Tents were set up in a substantial area outside the city walls;[25] inside the streets were packed. Passover commemorated the Exodus from Egypt, the time of Israel's liberation from bondage. Thus it was charged with political significance, and many doubtless felt anger and resentment at the Romans, whom they saw as the current equivalent of pharaoh. The bondage of Israel was light, as bondage goes, but still it was not freedom. Since trouble was likelier to break out at a pilgrimage festival than at any other time,[26] it was the custom of the prefect to come to Jerusalem from Caesarea, bringing extra troops.[27]

The scene changes in another sense. The scribes and Pharisees, so prominent in the story until now, almost vanish. In Mark, after Jesus enters Jerusalem, Pharisees are mentioned only in 12:13 (|| Matthew 22:15-22), where they join with others to question Jesus about paying taxes to Caesar. In Luke, they are numbered among the multitude watching Jesus enter, and they offer him advice (Luke

19:39). Pharisees also appear in Matthew 22:34,41, but not in a strongly hostile sense. They are denounced in Matthew 23, and they go with the chief priests to see Pilate in Matthew 27:62, to ask that Jesus' tomb be guarded. Even in Matthew, however, they are not the main adversaries. That role is played by the chief priests.

Jesus' last   There are five major events in the story of Jesus' last week.
week   1. He entered Jerusalem on a donkey; people welcomed him by shouting:

> "Hosanna! Blessed is he who comes in the name of the Lord! Blessed is the kingdom of our father David that is coming" (Mark 11:9-10).

According to Matthew and Luke, they explicitly called him "king" or "son of David" (Matthew 21:9; Luke 19:38).

2. He went to the Temple, where he turned over the tables of money changers and the seats of those who sold pigeons (Mark 11:15-19).

3. He shared a last supper with his disciples, saying that he would not drink wine again "until that day when I drink it new in the kingdom of God" (Mark 14:22-25).

4. The high priest's guards arrested him and took him before the high priest and his council. Witnesses accused him of having threatened to destroy the Temple, but he was not convicted. He admitted to the high priest, however, that he was both "Christ" (in Hebrew, "meshiaḥ") and "son of God," and he was convicted of blasphemy (Mark 14:43-64).

5. His captors sent him to Pilate, who interrogated him and then ordered that he be crucified for claiming to be "king of the Jews" (Mark 15:1-5,15,18,26).

There are two principal questions: "Why was he arrested?" and "On what charge was he executed?" The second question, which leads to the discussion of Christology (the Christian doctrine of who Jesus was), has drawn a great deal of attention. The first, however, the motive for his arrest, is historically more illuminating. The formal charge against him could have been trumped up, but there must have been some explanation for his arrest.

Some light is shed on the topic by the account of his arrest. Jesus and his disciples shared what would be their last supper, apparently on Passover evening (Matthew 26:17-29; Mark 14:12-25; Luke 22:7-20). After the meal, probably around midnight, he went to Gethsemane (usually placed on the Mount of Olives, a hill east of the Temple) to pray. After some time, but still well before dawn, he was arrested. Matthew gives what is doubtless the right explanation of the time of the arrest: The high priest ordered that it not be "during the feast, lest there be a tumult among the people" (Matthew 26:5). The secret arrest indicates that Jesus had become a public figure during Passover week, and that action against him might lead to upheaval.

Two previous events posed this threat: Jesus' entry to the city and his attack on money changers and bird sellers in the Temple. If the entry to Jerusalem, with people shouting about the kingdom of David, really took place and really involved a lot of people, it is surprising that Jesus was not arrested earlier. There are two possible explanations: (1) the demonstration was extremely small, was limited to the outskirts of Jerusalem and attracted little attention; (2) the high priest's security forces did not know where to find Jesus. It is likely that both of these are true. A large demonstration almost certainly would have attracted armed intervention. Even a small following, inspired by enthusiasm for the coming kingdom, would have alarmed the high priest. But he may not have known where to find the troublemaker and how to arrest him quietly. Later, one of Jesus' disciples, Judas, betrayed him (Mark 14:10f., 14:43-46), but earlier in the week Jesus was probably lost in the crowds.

The second incriminating action was Jesus' turning over seats and tables in the Temple area. This too was probably a small demonstration. The story does not mention the disciples, who may not even have been present. Had Jesus run rampant, upsetting tables and chairs over the whole area, the Temple guards would have intervened.

That both these incidents figured in the authorities' concern is evident from later events. When Jesus was taken before the high priest and his council, the first charge against him was that he had threatened the Temple. Pilate executed him on the charge of claiming to be "king of the Jews," which reflects his entry into Jerusalem. These charges may have been exaggerated; possibly he did not say "I will destroy the Temple" and "I am the king of the Jews." But, when one considers his teaching about the "kingdom," his view that accepting him was important for future membership in it and the shouts of his followers when he entered Jerusalem, the charge that he claimed to be king is perfectly understandable. Similarly, his statement about the coming destruction of the Temple, coupled with his act of physical violence, could be construed as a threat to destroy it.

Caiaphas and Pilate knew that Jesus did not have an army that could defeat the Temple guards and the Roman troops, much less the larger forces available in Syria. Had the high priest and the prefect suspected a real *Putsch*, Jesus' disciples would have been rounded up as well. What they feared was an uprising—the fear of all colonial powers. Especially in Jerusalem at Passover, talk about David's kingdom and a new or renewed Temple could inspire the populace to think that redemption was at hand. They might rise to strike a blow to hasten it, as they in fact did some 30 years later.

Jesus' arrest reveals that he was regarded as potentially danger-ous. Why was he not merely flogged as a warning and released? Josephus tells of another Jesus, the son of Ananias, about 30 years later. At the Feast of Tabernacles (Sukkoth), in a period that was otherwise peaceful, Jesus son of Ananias went to the Temple, where he cried,

> "A voice from the east, a voice from the west, a voice from the four winds; a voice against Jerusalem and the sanctuary, a voice against the bridegroom and the bride, a voice against all the people."[28]

This prediction of destruction—that it was such is clear from the reference to the bridegroom and the bride, taken from Jeremiah 7:34—led to his being interrogated and flogged, first by the Jewish authorities, then by the Romans. He answered questions by "un-ceasingly reiterat[ing] his dirge over the city," and was finally re-leased as a maniac. He kept up his cries for seven years, especially at the festivals, but otherwise not addressing the populace. Fi-nally, a stone from a Roman catapult killed him.[29]

Our Jesus' offense was worse than that of Jesus son of Ananias. Jesus of Nazareth had a following, perhaps not very large, but nevertheless a following. He had taught about "the kingdom" for some time. He had taken physical action in the Temple. He was not a madman. Thus he was potentially dangerous. Conceivably he could have talked his way out of execution had he promised to take his disciples, return to Galilee and keep his mouth shut. He seems not to have tried.

The trial In Matthew and Mark there are two hearings before Jewish au-
of Jesus thorities, but only one in Luke (Matthew 26:57-75, 27:1-2; Mark 14:53-72, 15:1; Luke 22:54-71). It is very likely that the long trial scene of Matthew and Mark is simply an expansion of the short one. In this case, the original report was simply that the chief priests and others consulted about Jesus, bound him and turned him over to Pilate.

It is the longer scene, however, that has always attracted atten-tion. According to Mark's version, witnesses testified that Jesus had threatened the Temple, but they did not agree (presumably on details), and so the charge failed. The high priest then asked Jesus, "Are you the Christ, the son of the Blessed?" Jesus admitted that he was, but immediately predicted that the Son of Man would come on clouds of glory. The high priest cried, "Blasphemy," and the council condemned Jesus (Mark 14:53-72).*

In a Jewish context, it is difficult to construe either "son of the Blessed [that is, God]" or "Christ" as blasphemy. Neither denigrates God. On the other hand, "Christ" and "son of God" became the two favorite Christian titles for Jesus, and some Christians understood them in a way that Jews might have regarded as blasphemous. That is, the combination "Christ," "son of God" and "blasphemy" fits the post-resurrection Church better than the lifetime of Jesus. The "false" charge that he threatened the Temple, on the other hand, is very close to what the Gospels tell us he did. If the trial scene is in any way accurate, it is more likely that the charge about the Temple was the telling one. Jesus was taunted with that accusation while on the cross (Mark 15:29f.), not with claiming to be the son of God. The authors of the Gospels, in a period when the Church was making its way in the Roman empire, did not want Jesus to appear as a rabble-rouser or as someone who threatened peace and good order. They toned down the threat to the Temple to a mere prediction (Mark 13:2 and parallels) and said that the accusation that he threatened it was false. His physical act against it they interpreted as "cleansing," as if the Temple personnel were corrupt ("a den of robbers," Mark 11:17). They preferred that he die for professing the Christology of the Church.

As we saw above, it is probable that we should reverse their preference: He was executed because he posed a threat to public order, not because he applied to himself the titles "Christ" and "son of God."

Our understanding of how it was that Jesus came to die does not, however, depend on a reconstruction of Mark 14:55-65. It is more instructive to focus on the main movement of events: Jesus' entry into Jerusalem, his demonstration against the Temple, his stealthy arrest by the high priest's guards, his crucifixion and the taunts about the Temple. One can understand the sequence of events without entering into the details of the trial scene.

The attack on the Temple seems to have been crucial in persuading Caiaphas and Pilate that Jesus should die. It confirmed his potential to make trouble, and it showed that he might use physical violence, even if of a very minor kind.

Since Jesus' action in the Temple had such drastic consequences, we need to return to the question of why he did it. We have seen

* Matthew has an interesting variant: After the high priest asks, "Are you the Christ, the son of God," Jesus replies, "You have said so, but I tell you that you will see the Son of Man . . . " (Matthew 26:63-64). It is not certain whether "you have said so" means yes or no.

that it was a symbolic gesture, as were some of his other deeds. If we consider them as a group, we may be able to better understand Jesus' intention.

As did many prophets before him, Jesus communicated by symbolic acts as well as by words. He called 12 disciples, apparently to represent the coming restoration of the 12 tribes of Israel. He ate with sinners, in order to indicate that they would be included in the kingdom. He entered Jerusalem on a donkey, perhaps to remind his followers of Zechariah 9:9 (cited at Matthew 21:5: "your king is coming to you, humble, and mounted on an ass"). When he overturned tables and stalls in the Temple area, he was probably also acting symbolically, perhaps indicating that the Temple would be renewed. His last meal with the disciples seems also to have been a symbol, one that pointed toward the coming kingdom, which would be like a banquet. (On the kingdom as banquet, see also the parables in Matthew 22:1-14 and Luke 14:15-24.)

Since the other symbolic acts reflect Jesus' expectation of a coming kingdom, it is probable that his demonstration in the Temple was intended in the same way. By both word and deed he proclaimed that the kingdom would come, that Israel would be restored, that the Temple would be rebuilt (or renewed), that he and his disciples would be leading figures in the kingdom and that people previously regarded as "last" (sinners and toll gatherers) would become the "first."

These expectations, however, were not fulfilled, at least not in any obvious way. What did happen was a surprise.

When Jesus was executed, his disciples, reasonably thinking that they would be next, hid. Some of his women followers—who were safer than the men and possibly braver—cared for his body. When they returned to the tomb a day and a half later (he died and was buried on Friday; they returned Sunday morning), they found that the tomb was empty. Jesus appeared to them and then later to the disciples in Galilee. The result of this was that they gathered in Jerusalem to wait for his return, which they expected soon. That is, they did not give up his idea that the kingdom would come; they now expected him to return from heaven to establish it. The movement grew and spread geographically. Twenty-five or more years later Paul—a convert, not an original disciple—still expected Jesus to return within his own lifetime. But the Lord tarried.

The "delay" led to creative and stimulating theological reflection, seen for example in the Gospel of John. Meanwhile, the man behind it all became remote. The synoptic material was by no means immune from this same kind of development. The consequence is that it takes patient spadework to dig through the layers of Christian devotion and to recover the historical core. Historical reconstruction is never absolutely certain, and in the case of Jesus it is often highly uncertain. Despite this, we have a good idea of the main lines of his ministry and his message.

A discussion of the resurrection is not, strictly speaking, part of the story of "the historical Jesus," but part of the aftermath of his life. A few words about the different resurrection accounts may nevertheless be useful. According to Matthew and Mark, the disciples went to Galilee and saw Jesus there; according to Luke they did not leave the environs of Jerusalem. The story of Jesus' ascension into heaven is slightly different in Luke 24:50-53 and Acts 1:6-11, though written by the same author. Equally striking are the differences between the stories of Jesus' appearances. In Matthew he appears only twice, once to Mary Magdalene and the other Mary (Matthew 28:1-10), once to the surviving 11 disciples (Matthew 28:16-20)—11 because Judas had committed suicide. In Luke, however, he does not appear to the women (see Luke 24:8-11), but comes first to two unnamed disciples (Luke 24:13-35) and then to all the disciples, before whom he ate (Luke 24:36-49). According to Acts, he was with the disciples for 40 days, appearing off and on (Acts 1:3f.).

The risen Lord

The earliest evidence, however, is not in the Gospels, but in one of Paul's letters. He offers, as part of what had been "handed down" to him, a list of appearances of the risen Lord: He appeared first to Cephas (Peter), then to the 12 (not the 11!), then to more than 500, then to James (Jesus' brother), then to "all the apostles" (apparently not just the 12), then to Paul himself (1 Corinthians 15:3-8).

Before commenting on the problems raised by these divergent accounts, let us first consider what the risen Jesus was like. According to Luke, he was not immediately recognizable; the first two disciples to whom he appeared walked and talked with him for some time without knowing who he was; he was made known "in the breaking of the bread," when they ate together (Luke 24:35). Although he could appear and disappear, he was not a ghost. Luke is very insistent about that. The risen Lord could be touched, and he could eat (Luke 24:39-43).

When Paul was engaged in a debate with his Corinthian converts about whether or not dead Christians will be raised, body and all, he tried to describe what the coming resurrection will be like. His answer is presumably based on his own firsthand experience when he saw the risen Lord ("Have I not seen Jesus our Lord?" [1 Corinthians 9:1]; God "reveal[ed] his Son to me" [Galatians 1:16]). In the resurrection, Paul explained, each individual will have a body, but it will be transformed: not a physical body, but a spiritual body. One fact is clear: flesh and blood cannot inherit the kingdom of God; in the resurrection, there will be no flesh and blood. This is directly applied to Jesus: "Just as we have borne the image of the man of dust, we shall also bear the image of the man of heaven" (1 Corinthians 15:42-50). Paul repeated: Everyone will be changed; when they are like the "man of heaven," they will no longer have their perishable bodies, but rather imperishable ones (1 Corinthians 15:51-54).

In the first century people knew about two experiences similar to resurrection. Luke and Paul both intend to exclude the possibility that the risen Jesus was either a resuscitated corpse or a ghost. A ghost then was what a ghost is now, or what a ghost was to Shakespeare:[30] a phantasm, especially one that appears late at night.[31] Sophisticated ancients, like their modern counterparts, dismissed ghosts as creatures of dreams, figments of the imagination. The less sophisticated, naturally, were credulous. Both Paul and Luke opposed the idea that the risen Lord was a ghost, Luke explicitly ("a ghost has not flesh and bones as you see that I have," Luke 24:39), Paul by implication: what is raised is a *body*. Yet they equally oppose the idea that Jesus was a resuscitated corpse. These were more common then than now, because embalming is now so widespread. It is, however, possible for a person to be dead to all appearances, and later to "regain" life. There are several such stories in ancient literature, some in the Bible and some elsewhere.[32] Paul and Luke, however, deny that the risen Lord was simply resuscitated. In Paul's view, he had been transformed, changed from a "physical" or "natural" body to a "spiritual body." Luke thought that he had flesh and could eat, but also that he had been changed. He was not obviously recognizable to people who saw him, and he could appear and disappear.

Both authors were trying to describe—Paul at firsthand, Luke at second or third hand—an experience that does not fit a known category. What they deny is much clearer than what they affirm.

Faced with accounts of this nature—sharply diverging stories of where and to whom Jesus appeared, lack of agreement and clarity on what he was like (except agreement on negatives)—we cannot reconstruct what really happened. We can, however, make some very general comments.

One is that the authors of the Gospels wanted to give *narrative stories* about the resurrection. They were probably not too worried about agreement or consistency. This may readily and convincingly be illustrated. In Acts there are three accounts of the Lord's appearance to Paul and the immediate aftermath, which differ at various points (Acts 9:1-30, 22:3-21, 26:12-20). For example, in one story (Acts 22:17-21), after the Lord first appeared to Paul,

Paul went first to Damascus and then to Jerusalem, where Jesus again appeared to him. It was at this second appearance that the Lord commissioned Paul to be apostle to the Gentiles. In Acts 9, however, the statement that the Lord appointed Paul to go to the Gentiles comes in Damascus (Acts 9:15). The author of Luke-Acts was not stupid; he doubtless knew that his stories varied. He could have told the same story in the same way, but that would not have been as interesting a narrative. Like many other authors, both ancient and modern, he disliked repetition; like other ancient authors, he would change events in order to avoid it.

Luke, like the other Gospel writers, wanted to tell stories in narrative form. They did not care about "accuracy"[33] in the way that we do. This makes it difficult to peer behind their accounts and describe what really happened.

Much about the historical Jesus will remain a mystery. Nothing is more mysterious than the stories of his resurrection, which attempt to portray an experience that the authors could not themselves comprehend. But we should remember that we know a lot, if we are content with a broad outline. We know that Jesus started under John the Baptist, that he had disciples, that he expected the kingdom, that he went from Galilee to Jerusalem, that he did something hostile against the Temple, that he was tried and crucified. Finally we know that after his death his followers experienced what they described as the "resurrection": the appearance of a living person who had actually died. They believed this, and within a few decades many of them would have given their lives for their belief.

THREE

After the Crucifixion–
Christianity Through Paul

HOWARD C. KEE

T HE NEW TESTAMENT IS THE PRIMARY SOURCE FOR OUR knowledge of Christianity in this period. The oldest sources that can be dated with reasonable certainty are Paul's letters and the reconstructed document known as Q* (used as a source by Matthew and Luke). In all probability, the Gospel of Mark can also be dated to this period. (These sources are discussed below, pp. 89 and 123-124.) Other early Christian writings included in the New Testament, although written later, provide supplemental—and, at times, divergent—bits of evidence.

Sources for a history of the Christian movement: 33 to 70 C.E.

Roman and Jewish sources of this period for the most part make only passing reference to Jesus and the Christian movement, but they do provide important confirmation and help to date some events connected with the rise of Christianity. Since the movement was initially so small, both in numbers and social impact, it is not surprising that non-Christian writers devoted so little space to it. Only in retrospect, as Christianity became a significant factor in the Roman world, did it merit sustained attention in Roman sources.

Even with the letters of Paul, we must distinguish between authentic letters written by him and other, later letters written in his name.

* See footnote on page 86.

Certain clues in Paul's authentic letters, when correlated with known outside events, enable us to date rather securely major points in his life. He tells us in 2 Corinthians that he escaped from the local authorities in Damascus during the reign of King Aretas (2 Corinthians 11:32-33). This must refer to Aretas IV, a puppet monarch of Nabatea (roughly equivalent to present-day Jordan), who administered this territory during the reign of the Roman emperor Caligula (37 to 41 C.E.). Aretas died sometime between 37 and 39 C.E. Since Paul's stay in Damascus lasted three years, it must have begun between 34 and 37 C.E. It was on the road to Damascus that Paul, after experiencing a vision of Christ, became a Christian, so we know within this chronological range when Paul, born Saul and a Jew, converted.

In Paul's letter to the Romans, he sends greetings to Priscilla and Aquila (Romans 16:3). Paul had first gotten to know Priscilla and Aquila in Corinth, as we learn from Acts 18:1-3. They had taken temporary refuge in Corinth after they and other members of the Jewish community had been driven from Rome by order of the emperor Claudius (41-54 C.E.). The expulsion of the Jews from Rome is also described by the Roman historian Suetonius.[1] According to Suetonius, someone named Chrestus—probably a reference to the Jesus movement, Chrestus being a corruption of Christos—caused a disturbance among the Jews of Rome; Claudius dealt with the disturbance by expelling *all* the Jews. The message about Jesus—that is, about Christos—had already reached Rome some time before this, since Priscilla and Aquila were converted to Christianity before Paul met them in Corinth.[2] These references to

---

* The designation of this source as Q (derived from the German word for source, *Quelle*) is common among international New Testament scholars for the non-Marcan material shared by Matthew and Luke. Since there is so much of their Gospels—mostly sayings, rather than narrative—that these two evangelists have in common, it is logical to assume they both have drawn from a single common source. This includes, for example, much of what is in the Sermon on the Mount (Matthew 5-7) as well as the parable of the joyous shepherd (Luke 15:4-7), the parable of the banquet (Luke 14:16-23) and the promise of a share in the rule of God (Luke 22:28-30). The major themes of the Q source are (1) discipleship: its privileges and trials; (2) the prophet as God's messenger; (3) the call to repentance or judgment; (4) Jesus as revealer and agent of God's rule. Details and analysis of this material are offered in the final section, pp. 123-124. Some recent studies of Q, such as that by John S. Kloppenborg, *The Formation of Q* (Philadelphia: Fortress, 1990), claim to be able to trace stages in the evolution of the Q material. The argument is purely circular, however: having decided from the outset that the message of the historical Jesus consisted of timeless wisdom and proverbs, these scholars assign to later editors all references to miracles, demons or the coming of an apocalyptic end to the present age. Their unannounced—perhaps unconscious—goal is to re-create a Jesus who fits more neatly with modern intellectual views and values. The Q document in its entirety, however, matches well with the understandings of Jesus and his message which are documented in our earliest Christian sources—Paul and the Gospel of Mark.

the Jesus movement also show that there was a Christian community in Rome long before Paul wrote mentioning Aquila and Priscilla and former co-workers by name (Romans 16:3-15). Paul arrived in Corinth about 50 C.E.; therefore, the Christian community in Rome had already been established in the 40s. Paul probably wrote the letter to the Romans in 60.

In his letter to the Galatians, Paul tells us that he returned to Jerusalem three years after his conversion on the road to Damascus, and that 14 years later he again went to Jerusalem (Galatians 1:18, 2:1). That second trip would be 17 years after his conversion. At that time, Paul seems to be still carrying out his ministry in Asia Minor, but also to have launched his outreach to Greece and beyond. The crucifixion of Jesus occurred no later than 33 C.E. If we add 17 years to that for the time between Paul's conversion and his second return to Jerusalem, this tallies nicely (i.e., within a few years) with the fact that Paul and his associates Priscilla and Aquila met in Corinth in about 50 C.E. This also suggests that Paul was converted within a year or two of the death of Jesus.

The Roman historian Tacitus describes the execution of Christians in Rome by order of the emperor Nero (54-68 C.E.),[3] which shows they were sufficiently numerous in the capital city by this time to attract the attention of the emperor, who used them as scapegoats for his own folly in having set fire to the city. Tacitus notes in passing that this movement had begun when Christos was executed in Jerusalem during the reign of Tiberius (14-37 C.E.), which confirms the evidence offered by the Gospels.

Although these dates lack precision, the evidence does provide us with a credible chronological framework in which to view the rise and spread of Christianity from Jesus' death to the fall of Jerusalem in 70 C.E. By the latter date, Paul had probably died in Rome as a Christian martyr, executed under Nero some time in the 60s—probably about 62 C.E.

In Philippians Paul writes as a prisoner of the Romans who expects to be executed by them, just as Jesus had been put to death at the hands of the Roman authorities (Philippians 3:20). Suetonius, the second-century Roman historian, describes the martyrdom of Christians in the early 60s in Rome,[4] which probably included Paul. The fourth-century Christian historian, Sulpicius Severus, states that Peter and Paul were among those publicly put to death by Nero.[5]

Chronological framework of Paul's life and letters	The approximate dates of key events in Paul's life are: [6]	
	Conversion to Christianity	34 C.E.
	Stay in Damascus	34-37 C.E.
	First visit to Jerusalem; approval of his activities by the Jerusalem apostles	37 C.E.
	Missionary activity in Antioch and Asia Minor	37-50 C.E.
	Arrival in Corinth	50 C.E.
	Departure from Corinth	51 C.E.
	Apostolic conference in Jerusalem (second visit)	Late 51 C.E.
	Missionary activity from Ephesus across Greece to Illyricum (Romans 15:19)	51-57 C.E.
	Return to Jerusalem from Philippi (third visit)	57 C.E.
	Two-year imprisonment in Caesarea	57-59 C.E.
	Taken to Rome by Roman authorities for trial as Roman citizen	59-60 C.E.
	Stay in Malta over winter	59-60 C.E.
	Arrival in Rome	60 C.E.
	Execution in Rome	62 C.E.

With this chronological framework in view, we may sequence and date Paul's letters as follows:

I. Written during Paul's first missionary tour of Syria, Asia Minor and Greece—about 50 C.E.:
1 and 2 Thessalonians

II. Written during his second tour of Asia Minor and Greece:
Galatians—about 54/55 C.E.
1 Corinthians—about 54/55 C.E.
2 Corinthians (from Macedonia) about 55/56 C.E.
Romans (he is planning journey to Rome and beyond)[7]—
about 57 C.E.
Philippians (written from prison in Caesarea [or Rome])—
about 58/59 C.E.
Colossians[8] and Philemon—58 C.E.

Other letters attributed to Paul, but differing in language, style and images of the Church are:

Ephesians (late first century)
1 and 2 Timothy, Titus (early second century)

This later material is relevant for the history of Christianity only beyond the limit of this chapter, 70 C.E.

The other two basic sources for our period are Q and the Gospel of Mark. Although no copy of Q has survived, its contents can be inferred with reasonable certainty by a careful comparison of the material common to both Matthew and Luke which does not derive from Mark, their other major source.[9]

Mark describes Jesus as merely predicting the fall of Jerusalem and its Temple in quite general terms (Mark 13). This contrasts with Matthew and Luke who refer to specific details of the fall of Jerusalem and its Temple which are known from other historical sources. This suggests that, unlike Matthew and Luke, Mark wrote his Gospel before the fall of the city, rather than afterward.

Another obvious source of information about this period is the Book of Acts, widely recognized to be by the same author as the Gospel of Luke. Estimates of the value of Acts as a reliable historical source have varied widely, ranging from dismissal as propaganda and pious fiction to full acceptance as historically reliable.[10] Literary and theological analyses of Acts in recent decades have shown that, while the author does preserve important and reliable historical details, his overarching aim is theological: to show the continuity between what God promised to his people through the Hebrew patriarchs and the prophets and what he has done through Jesus and is continuing to do through the work of the Spirit. In the service of this theological aim, details of the apostolic viewpoints and activities in Jerusalem, as well as Paul's reaction to them, are blended to offer a picture of basic unity among the early Christians. This image does not fit well with the evidence of disagreement among the first generation of Christians that is apparent in Paul's letters and the other first-generation Christian writings. Accordingly, we will use the historical evidence from Acts only where it is plausible and is compatible with information from Paul and other sources, taking into account the special aims of the author of Acts.

For the early Christians, the crucial event following the death of Jesus on the cross and his burial was that God raised him from the dead.

Mark simply announces that the risen Jesus will soon rejoin his disciples (Mark 16:7). The later Gospels, however, offer descriptions of his appearances: to the faithful women at the empty tomb (Matthew 28:9-10); to the disciples in Galilee, where Jesus commands them to go forth to the whole world and baptize "all nations . . . teaching them to obey everything I have commanded you" (Matthew 28:19-20);* to a group of his followers near Emmaus, west of Jerusalem (Luke 24:13-35); to the 11 faithful

Origins of the early Christian movement

---

* Matthew pictures Jesus as concentrating during his lifetime on a mission to Israel, and then turning the disciples to the wider mission to the world. The NIV and NRSV notes miss this crucial point.

disciples in Jerusalem (Luke 24:36-49); and then again just prior to Jesus' ascension (Luke 24:50-53). John's Gospel also has a series of these post-resurrection appearance stories: to Mary Magdalene (John 20:1-18); to the disciples in Jerusalem (John 20:19-23); to Thomas, the doubter (John 20:24-29); to the disciples in Tiberias (John 21:1-23). Indeed, in John it is claimed that Jesus *is* the resurrection (John 11:25-26), that the events of his crucifixion and resurrection were determined by God (John 12:20-36) and that through his impending death he would be glorified (John 13:31-35).

Jesus' resurrection on the third day after his crucifixion and his appearance to chosen witnesses is also affirmed in an earlier period by the letters of Paul (1 Corinthians 15:4). Moreover, although Mark does not report post-resurrection appearances, he does report Jesus' own prediction of his resurrection after three days (Mark 8:31, 9:31, 10:34).[11] The Synoptic Gospels reflect a consistent pattern of promises attributed to Jesus that, in addition to appearing to his followers after his death and resurrection (Mark 16:6-7; Matthew 26:64; Luke 24:6-7), he would be exalted by God to a position of honor (Mark 14:62; Matthew 26:64; Luke 22:69). In this way, the disciples are reported to have received firm promises that God would vindicate Jesus following his death,[12] including the specific assurance that he would be raised up and precede them to Galilee, where they would see him (Mark 14:28). Matthew even includes a detailed description of Jesus' role in the final judgment of the human race (Matthew 25:31-46).

Thus, the early Christian tradition—while differing widely in detail—has a common insistence that Jesus' followers were given full advance notice that his death would not bring an end either to his life or to God's purpose in acting through him.

At his final meal, according to the Gospel accounts, the disciples were told in symbolic language that was to become part of the eucharistic words employed by the Church down to the present day that Jesus would be taken from them for a time but that he and they would be reunited in the new age when God's rule would triumph over the world (Mark 14:25; Matthew 26:29). The disciples are initially skeptical, according to the tradition, as reflected both by their abandonment and denial of him in the hour of his crucifixion and by their fear after his burial and the reports of his resurrection (Mark 16:8; Matthew 28:17; Luke 24:21-25). But the experience shared by Paul and Jesus' disciples of seeing him alive again convinces them that God raised him from the dead.

These accounts, however, date from the latter half of the first century C.E. How many of these sayings attributed to Jesus derive from him and how many were developed by the early Church—

THE HOUSE OF ST. PETER. Under a fifth-century octagonal church in Capernaum are remains of a fourth-century house church on top of a first-century residence. This may have been the home of the apostle Peter, often visited by Jesus (Matthew 4:13; Mark 1:21,29). The house was located near the synagogue.

either through oral tradition or by the Gospel writers who offer the reports–is impossible to say with certainty. But one important line of evidence from outside the Gospels shows how very early this belief in the resurrection can be documented. In his first letter to the Corinthians (1 Corinthians 15:3-8), probably written in 54/55 C.E., Paul refers to the early tradition that he shares concerning the crucifixion, burial and resurrection appearances of Jesus. These appearances are presented as a series of events that began with Peter (Cephas); followed by appearances to "the twelve" (referring to the basic core of disciples of Jesus, even though Judas had defected); then to "more than five hundred" members of the Christian community; to James, the brother of Jesus who had become leader of the Jerusalem group of Christians; to "all the apostles" (which implies that the group of commissioned agents and messengers had increased beyond the original 12); and, finally, to Paul. In Galatians 1:16 (written about the same time as 1 Corinthians), Paul describes his personal experience of the risen Christ–in the midst of his efforts to destroy the Jesus movement, Paul had had a vision, or encounter, that he believed was an act of God revealing his son to him.

These reports of the post-resurrection appearances of Jesus, together with the chronological information that Paul offers in his letters concerning his conversion and his subsequent efforts to preach the gospel about Jesus, have important implications for the history of Christianity in the post-crucifixion period.

From his residence in Syria, Paul had learned of the spread of a movement that called itself the "community," or "assembly" (*ekklesia*), and that defined itself as God's people in such a way that Saul/Paul felt compelled to seek to destroy it (Galatians 1:13). Had the movement been merely a reform group within Judaism, such as the community pictured in the Manual of Discipline of Dead Sea Scroll fame, Paul would not have been troubled by claims that ran counter to his own Pharisaic beliefs. What troubled Paul was the inclusiveness of the appeal of the Christian group, which claimed to be heir to the covenant promises of the God of Israel.

A new covenant community Those whom Jesus had welcomed into the nucleus of the new covenant community called together by his preaching and actions— people who were ritually impure, the disabled who were also impure, men of lowly or outcast occupation, collaborators with the Romans—were basically offensive to a Pharisaic Jew like the unconverted Saul, whose major concern was to gain and retain the moral and ritual integrity of God's people. The presence of a community of this radical persuasion in Damascus, the largest city of the Decapolis, was especially offensive to him. Jesus himself was said to have visited Hellenized centers of Greco-Roman culture (Mark 5:1-20, 7:24-31; Matthew 4:25, 15:21-28). This indicates to the modern historian that Jesus' message must have evoked a response of faith among people living in these Hellenized cities, and that, as a result, groups of his followers were meeting in predominantly Gentile settings such as Damascus almost immediately after his death.

Some modern scholars would like to dismiss the reports in Mark of Jesus' journey through the regions of Tyre and Sidon and the Decapolis (Mark 7:24-37) as later Gentile Christian traditions read back into the time of Jesus. The Decapolis was a loose federation of ten cities in what are now Israel, Jordan and Syria. Each city, built on the Hellenistic model with a central market area, baths, stadiums and temples dedicated to the Greek gods, represented a major effort by Hellenistic rulers to foster Greek culture in the Near East. Included were Damascus, Philadelphia (modern Amman), Scythopolis (modern Beth-Shean) and Gerasa. The journeys Jesus made to Hellenized centers make perfect sense when viewed against the challenge to the Jesus movement by Saul/Paul, a dedicated Pharisaic Jew, who regarded the movement not as a Jewish sect, but as a threat to the very integrity of the covenant people. The constructive engagement of Jesus' followers with Gentiles was happening with such effectiveness as to alarm someone like the unconverted Saul, concerned as he was with carefully defining and delimiting God's people.

As we shall see, the issues that later developed between Paul and the Jerusalem-based apostles were not over the message to be preached or whether Gentiles were to be welcomed into the new community, but (1) whether the primary target for converts was to be Jewish (as with the Jerusalem apostles) or Gentile (as with Paul) and (2) whether there were to be different criteria for including Gentiles in the community. But Paul is clear that, although there may have been a dispute between him and the other apostles concerning a division of labor, there was no divergence among them regarding the basic principle of the inclusiveness—including Gentiles—of the newly defined covenant people.

All of the apostles, including Paul, shared the conviction that God had designated Jesus as the Messiah by raising him from the dead. As witnesses of the resurrection, they were under divine obligation to bear witness to that event and to invite all who were persuaded by their testimony to share in the new covenant community they believed God was establishing through the life, message, death and resurrection of Jesus. Jesus himself had set the pattern for participation in the community by building on prophetic tradition and on precedent in the history of Israel by inviting into the community all those who were ethnically, physically, morally or ritually outsiders to historic Israel. Without excluding those who already considered themselves members of the covenant, the earliest Christians made it clear that a share in the life of the new community was open to Gentiles. All who had faith in the God whose nature and purpose for humanity Jesus had disclosed were to be welcomed into this new covenant.

The central symbolic act of participation in the new covenant was the sharing of bread and wine inaugurated by Jesus at his last meal with his followers, as attested both by the Gospels in various forms (Mark 14:22-25; Matthew 26:26-29; Luke 22:15-20),[13] and by Paul (1 Corinthians 11:23-26).

Paul did not regard himself as an innovator. On the contrary, he acknowledged that the symbolic meaning of the Eucharist and the cultic formula associated with it were part of what he had "received" from his predecessors in the faith (1 Corinthians 11:23-25). Like the Gospel accounts of the Last Supper, Paul asserts that this ceremony is not merely a remembrance of a central event in the past, but also an assurance of what God is yet to do through "the Lord Jesus" in the future fulfillment of his purpose for his people (1 Corinthians 11:26).

MOSAIC OF LOAVES AND FISHES. This fifth-century floor mosaic in the Church of the Multiplication at Tabgha on the Sea of Galilee commemorates the "Feeding of the Five Thousand." In a story recounted in slightly different forms in all four Gospels (Matthew 14:13-21; Mark 6:30-44; Luke 9:10-17; John 6:1-15), Jesus, using a boy's offering of five barley loaves and two fish, fed a hungry crowd of thousands. By tradition, this isolated area not far from population centers was the site of the miracle.

The division of labor between Paul's mission to the Gentiles and that of the other apostles to the Jews was by no means absolute. In Paul's letters and in the account of his activity in Acts, he is pictured as working with Jews and taking part in their meetings. Conversely, Peter is portrayed by Paul as initially sharing table fellowship with Gentile Christians (Galatians 2:12). In Acts 10, Peter, in response to a series of divinely inspired visions, takes the initiative in opening participation in the new community to a Roman military officer, Cornelius. Peter's action is divinely confirmed by the outpouring of the Spirit on the believing Gentiles (Acts 10:44-48).

Was Mosaic Law binding on Christians? That the outreach of early Christians was primarily to Jews is supported only by shreds of evidence. In Paul's letters and in Acts, some people insist that male members of the new community must be circumcised (Galatians 2:12; Acts 11:2). Scholars have inferred, therefore, that a wing of the early Christian movement insisted on basic conformity among all Christians to the Mosaic Law, as symbolized by the rite of circumcision and Jewish dietary restrictions. Apart from passing references to those of this persuasion, we have no evidence for the existence of a distinctively Jewish Christian group, although of course many Jews did become Christians.

The clearest evidence of efforts by some early Christians to come to terms with details of the Jewish tradition is provided by the Gospel of Matthew. In Matthew's version of Jesus' teaching about the Law, in material found only in Matthew and only in this context, Jesus insists that his followers be strict in obeying the commandments of God ("Think not that I have come to abolish the Law and the Prophets; I have come not to abolish them but to fulfill them; for truly I say to you, till heaven and earth pass away, not an iota, not a dot will pass from the Law until all is accomplished" [Matthew 5:17-18]), and that their "righteousness" exceed that of the scribes and Pharisees (Matthew 5:20). This Gospel was probably written toward the end of the first century at a time when—following the destruction of the Temple and with it the functions of the priests—survival and reformulation of the Jewish tradition were in the hands of the scribes and Pharisees, who had been working since post-Maccabean times to show the relevance of Scripture for the life of God's people in the present. Now Christians were making similar claims about the Jewish Scriptures, and some of them reframed the Jesus tradition to support their claims in direct competition with emergent Rabbinic Judaism. These Christians were not claiming to be Jews, but to be God's true and truly obedient people. This is explicit only in Matthew, where Jesus is reported as placing his interpretation of Scripture over against Jewish interpretations which had become dominant in the post-70 period: "You have heard it said of old . . . but I say to you" (Matthew 5:21-22,27-28,31-32,33-34,38-39,43-44). It would be anachronistic, however, to read this process of competitive interpretation of Scripture back into the time of Jesus.

Eusebius, in the fourth century, describes the flight of Christians from Jerusalem just before the Romans attacked the city in 70 C.E. However, he does not indicate that these Christians were distinctively Jewish Christian. On the contrary, they are sharply differentiated from the Jews, who, according to Eusebius, had been seeking to drive them from the city by "thousands of deadly plots." Clearly the form of Christianity that took root among the Jerusalemites was not merely a mildly dissenting version of Judaism—although the members of the new movement in Jerusalem were principally Jewish. Guided by a revelation that forewarned them of the impending doom of the city and the destruction of the Temple, the Christians went, significantly, to Pella, one of the Hellenized cities of the Decapolis east of the Jordan River, not to a Jewish community.[14]

The differences between the Jesus movement and official Judaism as represented by the priesthood and the Temple are also attested by the importance within the Gospel tradition of the prophecy attributed to Jesus that the destruction of the Temple would be an act of divine judgment (Mark 13; Matthew 24-25; Luke 21).

The assumption that the early Christian movement was in effect a Jewish movement rests largely on 19th-century scholarship. Based on the philosophy of Hegel, it posited a gospel free of the Law as the antithesis to the supposedly original, Law-observant gospel of pre-Pauline Jewish Christians. The 19th-century scholars who created this paradigm simply read into the New Testament evidence of the workings of their own constructs.

The issue was not, "Who are the real Jews?" but "What are the criteria for participation in the life of God's covenant people?" A basic issue was whether ethnic and/or ritual links with Jewish tradition were essential requirements. Nearly all the early Christians rejected both of these criteria, while insisting that through Jesus and his teaching, his death and his resurrection, the way was open to share in the new covenant without respect to ethnic or ritual requirements. The Christians claimed that Jesus' words and actions had provided them with the divinely intended meaning of the Scriptures and their relevance for the life of God's people in the new age that Jesus had inaugurated. There were disagreements among early Christians about the extent to which the moral aspects of Jewish law were binding on them, but on the whole they insisted that Jesus had provided them with the moral essence and living example of God's will for his people as conveyed through the Scriptures of Israel.

Eusebius does mention one group of Christians—the Ebionites, or the "poor ones," so named because of their views on poverty— who insisted on complete observance of Jewish law. But Eusebius does not even hint that this group was the original nucleus of Jesus' followers, from which Paul was a radical deviant.

In the second century and later, certain Christians in Syria and Egypt rejected or radically revised the reports of Jesus in the canonical Gospels. They denied the virgin birth and insisted on full conformity to the Law of Moses. Their reworked gospels—they claimed their versions were the original Gospel of Matthew—are the apocryphal Gospel of the Hebrews and the Gospel of the Nazoreans, or Nazireans. Both of these survive only in fragmentary quotations in works attacking their views. The most plausible theory is that these groups developed within Christianity during precisely the centuries—second to fifth—when the Mishnah and the

Talmud were taking shape as post-Temple Judaism reconstituted itself. The contrast between such later splinter groups and the views of the first-century Christians is marked.

The documentation that has survived in the New Testament is uniform in indicating that from the beginning the Jesus movement included both those whose origins were within the tradition of the covenant of Israel and those who were outside that tradition. It was precisely this factor that was so troubling to the Pharisee Paul; that is why, initially, he set out to destroy the movement. Instead, however, he found himself called to give leadership within it.

Paul's outreach to the Gentiles is clearly seen in his letters; it is also recounted in narrative form in Acts, written a generation or two after Paul's time.

We will look first at his letters to see what they tell us about his message and his views regarding the issues in Christian communities comprised of both Jews and Gentiles. We will then turn to the description of his mission to the Gentiles in Acts.

Paul's career as messenger of Jesus Christ to the Gentiles

Paul's letters provide us with a fair amount of information about his origins, upbringing and religious life prior to his conversion. We learn that he had been born and reared within the Jewish tradition (Philippians 3:5-6). He had been circumcised on the eighth day, as the Law of Moses and precedent going back to Abraham required (Genesis 17:12; Leviticus 12:3). His ethnic origins were within Israel; he even claimed to know that he was descended from the tribe of Benjamin. Although he communicated easily in Greek, as is evident from his letters, he describes himself as having been raised in a Hebrew-speaking family ("a Hebrew born of Hebrews" [Philippians 3:5]). Archaeological evidence indicates that at this time Greek was widely used even among observant Jews. The majority of the inscriptions connected with Temple and Jewish burials of this period are in Greek. The earliest surviving synagogue inscription—the famous Theodotus inscription from late second-century Jerusalem—is also in Greek. Even the leader of the Second Jewish Revolt against Rome (132-135 C.E.), Bar-Kokhba, wrote in Greek—some of his letters have been found.[15]

So Paul was bilingual—or trilingual, he probably spoke Aramaic as well. His knowledge of Greek obviously gave him an advantage in his Gentile mission in the wider Roman world where the dominant language was Greek.

Paul was a Hellenized Jew. The cultural impact of Hellenism on Paul is evident in his interpretation of the Jewish covenantal tradition. For example, he writes to the Romans about the human conscience as the instrument through which the law of nature is communicated to all humanity (Romans 2:12-15); conscience is a

Hellenistic Greek, not a Jewish, concept. Similarly, when he enumerates the moral fruits of the Spirit at work in the life of Christians, he includes technical terms for virtues—such as *chrestes* (integrity, goodness) and *egkrateia* (self-control)—that come directly from Stoic moral philosophy (Galatians 5:22-23). This is not surprising. From Jewish writings such as the Testaments of the Twelve Patriarchs, we know that Stoic modes of moral thinking derived from Greek philosophy had penetrated Judaism.[16]

In his letters, Paul never mentions Tarsus as his native city though this is indicated several times in Acts (Acts 9:30, 11:25, 22:3). Tarsus, the capital of Cilicia (in modern-day Turkey), was a major intellectual center of the Roman world, known especially for Stoic learning. If indeed Paul was from Tarsus, the Stoic elements in his thought would be even more readily understandable.

Paul had chosen to identify himself with the Pharisees (Philippians 3:5) and, like other Pharisees, he defined his Jewish identity in terms of personal commitment to the Law of Moses in daily life. Though not opposed to the Temple rituals nor negligent of them, the Pharisees were convinced that their life as God's covenant people required reinforcing their group identity through meetings in homes and public halls.[17]

When Paul heard that groups—early Christians—were meeting for outwardly similar purposes, that their members claimed to be God's covenant people but allowed full participation by Gentiles and others who did not measure up to the purity requirements of Paul's Pharisaic standards, he could not permit such a movement to continue unchallenged. In Galatians 1:13, he describes how he attempted to destroy the early Church and refers to his zeal as its persecutor. Yet, even after his conversion, he seems to have felt no guilt for his persecution of Christians. His conversion arose from a profound personal encounter with the risen Christ, not guilt.

Paul's Paul's letters say little about his conversion experience, beyond
conversion the fact that he had seen the risen Lord. "Have I not seen Jesus our
and his Lord?" (1 Corinthians 9:1). Elsewhere he tells us the Lord "ap-
acceptance by peared to me" (1 Corinthians 15:8), and that "God was pleased to
the Jerusalem reveal his son to me" (Galatians 1:16).[18] This encounter must have
apostles taken place near Damascus, because Paul says he returned there
soon after this transforming experience (Galatians 1:17).

The Book of Acts, however, gives us a far more dramatic account: A light comes from heaven; he hears a disembodied voice ("I am Jesus whom you are persecuting"); he falls to the ground; he is temporarily blinded; he is led by his companions to Damascus; there another disciple, Ananias, has a vision in which Jesus appears and tells him that Paul is "a chosen instrument of mine to carry my name before the Gentiles and kings and the sons of Israel"; Ananias seeks out Saul of Tarsus (Paul) in the street called Straight and lays hands on him, restoring his sight (Acts 9:3-18). Then Paul is baptized and takes food and is strengthened (Acts 9:18-19).

Somewhat different versions of this incident are recounted in Acts 22:4-16 and Acts 26:9-18. The descriptions in Acts appear to be later embellishments of the basic event reported by Paul in bare outline in his letters.

Following his vision of the risen Christ, he went to Arabia (probably what was called Arabia Petraea, a region now included in Jordan) (Galatians 1:17), and then returned to Damascus. Since no other city is mentioned as his early base of operations, Damascus probably served as the center of his evangelistic outreach to Gentiles, for which he believed he had been commissioned by Christ (Galatians 1:16).

Then, three years after his conversion, he went to Jerusalem to confer with Peter and James and to obtain the approval of the Jerusalem-based apostles. Thereafter, he went farther north to the regions of Syria and Cilicia (Galatians 1:18-21), sometimes referred to as his first missionary journey. At that time, Antioch, on the Mediterranean coast near the present Turkish-Syrian border, became his base of operations (Galatians 2:11). Oddly enough, he makes no mention of Tarsus, the chief city of Cilicia and possibly his home town.

The initial approval given by Peter and James in Jerusalem for Paul's mission to the Gentiles was confirmed 14 years later (in late 51 C.E.) in a more formal Jerusalem meeting with all the apostles. The apostles were convinced that God was working through Paul—just as God was working through Peter in his mission to the Jews. It was then agreed that Paul and his associate Barnabas should seek to bring Gentiles into the new fellowship, while the other apostles would continue to concentrate on evangelizing Jews (Galatians 2:9). Only one requirement was made of Paul and the Gentile churches: "remember the poor"—which probably meant to provide support for the isolated and beleaguered Christian community in Jerusalem. (The members of the Jerusalem community probably identified themselves as "the poor" to whom God's good news had been preached; see Luke 4:18, quoting Isaiah 61:1.) That obligation is almost certainly what lies behind the collection for the Jerusalem Christians that Paul later made among the Gentile churches and was in process of delivering when he was arrested six years later in Jerusalem (Romans 15:25-29; 2 Corinthians 8:1-5, 9:1-2).

Paul's primary role from late 51 C.E., after the confirmation of his mission by the Jerusalem apostles, was as an itinerant messenger of the Christian gospel, founding and nurturing Christian communities in major cities across Asia Minor and on mainland Greece, from Macedonia to Corinth (called by some scholars his second missionary journey). Because only some of his letters have survived, we do not know all the places Paul visited or where he founded Christian communities. Acts gives an account of his journeys and activities that is on the whole compatible with what can be inferred from his letters. At several points, however, Acts portrays Paul in a somewhat different light, especially concerning the obligation of Christians to observe certain features of Jewish covenantal identity. For example, in Galatians 2, the Jerusalem apostles impose no cultic or moral requirement derived from Jewish sources on Gentile converts to Christianity. But in Acts 15, Paul is reported as agreeing with the Jerusalem apostles to require minimal dietary obligations for Gentile Christians: they are to abstain not only from idolatry and unchastity, but also "from what is strangled and from blood." Eating meat improperly slaughtered or still containing blood was prohibited by Jewish law (Leviticus 17).

Defining participation in God's covenant people

The question of how participation in God's covenant people was to be defined was central for both Jews and Christians throughout the first century. Neither group had a uniformly agreed upon answer. The variety of answers from the Christian side is evident in Q and Mark, as well as in Paul's letters. In Q, for example, to share in the covenant required acceptance of suffering and trials endured in Jesus' name (cf. Luke 22:28-30). In Mark, the basis of the covenant is Jesus' offering up of his life as a sacrifice ("My blood of the covenant") in expectation of God's vindication of Jesus and his followers ("sheep") in the age to come (Mark 14:22-28). For Paul, the death of Jesus formed the basis of the relationship to God in the new covenant, in contrast to conformity to the Law which had provided the basis of the relationship between God and his people as an interim arrangement between the time of Moses and the time of Jesus.

At the same time, there were differences among the various early Christian communities about how they were to be constituted organizationally. Was it enough to encourage spontaneous leadership, arising from the needs of the moment? Or should there be a planned structure, with assigned responsibilities and defined procedures for decision-making?

Modern sociologists have long noted that although religious movements may begin with spontaneity and even with a sense of expectancy of the end of the present order, they inevitably move toward organization and stabilization. The guidelines for admission and maintenance of status within the group come to be more and more sharply formulated. The responsibilities of leadership, which initially are spontaneous and *ad hoc*, come to be more precisely defined. In the post-70 period, the pseudo-Pauline letter to the Ephesians and the Pastoral Epistles, as well as the Gospel of Matthew, give clear evidence of a shift toward formal organization within the Christian movement. But developments in that direction are already apparent, as may be seen from Paul's letter to the Colossians in the pre-70 period. In the authentic letters of Paul, we get hints of the initial stages in this institutional development, as we shall see.

Paul's letters reflect the variety of settings in which he preached the gospel and where Christian communities arose in response. Sometimes the relationship of the new community to Jewish modes of covenantal definition was a major issue; Galatians and Romans are the prime examples of this. Elsewhere, the new communities were more concerned with the relationship of their community to the wider pagan culture, as in 1 Corinthians and 1 Thessalonians. In still other communities, the major difficulty involved personal relationships among individual members and small groups within the Church, as is evident in 2 Corinthians.

The spread of Christianity in the Greco-Roman world

Undergirding the arguments in all of his letters are two basic factors: (1) Paul's personal encounter with Christ and (2) his conviction that what God had done and was doing through Jesus Christ was in fulfillment of the promises made to his ancient covenant people through the patriarchs Abraham, Isaac and Jacob, and through Moses, David, Solomon and the Prophets. At the same time, Paul's letters show how deeply he was influenced by the Greco-Roman culture of his day, especially in relation to the Stoic philosophical teachings about natural law and moral accountability. The Stoics taught that the universe was maintained by certain natural laws on the basis of which all of life and the universe itself were ordered. Conscience was the universal innate capacity of human beings to recognize the laws of nature. Moral responsibility requires that we live in accord with natural law, even though, in the process, suffering and difficulties may result for the individual. Stoic philosophers taught that humans would be called to account in the future regarding the extent to which they fulfilled or failed to fulfill their moral obligations. Paul was able to incorporate elements of the Stoic philosophy into his understanding of (1) what God was doing for the human race through Jesus and through the working of the Holy Spirit, and (2) how God would hold his people accountable when the day of judgment came.

We can detect a certain tension in the claims of the early Christians concerning what is new in the message and meaning of Jesus: They insisted that through Jesus the Jewish Scriptures were being fulfilled and that what God was doing in Jesus would culminate in a new age, at which time the present world order would be transformed. However, this raised the question as to whether, on the one hand, Gentile culture was to be incorporated into the Christian worldview or, on the other hand, was to be denounced as demonic in origin. Paul's letters by no means resolve this issue. The issue remains important in the later writings attributed to Paul and in the narrative account in Acts of the movement of the gospel from the center of the Jewish world, Jerusalem, to the center of the Gentile world, Rome.

***Letter to the
Galatians***

Paul's letter to the Galatians reflects a sharp conflict within the Christian community of Galatia—probably in northwest Asia Minor—concerning the extent to which Jewish requirements for membership in the covenant community were obligatory for non-Jews who wanted to join. Paul is on one side; Peter, on the other. In Paul's arguments, we see how his training in Jewish law combined with his familiarity with the moral and philosophical insights of pagan philosophy enabled him to interpret Jesus' message in a way that communicated effectively and persuasively to people who had no background in Jewish life and thought. Yet his analysis only adapts Jesus' own redefinition of covenantal participation; it is not a completely innovative product of his own mind.

The issue also arises in connection with a visit of Peter to Antioch, where he declined to share a meal with Gentile Christians (Galatians 2:11-12). Other Christians of Jewish origin were influenced by Peter's withdrawal, and everyone was apparently confused by, and even divided over, the issue. Peter had previously agreed to the principle of Gentile inclusion. Paul points to Peter's inconsistency. He argues that one's relationship to God is not based on moral or ritual performance—even by such a venerable standard as the Law of Moses—but by trust in what God has done through Jesus Christ to free us from sin and death and from the powers of this world (Galatians 2:15-17).

Paul appeals to two factors to support his case. The first is that the Spirit that the Christians have received from God and that provides guidance and moral renewal for our lives is not something earned, but a gift God freely provides (Galatians 3:1-5). Second, Paul makes a historical argument: Abraham's relationship to God—as well as that of his heirs who shared in the covenant—was based not on how well Abraham behaved, but on the fact that he was willing to trust God to provide him a son and heir. That alone was the ground of his right relationship with God, and on that basis alone all the nations of the earth have the possibility of sharing in that relationship (Galatians 3:6-9). Paul argues that we deceive ourselves if we suppose that we can earn that standing before God by conformity to the Law. No one can fully obey the Law; therefore, no one can earn moral worth. If one were to approach God on this basis, the inevitable result would be condemnation for failure. But God has foreseen that universal human problem; he has provided a sacrificial offering through which that potential curse for failing to fulfill the Law has been removed: the sacrifice of Jesus and his death on the "tree" (Deuteronomy 21:23). As a result of this supreme offering on the cross, Jews and Gentiles alike–wholly apart from conformity to the Law of Moses–are invited to share by faith in the benefits that God has provided through Jesus for the inclusive covenant people (Galatians 3:10-14).

Even historically, Paul asserts, Abraham's relating to God by means of faith antedated by more than four centuries the giving of the Law through Moses. The Law given to Moses was an interim arrangement to avoid moral chaos among God's people until the ultimate solution for the human condition would be revealed through Jesus' death and resurrection; the Law served as a kind of baby-sitter for an immature people.[19] Now, however, a more mature relationship was possible between God and his "sons"–namely, through Jesus (Galatians 3:23-26).

A share in this new community or family of God, Paul argues, is open to all–across the traditional religious, sexual, ethnic and social boundaries. As Paul phrases it, in Christ "there is neither Jew nor Greek . . . slave nor free . . . male nor female" (Galatians 3:28).

While this new community is characterized by freedom, it is not irresponsible, unbridled freedom. It is liberation from hostile powers and from religious traditions that hold people in bondage to rules and regulations, rather than freeing them to enjoy life as God's sons and daughters (Galatians 4:1-7).

Paul's opponents have tried to persuade the Galatians that they must observe certain Jewish holy days to find acceptance with God (Galatians 4:10). Paul tells them that, without realizing it, they are making the same mistake Abraham made when he foolishly supposed he could help God out by having a son through intercourse with a female slave (Hagar) rather than relying on God to provide him a son and heir through Sarah (Galatians 4:21-31). Shifting his imagery, Paul says that we must choose between living in a center of slavery (Mt. Sinai) among those who seek to live in accordance with Mosaic Law or living as a citizen in God's city of freedom.

The freedom Paul refers to is experienced through the power of the Spirit that God gave to his own people. Through that Spirit, both the essence of Jewish law ("You shall love your neighbor as yourself"–Leviticus 19:18) and the highest virtues of Stoic morality (patience, goodness, kindness, faithfulness, gentleness, self-control) are attained by the members of the new community (Galatians 5:16-24). In this way, Paul combines his Jewish insights and his Greek philosophical leanings. It is his own unique adaptation of Jesus' message of covenantal participation, but it is by no means completely his own.

Letter to the   Paul's letter to the Romans, written toward the end of his career,
Romans   presents a more studied and nuanced argument of some of the issues discussed in Galatians. Romans was written in Corinth sometime between 55 and 57. Paul was planning to visit Rome (his so-called third missionary journey) after taking to Jerusalem the contribution of the Gentile churches of Greece and Asia Minor to the church there (Romans 15:22-29). Paul was well aware of the difficulties he might experience in Jerusalem, both from non-Christians and from Christians who were critical of his principles of Gentile inclusion.

All the evidence indicates that the church in Rome originally included primarily or even exclusively people with a Jewish background. By the time Paul was writing, however, it included Gentiles as well and represented a broad social and cultural mix (Romans 1:13-14). Paul seized the occasion of his planned visit to Rome to address in a more systematic way the issue of the relationship of Jewish legal tradition and ethnic identity to membership in the people of God: God's purpose was initially pursued through the Jews, but now Gentiles are fully included as well (Romans 1:16).

Both Jews and Gentiles suffer from the same gross shortcomings. Both have failed to reflect the glorious divine image in which God created male and female (Romans 3:23). Both have turned from honoring God their creator to devotion to created things. As a result, God has given them up, allowing them to follow their self-gratifying urges (Romans 1:18-2:11). Consequently both will be held accountable by God for their misdeeds. This judgment applies equally to those who know the law of nature through their conscience (non-Jews) and to those who know the Law of Moses–despite the enormous potential advantage that God had granted to the Jews (Romans 2:17-3:8). In short, both Jews and Gentiles can achieve a right relationship with God in the same way.

Indeed, God has already taken the initiative in making it possible for his creatures to stand in right relationship with him. This he has done by the sacrificial death of Jesus, his son, which constitutes a public demonstration of God's nature as loving and forgiving. All that humans need to do is to respond appropriately to this divine initiative by putting their faith in this divine solution to the problem of their alienation from God (Romans 3:21-31). That basic insight into how God works on behalf of the human race, Paul states, was disclosed to and through Abraham. Its benefits were effective before he accepted circumcision as the sign of the covenant relationship, despite the fact that Sarah's womb was then lifeless and unable to produce an heir. Now all who hear the good news about what God has done through Jesus can share in the community of faith (Romans 4).

According to Paul, all human beings are faced with a choice between two role models: Adam or Christ. Adam's self-seeking disobedience resulted in estrangement from God and the loss of his original blessedness; Christ's self-giving, on the other hand, was rewarded by God with life not only for Christ but for all those who rely on him to attain their place in the new covenant community (Romans 5). United with Christ symbolically through baptism, those who give themselves to him have already experienced the death of their old pattern of existence and their liberation into a new life that Jesus both exemplifies and makes possible (Romans 6). There are still obstacles to overcome, urges from the old style of life epitomized by Adam (Romans 7), but God's power through the Spirit transforms and renews human existence (Romans 8:1-30). Even suffering and death cannot separate the faithful from a share in the life of God's new people (Romans 8:31-39).

For Paul, historic Israel has had a special place in God's purpose. He longs for his Jewish contemporaries to enter into the new life that God has provided through Jesus (Romans 9:1-5). But throughout their history, many have failed to heed God's message. Indeed, those within Israel who have accepted God's message have always been a minority; witness Elijah's experience–he was the only one left in Israel still faithful to Yahweh their God (1 Kings 19:10,14; Romans 11:2-4). Paul notes that a remnant of traditional Israel has heard and heeded God's message through Jesus, just as in the days of the prophets only a minority heard the call. Yet Paul does not despair; that most Jews reject Jesus as the Messiah simply provides an added impetus to Paul to spread the news about Jesus to the Gentiles; they, he observes, respond in larger numbers (Romans 11:11-32). He hopes that at a later time more Jews will accept the Christian way of understanding and experiencing participation in God's covenant.

In the final chapters of his letter to the Romans, Paul considers how Christians should relate to one another and to the imperial power of Rome. True worship of God occurs within the community; there they are to present themselves to God, rather than offering the traditional sacrifices; there they are to accept their mutual responsibilities and share what God has given them for the benefit of the whole group (Romans 12). Nevertheless, they are subject to the secular state, because God has granted it power to maintain order in the interim before the coming of the kingdom of God (Romans 13). Meanwhile, the members are to live and work for the benefit of the community as a whole (Romans 14:1-15:13).

In other letters, Paul also discusses how Christians should relate to the Gentile culture that surrounds them and how they should behave toward each other (1 Corinthians; 1 Thessalonians) and considers questions of authority within local churches and relationships among churches in various population centers and with different cultural outlooks (2 Corinthians; Philippians). Before turning to these issues, however, let us consider the account in Acts; this conforms in general to what can be inferred from Paul's letters, but also differs from them.

Acts of the Apostles   Although the author of Acts wrote in the later years of the first century C.E. or even the early second century, he apparently had access to important early sources and traditions about the apostles, especially Paul. The author's stylized literary mode and use of rhetorical forms from the Greco-Roman world have led some scholars to minimize the historical value of the work. It is true that it reflects a later perspective—long after the first generation of Christians. Nevertheless, the accuracy of many details included in the narrative has long been recognized, and has been confirmed by recent scholarship on the subject.[20]

Acts not only describes the spread of Christianity in the Roman world, but shows this development as part of God's plan from the beginning, a plan confirmed by Jesus, by the Scriptures, by the apostles, by the Spirit and by the result of Gentile conversions from Judea to Rome. It is in Acts that Jesus, in a post-resurrection appearance, tells his apostles that their testimony about him is to extend from Jerusalem through Judea and Samaria to "the ends of the earth" (Acts 1:8). Acts 2 describes an event on Pentecost, which Jewish tradition associated with the giving of the Law on Sinai. On this first Pentecost after Jesus' crucifixion, we see the Christian equivalent of that gift: the descent of the Holy Spirit on the apostles. Unlike Israel's Sinai experience, on this Pentecost there are gathered at Mt. Zion not only Jews but devout people "from every nation under heaven" (Acts 2:5). The miracle is that the apostles' words are heard by these people of diverse tongues each in their own language (Acts 2:5-13). Peter explains that the ecstatic experience of God's Spirit and the comprehension of the message by all is the fulfillment of the prophecy in Joel 2:28-32: The Spirit will be poured out on all humanity—male and female, young and old, slave and free. The result is that "whoever calls on the name of the Lord will be saved" (Acts 2:21). Nevertheless, Peter's message is addressed to "all the house of Israel." Initially, then, the apostles' message was reportedly limited to Jews.

As the narrative progresses, however, we see indications of the potentially universal inclusiveness of the message about Jesus. In Acts 6:1-6, the apostles choose seven people from a group of "Hellenists"—all of them with Greek names—to oversee the serving of tables. This could involve presiding at the common meals of the Christians or it could mean caring for the common funds of the group. In the account that follows, however, one of the Hellenists, Stephen, denies that God is specially present in any humanly constructed building—including, implicitly, the Temple—and accuses the Jewish leaders of having resisted God's message and rejected his messenger, Jesus, just as their predecessors had resisted God's Spirit and persecuted the prophets (Acts 7:51-53).

The Hellenists reach out beyond mainstream Judaism, preaching the gospel to Samaritans.* The Samaritans respond in faith by receiving the Spirit through the laying on of hands of the apostles (Acts 8:2-17). Philip, another one of the Hellenists, converts an inquiring Ethiopian by pointing out to him that the description of the sacrificial lamb in Isaiah 53:7-8 is a prophetic picture of Jesus (Acts 8:26-40).

The inclusion of non-Israelites becomes an explicit issue when Peter questions the instruction he receives through a vision to "eat what is profane or unclean" (Acts 10:9-16). Peter soon understands that this is a symbolic instruction from God to associate with and invite into the fellowship of the new community people like Cornelius, a Roman military officer, and his entire household, who convert to Christianity. Peter concludes that "everyone who believes in Jesus receives forgiveness of sins through his name" (Acts 10:43). The accuracy of this perception is confirmed by the outpouring of God's Spirit on Gentile believers (Acts 10:44-48). The importance of this issue and of Peter's God-given insight is underscored by the fact that Peter later describes his experience in detail to the Jerusalem apostles (Acts 11:1-18).

The Hellenists persecuted by the Jewish leaders are scattered as far as northern Syria and Cyprus. This results in the evangelism of Jews as well as Gentiles at these locations. An emissary from the

---

* Samaria, a district north of Jerusalem, was where Jacob had first lived in the land and had erected an altar to God and where Joshua gathered the tribes of Israel on their entrance into the land (Joshua 24). On Mt. Gerizim across the valley from Shechem a temple of the God of Israel was erected in the Roman period, in direct competition with the Temple in Jerusalem. The Samaritans also had their own version of the Law of Moses.

Jerusalem apostles, Barnabas, seeks out someone to take leadership of the evangelism program in Antioch. The person selected is Saul, or Paul to use his Greek name. Here he is pictured as ideally suited for this work among the Gentiles, which is to move through the islands of the eastern Mediterranean to the southern coast of Asia Minor (Acts 13:1-14).

Paul's strategy follows a consistent pattern: The initial arena for proclaiming the message about Jesus is the synagogue. Only when this effort is met with hostility do Paul and his associates turn to the Gentiles. Their appeal to the Jews is based on their claim to have seen the risen Jesus and on the Scriptures (Acts 13:16-41). When Jewish hostility mounts (Acts 13:45), Paul and Barnabas announce that they have fulfilled their initial obligation to preach to Jews and are now turning to Gentiles, which is in accord with the prophetic instruction to be a "light to the Gentiles, that you may bring salvation to the ends of the earth" (Acts 13:46-47; cf. Isaiah 49:6).

The same pattern repeats itself, with variations, in Iconium (Acts 14:1-7) and in Lystra (Acts 14:8-19). Yet Paul returns to cities where he has been persecuted in order to confirm and instruct converts there, and to establish the basis for ongoing leadership in the community (Acts 14:19-23).

Reports of his successful results elicit fierce opposition from Christians in Antioch who insist that all members of the new community must obey the Mosaic Law, which alone defines participation in God's covenant people (Acts 15:1-3). We have already observed that the conference with the Jerusalem apostles described in Acts 15:4-35 confirms the inclusion of Gentiles. Nevertheless certain minimal ritual requirements are imposed on Gentile Christians—abstaining from "blood and from things strangled" (both of which were part of the dietary laws included in the Mosaic Law—Leviticus 17:10-14; Genesis 9:4), refraining from certain sexual violations found in Leviticus 18:6-26, and refraining from idolatry (as prohibited in Exodus 34:15). (In Paul's own account of this discussion, there is no mention of these requirements being placed on Gentile converts (see above). The principle of Gentile inclusion is then affirmed and documented by appeal to Scripture in a composite quotation (Acts 15:16-18) that derives from Amos 9:11, Jeremiah 12:15 and Isaiah 45:21. A letter confirming these principles is sent to the church in Antioch (Acts 15:22-29).

Returning to Asia Minor by way of Syria—but with a new co-worker, Silas, in place of Barnabas (Acts 15:36-41)—Paul resumes the basic pattern of his Gentile mission: making his initial approach to Jews, but ready to turn to Gentiles when he or his message is rejected. God guides each step of his endeavor (Acts 16:6-10).

This mixture of contacts with Jewish and Gentile hearers continues in Acts. In Thessalonica, both Jews and proselytes are brought into the Christian faith, although there is fierce Jewish opposition as well (Acts 17:1-15). In Athens, we learn of an impressive encounter with Greek intellectuals, with very little result (Acts 17:16-34). In Corinth, Paul is more successful, first with Jews, and then in a Gentile household next door to the synagogue (Acts 18:1-17). After a return visit to Syria and Palestine–apparently not including Jerusalem (Acts 18:18-22)–the basic pattern is resumed in Ephesus: initially in a synagogue, and then in a hired public hall (Acts 19:8-10).

The final section of Acts begins with Paul announcing his intention to return to Jerusalem before going on to Rome itself (Acts 19:21). Following a brief return visit to Macedonia (Acts 20:1-12), he sets out for Jerusalem, pausing at Miletus for a visit with the church leaders from Ephesus (Acts 20:17-38). His words to them combine instructions to local church leaders with an apparent prediction of his own martyrdom in Rome. He receives repeated warnings that danger awaits him in Jerusalem (Acts 21:4,11). Paul, like other Christians toward the end of the first century, felt caught between hostility from emergent Rabbinic Judaism, on the one hand, and an increasingly suspicious Roman authority that saw Christianity's potential for civil subversion on the other. Paul, we are told, obeys various forms of Jewish purity laws, including the circumcision of his young co-worker, Timothy (Acts 16:3). Paul himself takes Nazirite vows en route to Jerusalem (Acts 21:26). The Nazirites were Israelites who took vows described in Numbers 6:1-21 that included abstinence from wine, from cutting one's hair and from having any physical contact with the dead. Paul can thus claim to be fully observant of the Law (Acts 21:24).

Paul offers detailed defenses of himself before religious and civil authorities in Jerusalem and Caesarea. These took place before the Roman military officer who seized Paul in the Temple (Acts 21:27-22:29); before the chief priests and the Jewish council (Acts 22:30-23:10); at the initial hearing before the Roman governor in Caesarea, where Paul was taken by the Roman troops to protect him from a Jewish plot to kill him (Acts 23:12-35); at the formal hearings before the Roman governor, Felix (Acts 24:1-25); before his successor, Festus (Acts 25:1-22); and before the puppet king, Agrippa II (Acts 25:23-26:32). Paul's repeated assertions that he had not violated either Jewish or Roman law are confirmed by the governor's declaration: "This man has done nothing to deserve death or imprisonment" (Acts 26:30-31). Paul's case is turned over to Caesar, to whom Paul as a Roman citizen had formally appealed (Acts 26:32). In his final appearance in Acts—under house arrest in Rome—Paul once again insists on his own obedience to the Law of Moses (Acts 28:17-28), and asserts that the inclusion of Gentiles in the covenant community is in accord with Scripture (quoting Isaiah 6:9-10; Psalm 67:2). Acts gives us no account of Paul's martyrdom, but the issues with the state and with official Judaism are clearly drawn.

According to the author of Acts, Paul and the Christian movement have divine empowerment and scriptural justification for what they are doing, and the new community is in no way politically subversive. The author of Acts is careful to close with the assertion that Paul is not charged with violation of any Roman law; rather, he lives protected by an agent of Roman authority (Acts 28:16). This conforms with what is implied in Paul's letter to the Romans, where he advises the Christians in Rome to obey the secular powers and to regard them as instruments of God for maintaining law and order in the secular state.

That Paul expected to die soon is clearly indicated in his farewell talk with the leaders from the church in Ephesus who came to see him as he was on his way back to Jerusalem for the final time (Acts 20:17-38). Various theories have been offered for the failure of Acts to describe Paul's death. These range from the unlikely proposal that Acts was written before his execution occurred to the more plausible suggestion that by omitting a description of Paul's death, the author achieves two objectives: (1) to show that in the providence of God the gospel moved from its beginnings at the center of Jewish life in Jerusalem to the symbolic and political center of the Gentile world in Rome; (2) to make the case in the early second century (when Acts was probably written and when the Roman authorities were beginning to see Christianity as a threat) that this movement was not subversive of either Roman law or Jewish tradition.

**First
Corinthians** As indicated earlier, Paul's letters also address a number of issues relating to the emerging Christian community, its organization, administration and tensions.

First Corinthians, for example, addresses the new community's relationship to the surrounding culture. Apparently the Corinthian Christians were embarrassed by the fact that Paul's message seemed to lack intellectual substance—or at least was not communicated in the rhetoric that could place it on the same level as popular philosophy of the time. The situation was aggravated by the fact that a certain Apollos had come to Corinth and displayed an impressive mix of Jewish and Hellenistic wisdom of a kind that was well known in Alexandria, primarily from the extensive writings of Philo, a Jewish intellectual and prolific writer. Culturally, Paul's message was no match for that of Apollos. He addressed the issue by drawing a sharp contrast between the gospel, on the one hand, and human wisdom, on the other. The gospel may sound like foolishness to Gentiles, but in fact the Christ whom it proclaims is both the power of God and the wisdom of God. The gospel's lack of intellectual appeal cannot hide the fact that it has the power to renew and transform human life (1 Corinthians 1:18-24).

Paul is also troubled by reports that Corinthian church members are identifying with Apollos rather than with him. Paul argues that both he and Apollos have been commissioned and empowered by God for distinctive contributions; it is, therefore, destructive to choose up sides (1 Corinthians 3:1-5).

Paul also wrote about sex and marriage among members of the community. He roundly condemns a man who has mistaken Christian freedom for moral irresponsibility. To the unmarried, he counsels remaining unmarried—unless they cannot exercise self-control, for it is better to marry than to be aflame with passion (1 Corinthians 7:8-9). Those who are married—even if married to unbelievers—should remain married (1 Corinthians 7:12-13). His advice was predicated on his belief that the end of the present age was imminent (1 Corinthians 7:29-31).

The Corinthians were also troubled by whether or not to eat meat that had been offered to pagan idols: it was cheap, and they knew the idols were nonentities. Paul's answer was that they must consider the effect of their actions on others, rather than pride themselves on their liberation and superior insight (1 Corinthians 8).

Disputes among the members were to be settled within the community, rather than by appeal to the pagan civil courts (1 Corinthians 6:1-8).

Accepting an invitation to a meal in a pagan household was not in itself evil, but it might offend another member of the community who was not yet free from the appeal or impact of the Hellenistic religious traditions (1 Corinthians 10:27-29).

Paul also discusses the role of women in the community (1 Corinthians 11:2-16). This was an especially touchy issue, because within Judaism as well as within wider Roman society in the early centuries of the Common Era there seem to have been limitations on women's participation. The Jesus movement was more open to women's participation, as the Gospels show. For instance, women figure significantly in the Gospel accounts as essential members of the support group for the movement (Luke 8:1-3), as direct beneficiaries of Jesus' redemptive activities (Mark 7:24-30) and as the prime witnesses to the empty tomb (Mark 16:1-8; Matthew 28:1-10). Paul is ready to assign women important roles in the life of the community. For example, Phoebe is identified in Romans 16:1 as a deacon of the church at Cenchreae, the port city of Corinth, and in Romans 16:3 and 1 Corinthians 16:19 Priscilla is mentioned as the equal of Aquila, her husband, in their joint roles as co-workers with Paul and as co-hosts of the church which met in their house. Yet he also at some points limits the public role of women in the common life of the community, as is evident in 1 Corinthians 14:33-36.

The central event in realizing the commonality of the community was at the Lord's Supper (1 Corinthians 11:17-34). Here again, Paul appeals to the tradition about the meal that he traces back to Jesus; in this table-fellowship members from varied social and economic backgrounds meet as one in full mutual acceptance and respect.

The diverse gifts that are evident among them—ecstatic speech and its interpretation, prophecy, healing, spiritual wisdom (1 Corinthians 12-14)—are not matters for pride, but a recognition that God has provided a range of special capabilities so that the needs of the whole community might be effectively met. Inserted in this discussion of charismatic gifts is Paul's justly famous hymn to Christian love:

> "If I speak in the tongues of men and of angels, but have not love, I am a noisy gong or a clanging cymbal. And if I have prophetic powers and understand all mysteries and all knowledge, and I have all faith, so as to remove mountains, but have not love, I am nothing. If I give away all I have, and if I deliver my body to the burned, but have not love, I gain nothing.
>
> "Love is patient and kind; love is not jealous or boastful; it is not arrogant or rude. Love does not insist on its own way; it is not irritable or resentful; it does not rejoice at wrong, but rejoices in the right. Love bears all things, believes all things, hopes all things, endures all things.
>
> "Love never ends; as for prophecies, they will pass away; as for tongues, they will cease; as for knowledge, it will pass away. For our knowledge is imperfect and our prophecy is imperfect; but when the perfect comes, the imperfect will pass away. When I was a child, I spoke like a child, I thought like a child, I reasoned like a child; when I became a man, I gave up childish ways. For now we see in a mirror dimly, but then face to face. Now I know in part; then I shall understand fully, even as I have been fully understood. So faith, hope, love abide, these three; but the greatest of these is love" (1 Corinthians 13).

The power of love transcends human knowledge or religious achievement; it transforms self-seeking into full mutual acceptance.

Paul reminds the Corinthian Christians of the centrality of the hope of the resurrection, the tradition on which it is based—reaching back to the earliest apostles—and the human renewal that will accompany that final event, bringing to an end this evil-dominated age (1 Corinthians 15). The Corinthian Christians are to remain steadfast in their commitment to this faith and to the life of the new community.

Meanwhile, however, Paul has made an agreement with the church in Jerusalem to take up an offering for them from the Gentile churches of the eastern Mediterranean; he stands ready to collect and deliver that gift to the earliest Christian community, the one in Jerusalem (1 Corinthians 16). He discloses his plans to revisit the churches of Macedonia on his way back to Jerusalem. His greeting to the Corinthians from the churches of Asia implies that he is in Asia Minor—probably in Ephesus—as he writes this illuminating letter about the nature of Gentile communities in the early Christian movement.

Paul's first letter to the Thessalonians gives evidence that the composition of this church in Macedonia is quite different from that of the Corinthians. The Corinthian church was composed of an original nucleus of Jews; the Thessalonians had been converted to Christianity from idolatry (1 Thessalonians 1:9). **Thessalonians 1&2**

The Thessalonians were experiencing severe persecution; their fidelity in the face of this was admirable and widely known (1 Thessalonians 2:14-16). Paul is eager to learn more about how they endured their trials (1 Thessalonians 2:17-3:10). He gives them advice concerning the perennial questions of faithfulness and mutual concern (1 Thessalonians 4:1-12), but he also seeks to allay some perplexities that have arisen concerning the coming of Christ at the end of the present age. Members of the community had died, and there were doubts and confusion about their participation in the resurrection when Christ returned (1 Thessalonians 4:13-18). Paul assures them that those who died ("have fallen asleep") will share in this new life; he then reminds the living of their moral obligations in the interim before the end of the age (1 Thessalonians 5:1-11). Mutual encouragement of the members and moral transformation are to characterize the life of the community as they await their final deliverance through Christ.

Perhaps 2 Thessalonians is a corrective Paul later felt obliged to write in view of the seeming failure of his prediction in 1 Thessalonians about the end of the age. Or 2 Thessalonians may be a later apologetic composition written in Paul's name. The later letter to the Thessalonians emphasizes two points: (1) God's judgment will fall on unbelievers; (2) a period of unprecedented Satanic activity will precede Christ's return. The distinction between true believers and faithless members of the community is sharply drawn in 2 Thessalonians—more so than in the other letters of Paul. This may indicate that 2 Thessalonians was written in a later generation when the expectation of Christ's imminent return had waned, accompanied by a decline in moral responsibility. Or it may be that these factors were already at work within Paul's lifetime, and that this letter was a necessary warning.

Second Corinthians   The second letter to the Corinthians is probably the most intensely personal of all Paul's letters. He had been accused by some Corinthians of negligence and vacillation in his relationship to the church there. He responds by repeatedly recounting the afflictions that he has had to endure in Asia Minor (2 Corinthians 1:8-10, 4:7-12, 6:4-5, 11:23-33). Obviously, as the Christian movement became more visible and effective, its opponents—political, religious and economic—intensified their efforts to destroy it.

Despite his suffering and frustration, he reports—in the third person!—his mystical exaltation when he was taken up into the very presence of God and received certain divine communications he cannot reveal (2 Corinthians 12:1-4). This experience is a classic example of what was known in Jewish tradition as *Merkavah* mysticism,[21] through which an agent or messenger of God is lifted out of the trials and sufferings that he has endured and is given the assurance and confirmation of God's support.

Paul then describes what life is like in the new covenant community. He contrasts the old and new covenants (2 Corinthians 3): Even though splendor surrounded the tablets of stone on which the Law was written and radiated from Moses' face as he directly encountered God (Exodus 34:29-35), that glory has faded. Now the presence of God through his Spirit brings about the transformation of God's people "from one degree of glory to another" (2 Corinthians 3:18). In another passage, Paul discusses the essential role of believers in serving God's purpose (2 Corinthians 5:16-21). Just as God was at work in Christ in order to reconcile the world to himself, so now God is at work through the believing members of the community. To them, the ministry of reconciliation has been committed; they now embody the "righteousness of God"—that is, God's activity to restore the world to a right relationship with Himself.

Philippians   Paul's letter to the Philippians deals with three important matters: (1) the ideal relationship between the apostle and a new community for which he is responsible; (2) the relationship of Jesus to God; and (3) Paul's views on martyrdom.

On the first, he commends them for their participation in his work through their prayers, their concern and their generous financial support (Philippians 4:14-19), and he appeals to them to foster mutual concern among their members. As to the second, he reminds them of Jesus' self-giving commitment to God's purpose (Philippians 2:5-11). Although Jesus could have attained equality with God, he chose instead a servant's role, fully experiencing what it means to be human, culminating in his death as a crucified victim of human sin and misunderstanding. In the resurrection, however, God exalted Jesus and assigned him a royal role by which the entire universe would be brought into obedience to God's will, serving his purpose. Paul's task—and that of all Christians—is to proclaim that message so that all humanity will acknowledge Jesus as Lord.

Lastly, in the letter to the Philippians Paul confronts the prospect of his own death. To die is to gain, he says (Philippians 1:20-22). He is ready to be like Christ in his death (Philippians 3:8-10); he awaits the transformation of his body into something resembling the glorious body of the risen Lord (Philippians 3:20-21). This attention to death suggests that Philippians is probably Paul's last preserved letter. Reference to the imperial (praetorian) guard under whose watchful eye he is imprisoned (Philippians 1:12-13) may indicate that he was writing from Rome, although he was also imprisoned in Caesarea before being sent off to Rome (Acts 23-26). In either case, the letter is a fitting valedictory, illuminating the values and aims that motivated Paul to the end: his readiness to suffer and die, as Christ did (Philippians 2:6-18, 3:8-11); his expectation that beyond death lies vindication by God (Philippians 3:1-11,20-21).

Pseudo-Pauline letters

Several writings attributed to Paul stem from a subsequent generation of the early Church. These include Colossians and Ephesians, 1 and 2 Timothy and Titus. Colossians is written in a style close to Paul's; the other pseudo-Pauline letters differ significantly in both style and content from Paul's own writing. In these texts, Christian faith is treated as a body of propositions to be affirmed rather than as reliance on what God has done and is doing through Jesus. Phrased another way, in these pseudo-Pauline letters, faith is belief rather than trust. Instead of relying on more or less improvised roles to meet the immediate needs of the community, there are detailed descriptions of qualifications and responsibilities for deacons, bishops and others. Members of the community are classified according to their social roles: masters and slaves, heads of households and their wives. Clearly, by the beginning of the second century the Church was moving into new organizational patterns; these developments are justified, however, by the claim of these writers that the institutional developments go back to the first generation of the apostles.

The	According to Acts 4:13, the apostles Peter and John were illiter-
beginnings of	ate;[22] if this is true, we can understand why the disciples produced
the Gospel	no written records of Jesus. In any event, there appears not to have
tradition	been any written narratives about Jesus or his teaching by his

According to Acts 4:13, the apostles Peter and John were illiterate;[22] if this is true, we can understand why the disciples produced no written records of Jesus. In any event, there appears not to have been any written narratives about Jesus or his teaching by his immediate followers. Apparently the Jesus tradition was initially transmitted orally. The earliest collection of written materials, mostly sayings, seems to have been Q, discussed earlier (p. 00). Then, in the late 60s, came the Gospel of Mark. The author of this Gospel is not identified in the document itself and his identity is unknown. As late as the second century, some Church leaders continued to prefer the oral tradition about Jesus to literary accounts. For example, Eusebius quotes a second-century bishop as saying that "what was to be obtained from books was not so profitable . . . as what came from the living and abiding voice."[23] Q has been reconstructed by inference from Matthew and Luke who each used it independently as a supplement to their other common written source, the Gospel of Mark.[24]

In assessing these sources, it is essential to recognize that they were not prepared as objective historical documents for preservation of information about the recent past. Their purpose was to tell the reader about Jesus and his significance for the community of the author's *own time*. Both Q and Mark emphasize the sense of urgency in the Jesus tradition about the signs of the end of the present age and the imminent coming of God's kingdom. Both Q and Mark focus on the needs of those who are trying to proclaim the message of Jesus in order to enlarge the community of believers and, at the same time, they attempt to give insight and reassurance to those already within the movement who are facing opposition or discouragement.

The result is not a radical distortion of what Jesus said and did, but it is an adaptation to conditions that existed among his followers in the 60s. By taking these factors into account, we can see the probable original form of the tradition and how it was modified to meet the conditions of historical change through which the movement was passing. Thus studying Mark and Q is as essential for understanding Christianity in the mid-first century as it is for reconstructing the life and teachings of Jesus.

Although Q consists almost entirely of sayings, it does include one narrative section: the story of Jesus healing the servant of a centurion (Luke 7:2-10 || Matthew 8:5-13). Thus, Q reveals some details about Jesus' career. Q also supplements the account in

Mark of Jesus' struggle with Satan at the outset of his public career (Luke 4:2-12 ‖ Matthew 4:3-10). But mainly the sayings (1) portray Jesus in the prophetic tradition; (2) report Jesus calling his disciples to follow him; and (3) describe Jesus as the agent of God to free people from the power of evil and to call them to membership in God's new people.

What emerges is basically compatible with Paul's letters: Jesus is God's agent in overcoming the powers of evil; he is redefining the covenant people in a way that includes those excluded or moved to the periphery by the ritual and ethnic norms of Pharisaic and other forms of Judaism in the first century C.E.; suffering and death are not signs of divine disfavor or abandonment but are essential stages in the accomplishment of God's purpose in the world; the new age of God's rule is soon to come; when it arrives, God will vindicate the faithful who have received the message and shared it with others, awaiting its consummation.

Gospel of Mark

Mark is mentioned as a companion of the apostles in later New Testament writings,[25] but we do not know when his name was first associated with this text. Our earliest manuscripts, dating from the fourth century, however, already refer to the book as the Gospel of Mark. Although attributed to Mark, the book must be regarded as anonymous.

The text contains several indications that it was written at a time when members of the Christian community expected God imminently to bring to a conclusion his redemptive plan for the world. In Mark 9:1, Jesus states that some of his associates will not have died before the kingdom of God comes "with power." That same promise is repeated in a slightly different way in Mark 13:30: "This generation will not pass away before all these things take place."

The things that are to "take place" have been previously detailed. First is the destruction of the Temple (Mark 13:2). That occurred in 70 C.E. This has led many scholars to date Mark after the destruction. While that is possible, I believe other factors make it more likely that it was composed shortly before the destruction. A comparison with the other Gospels—which *were* written after the destruction—is instructive. In Jesus' prediction of the fall of the Temple in the other Gospels, we are given details that clearly seem to reflect a later time. For example, Luke notes that the city will become totally subjugated to Gentiles and surrounded by their armies (Luke 21:20-24), as in fact it was after the Roman siege and destruction. Matthew greatly expands the Marcan account in order to stress the antipathy between Jesus' followers and the Jewish leaders. Mark, on the other hand, seems to have been influenced by Daniel's vision of the pagan desecration of the Temple rather than by the events of 70. Mark refers to the "desolating sacrilege" (Mark 13:14), which echoes Daniel 9:27: "Upon the wing of abominations shall come one who makes desolate."

Mark does indicate, however, that the conflict between Jewish leaders and Jesus' followers has intensified (Mark 13:9) and that the mission to the Gentiles must be launched (Mark 13:10). The inclusion of explanatory notes about Pharisaic and scribal ritual regulations (Mark 7:3-4) are understandable if the text was written a generation after Jesus' time. They were needed in the context of the debates within the Jesus movement concerning the applicability of Jewish law to members of the new movement, many of whom were Gentiles and therefore needed an explanation of Pharisaic and scribal ritual regulations.

The persecution and tribulation that God's people are suffering cannot be indefinitely extended, or no one would survive. The sufferings of the faithful, however, are to be matched by cosmic disturbances heralding the end of the age and the triumph of God's purposes. The apocalyptic features in Mark go well beyond the more modest predictions and expectations in Paul's letters, but not as far as the later Gospels or the Book of Revelation. What is awaited is the coming of the Son of Man, which will be the signal to assemble the members of the community from throughout the earth (Mark 13:26-27).

These considerations lead me to date Mark to the late 60s. We are told that no one can predict when the climactic events will occur; that is a secret known to God alone (Mark 13:32). The members of the community, however, are to be constantly watching, in readiness (Mark 13:33-37). It seems wholly plausible that such an attitude would develop in the years prior to the fall of Jerusalem, say 67-70.

The surge of Jewish nationalism that led to the First Jewish Revolt against Rome also lies behind Mark's effort to distance himself and the early Christian community from political messianism. The priests and their supporters join the Roman officials in identifying Jesus as "King of the Jews" (Mark 15:2,9,12,18,26). This encourages the Roman officials to put him to death as a threat to civil order. Yet the charges leveled against him at the hearing before the high priest concern his threat to the Temple ("I will destroy the Temple") and his special relationship to God ("Are you the Messiah, the son of the Blessed?"), rather than any claim to a political role. Pilate opens the hearing by asking Jesus, "Are you the King of the Jews?"; the Jewish leaders had evidently raised this charge because, if confirmed, it would be a capital offense; by contrast, the claim to be the Jewish religious messiah would not. But there is no hint in Jesus' prophecies that he advocated a Jewish nationalist revolt. Indeed Jesus' counsel is that when the armies come, as they did in 67-70, his followers were to flee, rather than to offer nationalist resistance (Mark 13:14). Historically, many Jews, by contrast, sought to survive the Roman attack by sealing themselves up in the Temple area. These details fit well into the time and circumstances just prior to the Roman invasion.

Mark seems to offer a synthesis of the Jesus tradition, on the one hand, and apocalyptic imagery of the sort that from the time of Daniel emerged in times of crisis, on the other. Mark offers not merely advance information, but advice to the emerging Christian community on how to preserve its integrity in the impending crisis, and what mode of divine vindication it can expect through Jesus, God's agent of renewal of the covenant people.

Mark is also important as the first example of the genre we now call a gospel. Mark's Gospel embodies a literary style that provided a means for evaluating the life and teachings of Jesus and a model for interpreting Jesus that is considerably different from Paul's letters.

Unlike the later Gospels, Mark's narrative covers the career of Jesus only from the time of his baptism by John to the discovery of his empty tomb. The fact that the other Gospels diverge widely where they do not follow Mark confirms the priority of Mark and the basic reliability of his testimony. The convergence of Mark's portrait of Jesus with that offered in Q further strengthens the case for Mark's overall historical reliability. The other Gospels show how speculative and diverse the thinking of the Church was on such subjects (not addressed in Mark and Q) as the birth and childhood of Jesus and the nature of the post-resurrection appearances. Mark's picture of Jesus is obviously colored by Christian faith in Jesus as Messiah, but in time and substance it stands closer to the events it describes than do the later Gospels.

Mark offers a blend of biographical details, examples of the content of Jesus' teaching, Jesus' challenge to his Jewish contemporaries, his definition of the people of God and their role in the world and the outlines of his own place in God's plan.

"The beginning of the gospel of Jesus Christ" is the opening line (Mark 1:1). Then Mark immediately quotes a prophetic passage from the Hebrew Bible—an amalgam of Malachi 3:1 and Isaiah 40:3-4:

"Behold, I send my messenger, before thy face,
who shall prepare thy way;
the voice of one crying in the wilderness:
Prepare the way of the Lord,
make his paths straight."

Mark 1:2-3

Fulfillment of Mark is telling us that the prophets of Israel have predicted the
Hebrew plan that is in the process of fulfillment by God through Jesus. It
Scriptures has been launched by John the Baptist, whose function is to prepare for Jesus. Even John's garb and diet match the prophetic model
in the Hebrew Bible: He is "clothed with camel's hair, and had a
leather girdle around his waist" (Mark 1:6). In 2 Kings 1:8, we
read that Elijah, the traditional harbinger of the messiah, "wore a
garment of haircloth, with a girdle of leather about his loins." In
Mark 1:6 we are told that John eats "locusts and wild honey" while
living in the wilderness. In Leviticus 11:22, we are told that locusts are one of the few kosher insects.

John announces that someone superior to him is coming; John
prepares the superior one for his role by baptizing him.

When John baptizes Jesus, the heavens open, the Spirit descends
and a voice proclaims, "Thou art my beloved Son" (Mark 1:11).
Thus Jesus' role receives divine confirmation in words that recall
both Psalms and Isaiah: "You are my son; today I have begotten
you" (Psalm 2:7) and "Behold my servant, whom I uphold, my
chosen . . . I have put my spirit upon him" (Isaiah 42:1). In these
passages from the Hebrew Bible, the coming of God's agent is
announced.

The time of testing through which Jesus then passes resembles
the preparatory experiences that Moses the law-giver and Elijah
the prophet experienced (Exodus 34:28; 1 Kings 19:8).

The summary of Jesus' message in Mark 1:15 ("The time is
fulfilled, and the kingdom of God is at hand; repent, and believe
in the gospel") makes the astounding claim that God's purpose is
about to culminate; in order to share in this event, people must
believe the good news. Mark's account of Jesus' words and deeds
is in effect a challenge to the outlook of the Jews of the first century. What was believed to be essential in God's dealings with his
people is declared to be no longer effective; it is replaced by new
ways of understanding God's plan as disclosed in Scripture and
effectuated by Jesus in his life and teaching. This theme of the
inclusiveness of the new covenant community fits well with Q, as
well as with the message of Paul, and should be recognized as a
central, authentic feature of Jesus' own message and activity.

Jesus not only announces the new era that God is about to
establish but through healings and exorcisms exhibits an ability
to defeat the powers of evil. His disciples are called on to break
with their families (Mark 1:16-20); they are sent out to all Galilee
(Mark 1:39, 6:7-13). But Jesus sets the pattern for a wider mission
by traveling through the regions of Tyre and Sidon and to the
Decapolis (Mark 5:1, 7:24,31). His healing activity includes a de-

moniac from a Gentile city (Mark 5:2-20)[26] and the daughter of a Greek Syro-Phoenician (Mark 7:24-30). It also extends to Jews whose occupation or physical condition put them outside the bounds of purity or acceptability–the tax-collector called to be a disciple (Mark 2:13-17) and a woman who has "had a flow of blood for 12 years" (she touches Jesus and is healed) (Mark 5:25-34).

The multiplication of the loaves and fishes appears in Mark in two different forms: In both, a hungry throng in a wilderness area is fed with food produced by a miracle, recalling the Israelite trek through the Sinai wilderness where, through Moses, the people were also miraculously provided with food. In the first version of the story in Mark (6:30-44), the feeding of 5,000, the context indicates that Jews are involved; the second version (Mark 8:1-10) follows an account of Jesus' mission among the Gentiles, so presumably Gentiles are involved. The inclusion of Gentiles in the people of God is a consistent and pervasive feature of Mark's account of Jesus' ministry, although the repetition of the story (which does not appear in Luke) may indicate that it is a later modification of the tradition. Even so, its point about Gentile participation in the new community is fully harmonious with the oldest gospel tradition.

Confrontation with Judaism

The confrontation with Judaism has two aspects in Mark. The first is a challenge to the dominant understanding of the moral obligations of members of the community. Jesus lays down new guidelines on the issues of divorce and remarriage (Mark 10:1-12–"What God has joined together, let no man put asunder"), on the participation of children in the community (Mark 10:13-16–"Let the children come to me"), on wealth and family standing (Mark 10:17-31–"Sell all you have and give it to the poor"). He takes a stand on current Jewish debates such as (1) whether there is to be a resurrection at the end of days (Mark 12:18-27), (2) which is the greatest commandment (Mark 12:28-34), (3) how the Messiah of Israel is to be identified (Mark 12:35-37) and (4) whether the current standards of piety developed by the Jewish scribes in the first century are suitable for God's people (Mark 12:38-40). But he also presents a more fundamental challenge to Judaism: He challenges the Temple as a religious institution (Mark 11:15-19); he announces without regret that the Temple will be destroyed (Mark 13:1-3); by means of a parable, he predicts that the present claimants to ownership of God's vineyard (an allusion to Isaiah 5:2) are to be replaced by a new people (Mark 12:1-12). Although the apocalyptic words of Jesus in Mark 13 have been arranged and modified by Mark in light of conditions just prior to the fall of Jerusalem in 70, it seems that the prediction of the replacement of the Temple by a new community as the locus of God's presence among his people goes back to Jesus himself.

With increasing clarity and detail, Mark portrays Jesus as telling his followers that his death is central to God's plan of human redemption from sin, and that it will be followed by God's vindication of him through the resurrection (Mark 8:31, 9:31, 10:32-34,45). Each of these predictions of his death is followed by a reminder that the disciples too must share in the suffering and sacrifice; their role is not simply one of authority or prestige (Mark 8:34-38, 9:33-37, 10:35-45). Following his seizure by the mob and an inconclusive hearing before the regional council* (Mark 14:43-72), Jesus is turned over to the Roman authorities, who sentence him to death on the political charge of claiming to be king of the Jews (Mark 15:1-15). His hasty burial late Friday afternoon (Mark 15:42-47) is followed by the discovery early on Sunday morning—three days later by Jewish reckoning—of the empty tomb (Mark 16:1-8). The very early date of the third-day tradition for the resurrection of Jesus is evident from Paul's testimony in 1 Corinthians 15:4. Paul states that this was part of what he had "received" from his predecessors in the faith within a year or so of the crucifixion of Jesus.

The oldest manuscripts of Mark all end on an expectant note: The assurance that Jesus will fulfill his promise of renewing his association with his disciples in Galilee (Mark 16:7-8; cf. Mark 14:28). Longer endings of Mark exist in several forms from late manuscripts of this Gospel. The oldest and best manuscripts, however, end with 16:8, as did the copies of Mark that were used by Matthew and Luke, since it is precisely at this point that they diverge in their respective accounts of the post-resurrection appearances of Jesus.

Written sources before 70   Unfortunately, no written sources about the origins of Christianity have survived from before the year 50 C.E. Paul's letters tell us about an older tradition, although we cannot determine whether this indeed goes back to Jesus or how accurate it is. Q and Mark

---

* The regional council (in Greek, *synedrion*) was an essential feature of Greek and Roman rule in the Mediterranean world. The occupying power would organize local leaders of wealth and power into a council with a degree of local autonomy on strictly regional affairs, but with the function of helping the local governor or king to make and effect decisions on major policy and fiscal matters. This policy was followed in Palestine as well. After the destruction of the Temple and the crushing of the Jewish insurrectionists, Jews, who already had a tradition of a religious council of 72, were permitted to organize a regional council to guide religious affairs. The name chosen for this institution was a transliteration of the Greek term for council: Sanhedrin. It continued to have a major role in the subsequent development of Rabbinic Judaism from the second to the sixth century, as reflected in the Mishnah and the Palestinian Talmud.

also provide some evidence about the historical Jesus and his disciples. Although these two sources differ in detail and style, they present converging lines of evidence on many important points. All three sources—Q, Mark and Paul's letters—insist on the continuity between the Jewish scriptural tradition and the Christian movement. All three sources reflect a continuity between what Jesus inaugurated and what happened in the movement that was launched in his name.

Q and Mark also converge regarding important features of the Jesus tradition. Both agree on the close links between Jesus and John the Baptist, with emphasis on the coming of the new age and the need for repentance and renewal on the part of historic Israel. In both, suffering and even martyrdom are inevitable and, in the long run, positive features of the coming of God's rule. This theme is also prominent in Paul's letters.

In all three of our earliest sources—Paul, Mark and Q—the debates between Jesus and his followers, on the one hand, and Jewish authorities, on the other, involve ethical questions that arise in the context of the extended process in the first century of Pharisaic recasting and reappropriation of the Law. The Pharisees, who first appear in the latter part of the second century B.C.E. as a party opposing the Hasmonean family (the Maccabean rulers), shifted their energies in the first century B.C.E. to a fresh appropriation of the Scriptures and especially of the Law of Moses. Their aim was to provide a vital, relevant alternative to the Temple ritual as the ground of Jewish identity. They reinterpreted the laws concerning priestly ritual purity to apply to themselves, thus specifying and concretizing their special place as members of God's people. The center of their group activity was the informal meeting in private homes or public halls where they studied the Scriptures in order to discover their relevance for their own lives and celebrated their common identity in a shared meal.

Paul's thinking also reflects his exposure to Stoic philosophy and ethics, with the result that his moral norms are a blend of Jewish and Hellenistic traditions. For Paul, the Temple and its cultus are metaphors, to be replaced by the Christian community in whose midst God dwells. For the Gospel tradition, the Temple's destruction is the final sign of the end of the present order and the coming of the new age.

On one central point, the early sources are in agreement: The new community is open to all. Neither ethnic, ritual, social nor economic factors are significant as a qualification for admission to or status within this newly defined people of God.

As Judaism reshaped itself after the destruction of the Temple, the competition and conflict between Judaism and Christianity became more severe. As Christianity reached out ever wider into the Gentile world, the nature of its links with its Jewish heritage became more ambiguous and controversial. Yet all the evidence before and after 70 points to the insistence of the early Christians that they were the heirs, and had the proper keys to interpretation, of the covenant tradition of Israel embodied in the Jewish Scriptures.

What is missing from the pre-70 material are guidelines for leadership roles and distribution of responsibilities within the early Christian communities. An improvisational aspect manifests itself in the different ways Paul handles these issues in different communities. The later material written in his name, as well as the later Gospels—especially Matthew—addresses the organizational needs of the Church directly as its faces a future extending indefinitely.

The crisis of 70 C.E. forever altered the situation for both Jews and Christians. For the Jews, it meant a major challenge: How could the people Israel reconstitute itself in the post-Temple era. The loss of the Temple and its cultus required the Jews to redefine themselves even more sharply in contrast to the new competition—the Christians—who claimed to have the correct insights and to be the true heirs of the covenant promises.

For the Christians, the primary emphasis in the pre-70 material is on what God had already done through Jesus, how the community was to be defined and how God would accomplish what he began through Jesus—a new perception of what it means to share in the life of God's people. The principle of inclusiveness in the Christian community had already been laid down by Jesus, and firmly established both in the Gospel tradition and by Paul. The post-70 Christian literature devoted itself to the task of establishing a Christian covenantal identity in sharp distinction to the emergent pattern of Jewish definition.

FOUR

Judaism from the Destruction of Jerusalem to the End of the Second Jewish Revolt: 70–135 C.E.

LEE I. A. LEVINE

T HE 60-YEAR PERIOD BETWEEN THE FIRST JEWISH REVOLT AGAINST Rome (66-74 C.E.) and the Second Jewish Revolt (132-135 C.E.) was one of the most remarkable and complex in Jewish history. It was a time of defeat and rebuilding, of continued confrontation and conflict alongside major efforts toward adaptation and adjustment. Some Jews refused to abandon hope for national redemption and actively engaged in planning a military-political option; others sought a religious and communal *modus vivendi* with Rome and within the Jewish community generally. Major segments of the old guard had been obliterated; new directions began to emerge that would eventually dominate Jewish religious and communal life for centuries, even millennia.

Undoubtedly, Jews both in Israel and in the Diaspora were traumatized by the news of the destruction of the Jerusalem Temple. True, a similar catastrophe had occurred with the destruction of the First Temple in 586 B.C.E., but the Jews had then managed to return to Jerusalem and restore the Temple–a memory which was perhaps comforting and encouraging. Nevertheless, the Second

Aftermath of the destruction of the Temple

Temple had stood for almost 600 years and had acquired enormous prestige and centrality for Jews the world over; its loss was surely a shock.

Both Jewish and Christian traditions have emphasized the extent of this tragedy, each for its own theological reasons. The destruction of the Temple in later Jewish tradition signaled the beginning of exile, which was God's punishment for the sins of the people ("Because of our sins we have been exiled from our land"–from the traditional *Musaf* service for the festivals).[1] For Christians, the destruction of the Temple signified punishment the Jews deserved because of their refusal to accept Jesus and because of their alleged role in his crucifixion; it was the ultimate sign of God's rejection of the Jews.

However, theological considerations aside, the objective reality for the Jewish people following the destruction of 70 was far more complex. Indeed, much of Jewish life lay shattered: Jerusalem was totally destroyed; only the three great towers that had once guarded Herod's palace and remnants of the western city wall remained intact.[2] The Temple had been razed and the city's population massacred or exiled. The high priesthood and Jerusalem's aristocratic class, which had dominated Jewish religious and political life for much of the Second Temple period, all but disappeared. Judea had dared rebel against mighty Rome; having failed, she paid the heavy price of revolt.

Many of the Jewish sects that had played a central role in Jewish religious life during the first century disappeared: The Sadducees, centered around the Jerusalem priesthood in the days of the Temple, lost their base of political and religious authority; the Essene center at Qumran[3] was destroyed by the Romans in 68 C.E.; members of the various pre-70 revolutionary movements (Sicarii, Zealots, followers of John of Gischala and Simon Giora) either were killed, taken captive, fled to North Africa or went underground.

Nevertheless, it is easy to overstate the effects of the year 70. Contrary to popular opinion, the exile did not commence in that year–most Jews were already living in the Diaspora before the destruction–nor did the year 70 signal the loss of Jewish independence. In reality, Judea had been conquered 130 years earlier by Pompey in 63 B.C.E. Although much autonomy had been granted to Herod (37-4 B.C.E.), it had already been greatly curtailed following Judea's annexation as a Roman province in 6 C.E.

Moreover, the continuum between the pre-70 and post-70 periods was maintained by the ongoing rule of Rome; culturally, economically and even socially much of Jewish life was not seriously interrupted between the pre- and post-destruction era. Indeed, large parts of the Jewish people were unaffected or only marginally affected by the revolt and its aftermath. Few Jewish communities in the Galilee were destroyed—Jotapata and Gamla were the exceptions. The Roman military march had little, if any, effect on the large Jewish settlement in Perea east of the Jordan, on the communities along the coastal plain or even on many areas in Judea itself. Thus, beyond Jerusalem and some parts of Judea, the upheavals of the First Revolt were not all that widespread, either demographically or economically.

Roman reactions to the revolt were measured. There was no attempt to annihilate the Jewish people or their Judaism. Rome did not change the name of the province, as she was to do some 60 years later, following the Bar-Kokhba revolt (it then became Syria-Palaestina). The province of Judea was not reduced in size, but continued to function intact. The Roman authorities even moved to correct certain abuses in the system of administration that may have contributed to the unrest in the pre-66 period. Recognizing that the earlier prefects-procurators drawn from the equestrian class* had shown little interest in or talent for dealing with the local inhabitants, and were often interested only in their own self-aggrandizement, Rome now determined that the governors of Judea would come from the senatorial class, on the level of an imperial legate of praetorian rank. Alongside this legate, there would also be a procurator in charge of finances. The legate was there to prevent the procurator from using his office to increase his personal wealth, as had often occurred in the past. In addition, the auxiliary troops previously drawn from the anti-Jewish pagan residents of the province were judged inadequate for policing Judea. These military units were disbanded and replaced by the Tenth Legion. As part of Vespasian's redeployment of troops in the East, this measure was obviously calculated to serve as a deterrent to any future uprising.

Roman reaction in the wake of the revolt

Some have claimed that the legal standing of the Jews in the Roman empire suffered and that they were henceforth characterized as alien residents (*peregrini dediticii*). However, the evidence for this is meager. Josephus speaks about the confiscation of land and the imposition of a special tax,[4] but these statements—particularly the former—must be understood as limited in extent and application, referring principally to those who had been directly involved. We have no substantial evidence that the Romans persecuted Jerusalem Jewry generally in the wake of the revolt.[5]

On the other hand, a new tax (the *fiscus Judaicus*) was imposed

---

* Literally, "horsemen," members of the Roman middle class, second to the nobility, from which horsemen originally were drawn.

ZEV RADOVAN

JUDEA CAPTA COIN. One of a series minted to commemorate the fall of Jerusalem to the armies of Titus in 70 C.E., this coin depicts Judea as a woman mourning beneath a palm tree. The large number of *Judea Capta* coins in gold, silver and bronze indicate the importance the Romans attached to their victory over the Jews.

on all Jews in place of the annual contribution to the Temple. To add insult to injury, these monies were donated to the temple of Jupiter Capitolinus in Rome. Other than this general tax, however, no collective punishment was meted out to the Jews.

The Romans also initiated a series of coins known as *Judea Capta* (Judea the Conquered) coins, on which a woman representing Judea is depicted in a position of subjection and humiliation, a theme clearly intended for propaganda purposes to acclaim the Roman victory and to deter any future uprising.

Rome also tried to deter any future revolutionary thoughts by supporting Josephus' writing of his *Jewish War*, describing the enormity of the conflict and vindicating Rome by placing the blame squarely on irresponsible Jewish fanatics. Josephus clearly downplayed any role that Rome or her governors had played in the events leading to the revolt (compare the somewhat more balanced presentation of these same events in his *Antiquities of the Jews*, written some 20 years later).

Despite Rome's relatively measured reaction to Judea's revolt, when all is said and done, the Jewish body politic had been badly hurt. Both religiously and nationally, the morale and confidence of the people had been severely damaged. Nevertheless, they were not broken, and the healing process commenced almost immediately.

The early Jewish Christian community, especially those who resided in Jerusalem at the beginning of the revolt, fled to Pella, east of the Jordan, at the outbreak of hostilities. The destruction of the Temple ended any desire or possibility for this group to see itself as an integral part of the Jewish people.[6] The subsequent history of the Jewish Christians and their various sects is well-nigh impossible to reconstruct, but we know that henceforth they pursued a religious and communal agenda different from that of the Jewish community.

Within the Jewish community itself, reactions to the destruction of Jerusalem and the Temple were diverse. Some revolutionaries continued their activities until the fall of Masada, Herod's wilderness retreat near the Dead Sea, in 74 C.E.[7] Many Jews fled to Egypt to pursue their agitation against Rome. Still others doubtless went underground, continuing in one form or another to nurture hopes of a future uprising. Eusebius' statement that first Vespasian (69-79 C.E.) and then Domitian (81-96 C.E.) sought to destroy the remnants of the seed of David[8] may be an allusion to continued revolutionary activity.

These varied elements of dissension probably played a significant role in the unrest that engulfed Judea in the second and third decades of the second century, and perhaps in the eventual outbreak of the Second Jewish Revolt against Rome—the so-called Bar-Kokhba revolt—in 132 C.E.

In some circles—however small they may have been—there was a certain air of despair and abandonment. The Tosefta, a third-century rabbinic commentary/expansion of the Mishnah, gives expression to this distress: *Apocalyptic literature of despair*

"After the last Temple was destroyed, ascetics who would not eat meat or drink wine increased in Israel. Rabbi Joshua met them, saying, 'My sons, why do you not eat meat?'

"They said to him, 'Shall we eat meat, for every day a continual burnt-offering [of meat] was offered on the altar, and now it has been discontinued?'

"He said to them, 'Then let us not eat it. And then why are you not drinking wine?'

"They said to him, 'Shall we drink wine, for every day wine was poured out as a drink-offering on the altar, and now [this practice] has been discontinued?'

"He said to them, 'Then let us not drink it.' He said to them, 'But if this is so, we also should not eat bread, for from it did they bring the Two Loaves and the Show-Bread. We also should not drink water, for they poured out a water-offering on the Festival [of Sukkoth] We also should not eat figs and grapes, for they brought them as First Fruits on the Festival of the Atzeret [Shavuoth].' They were silent."[9]

Although several apocalyptic books that can be dated to the

post-destruction period also reflect distress and despair, they nevertheless express hope and comfort in a promising future.[10] For
example, the following poetic lament appears in the Syriac apocalypse of 2 Baruch:

> "Blessed is he who was not born,
> or he who was born and died.
> But we, the living, woe to us,
> because we have seen those afflictions of Zion,
> and that which has befallen Jerusalem.
> . . .
>
> "You, farmers, sow not again.
> And you, O earth, why do you give the fruit of your harvest?
> Keep within you the sweetness of your sustenance.
> And you, vine, why do you still give your wine?
> For an offering will not be given again from you in Zion,
> and the first fruits will not again be offered.
> And you, heaven, keep your dew within you,
> and do not open the treasuries of rain.
> And you, sun, keep the light of your rays within you.
> And you, moon, extinguish the multitude of your light.
> For why should the light rise again,
> where the light of Zion is darkened?
> And you, bridegrooms, do not enter,
> and do not let the brides adorn themselves.
> And you, wives, do not pray to bear children,
> for the barren will rejoice more.
> And those who have no children will be glad,
> and those who have children will be sad.
> For why do they bear in pain only to bury in grief?
> . . .
>
> "Henceforth, do not speak anymore of beauty,
> and do not talk about gracefulness.
> You, priests, take the keys of the sanctuary,
> and cast them to the highest heaven,
> and give them to the Lord and say,
> 'Guard your house yourself,
> because, behold, we have been found to be false stewards.'"
>   2 Baruch 10:6-7,9-15,17-18

But all was not despair; in this same book Israel was bidden to
await the redemption that was not far off:

> "And that period is coming that will remain forever; and there
> is the new world which does not carry back to corruption those

who enter into its beginning, and which has no mercy on those who come into torment or those who are living in it, and it does not carry to perdition. For those are the ones who will inherit this time of which it is spoken, and to these is the heritage of the promised time. These are they who prepared for themselves treasures of wisdom. And stores of insight are found within them. And they have not withdrawn from mercy and they have preserved the truth of the Law. For the coming world will be given to these, but the habitation of the many others will be in the fire" (2 Baruch 44:12-15).

A similar composition from this period is 4 Ezra,[11] the most widely circulated Jewish apocalypse in antiquity and continuing into the Middle Ages. In several of its seven sections, Ezra, who is regarded in this work as a second Moses, bemoans Israel's tragic fate in contrast to the prosperity enjoyed by Gentiles. Three sections consist of dialogues between Ezra and an angel; in each Ezra is assured that wickedness will soon cease, the dead will rise and the approaching end, brought about by God himself, will include the coming of the Messiah, the salvation of the few and the destruction of the many. The book's final four sections are visions related to issues raised in the dialogues—the rebuilding of Zion, the reinstitution of the Temple and its sacrifices, the advent of God who will redeem mankind, and the coming of the Messiah which will signal the end of godlessness and the approach of the day of judgment.

A number of works coming from the Diaspora almost completely ignore the effects of 70. One type of apocalyptic book written at about this time is exemplified by the Fourth Sybil,[12] which proclaims in the name of God that a series of catastrophes will befall the peoples and cities of Europe and Asia unless they repent; at the end of days, God will raise people from the dead, pronounce judgment and grant new life to the righteous. Surprisingly, however, Fourth Sybil reflects no particular concern with the destruction of the Temple or Jerusalem.

Similarly with regard to the intriguing *Liber Antiquitatum Biblicarum*, falsely ascribed to Philo of Alexandria.[13] This book covers biblical history from Adam to David, often integrating aggadic* themes and occasionally altering the biblical material in an original fashion. Although it is dated to the late first century C.E., this author, too, makes no mention of the events of the year 70, which appear to have had no significant impact on his outlook.

In a similar vein, the books written by Josephus several decades after the destruction of the Temple—*Antiquities of the Jews, Against*

---

* The *aggadot* (sing., *aggadah*) are non-halakhic (legal) expositions of biblical text.

Apion and *Vita*—discuss Jewish history, institutions, ideas and beliefs in the post-destruction period without any significant or dis-
cernible reaction to the destruction itself or to the trauma that it
caused. Not only in his writings, but in his personal life as well,
Josephus appears to reflect the ability of many Jews—both in Israel
and the Diaspora—to adjust to the new circumstances and to restructure their political and religious future in accord with conditions in the post-70 era.

Until his death in the mid-90s C.E., Agrippa II, the last of the
Herodians, continued to rule in the northeastern sector of Roman
Palestine (Trachonitis, Gaulanitis, Batanea, Auranitis) and in eastern Galilee. There is no indication that Agrippa II suffered from
the effects of the year 70; just the opposite may have been the case;
coins minted in the mid-80s with both Greek and Latin legends
seem to indicate a new flourish of activity in his realm, and the
initials *SC* (*Senatus Consultum* [Resolved by the Roman Senate])
may well reflect increased Roman recognition of his rule. The Talmud preserves a series of discussions between an Agrippa and
contemporary rabbis, especially Rabbi Eliezer ben Hyrcanus (late
first to early second centuries), in which Agrippa is referred to
approvingly. In the past it was generally assumed that these references were to Agrippa I, who ruled from 41 to 44 C.E., before the
destruction of the Temple. However, it is quite possible that they
refer to Agrippa II, who may have filled a part of the political and
communal vacuum within the Jewish community left by the destruction of the Temple and Jerusalem.[14]

The sages   Perhaps the most significant reaction to the events of 70 was the
and the   convening of a group of sages in the little town of Yavneh (Greek,
Yavneh   Jamnia), located near the coast between Jaffa and Ashdod. Their
academy   activities would leave an indelible mark on the future of the Jewish
people. In Yavneh, these sages began a process which eventually
led to the reconstruction of Judaism in the post-Temple period.

These sages, who had survived the traumatic events of the destruction relatively unscathed, continued the traditions of the Pharisees under new circumstances. In contrast to other pre-70 sects,
they had not been linked to the Temple nor had they been based
in any specific locale (as the Essenes were in Qumran); they managed to escape the fate of almost every other Jewish sect following
the destruction of Jerusalem.

Within this Pharisaic movement were two academies, Beth
Shammai (the House of Shammai) and Beth Hillel (the House of
Hillel), named for the pre-destruction sages who had founded them.
In the mid-first century, Beth Shammai had often adopted a stri-
dent nationalistic and religious position; the Hillelites, on the other

hand, often opted for a more moderate posture. For example, the Shammaites adopted a pro-revolutionary and anti-Gentile stance on the eve of the revolt, whereas the House of Hillel remained more tolerant and open.[15]

On the whole, the Yavnean sages proved to be very adept ideologically; they mitigated the disaster of 70 by offering alternate means of religious expression in the absence of the Temple. They were also adaptive in their reinterpretation and revision of the *halakhah* (Jewish religious law) and even introduced new patterns of behavior that addressed the social and religious conditions of the post-70 era.

The Yavnean period lasted for about 60 years, until the outbreak of the Second Jewish Revolt against Rome (70-132 C.E.).[16] It can be conveniently divided into two distinct stages, each associated with the sage who stood at the head of the Yavnean academy in successive generations—Rabbi Yoḥanan ben Zakkai and Rabban* Gamaliel II.[17]

The first stage—under Yoḥanan ben Zakkai—laid the foundations, established a general framework, set certain directions and forged guidelines along which rabbinic activity would develop and crystallize. In the second stage—under Gamaliel II—new initiatives were undertaken to provide the Jewish people with the political, religious and social alternatives around which they could restructure their lives communally and institutionally.

Rabbi Yoḥanan ben Zakkai

Little is known about Yoḥanan ben Zakkai's personal life. Reputedly a student of Hillel, he spent 18 years in Arav in the Lower Galilee,[18] and in the years prior to the outbreak of the revolt he lived in Jerusalem.

Later generations told of Yoḥanan's supposed mastery of Scripture, Mishnah, Gemara (Talmud), *halakhah*, *aggadah* and *midrash*,** as well as the subtleties of the scriptural text, mysticism and metaphysical speculation.[19] The historical reliability of such traditions is questionable; on firmer ground, see a number of traditions reporting on Yoḥanan's engaging the Sadducees in numerous disputes.[20]

If we know little about Yoḥanan before 70, what we know about him in the post-70 period is quantitatively greater, although here, too, several traditions are shrouded in layers of legend. Many of the traditions are contradictory and serve to teach us more about how later generations regarded him than about the historical circumstances of his day. He apparently escaped from Jerusalem during the Roman siege of the city and sought refuge in a Roman

---

* A title of especial esteem accorded to a very select number of sages.

** *Midrashim* are halakhic and aggadic expositions of biblical text.

camp. Eventually, he took up residence in Yavneh, perhaps remaining there voluntarily after his release from a local Roman detention camp. There he introduced a number of legislative enactments (*takkanot*).

Yoḥanan's general political, social and religious orientation may be summarized in several statements attributed to him (or, sometimes, to his student, Rabbi Joshua ben Hananiah) by later Jewish tradition. They reflect a position of moderation and accommodation:

> "Do not rush to destroy the altars of the Gentiles, lest you will have to rebuild them yourselves; do not destroy those of bricks, lest they say to you, 'make them of stone'; [nor those] of stone, lest they say to you, 'make them of wood.'"[21]

Yoḥanan praised those who "spread peace between city and city, between nation and nation, between government and government."[22] Whether Yoḥanan was a pacifist or simply a political realist cannot be determined from the available sources. What is clear, however, is that he adopted a nonbelligerent stance vis-à-vis the Gentiles and an accommodating one within the Jewish community itself. His position was based on a realistic assessment of the political and social factors of the time. Even in the pre-70 era, for example, he is reported to have advocated the abolition of the rite of drinking the "bitter water," a Temple ritual for determining whether a woman was guilty of adultery (Numbers 5:11-31). As it is said:

> "When adulterers multiplied, [the rite of] bitter water ceased, and Rabbi Yoḥanan b. Zakkai brought it to an end . . . ."[23]

He was similarly realistic with respect to the destruction of the Temple. In the absence of sacrifice and other Temple-related rituals, alternative forms of worship and atonement had to be found. In short, he avoided extremism in any direction; he sought to combine hope for the future with a recognition of the loss sustained in the present, at the same time addressing aspects of Jewish life in light of the changing times.

The following quotations reflect Yoḥanan's attitudes, first, toward messianic expectation and, second, regarding the destruction of the Temple:

> "If you have a plant in your hand and they say to you, 'The Messiah has come,' go and complete the planting and afterwards go out and receive [the Messiah]. If children will say to you, 'Come, let us build the Temple,' do not listen to them. If elders say to you, 'Come, let us destroy the Temple,' listen to them. For the building of the young is in actuality destruction

and the destruction [that is advocated] by the elders is indeed a rebuilding."[24]

"He [Rabbi Joshua, the student *par excellence* of Rabbi Yoḥanan] said to them: 'My sons, mourning too much is undesirable and not to mourn at all is undesirable. Rather, our sages have said, "A person should plaster his house and leave a small portion [unplastered] as a memory of Jerusalem. A person should make all the preparations for a meal and leave a little bit [unfinished] in memory of Jerusalem. A woman should make jewelry for herself and leave a little [part of herself unornamented] as a memory of Jerusalem." ' "[25]

Our sources, unfortunately, say little about Yoḥanan's public life in Yavneh. The thrust of his activity appears to have centered around the issuance of a series of *takkanot* (religious enactments). Tradition speaks of nine such *takkanot*;[26] they are of interest both for what they tell us and for what they omit. Three deal with an attempt to transfer Temple practices to an appropriate post-70 setting (the synagogue?). The practices addressed in these enactments had been associated specifically with the Temple. For example, before 70, the shofar (ram's horn) was blown on Rosh Hashanah (the New Year) only in the Temple (incidentally, in those days, it was blown even when Rosh Hashanah fell on the Sabbath). After 70, Yoḥanan declared that the shofar could be blown anywhere.[27] Similarly, in the pre-70 period the *lulav* (palm branch) was used in the Temple for seven days on Sukkoth (the Feast of Tabernacles), but in other places only for one day. Following the destruction of the Temple, Yoḥanan declared that the *lulav* could be used everywhere for seven days.[28]

Yoḥanan's takkanot (religious enactments)

Three other *takkanot* likewise dealt with practices associated with sacrifices in the Jerusalem Temple. With the destruction of the Temple and the cessation of sacrifices, requirements had to be changed. For example, in the pre-70 period, testimony for the appearance of the new moon[29] could be given only until the afternoon sacrifice was offered. Following 70, Rabbi Yoḥanan declared that such testimony was acceptable throughout the day.[30]

Another of Yoḥanan's *takkanot* abolished the requirement from Temple times that a convert set aside a quarter of a shekel (or, translated into the coinage of the day, a quarter of a dinar) in lieu of a sacrifice.[31] Still another annulled the requirement that the first fruits of a newly planted tree be brought to Jerusalem in the fourth year.[32]

What is striking about these *takkanot* is not only what they deal with—their concern for certain important ritual and procedural matters following the destruction of the Temple—but what they don't deal with. Many areas of Jewish life, such as the holidays generally, the Sabbath and prayer, are not addressed. Moreover, no *takkanah* deals with social, institutional or economic issues that undoubtedly beset the Jewish community at the time. These *takkanot* therefore may provide a good indication of the scope—and limitations—of Yoḥanan's activities in Yavneh.

This impression is reinforced by several other considerations. We have no evidence that Rome recognized Yoḥanan's leadership (this is in contrast to his successor Rabban Gamaliel). Nor do our sources reflect any kind of recognition by Jews generally, or by communal heads, of Yoḥanan's position. He is never reported to have visited Jewish communities, nor is there any indication that Jews consulted him on halakhic issues (again in contrast to Gamaliel).

Also striking is the limited number of people who seem to have joined Yoḥanan in Yavneh. There may very well have been opposition from certain Jewish circles to his attempts to restructure and redefine some aspects of Jewish life. Some may have resented Yoḥanan's abandonment of Jerusalem during the Roman siege; others may have opposed his readiness to make adjustments and "compromises" in Temple prerogatives and privileges. This was almost certainly true of many among the surviving Temple priesthood, who undoubtedly resented Yoḥanan's attempt to transfer Temple practices to other Jewish frameworks; they probably would have preferred preserving the uniqueness of the Temple with regard to central Jewish ceremonies, even in the post-70 era and even if this meant suspension of the rituals.

Yoḥanan's willingness to adapt traditional practices to radically new historical circumstances is reflected not only in his *takkanot* but in a number of his sayings as well. A much-revered comment of Simon the Just (c. 200 B.C.E.) stated that the three pillars on which the world rests are the Torah, Temple worship and acts of piety.[33] Yoḥanan dramatically reinterpreted one component of this statement. When asked, "Now that there are no sacrifices, how can we seek atonement?" Yoḥanan replied that good deeds (literally, acts of loving-kindness) will atone as sacrifices once did.[34]

Rabban   Yoḥanan was succeeded at Yavneh by Rabban Gamaliel II (c. 90-
Gamaliel II   115). Under Gamaliel, Yavneh changed radically. Most importantly, its rabbinic center achieved recognition and status, not only within the Jewish community but among the non-Jewish population as well. It became a center of most sages, some of whom lived there permanently, while others visited periodically. One source speaks of 85 rabbis who convened there,[35] another of a gathering of 138

sages.[36] Halakhic questions were brought to Yavneh from all parts of the country,[37] as well as from "Asia" (probably a locale in Palestine, although conceivably in Asia Minor). In addition to halakhic advice, Rabban Gamaliel and his court at Yavneh dealt with regulations regarding testimony of a new moon (the sign of the beginning of a new month) and the intercalation of years.[38]

Gamaliel, accompanied by other sages, often traveled to cities and towns throughout the country to visit colleagues, supervise religious practices and dispense halakhic advice.[39] He visited Jericho, Lod and Ashkelon in Judea;[40] Narbata and "Samaritan towns" in Samaria;[41] Kefar Othnai (Legio) in the Jezreel Valley; as well as Tiberias, Acco, Akhziv and the "Ladder of Tyre" in the Galilee.[42]

One rabbi (Rabbi Joshua ben Hananiah, a student of Yoḥanan ben Zakkai) traveled to Alexandria to discuss various halakhic issues;[43] another (Rabbi Akiva) ventured to Arabia, Africa, Gallia (probably Galatia in Asia Minor), Cilicia, Cappadocia, Nehardea (in Babylonia) and Medea.[44] Gamaliel himself traveled to Rome on a number of occasions.[45]

Rabban Gamaliel's status among the sages is evident. In the court of law, he sat in the middle, with elders sitting to his right and left;[46] his authority is reflected in the fact that he had the power to remove the mayor, or head, of Gader from office—and he used it.[47]

Gamaliel's high prestige, especially in light of the relatively low public profile held by his predecessor, Yoḥanan ben Zakkai, may be understood in light of two factors, one internal, the other external. The first had to do with his pedigree. For generations his family had held a rank of seniority and leadership, at least within Pharisaic circles; his great-grandfather was Hillel the Elder, who lived in the time of Herod the Great. His grandfather, Rabban Gamaliel the Elder had held a leading position in first-century Jerusalem; he was a prominent figure in the Sanhedrin in the 30s, when the priests and Sadducees contemplated bringing the early Christians to trial (Acts 5:34-39). The father of Rabban Gamaliel II was Rabbi Simeon ben Gamaliel, who played an active role in the moderate leadership of Jerusalem during the early stages of the revolt.[48]

We do not know what happened to Rabban Gamaliel II following the destruction of the Temple. Either he was too young to assume leadership immediately following the war or, owing to his father's participation in the rebellion, he had to seek refuge during this initial period, until a new political constellation allowed him to assume a role comparable to that enjoyed by his forebears. In any case, the high regard accorded the House of Hillel among the Pharisees specifically and within the Jewish community generally was clearly a key factor in Gamaliel II's assumption of a prominent position at Yavneh.

A second factor that sheds light on Gamaliel II's prestige and leadership, and that may have been no less crucial, was Rome's recognition of him as spokesman and leader of the Jewish community in Palestine, *de facto* if not *de jure*.[49] According to one source, Gamaliel went to Syria "to be granted authority by the Roman governor."[50] Although the precise nature of that authority is not spelled out, based on the context it may have had to do with the right to decide on calendrical issues.[51]

Why this recognition was conferred on Gamaliel by the Romans is another question. Perhaps the Romans were simply following their long-established policy of seeking support among the local aristocracy in order to maintain their rule over conquered provinces. Gamaliel became a logical candidate for the Romans to cultivate and nurture. This prestige and authority was probably conferred on Gamaliel some time close to the turn of the century.*

Roman recognition of Gamaliel may also have been connected to the death of Agrippa II in the mid-90s. As noted above, Agrippa—who ruled Trachonitis, Gaulanitis, Auranitis and Batanea in the northeastern part of Palestine—may have served as the link between the Roman government and the Jewish community generally during the decades following the destruction of the Temple. If this was the case, Rome would have looked elsewhere for this link when he died and would have found it in the head of the academy at Yavneh.

Neither the extent nor the nature of Rabban Gamaliel's position of leadership among the sages of Yavneh is clear. On a number of occasions his decisions were challenged by colleagues; on other occasions, he acted in an authoritarian manner. In several instances, Rabban Gamaliel chastised Rabbi Akiva (a younger contemporary and the leading sage in the first third of the second century) for acting contrary to one of his decisions[52] or for siding with an opinion of the sages that did not conform to Gamaliel's own view.[53] Gamaliel upbraided Rabbi Tarfon when he absented himself from deliberations of the Yavnean court.[54] He even banished his own brother-in-law, Rabbi Eliezer ben Hyrcanus, from rabbinic circles; Eliezer purportedly died in a state of humiliation.[55]

---

* It is unlikely that the Flavian dynasty would have accorded such recognition to a Jewish leader, especially during the reign of its last representative, Domitian (81-96 C.E.), who appears to have harbored a decidedly negative attitude toward Jews and Judaism. As previously noted, it was Domitian who reputedly made an attempt to hunt down Jews suspected of being from the Davidic line (*Eccles. Hist.* 3,19), and it was he who initiated a persecution of supposed converts to Judaism in Rome (Smallwood, *Jews under Roman Rule* [see endnote 5], pp. 376-385). Thus, it was probably only after Domitian's death that Rome was willing to consider cultivating a new type of leadership on which to base its rule in Judea.

Gamaliel's major opponent within rabbinic circles was Rabbi Joshua ben Hananiah, a student of Rabbi Yoḥanan and the elder statesman among the sages of Yavneh in the era of Rabban Gamaliel. The two clashed head-on on a number of occasions: Joshua was once critical of Gamaliel's treatment of a calendrical question. On that occasion, Gamaliel ordered Joshua to appear at the Yavnean court carrying his staff and money on the day that Joshua had calculated was Yom Kippur, the holiest day of the Jewish year, thus humiliating his opponent by having him perform acts prohibited by Jewish law on that day.[56]

On another occasion, Rabban Gamaliel and Rabbi Joshua disputed over whether the evening prayer ('*Arvit*) was obligatory. Gamaliel claimed that it was; Joshua and other sages argued that it was not. Gamaliel forced a confrontation at the academy. Having embarrassed Joshua in front of his colleagues, Gamaliel succeeded in angering them; according to tradition, they then deposed him as head of the academy. Only after expressing regret and acknowledging his misconduct was Gamaliel reinstated.[57] Apparently Rabban Gamaliel's position, at least among the sages, was not inviolate; given enough cause, the sages were able to take effective action against him. Nevertheless, it is doubtful that Gamaliel's temporary ouster affected his status as the Roman representative, or spokesman, of the Jewish community vis-à-vis the imperial government.

Under Rabban Gamaliel, the Yavneh academy dealt with numerous communal issues, as well as matters of Jewish life and practice. In some cases, the decisions on these issues have had an effect on Jewish tradition down to our own day. We will discuss four areas where this has been the case:

The origins of traditions still observed today

1. Prayer. The liturgy of the pre-70 synagogue—in Palestine at least—appears to have centered exclusively around the Torah-reading ceremony, and then mainly on the Sabbath and festivals.[58] Only after 70 was prayer developed and instituted on a daily basis. The obligation of daily prayer for all Jews, in private and communally in the synagogue, seems to have crystallized at Yavneh,[59] as did the basic structure of Jewish prayer.

2. Decisions regarding the canon. Canonization of the Hebrew Bible was a long process, stretching over centuries. The first part— the five books of Moses, the Torah—was canonized by the time of Ezra, when the Jews returned from the Babylonian Exile in the sixth century B.C.E. Not long afterwards, the second part—the Prophets—was similarly accorded sacred status. Many of the books that later comprised the third part of the Hebrew Bible—the Writings—were already universally accepted by the first century C.E.,

but the status of several books—Ezekiel, Ecclesiastes and the Song of Songs (Song of Solomon)—may have still been in doubt—at least in rabbinic eyes. In the language of the sages, did these books make the hands unclean? That is, were they divinely inspired? Under the leadership of Rabban Gamaliel, further deliberations occurred and several important decisions were made in this regard.[60]

3. Codification of Jewish law. The Yavneh academy devoted most of its time to clarifying and developing the received *halakhah*, or religious law. One issue was whether the *halakhah* be determined according to the moderate Beth Hillel or the stricter Beth Shammai. Acknowledging that both schools founded in the pre-70 period had, at least theoretically, an equal claim to legitimacy, Beth Hillel at Yavneh was ultimately accorded priority in determining matters of *halakhah*.[61]

4. Holidays. The rabbis of Yavneh also attempted to fill the vacuum created by the loss of the Temple. Before 70, neither Rosh Hashanah nor Yom Kippur had played a major role in the religious lives of Jewish communities outside of Jerusalem. Rosh Hashanah was important largely because it marked the beginning of the seventh month in the Jewish calendar.* Yom Kippur involved a ceremony of major importance, but its celebration was largely confined to the Temple precincts. After 70, the sages of Yavneh created an entirely new liturgy for the high holidays. New themes crystallized—the kingship of God, remembrance and redemption—and appropriate blessings and prayers were formulated. Special scriptural readings were introduced, along with a special ceremony for the blowing of the shofar. Yom Kippur was institutionalized as a fast day for all, when the individual, as part of the congregation, was to seek forgiveness.

The sages of Yavneh also filled a void with respect to the observance of Passover. Previously, the Passover celebration had been intimately connected with the Temple sacrifice; each household was bidden to participate in the Passover meal in the Temple precincts proper or anywhere in Jerusalem following the sacrifice of the Paschal lamb.[62] After 70, this was no longer possible, and so the home observance we know as the Passover seder was created. Much of the Passover *haggadah*, the service for the seder, took shape at Yavneh under the leadership of Rabban Gamaliel.

Jewish nationalist aspirations   The academy at Yavneh devoted itself politically to a policy of rapprochement and cooperation with Rome and religiously to the implementation of the necessary readjustments in ideology and practice so that Jewish life might thrive and develop in the post-

* The number seven has special symbolic significance in Jewish tradition (seventh day of creation, seven days a week, seven years to a sabbatical year, etc.).

Temple era. But a very different movement was operating elsewhere in Judea. In certain circles, Jewish nationalist aspirations were far from squelched by the defeat at the hands of Rome. While most Jews clung to the vague hope that somehow, sometime, Jerusalem would be reclaimed and the Temple rebuilt, there were others who continued to nurture the dream of obliterating (or at least drastically curtailing) Roman rule in Judea. The Second Jewish Revolt against Rome, also known as the Bar-Kokhba revolt of 132-135 C.E., was the political and military expression of this dream.[63]

Unfortunately, our knowledge of this revolt—the events leading up to it, its leadership and the succession of events during this three-and-a-half-year period—is woefully sparse and fragmentary. In contrast to the two other major Jewish revolts in antiquity—the Maccabean, or Hasmonean, uprising against the Seleucids in 166 B.C.E. and the First Jewish Revolt against Rome in 66 C.E.—no historical account describes the background and progress of the Bar-Kokhba revolt. Nothing comparable to 1 and 2 Maccabees, which chronicles the Maccabean uprising, or Josephus' *The Jewish War*, which gives an extraordinarily detailed account of the First Jewish Revolt, exists for the Bar-Kokhba revolt. All that has been preserved are scattered references in later pagan, Christian and Jewish sources.

Quite recently, archaeology has been able to contribute new evidence, offering us a greater understanding of certain aspects of this revolt. However, the coins, papyri, milestones, caves and fortresses dating from this period that have been uncovered by archaeologists fall far short of providing a comprehensive or coherent picture. And without a substantial literary source to offer an adequate context for these finds, it is often difficult to draw firm historical conclusions.[64]

Nevertheless, the new archaeological discoveries as well as recent reevaluation of the surviving literature have enabled us to correct—or at least challenge—some of the old assumptions about the Bar-Kokhba revolt.

Until relatively recently, scholars have assumed that the entire province of Judea and most Jews living there were mobilized and actively supported the Bar-Kokhba revolt. This view is based on highly exaggerated accounts that magnified the suffering, tragedy and loss of life during the revolt.[65] Later rabbinic tradition adopted a generally critical attitude toward Bar-Kokhba—referring to him as Bar Kosba (Son of Lies);* it sought to discredit him and to demonstrate the futility of armed rebellion. Similarly, the Church Fathers saw the Bar-Kokhba revolt as a futile attempt to restore the Jewish independence that had been taken away by God as punish-

---

* On Bar Kokhba's name, see endnote on page 196.

ZEV RADOVAN

BAR-KOKHBA REVOLT COIN. When Simeon bar Kosba, known as Bar-Kokhba, led the Second Jewish Revolt against Rome in 132 C.E., the insurrectionists minted coins to demonstrate their independence. Over 80 percent of these coins mention Jerusalem, and all symbols on the coins relate to the holy city, showing its importance as the center of national identity. This coin depicts the Temple in Jerusalem with the Ark of the Covenant, lost since the destruction of the First Temple in 586 B.C.E., restored to its proper place.

ment for the Jews' denial of Jesus. Even the Roman historian Dio Cassius greatly exaggerated the scope of the violence, thereby enhancing the significance of the Roman victory; he speaks of the destruction of some 50 fortifications and 985 villages and the loss of 585,000 lives![66]

All these claims notwithstanding, there is practically no description of hostilities except in southern Judea (the biblical area of Judah). The archaeological material clearly corroborates this picture. All remains of the Bar-Kokhba revolt, whether coins, caves of refuge, papyri or fortifications, have been found in that region. The Galilee, the second major area of Jewish population at the time, remained virtually untouched by the devastation of the revolt and thus was able to assume a position of leadership as it absorbed refugees from the southern part of the country after the hostilities ended.

The messianic nature of Bar-Kokhba's leadership has also been called into question recently. There is no doubt that the revolt was under the leadership of one Simeon bar Kosba, known to us as Bar-Kokhba. This is clear not only from the literary sources, but also from archaeological evidence. The coins and papyri (which record the name and title of Simeon bar Kosba) recently found in the Judean wilderness reflect a strong and unified leadership throughout the course of the revolt. Bar-Kokhba issued directives

BAR-KOKHBA LETTER IN GREEK. Simeon bar Kosba, the leader of the Second Jewish Revolt, was perhaps called Bar-Kokhba, or Son of a Star, an allusion to Numbers 24:17, "A star shall come out of Jacob." Bar-Kokhba's letters give evidence that he was a responsible organizer and devout observer of the commandments. Some of the correspondence found in the Bar-Kokhba caves was written in Greek, indicating the widespread use of that language even among nationalist Jews in Palestine. This letter is the only document that mentions Bar-Kokhba's name in Greek, inserted between the first and second lines to further identify the common name Simon. When written in Aramaic and Hebrew, the name has no vowels.

in a variety of matters ranging from religious and ritual concerns to taxation and military discipline. This situation, with Bar-Kokhba in clear command, stands in marked contrast to the First Jewish Revolt against Rome, which was characterized by anarchy among the Jewish forces and the lack of any overall planning or leadership before or during the revolt.

It is true that Rabbi Akiva, a leading figure at the Yavneh academy, hailed Bar-Kokhba as the messiah, but it is difficult to tell whether this belief was widespread. It may be that this was the view of Rabbi Akiva and his circle, not necessarily of the sages in general or of the people at large—or even of Bar-Kokhba himself. On his coins he called himself *Nesi Yisrael* (patriarch, or head, of Israel). The term has no overt messianic implications.

Moreover, Akiva's role in the uprising has very probably been exaggerated.[67] It is true that he apparently proclaimed Bar-Kokhba a messianic figure. It is often forgotten, however, that the Talmud records an immediate retort by a colleague, Yoḥanan ben Torta: "Akiva, grass will grow on your cheeks [i.e., you will long be dead] and the Son of David will still not have come."[68] Moreover, other rabbis cautioned against involvement with any kind of military or messianic aspirations. For example, Rabbi Joshua ben Hananiah, Yoḥanan's pupil, advocated peace and accommodation as against confrontation with Rome.[69] Certainly the principal thrust of the rabbinic endeavors at Yavneh before Bar-Kokhba (and in Usha*) was to forge a *modus vivendi* with Rome, eschewing any confrontation.

Rabbi Akiva's many trips outside Judea have often been seen as an effort to galvanize support for Bar-Kokhba's plans. This assumption, however, is entirely gratuitous, for in our sources these trips are associated only with legal questions or with sermons he delivered. Political concerns never appear in any of these traditions.

Causes of the Bar-Kokhba revolt
Perhaps the most frequent subject of discussion concerning the Bar-Kokhba revolt relates to its causes. In the past, scholars have focused almost exclusively on two causes. One was a decree of the Roman emperor Hadrian prohibiting the practice of circumcision; according to a fourth-century biography of Hadrian, this was the immediate cause of the outbreak of hostilities.[70] However, the Roman historian Dio Cassius, in his early third-century *History of Rome*, tells us that it was the announcement of Hadrian's intention to build a new city to be called Aelia Capitolina on the site of Jerusalem that triggered the rebellion.[71] As its name implies (Aelia after Hadrian Aelius; Capitolina after the temple of Jupiter Capitolinus to be erected on the site of the destroyed Jewish Temple), it was to be a thoroughly pagan city without any Jewish association.

Opinion has been divided over which was the real cause, or, alternatively, which was the primary cause of the revolt. Both may well have constituted indispensable ingredients leading to the outbreak of hostilities.

As we shall see, however, other basic conditions were also important in accounting for the revolt. Moreover, both of the decrees referred to above were part of Hadrian's more general policy of Hellenizing and acculturating the oriental East to the norms and accepted behavior of Greco-Roman society. Circumcision, for example, was not peculiar to the Jews: Egyptians, Ethiopians, Arabs and Phoenicians also circumcised young males. The prohibition almost certainly did not apply only to Jews. To reinforce Domitian's earlier legislation banning castration—and viewing circumcision as a barbaric custom that conflicted sharply with the Greek ideal of the perfection of the body—Hadrian banned circumcision as

---

* Sages gathered at Usha in Lower Galilee, near Haifa, in about 140 C.E. following persecutions after the Bar-Kokhba revolt.

ZEV RADOVAN

AELIA CAPITOLINA COIN. Minted in 131 C.E., this coin depicts the temple to Jupiter, flanked by statues of Juno and Minerva, which the Roman emperor Hadrian planned to build on the Temple Mount in Jerusalem. Hadrian's plan to transform Jewish Jerusalem to a Roman city named Aelia Capitolina sparked the Second Jewish Revolt against Rome in 132 C.E. The new Roman name for the city is inscribed on the coin: COL(onia) AEL(ia) KAP(itolina), a name combining one of Hadrian's names, Aelius, with a reference to the three deities of the Roman Capitolina, Jupiter, Juno and Minerva.

well. The Jews, however, regarded this decree as a severe blow to their religious self-definition and autonomy.

As to Hadrian's declared intention to build a pagan city on the ruins of Jerusalem, he had previously established Greek cities and institutions throughout the Roman East. Even in Palestine, he had built major institutions in cities like Caesarea, Gaza and Tiberias. Therefore, announcing the building of Aelia Capitolina in place of Jerusalem was by no means out of the ordinary. For the Jews, however, this move was undoubtedly traumatic, recalling, for them, the persecutions under Antiochus IV (167 B.C.E.), when pagan worship was introduced into Jerusalem. Moreover, Hadrian's plan dashed any immediate hopes the Jews may have had for the restoration of Jerusalem as a Jewish city and the rebuilding of the Temple.

While these decrees probably explain the specific timing of the outbreak of hostilities, Eusebius, the fourth-century bishop of Caesarea, in a passage often ignored, suggests that the revolt was not simply a sudden eruption of Jewish nationalist and religious fervor, but was rather the culmination of a decades-long period of discontent and unrest following the destruction of the Second Temple.[72]

Eusebius also notes that because the Romans were apprehensive of any type of messianic or royal claims, they sought to track down those Jews of Davidic descent.[73] This concern, which probably had some foundation, was evident throughout the late first century under the emperors Vespasian (69-79), Domitian (81-96) and Trajan (98-117).

The Diaspora revolts Under Trajan, a series of major revolts did in fact erupt, primarily affecting the Jews of the Diaspora.[74] In 115 C.E., Jews in Egypt and Cyrene (on the North African coast in present-day Libya) took advantage of Trajan's absence on a Mesopotamian campaign to attack their Greek neighbors. The devastation in both Greek and Jewish communities was enormous; the Jews gained the upper hand in rural areas of Egypt, but were defeated in Alexandria. The hostilities were so severe that as late as the year 199/200 an annual festival was celebrated in the Egyptian town of Oxyrhynchus to commemorate the victory over the Jews.[75] To subdue the revolt in Cyrene, where the hostilities were even more devastating—some 220,000 people were massacred according to Dio[76]—Trajan sent one of his prized generals, Marcius Turbo.[77] The leader of these Jewish uprisings—called Lucuas by Eusebius and Andreas by Dio—appears to have had royal, if not messianic, aspirations; he claimed the title of king.[78] Archaeological evidence from Cyrene seems to bear out the enormity of this revolt: milestones found here refer to the "Jewish rebellion."[79] A number of Roman temples in the city of Cyrene were found destroyed or damaged.

Cyprus was another area of violence involving Jews around 115 C.E. Some 240,000 pagans were said to have been killed; consequently Jews were banned from the island.[80]

Finally, as Trajan advanced southward along the Tigris, the Jews of Mesopotamia rose in revolt. Trajan's general, Lucius Quietus, was sent to quell this rebellion, which resulted in the death of thousands of Jews.[81]

Whether these revolts among Diaspora Jewry affected Palestine is a much-debated question. Hadrian's biographer notes that there was some kind of uprising in Judea at about this time.[82] Rabbinic tradition also records a war of Quietus,[83] who, after serving in Mesopotamia, became governor of Judea. Presumably this war of Quietus occurred in Judea.

Recent archaeological evidence seems to corroborate this picture of unrest in Judea for at least 15 years before the actual outbreak of the Bar-Kokhba revolt. The building of roads by the Roman army during the second and third decades of the second century undoubtedly had—as was usually the case—military implications.[84] Moreover, a number of legions, or parts thereof, appeared in Palestine during this period, probably in response to unrest among the local population—or in anticipation of it. These were the sparks that helped ignite the tinderbox.

What were the aims of the Bar-Kokhba revolt? On the one hand, there was no doubt a strong element of protest against the decrees that had sparked the hostilities. Beyond that, however, and judging from the coin inscriptions, it is clear that Bar-Kokhba was striving for the "freedom of Jerusalem" and the "redemption of Israel." What precisely this meant in political terms is not clear. It is hard to imagine that, with the Roman empire at its zenith, Bar-Kokhba aspired to overthrow Roman rule. Perhaps he sought to repeal recent imperial decrees (circumcision? the founding of Aelia Capitolina?) and to gain some kind of local autonomy. However, it is also possible that the leadership of this revolt was so intoxicated by religious dreams of national restoration that any kind of rational reading of the international political and military map was beyond its capacity. We simply don't have enough information to decide this question with reasonable certainty.

The aims of the Bar-Kokhba revolt

Similarly, it is difficult to track the course of the revolt. Clearly, the outbreak of hostilities caught Rome unprepared, as happened not infrequently under the empire. The Jews appear to have won a number of victories in the very early stages of the conflict, although they never captured fortresses or cities. Based on recent archaeological evidence, Jewish military activity seems to have been centered around subterranean caves in southern Judea, where Jewish soldiers would hide, venture out and attack the enemy and then retreat for regrouping. How grave the situation was in terms of Roman interests is difficult to tell, but Hadrian was forced to dispatch one of his best generals, Julius Severus, to bring the hostilities to a quick end. The Romans conquered Judea, leaving the rebels to gather for a last stand at Bethar (in the Judean hills, to the southwest of Jerusalem). This stronghold fell in the summer of 135 C.E.

The collapse of the Bar-Kokhba revolt spelled the end of active Jewish nationalism in antiquity. For 300 years, since the successful Maccabean revolt in the second century B.C.E., nationalist aspirations had been a significant factor in Jewish history, often finding expression in revolts or attacks on Gentile neighbors. With the end of the Bar-Kokhba revolt, a new period in Jewish history began in which active Jewish nationalist aspirations were in abeyance.

After the rebels' defeat at Bethar, the name of the province was changed to Syria-Palaestina in an effort to obliterate the name Judea as well as any other reference to the Jews. Aelia Capitolina was built on the site of Jerusalem. The city bore a decidedly pagan character for the next several centuries, and Jews were banned from the city.

The aftermath

After more than 1,000 years, the center of Jewish life now shifted from Jerusalem and Judea to the Galilee, which assumed a central role in Jewish Palestine for the next 800 years.

The end of the Bar-Kokhba hostilities also saw the beginning of an exodus of Jews from their homeland to countries of the Diaspora. For the first time, we read of sages who took up residence in Babylonia.

In Palestine, the Jews were forbidden to observe some of their most traditional and basic practices, including prayer, study, circumcision, holiday observance, etc., for a number of years.[85]

Cumulatively, the two major revolts—the First Jewish Revolt against Rome (66-74 C.E.) and the Second Jewish Revolt under Bar-Kokhba (132-135 C.E.)—had far-reaching effects on Jewish life, spiritually, institutionally and psychologically. Yet, at the same time the Jews of Palestine were undergoing these traumatic upheavals, the groundwork for a renewal of Jewish life, its norms and values was being laid, slowly and carefully in Judea itself. This, in the end, is the profound historical significance of Yavneh.

General Sources

The sources used in this essay vary in terms of their dates and historical reliability. Contemporary ideological statements are the most reliable, for at the very least they tell us what one author who lived at the time thought and felt (e.g., the author of 4 Ezra or 2 Baruch). Of course, the problems begin when we try to generalize these ideas with regard to society at large: How many people actually felt this way or identified with this particular line of thought?

Most of our sources, however, derive from a later period than we are treating, and here caution must be exercised. This is particularly the case as regards rabbinic sources although it holds true for Roman and Christian material as well. Rabbinic material was transmitted for the most part orally and was edited over a very extensive period—i.e., close to a millennium—commencing at the turn of the third century C.E. Several considerations must be brought to bear in the use of such material for the period we are discussing. Generally speaking, the earlier the redaction the better; the closer the material is to the time it purports to represent the more limited the editorializing by later generations. This does not mean, of course, that all early material is historically reliable or, for that matter, that later material is *ipso facto* unusable. Ultimately, what is necessary is the use of comparative data—at the very least from within the same corpus and ideally from other independent sources—in order to offer some sort of affirmation to the material at hand. Historical reliability is immeasurably increased when a number of different accounts point in the same direction and to the same supposed reality. In the many cases where outside material is unavailable, a measure of skepticism is in order, without necessarily leading to a wholesale dismissal of the historicity of the material at hand. If the reported event is inherently possible, if it is not contradicted by other sources and conforms to a literary pattern, and if it is not identifiably tendentious, then the source is deemed reliable—for its overall picture if not for each and every detail.

FIVE

Christianity from the Destruction of Jerusalem to Constantine's Adoption of the New Religion: 70-312 C.E.

HAROLD W. ATTRIDGE

T HE PERIOD BETWEEN 70 AND 312 C.E. IS BOUND BY TWO signal events, each of which was recognized by contemporaries as well as by later historians as having special significance. On August 30 in the year 70, Roman legionaries burned the Jerusalem Temple to the ground.[1] On October 27, 312, at the Milvian Bridge outside Rome two generals fought a decisive battle for dominion of the western half of the Roman empire. The victor was Constantine, who then entered the Eternal City, where he later erected a statue of himself, the remains of which may still be seen in the Capitoline Museum. In its hand, this colossal statue held a cross. Constantine claimed he had "saved and delivered the city from the yoke of the tyrant under this sign."[2]

The first of these two dates marks the end of an epoch in Jewish history as well as the limit of the first generation of the Jesus movement. At that time the Jesus movement was still a loosely knit, often despised, sect comprised of Jews and Gentiles excited by the anticipated establishment of the reign of God upon earth. The second of these two dates marks a critically important event in the increasingly triumphal advance of the well-organized Christian Church into a position of dominance in ancient Mediterranean society.

A COIN OF CONSTANTINE. This Roman coin depicts the emperor Constantine (306-337 C.E.), who brought an end to the Roman persecutions of Christians that were at their height from 303 to 311 C.E. Although he was not baptized until the end of his life, Constantine's support gave the new religion official status.

ZEV RADOVAN

CATACOMB OF PRISCILLA. Jesus was called the Good Shepherd both by himself (John 10:11) and his followers (Hebrews 13:20). This fresco is an example of the art used by early Christians to decorate the catacombs used from the second through the fourth centuries C.E. for burials and perhaps as meeting places. Some 600 miles of catacombs lie beneath the streets of Rome.

ALINARI/ART RESOURCE, NEW YORK

Between these two events, the Christian movement gradually solidified its internal organization and, after numerous challenges, formalized the structure of its beliefs. In the process it defined itself over against the people of Israel from which it had emerged and in tension with the larger Hellenistic-Roman society of which it became an increasingly important part.[3]

Evidence for the history of Christianity in the pre-Constantinian period is primarily literary,[4] although there is also some archaeological evidence, as we shall see.[5]

In the nearly two and a half centuries covered by this period, Christian writers produced a wide range of works—homilies and expositions of Scripture; tales of apostles and martyrs to instruct and inspire believers; hymns and poems to celebrate God's actions in Christ and in the Church; polemical tracts against Jews and pagans and against other factions within the Christian movement; *apologiae* (defenses) to deflect criticism and entice outsiders; and eventually more speculative works attempting to make coherent sense of Christian claims. Most of this large literary corpus was preserved by what emerged as the orthodox Church of the fourth century, although chance discoveries of the last century and a half have yielded important new evidence, particularly for versions of Christianity that did not succeed. In addition, a fourth-century bishop, Eusebius of Caesarea, composed an *Ecclesiastical History*, giving an account of the period from Jesus to Constantine that remains valuable, both for its overall framework and for the remnants of otherwise lost writers that it preserves.

By 70 C.E., Christian communities had formed not only in Israel, but also in many parts of the Mediterranean basin and beyond. As Paul's letters and the Book of Acts reflect, followers of Jesus were active in the Land of Israel—in Jerusalem and, no doubt, in Galilee. Missionaries from Jerusalem, apparently members of the Hellenist faction there, had founded a congregation in Antioch, the third major metropolis of the empire after Rome and Alexandria. Antioch in turn had served as the initial base for Paul's successful missionary activity in Asia Minor, particularly in Ephesus, and Greece. Missionaries had already visited Rome; as we have seen, their activity caused such turmoil in the Jewish community there that the emperor Claudius expelled Jews in the 40s. According to tradition preserved in Acts 8:26-40, Jerusalem Hellenists inaugurated African Christianity by converting an Ethiopian official.[6] Other missionaries may also have reached Egypt. An "eloquent" Alexandrian named Apollos appears in connection with Paul's missionary activity (Acts 18:24-28; 1 Corinthians 1:12, 3:4-5, 4:6, 16:12); there were undoubtedly other Christians in Alexandria. Paul himself, after his years in Greece and Asia Minor,

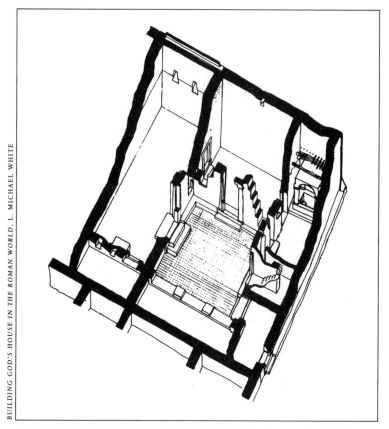

BUILDING GOD'S HOUSE IN THE ROMAN WORLD, L. MICHAEL WHITE

CHRISTIAN BUILDING AT DURA-EUROPOS. Dating to the third
century C.E., this is the earliest building thus far discovered specifically devoted to Christian assembly. It was located in a Roman
garrison town on the Syrian frontier that was destroyed in 256 C.E.
Early Christians met for fellowship, prayer and study in homes
(Acts 2-5), probably through the second century. In time, one room
of the house was modified into an assembly hall and another into a
baptistery. By 300 C.E., Christians were building structures specifically designed as churches.

intended to pursue missionary activity in Spain; at least one early
Christian source suggests that he was released from his Roman
imprisonment and actually made the journey to the far west.[7] By
70, then, there was a Christian presence throughout the Mediterranean, particularly in what were to become major ecclesiastical
centers of subsequent centuries—Alexandria, Antioch and Rome.

In the second century, Christianity continued to expand, from
the major urban centers of the Greek-speaking part of the empire
into the hinterlands of Syria, Asia Minor, Italy and Egypt. In the
early second century, Pliny the Younger, the Roman governor of

Bithynia-Pontus on the southern shore of the Black Sea, reported to the emperor Trajan the extensive presence of Christians in his province.[8] The movement also spread to the Latin West and the Syriac-speaking East. By the third quarter of the second century, we hear of major Christian communities in Gaul. At Lyons a group of Christians were martyred and a new bishop, Irenaeus, launched a vigorous literary defense of orthodoxy. At Carthage, the capital of North Africa, a Christian community with a strong sense of its separate identity also produced martyrs and a major literary figure, Tertullian, active in the late second and early third centuries (190-220). In the East, late second-century evidence of a Christian community comes from the Syrian trading city of Edessa. Christians apparently conducted missionary activity even farther to the east. Eusebius reports that a leading Alexandrian intellectual of the middle of the second century, Pantenus, traveled to the west coast of India. There he found a group of Christians who traced their origins to the apostle Bartholomew.[9]

Beginning in the late second century, Christians produced numerous legendary accounts of the missionary activities of the apostles; although often pious fantasy, some historical reminiscences may underlie reports that the apostle Andrew preached among cannibals on the Black Sea or that the apostle Thomas introduced a life of holy chastity in Parthia (modern Iran) and in the Indus Valley (modern Pakistan).[10] By 312, when Constantine triumphed at the battle of Milvian Bridge, Christians had become, if not a majority, then at least a substantial and fairly coherent minority throughout the Roman empire and beyond.

Organizing members of what Paul called the "body of Christ" so as to provide mutual aid and to confront an often hostile world was no simple matter. The Christian community soon formalized the ways in which it worshiped. As it did so, a leadership structure evolved in which authority was increasingly vested in functionaries of local communities—first in boards of elders, later in individual bishops. These local leaders eventually organized themselves into regional and, later, empire-wide networks, with the bishops of the principal sees playing an increasingly prominent role.

Development of the institutional Church

Succeeding generations could find various models of ecclesiastical organization in the history of the first apostolic generation. In Jerusalem, a troika of Peter, James and John eventually gave way to a community in which James, the brother of Jesus, played the leading role. Paul's community at Corinth met in the houses of wealthy patrons, such as Chloe (1 Corinthians 1:11) and Phoebe (Romans 16:1); but ecclesiastical functions, such as praying, "prophesying" (or delivering inspiring messages) and speaking in tongues, were gifts of the Spirit that fell on various members of the community, male and female, slave and free. By the end of the first century more stable forms of order begin to appear, but considerable variety and experimentation is evident.

In the area of Paul's missionary activity, itinerant missionaries were soon replaced by local bodies of elders. The situation is attested in Acts, written by a disciple of Paul,* perhaps in Asia Minor in the late first century. Before leaving the Aegean area on his final journey to Jerusalem, Paul bids farewell to a leadership cadre of presbyters (elders) (Acts 20:17). The account of this departure, with its formal farewell, may have served as a legitimization of the organizational structure that emerged after Paul's death.

Paul's disciples addressed the question of organization in a series of pseudepigraphical compositions (i.e., written in Paul's name)—the Pastoral Epistles, 1 Timothy, 2 Timothy and Titus.[11] These texts portray a hierarchical arrangement consisting of an apostolic figure with regional authority (Timothy and Titus) and, in the local churches, two tiers of elders—bishops and deacons (1 Timothy 3:1-13)—as well as an order of "widows" (1 Timothy 5:1-16). The latter were apparently real widows who both received support from the Church and assisted its leaders. The office of bishop remains poorly defined. The designation of the office, *episcopos* (overseer), indicates that its holders had some administrative or supervisory duties, but there is no indication that the bishops were yet the sole authorities in their communities.

The Pastoral Epistles reflect some of the social pressures that affected the formation of an ecclesiastical order. The author demands that leaders be men of good standing and repute, solid citizens who have been duly ordained (1 Timothy 4:14). Christianity is no longer an eschatological cult eagerly waiting the end of time, but a religious philosophy teaching its adherents virtues appropriate to the various states of civilized society. Women, slaves and children no longer learn the equality preached by Paul (Galatians 3:28) but the submissiveness appropriate to their subordinate social roles.[12] The Christian movement is accommodating itself to society; in doing so it loses some of its initial radical character.

The Didache The *Didache*, a handbook of church order, also reflects this development.[13] Claiming to be the "Teaching of the Twelve Apostles to the Gentiles," it depicts the organization of a Christian community in Syria in the late first century, and it formed the basis for numerous subsequent works of the same type. According to the *Didache*,

---

* Traditionally, both the Gospel of Luke and Book of Acts are attributed to Luke, a physician and Gentile convert, who was for a time one of Paul's companions.

community life is to be based on ethical instruction (chapters 1-6) about the "two ways": the way of sin leading to death; the way of the Decalogue interpreted through Jesus' teachings, leading to life.[14] The *Didache* also evidences a major concern with the proper celebration of the rituals that formed the focus of Christian community life. The initiatory rite of baptism (chapter 7) was effected by immersion in running water, as the celebrant invoked the names of Father, Son and Spirit as in Matthew 28:19. The eucharistic meal (chapters 9-10) had a decided eschatological tenor, in which the bread signified scattered people restored to unity at the end of time. The instructions for celebrating the Eucharist make no mention of Jesus' death, so prominent in Paul's description of the sacred meal (1 Corinthians 11:17-34); obviously, there was room for considerable diversity in Christian ritual at this stage.

The regulations for worship stipulate that the Christian liturgical celebration take place on the Lord's Day—not the traditional Jewish Sabbath but the first day of the week, the day of Jesus' resurrection. Other evidence from the late first and early second centuries suggests that Christians had shifted the focus of their sacred time. Reports of liturgical activity in the middle of the second century indicate that the practice of Sunday observance was well entrenched.[15]

Two structures of authority are mentioned in the *Didache*. On the one hand, churches must welcome and support (but also test) itinerant "apostles and prophets" (chapters 11-13). These individuals, reminiscent of Paul and other early wandering teachers, still enjoy pride of place. Alongside them, however, "bishops and deacons" (chapter 15) lead local congregations. These officials are hierarchically distinguished, but not in the rigid way they would be in later years. Men charged with specific functions hold both offices, and, as in the Pastoral Epistles, bishops are not yet the sole leaders.

The pattern of leadership in the Christian congregation in Rome is reflected in the anonymous Epistle to the Hebrews, an elaborate homily that interprets the death of Christ as a counterpart to the purification ritual conducted by the Israelite high priest on the Day of Atonement (Yom Kippur). The text was apparently sent to Rome late in the first century from an uncertain location, perhaps Antioch or Alexandria.[16] Its concluding admonitions to obey leaders (Hebrews 13:7,17) hint that a rather loose structure of governance led by elders was still in effect.

Both the presbyterial structure and the cultic symbolism are prominent in another late first-century document. *First Clement* purports to be a letter from the leaders of the church in Rome to the church in Corinth.[17] Tradition attributes the letter to Clement, who is mentioned in later succession lists as the third or fourth bishop of Rome.[18] The attribution to Clement may indicate that he was the "executive secretary" of the Roman council of elders. The letter indicates that leaders of the Roman church intervened in Corinth to settle a dispute that had resulted in some Corinthian church leaders being deposed. Relying heavily on examples from the Hebrew Scriptures and on Paul's epistles to Corinth and Rome, the letter urges reconciliation and obedience to the established structure of authority. As in the Pastoral Epistles and in the *Didache*, this structure consists of a two-tiered hierarchy: bishops and deacons.[19]

Ignatius of Antioch A new development in church organization appears slightly later, in the letters of Ignatius of Antioch.[20] This bishop ran afoul of Roman authorities and, probably about 115 C.E., was sentenced "to the beasts" in Rome. Escorted there by armed guards, he sent one letter ahead to Rome and six letters back to communities in Asia Minor that had assisted him along his way.[21] Ignatius expresses his ardent desire to follow Christ in suffering, and advises well-wishers against any efforts to save him. At times, he polemicizes against Christian factions, perhaps having in mind the situation back in Antioch. He castigates Judaizers, who resisted the growing gulf between Jews and Christians,[22] as well as Docetists, who doubted the full reality of Jesus' humanity and claimed that Jesus only appeared to be human.[23] Both issues—the relationship to Judaism and the nature of Jesus' humanity—remained troublesome in the second century. In criticizing these factions, Ignatius urged all Christians to cleave to their bishops, since union with God depends on union with the unique head of each community.[24] The urgency of his arguments suggests that leadership by a monarchical bishop was a recent innovation. The institution of the monarchical bishop increasingly became the bulwark of what Ignatius called, for the first time, "the catholic church."[25]

The principle enunciated by Ignatius eventually became the norm. By the end of the second century most Christian communities were headed by individual bishops. Not everyone agreed that this was a positive development, however. As the formality of ecclesiastical organization increased, rival groups emerged, and various Christian sects contested the overall hierarchical arrangement.

Followers of Marcion and Valentinus provide examples. Just before the middle of the second century, their followers formed influential communities in Rome. The development of a stronger episcopal office in Rome at this time may have been a response to the threat of Marcionites and Valentinians. More about them later.

The focal point of institutional development, however, was the liturgy. We get some sense of how Christians were worshiping in Rome around 150 from the apologetic writings of Justin Martyr. He describes baptismal rites and the Sunday assembly, held to read "the memoirs of the Apostles or the writings of the prophets," to hear the homily of the president, to pray and to partake of the eucharistic gifts of bread and wine, which are the flesh and blood of Christ.[26] The overall structure of the Roman Mass was thus already in place.[27]

The Episcopacy of Rome

Evidence of the emerging Roman episcopacy comes from Hegesippus, an easterner active in Rome in the latter part of the second century.[28] As part of an effort to combat heresy, Hegesippus traveled around the Christian world collecting traditions and lists of leaders in the principal metropolitan areas. He finally wrote up the results of his investigations in five books of *Memoirs*, giving the "unerring tradition of the apostolic preaching."[29] Fragments of Hegesippus' memoirs survive in Eusebius' *Ecclesiastical History*.[30]

The Quarto-decimans and the Easter controversy

The trend toward uniformity in belief and practice, as well as the growing power of the monarchical episcopacy at Rome, are evident in a controversy that erupted in the last years of the second century. The controversy arose because Christians in Asia traditionally commemorated Jesus' death and resurrection at the time of Passover, following the Jewish lunar calendar. Because Passover begins on the 14th day of the Hebrew month of Nisan, Christians who observed Easter according to this calendar were dubbed Quartodecimans, or Fourteeners. On the basis of this chronological reckoning, Easter, celebrated on the third day after the death of Jesus, could fall on any day of the week.[31] Christians in Rome, as well as in other areas of the Church, insisted on celebrating Easter on the Sunday following Passover, thus observing the day of the week on which Christ rose. In the mid-second century, leaders of the churches in Asia and leaders of the churches in Rome had agreed to disagree, but under Pope Victor (189-198) attitudes changed. The Roman bishop tried to enforce uniformity by excommunicating those who followed the Quartodeciman tradition of the Asian churches. Victor's initiative failed when other bishops, preferring to preserve ecclesiastical unity, refused to join him. One influential bishop, Irenaeus of Lyons, mediated the dispute in the interest of Church unity. Eusebius reports that, true to his name, Irenaeus acted "irenically" during the controversy, urging Victor to remain in union with the churches of Asia.[32] The dispute continued to smolder until finally settled by the Council of Nicaea in 325, which stipulated that Easter was to be celebrated on the

Sunday following the full moon after the vernal equinox. Nonetheless, Victor's attempt to enforce uniformity was a forerunner of later claims to widespread jurisdictional authority on the part of the Roman pontiffs.[33]

A reaction against the growing authority of the episcopal structure also appeared in the late second century in the Montanist movement. By 171,[34] in the province of Phrygia (in Asia Minor), a group emerged that styled itself the "new prophecy." A certain Montanus, along with two women, Priscilla and Maximilla, engaged in ecstatic prophecy and proclaimed that the Parousia (second coming of Christ) would soon take place in the Phrygian villages of Pepuza and Tymion, which they renamed Jerusalem.[35] This prophetic movement revived several features of primitive Christianity—an intense eschatological expectation and reliance on charismatic gifts working outside the established hierarchy. The Montanists tended to be ascetics who rejected contemporary society. The movement aroused the ire of the hierarchical establishment.[36] Although condemned by councils and suppressed by Church leaders,[37] Montanism and its moral rigor attracted many followers. These included the Carthaginian theologian and polemicist Tertullian.

In the early third century, the rivalry generated by growing episcopal power is evident. We are particularly well informed about developments in Rome through the writings of Hippolytus, a prolific author, heresiologist (expert on heresies) and antipope, martyred about 235. One of the major works attributed to Hippolytus, *The Apostolic Tradition*, deals with the practical questions of organizing ecclesiastical life, giving regulations for liturgical practice and for the installation of various ranks of the hierarchy.[38]

Penance and the forgiveness of sin Such works were becoming more common. At roughly the same time (the early decades of the third century), Christians in Syria produced a similar work, the *Didascalia*,[39] composed in Greek on the model of the *Didache*. This Syrian work gives instructions about the election and installation of bishops, priests and deacons; liturgical celebrations; the behavior of widows and deaconesses; organized charity; and the education of children. On an issue that was to become increasingly controversial during the third century, it takes the position that penance is allowed even for severe sins such as adultery and apostasy, although unrepentant heretics are to be expelled from the church.

In Rome, Hippolytus had taken a different position. When Callistus (also known as Calixtus I) ascended to the episcopacy, he adopted a lenient disciplinary policy: He was ready to forgive even serious sins, accepted as members of the clergy men who had been married more than once, tolerated socially unacceptable marital or quasi-marital arrangements between highborn women and slaves or freedmen and allowed a second baptism. Hippolytus found in Callistus' policies neither compassion nor egalitarianism, but only accommodation with evil.[40] He accused Callistus of merely setting up a sectarian school. Hippolytus himself became a rival bishop, continuing in schism under succeeding popes, Urban (222-230) and Pontianus (230-235). At that point a reconciliation apparently occurred. In 235 both Hippolytus and Pontianus were exiled by the new emperor, Maximinus Thrax, and they both died in exile. The united community of Rome elected a single new bishop, Anteros (235-236), and revered the memory of Hippolytus as a martyr.

At about this time, learned and vigorous bishops in the leading Christian centers attempted—with varying degrees of success—to forge a wide-ranging consensus on issues of doctrine and practice. One of the main issues on which the bishops united was the matter of penitential practice that had divided Callistus and Hippolytus. The rigorist position defended by Hippolytus had deep roots in early Christianity. The Evangelists recorded a saying attributed to Jesus excluding forgiveness for the "sin against the Holy Spirit" (Matthew 12:32; Mark 3:29; Luke 12:10; see also Gospel of Thomas 44). For a first-century writer like the author of the Epistle to the Hebrews, certain kinds of post-baptismal sin could not be forgiven (Hebrews 6:4). On the other hand, in the early second century a revelation recorded in a Christian apocalypse written in Rome, the *Shepherd of Hermas*, allowed for the possibility of a single act of repentance even for serious sin—such as adultery—committed after baptism.[41] Not all Christians could accept this innovation, and Tertullian, the North African controversialist of the late second century, derided the "shepherd who loves the adulterers."[42]

In the mid-third century, a series of events highlighted tensions on this issue. A key figure was Cyprian, the bishop of Carthage. Shortly after Cyprian became bishop in 248 or 249, the emperor Decius (249-251) inaugurated the first empire-wide persecution of Christians. During the persecution, Cyprian led his community from hiding. After the emperor's death, Cyprian confronted the problem of dealing with Christians who, during the persecutions, had sacrificed to the Roman gods or had purchased certificates (*libelli*) indicating that they had done so. Now they wanted to return to communion with the Church. Should this be permitted?

In response to the problem of "the lapsed," several factions emerged. One group favored immediate reconciliation, based on the forgiveness granted by martyrs or confessors. Cyprian, however, insisted on the necessity of a penitential discipline, supervised by episcopal authority.[43] This position was confirmed by a synod of bishops at Carthage in 251, the attendance at which shows how widespread the Church was in North Africa.

A more serious challenge came from rigorists who resisted granting any reconciliation to the lapsed. In Rome this faction, in the tradition of Hippolytus, formed a schismatic community headed by a presbyter named Novatian.[44] Bishops throughout the empire were called upon by Pope Cornelius (251-253) to take sides in the controversy over the lapsed.[45] Cyprian entered the fray with his *On the Unity of the Church*, insisting that Christians remain in union with their bishops, whose authority was bound up with the promise to Peter in Matthew 16:18-19. Cyprian even acknowledged a certain "primacy" to the successor of Peter in Rome, although this was apparently more temporal or honorific than juridical.

Whatever Cyprian thought of the importance of the Roman bishop in the controversy over the lapsed, he sharply differed with Pope Stephen (254-257) on another matter. Following the custom in North Africa, Cyprian insisted that persons baptized by schismatics and heretics, such as the Novatianists, needed to be rebaptized if they wanted fellowship with the Church. Pope Stephen defended the traditional Roman practice that recognized the validity of baptism no matter who administered the sacrament. He sharply rebuked Cyprian and a heated interchange ensued, at which time Cyprian apparently issued a revised version of his tract on unity, downplaying the role of Peter's Roman successor.[46] The controversy ended when both bishops died in 257, Cyprian as a martyr. Although Stephen's position eventually prevailed, Cyprian's ideal of a pure Church with worthy ministers continued to dominate North Africa and would fuel the bitter Donatist controversy that erupted in the fourth century.

The row between Cyprian and Stephen indicated both the strengths and weaknesses of the developing institutional Church. A vigorous bishop, particularly when acting in consort with other bishops organized in regional councils, could provide effective leadership and act as a strong unifying element for a community in a situation of crisis. Yet forceful bishops, convinced of the righteousness of their cause in a matter under dispute, could readily lead to schism in the universal Church.

Christianity's self-definition: Neither Jew nor Greek

As the Christian movement developed institutionally, it created its own ethos and evolved its own self-understanding. This occurred in varying ways in different regions, but several factors exerted widespread influence.

The roots of the Christian movement were obviously in the Hebrew Bible; and Christians claimed to be the authentic continuation of ancient Israel. This claim naturally led to tension with emergent Rabbinic Judaism.

Christians within the Roman empire, and even in the Syriac-speaking regions to the east, were heirs also of the Hellenic cultural tradition that had been shaping Mediterranean civilization for several centuries. Christians also needed to decide how they would relate to that culture, but the first pressing issue was the relationship with the people of Israel.

The Christian confrontation with Jewish traditions that developed after the destruction of Jerusalem is evident in those parts of the New Testament produced in the postwar generation, the period when, in fact, most of the Christian movement's sacred documents reached their final form. Within two decades after the destruction of Jerusalem (that is, by 90 C.E.),[47] Christians, probably in Antioch, produced the Gospel of Matthew, combining two strands of tradition: (1) accounts of Jesus' miracles, death and resurrection came from a version of the Gospel of Mark; (2) many of Jesus' teachings derived from a collection of sayings, now commonly labeled Q, which Luke also used.

The Gospel of Matthew

The anonymous author of Matthew gave a distinctive cast to his compilation, while claiming that Jesus was the anointed son of God, the agent of salvation for humankind. Jesus played that role as a descendant of David, who fulfilled the expectations of Israel's Scriptures. The first two chapters of Matthew's Gospel clearly express his perspective. A genealogy (Matthew 1:1-17) traces Jesus' Davidic descent, and legends about his birth and infancy cite Hebrew scriptural texts as prophecies (Matthew 1:23, 2:6,15,18). This device, found elsewhere in Matthew as well (Matthew 4:14-16, 12:17-21), is similar to the so-called *Pesher** commentaries found among the Dead Sea Scrolls, which also cite Scripture as prophecy.[48]

For Matthew, Jesus had not only been predicted by Scripture, he was also its definitive interpreter as a teacher of strict obedience to God's revealed will. Matthean Christians were summoned to follow the written Torah (Matthew 5:17-20) and the Pharisaic Oral Law, but not the Pharisees' personal example (Matthew 23:2-3). Matthew's observant followers of Jesus had a universal mission, to teach all nations to obey what had been commanded by their risen Lord, now expected as the ultimate and imminent judge of humankind (Matthew 25:31-46). Matthew thus maintains conti-

---

* *Pesher* means interpretation. The term is used in Qumran commentaries to introduce the interpretation of a biblical verse.

nuity with the faction that had opposed Paul in Antioch half a century earlier over the issue of whether or not to keep *kashrut* laws (determining what foods were kosher) (Galatians 2:11-14).

Matthew's author was concerned with maintaining a community composed of "weeds" as well as "wheat" (Matthew 13:24-30). He collected into one of Jesus' "discourses" traditional sayings on community life (Matthew 18:1-22), urging, for example, reconciliation among alienated members of the Church (Matthew 18:15-17). Although the precise structure of authority operative in the Matthean community is unclear, Matthew certainly revered Peter. Matthew's Gospel alone records Jesus' saying about the foundational "rock" of the Church ("You are Peter, and on this rock I will build my church" [Matthew 16:18]). There may be a connection between that saying and the later emergence in Antioch of a church organization centered on a single powerful bishop who would serve as the focal point for the local version of the New Israel.

Luke's Gospel and the Acts of the Apostles Another approach to the problem of continuity with Israel appears in the works attributed to Luke. Luke's Gospel, composed in the late first or early second century,[49] was the first of a two-volume set. Not content to tell Jesus' story, the author of the third Gospel recounted in his Acts of the Apostles the expansion of the Christian movement into the Mediterranean world. These two volumes, the largest component of the New Testament, constitute one of early Christianity's most sophisticated literary products. Luke's skill is particularly apparent in Acts, where vivid narrative alternates with the rhetorical appeal of dramatic speeches.[50]

Like Matthew, Luke's Gospel combines two major written sources, a version of Mark and the collection of Jesus' sayings (Q). Luke also drew on other sayings and stories, including a number of Jesus' parables.[51] While Matthew and Mark insisted on Jesus' imminent coming as divinely appointed judge, Luke portrays Jesus as a peripatetic teacher who, on his way to Jerusalem, instructs his disciples in appropriate conduct and attitudes (Luke 9:51-19:27). But Luke, too, suggests that the Way (Acts 9:2) inaugurated by Jesus is continuous with the traditions of ancient Israel. The scriptural allusions of Luke's carefully crafted infancy narrative (Luke 1-2) convey this conviction as effectively as Matthew's citation of prophetic texts in his infancy narrative.[52] Acts 5:27-42 makes a similar point: The apostles teach in the Temple and Gamaliel, a leading Pharisee, advises the Jewish leaders to take a "wait and see" attitude; if this movement "is of human beings, it will fail, but if it is of God, you will not be able to overthrow it" (Acts 5:38-39).

Despite emphasizing continuity with Judaism, Luke does not presume that Christians are strict observers of the Pharisaic Oral

Torah. Where Matthew's Jesus calls for a "higher righteousness" and for "perfection" (Matthew 5:48), Luke's calls for "mercy" (Luke 6:36). Jesus displays this quality in his consolation of grieving women (Luke 23:28) and in his assurance of salvation to the penitent thief (Luke 23:43). In Matthew, Jesus builds a fence around the Torah, in effect extending the reach of the commandments in order to avoid the possibility of transgressing them. In Luke, on the other hand, Jesus abstracts from the Torah an ethic of compassion.

Acts 15 recounts an apostolic council held in Jerusalem. At its conclusion, the council decrees that Gentiles may become Christians without circumcision, the sign of membership in the covenant community for Jews. In short, Gentile Christians need not follow Jewish religious law (*halakhah*) except that they must refrain from idolatry and unchastity and observe minimal dietary restrictions. But that is all. Whatever the historicity of this account,[53] it represents Luke's understanding of some of the practical obligations demanded of the Gentile Christians who apparently constituted the bulk of his readership.

For Luke, Christianity is a new and universally applicable religious and moral way of life. Acts emphasizes the distinction between Christians and Jews. In Acts' account of Paul's ministry, Jews appear as his major opponents and against them he directs his most fervent rhetoric (e.g., Acts 22:1-21). The fact that Jews did not accept Paul's proclamation distressed Luke, but he consoled himself by arguing that the prophets had foreseen this development (Acts 28:26-27).[54]

Luke's treatment of Israel and the Jews is part of his attempt to help a Gentile Christian community understand itself. Luke also does this by correlating Jesus' life with universal history (e.g., dating events with reference to Roman rule—Luke 2:1-2, 3:1-2), thereby laying the groundwork for later Christian periodizing of history. This correlation enables him to show the "fit" between the Christian movement and the Greco-Roman world. The emphasis on its Israelite roots certifies the new movement as part of an ancient and honorable tradition, a claim later to be developed by Christian apologists. On the other hand, distinguishing between Christians and Jews enables Luke to disassociate his community from politically dangerous Jewish nationalist sentiments. In Acts, Roman authorities repeatedly exonerate Christians, the consummate good citizens, from various charges.[55] Acts ends before Paul's execution, which, according to tradition, took place in Rome under Nero. Acts thereby avoids what might have been embarrassing evidence of Rome's negative judgment on Christians.

Luke-Acts formed an important basis for Christian self-defini-

RONALD SHERIDAN'S PHOTO LIBRARY

ROMAN EMPEROR NERO. Nero (54-68 C.E.) came to power on the death of his adoptive father, Claudius. Noted for his vanity and extravagance, Nero was suspected of causing the great fire of Rome in 64 C.E. to create space to build a grandiose new capital. Nero accused the Christians of the arson to divert attention from his own actions. Instead, his persecution of the unpopular sect created sympathy for them and more unpopularity for himself. By tradition, the apostle Paul was executed in Rome during Nero's reign.

tion in the second and following centuries. In its vision, Christians—including Gentile Christians—were a people chosen by God in light of His ancient promises to Israel; this new Israel was a people called to a high morality and a compassionate concern for the weak. This universal message would have a powerful and broad appeal.

Other Christians working within a Pauline heritage display analo- ***Pseudo-***
gous approaches to the issue of the relationship with Israel. ***Pauline***
Pseudepigraphical literature in the Pauline tradition flourished ***Epistles***
during the period that spawned Luke-Acts. Colossians is attributed to Paul and his co-worker Timothy (Colossians 1:1), but differences in nuance between Colossians and the major Pauline
epistles suggest that Paul was not, in fact, its author. Instead, the
letter is by an admirer in the succeeding Christian generation,
adapting Paul's heritage to a new situation.[56] Its portrait of Christ
as the "image of God," active in creation and now enthroned over
the cosmos, counters a religious movement felt to be problematic.
At issue is apparently some mystical practice ("self-abasement and
worship of angels, dwelling on visions" [Colossians 2:18]); perhaps this was derived from some form of speculative Jewish piety,
bound up with the liturgical cycle of "festivals, new moons and
sabbaths." Several oblique references (Colossians 2:6-19) criticize
this piety and propose as an alternative the ethical observances
(Colossians 3:1-4:6) appropriate to those who revere the cosmic
Christ. Details of the exhortation exemplify the tendency of Christian texts of this period to emphasize socially accepted moral
norms. Wives are to be subject to their husbands, children to their
parents, slaves to their masters (Colossians 3:18-22).

Another Paulinist drew on Colossians to compose Ephesians.
This text celebrates the mystery of the Church, Christ's body
(Ephesians 1:23) or bride (Ephesians 5:32), which had broken
down the barriers separating Jew and Gentile ("He is our peace,
who has made us both one, and has broken down the dividing
wall of hostility, by abolishing in his flesh the law of commandments and ordinances" [Ephesians 2:14-15]). The intense polemic
that characterizes Matthew and John over the separation from the
synagogue is not in evidence here.

In this same general period (90-110), the Gospel According to ***The Fourth***
John emerged in virtually its final form.[57] Tradition places John in ***Gospel***
Ephesus.[58] John's Gospel may have been edited there, though on ***and the***
the basis of traditions from Judea and Samaria. ***Apocrypha***

This complex work developed as an elaboration of a source
rather like Mark, recounting the miraculous activity of Jesus. Teachers, reflecting on Jesus' significance, gradually expanded this narrative, composing the lengthy discourses now set on Jesus' lips.
The result is what Clement of Alexandria in the late second century called the "spiritual Gospel,"[59] an evocative text that presents
Jesus as the Word (John 1:1), God's definitive revelation. Perhaps
in opposition to other speculative Christians who conceived of

Jesus in similar terms, including the Docetists combatted by Ignatius, the Fourth Gospel insists that Jesus is revealed not simply in his teaching, but on the cross: Jesus' death is an act of selfless love (John 15:13) by which he glorifies God and draws all people to Him (John 12:28-33).

Tensions that affected Christianity in the late first century are obvious in the Fourth Gospel. John clearly attests the rupture with the synagogue, perhaps caused by the reconstitution of Jewish life under the rabbis at Yavneh in the postwar period (see pp. 132-140).[60] The text anachronistically portrays people of Jesus' day being expelled from the synagogue for allegiance to Jesus (John 9:34), a scenario that reflects the Christian community's own experience. This experience led in turn to a bitter polemic against the Jews (John 8:44), who become generic symbols of unbelief.

The polemic in Matthew against emerging Rabbinic Judaism and the tensions between Jew and Christian apparent in texts such as Ignatius' letters attest the continuing rivalry between the two communities in Syria. Yet many Christian communities through the first several centuries of the Common Era retained a Jewish identity and left their mark on a considerable body of literature. It may have been such Christians who adapted and lightly reworked numerous apocrypha and pseudepigrapha of the Old Testament, works attributed to figures of the Hebrew Scriptures. One of the earliest is the Martyrdom, or Ascension, of Isaiah, which recounts the execution of Isaiah by being sawn apart.[61] Before his death he utters a prophecy describing the crucifixion of the "Beloved One"[62] and giving a warning appropriate to Christians in the early second century, a warning against "many who will love office. . .elders and shepherds who wrong their sheep."[63] This portion of the work is probably a Christian interpolation into an older Jewish legend. Similarly, the Testaments of the Twelve Patriarchs probably had a Jewish prehistory, although in its current form it is replete with Christian allusions. For example, the Testament of Benjamin 9:3 prophesies that "the unique prophet. . .will enter the Temple, and there the Lord will be abused and will be raised up on the wood." Most of the contents of the Testaments consist of ethical exhortations delivered by the sons of Jacob before death. Yet within these exhortations are allusions to Christian messianic beliefs. Thus, the Testament of Simeon 6:7 offers a blessing "because God has taken a body, eats with human beings, and saves human beings."

Some Jewish Christian groups traced their lineage to the Jerusalem Christians gathered around James, the brother of Jesus. Their tradition maintained that after James' martyrdom around 64 C.E.[64] the Christian community in Jerusalem fled to the city of Pella in the Transjordan. Whatever the report's historical value,[65] there did emerge in the Syrian area Christians who venerated the memory of James and observed the Torah as he had. Their works include the recently discovered First and Second Apocalypse of James, probably dating from the second century, containing accounts of James' martyrdom at the hands of the Jerusalem authorities.[66]

Some traditions about Jesus preserved in Jewish Christian communities were written down in the early second century. Later sources mention the Gospels of the Nazoreans, the Gospel of the Ebionites and the Gospel of the Hebrews. Like the Jewish Christian communities that produced them,[67] these gospels and other texts have vanished, with the exception of a few fragments.[68] Another Jewish Christian document, the *Book of Elchasai*, is a collection of sayings that claims to have been revealed to a prophetic figure named Elchasai. The work refers to the third year of Trajan (101 C.E.), so it was probably composed just at the turn of the century.[69] The fragmentary remains suggest that this group, like the Matthean Christians, maintained strong eschatological interests, along with a rejection of the Temple and its sacrificial rituals. The Elchasites would continue to be active at least into the third century,[70] when a prominent religious reformer, Mani, emerged from the sect. Mani's Jewish Christian background has been amply confirmed in a recently discovered Greek biography, known as the Cologne Mani Codex, dating to the third century, the decipherment of which began in 1969.[71] Mani eventually created a religious movement that attempted to synthesize the major religions of the Greco-Roman and Persian worlds. Manichaeism became a major competitor of Christianity in the fourth century. Eusebius comments that it was a "deadly poison" come from the land of the Persians;[72] he doubtless expresses a widespread Christian attitude.

The Gospel of Thomas

Another early gospel that incorporates some Jewish Christian traditions—the Gospel of Thomas—has also survived. This work is a collection of 114 sayings of Jesus, only some of which have parallels in the canonical Gospels. The text was previously known from Greek papyrus fragments, the earliest dating to 200 C.E. A translation into Coptic, the language of Christian Egypt, was discovered at Nag Hammadi in Upper Egypt in 1945.[73] Although the Gospel of Thomas expanded over time, a substantial portion was probably assembled in written form by the early decades of the second century.[74]

The Gospel of Thomas (Saying 1) presents the "living Jesus" as a source of divine wisdom whose sayings conceal mysterious teaching. It invites meditation and reflection on the nature and destiny of the self, as well as renunciation of the world. It thus gives evidence of an ascetic strain that consistently characterized Syrian Christianity. The attribution to Didymus Judas Thomas, traditionally venerated in the east Syrian city of Edessa, suggests an association with the East.[75] The Gospel of Thomas eventually attracted Christians with Gnostic predilections, who added touches reflecting their approach to religious questions. Nonetheless, among its ancient traditions are Jewish Christian elements, including a reverence for "James the Just . . . for whose sake heaven and earth have come to exist,"[76] as well as sayings of Jesus paralleled in the fragmentary Jewish Christian gospels.

Epistle to the Hebrews   In other parts of the Christian world, the polemics between Christian and Jewish groups continued. The notion that Christianity had superseded the Israelite cultic tradition is a presupposition of the Epistle to the Hebrews, apparently addressed to Rome, as we have noted. This homily, urging increased commitment to the Christian community, draws heavily on cultic images associated with the sacrificial rituals of the Jewish Day of Atonement and the solemn sprinkling of blood in the inner portion of the Temple (Hebrews 9:1-10).[77] Its portrait of Jesus, unique in the New Testament, depicts a heavenly high priest whose sacrificial death inaugurated the new covenant promised in Jeremiah 31. This portrait combines features of Jewish apocalyptic literature with language at home in the Platonic philosophical tradition. Hebrews intimates that in the life of covenant fidelity, rather than in piety connected with the Temple, Christians have access to ultimate reality.

The situation in Egypt may be reflected in the Epistle of Barnabas, which, incidentally, was cited as authoritative scripture by Clement of Alexandria at the end of the second century, although it ultimately failed to be included in the canon. Its prominence in Alexandria, and its allegorical approach to Scripture, suggest that it was composed there. It was certainly written after the destruction of the Temple in 70, and probably before the end of the Bar-Kokhba revolt in 135.[78] The text is concerned primarily with the Christian interpretation of the Old Testament. As in the Epistle to the Hebrews, institutions of ancient Israel, such as the Temple and the sacrificial system, are seen as symbolic types of Christianity, the true continuation of Israel.

The works of Justin Martyr mark a new stage in the Christian debate with Judaism. Justin was an apologist, a defender of the faith, active in Rome from about 140 to about 170.[79] According to his own stylized account, he engaged as a youth in a quest for truth and sampled various philosophical options.[80] Though attracted by Platonism, he finally rejected all philosophical solutions to life's questions in favor of Christian revelation. In Rome,

Justin established himself as a Christian teacher and engaged in controversies with enemies both inside and outside the Church. His *Dialogue with Trypho* is a record of a dispute with a Jewish sage. It reflects the continuing problems the Christian community had with the other heirs of Israel's religious traditions. The work is largely a discussion of biblical interpretation in which Justin argues for a Christian reading of Hebrew Scriptures, interpreting them as messianic prophecy fulfilled in Jesus.[81] Justin illustrates here the insistence in mid-second century "orthodox" Christianity on grounding Christian claims in Israel's holy Scriptures.

Christians in Egypt engaged in similar polemics. The third-century Church Father Origen reports on a *Dialogue Between Jason and Papiscus*, in which Jason, a Christian, debates with Papiscus, a Jew of Alexandria; Papiscus finally acknowledges Christ and asks to be baptized.[82] This type of debate literature would have a long history, often reflecting real rivalry between Jews and Christians.

Even more intense polemics against Jews surface in the writing of Melito, a late second-century bishop of Sardis in Asia Minor. Archaeological excavation of an opulent synagogue from several centuries later suggests that there had long been a strong Jewish community in Sardis, the ancient capital of Lydia. Melito's homily *On the Passover* was discovered only in 1932 on an Egyptian papyrus purchased by the Chester Beatty Library in Dublin. It is a florid piece of rhetoric that interprets the Passover as symbolic of the Passion of Jesus, and bitterly denounces Jews as responsible for Jesus' death.[83] Melito's hostility may be extreme, but his polemical stance toward Judaism is symptomatic of widespread Christian attitudes. Although relations between individual Jews and Christians could be amicable, intense religious debate would continue throughout the pre-Constantinian period and beyond.

By 70 C.E., Christian beliefs were already considerably developed. Although Christians may have disagreed about the precise nature of the salvation of which Jesus was the agent, they generally agreed that God worked through Jesus in a special way. They celebrated this saving event in story and song, conferring on the resurrected and exalted Jesus ever greater titles of honor. In New Testament documents composed in the last quarter of the first century considerable diversity remains in both the titles and functions attributed to Jesus. Matthew thinks of Jesus as the son of David, but also the son of God, whose special birth designates him as the eschatological agent of judgment (Matthew 25:31-46). Luke, like Paul in Romans 1:3, describes Jesus installed, by virtue of his resurrection, as the eschatological Messiah, destined to come as final liberator and judge (cf. Acts 2:32-36, 3:20).

Emergence of Christian orthodoxy

Early doctrinal controversy Neither Matthew nor Luke, however, regarded Jesus as somehow one with God from all eternity. Precisely that affirmation is made by the author of the Fourth Gospel (John 1:1-2, 10:30, 14:11) and the Epistle to the Hebrews (Hebrews 1:3, 7:3, 13:8).

These affirmations about Jesus were rooted in Israelite traditions, particularly in speculation about Wisdom (Proverbs 8:22-31; Wisdom of Solomon 7:22-8:1) or an angel as intermediary between God and humankind.[84] The first step in attributing divine status to Jesus involved equating him with such heavenly intermediaries. Regarding Jesus as one with God soon posed a new set of theoretical problems for Christian thinkers. First of all, affirming that Jesus is divine challenged traditional monotheism. What is the relationship between this divine being and the God known through Israel's scriptures? This affirmation also raised questions about the nature of the man Jesus. Was he human as other men are or did his divinity compromise his humanity in some way? These two fundamental issues, and several related questions, generated controversy throughout the pre-Constantinian period and on into the period of the great councils of the fourth and fifth centuries.

Some New Testament documents provide evidence of early doctrinal controversies. For example, the Fourth Gospel highlights a Beloved Disciple, an anonymous figure identified by later tradition as John the son of Zebedee. Whoever he may have been, this hero of the Johannine community is regarded as superior to Peter (John 13:23-25, 20:2-10), the latter perhaps symbolizing the mainline churches of the day. Yet an appendix (John 21) recognizes Peter's status and, by implication, the authority of the churches that revered him. What originally distinguished Johannine and Petrine Christians may have been certain doctrinal issues. John's Gospel, for instance, minimizes expectations of Jesus' imminent coming and emphasizes instead his abiding presence (John 15:4-8). The Gospel's insistence that Jesus is one with God from "the beginning" (John 1:1-3, 10:30) may also have been distinctive.

Continued friction among Christians regarding such issues is also evident in the so-called Johannine epistles, letters related to the Fourth Gospel but probably not written by its major author.*[85] First John criticizes "secessionists," who departed in a dispute over the fleshly (that is, human) character of Christ (1 John 4:1-3) and the reality of sin (1 John 1:8-10). Similar issues are at stake in 2

---

* The Johannine epistles are attributed to the author of the Fourth Gospel but are probably from a different hand. The relationship of the Gospel and epistles is much debated. Part of the problem lies in the fact that the Gospel is not the product of a single author.

John. Third John 9-10 reflects personal antipathy among Christian leaders. Some of this animosity may have stemmed from the development of hierarchical authority (one Diotrephes is opposed because he "loves first place").

Marcion and the Christian canon

A major rival of the emerging mainline Church in the second century was Marcion, a native of Asia Minor, whose teaching and organizational ability had far-reaching influence. Marcionite churches continued to the fifth century in the Syriac East. Heresiologists from Justin[86] through Clement of Alexandria,[87] Irenaeus,[88] Tertullian[89] and the fifth-century Ephraem of Syria[90] found it necessary to refute Marcion's theology. Unfortunately, Marcion's own writings have not survived. We know them only from the differing portraits by his critics.[91] This has resulted in varying assessments of his career and the character of his thought.[92]

A successful merchant who had been raised in a Christian home, Marcion came to Rome late in Hadrian's reign (137-138) and made a substantial donation of 200,000 sesterces to the church. In 144, however, he was expelled from the community, but he continued his religious activity and founded an enduring ecclesiastical organization. Marcion composed at least two influential works. One was an edition of what he considered authoritative Scripture, consisting of a version of Luke and the Pauline epistles.[93] The second was his *Contradictions*, where Marcion laid out differences between the Hebrew Scriptures and his own New Testament, and then articulated his controversial theology. At the core of Marcion's theology was a distinction between the God of goodness revealed by Jesus and an inferior God of justice operative in creation and in Israel's history. Jesus was the agent sent to bring human souls back to the true God.[94]

Marcion's rejection of the Hebrew Bible contributed to the emergence of another major Christian institution—Scripture as we know it. The fact that Marcion had radically limited authoritative Christian writing to Luke and the Pauline corpus was one factor in forcing the Christian community to define its more encompassing canon of Scripture, including both the Old and New Testament.[95] Some of the history of New Testament canonization is revealed in the Muratorian Canon, a fragmentary list of the books of the New Testament acknowledged as authoritative in Rome about 185.[96] The Muratorian Canon mentions the Gospels, Acts and the Epistles of Paul, including the Pastorals, but not Hebrews. In addition, Jude, Revelation and one epistle of Peter appear, along with the Wisdom of Solomon. The list excludes the apocryphal letters of Paul to the Laodiceans and the Alexandrians as well as the "recently composed" *Shepherd of Hermas*. Although at this time the

NAG HAMMADI. The base of the cliffs of Jabal al-Tarif, in Egypt near the Nile River, is the site of the 1945 discovery of the Nag Hammadi codices. The Nag Hammadi library consists of 13 codices, or books, written in Coptic, an ancient Egyptian language that used Greek letters and some Greek words. These fourth-century papyrus manuscripts contain 52 separate tractates, or essays, that reflect the views of the Gnostics, a Christian group declared heretics by orthodox Christian authorities.

contents of the New Testament were not yet fixed, as they would be in the fourth century, the outlines were beginning to become clear. Apocryphal works such as the Gospel of the Ebionites and the legends about the miraculous infancy and boyhood of Jesus,[97] in circulation at this time, might serve for edification, but, in the estimation of episcopal leaders, they were not to be accepted as authoritative Scripture.

Gnosticism—
A challenge to
mainstream
Christianity
Another challenge to mainstream Christianity (as radical as that of the Marcionites) was Gnosticism, which emerged with clarity in the second century. *Gnostic* means one who knows; the term is often loosely applied to various speculative or syncretistic move-

NAG HAMMADI CODEX II. The Gnostic Gospel of Thomas, attributed to Didymus Judas Thomas (Didymus is Greek and Thomas Aramaic for the word "twin"), is a collection of 114 sayings of Jesus known to have existed in written form in 200 C.E. Some have parallels in the canonical Gospels, but many do not. The book presents the "living Jesus" as a source of divine wisdom (*gnosis* is Greek for "knowledge") and invites meditation on the nature and destiny of the self. The sayings include proverbs, parables, aphorisms, prophetic sayings and community rules.

CLAREMONT GRADUATE SCHOOL/INSTITUTE FOR ANTIQUITY AND CHRISTIANITY

ments. The precise delineation of the Gnostic phenomenon and its development remain matters of debate.[98]

Church Fathers, who were familiar primarily with Christian Gnostics, assumed that the phenomenon was a Christian heresy,[99] ultimately deriving from the Simon Magus mentioned in Acts 8:9-24.[100] Despite the prominence of second-century Christian Gnostics, it is unlikely that the movement originated simply as a revision of Christianity.

In 1945 peasants near Nag Hammadi in upper Egypt discovered a collection of more than 40 Christian tractates, many of them Gnostic. Most had been composed in Greek in the first centuries C.E. and then translated into Coptic, the language of Christian Egypt. The Nag Hammadi codices, finally copied in the fourth century, contain such Coptic translations. These codices have shed significant new light on the phenomenon of Gnosticism both inside and outside Christianity.[101]

Among fringe elements of Judaism, perhaps in Syria-Palestine or in Egypt in the late first and early second centuries, certain individuals claimed a distinctive form of "knowledge." This

knowledge, or *gnosis*, found expression in a myth about the transcendent, spiritual world that was combined with a symbolic
interpretation of the creation stories in Genesis. Although details
vary, Gnostic texts regularly posit a primordial deity, utterly transcendent and unknowable. From that primal source flowed a
series of emanations, one of whom was Lady Wisdom described
in traditional Jewish sources.[102] This divine entity, for reasons vari-
ously defined, fell from the fullness of the godhead and produced
worlds made up of soul and matter. Over these worlds now reigned
a creator god who constantly struggled to control the spirit imprisoned within matter as a result of Lady Wisdom's fall. Gnostics
read the creation stories in Genesis as a record of the hostility of
the jealous creator. This hostility is manifest, for example, when
the creator prohibits Adam and Eve from eating of the tree of
knowledge. Gnostics wanted to escape from the prison over which
this creator god ruled. The first step was to attain awareness (*gnosis*)
of the true origin and identity of the self. Such knowledge made
final reintegration into the world of spirit possible.[103]

Whether this myth and the doctrine it spawned were originally
created by Christians or Jewish heretics is unclear. In any event,
its massive rejection of the God of the Old Testament appealed to
Gentile Christians radically disaffected from Jewish traditions or
stung by Jewish repudiation of their message.[104]

Christian Gnostics were especially active in Alexandria during
Hadrian's reign (117-138). Carpocrates inaugurated a sect that
apparently drew libertine consequences from the Gnostic denigration of the material world. In Carpocrates' view, if only spirit was
important, then what was done in the body hardly mattered.[105] On
the other hand, Basilides, a philosophically inclined teacher, combined Gnostic myth with more conventional Stoic ethics.[106]

Valentinus   Another Alexandrian teacher named Valentinus went to Rome and
and his   established there the most influential Christian Gnostic school of
disciples   the second century. Although he shared the popular Platonism of
his day,[107] Valentinus was also influenced by the speculative currents that characterized Alexandrian intellectuals. He was active in
Rome in the 140s and 150s[108] and, according to Tertullian, even
became a candidate for bishop in the Roman community.[109]

As with Marcion, Valentinus' writings have perished, with the
exception of a few tantalizing fragments and possibly one longer
tractate.[110] The fragments suggest that he taught a docetic
Christology that disparaged the reality of Jesus' humanity.
Valentinus may have been the author of a strikingly original work
found in the Nag Hammadi library, the Gospel of Truth.[111] This
text is not a narrative gospel but a meditative homily, obviously

the work of a sensitive literary artist. Its poetic imagery depicts a wretched human condition, sunk in ignorance and subject to Error. At the coming of revealing Truth, embodied in Jesus, people experience an awakening from sleep and become united with their divine source.

Valentinus extended his influence through several prominent disciples, active both in Italy and in the East. One of these followers, Ptolemy, himself produced disciples who encountered Irenaeus in Gaul in the 180s and stimulated his heresiological work. Ptolemy once wrote an epistle to a laywoman, Flora, expounding the principles of the Valentinian interpretation of Scripture; like other Valentinians, he did not reject the Old Testament, as had Marcion, but claimed that it derived either from human traditions or from beings inimical to the one transcendent God. Ptolemy thereby discovered different levels of meaning and truth in the text.[112]

Valentinus' disciples like Ptolemy developed doctrinal positions that may have been only implicit in Valentinus' thought. One distinctive claim was that there were three types of people: pneumatics, or spiritual people, who had full possession of the truth, that is, Valentinians; psychics, or soulful people, who had limited insight and were devoted to the God of creation, that is, ordinary Christians; and hylics, or material people, who were outside the ecclesiastical community altogether. Another distinctive feature was their complicated theory that the inner workings of the godhead were composed of eight bipolar entities. These entities constituted abstract, spiritual principles dimly imaged in the ordinary world. It was the Gnostic's destiny to rejoin them in the Pleroma, or the fullness of deity.

The Valentinians' general denigration of the created order and apparent determinism led to severe criticism by "orthodox" theologians. Nonetheless, Valentinian communities continued at least into the fourth century.[113]

Response to the Gnostic challenge

The Gnostic challenge produced a varied response. In Alexandria, the major hotbed of Gnosticism, the course of the debate is difficult to trace. Christian pseudepigrapha were apparently used in the anti-Gnostic struggle. For example, the *Epistula Apostolorum*, an anti-Gnostic encyclical attributed to the 12 apostles, utilizes, in addition to canonical texts, second-century works such as the Apocalypse of Peter, the Epistle of Barnabas and the *Shepherd of Hermas*. The *Epistula Apostolorum* purports to record the apostles' reminiscences of Jesus' activity during his life, as well as a post-resurrection dialogue between Jesus and his disciples. This dialogue describes the process of the incarnation, predicts the second coming in the "hundred and fiftieth year" and emphasizes the reality of the resurrection and judgment on sinners. Its polemical aims are clear, for the reminiscences are said to be composed to counter the teachings of false epistles of Simon Magus and Cerinthus, often regarded as the earliest Gnostics.

At least one of the works eventually included in the canon of the New Testament may have been composed as part of the debate with Gnosticism that developed in Alexandrian circles in the mid-second century. The clearly pseudepigraphical 2 Peter appeals to Peter's authority as an eyewitness of Jesus to condemn dangerous "false teachers" who made questionable use of Paul's letters. In response, 2 Peter insists on a hierarchy of religious values in which knowledge (*gnosis*) and ascetic practice are subordinated to love (2 Peter 1:4-7). The text, unlike the Gnostics, affirms traditional eschatological hopes (2 Peter 3:1-18).

The *Second Epistle of Clement* was also composed around the mid-second century, perhaps in Alexandria.[114] The work is not an epistle, nor does it refer explicitly to Clement. It is a hortatory treatise, calling for repentance, a life of virtue and loyalty to the Church. It strongly defends the reality of Jesus' incarnation and bodily resurrection, doctrines called into question by some Gnostics. The text illustrates the process of theological polemic that took place in the second century. It contains traditional sayings of Jesus, some of which are not found in the canonical Gospels.

In the West a principal adversary of Marcion and the Gnostics was Justin Martyr, whose *Dialogue with Trypho* has already been mentioned. He also wrote a treatise on heresies, criticizing the Marcionites and perhaps the Valentinians as well.[115] Unfortunately, the work has not survived. What has survived in his *First* and *Second Apologies* is Justin's Christological reflection on Christ as the Word (Logos), or Reason, of God.

Justin's notion of Christ as the Logos may owe something to John's Gospel, although he never explicitly cites it. Justin may also have been influenced by Hellenistic Jewish speculation, like that of the first-century Alexandrian Jewish philosopher, Philo.[116] The concept of the Logos enabled Justin to make several moves as he wrestled with the fundamental theological issues raised by a belief in Christ. On the one hand, he could rationalize the Christian affirmation of the deity of Jesus. Taking his cue from Stoic theories of language, he could affirm that the Son was the outward expression (*logos prophorikos*) of the thought (*logos endiathetos*) of the Father.[117] The concept of Logos also enabled Justin to explain the continuity of Christianity with the entire history of humankind. Again relying on a Stoic notion—rational principles are sown like a seed (*logos spermatikos*) in all matter, a sort of DNA code that makes development and growth possible—Justin argues that the

Son is a principle of rationality sown throughout human history but "brought to fruition" with the incarnation.[118] In such ideas we can see the beginnings of a speculative theology, that is, a systematic attempt to restate the meaning of Christian faith in a new set of categories.

Gnosticism was not the only problematic development in the second century. The Syrian East in the later years of the century was home to a version of Christianity that pursued asceticism to extremes that were viewed with suspicion elsewhere. Around 177, Tatian, a pupil of Justin who left Rome for his native Syria after his master's execution, composed a strident apologetic work called the *Oration Against the Greeks*, bidding a less than fond farewell to Greek culture.[119] Tatian also composed a harmony of the four Gospels, the *Diatessaron*, which remained extremely influential in the Syriac-speaking world, where it was widely used until at least the fourth century.[120] Unfortunately, the work has perished, apart from a small Greek fragment and traces that survive in later Gospel harmonies compiled in both East and West.[121]

Rise of asceticism in Syrian Christianity

Heresiologists claim that Tatian professed a doctrine similar to that of Valentinus.[122] Yet what was objectionable, especially for later orthodoxy, was not so much his doctrine but the lifestyle he espoused—that is, a radically ascetic form of Christianity known as Encratism, which even forbade marriage.[123]

Another example of the Encratism for which Tatian stood is the *Book of Thomas the Athlete,** a document found in the Nag Hammadi codices. The text vigorously condemns the "blazing fire" of sexuality and provides further evidence of the extreme views on sexual matters popular in Syria at this time. It urges disciples to escape the bond of desire that "has fettered them with its chains and bound all their limbs with the bondage of lust."[124] The asceticism of early Syrian Christianity continues in the *Acts of Thomas*, which advocates strict sexual abstinence.[125]

Another element of Eastern Christianity rejected Paul and Gentile Christianity. An anonymous Christian novel composed in the Syrian East in the early third century purports to recount the experiences of Clement of Rome with Peter on the latter's journey to Rome. The work, which survives only in fourth-century editions, the *Pseudo-Clementine Homilies* and the *Recognitions*, constitutes one of the most vivid documents of Jewish Christianity of the period.[126] Peter here proclaims a Christ who is the "true prophet";[127] Peter's great adversary, Simon Magus, becomes a transparent cipher for Paul, preaching a false gospel.[128]

* Thomas is an "Athlete" or "Contender" because of his struggle for mastery over passion.

Irenaeus and ecclestiastical orthodoxy	A comprehensive proto-orthodox vision of Christian doctrine emerges toward the end of the second century in the work of Bishop Irenaeus of Lyons, in Gaul, who assumed the leadership of the community after a major persecution in 177.[129] Although Lyons was a provincial city, Irenaeus played a significant role in the empire-wide network of Christian leaders. He composed, among several other works,[130] a treatise *Against the Heresies*, in which he sets the Valentinian Gnostic movement in a larger context and catalogues numerous Gnostic groups and their literary products.[131] Irenaeus goes on to offer a thorough critique of Gnostic theology, articulating the principles on which ecclesiastical orthodoxy was being based: first, Scripture. Although Irenaeus does not provide a complete list of the books that eventually became the canonical New Testament,[132] he insists on the importance of the four Gospels as the heart of the collection. His arguments for four—no more, no less—are, however, highly artificial. For example, he associates the four Gospels with the four figures of Ezekiel's visions (lion, calf, man, eagle).[133]

A scriptural canon was important in defining what was orthodox since it excluded appeals to secret traditions or apocryphal gospels. Yet, for Irenaeus, Scripture by itself was not sufficient, because the text could be interpreted in many ways. What guaranteed right interpretation was the ecclesiastical structure, consisting of a succession of bishops reaching back to the apostles.[134] The hierarchical organization supervised the liturgical tradition, where the ordinary Christian experienced the process of the formation of orthodoxy. Especially important was the baptismal liturgy; there the initiate was asked a series of questions about God, Jesus, the Spirit, the Church and the Christian's hope for the future.[135] This question-and-response procedure eventuated in the rules of the faith, or summaries of belief, to which Irenaeus alludes and which formed the basis thereafter for most formal creeds.[136]

For Irenaeus, Scripture, structures founded on the apostles' succession and formal statements of belief, or creeds, were the pillars of orthodoxy. According to him, they taught that God acted in human history through Jesus, who "recapitulated," or restored, God's original intention for humankind.[137] Through the incarnation of the son of God, it was possible for humans to be in communion with God and share divine incorruptibility.[138]

Rome as the center of theological debate	Rome became increasingly significant as a center of Christian theological debate in the late second and early third centuries. At the heart of these debates was the problem posed for traditional monotheism by the claim that Jesus is the son of God. Some Christian

teachers—labeled dynamic Monarchians—rejected the charge that Christians believed in two gods.[139] They explained their faith by affirming that Jesus was a human being on whom the power (*dynamis* in Greek) of God had descended at his baptism. Jesus was thus the "adopted" son of God. This position is occasionally known as adoptionism. Christians of this Monarchian persuasion apparently established an independent community and elected as their bishop a presbyter Natalius, whom they paid 150 denarii a month. In him we find the first recorded instances of an antipope and the first payment of an ecclesiastical salary.[140]

Another Christian teacher, named Noetus, originally from Smyrna in Asia Minor but later active in Rome, preserved the unity, or monarchy, of God by denying any real distinction between the Father and Christ. The divine element in Jesus was simply a mode of the one God.[141] Sabellius, who also taught this doctrine, was excommunicated from the Roman congregation under Pope Callistus (217-222).[142] Teachers like Noetus and Sabellius were derisively dubbed Patripassionists, since they seemed to affirm that in Jesus' crucifixion, God the Father had suffered and died. Theologians concerned with the Trinity in the third century constantly took as a starting point a denial of this position, regularly known as Modalism or Sabellianism.

Meanwhile, theologians in the Greek East continued to wrestle with the legacy of Gnosticism. The most prominent was Clement of Alexandria, who headed a catechetical school for the instruction of new Christians in the Egyptian metropolis in the last decade of the second century. Early in the third century a persecution of Christians erupted and Clement left Egypt for Cappadocia, where a pupil, Alexander, was bishop. Clement died there in approximately 215. **Clement of Alexandria**

With Clement, orthodox Alexandrian Christianity finally achieved forceful literary expression. Clement's major surviving works constitute a trilogy devoted to the explanation of the principles that governed his educational program. The first, the *Exhortation to the Greeks*,[143] uses a form familiar to Greek philosophy, the protreptic discourse—a discourse designed to encourage the audience to convert to the author's school. The form is as significant as the content. Clement, like other major Alexandrian teachers, was committed to the appropriation of philosophy in the service of Christianity. The *Exhortation*, like second-century apologies, appealed to the presence of the divine Logos, or Reason, active throughout history and finally incarnated in Jesus.

Clement's second important treatise continues to play with this notion. *Paidogogos*, or the *Tutor*, discusses the role of the divine

Logos in bringing people to moral and spiritual perfection, doing, that is, what Clement and other Christian educators considered their own task.[144]

The eight rambling books of Clement's *Stromateis* conclude his trilogy.[145] The title may be translated "Miscellanies," or "Carpets," and resembles other learned, but loosely structured works of the period. Here Clement delicately threads his way between the ecclesiastical factions of Alexandria. He defends the use of Greek philosophy by Christian theologians against the simpler believers who rejected such sophistication as dangerous to the faith. Faith, however, remains supreme, and philosophy only prepares for it. Through his insistence on faith, Clement resists the exaltation of knowledge by Gnostics, who have only what 1 Timothy 6:20 called "falsely called knowledge." True *gnosis*, Clement says, is to be found among Christians who cultivate the virtues of faith and charity. Clement not only rejects the theoretical claims of the Gnostics, but also some of their extreme ascetic practices. Thus, he defends the importance of marriage against an ideal of celibacy. He insists that marriage aims not only at procreation, but at the welfare of the married couple as well.

Heresiological Another eloquent spokesman for the faith and a trenchant polemi-
works of cist was the North African Tertullian.[146] His earliest writings, which
Tertullian appeared around 196, include apologies that defend Christians and denounce pagan immorality. Like Justin, he wrote a treatise *Against the Jews*, indicating that the rivalries between Christian and Jewish communities extended to North Africa. Like Irenaeus, he composed heresiological works. *On the Prescription of Heretics*, in 203, uses legal conceits to argue that heretics have no basis on which to argue for their doctrine. More positively, Tertullian, like Irenaeus, argues that the credal rule of faith and the apostolic succession guarantee orthodoxy.[147] His later *Against the Valentinians* and *Against Marcion* (written between 206 and 208) focus on the major heresies of the second century, although the former is more satire than argument.

In refuting his opponents, Tertullian engages in serious theological analysis. In *Against Hermogenes* he treats the doctrine of creation, defending the position that God created from nothing. In *On the Soul* he argues that the soul is corporeal and created with the body; hence, it does not preexist, nor does it transmigrate, as Platonists and some Gnostics held. In *On the Flesh of Christ* he insists on the reality of the incarnation of Christ and rejects Docetic notions of a purely spiritual body of Jesus. In *On the Resurrection of the Dead* he defends the analogous position concerning the believer's resurrected body against those who, like the Gnostics, denied or severely qualified any belief in corporeal resurrection.[148] In *Against Praxeas* he argues against the Monarchian position, popular in Rome in the early third century, that denied any substantial distinction between Father and Son in the godhead. Tertullian's response, which insisted on the unity of "nature" but distinction of "persons" within the Trinity, provided categories that would later define orthodox theology.

By far the most significant Christian intellectual of the third century was Clement's pupil and successor, Origen (c. 185-253).[149] Born in Alexandria, he early became an ardent enthusiast for the faith. The story is told that he tried to follow his father Leonidas to martyrdom in the persecution of 203, but was prevented when his mother hid his clothes. The earnest youth would not appear naked and so escaped death. Since his father's property had been confiscated, Origen supported himself by teaching, while he practiced a life of rigorous asceticism. According to one account, Origen went so far as to take Matthew 19:12 literally and castrated himself.[150] Shortly after his father's death, he assumed responsibility for the catechetical school, which he headed until 230. He rapidly acquired a reputation for theological acumen and was even called upon to resolve controversies outside Egypt. His travels took him to Palestine, Arabia, Antioch, Athens, Rome, and even an audience with the emperor's mother.[151]

Origen

Demetrius, the bishop of Alexandria, objected to the fact that Origen, a layman, had preached before Palestinian bishops. In 231, however, two Palestinian bishops—Alexander of Jerusalem and Theoctistus of Caesarea—ordained him. This led to a definitive break with Demetrius, who excommunicated him. Origen left Alexandria, where the school was taken over by his assistant, and the future bishop, Heraclas. Thereafter, Origen was headquartered in Caesarea, where he conducted a school for theological studies. He also continued to travel as a theological consultant. Origen appears to have been not only a master of theological reasoning, but also an individual with pastoral sensitivity. He died at Tyre in 253 or 254 as a result of tortures inflicted during the Christian persecution by the emperor Decius.

Origen's literary output is astonishing for its range and depth. As a Christian apologist, he composed a lengthy refutation of the philosopher Celsus.[152] As a biblical scholar, he produced an enormous reference work, the *Hexapla*, which compared six versions of the text of the Old Testament in parallel columns. He was also concerned with issues of interpretation and composed numerous homilies and commentaries, including treatments of John and Romans.[153] As a pastoral theologian, he wrote tracts *On Prayer* and an *Exhorta-*

tion to Martyrdom.[154] As a systematician, he produced *On First Principles*; this text presents a comprehensive vision of the drama of salvation and of the process of devolution from and return to God.[155]

Origen was convinced that all rational beings, angels as well as human beings, are endowed by their creator with freedom of choice. This helps explain the human condition. By a free act of will, some angels refused to serve God and "fell." This position contrasts with the Gnostic understanding of a fall within the godhead itself. The doctrine of free will also helps explain the union of humanity and divinity in Christ; Jesus' soul, which, like all human souls, preexisted his birth, freely chose from all eternity to contemplate the eternal Reason (Logos) that is the son of God. Finally, because all rational creatures are endowed with free will, it is possible even for some of the worst fallen angels to choose God in the end, an optimistic notion that scandalized many of Origen's critics.

While Origen was interested in theological speculation, he was above all concerned with the interpretation of Scripture, the source of revealed wisdom. According to Origen, Scripture can be understood in a variety of senses.[156]

Origen's legacy had enormous influence. His principles of interpreting Scripture were assumed by most Greek patristic authors. His complex doctrinal position, however, had a more checkered afterlife. Origen's understanding of the second person of the Trinity—the Logos, or Son—contained elements that could easily be appropriated by rival theologies of the next century. He insisted that the Son was eternally generated by the Father.[157] Theologians such as Athanasius of Alexandria, the great fourth-century defender of orthodoxy, would also insist on this point. Yet, like most theologians who used the notion of the Logos, Origen maintained that the Son was in some sense subordinate to the Father.[158] This position, carried to its extreme, would mark the Arian side of fourth-century debates.[159]

Dionysius, a pupil of Origen and bishop of Alexandria (248-265), played a leading role in ecclesiastical affairs in the third century. He headed the Alexandrian catechetical school after Origen's successor, Heraclas, had become bishop, then succeeded him in that episcopal post. The extant fragments of his works, preserved primarily by another Origenist, Eusebius, attest both to his intellectual and to his pastoral skills. In some of his letters Dionysius shows that the debate about the divine status of the Son, which would forcefully erupt in the fourth century, was already underway.

While Dionysius illustrates the continuing importance of sophisticated theological inquiry in Alexandria, other factors were at work in the hinterland. Late in the third century, certain individuals in Egypt, committed to an ascetic lifestyle long popular in various Christian communities, began a process of withdrawal (*anachoresis*) from society and thus became the first anchorites, or solitary monks. The paradigm for such people is often said to be Antony, whose biography was written by Athanasius, the fourth-century patriarch of Alexandria.[160] The situation was more complex than this heroic literary portrait suggests, but that a new style of Christian asceticism began to develop in Egypt in the late third century is clear.[161] Proponents of this lifestyle would play a major role in shaping orthodoxy in the next century.

The last years of the third century saw the emergence of critics of Origen, such as Methodius, bishop of Olympus, an erudite scholar and literary artist. His *Symposium* (or *Banquet*) imitated Plato's classic dialogue on love, but celebrated the Christian ideal of chastity.[162] In other works, he refutes elements of Origen's thought, such as his notions of the preexistence of the soul and the spiritual character of the resurrected body. Methodius met the fate that was denied Origen and perished as a martyr in 311. The controversy over Origen's views would continue as the doctrines of the Trinity and the union of God and man in Christ were refined in the fourth and fifth centuries.

For a movement that was to dominate the Roman empire, Christianity began inauspiciously—with the execution of its founder as a Roman criminal. That shady past, along with the rejection by Christians of significant elements of Greco-Roman religion, produced suspicions and hostilities that were not easily overcome. We have already seen in the work of the some of the later authors of the New Testament, particularly Luke-Acts and the deutero-Pauline epistles, a concern to reach some accommodation with Hellenistic society. Not all Christians in Asia Minor in the late first century approved of such tactics.

The Book of Revelation (or the Apocalypse) seethes with vehement hostility toward Rome.[163] Drawing on the rich symbolic language of Jewish prophetic and apocalyptic literature[164] and on Hellenistic myth, John the seer* creates a tapestry of vivid images. The work's surrealistic tableaux deliver a message of warning and of consolation for Christian churches in the Roman provinces of Asia in the last decade of the first century. John urges Christians to resist the threats of the "great beast from the sea"—a symbol of Roman imperial might (Revelation 13:1-10), and the blandishments

Confrontation with Rome

---

* The author of the Book of Revelation, who claimed experience of an ecstatic vision (Revelation 1:10) is clearly named John (Revelation 1:4, 1:9). He makes no claim to be John the son of Zebedee. His style and theological perspective are quite different from that of the Fourth Gospel.

of "the beast from the land"–a symbol of local magnates who supported Roman power (Revelation 13:11-18). The seer assures his readers that, despite trials and tribulations, they may be confident of ultimate victory, because the evil at work in Roman oppression has already been overcome. The "blood of the lamb" (Revelation 12:11) has conquered the transcendent source of evil and has inaugurated God's earthly reign. The fact that oppression continues means that mopping up operations are still underway, but Christians can anticipate the imminent realization of the divine kingdom (Revelation 19:11-22:5).

Revelation's imagery occasioned debate throughout antiquity. Eventually, teachers such as Origen, Eusebius and Augustine understood the thousand-year-long (millennial) kingdom of the saints (Revelation 20:4-6) to be a symbol for the Church itself. Yet many, including Justin and Irenaeus, took the promised imminent kingdom literally.

Revelation lavishes special concern on those who suffer and die for their testimony to Jesus. The actual number of people who had suffered by the time Revelation was written is unclear. Revelation mentions at least one individual by name–Antipas (Revelation 2:13). Other Christians in Asia Minor followed in Antipas' footsteps.

Correspondence between the emperor Trajan and Pliny the Younger, the Roman governor of Bithynia, provides an interesting picture of Roman policies toward Christian martyrs. Upon assuming his position as governor around 110 C.E., Pliny was confronted with the problem of people who had been denounced as Christians. He investigated the matter and found the Christians to be harmless. They gather, he reported, once a week and "sing hymns to Christ as to a God."[165] Nevertheless, when some Christians proved stubborn in their adherence to what Pliny considered a vile superstition, he had them executed. He then wrote to the emperor Trajan to review his actions. Trajan approved, although he discouraged Pliny from heeding anonymous accusations or from actively searching out Christians. Hadrian later confirmed the essentials of Trajan's policy.[166] There were oddities in the official policy, as later apologists pointed out.[167] The mere fact of being a Christian, a member of an unauthorized association, was itself a crime, whether or not Christians committed any of the acts of which they were often accused. Yet imperial policy at this period was not to actively search for members of the group. Until the middle of the third century, persecution of Christians was generally occasioned by local factors, rather than by the imperial government.[168]

Christian apologists,[169] beginning in Hadrian's reign, defended the faith. A certain Quadratus addressed a defense to Hadrian when he visited Athens in 124. From it a small fragment survives emphasizing the reality of Jesus' miracles.[170] Another early apologist, Aristides, defended Christianity as the true heir both of Jewish monotheism and of its strict morality.[171]

Justin Martyr, whom we have already encountered as a polemicist and heresiologist, played an important role as a spokesman for Christians at Rome in the mid-second century. In 156, the aged bishop of Smyrna, Polycarp, was martyred.[172] A graphic account of his martyrdom survives.[173] Justin's apologies may have responded to this event.[174]

Justin Martyr as Christian apologist

Justin, like many second-century apologists, attempts to refute anti-Christian slanders; on the offensive, he attacks traditional Greco-Roman religion as superstitious and defends the rationality of his own faith. The stereotypical slanders against Christians were obvious misperceptions or malicious distortions. According to their critics,[175] Christians partook of Thyestian banquets, named for the mythical figure who ate his own children. Christians also reportedly engaged in incestuous Oedipal sexual practices (named for the tragic Greek king who married his mother).[176] The charges of cannibalistic feasts were no doubt occasioned by reports of Christians "eating the flesh" of Jesus and "drinking his blood." The charges of sexual misconduct arose from their practice of having "love feasts"—nocturnal meals in which men and women mingled and exchanged "sacred kisses" with their "brothers and sisters." Justin and later apologists ridiculed such charges and asserted the lofty morality of the Christian community, while condemning the immorality of pagan life.[177] When Christianity was charged with being an innovation, Justin and his fellow apologists argued that their Christian faith was the authentic continuation of Israel. They turned the tables on their critics and, following the polemics of Hellenistic Jews, argued that Greek culture was derivative: Plato learned all he knew from the Torah![178] Finally, against the charge that Christians were irrational, Justin boldly claimed that they were the followers of Reason (the Logos) incarnate.

Justin's apologies aimed to prevent persecution of Christians, but in that he was unsuccessful. He himself was denounced by Crescens, a rival Cynic philosopher. As a result, Justin was hauled before the city prefect and tried and executed along with several companions about 165. The account of his trial has been preserved as one of the first "Acts" of the Christian martyrs.[179]

It was probably in Justin's later years that Roman Christians established memorials to the apostles Peter and Paul who had been martyred in Rome. One of these "trophies," as a third-century Ro-

Early Christian martyrs

THE BONES OF ST. PETER, JOHN EVANGELIST WALSH

MEMORIAL UNDER ST. PETER'S. Based on the Gospel of Matthew's account of Jesus saying, "You are Peter, and on this rock I will build my church" (Matthew 16:18), the Roman Church perceived the martyred disciple Simon Peter as the precursor of the authority of the bishops. Peter was revered by first-century Christians for his leadership and martyrdom. Around 165 C.E., Roman Christians established a memorial to him that was uncovered in the early 1940s beneath the high altar of St. Peter's basilica in Rome. It is probably not the site of Peter's actual grave, but rather the area where he was believed to have died. The photograph shows the *Tropaion*, which may be the monument to Peter mentioned in the writings of a priest named Gaius in 200 C.E.

man presbyter called them,[180] has been uncovered under St. Peter's basilica in the Vatican. Despite speculation that it marks Peter's actual grave, it is no more than a memorial of the area where he was believed to have died.[181] It is, however, testimony to the solidarity that second-century Roman Christians felt with the martyrs of the first generation.

The martyrdoms of Polycarp and Justin were not part of a systematic campaign against Christians, but neither were they totally isolated incidents. In both East and West the reign of the emperor Marcus Aurelius (161-180) witnessed considerable hostility toward Christians. Occasional local acts of persecution with the involvement of imperial authorities were supported by educated pagans who continued to treat Christianity with disdain or revulsion. The satirist Lucian ridiculed Christians and viewed them as religious fanatics typified by one Peregrinus Proteus, who committed a spectacular suicide by immolating himself at the Olympic games in 165.[182]

In the winter of 174-175, while Marcus Aurelius was subduing the Quadi and other Danubian tribes, Avidius Cassius, one of his leading generals and legate of the East, led an unsuccessful revolt. After the revolt was suppressed, several Christian apologists appeared, eager to show their loyalty to Rome and its emperor and at the same time to refute the slanders their enemies continued to raise. One Apollinaris of Hierapolis in Phrygia is remembered for claiming that a fortuitous thunderstorm that saved Marcus Aurelius' legions in his northern campaigns was the result of the prayers of Christian soldiers.[183] The message was clear: Christians are no danger to Rome; they are instead the cause of its security.

Sardis, the ancient capital of Lydia, was the home of Bishop Melito, who had traveled to Palestine to inquire about the works rightly included in the canon of the Old Testament.[184] Melito also composed apologies—only fragments of which survive—containing sentiments frequently echoed in subsequent apologies: that the Christian "philosophy" arose providentially under Augustus, that it grew with the empire and that only emperors generally recognized to be wicked had persecuted the Church.[185] Melito's approach was probably designed to appeal to the storied clemency of the philosophical emperor, Marcus Aurelius.

Another apologist, Athenagoras of Athens, addressed his *Embassy* to Marcus Aurelius and to Commodus, Aurelius' son and co-regent in his last years. Like all the apologists, Athenagoras exalts the lofty morality of Christians. His work also displays an openness to Greek philosophy, especially Platonism, and to Greek literature, which he mined to support Christian doctrine. All of this is not surprising in a university town like Athens.

EARLY COPY OF 2 PETER. One of the most important witnesses to the text of 2 Peter is this third- or fourth-century copy. Made before the New Testament canon was fixed, this copy concludes with a prayer for the scribe—not a professional if judged by the awkward handwriting—and the reader.

Another outpost of Christianity produced a crop of martyrs late in Aurelius' reign. In 177 persecution erupted at Lugdunum (modern Lyons), on the Rhone River. Surviving Christians sent an account of the affair to churches in Asia; that dramatic record has been preserved by Eusebius.[186] Christians at Lyons were subject not simply to mob violence or random denunciation; local Roman officials engaged in active prosecution of the illicit religion. Many Christians were arrested and tortured, including the bishop Pothinus. Those who remained faithful, called "noble athletes," experienced a variety of grisly tortures, which the account records in detail.

Near the beginning of the reign of the emperor Commodus (180-192), a Christian community in North Africa was persecuted: Christians from the village of Scillium near the provincial capital of Carthage were brought before the governor, Vigellius Saturninus, on July 17, 180, and executed when they refused to take an oath by the emperor's "Genius."[187] The deaths of these Scillitan martyrs mark the first skirmish in a long battle between native church and imperial government in North Africa.

Tertullian, inspired by the courage of these martyrs, wrote

tracts on various aspects of appropriate Christian behavior: Should Christians attend games and shows (*On the Spectacles*)? Should Christians engage in professions that involve intimate contact with pagan cult, such as the teaching of rhetoric or the military (*On Idolatry*)? What should Christian women wear (*On Women's Dress, On the Veiling of Virgins*)? What are the appropriate marital practices for Christians (*On Monogamy*)? In these and similar works, Tertullian shows himself a puritan, with an ideal of the Church as an undefiled community, radically distinct from its depraved environment.

In the early third century (202 C.E.) two young women, a 22-year-old nursing mother named Vibia Perpetua and her personal slave Felicitas vehemently rejected the North African society that had nurtured them; they became Christians. As a result, they were imprisoned, tortured and killed. The account of their travails is a gem of martyrological literature.[188] Their exemplary testimony to the faith served as a model for Christians in the following century.

The martyrs, incidentally, were by no means all orthodox Christians. For example, Perpetua and Felicitas, who died so bravely for the faith were probably adherents of Montanism.

Tensions between Christians and imperial authorities mounted in the third century. The tolerant Severan dynasty, which ruled from 193 to 235, was followed by a half century of military rulers, none of whom enjoyed a long or peaceful reign. Not all were inimical to Christianity. Eusebius transmits a report, probably erroneous, that at least one, Philip "the Arab" (244-249), was a Christian.[189] At mid-third century, however, hostile attitudes toward Christians prevailed in official circles.

Philip's successor, Decius, concerned to halt the disintegration of traditional Roman society, launched the first empire-wide persecution of those who refused to show allegiance to Rome by sacrificing to her gods. Some Christians refused and were martyred, including Fabian, bishop of Rome. Others, including leading bishops, such as Cyprian in North Africa and Gregory Thaumaturgos in Pontus, went into hiding. Some Christians did not sacrifice, but purchased documents (*libelli*) certifying that they had done so.[190] On the other hand, many Christians simply complied with the law.

Decius fell in a battle with the Goths in 251, inaugurating a two-year power struggle. When Valerian emerged victorious in 253 the persecution of Christians temporarily ceased, but was rekindled in 257 as the emperor, desiring a unified empire behind him, prepared for a new Persian campaign. This phase of persecution cost the lives of Pope Sixtus in Rome and Cyprian in Carthage.

After Valerian fell captive to the Persians in 260, his son,

Gallienus, reversed his father's policy and allowed Christians to go about their business.[191]

With the accession of Diocletian (284-305), the period of political turmoil that marked the mid-third century ended. Diocletian initiated sweeping reforms in imperial administration. The most important was the institution of the tetrarchy: The empire was divided into two halves, each of which was ruled by a senior emperor, the Augustus, assisted by a junior emperor, the Caesar. In the East, Diocletian was aided by Galerius; in the West, Maximian was assisted by Constantius. This cumbersome arrangement brought stability to the realm and a breathing space for recuperation. During most of Diocletian's tenure, the Christian movement continued to enjoy peace. Christians were tolerated and their churches flourished. The persecution that erupted in February of 303 was, for this reason, all the more shocking.[192] The abrupt change in imperial attitude was especially advocated by Diocletian's associate, Galerius, who revered Roman tradition and perhaps saw the policy as a way of gaining political leverage against Constantius. Galerius, who became Eastern Augustus when Diocletian abdicated on May 1, 305, continued in his war against the Church until shortly before his death, when in April 311 he issued an edict reversing the policy of persecution.

Constantine— defender of the Christian faith

From 303 to 311, then, persecution of Christians raged, at least in the East, and a long series of martyrs paid with their lives for their adherence to the faith. Conditions were better in the West, under Constantius I, who was first the Caesar, then, after 305, the Augustus. After his death in 306, a new political figure even more favorable to Christians emerged. Constantine, the son of Constantius, was reared at Diocletian's court, had served in Galerius' army and seemed destined for the purple, but he was threatened by the maneuvers of Galerius.

Galerius and Constantius became Augusti after Diocletian's abdication in 305, but Galerius arranged for the appointment of Caesars—East and West—closely allied to him. At an opportune moment, Constantine left the Eastern court and joined his father in Britain. There the legions proclaimed him emperor—on July 25, 306. At that point, he controlled Britain, Gaul and Spain. With his Western legions behind him, Constantine was recognized by Galerius as a Caesar in the West, but Constantine's ambition aimed higher. Shortly after Constantine's acclamation, Maxentius, the son of the former Western Augustus Maximian, revolted and gained control over Italy and North Africa. Maxentius emulated Constantine and ended persecution of Christians in his domain. Rivalry between Constantine and Maxentius continued. Constantine invaded Italy and was successful in a final confrontation that took place at the Milvian Bridge, a few miles north of Rome, on October 28, 312.

Before the battle Constantine, claiming to have seen a vision, ordered his troops to affix a new symbol to their equipment, a *labarum* that prominently featured the *chi-rho* monogram of Christ.[193] Constantine thus entered Rome, and took control of the Western empire, as the defender of the Christian faith.

In the East, Licinius, successor of Galerius, ruled in an unstable alliance with the Eastern Caesar, Maximinus Daia, who briefly renewed the persecution of Christians in 312. Constantine and Licinius met at Milan in January 313 to formalize their relationship as Augusti. They agreed on the formal end of persecution of Christians, extending throughout the empire the conditions that prevailed in the West. Once Licinius had defeated Maximinus (May 1, 313), he sent to all Eastern provincial governors copies of the decisions that he and Constantine had reached. This rescript has come to be known as the Edict of Milan.[194]

The rise of Constantine marked a major change in the relationship between the Church and the imperial government. Persecution was now a thing of the past. The Christian community was not simply tolerated but was protected. In 324, Constantine defeated Licinius. Henceforth, Constantine was in sole control of the empire; the relationship between Church and government solidified further. That process, however, will be discussed in a subsequent chapter.

In the early years of Diocletian (280-290), Eusebius, our major source for the period and future bishop of Caesarea, was a theological student at Caesarea.[195] There he studied under the Origenist scholar Pamphilus. In the peaceful years before the great persecution, Eusebius began the apologetic writing that was to occupy him for most of his adult life. His major project at this time was an ambitious one, inspired perhaps by Origen's massive biblical study, the *Hexapla*. Eusebius, however, was interested not in philology but in history. In his *Chronicle*, he attempted to synthesize into tabular form the dates of all known historical kingdoms.[196]

Eusebius of Caesarea, a major source of Christian history

Eusebius' *Chronicle* served as the basis for his major work, the *Ecclesiastical History*, which was to undergo several revisions during his lifetime. It began as a triumphal statement about the progression of Christianity until the time of Diocletian. The first seven books were probably completed in the early fourth century.[197] Eusebius later added to his history a version of his account of the great persecution, *The Martyrs of Palestine*. Ultimately, his *Ecclesiastical History* celebrated Constantine's triumph over his enemies, including Licinius in 324. Eusebius, as bishop of Caesarea, continued to admire the emperor and celebrate his combination of the Church and the empire until they both died in the late 330s.

Upon Constantine's victory, Eusebius hymned what he viewed as the dawn of a new age, when:

> "All things were filled with light, and men, formerly downcast, looked at each other with smiling countenances and beaming eyes; with dancing and hymns in city and country alike they gave honor first of all to God the universal King, for this they had been instructed to do, and then to the pious Emperor with his sons beloved of God; old ills were forgotten and oblivion cast on every deed of impiety; present good things were enjoyed, with the further hope of those which were yet for to come."[198]

SIX

Judaism to the Mishnah: 135–220 C.E.

SHAYE J. D. COHEN

THE PERIOD COVERED BY THIS CHAPTER—FROM THE END OF THE third Jewish revolt against Rome in 135 C.E.* to the publication of the Mishnah by Rabbi Judah the Patriarch in about 220 C.E.—was the time of the *Pax Romana*. It included the reigns of the "good emperors"—Antoninus Pius, from 138 to 161, and Marcus Aurelius, from 161 to 180. In the words of Edward Gibbon in his classic *Decline and Fall of the Roman Empire*, this was "the period in the history of the world during which the condition of the human race was most happy and prosperous."[1] What was good for the rest of the world, however, was not necessarily what was good for the Jews—as some of the aftermath of the revolt of 132-135 illustrates.

Unfortunately, our information about the Jewish history of this period is both scanty and one-sided. Practically all the literary evidence is rabbinic—which means we hear much about the rabbis and their concerns, but little about non-rabbinic and Diaspora Jews, and virtually nothing about "political" events. In short, our

---

* The First Jewish Revolt against Rome occurred in 66-70 C.E. Some scholars, including Professor Cohen, count the Jewish revolt in Alexandria and Cyrene (115-117 C.E.) as the second revolt. Therefore, the revolt in 132-135 C.E. becomes the third revolt. Other scholars refer to the revolt of 132-135 C.E. as the Second Jewish Revolt.—**Ed.**

sources do not allow us to write a complete history of the Jews and Judaism of the second and early third centuries.

The effects of With the fall of Bar Kosba* (or Bar-Kokhba) at Bethar in 135 C.E.,
the war of the third Jewish revolt against Rome was effectively ended. The
132-135 C.E. severity of this war and the intensity of the persecution that ac-
companied it and followed it are subjects of scholarly debate. But even if the conflict was more a rebellion than a war and even if the persecution was not as ruthless or systematic as it has sometimes been portrayed, nevertheless, the conflict clearly was a serious one and had serious consequences in both the long and short terms.

De-Judaization To punish the Jews for initiating yet another military action against
of Judea and the state–the third in 70 years–the Romans decided to de-Judaize
Jerusalem their country. Jerusalem became a pagan city–renamed Aelia Capitolina. According to various Christian sources, Jews were pro-hibited from entering the city, except on the 9th of Av, the national fast day commemorating the destruction of both the First Temple (the Solomonic Temple) and the Second Temple (destroyed by the Romans in 70 C.E.). Jews were permitted to enter the city only to lament these destructions.[2] This Christian tradition is not con-firmed by Jewish sources and may well be an exaggeration, but the facts were bad enough. Perhaps a modest Jewish community was reestablished in Jerusalem in the latter part of the second century, but its presence could not change the fact that Jerusalem was no longer a Jewish city.[3]

The Romans also changed the official name of the country from Judea to Palaestina. No longer was Israel the land of the Jews; it was the land of the Philistines, of which "Palaestina" is the Greek equivalent.

This legal and administrative change reflected a demographic change as well. The Jewish population of the district of Judea (the area around Jerusalem) was apparently severely diminished by the war (whether by death, capture or flight), and the Jewish popu-lation continued to decline (with occasional contrary growth spurts) in subsequent centuries. Few details are available, but the impres-sion of decline is unmistakable.[4] The center of Jewish life moved from Judea to towns and villages in Galilee that had survived the war unscathed. Perhaps there was a modest revival of the Jewish population in Judea at the end of the second century and later,[5] but the overall trend is clear.

---

* In various documents discovered in the Judean desert, the leader of the third revolt writes his name "Simeon b. KSBA." The name was probably pronounced either "Kosba" or "Kosiba."

With the emergence of Galilee as a major center of Jewish life, the **The** rabbinic leaders also moved there. From places like Yavneh and **weakening** Lydda in Judea, they migrated north. Indeed, the first rabbinic **of the center** literary works were redacted (that is, compiled and edited) in Galilee, not Judea.

Although in the short term the shift was from Judea to Galilee, in the long term the decline of Judea meant the decline of the entire Land of Israel as the center of Jewish life (again, with occasional contrary growth spurts).

Even in the period preceding 70, when the Temple still stood and the high priest still officiated in all his splendor, the central Jewish authority in Jerusalem had no real control over the Jewish communities of the Diaspora. With the developments that began in 70 and continued thereafter—the destruction of the Temple, the dissolution of the authority of the priesthood, the transformation of Jerusalem into a pagan city, the cessation of Jewish pilgrimage to the central shrine and the decline of the Jewish population of the country—the communities of the Diaspora acquired ever greater opportunities to develop as centers of Jewish life in their own right.

According to a story preserved in the Talmudim,* Rabbi Hananiah, the nephew of Rabbi Joshua (who figured prominently in the previous chapter), fled to Babylonia after the third Jewish revolt and there attempted to intercalate the calendar.[6] Control of the calendar was of immense importance in Jewish life because calendar intercalation determined the days on which all religious observances, including those mandated in the holy Scriptures, were observed. Calendar control thus involved the ultimate political authority in Judaism. During the Second Temple period (which ended in 70 C.E.), this authority was very probably vested in the high priest. In the period after 70 C.E., the rabbis arrogated this authority to themselves. In the story that appears in the Talmudim, Rabbi Hananiah, an emigré Judean scholar, tried to assert the supremacy of Babylonian Jewry by asserting its right (that is, his own right while in Babylonia) to intercalate the calendar. His attempt was unsuccessful because it was several centuries too early. This authority remained for some time with the rabbis in the Land of Israel (in Hebrew, Eretz Yisrael). But by the tenth century, Babylonia became the center of Jewish life, a position that would be inherited in turn by various North African and European Jewish communities. If Jerusalem had continued to exist as the center

---

* Plural of Talmud. The Talmudim are two massive commentaries on the Mishnah, one written in the Land of Israel between about 220 and 400 C.E., known as the Jerusalem, or Palestinian, Talmud and the other written in Babylonia between about 220 and 600 C.E., known as the Babylonian Talmud.

of Jewish life and the seat of Jewish political authority, would these developments have taken place? Probably not, and even if they had, surely the configuration of authority would have been far different.

Impact on
theology and
practice

Many scholars have suggested that the defeat of 135 C.E. had a major impact on Jewish theology and practice. The evidence, however, comes almost exclusively from the Talmudim and assumes that the Talmudim reliably quote the opinions of rabbis who lived in the second century, long before the Talmudim were written. (The Talmud of the Land of Israel [also known as the *Yerushalmi*, or Jerusalem Talmud, and as the Palestinian Talmud] was completed about 400 C.E. The more authoritative Babylonian Talmud [the *Bavli*] was completed about 600 C.E.) Nevertheless, the talmudic evidence for theological change makes sense in the context of the post-Bar Kosba period. We will consider a number of these post-Bar Kosba theological developments.

With the defeat of Bar Kosba, who may have had messianic pretensions (or, at least, who may have been looked on as a messiah by some of his followers), the belief that eschatological deliverance was imminent was replaced by more realistic expectations. The Messiah would come, the wicked Roman empire would be destroyed and the righteous would be vindicated—all this would surely happen, but it would happen later rather than sooner.

Precisely when the Jews began to realize that their Temple would not be rebuilt anytime soon is a matter of debate, but the process clearly begins after 135 C.E. In the fourth century, under the emperor Julian, the Jews almost regained their Temple, but the initiative for that remarkable episode came from the emperor, not from the Jews. In order to discomfit the Christians, Julian, the last pagan emperor of Rome, promised the Jews that he would rebuild their Temple. Unfortunately, he died in battle before the plan could be realized.

With the defeat of Bar Kosba, the Jews came to realize that the rebuilding of the Temple and the reassertion of their national independence were to be the work not of humanity but of God, and certainly not the work of a pagan king (like Julian—or even Cyrus, the Persian ruler who in the sixth century B.C.E. permitted the Jews to return from the Babylonian Exile and rebuild their Temple, the Second Temple). The Jews were to await the appointed hour of their deliverance, which would be hastened not by military or political action but by study and living a life of Torah.

In the Second Temple period, many Jews believed that the end-time (the eschaton) would be accompanied by the appearance of not one but two messiahs. For example, texts among the Dead Sea

Scrolls speak of "the messiahs of Aaron and Israel."[7] One passage in the Babylonian Talmud also reflects a belief in two messiahs, the messiah of the tribe of Judah and the messiah of the tribe of Ephraim.[8] What is striking about this talmudic passage, however, is that the messiah of Ephraim is a *failed* messiah. He fights the Gentiles in order to prepare the way for the Judahite messiah, who will be a son of David; but the messiah of Ephraim is killed in the process. This peculiar belief in a messiah who is killed while fulfilling his assigned task is probably a reflection not of Christian theology but of the disappointment felt after the defeat of 135 C.E. Bar Kosba, the messiah of the tribe of Ephraim, was killed fighting the Gentiles, but he prepared the way for the messiah of the tribe of Judah—sometime in the distant future—who will complete the process of initiating the eschaton.[9]

Paradoxically, the decline of the Jewish character of Judea (and ultimately of the entire Land of Israel) after the third Jewish revolt led to a kind of sanctification of the land. After 135, the rabbis living in the Land of Israel (Eretz Yisrael) began to speak of the special qualities of the land and the importance of dwelling there:

> "The settlement of the Land of Israel is equivalent to all the other commandments in the Torah. . . . Anyone who leaves the land [of Israel] at a time of peace and emigrates, is reckoned like an idolater . . . Jews dwelling outside the Land of Israel are idolaters."[10]

Such sentiments are absent from the traditions that rabbinic literature ascribes to the rabbinic masters before 135 C.E., but become more and more common in the generations after that date.[11] Rabbis who lived in Babylonia, on the other hand, clearly had a different view of the value of settling in the Land of Israel—they obviously valued it less highly than rabbis living there—but even among the sages in Israel, the ideological and metaphysical importance of the land began to rise only when its importance in reality began to fall.

The Jewish attitude toward martyrdom also changed after the Bar Kosba defeat. The new attitude that emerged had an enormous impact on the responses of medieval Jewry toward Christian and Islamic persecutions.

Changing attitudes on martyrdom

To appreciate this change in attitude, we must go back to the successful Jewish revolt against the Syrians in 167-164 B.C.E., which led to an independent Jewish state under the Hasmonean dynasty. That revolt featured both martyrs and martyrologies.[12] The first-century Jewish historian Josephus boasts that the Jews, unlike the Greeks, are ready, if necessary, to die for their laws and their sacred books, and Josephus is not alone in describing the martyr in glowing terms.[13] The Bar Kosba war too had its share of martyrs.[14] This enthusiastic endorsement of martyrdom was tempered by rabbinic legislation in the wake of the Bar Kosba revolt. According to one opinion, martyrdom was justified only if a Jew was being compelled to commit murder, idolatry or fornication; other prohibitions could be violated in order to save one's life. According to another opinion, martyrdom was justified only if a Jew was being compelled to violate Jewish law *in public*; in such circumstances death was preferable to the violation of any commandment, even the most trivial.[15] This debate, which in effect limited the precise conditions under which martyrdom was permitted or required, would echo and re-echo throughout Jewish society of medieval Europe and the Levant, as the Jews deliberated their responses to Christian and Islamic persecutions.

As we learned in the previous chapter, Hadrian's edict against circumcision was one of the major causes of the outbreak of the third Jewish revolt in 132 C.E. According to rabbinic accounts, during and after the war some Jews underwent an operation called epispasm to disguise their circumcision.[16] (This operation had also been practiced by some Jews under the influence of Hellenism in the second century B.C.E.) In an effort to halt such operations in the future, the rabbis after 135 C.E. ordained that *periᶜah* (the slitting of the inner lining of the foreskin) be part of the circumcision ritual, because the procedure renders epispasm extremely difficult. The ruling has had a continuing effect: to this day Jewish ritual circumcision includes *periᶜah*.[17]

The end of the third Jewish revolt also marks the end of more than three centuries of Jewish militancy. During the period from the Maccabees (160s B.C.E.) to Bar Kosba (132-135 C.E.), the Jews in both the Land of Israel and the Diaspora mounted a number of military campaigns against the state, sometimes successfully, sometimes not. Each of these campaigns had its own unique causes and circumstances, but what they had in common was their exceptional character. When the Jews were exiled to Babylonia in the first decades of the sixth century B.C.E., the prophet Jeremiah counseled them to:

> "Build houses and live in them . . . . take wives and beget sons and daughters . . . . seek the welfare of the city to which [God] has exiled you and pray to the Lord in its behalf; for in its prosperity you shall prosper" (Jeremiah 29:4-7).

The Jews of Babylonia followed the prophet's advice, even after they returned to the Land of Israel. The Jews had learned to live under foreign dominion, without their own national sovereignty.

This tradition was broken by the Maccabees when they rebelled against Antiochus and reestablished national sovereignty—until Rome imposed its rule in 63 B.C.E. Then came the disastrous defeats of 66-70 C.E., 115-117 C.E. and 132-135 C.E. Finally, the Jews once again realized the wisdom of a Jeremianic political stance. In the centuries after 135 C.E., the Jews both in the Land of Israel and in the Diaspora occasionally became restive and rioted against the state, but they no longer mounted any large-scale or sustained military action. Not until our own century would the Jews again resort to arms in order to control their own political destiny. The defeat of Bar Kosba was the defeat of Jewish militancy for the next 1,800 years.

The Jews and the state: 135-220 C.E.

Although the Jews were defeated in the war of 132-135 C.E., their struggle was not without accomplishments—for example, repeal of the prohibition against circumcision. The Roman emperor Antoninus Pius rescinded Hadrian's edict[18] and thenceforth the Jews were permitted to circumcise their sons without any interference from the state. Only the circumcision of slaves and proselytes would continue to be an issue well into Christian times.

The Romans must have recognized quickly that it was in their own interest to restore peace as soon as possible to the region; accordingly, they did not adopt punitive measures against the Jews. True, Judea was renamed Palestine and lost its Jewish character and Jerusalem became a pagan city renamed Aelia Capitolina; perhaps the head-tax on Jews was increased (thus paralleling the institution of the *fiscus Judaicus* after 70 C.E.).[19] But the Romans made no attempt to uproot Judaism from other parts of Palestine or to abolish Jewish privileges. The persecutions were over.

Nor is there any evidence that the Jews of the Diaspora were molested in the aftermath of the revolt. They continued living as before. Although the three emperors who followed the revolt (Antoninus Pius [138-161], Marcus Aurelius [161-180] and Commodus [180-192]) were not particularly pro-Jewish—indeed, Aurelius is reported to have had a decided antipathy toward Jews[20]—peace nevertheless reigned.

In intellectual circles, Judaism was not only tolerated, but even respected to a degree not documented previously. Galen, the second-century Greek physician, and Celsus, the second-century philosopher, wrote substantive critiques of Judaism as a philosophical system. Neither writer was attracted to Judaism, but each took it seriously.[21] Their contemporary, Numenius of Apamea, the Neoplatonist, went even further; for him Judaism and Greek philosophy were a fundamental unity, different expressions of the same truths. "For what is Plato but Moses speaking in Attic Greek?"

is a remark attributed to Numenius.[22] Whether this new-found respect for Judaism was a consequence of the war of 132-135 C.E. or of the growing prominence of Christianity or of internal developments in the paganisms of the late Roman empire or of some combination of these is not clear. What is clear is that Judaism's status in the empire did not suffer as a result of the war.

Unfortunately, we have no reliable evidence documenting the Jewish adjustment to the new Roman peace. According to a story that appears in the Babylonian Talmud and other collections, Rabbi Eleazar b. Simeon, a figure of approximately this period, was appointed a tax collector by the Roman government and in that capacity supervised the execution of several people "who were worthy of being executed." The story recounts how a fellow rabbi criticized him for such behavior. If the story is true, it shows that some Jews in the Land of Israel were willing to cooperate, even collaborate, with the Romans in the wake of the war of 132-135 C.E.[23] But is the story true? And, if it is true, was Rabbi Eleazar's action exceptional or typical? We do not know and we have no way of finding out. It is unfortunate for us that the Mishnah and other early rabbinic works (the tannaitic literature [see box, p. 219]) were not interested in contemporary history and politics. These works have other (and from their perspective far more important) items on their agenda. But the best argument that the Jews in the Land of Israel were able to reestablish a *modus vivendi* with the Romans is the argument from silence: There is no evidence for continued military conflict, resistance or persecution.

The Severan Dynasty: 193-235 C.E. Following Marcus Aurelius, Commodus reigned as emperor from 180 to 192 C.E. His reign ended in strife and civil war. In 193, Septimius Severus, an energetic and competent soldier but an outsider in the world of imperial politics, declared himself emperor, thus inaugurating the Severan dynasty, which lasted until 235 C.E. Severus was of Punic stock, from the province of Africa (modern-day Libya and Tunisia). He was succeeded by his son Caracalla (211-217 C.E.). Our sources are ambiguous and even somewhat contradictory regarding the relations of Severus and Caracalla with the Jews. According to the *Life of Severus*, on his way to Alexandria in 195 C.E. Severus "conferred numerous rights upon the communities of Palestine" and "forbade conversion to Judaism under heavy penalties and enacted a similar law in regard to the Christians."[24] Whether the recipients of his generosity were Jewish or pagan communities (or both) is not stated. Many historians, however, doubt the authenticity of this prohibition against Jewish conversion, because neither it nor the companion prohibition of conversion to Christianity is attested anywhere else.[25]

When Severus visited Palestine later in 195, the Jews of Kasyoun (in Upper Galilee) erected a Greek inscription "for the well-being of our masters, the emperors and Caesars, L. Septimius Severus . . . and M. Aurelius Antoninus. . . ."[26] (Marcus Aurelius Antoninus was Caracalla's official name.) The cold face of the stone does not reveal the emotions or motives of the Jews who erected it: Were they terrified at the approach of an emperor whose presence did not bode well for the Jewish community, or were they delighted to receive an emperor whom they regarded as their friend and for whose safety and success they entertained only the fondest hopes? Severus had just spent the previous two years suppressing a rival claimant to the purple, a man who had apparently received substantial support from some segments of the Palestinian population (including some Jews?); perhaps the inscription was meant to reassure Severus of the loyalty of the Jews. In any event, the inscription is exceptional: Of the thousands of Jewish inscriptions that have been discovered in the Land of Israel, whether Greek, Hebrew or Aramaic, it is the only one dedicated to the welfare of a reigning monarch. The feelings that motivated it must have been exceptional too. Unfortunately, we do not know what those exceptional feelings were.

In 197 C.E. there was a "Jewish and Samaritan war"—at least according to the Church Father Jerome (c. 342-420).[27] On its face, this passage could refer to a war between the Jews and the Samaritans or a war by Rome against the Jews and Samaritans. A passage in the *Life of Septimius Severus* may suggest the latter interpretation; the passage states that Severus "gave permission for his son (Caracalla) to celebrate a triumph; for the senate had decreed to him a triumph over Judea because of the successes achieved by Severus in Syria."[28] On the other hand, a triumph in or over Judea was not necessarily a triumph over the Jews, since the Jewish character of Judea (as opposed to Galilee) severely declined in the second century. If these passages demonstrate anything, they emphasize the paucity of historical data in the sources available to us, as well as their ambiguity. They help explain why it is so difficult to write a Jewish history of this period.

Aside from the questionable prohibition against conversion to Judaism, Severus and Caracalla enacted another significant law affecting Jews, the historicity of which is not in doubt. The new law permitted Jews to hold municipal offices, but also imposed on the Jews "liturgies such as should not transgress their religion."[29] "Liturgies" is a technical term for municipal or provincial offices that entailed substantial financial liabilities and were filled compulsorily. Thus this law granted the Jews a boon, but at a price: Jews could now achieve rank and power in their cities, but they

MENORAH PAINTED ON THE WALL OF A CATACOMB IN ROME.
Jewish symbols and inscriptions evident in numerous catacombs
demonstrate the presence of a large Jewish community with at least
11 different synagogues in Rome in the early centuries of the
Common Era.

could also be appointed to undesirable posts with financial liabilities from which they had previously been exempted. This law can
be labeled neither pro-Jewish nor anti-Jewish; nevertheless, in operation it meant that urban Jews of both Palestine and the Diaspora
could not escape the financial crisis of the empire in the third
century.[30]

The evidence we have surveyed thus far concerning the relationship of the Jews and the state under the Severans is ambiguous. Some of it seems to imply either tension or at least no love lost between the Jews and the Severans. In contrast, Jerome gives us a somewhat different view. In his commentary on Daniel 11:34 (the verse is "Now when they shall stumble they shall be helped with a little help"), Jerome writes that "Some of the Hebrews [that is, Jews] understand these things as applying to the princes Severus [that is, Septimius Severus] and Antoninus [that is, Caracalla], who esteemed the Jews very highly."[31] According to this interpretation of the biblical verse, after the Jews "stumbled," that is, after the wars of 66-70 and 132-135 C.E., they were "helped with a little help" by the Severans. The identity of the Jews who proposed this interpretation is unknown, but they clearly remembered Severus and Caracalla favorably.

Perhaps the Jews who provided this interpretation of Daniel were admirers or supporters of the patriarchal house. As I shall discuss below, the office of the Jewish patriarchate attained new prominence and importance at the end of the second century and beginning of the third century C.E. This was the period of Rabbi Judah the Patriarch (Judah ha-Nasi, in Hebrew; he is also known as Judah the Prince), who seems to have enjoyed excellent relations with the Roman government and who, as evidence of his power, edited the Mishnah, the authoritative rabbinic legal text that left an indelible imprint on the character of Judaism from his time to ours. According to Jewish tradition, Rabbi Judah was of such outstanding significance that he is often referred to simply as "Rabbi." For admirers of Rabbi Judah, for students of the Mishnah and for supporters of rabbinic political power, the period of Severus and Caracalla was indeed "good for the Jews." Those, however, who opposed the patriarch,[32] who objected to his creation of the Mishnah[33] and who competed with the rabbis for political power[34] may have entertained a somewhat different view of these Roman emperors. In any case, the Severans supported Rabbi Judah for reasons of their own,[35] believing that he would promote peace and stability in the land and further Roman interests. There is no reason to think that they were disappointed in their choice.

Unfortunately, the bulk of our evidence for the history of Jews and Judaism in the second century C.E. is provided by rabbinic literature, which does not represent all Jews or all varieties of Judaism. Rabbinic literature, beginning with the Mishnah, presents a decidedly partisan view of the world. Before we examine that view and the sources that document it, we should look at the life and culture of non-rabbinic Jews—those who lived in the Diaspora, those

Position of non-rabbinic Jews

HERSHEL SHANKS

OSTIA SYNAGOGUE. The city of Ostia, which served as the port of Rome, had a large Jewish community. The first synagogue was built on this site in the first century. This synagogue, however, dates to the fourth century. When the harbor silted up in the late fourth century, the city—and the synagogue—fell into a decline. The synagogue was abandoned in the fifth century. The photograph shows the Torah shrine on the right and a four-columned gateway to the synagogue. Synagogues like this attest to the widespread prosperity and vigor of Jewish life at this time.

who lived in the urban areas of the Land of Israel, the *'amme ha'aretz* (the people of the land) living in the Land of Israel, and, lastly, the "heretics."

The Jews of the Diaspora The Jewish communities of Alexandria in Egypt and in Cyprus and Cyrene were devastated in the revolt of 115-117 C.E. Other Jewish communities of the Roman Diaspora, however, remained vigorous throughout the second century. These included especially the community in Rome and numerous Jewish communities in Asia Minor (western Turkey). That Rome had a large and varied Jewish population is demonstrated by the Jewish catacombs,[36] the underground burial chambers used by the community. The inscriptions in the catacombs reveal a community with at least 11 synagogues (or congregations), each with its own officers and lead-

SARDIS SYNAGOGUE. This large synagogue in present-day Turkey was originally a Roman municipal building constructed when the city was rebuilt after an earthquake in 17 C.E. Over 100 yards long, the building was located next to the main square. The Jewish community then acquired the building and converted it into a synagogue. Extensively renovated around 400 C.E., the main hall could hold 1,000 people. When foreign invaders destroyed the city in 616 C.E., the synagogue too was destroyed, and the congregation dispersed.

At the far left is the peristyle atrium which served as an entrance. Flanking the doorway into the large hall are two niches, one for Torah scrolls and the other for a menorah. Pillar bases parallel the walls. On the right by the semicircular apse is a large table that was probably used for the Torah scroll during public readings.

ers, a vigorous population and a robust Jewish identity. Other cities on the Italian peninsula (notably Ostia and Venosa) also had a Jewish presence, as archaeological remains and inscriptions attest. But obviously these Jewish communities could not compete in importance with the one in Rome.

In Asia Minor Jewish communities also flourished. In the late second century, the Jewish community of Sardis, as archaeological excavations have shown, gained control of a large building that had been owned by the municipality and that fronted on the *agora* (the main city square). The Jews promptly converted this magnificent building into a synagogue. This synagogue was longer than a

SARDIS SYNAGOGUE. The supports of the massive table showing eagles grasping a tied bundle of rods are in secondary use in the synagogue. They were originally part of a Roman monument.

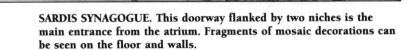

SARDIS SYNAGOGUE. This doorway flanked by two niches is the main entrance from the atrium. Fragments of mosaic decorations can be seen on the floor and walls.

SARDIS SYNAGOGUE. This stylized marble carving found in the synagogue at Sardis represents a menorah with a *lulav* (palm branch) on the left, shofar (ram's horn) on the right and a rolled-up Torah scroll seen from the end.

football field and opulent even by modern standards. It obviously reflects a Jewish community that was both wealthy and influential.[37] At nearby Aphrodisias a recently discovered inscription records the support that a Jewish charitable organization received from "the righteous Gentiles" (God-fearers) of the city. These Gentiles included nine members of the city council, a fact that shows that this Jewish community also was well-connected, secure and thriving.[38] The exact date of the inscription is uncertain (it may date to the third century rather than the second), but we may assume that other communities too, whether in Asia Minor or elsewhere and whether in the second century or the third, enjoyed a peaceful and happy existence in their Diaspora setting.

Although our evidence is meager, nothing in it suggests that the Jews of the Roman Diaspora looked to the rabbis of Palestine for guidance and support. Nor is there any indication that they practiced a rabbinic form of Judaism. Inscriptional remains of Diaspora Jewry contain virtually no references to rabbis; nor do other archaeological remains indicate the presence of Rabbinic Judaism.[39]

The linguistic barrier between Diaspora Jews and the rabbis of Israel

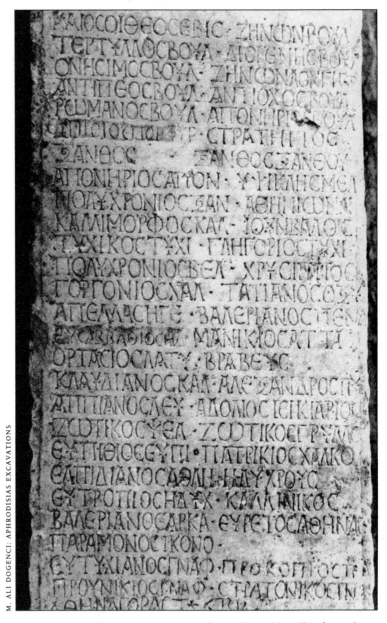

M. ALI DOGENCI: APHRODISIAS EXCAVATIONS

APHRODISIAS INSCRIPTION. This 6-foot-tall marble pillar from the third century C.E was part of a memorial building in Aphrodisias in Asia Minor. Inscribed with a list of donors or founders, the pillar includes nine members of the city council, showing that this Jewish community was well-connected, secure and thriving. Under the heading, "and those who are God-fearers," are Greek names of Gentiles sympathetic to Judaism who probably observed some, but not all, Jewish religious practices.

The Jews of the Roman Diaspora spoke Greek; their knowledge of Hebrew ranged from meager to nonexistent. In the first century C.E., Philo, the most literate and learned Jew produced by the Roman Diaspora, studied the Torah in Greek, thought about it in Greek and wrote about in Greek. As far as is known, the Diaspora Jews were no more fluent in Hebrew in the second and third centuries than they had been in the first. The rabbis, however, made no effort to translate their teachings into Greek and had no interest in Greco-Jewish literature. Josephus, Philo and all the other extant works of Greco-Jewish literature were preserved by the Church, not by Rabbinic Judaism. The languages of Rabbinic Judaism were Hebrew and Aramaic. Diaspora Jews knew little if anything of either of these two languages, so they could not have been part of the world of the rabbis. Perhaps a few rabbis of the second and third centuries knew enough Greek to speak to the local governor or other high-ranking officials, but there is no indication that such knowledge was widespread or was deemed useful for communication with the Jews of the Diaspora.

Furthermore, there is no evidence that the rabbis of the Land of Israel in either the second or the third century even made an effort to reach out to the Jews of the Diaspora. Rabbinic literature is filled with stories about the travels of the rabbis of the second century, especially of the pre-Bar Kosba period. These stories have not yet been systematically collected and evaluated, but whatever historicity they may have, they do not demonstrate that the rabbis of whatever period—whether the actors or the storytellers—were interested in spreading their message and hegemony to the Jews of the Diaspora. There is a persistent tradition in rabbinic literature that a convert to Judaism named Aquila revised the Greek translation of the Torah (the Septuagint, abbreviated LXX) under the supervision of Rabbi Eliezer and Rabbi Joshua, but the historicity of this claim is hard to establish.[40] In any case, there is no clear evidence before the sixth century that the Greek translation of Aquila was actually used by Diaspora Jewry.[41]

Thus, there was a serious linguistic barrier between the Jews of the Roman Diaspora and the rabbis in the Land of Israel, and there was little interest or ability on the part of these rabbis (at least in the second and third centuries) to become involved in the religious life of Diaspora Jewry. Diaspora Jews attended their synagogues; prayed and read the Torah; observed the Sabbath, holidays, food laws; believed in the one God who created heaven and earth and chose Israel to be his people; obeyed (or did not obey) their traditional authority figures—all, however, without the help of the lettered elite that was emerging in Palestine.

The Jewish Diaspora in Babylonia was Aramaic-speaking, and

therefore could communicate far more easily with the rabbis of
the Land of Israel than could the Greek-speaking Jews of the Roman Diaspora. Various rabbis of the second century were reported
to be of Babylonian extraction, and various Palestinian rabbis were
said to have traveled to Babylonia, but Babylonia was not yet in
the rabbinic orbit in the second century C.E. Although the
Babylonian Talmud reveals a great deal about the religious and
social life of Babylonian Jewry in the third to fifth centuries C.E., it
tells us almost nothing about life in the second century. We may
assume that the Jews of Babylonia, like their co-religionists in the
Roman Diaspora, continued to observe their traditional practices
without the help of the rabbis from the Land of Israel.[42]

The urban   Like the Jews of the Roman Diaspora, the Jews of the coastal cities
Jews of the   of Palestine lived in a Gentile, Greek-speaking environment. In the
Land of Israel middle of the third century, many rabbis began to make their home
in these cosmopolitan and mercantile centers, notably Caesarea,
but in the second century they did not. There were Jews in these
cities in the second century—one Jew even became the *agoranomos*
(market inspector) of the city of Joppa[43]—but not rabbis. In the
immediate post-135 period, the rabbinate was primarily a rural
phenomenon, located in the small towns and villages of Galilee
and Judea.[44] In the fourth century, the Greek-speaking Jews of the
coastal cities recited even the *Shema* (the fundamental declaration
of faith in the Lord as the "One God") in Greek in their synagogues,[45] and we may presume that they did so in the second
century as well. They were not part of rabbinic society.

The 'amme   Even in the rural heartland of rabbinic Palestine, not everyone was
ha'aretz of   a follower of the rabbis. Many Jews were *'amme ha'aretz*, "people
the Land of   of the land" (singular, *'am ha'aretz*), Jews who could not be trusted
Israel   to observe properly the laws of purity and tithing. Many rabbinic
texts contrast the *'am ha'aretz* with the *ne'eman*, someone who is
"trustworthy," that is, someone who is presumed to observe properly the laws of tithes, and, with the *haber*, or "associate," someone
who is presumed to observe properly the laws of purity. Here is
the Mishnah's formulation:

> "A. He that undertakes to become trustworthy [*ne'eman*] must
> tithe what he eats, what he sells and what he buys; and he may
> not be the guest of an *'am ha'aretz*.

> "B. R. Judah says: Even he that is the guest of an *'am ha'aretz*
> may still be reckoned trustworthy. . . .

> "C. He that undertakes to become an associate [*haber*] may not
> sell to an *'am ha'aretz* [foodstuff that is] wet or dry, or buy from

him [foodstuff that is] wet; and he may not be the guest of an
'am ha'aretz. . . .

"D. R. Judah says: Nor may he rear small cattle, or be profuse in
vows or levity, or become impure through contact with the dead,
but shall minister in the house of study."[46]

In this passage, the *'am ha'aretz* is presumed to observe the
laws of purity and tithing either unsatisfactorily or not at all; therefore, the trustworthy and the associate must absent themselves
from his table (paragraphs A and C). The laws of purity and tithing center on food, which is very susceptible to impurity. Therefore these laws (unlike, for example, the laws regarding Sabbath
observance) erect clear social barriers between those who observe
them and those who do not.* The emphasis on the laws of tithing
and purity as social markers is probably a vestige from the sectarian past of at least one strand of Rabbinic Judaism; sects encourage separation from the society around them and use the concepts
of purity and impurity to define who is in the group and who is
out. The table fellowship that is reserved exclusively for members
of the group is clearly reflected in paragraphs A and C of this
mishnah. The *'am ha'aretz* is clearly out.

The modifications advanced by Rabbi Judah (not to be confused with Rabbi Judah the Patriarch, who will be discussed below) in paragraphs B and D suggest that in his time (the middle of
the second century C.E.) the old structure was breaking down.
Rabbi Judah allows the trustworthy to sup with an *'am ha'aretz*.
His definition of an associate does not require separation from the
'am ha'aretz; it does not even center on the laws of purity. According to Rabbi Judah, the distinguishing characteristic of the associate is his readiness to follow rabbinic norms and serve the rabbis,
not his abstention from contact with the *'amme ha'aretz*.[47] In Rabbi
Judah's terms, an *'am ha'aretz* is simply someone who does not
follow rabbinic piety, i.e., a non-rabbinic Jew. Rabbi Judah's redefinition of the *'am ha'aretz* in paragraphs B and D of the quoted
mishnah reflects an effort to break down, or at least to soften, the
sectarian and separatist aspects of the more restrictive definition
in paragraphs A and C.

The social reality lurking behind these rules and this debate is
obscure. Did all rabbinic Jews properly observe these laws? If not,
what was the relationship between those who did and those who
did not? What percentage of the population did the *'amme ha'aretz*

---

* The laws of purity and tithing are separate from the laws of *kashrut*. The laws of
kashrut derive from Leviticus 11 and Deuteronomy 14:1-21; the laws of purity
derive from Leviticus 12-15 and Numbers 19; the laws of tithing derive from Numbers 18:8-32 (and various other passages).

constitute? What was their social status? What and who brought about the deemphasis of the sectarian and separatist elements in the definition of *'am ha'aretz*? Unfortunately, we cannot answer these important questions.

But the rabbinic legislation on the *'am ha'aretz* shows that the rabbis were well aware that there were Jews "out there" who did not attend upon the rabbis' every word and who did not follow a rabbinic way of life. Elsewhere too the rabbis reveal their awareness of such Jews. Every day a rabbinic Jew was supposed to thank the Lord for not creating him "a gentile, an 'outsider' [*bur*], or a woman," three categories of people who could not experience rabbinic piety.[48] When Rabbi Akiva remembered what he had done in his youth before becoming a rabbi, he said, "I thank you, Lord my God, that you have placed my lot among those who sit in the house of study (*bet hamidras*) and you have not placed my lot among those who sit on the corners [?] in the marketplace."[49]

Since these Jews did not look to the rabbis for leadership—and were in turn spurned by the rabbis[50]—to whom did they turn for religious guidance? Still again, the answer is not clear. What is clear, however, is that these Jews, like the non-rabbinic Jews of the Diaspora and the Greek cities, were neither "sectarian" nor "deviant." The rabbis had to admit that the *'amme ha'aretz* did observe many of the commandments, notably the prohibition against eating food grown during the sabbatical years. They also observed the Sabbath.[51] We may presume that they observed the explicit commandments of the Torah and continued to practice Judaism as they had always done.

The place of prayer We may presume too that private and public prayer was part of the traditional piety of the *'amme ha'aretz*. Little is known of the synagogue in the second and early third centuries C.E. Various synagogues are attested archaeologically for the Second Temple period, and numerous synagogues are attested archaeologically for the late third century and onwards, but not a single synagogue is attested archaeologically for the period under review here.[52] Perhaps in the wake of the destruction of the Temple the Jews hesitated to erect buildings that might seem to be replacements for that which was irreplaceable.

In the absence of permanent buildings, public prayer probably took place in town squares or other open, accessible areas. In Jewish circles known to the author of the Gospel of Matthew, the Pharisees took the best seats (or "the seats in front") in synagogues, that is, public assemblies (Matthew 23:6), but the rabbinic texts that took shape during the second century seldom claim rabbinic leadership of public prayer. In fact, the Mishnah and related documents show remarkably little interest in public prayer or in the gatherings (the synagogues) in which this prayer took place. The simplest explanation for this phenomenon is that the synagogue was not a rabbinic institution. The rabbis neither created nor supervised the institution of public prayer, and it would be some time before the rabbis would become communal authorities in matters of liturgy and liturgical practice. The Jews, many of them *'amme ha'aretz*, who frequented public prayer assemblies in the second century C.E. had no need for rabbinic leadership. They had neither time for, nor interest in, the demands of the "fanatical" rabbis. The feeling was mutual; "sitting in the assemblies [or synagogue] of the *'amme ha'aretz* drives a man from this world" was a rabbinic saying.[53]

"Heretics"

Just as the rabbis used the term "Gentiles," *goyim*, to refer to all non-Jews, whatever their ethnic origin, theological belief or ritual practice, so too the rabbis used a single term "heretics" (*minim*) to designate a wide variety of Jews whose theology or practices the rabbis found offensive. The Mishnah refers in a few passages to these heretics and their heresy (*minut*), and later documents supply numerous additional references.[54] Rabbinic texts also refer to "apostates," *meshumadim* or *mumarim*. The rabbis sometimes label a specific practice or belief as "the way of outsiders" or "the way of the Amorites" and other similar expressions.[55] Thus the rabbis of the second century seem to have known not only *'amme ha'aretz*, the great unwashed, but also heretics, who decidedly rejected beliefs or practices that the rabbis, at least, regarded as normative, and apostates, who removed themselves from the social control of the Jewish community.

The precise identity of these deviant Jews (deviant, that is, from the perspective of the rabbis) and their non-normative ways (non-normative, that is, from the perspective of the rabbis) is an intriguing question that has aroused much speculation. Many scholars have suggested that Christian Jews (that is, ethnic Jews who accepted the divinity or messiahship of Jesus and modified their Judaism accordingly) were the likeliest target of these rabbinic polemics, but the question is open.

More important than the precise identity of the *minim* is the fact that the rabbis paid so little attention to them. The rabbis in the Mishnah and later documents did not formulate creeds and dogmas that would serve as touchstones to distinguish between the true and the false. Nor did they create social mechanisms and institutions that would allow them to exclude those whom they did not like. Perhaps the rabbis were not interested in doing any of these things because no one would have listened to them even if they had, but it is striking that the rabbis went about their work all but oblivious to the varieties of Judaism around them. Christian writers of the second century were interested in normative self-definition, and wrote numerous treatises against both heretics and Jews, but the rabbis of the period were interested neither in heresy nor in Christianity. We may be sure that heretics and Christian Jews were out there in the second century, but the rabbis paid them little attention.[56]

Rabbinic Judaism   Having discussed categories of non-rabbinic Jews, let us turn to Rabbinic Judaism.

The rabbis, or sages, emerged as a distinctive group in the decades after the destruction of the Temple in 70 C.E., as we have seen in a previous chapter. But only at the end of the second century C.E. and the beginning of the third century C.E. did the rabbis begin to find a place for themselves in Jewish society at large in the Land of Israel. This change was the work of Rabbi Judah the Patriarch (c. 175-220 C.E.).

The leader of the rabbis was the patriarch (this was his title in Greek and Latin; in Hebrew the title is *nasi*).[57] The clearest expressions of his authority were his right (1) to appoint (or ordain) judges in the rabbinic judicial system and (2) to supervise the intercalation of the calendar. The first patriarch about whom we have any reliable information is Rabban Gamaliel, one of the dominant figures of the Yavnean period after the First Jewish Revolt.* But it was only in Rabbi Judah's time that the patriarch became more than just the first among equals. Rabbi Judah was the first patriarch to develop rules of etiquette governing behavior at his court, to amass substantial personal wealth and to claim (or, perhaps more accurately, to allow others to claim on his behalf) descent from the royal house of King David.

One rabbinic tradition has R. Gamaliel, the patriarch of Yavneh and R. Judah's grandfather, "receive authorization" from a Roman governor in Syria. But there is not a single rabbinic tradition bringing Rabbi Simeon b. Gamaliel, Rabbi Judah's father and predecessor, into contact with a Roman official; perhaps the Romans suspected the rabbis generally, or the patriarchal house specifically, of supporting the third Jewish revolt of 132-135 C.E., and the two sides kept their distance. In stark contrast, numerous rabbinic traditions report that Rabbi Judah was befriended by a Roman official—Antoninus, sometimes called King Antoninus. The legendary character of many of these traditions is obvious, but some of them may well have a historical core. Even if the identity of this Antoninus is uncertain (the most plausible conjecture is

* On Rabban Gamaliel and his influence, see pages 136-140.

that he is the emperor Caracalla, i.e., Marcus Aurelius Antoninus),[58] the stories show that Rabbi Judah enjoyed some measure of recognition from the Roman government and, as a result, gained certain benefits both for himself and for the Jewish community.

Rabbi Judah's tenure as patriarch also had a major impact on the development of the rabbinate. The tension between the rabbis and non-rabbinic Jews did not disappear, but, as a result of the work of Rabbi Judah, the rabbis became much more involved in the society around them and aspired not only to religious virtuosity but also to communal leadership. Here are several examples of ways by which Rabbi Judah sought to bring the rabbis into Jewish society at large. *Rabbi Judah ha-Nasi*

• He greatly enhanced the power of the patriarchate and thereby the power of the rabbinate. Rabbi Judah was asked by the people of Simonias (in Galilee) to appoint for them a man who would "deliver sermons; serve as judge, deacon (*hazzan*) and scribe (or teacher of children, *sofer*); teach us (rabbinic tradition); and fulfill all our desires"—quite a request! Rabbi Judah also sent Rabbi Romanus to check the family purity of the Jews in a certain distant place.[59] No such traditions are recorded for any of the previous patriarchs.[60] It was only from the time of Rabbi Judah the Patriarch and afterward that rabbis became communal functionaries under the authority of the patriarch.

• The two major rabbinic institutions in antiquity were the school and the judicial court (not the synagogue). Most rabbinic schools in antiquity, in both Palestine and Babylonia, were disciple circles (a master attended by his faithful students) rather than academies (perpetual institutions with a corporate identity). These disciple circles were small and reached only small numbers of people; they were not intended to promote Rabbinic Judaism among the broad reaches of the population.[61]

Interaction between rabbis and plain Jews took place primarily not in schools but in courts. A study of all the legal cases reported in tannaitic literature (principally the Mishnah and its supplement, the Tosefta) reveals that the scope of authority of the rabbinic judges in the second century was rather narrow. They were consulted most often in cases dealing with the laws of purity and marriage law. In these areas the rabbis were apparently acknowledged as experts, but in other areas—civil law, the laws of *kashrut* (dietary laws), the laws of the Sabbath and the practices of the synagogue—the rabbis were rarely consulted, either because people had other authority figures to whom to turn or because the people simply followed traditional pre-rabbinic precedents. However, the legal cases in which Rabbi Judah the Patriarch and later rabbis became involved show a somewhat different topic profile. Here marriage law, civil law, the laws of *kashrut* and the laws of the Sabbath all figure prominently. This demonstrates that the scope of rabbinic jurisdiction expanded significantly during Rabbi Judah's tenure, and that the rabbis were becoming more involved in the lives of the general population.[62]

• In the period before Rabbi Judah, the rabbis had been well-to-do, had associated with the well-to-do and had interested themselves in questions that were important to the landed classes. Perhaps some of the sages were poor, but their poverty has been rendered invisible in tannaitic literature.[63] Those rabbis about whose economic status anything is known seem to have been land-owners. They even shared the eternal prejudice of landowners against shepherds and goatherds, whom the rabbis regarded as inveterate thieves and contumacious liars.[64] Although traditions in the later Talmudim refer to the poverty of some second-century rabbis, who allegedly were employed in menial occupations, these traditions receive no confirmation from the Mishnah itself, or from the rest of tannaitic literature. They are probably retrojections, or throwbacks, from the conditions of later times. The rabbis of the second century encouraged Jews to support the poor, tried to regulate the collection and disbursement of charity and perhaps even served as charity agents themselves, but they never say that charity should be given to needy rabbis and never report that poor students actually received any charity.[65]

By contrast, in the period of Rabbi Judah the Patriarch, we observe the beginnings of tension between the well-to-do and some rabbis. Rabbis are appointed to salaried posts; these are not wealthy, landed people. In Rabbi Judah's tenure, a "poor tithe" is distributed for the first time to needy students. During Rabbi Judah's tenure and afterwards, as the patriarchate enlarged its power, the rabbinic movement expanded its social horizons in order to find ways to include the poor among its numbers. The links between the rabbis and the people were becoming closer.[66]

• Before Rabbi Judah, the rabbinate had been primarily a rural phenomenon in Judea and especially in Galilee. Most of the legal cases presented to the *tannaim* originated in rural settlements, not in cities. Rabbinic traditions consistently place the rabbis of the second century, both before and after the war of 132-135 C.E., in rural towns and villages. The urbanization of the rabbinic movement is also the work of Rabbi Judah. When Rabbi Judah moved the seat of the patriarchate from Beth Shearim to Sepphoris (both in Lower Galilee), the rabbinic movement was headquartered in a city for the first time since its early days in Yavneh and Lydda (in the generation immediately after 70 C.E.). Rabbi Judah attempted

Tannaim and Amoraim

The rabbis who lived in the generations before about 220 C.E. when the Mishnah was completed are known as *tannaim*, "teachers" (singular, *tanna*). Most of the *tannaim* lived between about 80 and 200 C.E. The rabbinic works that contain the sayings of, and stories about, the *tannaim*, and that do not cite any named authority who lived after about 220 C.E., are known as tannaitic literature. The first and most important of these works is the Mishnah (literally, "repetition" or "instruction"), described on pages 219-223; other works in this category are the Tosefta, a supplement to the Mishnah, and a set of commentaries on Exodus through Deuteronomy (the *Mekhilta*, the *Sifra* and the *Sifre*).

Although they contain many sayings of, and stories about the *tannaim*, the two Talmudim are not tannaitic works, because they cite numerous authorities who lived after the *tannaim*. These authorities, who lived from about 220 to 500 C.E., are known collectively as *amoraim* (singular, *amora*), and therefore the two Talmudim and various other works are called amoraic literature.

to establish the ritual purity of the cities of Palestine and to free their inhabitants from the requirement of giving the priestly tithes. Both reforms were clearly intended to facilitate the entrance of rabbis and rabbinic Jews into the cities. Probably not by coincidence, Palestine entered a new phase of urbanization during Rabbi Judah's tenure.[67]

Rabbi Judah's crowning achievement, however, was the Mishnah, the font of rabbinic literature.

The organization of the Mishnah

The Mishnah is a large work, some 800 to 1,000 pages in English translation.[68] It consists of laws, debates on legal questions and brief narratives on legal subjects. Strangely enough, it contains few citations to, or explanations of, Scripture. Moreover, with the exception of an atypical tractate called *Pirqei Avot* (The Sayings of the Fathers), the Mishnah contains very little homiletical or ethical material. Nor does it contain explicit theology or eschatology. In short, the Mishnah is a book of laws.

It is divided into six orders, or divisions, which are in turn subdivided into 63 tractates. Each tractate is in turn divided into chapters, and each chapter into individual pericopes or sections, each of which is often called, simply, a mishnah.

Each of the orders is devoted to some overarching theme or set of issues, and each of the tractates in turn addresses an aspect of the theme. The first order, *Zera'im*, or "Seeds," concerns the obligations incumbent upon an Israelite before he—for the Mishnah the paradigm of normality is the Israelite male—may partake of the bounty brought forth from the earth. The earth is the Lord's, and the Israelite, in return for tenancy on the Lord's domain, must either recite benedictions or separate some of the produce for the poor or for the priest or for the Levite, or present some of it at the Temple. The second order, *Mo'ed*, or "Appointed Times," concerns Holy Times, the sacred times of the year and their rituals, especially the rituals that were enacted in the Temple (even though it had been destroyed long before). The third order, *Nashim*, or "Women," concerns marriage law and the authority of a husband to cancel his wife's oaths. The fourth order, *Nezikin*, or "Damages," is devoted to interpersonal relations: civil law, torts, contracts, bailments, the authority of the judiciary, relations between Jews and Gentiles and relations between one Jew and another (here appears the anomalous tractate *Pirqei Avot*). The fifth order, *Kodashim*, or "Holy Things," concerns the sacrificial cult, the structure of the Temple, the misuse of animals and objects dedicated to the cult and the slaughter of nonsacrificial animals. The sixth order, *Tohorot*, or "Purities," concerns the purity system: sources of impurity, the means by which impurity is transferred, objects susceptible to impurity and modes of purification.

This large and complex work is highly edited and stylized, suggesting the existence not only of a strong editor but also of a sustained period of peace and stability (from after the revolt of 132-135 C.E. to about 220 C.E.). The Mishnah demonstrates a passion for classifying things, for numbering the resulting categories and for exploring the precise contours of the boundary that separates one category from another. The Mishnah also shows a passion for stating abstract principles and demonstrating how the principles are to be applied with different results in different cases.[69] But for all its abstraction and formal precision, the Mishnah is not a collection of Aristotelian treatises. It is highly digressive and often links one pericope to the next by verbal association or some other literary criterion. Most important, the Mishnah is not arranged logically. It has no beginning or end; it has only a middle. The closest thing to an introduction to the work is tucked away in the fourth order in the opening chapters of the tractate *Pirqei Avot*; there we learn that the authority assumed by the Mishnah can be traced back to Moses at Sinai. For the rest, however, the Mishnah starts where it wants and ends where it wants; it treats in great detail fragments of themes, but seldom treats an entire theme.

Thus for example, the very first mishnah addresses the question "From what time in the evening may the *Shema* be recited?" (*Berakhot* 1:1). But how do we know that this prayer is to be recited in the evening at all? And by whom? And why? All these questions are logically anterior to the question posed by the mishnah, but the mishnah ignores them completely.

The Mishnah is, as I said, a book of laws; yet it is not a law book. Unlike most law books, it contains numerous disputes and divergent opinions without giving any obvious indication which opinion is the one to be followed. Unlike most law books, it often omits the penalty for infractions of its rules or the manner in which a wrong is to be righted. Unlike most law books, it describes institutions (the Temple, the Sanhedrin) and authorities (the high priest) and rituals (the sacrificial cult) that no longer existed when the book was written. Unlike most law books, it all but ignores the institutions (the synagogue) and authorities (the Roman government, the municipal governments in Palestine, the rabbis themselves[70]) and rituals (public prayer, public and private study of Torah[71]) that did exist when the book was written. The Mishnah thus is not a law book.[72]

The Mishnah as a book of laws, not a law book

If not a law book, what is it and why was it written? The answer remains elusive. The Talmudim, which are in effect commentaries on the Mishnah, state on several occasions that the Mishnah was edited or arranged by Rabbi Judah the Patriarch.[73] This assertion is universally accepted as true, although it is nowhere advanced by the Mishnah itself.

Why did Rabbi Judah edit the Mishnah? The publication of the Mishnah was an integral part of his program to extend the power of the patriarchate. By superseding previous legal collections and incorporating them into a single Mishnah, Rabbi Judah asserted his authority over the rabbinic movement, the intended audience of the new book: From now on all rabbinic study would focus on one collection only—*his*.

Yet the Mishnah is more than an implicit assertion of power by the patriarch. It is the core document of Rabbinic Judaism, forming the foundation for virtually all rabbinic literature that would follow it, from the third century C.E. to our day. Although the Mishnah has become a "classic," safely located within the confines of the sacred traditions of Rabbinic Judaism, the Mishnah was (and to some extent still is) a radical work.

The Mishnah is radical in that it is the first Jewish work, whether biblical or post-biblical, whether in Hebrew or Greek or Aramaic, whether Palestinian or from the Diaspora, to attribute conflicting legal opinions to named individuals who, despite their differences, belong to the same group. The legal materials in the Hebrew Bible are not uniform, to be sure. The Holiness Code (Leviticus 19-20 and related passages), the Covenant Code (Exodus 21-24), the priestly laws, the laws of Deuteronomy, etc. are products of different schools and different philosophies, and those differences are often manifest in legal contradictions. But the editor of the Torah combined these codes anyway, without even hinting to the reader that the collections do not always agree, thus allowing later Jews to pretend (or rather, to *insist*) that the collections always do agree. But the Mishnah allows no such pretense.

The very first mishnah opens with a question ("From what time in the evening may the *Shema* be recited?") which leads to a second question ("Until what time in the evening may the *Shema* be recited?") that receives three different answers, each one ascribed to a different authority. The Mishnah not only tolerates legal disputes, it relishes them. Legal dispute is the core of Mishnaic discourse. And the disputes are open-ended: The Mishnah does not contain any explicit rules by which the winning position can be determined.[74] Whether these disputes are entirely rhetorical (in other words, the Mishnah is the record of a debating society) or whether they mirror real diversity in practice is not clear; if the latter, the social mechanisms that held this disputatious and fractious group together must have been remarkable, but they too are unclear.

The Mishnah is radical in another respect, too. With few exceptions it does not attach its legal rulings to Scripture. In the opening chapter of the tractate *Pirqei Avot*, we are told of a chain of tradition that links Moses at Mt. Sinai to the rabbis of the Mishnah, specifically the patriarchal house of Rabbi Judah. *Pirqei Avot* thus asserts that rabbinic authority derives from Moses and God. But the Mishnah itself is not interested in proving this assertion. In the Mishnah, rabbis debate numerous points of law but seldom cite the biblical authority that would substantiate their positions. Many of their rulings probably were derived from a close reading of the laws of the Torah, but the Mishnah obscures this fact by omitting the scriptural source.

As a result, it is impossible to tell from the Mishnah whether a given ruling is derived from Scripture or not. Nor does the Mishnah reveal whether a given ruling is ancient or modern, traditional or innovative. The authority for the Mishnah's statements is entirely internal to the Mishnah itself: anonymous sages as well as named sages speak, and the reader is supposed to respect their words. By ignoring all external sources of authority, including Scripture, the Mishnah implicitly presents itself as a source of authority, endorsing the right of its human authors to debate and legislate. (Presumably such a view would also enhance the power of the patriarch to legislate.)

This radical and unsettling thesis was rejected by virtually all of the Mishnah's commentators, beginning with the Talmudim and the tannaitic commentaries on the Torah.[75] These works attempt to demonstrate that the Mishnah—not just the Mishnah in general or in theory, but the specific rulings of the Mishnah, one by one— derives from Scripture: law must be subordinate to revelation, and must somehow be derived from the Torah of Moses. In this conception the only innovation allowed is the innovation that claims to be traditional, that claims to be the working out of what had been revealed to Moses long before. Thus in one sense the Mishnah lost; its implicit defense of the autonomy of human reason was rejected. But in another and much larger sense the Mishnah won; it gave rabbinic learning a secure base on which to build for the future.

SEVEN

The World of the Talmud: From the Mishnah to the Arab Conquest

ISAIAH M. GAFNI

T O SOME EXTENT, THE FOUR CENTURIES OF JEWISH HISTORY surveyed in this chapter—from the completion of the Mishnah (c. 220 C.E.) to the Arab conquest of the East (early seventh century)—represent a continuation of the post–Bar-Kokhba period. No longer do we encounter major political or military opposition to the empires that ruled over those lands where the vast majority of Jews lived—whether in Palestine or the Diaspora. While the yearning for messianic redemption still asserts itself at certain major junctures, this messianism evinces itself in a far more spiritualized way (as it did in the previous period when the Mishnah was produced), rather than being centered around another Bar-Kokhba-like Jewish military figure. Indeed, these messianic passions henceforth arise primarily as a Jewish reaction to events totally beyond the control of the Jewish community itself—whether it be the pagan-Christian clash in the days of the Roman emperor Julian (361-363 C.E.) that almost led to the restoration of Jewish Jerusalem, or the three-way struggle for control over the Land of Israel (Byzantium-Persia-Arabia) that paved the way for the Muslim conquest.

More radical in its ultimate consequences is the slow but constant shift in the delicate relationship between the Jewish center in Palestine and the emerging Jewish community of Babylonia. While

A PAGE FROM THE TALMUD. The Talmud (Hebrew for instruction) is an authoritative collection of rabbinic commentary that includes the Mishnah (a collection of Jewish laws compiled by Judah ha-Nasi at the beginning of the third century C.E.) and the Gemara (an elaboration and commentary on the Mishnah). Here we see part of the tractate *Avodah Zarah*, copied in Spain in 1290 C.E.

the unchallenged status of the Mishnah as the definitive compilation of Jewish law still suggests a preeminent role for Jewish leadership in Palestine, this in itself served as a watershed in Jewish communal life. For the Mishnah represents the last such case of a uniquely Palestinian dominance over the legal development within Rabbinic Judaism. The subsequent parallel development of the two monumental corpora of rabbinic discussions and interpretation of the Mishnah, that is, the Palestinian Talmud (also known as

Yerushalmi or the Jerusalem Talmud, JT) and the Babylonian Talmud (BT)—with the ultimate superior status attached to the latter—is only the most obvious of a growing number of signs pointing to changes on a worldwide scale that reshaped the face of the Jewish community.

At the beginning of the third century, the Jews were still the predominant ethnic community in the Land of Israel,[1] notwithstanding the fact that Hadrian had already attempted to blur this reality by changing the name of the Roman province from Iudaea to Syria Palaestina.[2] If there was another major community for the Jews of Palestine to contend with, it was still probably the Samaritans,[3] not the fledgling Christian community, which had not yet begun to multiply in the Land of Israel at the same swift pace apparent in the rest of the empire. Even by the year 325, one year after all of the Eastern empire came under the rule of the first Christian emperor, it is still evident that the vast majority of Christians in Palestine continued to reside primarily in the Greek cities of the land, and had a long way to go before emerging as a major demographic force.[4] Within one century, however, these proportions slowly began to reverse themselves; by the end of the fourth and the early fifth centuries, the Jews comprised barely one-third of the total population, while the Christian community gradually emerged as a dominant demographic factor. Toward the latter part of the period surveyed in this chapter, and certainly by the sixth century, the Christian community of Palestine had grown to become the overwhelming majority among the inhabitants of the land.[5]

This new demographic reality naturally influenced the nature of Jewish-Christian confrontation and polemics, at least as reflected in the writings of the religious leaders of both groups. Beginning in the third century, the rabbinic attitude toward Christianity was no longer expressed as one dealing with an internal Jewish social and religious schism that must be resolved through a reappraisal or redefinition of what was legitimately "Jewish."[6] What emerged now, and remained a constant factor in the Palestinian rabbinic literature of the talmudic era, was a confrontational attitude toward Christianity as a distinct religion, which nevertheless required the attention of the rabbis in light of its growing strength and influence in the Land of Israel as well as throughout the empire. By the fourth century the rabbis, like most Jews, were aware of the fact that "the Kingdom [Rome] had become a heresy (*minut*),"[7] and this dramatically affected the status of the Jews. With the Church now able to assert a major degree of authority over the empire's administration, the Jews in Palestine and the empire at large found themselves—for the first time—at the mercy of their religious rival.

While the official status of Judaism as a legitimate religion did not change overnight, it was only a matter of time before the antagonism and hostility between the two groups erupted on various levels: legislation, religious decrees aimed at separating the Christian masses from all Jewish influence, even physical clashes.

Beyond all this, the third century served as yet another turning point—one in the realignment of Jewish leadership. After centuries of almost total absence from the historical scene, save for isolated first-century anecdotes recorded primarily by Josephus,[8] the Jewish community beyond the Euphrates River resurfaced, ultimately laying claim to a growing degree of independence, if not outright hegemony, regarding all aspects of Jewish communal life dependent on rabbinic leadership. This reemergence coincided dramatically with the political changing of the guard in Persia. After hundreds of years of Parthian Arsacid rule, the Jews (as well as others) found themselves not only under the rule of a new Persian dynasty founded by the Sassanians (c. 224 C.E.), but also in the midst of a major religious revival of the Zoroastrian church and a political radicalization that led to the outbreak of new hostilities between Persia and Rome. And thus, while scholars argue, not without some justification, the merits of designating the period of Jewish history beginning in the third century C.E. as the "Talmudic Era,"[9] the fact is that the new literary development that followed the compilation of the Mishnah dovetails precisely with major political and religious developments that reshaped for all time the history of all the peoples of the Near East, and to a very large degree that of the Jewish people among them.

The Jews of Palestine in the Late Roman period: 220-324 C.E. The first years of the post-Mishnaic period in Palestine coincided with the reign of the last of the Severan emperors, Alexander Severus (222-235 C.E.). Following his death, the Roman empire sank into 50 years of political chaos and economic crisis. Emperors rose to power only to be assassinated within a few months, or a year or two at most; rampant inflation rendered Roman coins worthless; ultimately, the *principate* system of government that had existed for over two centuries collapsed, thus requiring a total restructuring of imperial administration.[10] (This was carried out by Diocletian in the final decades of the third century.) The Jewish nation was just one of many passengers on this storm-tossed ship. The vicissitudes of Roman rule in the third century were as strongly felt in Palestine as in the rest of the empire.

Jewish life under the Severan dynasty can arguably be considered the high point of Roman-Jewish relations,[11] which dated back to the initial contacts between the two nations during the early stages of the Hasmonean uprising. Moreover, while the pact between Rome and Judah Maccabee was essentially nothing more than a declaration resulting from common political aims and interests, the favorable relationship between the Jews and the empire under the Severans was far more striking. Not only did it yield practical advantages for the Jewish side, but it evolved a mere two generations after the terrible devastation wrought by Roman legions upon the land and people of Israel during the Second Jewish Revolt.

The most obvious result of the improved relations with Rome was the enhanced status of the patriarchate in the days of Judah ha-Nasi—which is frequently translated as Judah the Prince—(c. 180-220 C.E.), the redactor of the Mishnah as noted in the previous chapter. Judah's unique position, combining political power with rabbinic authority, did not go unnoticed by the rabbis ("From the days of Moses until Rabbi [Judah] we have not found Torah and [political] greatness in one place [i.e., in one person]"),[12] and while the spiritual and halakhic power wielded by subsequent patriarchs may have wavered, the political role of the patriarch remained a constant factor in Jewish life until the abolition of the office in the early fifth century. While our knowledge of the patriarchs in the fourth and fifth centuries derives exclusively from non-Jewish sources, the third-century patriarchate is well documented in rabbinic literature, and thus we enjoy certain insights into the nature of Jewish communal leadership of this period in Palestine that tend to become somewhat obscured in later centuries.

The growth of the Patriarchy

The patriarch was the Jewish representative before imperial authorities.[13] Simultaneously, he provided a unifying factor within the Jewish community. Rabbinic as well as non-Jewish sources attest to the fact that messengers (*apostoli*) were dispatched to Diaspora communities for purposes of collecting funds as well as supervising local communal authorities.[14] It was this role, together with the fact that the patriarchs claimed Davidic lineage, that ultimately rendered the office a major target of ecclesiastical pressure.

As we proceed into the third century, a number of changes in the nature of the office emerge, as well as in the expressed attitudes of the rabbis toward the various patriarchs. One major departure from the days of Judah is the physical removal of the court of the patriarch from Sepphoris to Tiberias (c. 250 C.E.). This move of the focal point of Jewish leadership appears to have taken place in two stages, and is indicative of a major development within the rabbinic class. Following the death of Judah we can clearly discern a decentralization of the all-embracing powers maintained by the patriarch.[15] Under Judah, for instance, ordination of rabbis was the sole prerogative of the *nasi*, or patriarch; afterwards this authority was divided between the office of the patriarch and the rabbis.[16] The wish to assert their independence as a distinct class may have induced the rabbis, following Judah's death, to remove their central academy from Sepphoris to Tiberias. Apparently, only later, during the days of Judah's grandson Judah II (c. 250 C.E.), did the patriarch's court move to Tiberias.[17] While this move rendered Tiberias the main center of Jewish Palestine for the next few centuries, it also suggests a heightened degree of tension in the relationship between the patriarchs and the rabbinic class.[18] In fact, numerous sources raise serious questions surrounding the propriety of patriarchal behavior during the third century, in particular regarding the ordination—"for money"—of unqualified judges.[19] Rabbinic criticism of the patriarchs sometimes alludes to other examples of improper behavior, especially their heavy-handedness in the collection of various taxes from an already overburdened population.[20]

From a purely historiographical perspective, it must be stated that we have only one side of the story—that of the rabbinic class as reflected primarily in the Talmud and Midrash, and we can only speculate on what response the patriarchs might have made to these attacks. Nevertheless, the weakening of the central power structure within the Jewish community should not surprise us, for, as we have seen, it coincided precisely with the collapse of central Roman authority throughout the empire.

New forms of taxation Social tensions were of course linked to the difficult economic situation. With Roman currency in essence rendered worthless, it was now meaningless to exact taxes in fixed sums. Rabbinic literature introduces us to a whole new system of painful taxation: forced labor (*angaria*) in the service of the Roman administration; billeting of soldiers and Roman officials (*akhsania*), which frequently created various religious problems; supplying food and clothing to the army (*annona*); and a host of other levies.[21] The well-known phenomenon of *anachoresis*, whereby members of a municipal council, individuals or even whole communities simply abandoned their homes and fled to avoid taxation is vividly documented in rabbinic literature.[22] Appointment to the municipal council took on a new and ominous significance, for members of the *boule* (council) were responsible for the full payment of local tax assessments, even if this meant paying it out of personal funds. Thus we understand Rabbi Yoḥanan's warning to the potential appointee to the council: "If you have been named to the *boule*, let the Jordan become thy neighbor [i.e., take flight across the Jordan]."[23]

The economic situation notwithstanding, the multifaceted spiritual activity of the rabbinic class seems to have flourished during

WERNER BRAUN

CAPERNAUM. In this aerial view of the ruins of Capernaum, the columns of a synagogue can be seen on the right. This structure dates from the fourth or fifth century C.E., but almost certainly stands on the site of the first-century synagogue in which Jesus worshiped when he was in Capernaum. A short distance in front of the triple doors of the synagogue is a fifth-century octagonal church believed to be built above the first-century home of the apostle Peter. In the foreground is the Sea of Galilee.

the third century. Indeed, the most outstanding authority of the second half of the third century, Rabbi Yoḥanan bar Napha (d. 279 C.E.), may be considered the supreme Palestinian sage of the entire talmudic era.[24] His influence as head of the Tiberian academy transcended the boundaries of Palestine. Even in the Babylonian Talmud, almost every page bears his name or reflects one of his traditions. Together with his colleague (talmudic tradition makes him a brother-in-law as well) Resh Laqish, as well as a host of other sages—many of whom were recent arrivals from Babylonia—the rabbinic movement of third-century Palestine seems to have played a major role in transforming the rabbis from a somewhat elitist and remote group of scholars into an influential, community-oriented class of social leaders. Whether this was the result of the creation and spread of permanent academies in numerous urban centers,[25] or possibly a consequence of the economic plight of the time which served as a great equalizer, contributing to the removal of social barriers, is unclear. Other factors, such as a growing need for intellectual leadership capable of fending off confrontation with the growing Christian community may also have played a role, but what is clear is that the rabbis now assumed a heightened degree of communal responsibility, primarily on a local scale, but sometimes as national figures as well.[26]

The role of the sages in Jewish-Christian confrontations One of the roles played by certain sages in the Land of Israel was as disputants in the growing debate between Jews and Christians. Sometimes the dispute was carried on by the dispensation of responses to hypothetical questions before purely Jewish audiences, most likely in the synagogue. But live confrontations also occurred, probably in major cosmopolitan centers such as Caesarea. It is not by chance that one of the major figures involved in these disputes was Rabbi Abbahu of Caesarea. One need not tax the imagination to uncover the targets of some of Abbahu's statements,[27] frequently based on an exegetical interpretation of Scripture:

> "Rabbi Abbahu said: If a man says to you: 'I am God'—he lies; 'I am the son of man'—in the end he will regret it. 'I will rise up to heaven'—he says this but will not do it."[28]

> "Rabbi Abbahu said: A parable of a mortal king: he reigns and has a father or a son or a brother. Said the Holy One Blessed be He: I am not like that. 'I am first' (Isaiah 44:6)—I have no father. 'I am last'—I have no son. 'And beside me there is no God'—I have no brother."[29]

The implications of these confrontations and the need of Palestinian sages to be well versed in Bible and biblical exegesis for just such occasions, may help to explain an important literary phenomenon as well. The rabbis of Palestine were responsible not only for the formation of the Palestinian Talmud, but also for the birth of a different literary genre—aggadic *midrash* (see pp. 255-256). These works reflect the broad spectrum of social and spiritual activity in third- and fourth-century Palestine. Oddly enough, no equivalent midrashic corpus was produced by the sages of Babylonia. This fact has led to much speculation. One solution may be supplied by Rabbi Abbahu himself: In the course of explaining to his apparently Christian co-residents of Caesarea why he, Abbahu, was well versed in the Bible while his Babylonian colleague Rav Safra was not, the Palestinian sage replied: "We [in the Land of Israel] live among you, hence we take it upon ourselves to learn."[30]

The nature of the debates between Christian figures such as Origen (and later Eusebius) and the rabbis of the day can be seen most clearly by comparing the contemporaneous writings of the two groups regarding the very same Scriptures. Such a comparison makes it clear that each side was well aware of the attacks launched against it by its adversary. Indeed, the comparison makes one wonder whether the two disputants were not in fact arguing face-to-face "before a live audience."[31]

These debates—and other contacts between certain sages and their non-Jewish counterparts—assume not only a familiarity with the adversary's theological claims, but also a shared knowledge of language, folklore and popular culture. It is not by chance that of all the sages it was Rabbi Abbahu who claimed it was permissible to teach one's daughter Greek "for it is an ornament on her";[32] nor should we be surprised that this sage was capable of repeating riddles based on knowledge of the Greek language and the numerical values of the Greek letters of the alphabet.[33] Rabbinic familiarity with "Greek wisdom" has been amply discussed in modern scholarship.[34] The brilliant studies of Saul Lieberman[35] have shown that although there is no explicit citation in rabbinic works to specific Greek literature, and although no Greek philosopher is discussed by name, it is clear that knowledge of Greco-Roman ideas, phrases and parables—as well as grammatical and rhetorical systems—infiltrated not only rabbinic literary work, but even religiously motivated deliberations.[36] We assume that these Greco-Roman elements were transmitted through a variety of intermediaries, most probably in oral rather than written form. Thus, the rabbis had no trouble comparing the stages of the Jew's daily *Amidah* prayer (as well as the praises of Moses, David and Solomon) with the structure and sequence found in the presentations of Roman rhetors.[37] Nor did Resh Laqish think it improper to compare the activity of the public preacher in the synagogue with that of the Greek mime in the theater.[38]

Obviously, these Greek influences were more pronounced among certain social strata within the Jewish population of Roman Palestine. Geographical proximity to large urban centers also played a role in determining the degree and intensity of such influences. While the use of Hebrew may have receded somewhat following the Bar-Kokhba uprising, it appears that many Jews in the land were bilingual, with Aramaic and Hebrew serving as their primary languages. But this situation was not uniform throughout the land. The number of Greek synagogue inscriptions found in Galilee, for instance, greatly exceeds those found in the synagogues of Judea and southern Palestine,[39] where Aramaic (and Hebrew) inscriptions were the norm rather than the exception. For our purposes, it is important to note that these Greek influences seem to have intensified in the third and fourth centuries as opposed to their prevalence in Mishnaic times. It is a good guess that *amoraim* (the sages of the Talmud) knew more Greek than *tannaim* (the sages of the Mishnah). The post-talmudic Jewish population became even more familiar with aspects of Greek-pagan culture than their predecessors.[40]

Transition to Roman-Byzantine era	The 50 years of Roman anarchy came to an end with the reign of Diocletian (284-305 C.E.), but in a larger sense Diocletian's rule represents a period of transition from the Late Roman period to the Roman-Byzantine era. While the religious upheaval brought about by Constantine affected Palestine only from the year 324 C.E., many of the administrative practices of Roman rule in the Byzantine period had their roots in the reforms introduced by Diocletian.[41] It was he who finally realized that the very size of the Roman dominion would ultimately be its undoing, and thus he decided to divide the empire into East and West. This division did not become permanent until the end of the fourth century, but its very inception had an impact on the administrative framework in which the residents of Palestine found themselves. Added to the basic geographical division was the innovative system of imperial rule known as the tetrarchy: Each of the two sections of the empire was ruled by an Augustus, under whom served a Caesar, who was designated as his eventual heir. The empire was thereby in effect divided into four sections, or prefectures, and these in turn were divided into dioceses. Palestine would henceforth be part of the prefecture of the East, with the seat of the governor of the prefecture (*praefectus praetorio*) situated in Constantinople.

The diocese in which Palestine was included was also called Oriens. Among its other provinces were Arabia and Egypt. This subdivision was designed not only to create a more efficient administration, but also to weaken the military power of any local governor. Interestingly, while the tendency under Diocletian was to limit the size of the provinces, the boundaries of Palestine in fact grew; major territories were added to the province in the south—the Negev and central and southern Sinai—at the expense of the province of Arabia. However, within the next century the province of Palestine would be divided twice. In 358 Palestine was split into two provinces, with much of its southern territory as well as parts of southern Transjordan becoming Palaestina Salutaris, with its capital first in Haluza in the Negev and then in Petra. The capital of the northern province of Palestine remained at Caesarea, but in 409 this province was itself split in two: Palaestina Prima comprising the central portion of the land (Judea, Samaria, the coast and parts of Transjordan), with the capital remaining at Caesarea; and Palaestina Secunda comprising the Jezreel Valley, the Galilee, portions of the Golan, and northern Transjordan. The capital of Palaestina Secunda was Scythopolis (Beth-Shean). It is this province that was home to the greater portion of the Jewish population in the Land of Israel.

Diocletian's fiscal and administrative reforms were favorably received by the Jews of Palestine. Moreover, under his rule, the Jews apparently maintained the status of a *religio licita* (permitted religion): "When King Diocletian came up here[42] he decreed and proclaimed: 'All the nations will pour libations save for the Jews.'"[43] This passage is particularly noteworthy, in that it contrasts sharply with the steps taken by Diocletian against the Christian community in the final years of his reign.

The third century in general introduced some of the harshest persecution of Christians, particularly in the days of Decius (249-251). Although Diocletian seems to have tolerated Christian communities during the earlier years of his reign, events took a sharp turn for the worse in the year 303, possibly at the urging of the Caesar Galerius. That year saw the beginning of what may have been the severest persecution of Christians in all of the Late Roman empire, lasting until the year 311. From an edict requiring the burning of all Scriptures and the dismantling of churches, events quickly turned to the torture and execution of Christians. Eusebius, bishop of Caesarea, was eyewitness to these events in Palestine and in other portions of the Eastern empire. He recorded them vividly in his *Ecclesiastical History*, as well as in a special treatise on the Palestinian martyrs. For those acquainted with the Jewish martyrdom stories of 200 years earlier, during the Bar-Kokhba uprising, Eusebius' descriptions are strikingly similar, even to the system of torture employed by the Romans.[44]

One can only wonder how Jews in Palestine reacted to the punishment of Christian martyrs by descendants of the very same rulers who had used the same modes of torture against the generation of Rabbi Akiva and his colleagues. If Saul Lieberman, in his famous study on "The Martyrs of Caesarea," is correct, there is testimony in rabbinic literature to a degree of respect and admiration expressed by the rabbis for these martyrs, displayed just a few years before the "kingdom would become a heresy,"[45] and Jews suddenly found themselves subject to Christian rule.

The Jews under early Roman-Christian rule: 324-361 C.E. Constantine's victory over his last major opponent, Licinius, on September 18, 324, at Chrysopolis, near Chalcedon, effected not only a reunification of the Roman empire under one ruler, but for the first time placed the Land of Israel, as well as the Jews of the entire empire, under Christian domination. The social and legal status of the Jews underwent a steady redefinition in Roman eyes. While it would be mistaken to suggest that Judaism was immediately rendered illegitimate and subjected to outright persecution,[46] it clearly found itself the target of a series of declarations issuing from ecclesiastical as well as legal sources. Indeed, it is in the various decrees of the Church councils of the fourth century, on the one hand, and the laws promulgated by Constantine and his successors, on the other, that one notes the dual nature of the steps now taken to define the role of Jews within society. Already in the decisions of the pre-Constantinian Church council at Elvira, Spain (306 C.E.), one senses the efforts of the Church authorities to isolate the Jews and remove any influence they might still possess over the growing numbers of adherents to Christianity. The thrust of these decisions, the long list of decrees that followed in the various Eastern councils, was to create as great a distance as possible between the old Israel and the followers of the Church.

At Elvira, for instance, special attention was given to the prevention of intermarriage between Jews and Christian women, as well as any sort of concubinage wherein a Christian male might have relations with a Jewish (or pagan) woman. Accepting any sort of Jewish hospitality was forbidden. Jews were even prohibited from blessing the fields of a Christian.[47]

It was in the East, however, that the Church authorities felt the greatest need to separate Jews from Christians. Not only were Jews far more numerous in this part of the empire, but they apparently still wielded influence over the religious behavior of certain Christian communities.

The most obvious and sensitive example of ongoing ties between the two religious groups was related to the celebration of Easter and its undeniable ties to the Jewish feast of Passover. Different Christian groups celebrated Easter on different days, many of them in conjunction with the Jewish Passover. For these groups, the intolerable reality was that the Jewish leadership in Tiberias (the patriarch and the Sanhedrin), by virtue of its ongoing intercalation of the Jewish calendar, in effect determined when Christians celebrated Easter. The agenda of the Council of Nicaea (325) therefore included, possibly at the request of Constantine himself, not only issues of theological differences within the Church, but also the need to establish a new system for determining the date of Easter. As stated by Eusebius, "It seemed very unworthy of this most sacred feast, that we should keep it following the custom of the Jews."[48]

Various other councils in the East forbade any participation of Christians in Jewish worship or attendance at Jewish synagogues. One intriguing decree explicitly forbade Christians to tend the lamps in Jewish synagogues on certain holidays, apparently alluding to a practice whereby non-Jews performed certain services forbidden to Jews themselves.[49]

Parallel to this new ecclesiastical demarcation between Jews and Christians, Constantine's victory also brought in its wake new legislation intended to define the status of the Jews. In certain instances a degree of continuity was maintained under Constantine,[50] but this could not overcome the basic fact that in embracing Christianity the empire would be left with no choice but to redefine the legal status of its Jewish subjects. Thus, while the state continued to recognize Judaism as a *religio licita*, it nevertheless created the impression that Jews would not be encouraged to play a major role in society.

Protection was granted to Jews who abandoned their religion; the legislation to this effect under Constantine suggests that the process of Jewish conversion did not go uncontested by the Jewish community:

> "We want the Jews, their principals and their patriarchs informed, that if anyone . . . dare attack by stoning or by other kind of fury one escaping from their deadly sect and raising his eyes to God's cult, which as we have learned is being done now, he [the attacker] shall be delivered immediately to the flames and burnt with all his associates."[51]

Roman legislation also made it more difficult for Jews to own Gentile slaves.[52] In this way, a religious scruple (lest the Jew convert the slave) had a major economic impact. It has even been suggested that this prohibition led the rabbis to rethink Jewish law regarding the conversion of Gentile slaves, with the aim of circumventing the new legislation.[53]

Other Roman laws enacted during the first decades of Christian rule seem to have steered a middle path. Thus, while Jews were now required in principle to participate in curial liturgies (compulsory functions imposed on local council members), certain exemptions were granted to leaders of the community "in order to leave them something of the ancient custom as a solace."[54] In the

late fourth and fifth centuries, however, the situation became progressively worse, although variations evolved in different parts of
the empire: Legislation in the West followed a more rigid approach
in its attitude toward the Jewish community than in the East, where
possibly out of deference to the far greater concentration of Jews
in that part of the empire, a more moderate policy was embraced.[55]

It is unclear whether the legal status of the city of Jerusalem
was redefined, or whether the Jews were again—as in the days of
Hadrian—denied access to the city, both as pilgrims and as residents.[56] However, it is clear that the character of the city changed.
Christian pilgrims began to flock to the Holy Land in general and
to Jerusalem in particular. One of the most prominent of these
pilgrims, Helena, mother of Constantine, established several
churches in the city. If indeed Jews were forced to reside beyond
the confines of the city, it is possible that this regulation took
effect in 335, coinciding with the consecration of the Church of
the Holy Sepulchre.[57] But the large concentrations of Jews in other
parts of the land, most particularly in the Galilee, prevented a
similarly swift introduction of Christianity and its symbols into
those regions.

Testifying to this Jewish communal vitality is the unique story
of the Jewish apostate Joseph. At first a high official in the court of
the Tiberian patriarch, Joseph clandestinely embraced Christianity but was ultimately discovered and removed from the Jewish
community. As a friend (*comes*) of the emperor, however, Joseph
was granted permission to establish churches "in the cities and
villages of the Jews, where *heretofore* no man could erect churches,
for they [the Jews] do not have [living] among them either a pagan
or a Samaritan or a Christian [but only Jews]."[58] Joseph's attempts
to build churches in the Galilee proved unsuccessful; in the end
he removed himself to Beth-Shean, where, as a somewhat bitter
old man, he managed to tell his story to Epiphanius.

***Clashes
between
Romans and
Jews; the
Gallus revolt***
The determination of the Galilean Jews to assert themselves came
to the fore again in the middle of the fourth century, in the so-
called Gallus revolt. Following the death of Constantine in 337,
the empire was divided among his three sons, with the East, including Palestine, falling to Constantius. After a series of civil wars,
by the middle of the century Constantius was the sole ruler of
Rome. While he was off in the West, however, delivering the decisive blow to his opponent Magnentius, events in the East once
again led to a Jewish uprising in Palestine, albeit of limited proportions. Before leaving for the West, Constantius had appointed
his cousin, Gallus, to the rank of Caesar.

If we are to believe the Roman historian Ammianus Marcellinus,

RICHARD NOWITZ

THE NECROPOLIS OF BETH SHEARIM. Three limestone arches frame the entrance to catacomb 14 at Beth Shearim, a complex of 26 catacombs cut into a limestone hillside in the Galilee. Judah ha-Nasi, called Judah the Prince or simply "Rabbi," was buried here in the third century C.E.; indeed, the cemetery became the final resting place for pious Jews from all over the Diaspora as well as Palestine. In the fourth century, Roman armies destroyed the city of Beth Shearim and use of the necropolis came to an end.

ZEV RADOVAN

INSIDE THE CATACOMBS OF BETH SHEARIM, a menorah is on top of the head of a man in a Roman military tunic. Jewish symbols such as the menorah are side by side with pagan motifs of eagles, bulls' heads and garlands in the tomb carvings.

Gallus was ill-equipped for the job, and his ineptness soon became apparent. The pagan historian Aurelius Victor relates that "at that time a revolt of the Jews, who nefariously raised Patricius to the royal power, was suppressed."[59] To this brief report, which leaves vague not only the question of Patricius' identity but also the causes of the revolt, a number of Christian historians add some details. Jerome relates that the Romans, in suppressing the revolt, destroyed not only Sepphoris, but also Tiberias, Lydda and "many other fortresses."[60] This report, with certain variations, is repeated in the writings of other Church historians.[61] Interestingly, while mention is made of Jewish slaughter of Roman soldiers as well as of "Gentiles, Hellenes and Samaritans," no mention is made of any attack on the Christian community. If such an event had occurred, it would surely not have gone unnoticed by Christian historians. We may therefore conclude that religious tension between the two communities was not the cause of the uprising. Furthermore, we would expect a Christian reaction, if "Patricius" were in fact a Jewish pretender to the throne, thereby suggesting messianic overtones. Since this was not the case, it seems likely that the Gallus revolt of 351-352 was the result of some local disturbances in the eastern part of the empire, when various local commanders appear to have tried to capitalize on the absence of Constantius and the presence of an ill-equipped Caesar, Gallus, to assume positions of power.

Rabbinic sources, as well as archaeological evidence, suggest that various clashes occurred at this time between Roman forces and Jewish civilians. Some Jewish towns may have been destroyed, the most important of which was Beth Shearim.[62] But the disturbances seem to have been local in nature, probably in reaction to certain isolated injustices rather than the result of a new quest for national independence. It is difficult to point to any lasting result of the Gallus uprising.[63]

The Jews and Julian: 361-363 C.E. Gallus was executed by order of Constantius in 354. One year later, Constantius appointed his younger stepbrother, Julian, as Caesar of the western provinces of the empire: Spain, Gaul and Britain. To everyone's surprise the young caesar, who until then had been occupied with intellectual, rather than administrative, endeavors, proved an overwhelming success in defeating the various invading tribes in Gaul and in restoring a measure of tranquility to the western provinces. Slowly Julian gained the enthusiastic support of the legions under his command. By the year 360, word reached Julian's legions of Constantius' plans to invade Sassanian Persia. Julian's legions thereupon revolted and declared Julian the new Augustus. Constantius' sudden death in 361 saved Rome from a civil war; the empire was united under the rule of Julian, a 30-year-old descendant of Constantine who suddenly declared his total opposition to Christianity and the marriage of Church and empire that had begun to evolve just a few decades earlier.

Julian did not abandon plans for a Roman invasion of Persia, and in 362, after having made his way to the East, he spent some nine months at Antioch preparing for a military campaign. Here the young emperor issued a startling declaration, which must have caught Jews as well as Christians totally off guard—he offered to restore the Jewish Temple in Jerusalem!

Julian had already made public, in late 361, his wish to abandon Christianity and restore pagan religion to its rightful position in the empire; to this end he had declared a renewed religious tolerance throughout the empire. He had restored the status of pagan temples to their pre-Constantinian position and reintroduced pagan ceremonies into the military. He even went so far as to remove all Christian clerics from their positions as teachers of literature. His justification for this is interesting: How could anyone teach a literature replete with allusions to Greek deities while concurrently denying the very existence of the entire Greek pantheon. The true aim of the decree was not lost on his contemporaries, for in fact it was intended as a means of removing all Christian influence from the educational institutions of the empire.

Only in this larger context can we understand Julian's turning to the leaders of the Jewish community with an offer to restore the Jewish Temple in Jerusalem. Julian, it must be remembered, was only one link in the chain of Neoplatonic philosophers who—beginning with the likes of Celsus in the second century, Plotinus and Porphyry in the third century and Julian's own (albeit indirect) mentor Iamblichus in the fourth century[64]—either championed a revival of Hellenistic philosophy and religion, or went further and, like Celsus, considered Christianity something of a barbarian superstition, which now threatened the very existence of the empire. The mystic element of Neoplatonic thinking led directly to an appreciation of sacrifices and temple worship; thus Julian (along with his spiritual predecessors) attacked Christians for abandoning sacrificial worship. This attack on Christianity did not really need the Jews for support. Recent scholarship suggests that, although the Jewish phenomenon of sacrificial worship in the Temple was introduced into this essentially pagan-Christian conflict, Jews themselves were not really an integral or active part in the confrontation.[65] Yet the Jews could not have totally ignored these developments. The paucity of our sources relating to their reaction is probably due more to the nature of extant Jewish literature from the period than a total ignorance of, or indifference to, the events surrounding them.

In any event, during his stay at Antioch in 362, Julian apparently invited a Jewish delegation to meet with him and inquired why they did not resume sacrificial worship in their accustomed manner. This question, as well as the reported reply (i.e., that they were forbidden to perform these rituals outside the Temple of Jerusalem), smacks of a degree of innocence or poetic license that may be attributed to Christian sources for the story.[66] Nevertheless, as a result of this meeting Julian promised to restore the Jewish Temple. Two letters written by the emperor himself attest to the nature of his promise. Only one of the letters has survived in its entirety, and much has been written surrounding its authenticity,[67] which today is accepted by the broad majority of scholars. The critical portion of the letter reads:

"To the Community of the Jews:

"In times past, by far the most burdensome thing in the yoke of your slavery has been the fact that you were subjected to unauthorized ordinances and had to contribute an untold amount of money to the accounts of the treasury. Of this I used to see many instances with my own eyes, and I have learned of more, by finding the records which are preserved against you. Moreover, when a tax was about to be levied on you again I prevented it. . . .

"And since I wish that you should prosper yet more, I have admonished my brother Iulus [Hillel], your most venerable patriarch, that the levy which is said to exist among you should be prohibited, and that no one is any longer to have the power to oppress the masses of your people by such exactions; so that everywhere, during my reign, you may have security of mind, and in the enjoyment of peace may offer more fervid prayers for my reign to the Most High God, The Creator, who has deigned to crown me with his own immaculate right hand. For it is natural that men who are distracted by any anxiety should be hampered in spirit, and should not have so much confidence in raising their hands to pray; but that those who are in all respects free from care should rejoice with their whole hearts and offer their suppliant prayers on behalf of my imperial office to Mighty God, even to him who is able to direct my reign to the noblest ends, according to my purpose. This you ought to do, in order that, when I have successfully concluded the war with Persia, I may rebuild by my own efforts the sacred city of Jerusalem, which for so many years you have longed to see inhabited, and may bring settlers there, and, together with you, may glorify the most High God."[68]

To understand the reasoning behind this letter and its promise to rebuild Jewish Jerusalem and the Temple, one need go no further than Julian's major literary attack on Christianity, *Against the Galileans*.[69] Julian's admiration for Jewish ritual is manifest in that work, as is his disdain for the Christians who, while professing to have inherited Israel, have in fact abandoned the loftiest components of that religion, only to have preserved the one unacceptable tenet of biblical Judaism, which is the claim that God is an exclusive deity, jealous of all other Gods:

> "For envy and jealousy do not even draw near the most virtuous of *men*; they are all the more remote from angels and gods. . . . Like leeches, you have sucked the worst blood from that source [i.e., the Jews] and left the purer."[70]

Julian's claim, then, is that in fact biblical Judaism is praiseworthy; Christianity, on the other hand, has ignored the positive elements of Judaism:

> "Why is it, I repeat, that after deserting us [pagans] you do not accept the law of the Jews or abide by the sayings of Moses? No doubt some sharp-sighted person will answer, 'The Jews too do not sacrifice.' But I will convict him of being terribly dull-sighted, for in the first place I reply that neither do you also observe any of the other customs observed by the Jews; and secondly, that the Jews do sacrifice in their own houses, and even to this day everything that they eat is consecrated . . . but since they have been deprived of their temple, or as they are accustomed to call it, their holy place, they are prevented from offering the first fruits of the sacrifice to God."[71]

This argument, of course, serves as the theoretical underpinning for providing the Jews with precisely what they are now lacking. In Julian's eyes a natural coalition ought to exist between pagans and Jews, with Christians being odd man out:

> "I wished to show that the Jews agree with the Gentiles [pagans] [in that the Jews too would sacrifice if their Temple were restored], except that they believe in only one God. That is indeed peculiar to them and strange to us [pagans]; since all the rest we have in a manner in common with them—temples, sanctuaries, altars, purifications and certain precepts. For as to these we differ from one another not at all or in trivial matters. . . ."[72]

Needless to say, Julian was well aware of the fact that by restoring the Jews to Jerusalem he would also be destroying the Christian argument that placed so much importance on the destruction of the city (Matthew 24:2; Mark 13:2; Luke 21:6) and the removal

ZEV RADOVAN

ISAIAH INSCRIPTION found in the retaining wall of the Temple Mount in Jerusalem. When the Roman emperor Julian, called "The Apostate," sought to reduce the power of the Christian church in 363 C.E., he allowed Jews to return to Jerusalem. Work began on a new Temple, only to be halted by Julian's death within the year. This inscription, "You shall see, and your heart shall rejoice; your bones shall flourish like the grass" (Isaiah 66:14), may date from that year of hope when the Jews began construction of a new Temple.

of the Jews from it.[73] Subsequent Christian authors who described the events caught the message perfectly, and Sozomen, for instance, was absolutely correct when he claimed that Julian "thought to grieve the Christians by favoring the Jews."[74]

The whole affair ended as abruptly as it began. Although the Roman historian Ammianus Marcellinus relates that the building of the Temple was undertaken,[75] and certain archaeological discoveries, including an inscription from the prophet Isaiah, unearthed at the recent excavations of the Temple Mount, may indeed date to the years of Julian,[76] his death in 363 during the campaign against Persia—legend attributes the fatal spear to one of his own Christian soldiers—put an end to any hopes the Jews may have entertained for rebuilding their Temple.[77]

From Julian's death to abolition of patriarchate: 363–c.425 C.E.

Julian's immediate successors did not retaliate with any anti-pagan or anti-Jewish reaction. Following Jovian's brief rule (died February 364), the empire was again divided, this time between brothers—Valens in the East and Valentinian in the West. These rulers continued to grant a degree of tolerance to the Hellenistic religions, and Judaism benefited from this moderation. As an Arian Christian, Valens had enough on his hands just maintaining his position versus the growing orthodox majority within the Church; this probably explains why he was careful not to arouse opposition among the other minorities in the East, including the Jews.

The two brothers promulgated the first law by Christian emperors relating to the status of the synagogue. The law exempted the synagogue from the forced imposition of *hospitium*, i.e., the requirement to lodge either soldiers or officials.[78]

In another, later law the brothers extended the exemptions of "the elders and others occupied in the rite of that religion [Judaism]" from serving in the curial liturgies.[79] The Jewish officials mentioned in this law, we are told, are "subject to the rule of the Illustrious Patriarchs." This point is important. From a variety of sources—all of them non-Jewish—it appears that the Palestinian patriarchs of the late fourth century were a potent force in the Jewish community, both in Palestine and in the Diaspora communities.[80]

This situation soon came under attack by various leaders of the Church. Beginning with Theodosius I (383-408), both the synagogues and the patriarchal leadership were subjected to a variety of pressures. Legislation took a decidedly negative turn. Outspoken attacks came from prominent personalities in the Church; these verbal attacks soon led to physical attacks on Jewish synagogues.

Why did the synagogue become a prime target in the late fourth century? First, because, more than any other institution, the synagogue was the focal point of Jewish communal life. Here the Jew not only prayed, but here he was also the recipient of a varied Jewish education: On any given Sabbath he would hear a reading of the Scriptures (from the Prophets as well as from the five books of Moses), together with a translation (*targum*) which was frequently not just a verbatim rendition of the texts into the local Aramaic vernacular, but also an enhancement of the text intended to enrich the message of the Scriptures.[81] To this was added a sermon (*derasha*) that probably served as the major vehicle for the transmission of rabbinic oral tradition, encompassing legal as well as moral guidance for the masses. So the synagogue provided the most immediate source of spiritual enrichment to the common Jew.

The synagogue as a focus of attack

But to all this was added, at least in the minds of certain Church authorities, the knowledge that Gentiles too, whether Christians or those with leanings in that direction, might also be attracted to the activities in the synagogue. Thus the need to restrict the institution by rendering it unattractive in the minds of the masses. At the same time, Church leaders sought legislative steps to prevent the synagogue from continuing to flourish.

In 386 C.E. John Chrysostom, presbyter at Antioch (later bishop of Constantinople), delivered the first of a series of sermons against the Jews. While his words may be an extreme example, they reflect the growing distrust and even fear of the powers of the synagogue:

> "A place where a prostitute offers her wares is a house of prostitution. But the synagogue is not only a house of prostitution and a theater, it is also a hideout for thieves and a den of wild animals."[82]

Chrysostom knew that Christians sometimes frequented synagogues:

> "When they see you, who worship the Christ who was crucified by them, observing Jewish customs and reverencing Jewish ways, how can they not think that everything done by them is the best? How can they not think that our ways are not worth anything when you, who confess to be a Christian and to follow the Christian way, run to those who degrade these same practices?"[83]

Two years after Chrysostom delivered this sermon, a Christian mob, led by the local bishop, destroyed the Jewish synagogue at Callinicum on the Euphrates. The emperor Theodosius demanded that the offenders be punished and the synagogue rebuilt, but Ambrosius, bishop of Milan, convinced him to rescind this decree.[84]

Subsequent Roman legislation makes it clear that this was not an isolated case. A law issued in 393, defending the synagogues, referred to the "excesses of those persons who, in the name of the Christian religion, presume to commit unlawful acts and to despoil the synagogues."[85] Such warnings continued into the early fifth century, but by then they were joined with threatening statements intended to project a more "even-handed" approach:

> "No one shall be destroyed for being a Jew . . . their synagogues and habitations shall not be indiscriminately burnt up, nor damaged without any reason. . . . But just as we wish to provide in this law for all the Jews, we order that this warning too should be given, lest the Jews, perchance insolent and elated by their security, commit something rash against the reverence of the Christian cult."[86]

Another law, issued in 423, prohibited the indiscriminate seizure or burning of a synagogue, but also stated that if the structure was dedicated to the Church, "they [the Jews] shall be given in exchange new places."[87] This could well be interpreted as encouraging the confiscation of synagogues; indeed, so as not to leave any doubt as to the ultimate intentions of the legislators, the law concluded by proclaiming: "No synagogue shall be constructed from now on, and the old ones shall remain in their state."[88]

The archaeological evidence of synagogues in Palestine during the Byzantine period makes it evident that these laws were frequently more symbolic than practical. Not only did Jews continue to build synagogues in the land, but they felt no qualms at incorporating into those structures elements obviously borrowed from the scores of churches that were now part of the Palestinian scene. These contacts were preserved "in the detailed construction, ornamentation, furnishing, stone-carving, and mosaics of [the] respective houses of worship in the Byzantine period."[89]

The decline of the Patriarchy

The office of patriarch did not fare as well. By the late fourth century the patriarchs found themselves under growing pressure, again obviously coming from ecclesiastical circles. Church leaders attempted to influence the emperors to limit the powers of the Jewish leaders. Given the fact that the patriarchs provided a convenient link between the Jewish community and the Roman administration, it was not in the latter's interests to limit the influence of the patriarchs.

In 396 a law was issued that prohibited public insults to the patriarchs: "If someone shall dare make in public an insulting mention of the Illustrious Patriarchs, he shall be subjected to a vindicatory sentence."[90] Three years later, however, a series of attacks on the Jewish leader began. He was referred to in one law as the "despoiler of the Jews"; he was warned, as were his messengers, to desist from gathering funds from the Jewish communities to be sent to the patriarch.[91] Chrysostom referred to the patriarchs as "merchants" or "traders," stressing their greed.[92]

At least in the East, these anti-Jewish laws met with considerable opposition, probably from the Jews themselves. Their efforts were initially successful. In a law promulgated in February 404, the privileges of the patriarch were reinstated.[93] A few months later, another law renewed permission to send funds to the patriarch.

This, however, was the last law that gave unqualified support to the office of the patriarch. With the ascension to the throne of Theodosius II (408-450 C.E.) pressure against the patriarch began to mount. In 415, a number of new restrictions were imposed on the Jewish community: New synagogues were prohibited. The patriarch was encouraged to destroy synagogues in places that had been deserted, provided this would not cause a disturbance. Patriarchs and Jews in general were prohibited from converting non-Jews. Any Christian slave belonging to the patriarch was to be transferred to the Church. This detailed law was, in effect, a direct attack on the patriarch, beginning with a personal reference—"Since Gamaliel supposed that he could transgress the law with impunity"—and proceeding to demote Gamaliel to a lower rank than he had hitherto enjoyed.[94]

This was not simply another attempt to weaken the unity of the Jewish community. Much more was involved. The patriarchs still claimed Davidic lineage. Although the messianic implications of this pedigree played no practical role in Jewish life, it did reflect Jewish commitment to the claim that the House of David still had a prophetic role to play in history's unfolding drama. Beyond this, a blow to the patriarchate was interpreted as a major step toward the ultimate dissolution of the Jewish community.

We do not know precisely what led to the final abolition of the patriarchate. A law in 429 stipulates that the Primates of the Jews, whether in the provinces of Palestine or in the other provinces, must transfer to the imperial treasury those funds that they have received "since the cessation of the patriarchs."[95] True, this law makes no direct mention of an imperial act that had eliminated the office of patriarch, but it is difficult to suppose that a lack of legitimate heirs brought an end to an office that had existed for centuries and had played such a crucial role in Jewish history since at least the destruction of the Second Temple.[96] Accordingly, many scholars believe that sometime between 418 and 429 C.E. some event sufficiently aroused the imperial administration that it forcibly brought an end to the office of patriarch. Yaron Dan notes that according to one source a rebellion broke out in Palestine in 418 and was put down by the Goth *comes* Plinta, who was later appointed consul.[97] If the Jews were believed to have played a role in this rebellion, this might have served as a pretext for the abolition of the patriarchate.

The law of 429 quoted above points to the existence of two Sanhedrins in Palestine. This too may have been the result of a Roman attempt to decentralize Jewish communal life and thereby weaken it.

The Palestinian Jewish community was not really devastated by the cessation of the patriarchate. Other institutions of Jewish leadership in Tiberias continued to exercise influence not only over the Jews of Palestine, but, in certain cases, in the Diaspora as well.[98]

The final two centuries of Byzantine rule in Palestine: 425-614 C.E.
The effects of the last two centuries of Roman-Christian rule in Palestine on the Jewish community are enigmatic, and even somewhat surprising. All signs should have pointed to the slow demise of the Jewish community's vitality: Central leadership in the form of the patriarchate had been abolished; beginning with Theodosius II, the legal status of the Jews came under renewed pressure; de-

mographically, the Jews of Palestine were clearly outnumbered by their Christian counterparts. And yet an apparently active and vital Jewish community continued to exist in the Holy Land.[99]

Synagogue building and restoration continued at full steam. Many of the synagogue structures that can be securely dated by means of inscriptions were either constructed or restored precisely at this time. The mosaic floor at Beth Alpha was produced during the reign of "King Justinus" according to the Aramaic inscription at the entrance to the main hall, almost certainly referring to the reign of the emperor Justin I (518-527 C.E.). The mosaic in the synagogue of Gaza was laid in 508. What is possibly the most interesting synagogue dedicatory inscription was found on the lintel from what must have been the the entrance to the synagogue at Kfar Naburaya: "In the year 494 to the destruction [of the Second Temple, i.e., in 564 C.E.], the house was built under the leadership of Hanina ben Liezer and Luliana (Julian) bar Judan."[100] Other impressive dated synagogue inscriptions come from Rehov, Ein Gedi and elsewhere. Clearly this was not a period of decline in the building and refurbishing of Palestinian synagogues.

All sorts of reasons have been proposed to explain the continued viability of the Jewish community in what should have been a period of decline. In purely economic terms, the late Byzantine period in Palestine was a prosperous one.[101] Christian pilgrims in ever-growing numbers continued to make their way to the Holy Land, not only spending money while there but frequently bringing with them donations for a variety of religious institutions, primarily churches and monasteries.[102] Moreover, the religious inclinations of some of these pilgrims were at times quite friendly toward the Jews. For example, Eudocia, the wife of Theodosius II, visited Palestine in 438. During her stay[103] she evinced much sympathy for the Jewish community. She may even have revoked the prohibition against Jews residing in Jerusalem, much to the consternation of Church leaders, such as Barsauma of Nisibis, who visited Palestine at the time.[104] According to Barsauma's biography, as a result of the empress' benevolence, the Jewish leadership issued the following proclamation to their people:

> "To the Great Nation of the Jews, from the Priests and Leaders in Galilee, Peace: Know you that the end of the dispersion of our people has arrived and the day of the ingathering of our tribes is upon us. For the Kings of Rome have decreed that our city of Jerusalem shall be restored to us. Hurry then to come to Jerusalem for the feast of Sukkoth, for our Kingdom is destined to arise in Jerusalem."[105]

While the authenticity of this letter, in precisely this version, is not above suspicion, there is no reason to doubt Eudocia's generosity, nor the existence of a certain degree of messianic fervor among the Jews.

This proclamation also indicates that a recognized Jewish leadership existed in Galilee even after the abolition of the patriarchate. Testimony to this leadership appeared again in the sixth century. Then its influence extended beyond the borders of Palestine, reaching as far as southern Arabia. Numerous Christian-Byzantine authors attest to the fact that the tribe of Himyarites in southern Arabia—modern Yemen—adopted Judaism in no small measure as a result of the activities of Jews sent from Tiberias. In the sixth century, the Himyarite Jews, in cooperation with Jews from Palestine, came to the aid of the local king, Dhu-Nuwas, who had also converted to Judaism and was resisting Ethiopian efforts to dominate the area. Southern Arabia was critical because it controlled important trade routes to the east. The Jewish leadership in Tiberias apparently felt it could alleviate its own plight under Byzantine rule by using the Himyarites as leverage.[106] The Christian author, Simon of Beth Arsham, describes how "these Jews of Tiberias send priests every year and all the time and arouse disputes with the Christians of Himyar"; Simon clearly understood the intentions of the Jews. He therefore warned them that "if they do not cease, their synagogues will be burnt and they themselves will be molested in all places where the Crucified one is reigning."[107] The allusion to priests in Arabia is all the more meaningful in light of a discovery made in 1970 in a mosque some ten miles east of the Yemenite capital of San'a. There, on a portion of a column, Dr. Walter Miller discovered a list of the 24 priestly orders (*mishmarot*), similar to the lists that existed in Palestinian synagogues at the time.[108]

The nature of the Jewish leadership in Tiberias is far from clear. One medieval source claims that a descendant from a different branch of the House of David appeared in the city approximately 100 years after the end of the patriarchate. A ninth-century Babylonian chronicle (*Seder Olam Zuta*, apparently produced to support the claim to Davidic lineage of the exilarchs in Babylonia) describes a Jewish uprising against the Persian Sassanian monarchy approximately during the years 495-502 C.E. The leader of the insurrection, the exilarch Mar Zutra, was ultimately executed by the Persians, but his son Mar Zutra managed to flee to Palestine, where he was appointed *resh pirka* (head of the academy [?]) and/or *resh sanhedrin* (head of the Sanhedrin) in Tiberias.[109] It is not clear whether these titles refer to two distinct offices and thus designate stages in Mar Zutra's Palestinian career,[110] or whether they are synonymous phrases. In either case, the source seems to suggest that Tiberias in the early sixth century did not suffer a void in the leadership structure of the Jewish community.

The fact that the community continued to be led, or at least taught, on a regular basis, primarily in the synagogue, by a circle of spiritual leaders is evident from a law introduced by the emperor Justinian in 553. Preserved in the Greek *Novellae*,[111] the law deals ostensibly with the language to be used by Jews in the synagogue, specifically when reading the Scriptures. In effect the law permitted the Jews to use Hebrew, Greek or any other language, although when reading the Bible in Greek they were encouraged to use the Septuagint version, but were also permitted the Greek translation of Aquila. Regarding the oral Jewish tradition, the law took a harsher tone, however: "What they call *deuterosis*, on the other hand, we prohibit entirely, for it is not included among the holy books."[112] Scholars are divided as to the precise meaning of the outlawed material. Some translate it as "Mishnah."[113] But what connection is there between the Mishnah and synagogue activity? I believe that *deuterosis* is a general term for oral tradition, which indeed is *deuterosis*, that is, secondary to the written Bible. The intention here seems quite obvious: it is the corpus of rabbinic tradition in its entirety, legal as well as homiletical, that could never be accepted by the Church; "It was not handed down from above by the prophets, but it is an invention of men in their chatter, exclusively of earthly origin and having in it nothing of the divine."[114] This is but a thinly veiled attack on the leadership of the Palestinian sages and their representatives, who were still, it appears, a potent force on the Jewish scene even in the middle of the sixth century.

The sages of Palestine in the post-Mishnaic period were not only an influential spiritual factor in their own day, they also left behind an impressive literary heritage.

The literary achievement in Palestine: Talmud and Midrash

Elements of continuity as well as innovation are to be found in the works of the Palestinian *amoraim*. But a word of caution and qualification must precede any discussion of this corpus, or corpora, of rabbinic literature. We commonly refer to the sages of the third and fourth centuries (and in Babylonia the fifth century as well) as *amoraim*, and to the talmudic works they produced as amoraic literature. This is, however, correct only in the sense that the books we are about to examine contain the statements, ideas and homiletics of those rabbis. The final redaction of almost all of these works came later, sometimes decades or even a century or two after the amoraic period. In some cases—including books that provided much of the source material for this chapter—they underwent a final redaction process hundreds of years after the deaths

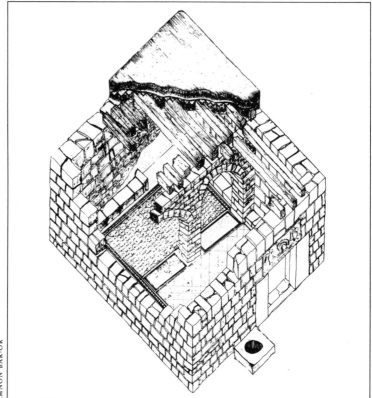

AMNON BAR-OR

THE HOUSE OF STUDY—BETH MIDRASH—AT MEROTH IN NORTH-ERN ISRAEL. This small house by the synagogue at Meroth was probably set aside for adult study of the Mishnah, the earliest collection of rabbinic laws. Stone benches lined the walls and mosaics depicting pomegranates and date clusters as well as specifically religious symbols (shofar on either side of a Torah ark, and a wolf and lamb illustrating Isaiah 65:25) covered the floors. Above the entrance was an inscribed stone lintel about 6 feet long. Originally built in the late fourth or early fifth century, the synagogue was destroyed by an earthquake and rebuilt in the seventh century. The House of Study may date from the seventh century rebuilding.

of the people whose deeds they recount. This is a result of the unique process of transmission and preservation of rabbinic material, which in many cases was not put into writing in a formal sense until the early Middle Ages.[115] Thus, for instance, we speak of books such as *Genesis Rabbah* or *Leviticus Rabbah* as amoraic *midrashim*, but this is only true in regard to the persons whose statements are quoted therein. In these two cases the final literary redaction probably did not take place until more than a century or two following the talmudic period, i.e., in the fifth to seventh cen-

BETH MIDRASH. This stone lintel is inscribed in Hebrew, "Blessed
shall you be in going in and blessed shall you be in going out"
(Deuteronomy 28:6). A large Roman-style wreath with a knot of ivy
tendrils was once flanked by two eagles, probably destroyed by
iconoclasts in the eighth century C.E. The lintel from Meroth is
similar to the only material evidence specifically mentioning a *beth
midrash,* a lintel found in Dabbura in the Golan that is inscribed,
"This is the *beth-midrash* of Rabbi Eliezer Ha-Kappar [a rabbi frequently cited in the Mishnah]."

turies.[116] Other *midrashim* make obvious references to the period
after the Islamic conquests. *Numbers Rabbah,* for example, was
probably not finally edited until the 12th century! So we must be
careful how we use this material.

The amoraic literature of Palestine differs markedly from the
literature of the earlier, Mishnaic period. While the Talmudim
of both Palestine and Babylonia are in a sense discussions and
elaborations of the Mishnah text, and in that sense are a direct
continuation of earlier rabbinic endeavors, the nature of these deliberations as recorded is totally different from the presentation of
the Mishnah. The corpus of law in the Mishnah emerged at some
time following its redaction as the definitive code of Jewish law, to
be studied in fine detail. But its structure is that of a legal code,
organized topically and systematically, and with very little nonlegal
material or digression from the main theme of each tractate. Not
so the Talmudim. While constantly building on the Mishnah, the
Talmudim nevertheless provide the student with a much more
fluid and elaborate context. The highly associative or suggestive
nature of talmudic discussion enables it not only to digress, but
also to introduce into supposedly legal discussions lengthy
nonhalakhic material: legend, folklore and popular wisdom. In a

sense, one feels far more "in the real academy" when studying
Talmud as opposed to Mishnah. The doubts and misgivings of
named rabbis appear alongside absolute *halakhah*. Sometimes we
are witness to lengthy deliberations that precede the final formulation of a legal statement.

***Differences
between
Palestinian
and
Babylonian
Talmudim***   Within this framework scholars have searched for signs peculiar
to the Palestinian Talmud, as opposed to that of Babylonia.[117] It is
assumed, to begin, that a major chronological difference exists.
Whereas the last generation of Babylonian *amoraim* referred to in
the Babylonian Talmud belong to the late fifth century (the last
Babylonian sage, Ravina, died in 500 C.E.), the names and events
mentioned in the Palestinian Talmud suggest a work whose development ceased approximately 100 years earlier.[118]

But beyond this difference is one of style as well. The discussion of the same Mishnah passage is almost always more concise
in the Palestinian Talmud, which frequently does not contain a
detailed analysis of each and every word in the Mishnah, as is
common in the Babylonian Talmud. Thus the Babylonian Talmud
frequently suggests an emendation of the Mishnah text, or at least
of our understanding of that text.[119] The question is whether these
discrepancies between the Talmudim are attributable to varying
styles and systems of study, or, on the other hand, to the historical
contexts in which the two works underwent the final stages of
their respective redactions. Some scholars would attribute the brev-
ity, and sometimes even abruptness, of the Palestinian Talmud to
the difficult political situation that pressed upon the Jews of Palestine during the Byzantine period.[120] While this might not be the
only solution, it is clear that the different conditions under which
the two works were composed played a major part not only in the
language (Palestinian Aramaic with a major dose of Greek in the
Palestinian Talmud; Babylonian Aramaic and numerous Persian
loanwords in the Babylonian Talmud) but in diverging attitudes
toward a number of the main issues of the day.

One enlightening example relates to the attitude of the two
Talmudim to the Gentile governments under whose rule the local
Jewish communities found themselves. The underlying perception
of many Palestinian sages, already evident in the Mishnah[121] and
later even more so in the Palestinian Talmud, is that Roman rule
of Palestine is not only evil but in fact illegitimate, at least within
the boundaries of Eretz Israel—thus encouraging, for instance, anyone who might wish to refrain from paying taxes to do so by any
means at their disposal. The accepted attitude in the Babylonian
Talmud, on the other hand, is that "the law of the kingdom is law"
(*dina de-malkhuta dina*), with all the concomitant requirements to

remain a law-abiding citizen.[122]

In addition, the manner in which the Mishnah was studied in the two Jewish centers may also have determined the differences between the finished products. Neither of the Talmudim contain discussions attached to all six orders of the Mishnah. This may be a consequence of different curricula in the academies of the two centers.[123] Indeed, not all portions of each of the Talmudim emanate from a single center in each land. Saul Lieberman has attempted to prove that certain tractates of the Palestinian Talmud were redacted in Caesarea rather than in Tiberias, where the bulk of the work seems to have been edited.[124]

As noted above, in Palestine a second genre of rabbinic literature emerged alongside the Talmud, that is, the amoraic *midrashim*. These works are frequently referred to as aggadic *midrashim* because the literary components of these books address themselves primarily to the vast and varied world of Jewish thought, morality and biblical exegesis, rather than legal material. When all is said and done the only really acceptable definition for *aggadah* is anything (and everything) that is not *halakhah*.

The aggadic midrashim

The aggadic material in the *midrashim* finds its genesis in a number of contexts. Discussions relating to the patriarchs and the ancient heroes of the nation could easily have developed out of constant rabbinic involvement in biblical exegesis. This, we have already seen, might have played a social role in the synagogue, as well as a purely academic one in the academies of the third and fourth centuries in Palestine. Even when the rabbis dealt with post-biblical persons or events, up to and including the events of their own generation, this was not done out of any critical need or intellectual desire to preserve "history" as we conceive of it. Rather, the past played a role only if it could be used to support some moral or ethical motive whose relevance was above time or place. Rabbinic history, then, is subservient to a higher goal, and we must never lose sight of this when using rabbinic *aggadah* for the purpose of deriving historical realities.[125] Thus, for example, the sages were not all that interested in ascertaining *what* happened during the Bar-Kokhba war (or any other major catastrophe), in the manner of a Dio Cassius, but rather they wanted to discover what improper behavior on the part of the Jewish people had led to the calamity. In the words of the Palestinian sages themselves:

"If you wish to know Him who decreed and [as a result] the world was created, study *aggadah*. For through this [*aggadah*] you know Him . . . and attach yourself to His ways."[126]

Two distinct types of aggadic *midrash* survived. One would appear to be the product of the academy. It is learned, and—most important—follows the Scriptures, word for word. We can regard these *midrashim* as commentaries on the Bible; indeed, they are frequently referred to as exegetical *midrashim*. One of the most prominent of these is *Genesis Rabbah*, which, together with *Lamentations Rabbah*, is possibly the best example of a *midrash* redacted not long after the end of the amoraic period.

The second genre, while obviously having undergone a literary redaction, nevertheless impresses us as being closer to the sermons that might have been delivered in synagogues on any given Sabbath or holiday.[127] Rather than explaining each biblical verse, these works focus on a major issue or theme, usually linked in the opening of the discussion to a scriptural passage. This passage is then linked, during the course of the discussion, with many other passages from all over the Bible, interspersing these references with stories and parables, many from everyday life. Slowly, the *midrash* weaves a case on any given issue, until finally returning, in a most acrobatic fashion at times, to the scriptural passage with which the discussion opened. Such *midrashim* are often referred to as homiletical *midrashim*. One of the best and earliest examples of this genre is *Leviticus Rabbah*. Some of the most beautiful specimens of rabbinic teaching can be found in these *midrashim* and, if nothing else, they make it abundantly clear why the emperor Justinian would consider the propounders of this kind of *deuterosis* to be the truly influential teachers of the Jewish community.

Halakhic and liturgical literature   The post-talmudic era (fifth to seventh centuries) in Byzantine Palestine does not mark a regression in the literary output of the country's spiritual leaders. Rather, we begin to encounter new literary genres in two specific categories of spiritual endeavor: *halakhah* and liturgy.

Discoveries in the Cairo Genizah now make it apparent that the late Byzantine period saw the emergence of a unique type of halakhic literature: collections of halakhic rules on particular issues of religious law, such as the laws of ritual slaughtering, blessings, formulas for documents and the like.[128] Compilations of halakhic decisions apparently became quite popular during the late Byzantine period. Known as books of *ma'asim*, these compilations supply us with a unique collection of sources on daily life in late Byzantine Palestine, touching on a variety of economic, social and religious issues.[129]

Alongside these halakhic works, the Byzantine period appears to represent the first major historical context for the appearance of the unique liturgical poems known as *piyyutim* (singular, *piyyut*). The first renowned *paytanim* (authors of *piyyutim*), such as Yosi b.

Yosi and Yannai, made their appearance at this time. *Piyyutim,* which accompanied the regular prayers in the synagogue, frequently address the issues and hopes of the time. They are a unique expression not only of a renewed yearning for redemption, but also of a return on a popular level to the use of the Hebrew language throughout the Land of Israel.

The first four decades of the seventh century—more precisely 614-638 C.E.—were tumultuous years in the history of Palestine. In that brief span the rule over the land changed hands at least three times, messianic hopes were raised, cruelly dashed, raised once again—and similarly crushed a second time. In this short time, two monotheistic religions—Judaism and Christianity—and a fledgling third religion—Islam—all focused their spiritual and political attentions on this small territory. In Palestine, the two great empires of the Near East clashed once again, the culmination of 400 years of strife between Rome and Sassanian Persia. Each enjoyed astounding victories and suffered terrible defeats. The ultimate consequence of these clashes was the complete exhaustion of both sides, opening the way for relatively easy conquests by a third party, conquests that determined the dominant character of this part of the world for the next 1,300 years.

Late Byzantine rule in Palestine; the Persian invasion and Arab conquest of the Holy Land

Over the centuries, the confrontation between Rome and Persia had amounted to something of a standoff. Persia ruled as far west as the Euphrates, Rome got as far as the Near East. The unfortunate buffer states—Armenia, Mesopotamia, Syria and Palestine—served as battlefields when one side or the other tried to gain advantage. By the late sixth century a *modus vivendi* had emerged between the two empires. Correspondence between the emperor Mauricius (582-602 C.E.) and the Persian king Chosroes II (590-628) points to their shared interest in achieving stabilization, if only as a means of freeing their respective armies to fight on other fronts. An "eternal" pact was signed between the two, which almost reflects their self-perception as the bearers of a shared role to preserve peace. Interestingly, this idea found its way into Jewish sources as well, such as the midrashic statement that "God did not divide the world among two nations and two kingdoms, except for the purpose of watching over Israel."[130]

The pact itself remained in effect for about ten years. The situation became destabilized, however, when the Roman army rebelled, placing one of its own, a man named Phocas, at the helm. Phocas proceeded to engineer the death of the emperor Mauricius (602 C.E.). This in turn freed the Persian king Chosroes to go to war against Byzantium. In the spring of 604 the Persian king took the border city of Edessa. A year later (605) the Persian army defeated

a Byzantine force in Mesopotamia. The following year (606) the
Persian forces conquered Byzantine Armenia. By 607 Roman fortresses along the Euphrates began to collapse, and Persian raids
reached territory in Syria, Phoenicia and even Palestine. This pressure led to the assassination of Phocas (on October 5, 610). He
was succeeded by Heraclius, the son of the Roman governor of
Africa. At first, Heraclius fared no better at stopping the Persian
forces. Antioch and then all of Syria fell. With the fall of Damascus
in 613, the road to Jerusalem was open.

It is not hard to imagine how these events were interpreted by
the Jews of Palestine. For years, and indeed for centuries, Jewish
eyes always turned eastward when they considered how the Holy
Land might be wrested from Rome. In the second century one
noted Palestinian sage, Rabbi Shimon b. Yohai, was recorded as
saying: "If you see a Persian horse tied to graves in Eretz Israel,
wait for the feet of the King, the Messiah."[131] A contemporary,
Rabbi Judah b. Illai, stated outright: "Rome is destined to fall to
Persia."[132] And now, Jews were apparently taking a more than
passive interest in the events. According to some reports, Jews
aided the Persian advance near Antioch, and even served as soldiers in the Persian army.[133]

To what extent the Jews of Palestine were actually willing to aid
the Persians is not entirely clear. But at least in Christian eyes
there was no doubt as to where the Jews stood: Sabeos, the Armenian historian of the late seventh century, stated,

> "All of Palestine surrendered willingly to the Persian king; in
> particular the remnants of the Hebrew nation rose up against
> the Christians and out of national zeal perpetrated great crimes
> and evil deeds against the Aryan community. They united with,
> and acted in total conjunction with, the Persians."[134]

According to another source, attributed to a Jewish convert
named Jacob (c. 640 C.E.), the leader of the Jews of Tiberias had
prophesied that in eight years the Messiah would appear and restore the kingdom of Israel.[135] Such messianic expectations are
also reflected in a unique new literary genre commonly referred to
as *midreshei ge'ullah*, that is, *midrashim* of redemption.[136] That the
kingdom of Persia was to usher in the messianic age, made it even
easier for Jews to identify this age with the return to Zion following the Babylonian Exile 12 centuries earlier. That the current
Persian king's name, Chosroes, was similar to Cyrus obviously
didn't hurt either.

It was this ferment that greeted the Persians as they entered Palestine. In the early summer of 614 the Persians entered Jerusalem and for three days conducted a mass slaughter of the local population. This was followed by a respite, during which those in hiding were encouraged by the captors to come out. Here our sources are divided as to what befell Christian captives, and in particular what role was played by the local Jewish population. Some have claimed that the Jews were proclaimed rulers of the city, invested with full powers of government. This of course played into the hands of those who then blamed the Jews for the systematic destruction of all the churches in the city. Pent-up hostility between the two religious communities so impressed our sources that it is difficult to form any clear picture of what actually happened. One anonymous source has the Jews informing the Persians of an enormous treasure of gold and silver under the Church of the Holy Sepulchre. The aim was clear in the eyes of the reporter: A Jewish attempt to have the church destroyed.

At the same time Jewish sources, e.g., one of the *midreshei ge'ullah* known as *Sefer Zerubavel*, describe a process of Jewish Temple restoration: sacrifices, building a tabernacle on the Temple Mount, prayers at the gate of the Temple Mount and the like.[137] But that same source goes on to describe what appears to have been a change of heart by the Persians. It is possible that after their initial successes in Palestine, the Persians realized that the Jewish population in the land, as well as in Jerusalem, was by now a small minority, and decided to come to terms with the far more powerful Christian community. As a result the Jews appear to have lost any control they may have initially enjoyed in Jerusalem, and Sabeos now quotes Modestus, the leader of the local Christian community:

> "They [the Jews] that dared to fight and destroy this true site, the mercy of God led to their banishment from His holy city. Those who hoped to become its citizens heard themselves banished . . . they were not deemed worthy to see . . . the holy grave . . . nor the gloriously renewed Golgotha. For others witnessed the return of their glory. . . ."[138]

Jewish sources allude to a messianic figure named Nehemiah ben Hushiel (or ben Joseph) who appears to have resisted this change in Persian policy, but, we are told, the king of Persia "went up against Nehemiah and all Israel . . . and he pierced Nehemiah through and they exiled Israel into the desert and there was woe in Israel like never before."[139]

Whatever messianic hopes the Jews had as a result of the Persian conquest were soon dashed. Indeed, they realized that among the three powers converging on Palestine and Jerusalem, only the Persians were devoid of any religious motivation. Thus, the Persians were the only force likely to grant the Jews autonomous existence in their land. As Michael Avi-Yonah analyzed it:

> "The deception, which the Jews suffered in their alliance with the Persians, marks therefore the real end of the political history of Judaism in Palestine."[140]

The defeat of the Persians
Persian fortunes, however, also began to suffer. The Byzantine empire under Heraclius launched a major counterattack. By 627 this offensive reached almost to Nineveh, where the Persians were again defeated. Their capital, Ktesiphon, soon came under attack. Chosroes was then deposed and murdered; his son died before he could strike a deal with the besiegers. Finally the Persian general Shar-baraz made a deal with Heraclius: Heraclius would recognize Shar-baraz as the Persian monarch in exchange for a Persian retreat from Mesopotamia, Egypt, Syria and Palestine; in addition, the remains of the Holy Cross—which the Persian army had seized—would be restored. On March 21, 629, Heraclius entered Jerusalem in a splendid procession; the return of the cross was regarded as a miracle.

It was the last great moment of glory in Byzantine Jerusalem. Within five years (634 C.E.) the Arabs attacked Gaza. Four years later Jerusalem was in Arab hands; the city surrendered in the spring of 638.

The appearance of yet a third force on the horizon could only have rekindled desperate Jewish hopes. Testimony to this is obviously reflected in the following *midrash*:

> "The year when the King Messiah will be revealed, all the nations of the world will be at strife with one another. The King of Persia will arouse the King of Arabia. And the King of Arabia will go to Edom [Rome] to take counsel with them. And the King of Persia will again lay the whole world waste. And all the nations of the world will clamor and be frightened . . . and Israel will clamor and be frightened and say 'to where shall we go and to where shall we turn.' And He says to them: My sons, do not fear . . . the time of your redemption has arrived."[141]

The events of this time found equally dramatic expression in *piyyutim*. One of the most beautiful and touching of these liturgical poems, written to be recited on the 9th of Av (commemorating the destruction of both the First and Second Temples), was apparently read during the year that the Arabs concluded their conquest of the Holy Land:

"On that day when the Messiah, the scion of David comes to a
　people pressed
these signs will be seen in the world. . . .
And the King of the West and the King of the East each other
　will pulverize. . . .
And the King of the West will establish his soldiers in the
　Land. . . .
And from the land of Yoktan [Arabia] a King shall appear and
　his camps in the land will be strengthened. . . ."

The poet goes on to describe how Israel will first be cleansed of
its sins and then, realizing it is on the verge of the messianic era,
gather in Jerusalem where the messiah will proclaim himself:

"And the Priests on their orders will stand;
And the Levites on their platforms will be raised;
And He will declare: I have returned to Jerusalem in mercy."[142]

The sages of the Babylonian Talmud list the successive births and
deaths of prominent rabbis:

Beyond the Euphrates: The Jews of Babylonia

"When Rabbi Akiva died, Rabbi [Judah the Patriarch] was born,
when Rabbi died Rav Judah [b. Yehezkel] was born. . . .
This teaches that a righteous man does not depart from the
world until [another] righteous man like himself is created,
as it is written: 'The sun riseth, the sun goeth down' [Ecclesiastes 1:5]."[143]

One can only wonder whether in the backs of their minds the
Babylonian sages did not interpret this theme as part of the larger
history of Israel as well. For as the Jews of Palestine began their
slow decline, the Jewish community of Babylonia was about to
embark on its own great chapter in Jewish history, beginning in
the third century C.E. down to the end of the geonic* period, in
the 11th century (see p. 63f.).

Jews had reached Babylon even before the destruction of the
First Temple. Their numbers substantially increased after the
Babylonian destruction of Jerusalem in 586 B.C.E. and the ensuing Exile. But in one of those inexplicable twists of history, we lose
track of the Babylonian community almost immediately, save for
bits and pieces of isolated information in the later books of the
Bible, and scraps of archaelogical evidence.[144] In the late sixth
century B.C.E., a minority of Jews returned from the Babylonian
Exile under the benevolent rule of the Persian monarch Cyrus the

---

* The *geonim* (singular, *gaon*) were the heads of the Babylonian rabbinic academies. *Gaon* is probably a shortened form of *rosh yeshivat gaon Ya'akov* with the final two words taken from Psalm 47:4—"the *pride* of Jacob."

Great. But until the Roman destruction of the Second Temple in 70 C.E., we need to be, and are, constantly reminded that Jews are still in Babylonia, indeed in numbers "so great that no one knows their precise number."[145] But the fact remains that for approximately 1,000 years the Jews of Babylonia were isolated from the mainstream of Jewish history—or at least from that history for which we have any substantial documentation. This paucity of documentation includes literary sources, such as the writings of Josephus, as well as archaeological evidence, especially when we compare the relative wealth of Jewish inscriptions from the Hellenistic-Roman world with that of the East.

Yet, we know the Jews of Babylonia were numerous and powerful, for Jews in the Hellenistic-Roman world repeatedly take into consideration the powerful potential support of their brethren in Babylonia before embarking on any major uprising, usually against the Romans.[146]

Every now and then a Babylonian Jew pierced the wall of silence and made his way onto the stage of Jewish history, in Palestine or elsewhere in the Greco-Roman world. The best-known example is Hillel the Babylonian, who made his way to Jerusalem, probably during the reign of Herod, and ultimately became the founding father of a school of rabbinic teaching (see pp. 11-12). But these are exceptions; the truth is that until after the Bar-Kokhba revolt (132-135 C.E.) the Jewish community in Babylonia made almost no impression on the life or the leaders of Palestinian Jewry.

When a sage in Babylonia attempted to intercalate the Jewish calendar following the devastation in Palestine of the Bar-Kokhba uprising, this was considered almost tantamount to heresy; the threat to Palestinian hegemony was thwarted.[147]

All this began to change in the third century C.E. Ultimately the rabbis of Babylonia themselves cited, in retrospect, the return of one of their own, Rav (Abba), to Babylonia in 219 C.E.,[148] as the beginning of a new era in the relative status of the two great Jewish communities: "We have made ourselves [or, consider ourselves] in Babylonia like Eretz Israel—from when Rav went down to Babylonia."[149] While this may seem to telescope a long drawn-out process into one identifiable event, the fact is that the date designated in that statement indeed points accurately to the early third century, when Babylonia's star began to rise.

Why was Babylonian Jewry unique? To begin, this was not only one of the largest concentrations of Jews in the world, but the one major community that did not find itself within the framework of the Hellenistic and Roman world. As such, it was impervious to the impact of the assimilatory nature of Hellenistic culture, and instead thrived in a much more feudalistic environment, wherein the wide variety of ethnic communities were granted a major degree not only of political self-rule but of cultural autonomy as well.

As we enter the third century, we find that the Jews of Babylonia have at their head an exilarch (*resh galuta*, "head of the Diaspora") with claims to Davidic lineage. To be sure, there is absolutely no mention of this position before the late second or early third century, and it was only in medieval times that apologists would find it necessary to invent genealogical tables to prove the Jewish leader's pedigree.[150] But the exilarchate was undoubtedly a potent force throughout the talmudic period in Babylonia—the period which began as the Sassanian dynasty assumed the local throne from their predecessors, the Arsacids in 224 C.E. In the face of the centralizing tendencies of the new monarchy, which probably threatened (or was feared to threaten) the autonomous framework of Jewish life,[151] the exilarchate represented the Jewish community before the authorities. At the same time it regulated much of the economic and social life of the Jews of Babylonia.[152] Their success was probably a major factor in the continued thriving of the Jewish community on the banks of the Euphrates and Tigris rivers.

But the exilarchate did not rule the Babylonian Jewish community single-handedly. Alongside the exilarch a new framework of leadership—the rabbis of Babylonia—emerged.

Much has been written about the stages of development of rabbinic leadership, as well as the degree to which the Jewish "man in the street" was actually affected by rabbinic influence. Clearly rabbinic academies (*yeshivot*) did not spring up overnight in third-century Babylonia;[153] such institutions usually undergo protracted periods of development before assuming roles of recognized communal leadership. A marked difference, however, characterizes the emergence of Babylonian rabbinic leadership, as compared to Palestinian leadership. The Palestinian patriarchs began their history as "rabbis," that is, central figures within the religious circles that disseminated religious teaching; but gradually they accreted political power. In Babylonia, the exilarch ruled, exercising political power within the community by virtue of his Davidic lineage. The Babylonian rabbis confined their concerns to moral and religious responsibilities, ever careful not to overstep their position and thereby offend the exilarch.[154]

If the rabbis of Babylonia were prudent in their relations with the exilarch, they were even more cautious in defining and publicly stating their attitude toward the government. As we have already noted, it is in Babylonia that we encounter the well-formulated principle that "the law of the government is law." Even when the revitalized Zoroastrian religious establishment took extreme steps to ensure that the major tenets of its religion not be debased,[155] these steps were not construed by the local Jewish community as persecutions. In fact, the Zoroastrian-Sassanian religious establishment avoided any sort of forced missionary activity that might impinge on Jewish behavior.[156]

In the fourth century it was the local Christian community whose loyalties were suspect. For that community was thought to automatically ally itself with the Roman-Christian empire. The Jews were clearly beyond such suspicion; it was assumed that they hated Rome—the destroyer of the Jewish Temple. Indeed, as we have seen, the rabbis of Babylonia even suggested that in the future Persia would defeat Rome. After all, Persia not only defeated the destroyers of the First Temple (Babylonia) but allowed the building of the Second Temple under Cyrus. Because Rome destroyed the Second Temple, "Is it not reasonable that Rome fall to Persia?"[157]

Athough not all Babylonian Jews were enamored with the new Sassanian regime (for example, Rav), the *modus vivendi* that emerged was the decisive factor in the subsequent success of Babylonian Jewry. Here, not surprisingly, we can observe a kind of reversal of roles between the Jewish community and the Christian Church. The bishop of Mar Mattai (near Mosul) in the first half of the fourth century, told his Christian flock not to heed the scoffing of the apparently more secure Jewish community:

> "The impure say that this church has no God . . . for if it had a God why doesn't He fight their battle . . . and even the Jews scoff at us and lord it over our people."[158]

The bishop knew of Jews who had succeeded in converting Christians; he delivered sermons against this danger.

While the conversion to Judaism does not seem to have been a major issue in Jewish Babylonia, it is true that there was little fear of Christianity among the local Jewish community. The rabbis of Babylonia evinced little insecurity regarding the viability of their community. In time, this self-assurance of the Babylonian Jewish community affected relations between Babylonian Jewry and Jewish Palestine. The Babylonian Jews came to regard themselves as the "purest" of the Jewish communities in terms of their pedigree, even when compared with Palestine.[159] By the late third century rabbinic authorities in Babylonia advised their disciples against "going up" to Palestine.[160] For many Jews—at the time and subsequently—Babylonia served as the prototype of the successful Diaspora, a place where one ought to remain until the ultimate redemption and deliverance. This obviously did not sit well with the Jewish leaders in Palestine. But Babylonian local patriotism continued to thrive. By the post-talmudic era we encounter

Babylonian apologists who suggest that their land is the real land of Torah, rather than Palestine.[161]

Babylonian Jewry thus shaped Jewish life and religious behavior at a definitive stage in the development of Judaism. The Babylonian Talmud ultimately attained overriding authority, in striking contrast to its Palestinian counterpart. For centuries it remained the central and most universally studied religious text among those Jews who devoted their lives to the study of "Torah." Moreover, the Babylonian *geonim* succeeded in spreading Babylonian tradition and legal decisions throughout much of the Jewish Diaspora. All this was true notwithstanding the central role filled by the Land of Israel in Jewish thought, as well as in so many other spheres of Jewish religious behavior.

EIGHT

The Religion of the Empire: Christianity from Constantine to the Arab Conquest

DENNIS E. GROH

THE BREATHTAKING RISE AND DEVELOPMENT OF CHRISTIANITY before the fourth century was equaled and even surpassed in the years 312 to 640 C.E. Constantine became the sole ruler of the Roman empire in 324 C.E.—just 13 years after the last systematic imperial persecution of the Christian churches in the East. From Constantine to the end of antiquity, with the exception of the brief reign of Julian (361-363), the empire would be continuously ruled by Christians.

Until the conversion of the emperors, Christianity had no true political center for its ambitions and no comprehensive agenda for the public ordering of its life. The continuous succession of Christian emperors provided the necessity, the machinery and the financing for the creation of a Christian empire.

Thus the ecclesiastics who had portaged through the turbulent persecutions of 303 to 311 C.E.[1] found themselves suddenly sailing on a great new public lake. The prestige of legitimacy and the largess of rich donors now showered upon the bishops of the Church who, for the first time in Christian history, became powerful figures in society. These centuries gave to Western history, as articulated by both imperial and ecclesiastical spokespersons, the dream of an entirely Christian world—ruled by Christian princes, decorated with a newly developing Christian art and architecture and held together by unanimity of doctrine.

In fact, when we look closely, we see that these centuries were also characterized by an enormous diversity in all areas—differences in language, doctrine, wealth and lifestyles. But for all the diversity and difference, we nevertheless see a gradual confluence of this new public religion with much older Mediterranean customs and traditions. By the sixth century C.E., there is a clearly recognizable commonality in pottery, mosaic styles, small artifacts, public works and roads. This is especially true of city culture. If you missed the name on your way in, you would be hard put to know exactly in what city you were.

In this sense, civilization meant standardization—uniform weights, measures, etc. By the sixth century, there existed an integral culture across the Mediterranean that can properly be called Byzantine. As we move into the welter of detail and dissent that forms the inevitable subject of history, it is good to remember that a Byzantine Christian civilization, centered in Constantinople, is being born that will endure and grow for at least the next 1,000 years, long after the Islamic conquest removes the old Eastern provinces from Roman rule.

Constantine becomes sole ruler in the East Until recently, when Constantine became a Christian or whether, in fact, he was ever a Christian, was open to debate. The question has now been largely settled by the authentication of a sermon he preached sometime in the years 317-324 C.E.[2] In that sermon Constantine publicly declared the Christian God to be his sponsor and the author of all his exploits:

> "When people commend my services, which owe their origin to the inspiration of Heaven, do they not clearly establish the truth that God is the cause of the exploits I have performed? . . . and surely all persons know that the holy service in which these hands have been employed has originated in pure and genuine faith toward God. . . . Hence, it becomes all pious persons to render thanks to the Savior of all, first for our own individual security, and then for the happy posture of public affairs: at the same time entreating the favor of Christ with holy prayers and constant supplications, that he would continue to us our present blessings."[3]

In 324 C.E. Constantine defeated and killed his pagan rival Licinius and took possession of the East; he could then drop all pretense of interest in other religions and, he hoped, take his rightful place among the "saints" of the Christian Church.[4]

Immediately after Licinius' defeat, Constantine began laying out a new capital for himself, which later writers would call "the new Rome," but which we know familiarly as Constantinople (Constantine's city).[5] Constantine included Christian churches within the very plan of the new city–without running afoul of vested pagan interests of the old Roman Senate, as he might have if he had built his city in the West.

Like so many aristocrats of the East in the fourth century, Constantine was not baptized until his deathbed, fearing that during his lifetime the judicial and military duties imposed on officeholders might require him to break one or more of the commandments. At his death in 337, he was buried in Constantinople in the Church of the Holy Apostles, where he had erected six coffins, symbolizing the apostles, on either side of his resting place.[6]

The world that Constantine's sons inherited was a far different world than their father had entered as a young soldier. Constantine had tied the fortunes of his house to the Christian Church and its prosperity. He had been no friend of other religions; but, although he fulminated against other faiths, he did not actually persecute them.[7] We can see this tone of distaste for other religions in his legislation regarding the Jews. Constantine's relation to the Jews, as judged by his legislation, conforms to that of his predecessors.[8] Jews continued to exercise their full civil rights, even serving on municipal councils. Jews since Hadrian's day (c. 135 C.E.) had been prohibited from visiting Jerusalem. Constantine both lifted this prohibition and allowed Jews to mourn the loss of the Temple annually.[9] What is new in his legislation regarding the Jews is the nasty tone of the language about Judaism,[10] in keeping with Constantine's distaste for non-Christian religions: It is described as a "deadly sect," "a nefarious sect":

The New Christian mind of the East

> "It is our will that Jews and their elders and patriarchs shall be informed that if, after the issuance of this law, any of them should dare to assail with stones or with any other kind of madness–a thing which We have learned is now being done– any person who has fled their feral [deadly] sect and has resorted to the worship of God, such assailant shall be immediately delivered to the flames and burned, with all his accomplices. Moreover, if any person from the people should betake himself to their nefarious sect and should join their assemblies, he shall sustain with them the deserved punishment."[11]

As we can see from the above law, Constantine wished to protect converts to his new faith which he considered to alone practice the true "worship of God." But he and his successors had "adopted" a religion that had grown teeth even before his advent in the East. The early Christian emperors were under continuous pressure from Christian bishops in the East to silence all other cults. The roots for this lay, we now know, in the Christian reaction to the last great persecution of the Church by the emperor Diocletian and successors in the years 303 to 311 C.E. The details of that persecution need not detain us, but the results of it sealed the fate of all other religions in the East. Christians who had been willing to consider coexistence with pagans found the pagan state turning on them in the worst persecution of Christians to date. They adopted a "never again" attitude toward paganism and, when the opportunity arose, sought to make Christianity the only legally permitted religion.

The writings of Eusebius of Caesarea, one of the most influential bishops of the East, allow us to trace the progress of this new hard-line policy toward non-Christians: Early in his writing career, Eusebius seemed to think of Christianity as the true religion, but not the *only* religion that should exist in the Roman empire. By late in Constantine's reign, Eusebius became convinced that other religions should be suppressed; and by the time of Constantine's death, Eusebius was demanding that the new emperors eliminate all other religions.[12]

A long campaign was beginning that would culminate in Christianity's being recognized as the official religion of the Roman empire. By 392 edicts were issued closing all temples and ending sacrifices at pagan shrines.[13] Thus in the reign of Theodosius I (379-395) Christianity became the official religion of the empire. Theodosius himself was raised suddenly to the throne as co-emperor by the emperor Gratian (375-383), who needed his help in ruling the Eastern portion of the empire. Historians have suggested this sudden, almost miraculous elevation contributed to Theodosius' commitment to Christianity; moreover, as a result of an illness early in his reign, Theodosius was baptized. Thus, unlike his predecessor-emperors who were baptized at the end of their lives, Theodosius sat on the throne as a baptized Christian.[14] Early in his reign he issued a famous edict (*Cunctos Populos*) bringing all peoples under the orthodox (or "catholic") view of the Trinity, identifying Christian imperial orthodoxy with Roman citizenship.[15] It was Theodosius who empowered Christian consensus on the doctrine of the Trinity at the Council of Constantinope in 381 (see below) and followed his commitment to orthodoxy by laws depriving dissenters and heretics of civil rights.[16]

Yet Theodosius, with the exception of laws restricting Jewish ownership of Christian slaves and prohibiting intermarriage between Jews and Christians, was careful to protect the previous

THEODOSIUS I. Roman emperor of the East from 379 to 395 C.E., Theodosius I was a vigorous champion of orthodox Christianity, making it the official religion of the empire. Unlike previous Christian emperors who were baptized at the end of their lives, Theodosius was baptized early in his reign. Also, he may have credited his religion for his unexpected rise to the throne. Although he deprived dissenters and heretics of civil rights and outlawed marriages between Christians and Jews, Theodosius protected most Jewish legal rights and tried by law to protect synagogues from hostile Christians.

© ERICH LESSING

legal rights of Jews and to try to contol by law hostile Christians who on occasion sought to destroy or despoil synagogues.[17]

The fourth century also saw the gradual conversion of the upper classes to Christianity. Frequently upper-class women converted first; the men followed, often pushed by the women or lured by the promise of imperial preferment. Both men and women found the transition easier because of the gradual assimilation into the new faith of many of the old Roman traditions.[18]

The persecution of 303 to 311 left another signal mark: People were cautious in giving unreserved praise to any Christian, even an emperor. In that persecution Christians had witnessed betrayal by many prominent Christian officials, even bishops. (Eusebius does not give us the name of his predecessor as bishop in the see of Caesarea, probably because his predecessor abandoned Christianity in the face of the persecutions.)[19] Thus Constantine came to an East where Christians were preoccupied with the problem of people who seemed to be solid and secure Christians and yet might turn and fall away from their baptismal vows, backsliding into pagan idolatry.[20]

Only after Constantine died, still safely a Christian, could Eusebius pull out all the stops in praising the Christian emperor. This he did in his panegyric *Life of Constantine*.[21] The care with which he ties Constantine's "happy" life to his loyalty to the Christian God shows Eusebius' anxiety that the sons might not follow their father's religious example.

Despite the privileges showered on the Christian Church by the emperors, Christians retained an ambivalent attitude toward living emperors. That ambivalence was further accentuated when Julian (361-363) came to the throne and, throwing off his Christian background, in fact attempted an actual, though brief, reestablishment of paganism.[22]

The Arian controversy and the Council of Nicaea   In the years 324 and 325, when Constantine, fresh from his triumph over his rival, rushed into the arms of the Christian bishops, he found himself embroiled in an enormous doctrinal controversy among Christians in the East, a controversy that dogged his last years and preoccupied his successors for the next half century: the Arian controversy.

Even before his arrival in the East after his victory over Licinius, Constantine sent his ecclesiastical troubleshooter, Hosius, bishop of Cordova, to make contact with the Christians of the East.* Hosius found not a peaceful people awaiting the triumphant approach of their first imperial coreligionist, but a Church rocked by controversy over questions involving the nature of Christ and Christ's relation to God the Father.

The controversy began in Alexandria, Egypt, in 318 C.E. when a presbyter named Arius challenged Bishop Alexander's teaching on the subject. After briefly hesitating, Alexander took disciplinary steps against Arius, who in turn appealed to the powerful bishop of Nicomedia, Eusebius. (Don't confuse Eusebius of Nicomedia with the church historian, Eusebius of Caesarea. Although both originally may have supported Arius, their courses diverged after the Council of Nicaea.) Eusebius of Nicomedia owed his power and prominence not to his writing ability (only one letter survives from his hand),[23] but to his position as bishop of Nicomedia, then the imperial capital of the East, and to the fact he was a member of the patrician class.[24] He belonged by birth to imperial circles, followed Constantine to Constantinople and baptized him just before his death in 337. Despite the rule enacted by the Council of

* The terms "East" and "West" are somewhat confusing in Roman studies. The western portion of the empire was comprised of the territory on both sides of the Mediterranean north and west of the Adriatic Sea, in which area people spoke Latin. East and south of the Adriatic on both sides of the Mediterranean, Greek was the spoken language. In 293 C.E. the emperor Diocletian formalized the division of the empire into western and eastern provinces, though the rule was considered to be one. Constantine's uniting of the *imperium* did not, however, affect those signal linguistic and geographical distinctions. Thus the later emperors of the fourth and fifth centuries were assigned certain "spheres" of their rule corresponding to this subdivision of the empire into East and West.

Nicaea in 325 prohibiting bishops from changing their sees, Eusebius became the bishop of that new city in 338 under Constantius.[25] Eusebius of Nicomedia was influential not only as an adviser to Constantine but also to Constantine's sons, thus guaranteeing that the Arian case would have a more than sympathetic hearing at the imperial court. The settlement of the controversy would have to await the formation of a true consensus of Eastern bishops and a change of imperial sentiments.

The controversy spread to Caesarea, where Eusebius of Caesarea also seems to have supported Arius.[26] In Antioch, a council to elect a new bishop took up the Arian controversy under the urging of Hosius.[27] The Council of Antioch in February 325 C.E. wrote a statement of faith (condemning Arianism),[28] and seems to have placed the church historian Eusebius of Caesarea in disrepute for his support of Arian views.

By now the matter had grown both so serious and so divisive that it became apparent to Constantine that it could only be settled by calling a full council of the Eastern bishops. They met in May of 325 at the town of Nicaea in Bythnia (modern Turkey) near Constantine's palace. The exact number of bishops in attendance is not properly recorded—nor the progress of the three-month-long discussions. The results of the Council of Nicaea, however, have been normative for Christians—both East and West—to the present day. A creed was produced at this first ecumenical (universal) council which Hosius and Constantine hoped would unify Christians of the East in their doctrinal thinking about Christ's relation to God the Father.[29] They failed.

What was a stake at the Council of Nicaea that made this early Christian discussion so universally important and so potentially explosive?

Bishop Alexander of Alexandria, whose views Arius opposed, had maintained a doctrine of the eternal and essential sonship of Christ. For the Alexandrian bishops, it was inconceivable that Christ was not eternally the son of God who possessed all the natural properties of the Father.[30] When Alexandrian bishops like Alexander and his successor Athanasius (328-373) read about Christ's sonship in the Scriptures, they saw a natural and biological kind of sonship, which differed from the adoptive sonship conferred on believers who were being redeemed by God (cf. John 1:12; Galatians 4:5-7).[31]

When the Arians read the same Bible, they focused on the similarity of Christ's sonship to ours. Thus they saw Christ's life as the perfectible model of our redemption—an adopted and obedient redeemer, created by God to increase in wisdom, stature and favor (grace) (Luke 2:52).[32] Thus the Arians stressed the changeable (improvable) nature of Christ as redeemer.

This view horrified the Alexandrian bishops. If Christ could change for the better, he could also change for the worse, thus jeopardizing human salvation. Church people who had witnessed the backsliding of lifelong Christians during the persecutions of 303 to 311 C.E. could not pin human salvation to so shaky a model as a changeable redeemer.

A secular age that had seen too much change in the crises of the third century could not abide much change of any kind.

During the reigns of Constantine and his successors, farmers were bound to the land by imperial legislation in order to end dramatic shifts in the agricultural tax base. Constantine set a new stable value for the gold coin, the solidus (which held against inflation and devaluation for the next seven centuries). Frontier armies and borders were rearranged to regularize their lines (if there was anything a Roman hated, it was a sloppy border). Another imperial fiat prevented transfer from one governmental agency to another; this applied to civil bureaucrats of all ranks, because the lucrative Palatine ministries tended to clump and glut with warm bodies, while the less remunerative (but also important) desks went begging—all this in an effort to bring order and stability to a too-changing world.[33]

It should be no surprise then that the bishops who came to the Council of Nicaea in 325 condemned Arianism and voted in favor of a creed that conceived of Christ's relationship to God in stable, unchanging, essentialist terms:

> "One Lord Jesus Christ, the Son of God, begotten from the Father as only-begotten, that is from the substance of the Father, God from God, light from light."

Nor should it surprise us that they rejected anyone who claimed that Christ was "of another hypostasis or a creature, or *mutable or subject to change*" (emphasis added).[34]

The doctrine of homoousios as one substance What was surprising was that all but two bishops signed a creed *that contained a nonscriptural term for the first time in Christian history*—homoousios, of the same substance. Christ was said to be "of the same substance" with the Father.

Although previously Eusebius of Caesarea had been accused of Arianism, he voted against it at the Council of Nicaea. Eusebius wrote home to his church in Caesarea (Caesarea Maritima in Palestine) to explain why he voted for the term *homoousios*. Eusebius goes on to say:

> " '*Homoousios* with the Father' indicates that the son of God bears no resemblance to originated creatures but that he is alike

in every way only to the Father."[35]

Constantine, who had called the synod, assured the bishops that the term did not imply anything heretical, such as that God had a substance which could be divided between Father and son. If we accept Eusebius' explanation for endorsing this bizarre and unforeseen turn of events, the council, lost in the luster of unprecedented imperial attention, thought they were simply using a term that made unequivocally clear that Christ was more like God than he was like us.

After concluding some additional business, the bishops were free to celebrate the 20th anniversary of Constantine's reign as his special guests.

Later in the century some Arians admitted they signed the Creed of Nicaea to please Constantine; they dismissed their action with these words:

"The soul is none the worse for a little ink."[36]

But a time bomb had been planted at the heart of the Christian proclamation. Constantine's unity was both illusory and dangerous, as the next 50 years of Church history show.

When Constantine died in 337 C.E., he was succeeded by his three sons, Constantius (337-361), Constans (337-350) and Constantine II (337-340), whose separate spheres of rule divided the Constantine political unity. War between Constans and Constantine II in 340 resulted in the death of the latter; Constans, the Western emperor, was killed in battle by a usurper named Magnentius in 350 C.E. Thus Constantius inherited his father's Eastern empire and ruled it for 24 years. He also inherited the influence of Eusebius of Nicomedia, now bishop of Constantinople, who had moved in as a key adviser to Constantine the Great immediately after Nicaea. Thus the court was under Arian influence. Until his death in 340/41, Eusebius of Nicomedia maneuvered to remove and reverse the Creed of Nicaea and to remove its supporters. Foremost among his enemies was Athanasius of Alexandria, who succeeded to the bishopric there in 328.

Of all the people at Nicaea, Athanasius (present as Bishop Alexander's secretary) was the clearest in his anti-Arian insistence that Christ was the eternal son of God, the very Word of the Father, an essential offshoot of God's deity. As the first bishop of Egypt who spoke the native language, Coptic, Athanasius was able in his 45-year reign as bishop of Alexandria to marshal the people of Egypt and the monks of the desert (see below) behind his adherence to the Nicene cause, as he interpreted it. Exiled five times for his opposition to the Arians and for his failure to reestablish

The aftermath of Nicaea

communion with them, Athanasius proved himself a master politician.[37] On one of his exiles, in 339 C.E., he fled to Rome where he won the support of the bishop of Rome, Pope Julius (337-352)—though he weakened his standing among Eastern theologians because of his support in Rome of a too-radical Nicene supporter, Marcellus of Ancyra.[38]

Two interrelated factors prevented an early resolution of the Arian crisis. First, the active interest of Constantius and subsequent emperors meant that any theological discussion in a synod or council was followed by imperial fiat enforcing, as a matter of law, the decisions of that council on churches of the East. Thus, in an attempt to find that uniformity of doctrine which the rapidly "Christianizing" empire required, a huge number of councils were held from 325 to 381 C.E. But each synod tended to reproduce the current theological sentiments of the reigning emperor.[39] Not until Theodosius I (379-395 C.E.) did an emperor with Nicene sentiments reign long enough to call a council that would genuinely enforce the anti-Arian doctrinal settlement of Nicaea.

Second, the conversion of the emperors to Christianity created a central forum for Christians to discuss issues face to face. No such ecumenical forum had existed in the days before Nicaea; thus Christians could no longer take doctrinal agreement for granted. Forced to talk with each other, they had to come to grips with the vast variety of beliefs that Christians actually held.

Thus the East was divided into a variety of doctrinal positions. Though the majority of Christian bishops were not Arian in their sympathies, they could not agree on terminology to express their view of the relation between God and Christ.

Urban unrest, always a danger in late antiquity (c. 300-640 C.E.), added to the inflammatory atmosphere. Forced councils, depositions and deportations of disgruntled Church leaders, with new bishops imposed on local populaces—all this reflected the high degree of imperial meddling in ecclesiastical affairs. For example, in 356 C.E. a radical Arian, George of Cappadocia, was imposed by Constantius on the Christians of Alexandria in place of their beloved bishop Athanasius, who was radically anti-Arian. At Constantius' death in 361, the citizens of Alexandria rose up and murdered the usurping bishop.[40]

The doctrinal breakthrough came when Athanasius began to talk with the theologians of Asia Minor—especially Basil of Caesarea (c. 330-379), his younger brother Gregory of Nyssa (c. 335-395) and their close friend Gregory of Nazianzus (c. 330-390)—who were respected by a large number of anti-Arian bishops of the East.[41] It was these theologians of Asia Minor, principally Cappadocians, who were able to bring two kinds of theological language back together. Theologians of the previous centuries had spoken of the redeemer in scriptural terms that emphasized his obedience to God's will. They had also described him as divine by nature. The Arian controversy had broken this theological language into two camps—Nicene supporters who emphasized Christ's divinity by nature and Arians who emphasized Christ's willing obedience. The Cappadocians were able to use both ontological and volitional language in such a way as to satisfy the wider East's desire for a redeemer both divine by nature and obedient to his Father's will.[42]

The Cappadocians also effected a major advance in the doctrine of the Trinity, building on the work of the anti-Arian Athanasius: Earlier thinkers had located the point of mediation between God and the world in the doctrine of the preexistent Logos (Word) of God, which they identified with the preexistent Christ (cf. John 1:1-3). But Athanasius in his numerous writings had laid stress on the incarnation of the very Word of God as the meeting point between God and creatures. The Cappadocians more clearly shifted that point of mediation to the incarnate (that is, the divine made flesh) Son[43] (cf. John 1:14), thus producing a connection between God and the world which focused attention on salvation rather than on cosmology. This new focus on the incarnation and away from the preexistent Logos took Christian theology into a distinctive arena where neither pagan philosophers nor philosophically inclined Jews could participate.

The doctrine of the Trinity

Basil's work stressed the essential divinity of the Holy Spirit;[44] he thus completed Christian thinking about the doctrine of the Trinity, and helped to pave the way for the Council of Constantinople in 381 C.E. This council produced a creed affirming the essential natural unity of Father and Son, applying the term *homoousios* (of the same substance) to the Son, while at the same time speaking of the Spirit's "proceeding" from the Father.[45]

The importance of the exegesis of Scripture, especially the New Testament, in the Arian controversy invites a brief comment on the canon of the New Testament. The term "canon" (measure, rule) refers to those books of the New Testament which are authoritative as Scripture for Christians. Such canonical books were not the only beneficial, or even "inspired" writings which could be employed by Christians for devotional or ecclesiastical purposes, but they were the books by which the inspiration and orthodoxy of other writings were to be "measured," or judged.

The canon of the New Testament

The last generation of Protestant scholars (especially) maintained that the canon of the New Testament was largely identified by the

LEAVES OF THE CODEX SINAITICUS. Discovered in the last century in St. Catherine's Monastery at the foot of Mt. Sinai, the Codex Sinaiticus is a fourth-century C.E. copy of the Septuagint, the earliest translation of the Hebrew Scriptures—from Hebrew into Greek. It is written in an uncial script, a curved form of capital letters.

A PAGE FROM CODEX VATICANUS B. This copy of the Septuagint has been in the Vatican since before the 15th century C.E. It probably dates to the fourth century. Like the other two famous early copies of the Septuagint (Codex Sinaiticus and Codex Alexandrinus), it is written on vellum. All three have erasures, alterations, interlinear markings and marginal notes.

beginning of the third century C.E.[46] That contention was based primarily on a misdating of a famous list of New Testament books (called the Canon Muratori) to the end of the second century, instead of to the late fourth century where it properly belongs.[47] Thus, although "Paul" and the Gospels plus some other books of our present New Testament had long been accepted as canonical, it was not until the fourth century that a Christian writer gave us a list of New Testament books that exactly matches ours. The list is contained in Athanasius of Alexandria's Easter Letter of 367 C.E.[48] By the early fifth century, the Council of Carthage (419) adopted the list of New Testament books used by the West.[49]

The great theologians who participated in the councils of the fourth century were functionaries of a Christian Church whose social composition and obligations had been transformed along the lines of the wider society. If one could characterize this transition in a single line, it would follow Ramsay MacMullan's dictum about the later empire: "Fewer have more."[50] In the closing years of the third century a wave of prosperity had settled on selected provinces of the eastern Mediterranean—especially Egypt, Syria and Palestine.[51] The new prosperity was accompanied by the rise of a class of people determined to garner this new wealth for themselves and their families and to wield for their own benefit the power that flowed from this wealth. Fourth-century texts call these people *potentiores*, the "more powerful ones." This focus on power was entirely appropriate in differentiating them from their second- and third-century forebears, who were termed *honestiores*, the "more honorable ones."[52]

Christian social life in the fourth century

We can sense their power and smell their greed in countless early Christian sermons denouncing abuses of wealth and counseling mercy for the poor. John Chrysostom (354-407), priest of Antioch—and later, bishop of Constantinople—at the end of the fourth century, for example, repeatedly warns against the risks of attachment to money and power:

> "He who loves money harbors countless suspicions of others, and there are many who are ready to accuse him of wrong-doing, many who envy, slander, and plot against him because they have been wronged. . . . Moreover even those more power-ful than he, because they are resentful and indignant at his treatment of inferiors, yet envious of him too, are likewise hos-tile and hate him."[53]

Thus the *potentiores* called forth Christian invective and also evoked one of the most characteristic fourth-century sins and fears—*envy*.[54] Envy was aroused—and wallowed in—by this class particularly because of its determination to enjoy wealth and power publicly at the expense, and to the detriment, of the wider community.[55] Nowhere is the *potentior* class' ostentation more apparent than in the private "palaces" they built in towns and cities. Their large houses ramble across whole quarters of a city, encroaching on both neighbors' and public space, significantly and contemptuously changing plans of quarters and even streets.

The private houses of Ostia, seaport of Rome, spread out across former apartment houses, reusing earlier walls.[56] The House of the Hunt at Bulla Regia in North Africa, completed before 350 C.E., covered several lots from an earlier period. Its walls moved out toward the public street when a repaving operation was underway, apparently with the connivance of local officials.[57] The house contained a basilica (or reception hall) where the *dominus* (or lord) received the homage of dependents and clients.[58] Such homage paid to the great landowners is depicted in the House of Julius mosaic from Carthage, in which tenants bring first fruits of the land to the *potentiores* who own the large rural estates. Houses ten times larger than the *insulae* (or blocks) of the central city were built in the North African town of Timgad.[59] Frequently, the great urban house owners would take over portions of the public street, squeezing down traffic patterns.

When the *potentiores* left home, they took symbols of their importance with them in the very clothes and ornamentation they wore. The plain toga of the earlier empire gave way to long tunics of fine linen with banded insignias of rank or to gaily colored silk robes.[60] When some of these people converted to Christianity they may have changed the patterns of their clothing, but not the quality. Wealthy Christians sometimes had depictions from the life of Christ or the Gospels woven into their tunics. The dour fourth-century bishop Asterius of Amaseia in Turkey dryly quipped: "When they come out in public dressed in this fashion, they appear like painted walls to those they meet."[61]

To light their way when they went out at night, they carried clay lanterns that held ceramic lamps with molded figures of praying saints or other cult figures.[62] By the fifth century, their fine tableware was decorated with stamped representations of crosses and saints, churned out in large quantities by pottery factories in Carthage and Asia Minor.[63] Even when the *potentiores* came to church, they got the front seats in the basilica. The rest of the congregation tended to arrange itself by class, with the poor toward the rear.[64] Those who had run afoul of Church law, the penitents, were in a special section at the very rear.[65]

On the other side of this great social watershed lay the *tenuiores*—the millions of ordinary citizens, the urban and rural poor, whose numbers and desperation begin to blur even so firm a Roman boundary as the one between slave and free.[66] By the end of the fourth century, the plight of the poor had worsened to the point where contemporary and later Christians revived an old classical and biblical distinction between the "indigent" poor and the "improvable" poor,[67] so that Christian largess could be properly distributed where it would do the most good. The bishops of the Church undertook the care of the lifelong helpless or "indigent" poor. Just as slaves and free tended to merge within the class of *tenuiores*, small rural landholders tended to be squeezed out by high taxes and wealthy neighbors, further swelling the ranks of the poor.[68] The true state of rural life in the fourth century is often difficult to gauge because of the paucity of inscriptions, and the picture varies from province to province. The small landowners of Syria tended to hold on well,[69] but those in Palestine rapidly lost ground, were bought out or simply fled their holdings after the middle of the fourth century.[70]

Rise of the holy ones and the monastic movement

Such a vast redistribution of wealth and power in the social order had its correlates in the spiritual realm. Here too "fewer have more" power.[71] By the fourth century, religious leaders emerged whose claim to special intimacy with the divine buttressed their gift of special spiritual powers which they wielded on behalf of the divine. Constantine was one of those new fourth century "friends of God." The increasing importance of the Christian bishops, as we have already seen in the councils of the Church, was also part of this general movement toward identifying *spiritual potentiores* who could mediate between heaven and earth and, especially, between human neighbors and groups caught in the morass of secular conflict.[72]

The bishops came to be regarded as the special protectors of the poor in the fourth century. In addition, an entirely new group of Christian spiritual *potentiores* arose who were themselves imitators of the poor: the Christian monks.

The origins of the monastic movement are shrouded in obscurity. In the closing decades of the third century a new kind of ascetic hero and heroine appeared in the deserts of Egypt. The first name associated with this new practice of departing the local congregations in towns and villages for the solitary life of prayer and fasting in the desert is St. Antony (c. 270-356 C.E.). But Antony had predecessors inasmuch as he learned this way of life from a long-practicing ascetic in a neighboring village.[73] Antony was a *monachos*, a solitary, or monk. The earliest appearance of the term in this sense occurs in an early fourth-century papyrus from Egypt, in which an anonymous monk is making peace between contend-

ST. GEORGE MONASTERY. Clinging to the cliffs overlooking the ravine of Wadi Qelt, this monastery in the Judean hills between Jerusalem and Jericho is close to the traditional sites of Elijah's wilderness sojourn (1 Kings 17: 1-8) and Jesus' temptations. (Matthew 4:1-11). The current monastery dates only to 1880, but is on the site of a laura—a worship center for anchorites—built by the early hermit St. George of Coziba in the late sixth century, destroyed in 614 and rebuilt by the Crusaders in the 12th century.

ing neighbors.[74] That power to reconcile contending parties, to resolve complicated political and theological disputes, to predict the future and to wield other powers ascribed to Christian solitaries depended on the degree to which ascetics had cut all social bonds with the community and had "died" to themselves that they might live only to God.

Thus Antony moved by stages deeper and deeper into the desert where he could carry on warfare with the demons and emerge victorious in virtue. Throughout the fourth century, monks filled the Egyptian and Syrian deserts—and crowds of townspeople followed them to seek their spiritual help and intercession with God.[75]

The hermit-figure, surrounded, often unwillingly, by his entourage, reflects a deep Roman commitment to life in the human community. The solitaries could not completely shake this off. A former soldier named Pachomius, converted by the kindness of Christian villagers, ultimately founded a *community* of monks in the Thebaid (Upper Egypt), south of Antony's hermitage. An angel appeared to Pachomius while he was still a solitary and told him, according to a fifth-century account, that he had "done well those things which pertain to your own affairs" but urged him on to found a community of monks.[76] This he did. Each monk had his own cell, but the monks were housed together behind a wall with a gatekeeper, assembling for the saying of a few psalms.

This communal (cenobitic) style of monasticism was the type that many Christian aristocrats preferred, especially in provinces like Cappadocia in Turkey. There the Cappadocian fathers (Basil of Caesarea, Gregory of Nyssa and Gregory of Nazianzus) would practice "withdrawal" from the world into a small community gathered on their rural estates. The old Mediterranean love of one's friends was wedded with a Christian principle. As Basil of Caesarea, whom we have already met in discussions on the Trinity, put it: "If you always live alone, whose feet will you wash?"[77] While the solitary remained the highest ideal for many Christians of the East, communal asceticism tended to lure educated or wealthy Christians.

Such asceticism called the rich to a life of poverty. The greatest miracle in that age of "getting and spending" was the presence of thousands of ascetic "voluntary poor," who simply withdrew from public and family life and gave their money to the poor. Such a stunning *anachoresis* (withdrawal)[78] from wealth allowed a special freedom to aristocrats, and, above all, to aristocratic women. Women like the patrician Melania the Elder could exert enormous power and influence *as a woman*, uncontrolled by the otherwise obligatory male guardian of patriarchal society:

"A woman of more elevated rank, she loftily cast herself down to a humble way of life, so that as a strong member of the weak sex she might censure indolent men, so that as a rich person appropriating poverty, and as a noble person adopting humility, she might confound people of both sexes."[79]

Among these holy persons were not only prominent women but also the first prominent black ascetic, the great St. Moses, whose sayings are preserved among the *Sayings of the Desert Fathers*.[80]

On Constantine's death, the empire was again divided into East and West. Although the West was linked in many ways to Constantinople, it was basically quite independent of the East—and far less prosperous. While wars in the western half of the empire between factions backing usurping emperors in 350-353 and 383-387 disrupted daily life,[81] on the whole the pattern of villa life continued, even evincing some prosperity, especially in Britain and the region of Trier,[82] though trade between the continent and the eastern Mediterranean was generally down in the late fourth

The West in the age of Augustine

century.[83] The major factor in the West's beginning to go its own way was the presence on its frontiers of the Germanic barbarian tribes seeking entry into the western provinces.

In the second century, the barbarian was seen as a noble figure. Unspoiled and uncorrupted by civilization, the barbarian was considered "wise," the possessor of a certain "natural" wisdom. Second-century Christian apologists often describe their own Christian sentiments as "the philosophy of the barbarians."[84] By the fourth century, however, the barbarian had become a threat to civilization. Late-antiquity texts refer to such a one as a "wild beast."[85] The most notable of late-antiquity barbarians, the Visigoths, were converted to a heretical, Arian, brand of Christianity sometime around 382-395.[86] Now twice damned—both as barbarians and as heretics—they migrated from their temporary home in Dacia (Romania) to Italy. In 410 C.E. they sacked the city of Rome. Although it had long since ceased to be the imperial capital of the West (the capital was at Ravenna, where the marshes of the city protected it from the barbarians), the sack of Rome was, nevertheless, an enormous blow to Christians of the West. In the works of the two greatest Eastern church historians, Socrates Scholasticus and Sozomen only a brief paragraph or two is devoted to the sack of Rome;[87] but St. Augustine's *City of God* consists of 22 books occasioned by the destruction of Rome at the hands of the Visigoths.

The Visigoths continued on their western migration, finally settling in Spain and establishing a kingdom there. But the disruptions caused by the migrations of a number of such tribes on numerous frontiers isolated Gaul (France) and brought an end to the Roman cities of eastern Britain, who threw off Roman control between 408 to 410 C.E. in despair of receiving help from the empire. The Britons themselves succumbed to the invasion of the Saxons in 428.[88] In 596, the pope sent a number of missionaries, including one Augustine to Britain, which helped ensure that medieval Britain would not only be Christian, but Roman-rite. Similar contacts were maintained with Gaul.

Augustine of Hippo In the closing decades of the fourth century, North Africa was also rapidly Christianized. In 354 Aurelius Augustinus (St. Augustine) was born into the crossfire between Christianity and paganism. Augustine's mother, Monica, was a devout and relentless Christian; his father, Patricius, a genial pagan. We know a great deal about Augustine's home life, education and early career from his *Confessions*, written between 397 and 401. By that time he had become the middle-aged bishop of Hippo Regius (modern Bonê in Algeria), where he served until his death in 430 C.E.[89]

Augustine's heart was a battleground for his parents until, in 387, he converted to Christianity. Both parents agreed, however, that he should have the best education possible. As a professor of rhetoric (speech and literature), he eventually found himself in the imperial capital of Milan. It was a fateful move for the young man, for there he encountered the preaching of Bishop Ambrose of Milan. The mid-life Augustine would trace God's providential hand in all this:

> "All unknowing, I was led to him by you, so that through him I might be led, while fully knowing it, to you [God]."[90]

As he would later tell the story, Augustine spent his first three decades running for the prizes of honor and glory and from his mother's faith and her God. Neither the low literary style of the Christian Scriptures nor Christianity's high moral claims on his sexuality interested him.[91] Influenced by the high standards of the ascetic movement, Christians of Augustine's circle thought of the conversion to Christianity as a simultaneous conversion to the most rigorous kind of asceticism—namely, sexual continence. A man both as warm and as sexually active as Augustine could not bear to walk such a celibate path.

As a young searcher after truth, Augustine had fallen in with the Manichaeans, an underground pagan sect favored by a powerful circle of Western aristocrats. Attracted by the promise of scientific knowledge, he remained a Manichaean long after his disappointment with its doctrine because of the boost to his career that its aristocratic connections provided.[92] Ambrose of Milan's preaching steadied Augustine's resolve to leave the Manichaeans and started him on his odyssey toward an intellectual Christianity heavily tinged with late Platonism.[93] It was, as for so many people of his day, a simultaneous adult conversion to sexual continence.

Returning to his native North Africa after his mother's death, Augustine became a priest and then bishop of the large city of Hippo Regius. A changed man, the Augustine of the *Confessions* was on the verge of making most of the great intellectual discoveries of his life, especially those concerning the nature of grace in Christian life.

As a late convert to Christianity, he hoped to make up for lost time and to achieve—through study, prayer and contemplation—that vision of God reserved to those perfected in grace. By the time of the *Confessions*, he realized that perfection in this bodily life remains an impossibility.[94] The middle-aged bishop, bruised in the conflict-ridden world of pastoral ministry, deepened in his understanding of the Scriptures and more aware of himself, now portrayed the Christian life as a pilgrimage, a lifelong journey that awaits the resurrection for completion and final healing. In words echoing St. Paul, who was a decisive influence, he wrote: "Yet with us it is still by faith and not yet by sight."[95]

The Donatist   Augustine needed all the faith he could muster in dealing with
heresy   his large seaport town and the surrounding countryside. Not only were the churches of North Africa filled with scores of new converts driven to the Church by imperial decrees ending paganism (Augustine called these pagan converts "ficti"-fakes),[96] the Church itself in North Africa was divided into two major wings—Catholic and Donatist. When Augustine became the Catholic bishop of Hippo Regius he inherited the leadership of only a minority of the Christian populace.[97] The more popular church was the so-called Donatist church, which traced its roots to a schism in 311 C.E. in the aftermath of the last persecution.[98] The Donatist church, which regarded itself as the "pure church," held sway in the countryside and in the towns.[99] Claiming descent from bishops who had not abandoned Christianity in the great persecutions of 303-311 C.E. and rejecting cooperation with the Roman state, especially the Christian emperors who had persecuted their founders, the Donatist "saints" formed a separatist church uncorrupted by the sinful contagion of their Catholic neighbors. They even practiced rebaptism (sometimes forcibly) upon unwary Catholics who crossed their path.

For a Catholic like Augustine, who was in the process of tracing human descent from sinful Adam, not saintly martyrs, the Donatists posed a grave theological difficulty. Augustine and his circle of Latin-speaking bishops were classicists, far removed from the rude Berber-speaking peasantry who were led by Donatists opposed to Roman values.[100] Beginning in 393, Augustine began attacking the Donatists in pamphlets, discussions and sermons.[101] By 405 he persuaded the Western emperor Honorius (395-423), whose capital was at Ravenna, to outlaw Donatism.[102] In 411 a great council was convened at Carthage where the imperial commissioner, after hearing the debates, ruled against the Donatists. A law was soon enacted prescribing severe penalties for adherence to the sect. This did little more than drive the Donatists underground[103] where, like so many of the old Roman religions,[104] Donatism survived to the Muslim conquest in the seventh century.

Augustine now turned his attention to a new controversy. A young British ascetic named Pelagius, who had been teaching the epistles of St. Paul to Christian aristocrats in Rome,[105] arrived in Hippo Regius in 411 C.E. while Augustine was attending the council on Donatism. Pelagius paid a call on Augustine, but was unable to see him.[106]

Pelagius and Augustine had heard about each other, but not favorably. When Pelagius had heard a famous passage of the *Confessions*, he had thrown a fit.[107] Augustine had there begged God to "Give what you command, and command what you will."[108] It was exactly the kind of theology that Pelagius and his party feared would undercut their belief that adults could turn to good works and break the ties with the sinful habits of the old life. To see God as the sole supplier of the power to do good works seemed to counter the moral injunctions of the New Testament and the old classical belief in the perfectibility of human nature.[109]

By 412 Augustine had moved even further along the road toward ascribing the power to do good solely to God. Death and the continuing struggle with sexuality which all Christians, even celibates, underwent, had convinced Augustine of the incurable frailty of Adam's descendants.[110]

This vast divergence on so momentous a subject exploded in 412 when Augustine fired off an anti-Pelagian tract *On the Merits and Remission of Sins and on the Baptism of Infants*, in which he championed the taint of Adam's sin in infants (1.13,68), denied that persons can fulfill the commandments (2.23), attacked the perfection of the favorite Pelagian biblical saint, Job (2.17), and reiterated his belief that none can be perfect in this life (2.2). Augustine even insisted that free will must be ascribed to the grace of God (2.7). **Hereditary sin**

Augustine had begun to discover the involuntary dimension, what Freud would call the Unconscious, in human beings. In Augustine's view there is a flaw (*vitium*) at the core of the self that sets our conscious desire to do good against our actual ability to perform the good (cf. Romans 7:21-23). This flaw inevitably results in failure to fulfill God's commandments unless God's grace intervenes and assists the self.[111]

Many people beside the Pelagians smelled something very new in this interpretation of St. Paul and its harsh new doctrine of hereditary sin. Augustine was—and continues to be—relentlessly criticized for breaking with classical Christianity on the doctrine of perfection.[112] But his continuous tracts against the Pelagians carried the day and convinced the Church that this was what it had always taught. Thus the doctrine of original sin, the obligatory baptism of all Christians and the necessity of grace for the performance of the good entered the West's theology.[113]

In the years 413 to 426, Augustine turned his attention to the problem that had set Pelagius, like so many other Christians of the day, in motion—the sack of Rome. Pagans pointed to the event as **Augustine's The City of God** proof that Rome's apostasy from the old religion had caused its fall. *The City of God* was Augustine's response. The work reflected the maturation of a thinker who encompassed the entire sweep of biblical and Roman history within his theological agenda. For Augustine, all humanity has been divided into two great "cities" or "societies"—the city of God and the human or earthly city (the city of the devil). Late in the work, Augustine gives his definition of a city, or society or people, a distinctly Christian definition:

> "[A] people is an assemblage of reasonable beings bound together by a common agreement as to the objects of their love; then, in order to discover the character of any people, we have only to observe what they love."[114]

The primary characteristic of the earthly city is its love of dominating others.[115] The primary characteristic of the city of God is its love of God and its subjugation to God's will; thus its primary virtue is humility.[116]

Here on earth the city of God shares turf with the damned and the unjust. The great Roman state, so praised by other writers for its benefits to humanity, is reduced to a utilitarian role: At its best it can only cooperate with the Church in helping humanity. The Church itself is but a mixed body of saints and sinners. But in life after the resurrection, the city of God will rise unmixed from the mists of human history that make sinner and saint unrecognizable from the outside. That great eschatological city shimmers over book 22 of *The City of God*, a holy communal pyramid drawing Christians to the end of history:

> "But, now, who can imagine, let alone describe, the ranks upon ranks of rewarded saints, to be graded, undoubtedly according to their variously merited honor and glory. Yet there will be no envy of the lower for the higher, as there is no envy of angel for archangel—for this is one of the great blessednesses of this blessed city. The less rewarded will be linked in perfect peace with the more highly favored, but lower could no more long for higher than a finger . . . could want to be an eye. The less endowed will have the high endowment of longing for nothing loftier than their lower gifts."[117]

In that passage Augustine foresees the healing of so many of Rome's political problems—the demise of the struggle for glory and honor, two of the most crucial concepts in the Roman political vocabulary,[118] and the healing of that most characteristic sin of late antiquity—envy.[119]

The passage also highlights the hierarchical thinking that subjugates individual interests to a community and a community to a single head—whether bishop, pope or abbot. When St. Benedict, the founder of the Benedictine monastic order, wrote his *Rule* sometime in the 530s in Italy, he embodied in the Western monastic system the ranking of the community in humble submission to a single ruler, the abbot. It is through such a monastic community on earth, living in love by submission to the *Rule*, that monks will arrive at that greatest of late antiquity Christian paradoxes: the height of humility.[120]

Book 22 of *The City of God* also heralds the triumph of the cult of the saints. Their healings and other miraculous events testify to that greatest of miracles, the resurrection (the sheer number of these miracles almost swamps the book). These miracles make common cause with the rise of elaborate ceremonies in the West venerating local saints and describing the benefits derived from such observance at their shrines.[121]

As Augustine lay dying in August of 430, Hippo Regius was being besieged by Vandal barbarians. Africa was thereafter detached from the empire for the next 100 years.

The West at the end of antiquity

Christians in the old imperial city of Rome, left to find their own way with the new barbarians, turned to the bishops of Rome as their guides and protectors. The church at Rome had long enjoyed a unique position in the West. It was the only church in the West that could claim apostolic foundation (e.g., St. Peter) and that was located in the imperial capital. The bishop of Rome had, by the third century, used the title "pope" (*pappa*), but bishops of the major cities of the empire (e.g., Carthage, Antioch, Alexandria) were also so styled. During the Arian controversy (318-381), various bishops of Rome had served as the theological voice of the West; but in the Donatist controversy the bishop of Rome had played an important role as the final ecclesiastical court of appeal for the West. As imperial power waned in the fifth century, a new political sovereignty, buttressed by a heightened religiosity, emerges in the Roman episcopate.

During the reign of Pope Leo I (440-461), we see the shape of the new papacy. The power and voice of the great apostolic martyr Peter, who watches over people everywhere, but especially over those who hold his see, energized Leo's papacy.[122] Over a century later, Pope Gregory the Great (590-604) put the matter charmingly. Telling the story of an appearance of St. Peter to a deacon of a church in Palestrina, Gregory says:

> "With this vision, the blessed Apostle wished to assure his followers that he was watching over them constantly and would always see to it that what they did out of veneration for him would be repaid with an eternal reward."[123]

ALINARI/ART RESOURCE, NEW YORK

TOMB OF THEODORIC. King of the Ostrogoths, Theodoric (c. 475-526 C.E.) invaded Italy in 489, defeating the barbarian ruler Odoacer and leading to a long period of prosperity. Although a follower of the Arian sect, Theodoric established a policy of religious tolerance. When he established his capital at Ravenna, he built several structures famous for their mosaics, including St. Apollinare Nuovo and the Arian Baptistery (see pp. 292 and 300). His tomb, also in Ravenna, has a monolithic dome 36 feet in diameter.

The Western popes' stress on Petrine authority gave further muscle to their arguments with the bishops of Constantinople. Tensions between Western and Eastern Christians increased. When Pope Leo wrote his famous *Tome to Flavian* (see below, p. 294) to help clarify an Eastern Christological controversy, the bishops at the Council of Chalcedon in 451 C.E. accepted it as orthodox, but not solely because it came from Peter's successor; rather because "it *agrees* with the confession of the great Peter and is a common pillar against those who think wrongly"[124] (italics added).

Western bishops struggled to maintain their authority in the cities, but the major event in the eventual Christian continuity of the West was the conversion of the Franks to "orthodox" rather than Arian Christianity at the end of the fifth or beginning of the sixth century.[125] Especially in Gaul (France), the orthodox bishops were members of the old Roman aristocracy and their followers were devoutly Catholic (= Nicene). To be ruled not only by barbarians, but heretical Arian barbarians was untenable politically. The conversion of the Franks helped ease the difficulty of Arian (heretical) barbarians ruling a Catholic populace. Traces of the unseemly hatred of the Catholics for such Arian rulers and for the Jews, who made common cause with them, appear in the sixth century *Life of St. Caesarius of Arles*.[126]

While the cities declined and governments shifted, the building of churches continued as other structures were falling into ruins. In Rome, for example, the beautiful Church of Santa Maria Maggiore was built in the fifth century with a triumphal arch adorned with mosaics proclaiming the divinity of Christ in accordance with the doctrine adopted at the Synod of Ephesus in 431.[127] In the first quarter of the same century, the apse of the *titulus* (title, or land-deed) church in Rome, Santa Pudenziana, was outfitted with a polychrome mosaic of Christ seated on a throne, dressed as an emperor, between representations of the 12 apostles dressed as senators.[128] The panoply of imperial imagery and ceremony was passing from the old pagan city of Rome to the Rome of the Christian Church.[129] In the splendid group of monuments found at Ravenna, the last Roman imperial capital of the West, we can see the glitter of this new age: The mausoleum of Empress Galla Placidia (d. 450 C.E.), built in the shape of a cross, was both a shrine to the martyr Saint Lawrence and an imperial tomb.[130] The entire upper zone is covered with shimmering mosaics, pointing toward that upper world that saints achieved and emperors aspired to.[131]

In 476, the last Roman emperor, ironically named Romulus, was pensioned off by Odoacer, the Visigoth master of the palace. To Renaissance scholars, this marked a great tragedy, for to them it symbolized the end of Rome. In fact, the barbarian rulers carried on many of the old imperial traditions, adapted to the new Christian world. When the Ostrogoth king Theodoric (493-526) died, he was buried at Ravenna in a round tomb, just as earlier Roman emperors had been.[132]

The Catholics also built a new baptistery at Ravenna when the town passed to the Eastern empire after 540 C.E. Because Arians did not baptize in the name of the Trinity,[133] the Arian baptistery would not suffice for the Catholics of the sixth century, and it was transformed into an oratory, or chapel.[134] A similar Catholic transformation occurred with the basilica of San Apollinare Nuovo, built as Theodoric's palace church; the mosaics of Theodoric and his court were covered up and replaced with mosaic curtains; a

ERICH LESSING ©

JUSTINIAN. This mosaic from the sixth-century basilica of St. Apollinare in Classe in Ravenna depicts the emperor Justinian (c. 527-565 C.E.) who, along with his wife Theodora, presided over a brilliant period of the Late Roman empire. In addition to significant military victories, he was responsible for the Code of Justinian, a major codification of Roman law, for the construction of the Hagia Sofia in Constantinople and of the Nea in Jerusalem (see pp. 296 and 298).

procession of virgins and saints leading to Christ and Mary enthroned as Byzantine rulers was created above the side aisles of the nave.[135]

The apex of mosaic art in Ravenna is the beautiful Byzantine Church of San Vitale. In a mosaic of extraordinary quality, the great Byzantine emperor Justinian (527-565) and his empress

Theodora stare out at the high altar in regal and liturgical atten-
tiveness from this last great work of imperial Western antiquity.[136]

The triumphant formulation of the doctrine of the Trinity by Basil ***The East***
and his party at the Council of Constantinople (381 C.E.) left a ***to the***
large problem unresolved: How does one describe the incarnation ***Council of***
of Jesus Christ if the historical Jesus shares in the eternal deity of ***Chalcedon:***
God? One solution was proposed by Apollinaris of Laodicea, who ***451 C.E.***
substituted the Word of God (the Logos) for the human mind of
Jesus. Fearful that if the Savior had a human mind he would be
unable to resist the power of sinful flesh, Apollinaris substituted
the unconquerable Logos to ensure Christ's victory over sin.[137]
Apollinaris was condemned at the Council of Constantinople on
the mere say-so of Basil of Caesarea.[138] But this condemnation did
not deal with a whole school of Christological thinking that emphasized Christ's single divine nature even after the incarnation.
That school included the great bishops of Alexandria.

The doctrinal situation was complicated by the presence of an
opposing school of thought represented by another great apostolic see, Antioch.[139] If the Alexandrians tended to emphasize the
monophysite (one nature) dimensions of the incarnation, the
Antiochenes stressed the dual nature of Christ—both divine and
human—and the voluntary (rather than natural or divinely brought
about) character of Jesus' work. Moreover, the Antiochenes tended
toward a more contextual and historical style of biblical exegesis,
which made much of the human temptation and sufferings of
Christ.[140] They bitterly opposed the Monophysite teachings of the
Alexandrians. In a later attempt to win over the Monophysites, the
emperor Justinian had the great Antiochene exegete Theodore of
Mopsuestia posthumously condemned in the Three Chapters Edict
(553/54 C.E.).[141]

In 428, Theodore's pupil, Nestorius, became bishop of Constanti- ***The***
nople. Nestorius criticized the use of the term *theotokos* (mother of ***Nestorian***
God) as applied to Mary. "I cannot term him God who was two ***heresy***
and three months old," said Nestorius.[142]

Nestorius' attempt to placate his enemies by calling Mary
christotokos, the "mother of Christ," fell on deaf ears. The dynamic
and irascible bishop Cyril of Alexandria (412-444) immediately
took exception to Nestorius' new formulation. At the heart of Cyril's
theology was the birth of the divine Word:

> "We do not say that the flesh was changed into the nature of
> Godhead, nor that the ineffable nature of the Word of God was
> transformed into the nature of flesh, for he is unchangeable
> and unalterable, always remaining the same according to the

Scriptures. But when seen as a babe and wrapped in swaddling clothes, even when still in the bosom of the Virgin who bore him, he filled all creation as God, and was enthroned with him who begot him."[143]

Despite the fact that the best historian of the century, Socrates Scholasticus, did not consider Nestorius' views heretical,[144] his work was condemned by the Synod of Ephesus (431) and the Council of Chalcedon (451); Cyril's position was approved by both.

Nestorius' condemnation and subsequent exile provided only a momentary breathing spell in a long and complicated advance toward the formation of Christian dogma regarding the person of the incarnate Christ. The period from Ephesus to Chalcedon is checkered with theologians and councils attempting to settle the issue.[145] In 451 a great council was assembled at Chalcedon to resolve the matter. The emperors Marcian and Pulcheria instructed the fearful bishops to write a creed that would definitively end the controversy.[146] We do not have a copy of the first draft that the bishops produced,[147] but their final *Definition of Faith* justified all their fears. Far from producing unity in the Church, the final *Definition* offended theologians of both the Antiochene and the Alexandrian schools. The creed established the duality of Christ's unmixed and unconfused natures—the presence of both the divine and human in the redeemer. The key phrase—"in Two Natures" that underscored this was borrowed, not from the then-current Eastern discussion, but from the *Tome to Flavian* of Pope Leo of Rome written in 449 to Flavian, bishop of Constantinople. That Christ was "acknowledged in Two Natures," seemed a sellout of the Antiochene or Nestorian position to the Monophysites. On the other hand, the connection of the term *theotokos* with Christ's humanity, rather than his deity, infuriated the Antiochenes as a sellout to the Alexandrians.[148]

The bishops also reiterated Canon 3 of the Council of Constantinople, which raised Constantinople to primacy in the East[149] over apostolic sees like Alexandria and Antioch. This further deepened the schisms within the Church. Jerusalem was raised to the fifth patriarchate of the Eastern Church.[150]

The Monophysite Christians then split off from the Church to go their own way in the East.[151] Later attempts by the emperor Justinian to win them back failed.[152] A hundred years after Chalcedon, dozens of Monophysite bishops were consecrated as a new church formed across the East from Asia Minor to Mesopotamia.[153] Nestorian Christians also remained outside the Chalcedonian settlement. Traces of their churches and monuments may be seen all the way east to China.[154]

GARO NALBANDIAN

ANASTASIS OF THE CHURCH OF THE HOLY SEPULCHRE. Supposedly the site of Jesus' burial and resurrection (*anastasis* means
"raising up" in Greek), this ornate construction in the Church of the
Holy Sepulchre in Jerusalem includes remains of the original fourth-
century structure over the tomb.

***Church and
society in the
later Eastern
empire to the
Islamic
conquest***

The early part of the fifth century was a golden time of church
construction in the East, especially in Palestine. The empress
Eudocia, following the earlier example of Constantine and his family, inaugurated a great building program in Jerusalem.[155] That
program had a darker side–the claiming of Mt. Zion, abandoned
since the second century, as Christian territory. The fight was on
to determine whether Jerusalem was to be a Christian or a Jewish
city.[156]

Recent studies of legislation against the Jews indicate a more
lenient attitude toward Jews in the Roman empire than had been
previously thought from a reading of the Church Fathers alone.[157]

HAGIA SOPHIA IN ISTANBUL. The first basilica on this site was built in 360 C.E., soon after Constantine the Great (306-337 C.E.) made the city on the Bosphorus his capitol, calling it Constantinople. After the basilica was destroyed by fire in 532, it was rebuilt by the emperor Justinian and consecrated in 537. Its central dome rises 180 feet and is over 100 feet in diameter. The Ottoman Turks, after capturing Constantinople in 1453, converted the church into a mosque, adding the minarets. Since 1935, it has been a museum.

Yet the Jews certainly experienced diminished civil rights, such as the prohibition of intermarriage between Jews and Christians,[158] a ban on building new synagogues (never enforced) and the elimination of the Jewish patriarchate in 425 C.E. (see pp. 247-248).[159] Especially nasty rhetoric comes from Christian pens in the first half of the fifth century concerning Jewish/Christian relations in Syria, Constantinople, Crete and Alexandria.[160]

In early fifth-century Antioch, John Chrysostom's sermons against the Jews focused on Christians in Antioch who were observing the Jewish law and tying Christianity to Sabbath attendance at synagogues and to other Jewish observances, such as ritual bathing.[161] As Robert Wilken has shown, Chrysostom's rhetoric against Jewish practices by Christians was tied to the issue of which religion—Judaism or Christianity—was the true religion: "If the Jewish rites are holy and venerable, our way of life must be false."[162]

The attempt of the apostate emperor Julian (361-363) to rebuild the Temple at Jerusalem, cut short by his early death, had

DAVID HARRIS

MADABA MAP OF JERUSALEM. This sixth-century Byzantine mosaic map found in 1884 in a church in Madaba, Jordan, shows prominent features of Byzantine Jerusalem including the Cardo, the broad column-lined street running horizontally through the center of the oval map. The large domed structure upside down at the bottom center of the map represents the Church of the Holy Sepulchre. The city's main gate, at left, opens into a plaza with a column in the center. The Nea church (see p. 298) opens onto the Cardo on the right.

affected Christian thinking deeply. The fact that the Temple was in ruins had been used by Christian apologists for centuries to prove that the old Israel was disinherited and Israel's mantle had passed to the Christian Church. By the early fifth century, as the empire moved toward the suppression of all other religions besides Judaism and Christianity, Christian writers had determined to lay final claim to Israel's inheritance.

This desire to deny Judaism's claim to the Old Testament and to the land of the Bible lies behind the huge number of polemical and outrageously negative references to Jews and Judaism in Bishop Cyril of Alexandria's writings (412-444 B.C.).[163] Cyril's virulent anti-Semitism, and the anti-Judaism of Christian theologians of his day, seems to have been inflamed by fears of Judaism's legitimate claim to be the continuation of the biblical Israel.

NEA VAULTED FOUNDATIONS. The emperor Justinian built the large, impressive Nea (New) church and an adjoining hospice in Jerusalem in the early sixth century. One of the identifiable features on the Madaba map of Jerusalem (see p. 297), the Nea church had massive vaulted foundations to support the structure on the sloping terrain of the southern edge of the Byzantine city.

AN INSCRIPTION (below) found on a support pier of the Nea church, firmly dating it to 540 A.D., reads, "And this is the work which our most pious Emperor Flavius Justinianus carried out with munificence, under the care and devotion of the most holy Constantinus, Priest and Hegumen [a head of a monastery] in the thirteenth year of the indiction."

NAHMAN AVIGAD

ZEV RADOVAN

The vibrant Jewish synagogue life of the fourth and fifth centuries, both in Israel[164] and in Diaspora cities like Alexandria, Antioch and Apamea (in Syria),[165] testifies to the prosperity of late Judaism.

The seriousness with which Christian authors and Christian emperors regarded Judaism also reflects the powerful place held by Jews in the fear/esteem of this rapidly developing Christian empire.

Yet, for all the respect, points of genuine contact and positive interchange between Christians and Jews do seem to have diminished in the Byzantine period. For example, in earlier centuries, Jews and Christians had engaged in dialogue on scriptural texts and various exegetical points common to the two faiths. By the fifth century Jews and Christians followed parallel, but not often intersecting, paths in their exegesis. Newer studies indicate that Christian knowledge of the rabbis and the Jewish world in this period was less than previously supposed, although a great deal of work still needs to be done in this area before any firm conclusions are drawn.[166]

In the Holy Land itself, pagans were persecuted—and taken over—far more than Jews. For example, Emperor Justin I (518-527 C.E.) transformed the temple of Hadrian at Caesarea into a church,[167] his nephew and successor Justinian promoted the Christian academy at Gaza and at the same time prohibited (in 529 C.E.) anyone who was not a Christian from teaching classical philosophy.[168] Nevertheless, Jews living in the Holy Land also felt "crowded" by a new Christian populace.

Pilgrimage and growing Christian presence in the Holy Land

Christian pilgrimage to the Holy Land steadily grew during the fourth and fifth centuries. Numerous Western Christians like Jerome, the translator of the Bible into Latin, came to settle there.[169] The Negev was Christianized at a time when there was a great burst in agricultural technology that made this possible. Entire Christian cities, festooned with multiple churches, sprang up.[170] These cities served the needs both of the new Christian empire and the needs of Christian pilgrims en route to and from Jerusalem.

Even traditional Jewish "turf," such as the Galilee, tended to be encroached on by Christians in the Byzantine period. From a fourth-century narrative, we learn of the attempt of Count Joseph of Tiberias, a converted Jew, to place church buildings in Sepphoris, Tiberias, Nazareth and Capernaum; this proved to be merely a straw in the wind.[171] By the mid-fifth century, the city of Sepphoris (Diocaesarea), a traditional Jewish stronghold, had a Christian bishop in attendance at the Council of Chalcedon.[172] A church shrine was raised over the House of St. Peter in Capernaum. A basilica was placed over the site of the Annunciation at Nazareth.[173]

ZEV RADOVAN

CROSS-SHAPED BAPTISTERY. This baptistery next to an early Byzantine church at Subeita (Shivta) in the central Negev is made from a single block of stone. Steps are carved in the east and west arms of the cross. The initiate descended into the water by one set of steps and "died to sin," then emerged by the other set of steps, symbolizing a new life.

Even at Hebron, a Jewish settlement area in the Byzantine period,[174] a Christian church was erected.[175] Around the Sea of Galilee, pilgrimage churches arose to serve Christians who traveled to venerate Christ's miracles at places like Tabgha and Kursi.[176]

The invention of the pendative (a triangularly shaped part of a sphere placed at the cornering of walls) by architects of Justinian's

HERSHEL SHANKS

THE CARDO. The principal street of Roman and Byzantine Jerusalem (this part dates to the Byzantine period), the Cardo was a 40-foot-wide road running north and south flanked by covered colonnades that were 10 feet wide. Drainage channels covered by stone slabs run between the road and walkways. The emperor Hadrian built Aelia Capitolina on the site of the destroyed Jerusalem along the lines of a Roman military camp with two main streets, the Cardo and the east-west Decumannus, remains of which have not yet been found.

day enabled a round dome to be placed on a square building. This provided Byzantine ecclesiastical architecture with a new form. The round dome was pioneered in the Church of St. Irene and perfected in Hagia Sophia, both in Constantinople.[177] In Jerusalem, Justinian had a round dome placed over the basilical church at Siloam.[178]

Recent archaeological excavations in Jerusalem reveal how extensive Justinian's building program was. Literary sources had preserved references to a huge church called the Nea that Justinian had constructed in Jerusalem. The mosaic Madaba map of Jerusalem had actually depicted such a large basilical structure. The Madaba map also detailed a long, porticoed street thought to be the *cardo maximus* of Byzantine Jerusalem. Nahman Avigad's excavations in Jerusalem have exposed the few remains of the Nea Church, as well as a long stretch of the southern *cardo* with its portico for shops and stores running along the line of Jewish

Quarter Street in modern Jerusalem.[179] The Nea Church was securely identified by an inscription found in a huge vaulted cistern attributing the work to Justinian and dating its construction to 549/50 C.E.[180]

Such a huge Christian building complex in the heart of Byzantine Jerusalem indicates the degree to which the emperor at Constantinople regarded Jerusalem as a Christian city. This notion of Jerusalem as a Christian city and the Holy Land as a Christian place also had a wide following among both clergy and laity. Imperial donations to found churches in the Holy Land did leave their mark on the landscape, but the burgeoning of new churches across Palestine was overwhelmingly due to clerical and lay donors, not merely to imperial donations.[181]

Prosperous Jews of Palestine responded both passively and actively to this new Christian presence. Passively, they stopped doing some things they had practiced for centuries, such as ossuary burial (secondary reburial of desiccated bones in boxes called ossuaries, about a year after death). The Jews abandoned this practice because it had been taken over by Christians.[182] On the active side, the Jews built a beautiful new synagogue at Capernaum, dated now to about 370 C.E. This white limestone synagogue can be interpreted as a restatement of the Jewish community's solidarity in the face of Christian encroachment at the House of St. Peter, just a few yards away.[183] That Greek-speaking Jews still claimed the classical tradition for themselves, not surrendering it to Christians, can be seen in the floor of the fifth-century house of Leontius, a Jew of Beth-Shean, with its scenes from the *Odyssey* and quotation from Homer.[184]

The continuous pressure from the Christian populace and the occasional destruction of synagogues drove Palestinian Jews into the arms of their old enemies the Samaritans. Together they made common cause and rioted at Caesarea in 556 and commenced an unsuccessful revolt in 578.[185] When the Persians invaded the Eastern empire (613-619), many Jews collaborated with them in hope of deliverance from Christian oppression.[186]

By the time the Byzantine emperor recovered the Holy Land from the Persians in 628, a number of churches had been destroyed and, indeed, the city economy of the wider eastern Mediterranean region had been considerably disrupted.[187] Yet life continued as usual in most places right up to and beyond the Muslim conquests of 634-640 C.E.[188] Both churches and synagogues were built and used throughout the seventh and even the eighth centuries and beyond under Muslim rule.[189]

The end of Judeo-Christian antiquity is measured not so much by a destruction as by a disruption—of trade and allegiance. With the Islamic conquest, trade with the West ceased; people relied on local products and then turned their allegiance and purchasing power toward the East. On sites across Palestine, ceramic products from North Africa and Asia Minor[190] were replaced by local wares. Byzantine coinage gave way to transitional Latin/Arabic coins minted in Damascus.[191] A great watershed in the history of Mediterranean civilization had been crossed. From the sixth century B.C.E. to the early seventh century C.E., Palestine had traded and faced towards the West.[192] When the sun rose again over Palestine in the seventh and eighth centuries, all the people of the East–Christians, Jews, Samaritans, Muslims–faced east toward a new medieval world.

NINE

Christians and Jews in the First Six Centuries

JAMES H. CHARLESWORTH

URING THE FIRST SIX CENTURIES OF THE COMMON ERA, BOTH Christians and Jews developed a clear and formative self-definition. This self-understanding enabled Christians to explain to themselves and to others who they were and why they were that way. Exactly the same was true of Jews. For both peoples it was a slow and often costly process. Precious lives were sometimes lost; creative traditions were sometimes sacrificed.

Were all these sacrifices necessary? Did survival require them? Should only secularists today face the shocking possibility that each survives only by sacrificing some of his or her heart? The Danish Christian philosopher Søren Kierkegaard, for example, asserted that much was sacrificed in the transference from Jesus to Peter, and that all was abandoned when the erstwhile purity became contaminated with enthronement as "the Holy Roman Empire."[1]

As a Christian, I must confess that this "elevation" of Christianity as the Holy Roman Empire is in some ways less attractive than the Jewish world of thought that led to the enthronement of Moses (in *Ezekiel the Tragedian*) and Enoch (in 1 Enoch). Why did each "religion" (or better, each social unit) feel the need to eliminate some old traditions and to focus on new formulas? Why was delimiting self-definition so important? And why did Christianity and

Judaism become so different from each other? Clearly, Christianity and Judaism did not develop in isolation from one another. This new perspective will focus the present discussion (the following historical periods will not be separated into self-contained nonoverlaping categories).

The age of variety and standardization: 167 B.C.E.- 70 C.E.

In Judaism, two overarching trends can be discerned during the period from 167 B.C.E. to 70 C.E.: variety and, at the same time, standardization.

In 167 B.C.E. the desecration of the Temple by Antiochus IV Epiphanes led to the famous Maccabean revolt. Sacrifices in the Jerusalem Temple were restored in 164 B.C.E. through the majestic victories of Judas Maccabee. His exploits are still celebrated today, notably by Christians in Handel's opera and by Jews in the festival of Hanukkah.

Sometime between 152 and 140 B.C.E., however, the Zadokites, the descendants of Aaron and the legitimate high priests, were expelled from the Temple, to be superseded by the Maccabees (1 Maccabees 10-14). Many of these Zadokite priests—and perhaps others—withdrew to the wilderness of Judea and settled at what is now called Qumran. There, west of the Dead Sea, they founded a community that preserved old "apocryphal" writings, like the earliest books of Enoch and other pseudepigrapha only now being edited. It was these priests who wrote the "secular" Dead Sea Scrolls. Using the rhetoric of the ancient world, but in a unique and powerful way, they castigated the officiating priests in the Jerusalem Temple as prostitutes and fornicators.

Their writings revealed how much Jewish thought was dependent not only on ancient sacred writings, like Isaiah, but also on the creative and challenging new thoughts from other cultures, especially Persian metaphysics. For example, their hymnbook (Thanksgiving Hymns, or *Hodayot*) shows the mixing of the concepts of Eden (from the Hebrew Scriptures) and paradise (from the Old Persian *pairidaêza*). This pre-Christian hymnbook also emphasizes that salvation is possible only by God's grace (a concept once attributed to the creative genius of Paul).

The Qumran community

The Qumran community was united and led by a charismatic and prophetic man called the "Righteous Teacher." He (or his followers) claimed that all the mysteries of the prophets were disclosed to the Teacher, and to him alone.[2] Apparently a similar claim was later attributed to Jesus in the canonical Gospels (viz., Luke 4:16-22; Mark 1:22,27; Matthew 7:29; John 7:46), and even later to the Jewish sage Akiva.[3]

Adapting and mixing ideas from Jewish Scriptures and from

FRAGMENTS OF ENOCH FOUND AMONG THE DEAD SEA SCROLLS. The apocalyptic Book of Enoch is quoted in the New Testament Epistle of Jude (Jude 14-15) which was written around 100 C.E. The Enoch fragments among the Dead Sea Scrolls are in Aramaic (below). Fragments of Enoch in Greek have long been known, but the most complete text is found only in Ethiopic.

ETHIOPIC ENOCH (right).

THE ETHIOPIC BOOK OF ENOCH, MICHAEL A. KNIBB

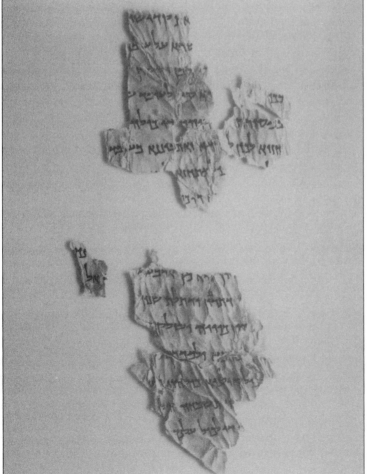

COURTESY ISRAEL ANTIQUITIES AUTHORITY

cultures to the East, the Righteous Teacher probably thought of himself as the "gardener" who was commissioned by God to plant "the shoot for the eternal planting,"[4] which was for God's glory. He or his followers developed the belief that they were living at "the end of days," and that God would soon send two messiahs, a priestly messiah and a kingly messiah. Their community was like an antechamber of heaven. The angels were present in their worship services. It was possible, they fervently believed, for a Qumran covenanter to move beyond the limitations of the human and to approximate angelic status.

The Qumran covenanters were anti-Hasmonean. That dynasty, established after the Maccabean revolt, declined distressingly. The Hasmonean king Alexander Janneus (103-76 B.C.E.) was pelted with citrons in the Temple during the feast of Tabernacles by his Jewish subjects.[5] At one point, he crucified 800 Jews and murdered their wives and children before their eyes, while he and his concubines feasted.[6]

The demise of the Hasmonean dynasty was accompanied by severe splits within Judaism: the Essenes (some of whom were responsible for the Dead Sea Scrolls), the Pharisees, and the Sadducees. Tragically, Roman forces were introduced into Palestine. In 63 B.C.E. Pompey and his troops were actually invited into Palestine because of a civil war between Jewish rivals for the throne. The Jewish hatred of Pompey is attested in the Psalms of Solomon.

In 40 B.C.E. the Romans declared Herod to be king. He murdered his way to actual enthronement in 37. He befriended Mark Antony and then Octavian (Caesar Augustus) after the great nonbattle at Actium in 31 B.C.E. When Herod died in 4 B.C.E. he had proved himself not only the greatest builder ancient Israel ever knew, but also a ruler who (by overtaxation) had enslaved and robbed many Jews, turning them from landlords into tenant farmers under heathen landlords.

Jewish factionalism and Hellenistic rhetoric

It was a time of terrible factionalism among the Jews. The authors of the Psalms of Solomon called other Jews "sinners." Pharisees and Essenes also castigated other Jews as sinners. Even before 63 B.C.E., the Jewish miracle worker from Galilee, Honi, was stoned outside Jerusalem by Jews who could not persuade him to curse the Jews they opposed.

According to the Gospels, Jesus of Nazareth called many Pharisees hypocrites and sinners. He was opposed by some leaders in the Jerusalem sacerdotal aristocracy. Some of these leading priests may well have turned Jesus over to the Romans; but it was Roman soldiers who crucified him. Sometime around 33 C.E. Stephen, a brilliant but tactless follower of Jesus from the Diaspora, was stoned by other Jews. Around 44 C.E. James the son of Zebedee was be-headed by Herod's grandson Agrippa I (Acts 12:2). James, Jesus' brother, was killed by some misguided Jews in 62.[7]

This Jewish factionalism was a reflex of the Hellenistic age. The polemics of the Hellenistic world are filled with extreme rhetoric. Dio of Prusa called the sophists "ignorant ones," "liars," and "flat-terers." Colotes, an Epicurean, branded some philosophers "pros-titutes." Romans castigated Christians for being fornicators and cannibals. Such was the rhetoric and the *topoi* of the ancient world.

This particular feature of Hellenistic life, unfortunately, was for-gotten when the Christian canon was closed. The Gospel accounts of the Pharisees as "hypocrites" were taken as reliable descrip-tions, especially since the Pharisees were the only other surviving branch of Early Judaism. At this point in history, Jesus is misrepre-sented; he is portrayed as anti-Pharisaic (yet the Christian canon indicates that many Pharisees admired him, cf. Luke 11:37, 13:31); but his death in the Gospel of John is attributed to the *Ioudaioi*, which was misinterpreted to mean "Jews" (as if there were a mono-lithic Judaism and he was not a Jew).

Only in the last few decades has it become clear that a mono-lithic Judaism did not exist before 70 C.E., and that the period from the first century to the fifth was a time in which "Judaism" and "Christianity" each developed a coherent self-definition. To attempt to reconstruct the history of Judaism and Christianity with-out warning about this age-old misrepresentation does violence to history. (It also perpetuates an atmosphere of fear that separates Jews and Christians, the twin sisters of Early Judaism, and under-mines historiography which must be practiced by Jews and Chris-tians working together, as in this book.)

While Jesus, in many sayings, felt his mission was only to the lost sheep of Israel, Peter and then Paul perceived that Jesus' Palestinian Movement had a world mission. Paul argued for aban-doning the Jewish dietary laws, rules of exclusion, the rite of cir-cumcision, and the observance of festivals. In so doing he removed most of the barriers separating Jews from Gentiles, and made it far easier to convert to the new religion. His emotional apocalyptic claims and soteriology (a theology of salvation that offered free and full forgiveness) won many converts to Christianity.

The First Jewish Revolt of 66 C.E.—which was squelched by two future emperors (Vespasian and Titus)—effectively ended in 70 C.E. with the burning of Jerusalem and the destruction of the Temple. This, in effect, marked the end of the history of ancient Israel. Large numbers of Palestinian Jews were killed or sold into slavery. Some were paraded through the Roman Forum, and then forced to build the Colosseum. Various legends relate that in the mid-60s (perhaps sometime between 62 and 66) Peter and Paul were martyred in Rome by Nero.

Before the destruction of the Temple, Jews enjoyed a rich and creative vitality. They were stimulated by all surrounding cultures, especially the Greeks, Persians, Egyptians, and Romans. The essence of Judaism, monotheism, was threatened by deifications—or better, angelifications—of Adam, Enoch, Jacob, and Moses. But angelolatry was not feared as much as idolatry, which was polemicized against by many Jewish authors.

The concept of paradise that emerged during this period (250 to 100 B.C.E.) was a mixture of Persian and Edenic (that is, Hebrew) traditions, and enriched by Platonic and related myths about the Isles of the Blessed Ones. The good life was somewhere else. The future held the answers; in the age to come God's promises would be fulfilled.

Standardization of the content and canon of Scripture

While this varied thought was developing, another phenomenon, appreciably antithetical to it, was progressing. It was the process of *standardization*. The content of Scripture was being defined. Because of Hebrew fragments of biblical books found among the Dead Sea Scrolls, we now know about some appreciably different versions of some biblical books—especially Jeremiah and 1 and 2 Samuel. Before 70 these books were standardized into the versions known today.

Standardization also progressed in the Hebrew script itself. It moved from archaic and Hasmonean forms to the Herodian form that is so similar to today's Hebrew script that children in Israel can easily read it.

Finally, like content and script, the canon of Scripture was being standardized. The number of books to be labeled "scripture" was delimited. Almost all these standardizations were settled by the first century C.E. (with the exceptions of Ben Sirach, which was eventually excluded, and Esther, which was included).

Liturgy too began to take the form known to Jews and Christians today. The Psalter was obviously the hymnbook of the Second Temple. We now have two early versions of the Aaronic blessing preserved in tiny silver scrolls from about 600 B.C.E., found in a burial cave west of the walls of Jerusalem.[8] These early versions became standardized in the priestly blessing we know from Numbers 6:24-26. This very form continues to be said by "the priest" today in synagogues and churches throughout the world.

The *Amidah* prayer (especially the 18 Benedictions said during the weekdays) took a standardized shape similar to the prayer said today in synagogues—even though later rabbis cautioned that spontaneous prayer is more desirable.[9] It is startling for many to realize that the synagogal prayers recited by Jesus and his earliest followers are said today only by devout Jews. Jesus and his followers also affirmed the widely recited credo from Deuteronomy 6:4, the *Shema*. During the pre-70 period the followers of Hillel and Jesus shared the same Scriptures and liturgies.

During this process of standardization the sacred language of the Jews moved from Hebrew only to Hebrew and Aramaic. Then for many Jews it included some Greek Scriptures (the Septuagint and the so-called Apocrypha which were composed in Greek). Finally, with rabbinic literature, the move was back to Hebrew and Aramaic. *The languages of Scripture*

The earliest Christians may have written some traditions of and about Jesus in Aramaic, but the earliest extant records are only in Greek. This remained the language for the composition of the New Testament, and many apocryphal, books. Beginning with Tertullian (c. 160-c. 220), who also wrote in Greek, the language of Rome, Latin, became the major vehicle for discussing the essence of Christianity. It was in Latin that St. Augustine (354-430) composed his famous and influential tomes.

Christian scholars in the East composed their works in Syriac, from perhaps the late first century C.E. until after the Arab conquest of the seventh century. Syriac Christianity developed alongside Jewish centers. Many brilliant Eastern Christian scholars, notably Ephraem Syrus (c. 306-363), knew and preserved early Jewish writings. In the East both Jews and Christians were free from the politics of the Roman Church. They were driven together by a sea of "paganism," and were united by shared Scriptures and a Semitic language.

Discussing the process of standardization has moved us beyond the historical period of the age of variety and standardization (167 B.C.E. to 70 C.E.). The year 70 marks the end of a singularly important period in Jewish and Christian history and the beginning of another age in history.

If variety and standardization characterized the period from 167 B.C.E. to 70 C.E., the period between the two Jewish revolts—from 70 to 132 C.E.—was marked by centralization. *The age of centralization: 70-132 C.E.*

A pupil of Hillel named Yoḥanan ben Zakkai, according to legend, miraculously escaped from Jerusalem during the siege of 70 because he told the Roman general Vespasian that he was about to become emperor. This rabbi established the first rabbinic academy at a place called Yavneh (Jamnia) in the fertile coastal plain (where once the Philistines lived).

At Yavneh about 84 C.E. two major decisions were made: First,

Judaism would be shaped primarily by the remembered insights of Hillel; second, the Jewish canon, which had been developing for centuries, was closed, except for some decisions regarding "the Writings" (especially Ben Sirach and Esther). These early Jews were not only the People of the Book. They also gave the Book to the People.

The Gospels—Mark, then Matthew, Luke, and John—were composed between 69 and 100. In them the blame for Jesus' crucifixion was shifted progressively from Pilate and the Romans to the Jewish high priest Caiaphas and the Jews. Unfortunately, later generations of Christians forgot the social context of these charges. The setting was the factionalism within Judaism and the struggle for self-identification by Christians and Jews.

The Gospel of Matthew remained on the fringes of Judaism. It was composed by a "school" that included some well-trained Jews. John was produced by a school in which there were many Jews. Some were apparently expelled from synagogues where they wished to continue to worship (the Greek word *aposunagogos* [expelled from the synagogue] appears only in John).

Minim is the rabbinic term for heretics. It is unclear when a curse on the *minim* was added to the daily *Amidah* prayer recited in synagogues. Some Jews influenced by Yavneh may have considered Jews who professed Jesus as Christ outside their acceptable boundaries, that is, *minim* (but certainly not apostates). Between the two Jewish revolts against Rome some of the major Jewish apocalypses were composed. These included, probably in this order, 4 Ezra, 2 Enoch, 2 Baruch, and the Apocalypse of Abraham. These apocalypses are contemporaneous with the canonical Gospels, which also contain some deeply apocalyptic sections, like Mark 13 (and 8:38); Matthew 24-25; some sections of Luke (9, 12, 17, 19, 21), and some old traditions in John (cf. 5:29, 14:26, 15:21, 16:2).

Under the influence of the School of Hillel and the fear of further rebellion (as well as the attempt to define itself over against Christianity), post-70 Judaism—especially after 135—attempted to eliminate the apocalyptic elements from its traditions. Christianity, on the other hand, would be sustained by apocalypsology (apocalyptically focused reflection), especially by the two most important dimensions of Jewish apocalyptic thought: the concept of the resurrection of the body after death (at the end-time) and the dawning of a new and glorious age. When Rabbinic Judaism decided largely to eliminate the apocalyptic perspectives and, at the same time, ecclesiastical Christianity embraced them, the two movements took different forks on the road to self-definition.

The first century C.E. was clearly the most important of the first six in both Judaism and Christianity. No discussion of this century would be complete without mentioning three significant Jews—Philo, Paul, and Josephus. Each provides important data regarding customs, festivals, historical events (especially the relations between Judaism and Rome), and the evolving and dynamic world of Early Judaism. To include them together now safeguards us from perceiving 70 C.E. as an absolute barrier.

The contributions of Philo, Paul and Josephus

The great bookends to first-century Judaism are Philo (c. 20 B.C.E.-c. 50 C.E.) and Josephus (c. 37-c. 100 C.E.). Paul is the creatively controversial thinker in the middle.

Paul was possibly martyred in Rome and Josephus died in Rome; much earlier Philo joined an embassy from Alexandria to Rome in 39. Each Jew was a prolific and fertile writer.

Philo makes no mention of Jesus, his contemporary in Palestine. Paul followed Jesus as cosmic "Lord." In a controversial passage, Josephus probably mentions Jesus, perhaps with respect, although he is included among those who were stirring up the Jews in Galilee and Judea.[10]

Philo of Alexandria developed an allegorical interpretation of Torah, the source of truth, by which he was able to collect syncretistically what he considered the perspicacious insights of non-Jews, especially Greeks like Plato (see chapter 1).

Paul (Saul of Tarsus) was converted from Pharisaism (into which he was born) to the Palestinian Jesus Movement sometime in the mid-30s. He zealously traveled westward to proclaim the gospel of Jesus Christ, the crucified Messiah and resurrected Lord through whom God had saved all (male and female, slave and free, rich and poor). Paul's thought is complex and nonsystematic; it was shaped by the contingencies and needs of the churches. We have some of Paul's letters, but we can only infer the issues and questions that evoked them. His letters perplex most exegetes. His thought nevertheless remains theocentric. He may have studied in Jerusalem under the great Gamaliel (Acts 22:3); he certainly continued to be indebted to Pharisaic Judaism of an apocalyptic strain. In ways difficult to comprehend in light of his conviction that salvation is solely through faith in Jesus, he claimed both that God has by no means forsaken his covenant with the Jews and that eventually "all Jews" will be saved (Romans 9-11).

According to his autobiography (*The Life*), Josephus became a member of the Pharisaic party, and was awarded Roman citizenship by the emperor Vespasian. Josephus' historical works—*The Jewish War* (c. 77-78 C.E.) and *Jewish Antiquities* (c. 94)—are invaluable to our attempts to understand the social and intellectual forces that led to the great First Jewish Revolt against Rome (66-70).

Josephus' works are a mixture of truth and distortion. His topographical descriptions are often amazingly accurate, as anyone can attest standing east of Gamla and reading his narrative composed in Rome. His descriptions of the war are often confirmed by related research, although he distorts the position of Zealots and messianic movements, essentially blaming their hotheadedness as much as the corrupt Roman procurators for the ill-conceived revolt. His praise for the grandeur of the Temple is not nearly so exaggerated as once thought. The Temple was a stupendous wonder; archaeologists have uncovered a stone that weighs well over 400 tons.[11] Josephus' depiction of Jewish thought is slanted, but not distorted; he wanted to persuade the Romans of the beauty of Jewish customs and thought and couched Jewish concepts in Greek terms.

The apocryphal gospels In Christianity in this period, we see the beginning of the glorification of Jesus' mother Mary. In Matthew and Luke she is hailed as the virgin who gave birth to the long-awaited Messiah, Jesus. In one of the earliest so-called apocryphal gospels, The Birth of Mary (also called the Infancy Gospel of James), she is portrayed as the fairest virgin in the Temple. In this work, her virginal nature, after giving birth to Jesus, is confirmed by a physical examination conducted by Salome. With this new tradition "the virgin birth" shifts from a concept symbolizing Jesus' divinity to a gynecological examination.

Numerous "apocryphal" gospels were composed before the Second Jewish Revolt began in 132 C.E., possibly including the Jewish-Christian gospels of the Hebrews, the Ebionites, and the Nazareans. For understanding Jesus' sayings, the most important of the apocryphal gospels is the Gospel According to Thomas. Although it contains some teachings that were later considered heretical, this document provides a record of the transmission of Jesus' sayings that is independent of the canonical Gospels. It is conceivable that in some passages the Gospel of Thomas preserves Jesus' words more accurately than the canonical Gospels. The Gospel According to Thomas is also closely linked with Judaism; for example, Peter says to Jesus: "You are like a righteous angel [*enouangelos endikaios*]" (Saying 13), which comports well with Jewish angelology.

During the years 100 to about 150, the latest documents in the New Testament were completed. At this same time apocryphal works like 2 Baruch, the Apocalypse of Abraham, the Odes of Solomon, and 3 and 4 Baruch were being composed. Ignatius (died

111) was writing his letters, Polycarp (69-155) and Papias (flourished c. 140) were preserving early traditions, and at least 13 versions of the Mishnah were taking shape for Rabbi Judah ha-Nasi later to edit. At the same time, Plutarch (46-125) was composing his *Parallel Lives*, the Stoic Epictetus (60-117) was completing his *Discourses*, and, a little later, Marcus Aurelius (121-180) completed his Stoic *Meditations*. Galen (130-200) would publish the first medical work since Hippocrates (c. 469-c. 399 B.C.E.), despite the appearance of the *De re medicina* of Aulus Cornelius Celsus (25 B.C.E.-50 C.E.). Christianity and Judaism were struggling for existence against impressive odds.

Before the fourth century, it is misleading to refer to Christian "heresy" because there was no dominant orthodoxy before this time. It is also misleading to use (without quotation marks to warn the reader) the terms "apocryphal" and "canonical" because the New Testament canon was not closed until the fourth century, at the earliest.

The most dangerous theological tendency during the first six centuries—one which still threatens Christian theology today—was Docetism. Docetism claims that Jesus only seemed (Greek, *dokeo*) to be human, but was actually a being of celestial substance. Docetism explains away Jesus' suffering: only the human apparition suffered, while God remained removed from the world of suffering.

Docetism was opposed by the Johannine School: "Deceivers [are those] who will not acknowledge the coming of Jesus Christ in the flesh [*en sarki*]" (2 John 7). Yet Docetism was advocated in the second-century Acts of John, in which John, weeping in Gethsemane over Jesus' crucifixion below him to the west, is told by a celestial Jesus, who saunters up to him, that what is happening down there is only illusory. According to another pericope in the Acts of John, John fails to see Jesus' footprints in the sands, as they walk together: Jesus was not human.

In the period from 70 to 132 Christianity and Judaism became centralized. Jesus' teachings, as remembered by those who proclaimed him, were collected into the first Gospels. After about 85 Paul's letters were collected and read in Christian services as if they were part of Scripture (2 Peter 3:16), and all the New Testament documents were composed. Judaism moved toward Rabbinic Judaism with emphasis on the themes (especially the *halakhah* [rules for living in the present world]) found in the Mishnah, which was taking shape during this period. Christians claimed that all problems were solved by faith in Jesus Christ, Jews stressed that all answers were revealed in the Torah (see 2 Baruch, Akiva, and the early portions of the Mishnah).

The age of canonization and codification: 132-200 C.E. The period from the Second Jewish Revolt (132-135 C.E.) to 200 C.E. can be described as the period of canonization for Christianity and codification for Judaism.

The first moves toward a canonical New Testament occurred in the second century. Irenaeus (c. 130-c. 200), for example, claimed that there must be four gospels, as there are four winds. He may have been reacting to Tatian, who compiled the first *Harmony of the Gospels* around 175.

Before considering how Judaism was codifying its Scriptures, we must discuss the revolt of 132-135. Events are impossible to reconstruct confidently. Whether the greatest rabbi of the time, Akiva (c. 50-132), actually declared that Simon bar Kosiba, the leader of the revolt, was none other than Bar-Kokhba, the "Son of the Star," the messiah, is a moot question. Nevertheless the revolt clearly had its messianic aspects. Christians did not join the forces of Bar Kosiba, but they should not be criticized for this apparent lack of loyalty. According to later rabbinic judgment he had been a false messiah. The schism between Judaism and Christianity had widened; that is clear. But it is inaccurate to objectify it and say, as is claimed in so many books, that Judaism and Christianity separated completely after 132 (see the judicious insights in chapter 8). Such a reconstruction fails to note that Christians continued, at least in some places, to frequent synagogues despite the protestations of John Chrysostom (c. 347-407). Origen and Jerome knew at least some Hebrew (and were presumably taught by Jews). Christians shared with Jews a major portion of their Scriptures. And almost all of the other section—the New Testament—was written within Early Judaism by Jews.

The need for "Christians" to define "Christianity" is apparent from the situation in Rome about the middle of the second century. The following leaders were there, and all were claiming to be Christians: Justin Martyr (c. 100-c. 165), the erudite and highly influential scholar who admired the Greeks and was the first Christian to attempt to reconcile reason and faith; Justin's student, Tatian (second century), who hated the Greeks (see *Address to the Greeks*, especially chap. 26); Valentinus (in Rome from c.136-c.165), one of the founders of Gnosticism as a philosophical system; Justin's other famous student, Rhodo (second century), an anti-Gnostic apologist; Marcion (died c. 160), who seems to have compiled the first "canon," and threatened the coherency of Christianity.

The "orthodox" Justin claimed that God's covenant with the Jews was no longer valid, and that Gentiles had replaced Jews. Marcion argued that the canon should be expunged of everything "Jewish," and contended that the God of Law of the Old Covenant had nothing in common with the God of love revealed in Jesus the Christ. Each abandoned Paul's solution (cf. Romans 9-11). It is significant, however, that Paul's letters were included in the canon and the works of Justin and Marcion were not. Christianity clearly needed normative self-definition (see chapter 5).

At this time and in this same process, Judaism was ahead of Christianity. After the two great revolts the Zealots vanished, as did the numerous "sects." The revolts had revealed the dangers of baseless dreams and false messiahs. The academy was transplanted to Yavneh in Judea, and then to Usha and Tiberias in Galilee.

The first attempts to codify the Mishnah (Hebrew, "instruction") had already begun. The leaders in this process were the heirs of a single group, the Pharisees. No longer was power divided between opposing camps (i.e. the Hillelites and the Shammaites). The followers of Hillel had triumphed, and a unified concept had emerged. Deviants were excluded from synagogue services. The canon was closed at Usha (c. 140), with the exclusion of Ben Sirach and the inclusion of Esther. Messianism and apocalypticism were largely excised, or at least diminished.

The process was completed by a descendant of Hillel, Rabbi Judah the Prince (also known as Judah ha-Nasi; 135-c. 220) around 200, when he gave the Mishnah its final, well-known form. This collection of Jewish Oral Law defined the proper conduct of the faithful in their daily lives, explaining even minutiae so that the boundaries for acceptable conduct would be prescribed. The Mishnah, the basis for the Talmudim, focused Judaism. Its powers for self-definition derived from the claim that both the written and Oral Law were divinely delivered to Moses at Sinai.

From the second-century Christian perspective, what was lacking in Judaism was a gospel, a proclamation of God's good news to all about Jesus, the One Promised, and a coherent dream for the future. Apocalyptic Christianity embodies the dream of the One resurrected by God.

In Judaism, messianism, apocalypticism, and belief in another world were never completely expunged by the rabbis. Hence, we hear the continuing volcanic explosions in Jewish literature represented by 3 Enoch, the *Hekalot* literature, the Zohar, the pseudo-messiah Sabbatai Sevi (17th century), and the complex forces that created, in our time, the dream of a Jewish state in the land.

Between 200 and 313 C.E., Judaism and Christianity followed different—but intertwined—courses. Each added something very different to their shared Scripture—the Hebrew Scriptures (or Old Testament). During this period the rabbis completed scripture with the Mishnah, then the Tosefta; much later in the fifth century they

The age of differing scriptures: 200-313 C.E.

completed scripture with the Talmudim. Christian scholars completed scripture with the 27 writings in the New Testament. The shared allegiance to the "Old Testament" is remarkable, even if Christians were by this time dependent on the Greek translation, the Septuagint (which Akiva wished to replace and so supported Aquila's translation).

A growing disdain for "the outside books" was shared by many Jews and Christians alike. Such was the unfortunate cost of self-definition based on a closed canon.

The third century also saw the flowering of Gnosticism. Its beginnings can be traced to the pre-Christian era in Platonic, Jewish, and Persian emphases on *gnosis* (knowledge) as the key to salvation; it reached the stage of a philosophical system during the middle of the second century C.E., especially in the work of Valentinus. The Gnostics thought that salvation was possible only for those who had fallen from a primordial stage of purity and who, through introspective "knowledge," could ascend again to the heavenly realm, often with the help of a descending godlike figure.

In 1945 in Egypt at Nag Hammadi a gnostic library was recovered; in it were preserved Coptic treatises that preserved gnostic works. One of them, the Apocalypse of Adam, may be a gnostic reworking of an earlier Jewish work that mirrors the baptist groups of the first century C.E. that congregated near the Jordan River.

Gnosticism was deeply influenced by many writings. Various gnostic compositions are deeply indebted to Christianity (especially the Gospel of John), to the neo-Platonists (especially Plotinus [205-270]), and to Jewish apocalypticism (especially the Enoch and Adam cycles).

Gnosticism proved to be a major threat to Christianity. Most scholars of the Church were forced to refute it. The most influential scholar in Rome, Hippolytus (c. 170-c. 236), directed his famous *Refutation of All Heresies* against it. Clement of Alexandria (c. 150-c. 215) agreed with the Gnostics that *gnosis* was the key to salvation, but he defined it as "illumination," which presupposed the "faith" of the apostolic scriptures and the continuing revelation to the Church. For Clement ignorance, not sin, was the fundamental evil.

His protege was none other than the genius Origen (c. 185-c. 254), who was so committed to his beliefs that he yearned (unsuccessfully) for martyrdom[12] and castrated himself because of a literal, and false, interpretation of Matthew 19:12 (it speaks of those "who have made themselves eunuchs for the sake of the kingdom of heaven"). Exiled by the bishop of Alexandria because of alleged improper ordination by bishops in Caesarea Maritima, he fled back to Caesarea where he founded a school in 231 that would become renowned and that would have an immense library, rivaling the one in Alexandria (both of which are lost).

In my judgment, Origen is the first biblical scholar. His most valuable work is the *Hexapla*, which places in six (sometimes nine) columns the text of the Old Testament according to six (or more) versions, beginning with the Hebrew. He was seeking to obtain the accurate text and meaning. His method of studying Scripture was literal, moral, and especially allegorical. Although his thought is sometimes contradictory and some of his major works are not preserved (at least in the original), he believed that God is One and transcendent.

Like many early scholars of the Church, Origen could not comprehend the relation between Father, Son, and Holy Spirit. Some of Origen's thoughts are mysterious; he was a mystic.

In the first two centuries Christians appropriated Jewish scriptures, especially the Septuagint, without reediting them. In the second and third centuries, however, they felt compelled to reedit what was being borrowed, namely the Testaments of the Twelve Patriarchs, which was used to teach morality; the Martyrdom or Ascension of Isaiah, which was expanded to clarify the descent of Christ into this world; the Testament of Adam, which was augmented to clarify time and the cosmos; and the *Hellenistic Synagogal Hymns*, which was interpolated so that the creative powers of Christ—not Wisdom—could be chanted in the churches (earlier Christ was identified with Wisdom; see Matthew 11:19 and the Odes of Solomon). All these redactions, interpolations, and expansions served the need of the self-defining Christian community. After such editorial work, which delimited the possibilities for speculation, only a Christian could use them; they reflected a Christian perspective.

Other "Christian" thinkers were veering off in wild directions. Montanus (late second century) claimed that the heavenly Jerusalem would descend to earth near Pepuza in Phrygia. Manes (c. 215-275), a dualist, contended that portions of light and darkness that had been imprisoned in human brains by Satan were released only by messengers: the biblical prophets, Jesus, Buddha, and—of course—Manes, who was rewarded for such weird thoughts by being flayed alive by the head of the Persian empire.

The recently researched Cologne Mani Codex[13] contains excerpts from numerous Jewish apocalypses otherwise unknown; they seem to be authentic and another indication of Judaism's continuing influence on almost all aspects of Christianity. Bardsanes (154-222), the father of Syriac hymnbooks, affirmed that Christ's body was a phantom (cf. Acts of John) but denied a future resurrection.

These wild offshoots resulted from a volatile mixture of mysticism and apocalypticism. Before the fourth century, Christianity was like a puppy that knows no boundaries.

This condition could not continue. It had to be outgrown.

The age of councils: 313-451 C.E.   The first century was obviously the most important of the first six, since origins dictate the spirit of a movement. The next most important century was the fourth, since in it the mentality of Christianity was clarified. Three dates in the fourth century are especially significant: 313, 325, and 367.

In 313 Constantine the Great (c. 288-337) declared all religions free from Roman persecution (see chapter 8). This edict (the misnamed Edict of Milan) did not elevate Christianity; it signaled Christianity's triumph over persecution, which was severe, as is well known in cliches about lions and Christians. Only on his death was Constantine himself baptized as a "Christian"; but it was not clear what constituted Christianity.

In 325 at Nicaea Constantine summoned the leaders of the Church. He ordered them to define the essence of Christianity, not because he was interested in theology, but because he needed ecclesiastical unity. As with Yavneh (Jamnia), there are no records of what actually took place. The most famous scholar in attendance was Eusebius (c. 260-c. 340), the father of Church history. Since the major issue was Christology, in particular the relationship between Father and Son—and in response to the challenge of the brilliant Arius—Eusebius submitted a creed that when enriched by the word "of one substance" (Greek, *homoousios*) was judged to be "orthodox." The creed finally adopted, however, was another one; it is the popular "Nicene Creed" said universally today in all churches claiming to be "catholic" and "apostolic." Arius' perception that Father and Son were not absolutely identical was rejected by the Nicene decision that they were of one substance (*homoousios*).

Here we see another major break with Judaism; Jews could not remain within Judaism and believe that Jesus is God. Many followers of Origen preferred the term *homoiousion*, "of like substance"; it provided the possibility for some distinction between Jesus and God. But in any discussion of substance we move from the world of Judaism in which Christianity originated to a different level of discourse. Never in Jewish apocalypticism, for example, is Adam, Enoch, or Moses considered of one substance—or even of like substance—with God. Rather, they are enthroned and elevated to angelic status.

We may ask whether, in these Christian debates, too much has been defined. Has the supracategorical dimension and ineffableness of God been sacrificed by the need to think in logical and philosophical categories? Did the success and popularity—and the unity—of Christianity (in the West) demand such logical precision?

In 367 Athanasius (c. 296-373), an influential opponent of Arianism, wrote a festal letter that listed, for the first time, the 27 books of the New Testament and in the order known today. Yet, after that time, and until about the sixth century, numerous books in the New Testament—Hebrews, 2 Peter, Jude, and Revelation—were still considered unacceptable.

Canonization was a process. It was not tied to a particular council. It resulted from four centuries of experience. Moreover, the contents of the canon continued to be debated in the Greek Orthodox Church, the Ethiopian Church, and the Syrian Church long after the fourth century. Even in the West the canon was not universally accepted in the fourth century.

The date 367, the date of Athanasius' list, is, nevertheless, important. From that date, we can talk about the existence of a canonical list of the New Testament that is shared today by Roman Catholics and Protestants.

Relations between churches and synagogues in Palestine

During the fourth and fifth centuries, despite what is taught today in some universities and claimed in numerous publications, Christians did relate with Jews (as chapter 8 demonstrates). Christians often attended synagogue services. John Chrysostom (c. 347-407), who referred to the Jews as "wretched and miserable," was forced to admit that "many" of the members of his church who claimed to accept his teachings did "attend their [Jewish] festivals, and even share in their celebrations and join in their fasts."[14] The synagogue, he said, is "a house of prostitution" and "a dwelling place of demons," yet some Christians "go to these places as though they were sacred shrines."[15] He calls such a Christian "a jackass" and perpetuates the foul myth that the Jews crucified Jesus. He misinterpreted the New Testament writings, especially John and Revelation; but his writings are still revered throughout much of Christendom.

Fortunately, there is abundant evidence of a positive relation among Jews and Christians. With the legalization of Christianity in the fourth century, Constantine initiated massive building programs in Palestine. Some of his work is still visible today. Yet, in the fourth and fifth centuries, impressive synagogues were built in Palestine. In Galilee, especially in Capernaum, these synagogues stood in close proximity to the churches. Sometimes the new synagogue was built above an older one so that the church was built near a synagogue. Sometimes the synagogue is later and so was built near a church. Obviously Jews and Christians often chose to worship close to each other.

Additional evidence of a positive relation is found in the life and work of Jerome (c. 342-420). He probably learned Hebrew from Jews. He was devoted to the Hebrew Scriptures; he translated the Hebrew Bible (Old Testament) and the Greek New Testament into Latin. His work assisted in the process of Christian self-definition; now Christians in the West had one accepted text of Scripture: the Vulgate.

Jerome's famous contemporary was Augustine (354-430). This fertile and influential thinker argued that God is the creator of all, that creation is essentially good, and that evil is to be explained as the absence of some good. He experienced God's grace in a profound way. He set for the next millennium a paradigm for thought: "the city of God" versus "the city of the world." His vision was of the final triumph of the city of God. He may well have been indirectly influenced by early Jewish thinkers (cf. 4 Ezra).

The year 451 is important for three reasons. It was the year of the fourth ecumenical council, held at Chalcedon. Only seven councils are universally considered ecumenical, that is, producing judgments on doctrine and discipline that are binding for all Christians. These seven were held at Nicaea (325), Constantinople (381), Ephesus (431), Chalcedon (451), Constantinople II (553), Constantinople III (680-681), and Nicaea II (787). The ecumenical councils were all held in one small section of the civilized world (Asia Minor). They reflect the fact that by the fourth century Christianity was such a powerful institution that the only means of defining itself was the rigid bureaucracy of a council.

The year 451 is also important because it is probably the year Nestorius died. Nestorius' own theology is difficult to ascertain, because his thought was so altered by the Nestorians. It is evident that he rejected the title "*Theotokos*" (God-bearer) for Mary, because he could not accept the idea that she was the bearer of God; Nestorius rejected any title or concept that would undermine the full humanity of Jesus. Nestorius was declared a heretic and exiled in 436 to Upper Egypt. The growing devotion to Mary would lead beyond *Theotokos* to *Dei Genitrix* (Mother of God). This trend was more typical of the West than the East.

The Eastern bishops who supported Nestorius broke free from the councils and established the Nestorian Church. Centered in Persia, this Syriac-speaking church became powerful, controlling the great school (really a university) at Nisibis. The Nestorians actually occupied the largest part of the civilized world. Before the Arab conquest in the seventh century, the Nestorians were powerful and influential from Famagusta, Cyprus, to Peking, China, and from southern Russia to the Malabar Coast of India.

Finally, the year 451 is important because that was the year of the Battle of Troyes (Battle of Châlons). Attila the Hun, after overrunning Europe and entering France, was defeated at Troyes. Europe nearly became a part of Asia. After his defeat at Troyes, Attila retreated to Italy were he suddenly died. The Huns, now without leadership, disappeared from history, but the West would take centuries to recover. The feudal ages were not far off.

The last half of the fifth century and all of the sixth century saw the institutionalization of Christianity. In short, Christianity solidified its position. Paganism was branded and banished. Christianity triumphed as the Holy Roman Empire. By the fifth century Rome had established herself as the head of the Church, the place of the pope ("Father," from Greek *papas*, through Latin *papa*). One reason was the universal recognition that Peter and Paul had been martyred and were buried in "the eternal city." In 385 the pope was accorded power to issue decisions without a council. Pope Gelasius I (492-496) declared Rome's superiority over all other churches, including Constantinople.

The age of Final Institutionalization: 451-571 C.E.

In the sixth century Dionysius Exiguus (c. 500-550) compiled the first collection of canon law. It was he who established the "Christian Era," but he incorrectly calculated the year for the birth of Jesus. Today the Western world follows his dates (which requires us to place the date of Jesus' birth before 4 B.C.E.).

The Roman emperor Justinian I (527-565) sought to unify West and East through his legal code and his energetic building campaigns. Among his best-known buildings are Hagia Sophia in Constantinople and the fortress-monastery at the foot of Mt. Sinai. He also closed the philosophical schools in Athens in 529.

Something else was also happening. Those whose ancestors in the faith had been fed to the beasts were now vengefully placarding Jews as "Christ killers."

Before 600 four important bodies of law affecting Jews had been promulgated: (1) Constantine's laws (315), which compromised the full equality of Jews as citizens; (2) Constantius' laws (399), which forbade a Christian woman to marry a Jew; (3) Theodosius II's laws (439), which closed leading government offices to Jews; and, finally, (4) Justinian's laws (531), which prohibited Jews from testifying against Christians.

These injustices, however, were shared by almost all non-Christians. The historian Max I. Dimont has perceptively argued that these laws must be grasped in terms of the pre-sixth-century world. In *Jews, God and History* he offers this sane advice:

"These laws had two purposes: to protect the infant religion from the competition of other religions, and to protect key posts for co-religionists. When Jews are singled out by historians as the only victims of these laws, we are given a false picture of their intent."[16]

How, then, did anti-Judaism evolve? When one forgets the social context of the documents in the New Testament, one may see its beginnings in the anti-Judaic passages in the New Testament, especially in the Gospels of Matthew and John and in the Revelation of John. As early as the second century, Melito of Sardis (died c. 190) defended the unity of the two Christian testaments by abolishing "law" in contrast to "gospel." Melito used his obvious poetic genius to vehemently denounce the Jews:

> "He who hung the earth is hanging; . . . he who fastened the universe has been fastened to a tree; . . . the King of Israel has been put to death by an Israelite right hand."[17]

No wonder that, hundreds of years later, at Easter time, the great pogroms would erupt. Melito's thoughts were anathema to the essential Christian preaching as it developed in the early years; but his ideas would become explosive in later centuries in the hands of those with absolute power and in need of a myth for hatred.

Might it now be possible to ponder to what degree the persecution of "Jews" was at least somewhat linked with the claim to be exclusively "God's chosen people," and with the charge that Mary, Jesus' mother, had conceived Jesus through sex with a Roman soldier named Panthera?[18] Some Jews obviously thought that Jesus was a demonic magician.[19] Some Jews claimed that the disciples had stolen Jesus' corpse (cf. Matthew 27:22-26), denying the resurrection. Understandably, by these polemics some Jews explained away Christian claims regarding the virgin birth, Jesus' miracles, and the resurrection. By this time in the sixth century Judaism and Christianity had parted.

In the first six centuries, Rabbinic Judaism was developing in different ways. After Rabbi Judah's compilation of the Mishnah (c. 200 C.E.), rabbinic writings continued to pour forth. These included the Tosefta (a post-Mishnaic work of uncertain date), but most importantly the massive volumes of the Talmudim, first in Palestine (c. 450) and then in Babylonia (c. 500). These writings complete the Torah and are considered scripture. Together they are reputed to contain the written and Oral Law delivered by God to Moses. These writings, and the Targumim (translations of the Hebrew Bible into Aramaic), preserve very old traditions, but they are edited in line with the needs and perspectives of these later centuries. Cumulatively, Judaism succeeded in defining itself so that it could survive outside the Land of Israel and without the Temple.

According to Christian perception, the development of ortho-doxy and the results of the councils were always by the guidance of "the Holy Spirit." Neither this concept, nor the title, is found in the Hebrew Scriptures. It does appear, although infrequently, in Jewish apocryphal works[20] and in the Mishnah.[21] It is also frequently found in the Dead Sea Scrolls.[22] Jesus probably knew the term "Holy Spirit," and his followers certainly developed and emphasized this Jewish title for a divine person. Jesus, or at least his followers, probably inherited the concept of the Holy Spirit from the Essenes.[23]

Rabbinic thought is appreciably different. Although far from presenting a unified concept, the sages stressed the idea that the Holy Spirit left Israel with the cessation of prophecy.[24] It was impossible, therefore, to claim that Hillel was blessed by the presence of the Holy Spirit.[25] What could be, and was, claimed, however, was that he alone of his generation was worthy of receiving the Holy Spirit.[26] Since Judaism and Christianity did not evolve without some knowledge of the other, the rabbis may have been subtly rejecting the triumphant Christian claim that Christians alone were guided by the Holy Spirit.

In 571, the prophet Mohammad was born. He succeeded in giving the Arabs a book of revelations—like the ones cherished by Jews and Christians—that would unite and strengthen them. A new age would begin, but it is beyond the scope of this book.

The history of Christianity has been written, with few exceptions, by historians trained only in Greek and Latin, who myopically focused solely on the records of the triumphant Western majority. The result is a tendency toward theological triumphalism, Western parochialism, and an anti-Jewishness that shreds, if it does not cut, the umbilical cord of Christianity. These historians fail to perceive that Christianity's road to self-definition was shaped in a social, and often polemically reactionary, arena that included Judaism.

Endnotes

O N E
Palestinian and Diaspora Judaism in the First Century

1. See particularly, Virgil's *Aeneid*, esp. 8.678-681 and 714-728.

2. On Herod as messiah, see Epiphanius, *Panarion* 1.1, 20.1. On Herod's strong-arm measures and popularity, see *War* 1.204-205; *Antiquities* 14.159-160.

3. *Antiquities* 15.96-103.

4. *War* 2.1-3; *Antiquities* 17.188.

5. *War* 2.111-117; *Antiquities* 17.342-355.

6. Tacitus, *Histories* 5.10.1.

7. *Antiquities* 19.236-247.

8. *Antiquities* 19.341.

9. See Josef Meyshan, "The Coinage of Agrippa the First," *IEJ* 4 (1954), p. 187, n. 2. Wolf Wirgin (*Herod Agrippa I. King of the Jews* [Leeds, UK: Leeds Univ. Oriental Soc., 1968]) suggests that Agrippa regarded himself as the messiah; but this seems unlikely since Josephus would hardly have praised him if that were so, inasmuch as a messiah, by definition, would have been a rebel against the ruling power of Rome. On Agrippa, see the definitive work by Daniel R. Schwartz, *Agrippa I: The Last King of Judaea* (Tübingen: Mohr, 1990).

10. Mishnah *Sotah* 7:8.

11. *Antiquities* 19.330-331.

12. See Uriel Rappaport, "The Relations between Jews and Non-Jews and the Great War against Rome," *Tarbiz* 47 (1977-1978), pp. 1-14 (in Hebrew).

13. *Antiquities* 18.6.

14. See Shimon Applebaum, "Josephus and the Economic Causes of the Jewish War," pp. 237-264, and Heinz Kreissig, "A Marxist View of Josephus' Account of the Jewish War," pp. 265-277, as well as comments on these two essays by Louis H. Feldman, "Introduction," pp. 37-41, all in *Josephus, the Bible, and History*, ed. Feldman and Gohei Hata (Detroit: Wayne State Univ., 1989). For a critical survey of the bibliography on Josephus as a historian of the Jewish war, ibid., pp. 385-393.

15. *Antiquities* 20.181.

16. Peter A. Brunt ("Josephus on Social Conflicts in Roman Judaea," *Klio* 59 [1977], pp. 149-153) argues that the revolt was directed almost as much against native landlords and usurers as against the Romans. Martin Goodman ("The First Jewish Revolt: Social Conflict and the Problem of Debt," *JJS* 33 [1982], pp. 417-427) concludes that the main cause was the rotting away from within of Judean so-

ciety due to social imbalance resulting from excessive wealth attracted to the city during the *Pax Romana*. Consequently, both the small, independent farmers and the craftsmen and urban plebs of Jerusalem fell heavily into debt and turned to banditry. Richard A. Horsley ("Josephus and the Bandits," *JSJ* 10 [1979], pp. 37-63, and "Ancient Jewish Banditry and the Revolt against Rome, A.D. 66-70," *CBQ* 43 [1981], pp. 409-432) emphasizes social banditry as a major cause of the revolt.

17. *War* 2.427.

18. *Life* 235; cf. Magen Broshi, "The Population of Western Palestine in the Roman-Byzantine Period," *BASOR* 236 (1979), p. 1.

19. *War* 3.43.

20. *War* 6.420.

21. *War* 2.295. See the excellent discussion by Martin Goodman, *The Ruling Class of Judaea: The Origins of the Jewish Revolt against Rome A.D. 66-70* (Cambridge, UK: Cambridge Univ. Press, 1987), pp. 170-172.

22. *War* 2.305-308.

23. *War* 6.425.

24. *War* 2.169-174; *Antiquities* 18.55-59.

25. *Antiquities* 18.121-122.

26. *War* 2.184-203; *Antiquities* 18.261-309.

27. R.J. Coggins ("The Samaritans in Josephus," in *Josephus, Judaism, and Christianity*, ed. Louis H. Feldman and Gohei Hata [Detroit: Wayne State Univ., 1987], pp. 257-273) stresses both the hostility and the ambiguity in Josephus' attitude toward the sect. On the other hand, Rita Egged (*Josephus Flavius und die Samaritaner: eine terminologische Untersuchung zur Identitätsklärung der Samaritaner* [Göttingen: Vandenhoeck and Ruprecht, 1986]) concludes that there is no ground for asserting that Josephus was anti-Samaritan, but that he failed to differentiate among the terms for Samaritans, and suggests that it was his assistants who had confused the terms. We may respond, however, that the major references to the Samaritans are in *Antiquities*, and that it is in *War*, as we learn from Josephus himself (*Apion* 1.50), that he had assistants.

28. See Clemens Thoma, "The High Priesthood in the Judgment of Josephus," in Feldman and Hata, *Josephus, the Bible, and History* (see endnote 14), pp. 196-215.

29. *War* 4.153-157.

30. For a critical bibliography of the messianic background of the Jewish war, see Louis H. Feldman, *Josephus and Modern Scholarship (1937-1980)* (Berlin: de Gruyter, 1984), pp. 489-491.

31. Suetonius, *Vespasian* 4.5.

32. Tacitus, *Histories* 5.13.2.

33. *War* 6.312.

34. *War* 6.423-425.

35. *Antiquities* 20.97-98; cf. Acts 5:36.

36. Salo W. Baron, "Population," *EJ*, vol. 13, col. 869, and *A Social and Religious History of the Jews*, 2nd ed. (New York: Columbia Univ. Press, 1952), vol. 1, p. 170, and esp. pp. 370-372, n. 7.

37. For a critical bibliography on Josephus' views concerning the Temple, see Feldman, *Josephus and Modern Scholarship* (see endnote 30), pp. 438-448.

38. *Apion* 2.165.

39. *Antiquities* 20.251.

40. *Antiquities* 20.180-181.

41. See Hugo Mantel, *Studies in the History of the Sanhedrin* (Cambridge, MA: Harvard Univ. Press, 1961). For other views, see Feldman, *Josephus and Modern Scholarship* (see endnote 30), pp. 463-467.

42. Mishnah *Sanhedrin* 1:5.

43. Tosefta *Sanhedrin* 3:4.

44. See Hugo Mantel, "Sanhedrin," *EJ*, vol. 14, col. 837.

45. Mishnah *Hagigah* 2:2.

46. *Antiquities* 20.200.

47. Josephus, however, mentions only one Sadducean high priest, Ananus the Younger, in connection with the condemnation of James, the brother of Jesus; *Antiquities* 20.199.

48. See Mantel, "Sanhedrin" (see endnote 44), col. 838.

49. So Haim Cohn, *The Trial and Death of Jesus* (New York: Harper & Row, 1971).

50. *War* 2.285-289, in Caesarea; *Antiquities* 19.305, in Dora; *Life* 280, in Tiberias.

51. JT *Megillah* 3:1.

52. BT *Ketubbot* 105a.

53. Mishnah *Sotah* 7:7-8; *Yoma* 7:1.

54. The Theodotus inscription is generally dated to the first century C.E. It refers to an earlier synagogue official who was Theodotus' grandfather. See Hershel Shanks, *Judaism in Stone: The Archaeology of Ancient Synagogues* (New York: Harper & Row, 1979), pp. 18-20.

55. See Shmuel Safrai ("The Synagogue and Its Worship," in *The World History of the Jewish People*, vol. 8: *Society and Religion in the Second Temple Period*, First Series, ed. Michael Avi-Yonah and Zvi Baras [Jerusalem: Massada, 1977], pp. 65-98, 338-345), who surveys the sources: the beginnings of the synagogue and its spread in the late Second Temple period; the names of the synagogues in Palestine and in the Diaspora; the character of the synagogue and its form of divine worship; assemblies on

Sabbaths, festivals and weekdays; prayer, Torah reading and sermons; the conduct of the synagogue and its officials; the location and structure of the synagogue; and various uses of the synagogue. See also Bernadette Brooten, *Women Leaders in the Ancient Synagogue* (Chico, CA: Scholars Press, 1982).

56. Baruch Lifshitz, *Donateurs et fondateurs dans les synagogues juives* (Paris: Gabalda, 1967), pp. 70-71.

57. Elias J. Bickerman, *The Jews in the Greek Age* (Cambridge, MA: Harvard Univ. Press, 1988), p. 139.

58. *Sifrei Deuteronomy* 357.

59. BT *Shabbat* 31a.

60. BT *Sukkah* 28a.

61. *War* 7.399.

62. *Antiquities* 4.219.

63. See Cheryl Anne Brown, *No Longer Be Silent: First Century Portraits of Biblical Women: Studies in Pseudo-Philo's Biblical Antiquities and Josephus' Jewish Antiquities* (Louisville, KY: Westminster/John Knox, 1992).

64. For a critical bibliography on the Jewish sects, see Feldman, *Josephus and Modern Scholarship* (see endnote 30), pp. 542-672.

65. JT *Sanhedrin* 10.6.29c.

66. *Antiquities* 13.171-173.

67. *Antiquities* 18.23-25.

68. Philo, *De Vita Contemplativa* 8.64-11.90.

69. See also Epiphanius, *Panarion* 20.1.

70. Mishnah *Demai* 2:2-3.

71. The *'am ha-'aretz* did not give the prescribed tithes, did not observe the laws of purity and were neglectful of the laws of prayer. So great was the antagonism between them and the learned Pharisees that, in an anonymous statement, their wives are called vermin, and to their daughters was applied the verse (Deuteronomy 27:21): "Cursed be he that lieth with any manner of beast" (BT *Pesahim* 49b). Rabbi Akiva (ibid.), referring to his youthful days in the middle of the first century, notes the bitter antagonism which the *'am ha-'aretz*, in turn, felt toward scholars: "When I was an *'am ha-'aretz* I said: 'I would that I had a scholar, and I would maul him like an ass.'"

Perhaps the nonobservance of the *'am ha-'aretz* has been exaggerated: See Mishnah *Tevul Yom* 4:5; *Tohorot* 8:5; *Hagigah* 3:4-5. See also Cohen, pp. 212-215.

72. This will help to explain why the Essenes, who are described at such length in *War* (2.120-161), get so much less space in the discussion of sects in *Antiquities*. *War* was written somewhere between 79 and 81 C.E., shortly after the destruction of the Temple; by the time

that *Antiquities* was written, in the year 93, the memory of the Essenes had faded.

73. See Günther Baumbach, "The Sadducees in Josephus," in Feldman and Hata, *Josephus, the Bible, and History* (see endnote 14), pp. 173-195.

74. *Antiquities* 18.17.

75. Cf. Acts 5:17: "The high priest stood up and those that were with him (which is the sect of the Sadducees)." It seems strange that Josephus says nothing at all (except for the fact that one high priest, Ananus [*Antiquities* 20.199] belonged to the Sadducees) about the connection of the Sadducees with the high priesthood and the Temple. The explanation may be that Josephus, as a priest himself, felt embarrassed by the predominance of priests in the ranks of the Sadducees and hence played down this relationship. Victor Eppstein ("The Historicity of the Gospel Account of the Cleansing of the Temple," *ZNW* 55 [1964], pp. 42-58), stressing the fact that only one high priest is specifically mentioned by Josephus, concludes that the Temple was not the headquarters of the Sadducees and that they were not, in fact, the party of the sacerdotal establishment. But to some degree this is an *argumentum ex silentio*, since Josephus' comments about the Sadducees are extremely brief.

76. *Antiquities* 18.17.

77. Mishnah *Avot* 3:2.

78. *Antiquities* 20.201-203.

79. *Antiquities* 18.23.

80. It may seem surprising that Josephus mentions this distinction only once (*Antiquities* 13.297-298), whereas to the rabbis this is the major point of difference between the Pharisees and the Sadducees. The explanation may be that Josephus is writing primarily for a non-Jewish audience, as we can see from the proem to *Antiquities* (1.10), where he cites as the precedent for his work the translation of the Torah into Greek (the Septuagint) for King Ptolemy II Philadelphus; and Gentiles would appreciate a distinction based on the attitude toward fate, since this was so central a point of argument between the two leading philosophical schools of the time, the Epicureans and the Stoics. Secondarily, the nonacceptance of the Oral Torah may not have been such a major difference, since we hear that the Sadducees had their own oral law in the form of a *sefer gezerata* (book of decrees) (*Megillath Ta'anith* 4). Jesus, we may note, denounces the Pharisees and the Sadducees together (Matthew 16:6-12); but we may suggest that perhaps Jesus agreed with the Sadducees in not washing his

The Rabbinic Sources
(pages 14-15)

1. See list in Emil Schürer, *The History of the Jewish People in the Age of Jesus Christ (175 B.C.-A.D. 135)*, rev. Geza Vermes and Fergus Millar (Edinburgh: T & T Clark, 1973), vol. 1, pp. 74-75.

2. Jacob Neusner, *Judaism: The Evidence of the Mishnah* (Chicago: Univ. of Chicago Press, 1981).

3. See Eliezer Berkovits, "Talmud, Babylonian" and Louis I. Rabinowitz "Talmud, Jerusalem," *EJ*, vol. 15, cols. 755-768 and 772-779, respectively.

4. See Moshe D. Herr, "Midrash," *EJ*, vol. 11, cols. 1507-1514.

5. See, in particular, Bernard J. Bamberger ("The Dating of Aggadic Materials," *JBL* 68 [1949], pp. 115-123), who notes, for example, that inasmuch as the second-century Rabbi Meir (*Megillah* 13a) states, as does the Septuagint (Esther 2:7), that Mordecai had married Esther, it is more likely that the translators were acquainted with this ancient tradition than that Rabbi Meir consulted the Septuagint.

6. For Josephus' knowledge of midrashic tradition, see Salomo Rappaport, *Agada und Exegese bei Flavius Josephus* (Vienna: Alexander Kohut Memorial Found., 1930),

and Louis H. Feldman, various articles on Josephus, notably "Josephus' Version of Samson," *JSJ* 19 (1988), pp. 171-214.

7. Jay Braverman (*Jerome's Commentary on Daniel: A Study of Comparative Jewish and Christian Interpretations of the Hebrew Bible* [Washington, DC: CBA, 1978]) notes 16 such Jewish midrashic traditions in Jerome's commentary on Daniel, only four of which have definite parallels in extant rabbinic literature.

8. Shaye J.D. Cohen, "Parallel Historical Tradition in Josephus and Rabbinic Literature," in *Proceedings of Ninth World Congress of Jewish Studies*, Jerusalem, Aug. 4-12, 1985, Div. B, vol. 1: *The History of the Jewish People (From the Second Temple Period until the Middle Ages)* (Jerusalem: World Union of Jewish Studies, 1986), pp. 7-14.

In view of the distrust that Cohen (*Josephus in Galilee and Rome: His Vita and Development as a Historian* [Leiden: Brill, 1979], pp. 38-39) has for Josephus' paraphrase of the Bible, as well as for his account of the Jewish war, his general preference for Josephus in episodes that parallel the rabbinic accounts seems surprising.

9. BT *Megillah* 15a.

10. See Shraga Abramson, ed., *Abodah Zarah* (New York: JTSem, 1957), pp. xiv-xv.

hands before eating (Luke 11:37ff.), a requirement according to the Oral Torah. When Jesus is rebuked by the Pharisees for not censuring his disciples, who ate without washing their hands, he replies, "Hypocrites, you give up what God has commanded, and hold fast to what men have handed down" (Mark 7:9), an allusion, it would seem, to the Oral Torah, which was transmitted orally from generation to generation.

Of course, the question of why we never hear of the excommunication of the Sadducees presupposes that the Pharisees, prior to 70, were in an authoritative position to set the boundaries of the Jewish community. To be sure, E.P. Sanders (*Judaism: Practice & Belief 63 BCE-66 CE* [London: SCM, 1992], esp. pp. 458-490) argues that the Pharisees governed neither directly nor indirectly; but as Steve Mason (*Flavius Josephus on the Pharisees: A Composition-Critical Study* [Leiden: Brill, 1991]) has convincingly shown, there is ample evidence in Josephus' writings that the Pharisees enjoyed the steady

and eager support of the ordinary people. This is all the more convincing inasmuch as Josephus himself actually disdained the Pharisees. Though some have disputed the later rabbinic claim that the Pharisees dominated the ritual of the Jerusalem Temple, texts soon to be published from the Dead Sea Scrolls indicate that the views assigned to the Pharisees in a number of mishnaic disputes are precisely those that were practiced in the Jerusalem Temple. See Lawrence H. Schiffman, *From Text to Tradition: A History of Second Temple and Rabbinic Judaism* (Hoboken, NJ: Ktav, 1991), p. 107, and his "New Light on the Pharisees—Insights from the Dead Sea Scrolls," *BR*, June 1992, pp. 30-35, 54.

81. *Antiquities* 18.17.

82. See William R. Farmer, *Maccabees, Zealots, and Josephus: An Inquiry into Jewish Nationalism in the Greco-Roman Period* (New York: Columbia Univ. Press, 1956). Farmer argues that Josephus deliberately omitted the connection because he was descended from the

Hasmoneans, the family of the Maccabees, who had been allies of Rome, and hence praised them, whereas he bitterly opposed the revolutionaries. Of course, there is a major difference between the Maccabees and the Zealots; namely, that the former revolted, at least initially, because of the suppression of the Jewish religion, whereas the latter sought political liberty, which, to be sure, they viewed in religious terms as the *sine qua non* for Judaism.

83. *War* 7.259-274.

84. The relationship of the Sicarii and the Zealots has been much debated. In a sharply worded article, Morton Smith ("Zealots and Sicarii: Their Origins and Relation," *HTR* 64 [1971], pp. 1-19) insists that the Sicarii must be distinguished from the Zealots in date of origin, locale, leadership and philosophy. We may suggest, however, that the fact that the name "Sicarii" is Latin while the name "Zealots" is of Greek origin is an indication that the names were given to these groups by their opponents. Moreover, the fact that the names "Sicarii" and "Zealots" do not occur in *Antiquities* and that the strange name "Fourth Philosophy" does not occur in *War*, even in the enumeration of the five revolutionary groups (*War* 7.259-274), may be an indication that the latter is a term for an umbrella organization that embraced the various revolutionary groups. Indeed, Menahem Stern ("Zealots," *EJ Yearbook* 1973, pp. 135-152) persuasively concludes that only a hypothesis connecting the Fourth Philosophy, the Sicarii and the Zealots can explain the significance that Josephus assigns to the first.

85. See Valentin Nikiprowetzky, "Josephus and the Revolutionary Parties," in Feldman and Hata, *Josephus, the Bible, and History* (see endnote 14), pp. 216-236.

86. *War* 2.434.

87. *War* 2.444.

88. *War* 7.29.

89. *Antiquities* 18.63-64.

90. For a discussion of this issue at length, see Louis H. Feldman, "The *Testimonium Flavianum*: The State of the Question," in *Christological Perspectives*, ed. Robert F. Berkey and Sarah A. Edwards (New York: Pilgrim, 1982), pp. 179-199, 288-293. See also John P. Meier, "The Testimonium Evidence for Jesus Outside the Bible," *BR*, June 1991, and his *A Marginal Jew: Rethinking the Historical Jesus*, vol. 1: *The Problem and the Person* (New York: Doubleday, 1991), pp. 56-88.

91. *War* 2.235-236, 253; *Antiquities* 20.121, 161.

92. Midrash, *Song of Songs Rabbah* 2:18.

93. See James C. VanderKam, "The People of the Dead Sea Scrolls: Essenes or Sadducees?" *BR*, Apr. 1991, pp. 42-47.

94. See Lawrence H. Schiffman, "The Significance of the Scrolls," *BR*, Oct. 1990, pp. 18-27.

95. See Hershel Shanks, "Dead Sea Scrolls Update," *BAR*, Jan./Feb. 1992.

96. See Frederick E. Greenspahn ("Why Prophecy Ceased," *JBL* 108 [1989], pp. 37-49), who concludes that the claim that prophecy had ceased was made by the rabbis in order to remove a real threat to their authority.

97. See Louis H. Feldman, "Prolegomenon" to M.R. James, *The Biblical Antiquities of Philo* (New York: Ktav, 1971), esp. pp. xxxviii-xlv.

98. See, in particular, Martin Hengel, *Judaism and Hellenism: Studies in Their Encounter in Palestine during the Early Hellenistic Period*, 2 vols. (Philadelphia: Fortress, 1974). I have challenged this view in "Hengel's *Judaism and Hellenism* in Retrospect," *JBL* 96 (1977), pp. 371-382, and "How Much Hellenism in Jewish Palestine?" *HUCA* 57 (1986), pp. 83-111.

99. *Apion* 1.60.

100. On the low level of Greek among Palestinian Jews, see Jan N. Sevenster, *Do You Know Greek? How Much Greek Could the First Century Jewish Christians Have Known?* (Leiden: Brill, 1969), pp. 65-71; Joseph A. Fitzmyer, "The Languages of Palestine in the First Century," *CBQ* 30 (1972), pp. 501-531.

101. *Antiquities* 20.263-264.

102. *War* 5.361.

103. *Life* 65-67.

104. Erwin R. Goodenough, *Jewish Symbols in the Greco-Roman Period*, 13 vols. (Princeton, NJ: Princeton Univ. Press, 1953-1968). See Morton Smith, "Goodenough's *Jewish Symbols* in Retrospect," *JBL* 86 (1967), p. 60.

105. See Victor Tcherikover, "The Greek Towns of Palestine," in *Hellenistic Civilization and the Jews*, ed. Tcherikover (Philadelphia: JPS, 1959), pp. 90-116.

106. See Magen Broshi, "Estimating the Population of Ancient Jerusalem," *BAR*, June 1978, pp. 10-15.

107. *Life* 235.

108. *War* 3.43.

109. Cf. Eric M. Meyers, "Galilean Regionalism as a Factor in Historical Reconstruction," *BASOR* 220-221 (1976), p. 97.

110. *Life* 40.

111. On Hellenizations in Josephus, see Louis H. Feldman, "Hellenizations in Josephus' Account of Man's Decline," in *Religions in An-*

Who Was Josephus?
(pages 22-23)

1. For critical bibliographies of scholarship on Josephus, see Louis H. Feldman, *Josephus and Modern Scholarship (1937-1980)* (Berlin: de Gruyter, 1984); "Flavius Josephus Revisited: The Man, His Writings, and His Significance," *ANRW* 2.21.2 (1984), pp. 763-862; "A Selective Critical Bibliography of Josephus," in *Josephus, the Bible, and History*, ed. Feldman and Gohei Hata (Detroit: Wayne State Univ., 1989), pp. 330-448. Per Bilde, *Flavius Josephus between Jerusalem and Rome: His Life, His Works, and Their Importance*, JSP Supp., series 2 (Sheffield, UK: Sheffield Academic Press, 1988).

2. *Life* 2.

3. *Life* 9.

4. *Life* 10-12. See Steve Mason (*Flavius Josephus on the Pharisees: A Composition-Critical Study* [Leiden: Brill, 1991], pp. 342-356), against the commonly held view that Josephus actually underwent a conversion to Pharisaism, has argued convincingly that Josephus was not and never claimed to be a Pharisee and that he actually disdained the Pharisees.

5. *Life* 13-16.

6. *Life* 28-29; *War* 2.562-568.

7. *War* 3.392.

8. BT *Gittin* 56a.

9. *Life* 423. For a critical survey of the literature dealing with Josephus' life, see Feldman, "Selective Critical Bibliography" (see endnote 1), pp. 340-344.

10. Seth Schwartz ("The Composition and Publication of Josephus' *Bellum Iudaicum* Book 7," *HTR* 79 [1986], pp. 373-385) argues persuasively that parts of Book 7 were composed as late as the early part of Trajan's reign (c. 100 C.E.).

11. *War* 1.3.

12. *Apion* 1.50.

13. For a critical bibliography dealing with Josephus' works, see Feldman, "Selective Critical Bibliography" (see endnote 1), pp. 393-400.

14. See the essays by individual scholars in *Josephus, Judaism, and Christianity*, ed. Louis H. Feldman and Gohei Hata (Detroit: Wayne State Univ., 1987), and *Josephus, the Bible, and History* (see endnote 1), esp. my comments on those essays in my introductions, pp. 23-67 and 17-49, respectively.

tiquity: Essays in Memory of Erwin Ramsdell Goodenough*, ed. Jacob Neusner, Studies in the History of Religions 14 (Leiden: Brill, 1968), pp. 336-353; "Abraham the Philosopher in Josephus," *TAPA* 99 (1968), pp. 143-156; "Hellenizations in Josephus' Version of Esther," *TAPA* 101 (1970), pp. 143-170; "Josephus as an Apologist to the Greco-Roman World: His Portrait of Solomon," in *Aspects of Religious Propaganda in Judaism and Early Christianity*, ed. Elisabeth Schüssler Fiorenza (Notre Dame, IN: Univ. of Notre Dame, 1976), pp. 69-98; "Josephus' Portrait of Saul," *HUCA* 53 (1982), pp. 45-99; "Abraham the General in Josephus," in *Nourished with Peace: Studies in Hellenistic Judaism in Memory of Samuel Sandmel*, ed. Frederick E. Greenspahn et al. (Chico, CA: Scholars Press, 1984), pp. 43-49; "Josephus as a Biblical Interpreter: The 'Aqedah," *JQR* 75 (1984-1985), pp. 212-252; "Josephus' Portrait of Deborah," in *Hellenica et Judaica: Hommage à Valentin Nikiprowetzky*, ed. André Caquot et al. (Paris: Editions Peeters, 1986), pp. 115-128; "Hellenizations in Josephus' *Jewish Antiquities*: The Portrait of Abraham," in Feldman and Hata, *Josephus, Judaism* (see endnote 27), pp. 133-153; "Use, Authority, and Exegesis of Mikra in the Writings of Josephus," in *Mikra: Text, Translation, Reading and Interpretation of the Hebrew Bible in Ancient Judaism and Early Christianity*, ed. Martin Jan Mulder and Harry Sysling, sec. 2, vol. 1 (Assen, Neth.: Van Gorcum, 1988), pp. 455-518; "Josephus' Portrait of Noah and Its Parallels in Philo, Pseudo-Philo's *Biblical Antiquities*, and Rabbinic Midrashim," *PAAJR* 55 (1988), pp. 31-57; "Josephus' Version of Samson," *JSJ* 19 (1988), pp. 171-214; "Josephus' Portrait of David," *HUCA* 60 (1989), pp. 129-174; "Josephus' Portrait of Jacob," *JQR* 79 (1988-1989), pp. 101-151; "Josephus' *Jewish Antiquities* and Pseudo-Philo's *Biblical Antiquities*," in Feldman and Hata, *Josephus, the Bible, and History* (see endnote 14), pp. 59-80; "Josephus's Portrait of Joshua," *HTR* 82 (1989), pp. 351-376; "Josephus' Interpretation of Jonah," *AJS Review* 17 (1992), pp. 1-29.

112. *Apion* 1.50. Henry St. John Thackeray (*Josephus the Man and the Historian* [New York: Jewish Institute of Religion, 1929], pp. 107-118), on the basis of a close study of Josephus' vocabulary and style, theorized that in books 15 and 16 of *Antiquities* Josephus utilized an assistant who had a particular love of Greek poetry, especially Sophocles, and that in books 17-19 he had an assistant who was particularly fond of Thucydides. In response to this "higher" criticism of Josephus, however, we may note

that Sophoclean and Thucydidean traces are to be found throughout *War* and *Antiquities*. Moreover, the presence of many similar phrases in other Greek works of the period, notably in Dionysius of Halicarnassus, shows that they are characteristic of first-century Greek rather than that they are the work of a special assistant.

113. *War* 1.3.

114. *Antiquities* 1.5.

115. See *Genesis Rabbah* 68.20.

116. Baron, *Social and Religious History* (see endnote 36), vol. 1, p. 170.

117. *Antiquities* 18.314-371.

118. *Antiquities* 18.376.

119. *Antiquities* 12.119; *Apion* 2.39.

120. *War* 7.45.

121. *War* 7.45.

122. *War* 2.477-478.

123. *War* 2.479.

124. *War* 7.100-111.

125. Cicero, *Pro Flacco* 28.68.

126. Cf., for example, *Antiquities* 14.213, 244-246. On the vertical alliance of the Jews with governments in antiquity, see Louis H. Feldman, "Anti-Semitism in the Ancient World," in *History and Hate: The Dimensions of Anti-Semitism*, ed. David Berger (Philadelphia: JPS, 1986), pp. 16-21. Horst R. Moehring ("The 'Acta Pro Judaeis' in the *Antiquities* of Flavius Josephus: A Study in Hellenistic and Modern Apologetic Historiography," in *Christianity, Judaism and Other Greco-Roman Cults: Studies for Morton Smith at Sixty*, part 3: *Judaism Before 70*, ed. Jacob Neusner [Leiden: Brill, 1975], pp. 124-158) contends that the documents quoted by Josephus were forged, and that since the fire of 69 C.E. destroyed about 3,000 documents in the Roman archives, no one was in a position to challenge him. We may reply that even if the documents in Rome had been burnt, it is hard to believe that there were no copies in the cities of Asia Minor affected by them or that people were not still alive who had an oral tradition as to their contents.

127. *Antiquities* 16.163.

128. *Antiquities* 14.188.

129. Philo, *In Flaccum* 7.47.

130. This is the conclusion of a recent treatment of the subject, Aryeh Kasher, *The Jews in Hellenistic and Roman Egypt: The Struggle for Equal Rights* (Tübingen: Mohr, 1985). This conclusion has now, however, been challenged by Constantine Zuckerman, "Hellenistic *Politeumata* and the Jews: A Reconsideration," *Scripta Classica Israelica* 8-9 (1985-1988), pp. 171-185. For a discussion of the scholarly literature on the subject, see Feldman, *Josephus and Modern Scholarship* (see endnote 30), pp. 331-338.

131. On this riot and its aftermath, see Philo, *In Flaccum*, passim, and *Legatio ad Gaium* 18.122, 19.131-20.132.

132. *Antiquities* 18.257-260.

133. Victor Tcherikover, *Corpus Papyrorum Judaicarum* (Cambridge, MA: Harvard Univ. Press, 1957), Prolegomena, vol. 1, p. 67.

134. *Antiquities* 19.280-285.

135. *War* 2.487-498.

136. *War* 2.497.

137. Cicero, *Pro Flacco* 28.66.

138. Suetonius, *Julius Caesar* 84.5.

139. Philo, *Legatio ad Gaium* 23.158.

140. *Antiquities* 18.143-168. There is good reason to doubt the statement of Suetonius (*Claudius* 25.4) that Claudius expelled from Rome the Jews who persisted in rioting at the instigation of Chrestus. Most scholars think that the reference is to Christos, that is Jesus, and to a Christian group in Rome. But Dio Cassius (*Roman History* 60.6.6) specifically says that Claudius did not expel the Jews; and Josephus and Tacitus, who have detailed accounts of this period, do not mention it at all. See Harry J. Leon, *The Jews of Ancient Rome* (Philadelphia: JPS, 1960), pp. 23-27.

141. Suetonius, *Titus* 7.1.

142. Suetonius, *Titus* 7.1.

143. *Life* 16.

144. *Antiquities* 20.195.

145. See Diana Delia, "The Population of Roman Alexandria," *TAPA* 118 (1988), pp. 287-288, who bases this estimate on a passage in the *Acta Alexandrinorum*.

146. Philo, *In Flaccum* 57.

147. BT *Sukkah* 51b.

148. BT *Yoma* 38a.

149. BT *Yoma* 38a.

150. BT *Arakhin* 10b.

151. Onias and Dositheus (*Apion* 2.49); Helkias and Ananias (*Antiquities* 13.349).

152. *Antiquities* 20.100.

153. Philo, *Legatio ad Gaium* 31.210.

154. Philo, *Legatio ad Gaium* 216.

155. *Antiquities* 14.110.

156. Mishnah *Yadayim* 4.3.

157. Horace, *Satires* 1.5.100.

158. Horace, *Satires* 1.9.69-70.

159. Tibullus, *Works* 1.3.18.

160. Ovid, *Ars Amatoria* 1.76,415-416.

161. For example, Suetonius, *Octavius Augustus* 76.2.

162. Strabo, *Geography* 16.2.40.763.

163. See Louis H. Feldman, "The Orthodoxy of the Jews of Hellenistic Egypt," *JSS* 22 (1960), pp. 212-237.

Who Was Philo?

(pages 30-31)

1. For the evidence, see Jacques Schwartz, "Note sur la famille de Philon d'Alexandrie," *Annuaire de l'Institut de Philologie et d'Histoire Orientales de l'Université Libre de Bruxelles* 13 (1953; Mélanges Isidore Levy), pp. 591-602.

2. See Alan Mendelson, *Secular Education in Philo of Alexandria* (Cincinnati, OH: Hebrew Union College, 1982), and Louis H. Feldman, "Philo's Views on Music," *JJML* 9 (1986-1987), pp. 36-54.

3. See Joshua Amir, "Explanations of Hebrew Names in Philo," *Tarbiz* 31 (1962), p. 297 (in Hebrew), and David Rokeah, "A New Onomasticon Fragment from Oxyrhynchus and Philo's Etymologies," *JTS* 19 (1968), pp. 70-82.

4. Philo, *De Specialibus Legibus* 2.15.62.

5. Philo, *De Migratione Abrahami* 16.89.

6. *Antiquities* 18.257-260.

7. E. Mary Smallwood, "Philo and Josephus as Historians of the Same Events," in *Josephus, Judaism and Christianity*, ed. Louis H. Feldman and Gohei Hata (Detroit: Wayne State Univ., 1987), pp. 114-129. For the view that Philo has an apologetic bias and that Josephus' account is simpler and more convincing, see Daniel R. Schwartz, "Josephus and Philo on Pontius Pilate," *Jerusalem Cathedra* 3 (1983), pp. 26-45.

164. BT *Bava Batra* 21a.

165. Philo, *De Specialibus Legibus* 2.15.62.

166. Philo, *De Providentia* 2.64.

167. *War* 7.420-436; *Antiquities* 12.387-388, 13.62-73, 20.236.

168. *War* 7.421. The Temple at Leontopolis is also mentioned in the Mishnah (*Menahot* 13:10) and in the Gemara (*Avodah Zarah* 52b, *Megillah* 10a), but the extant works of Philo make no mention of it, either because of its unimportance or because Philo remained loyal to the Jerusalem Temple.

169. Philo, *De Specialibus Legibus* 1.35.186

170. Philo, *De Specialibus Legibus* 3.5.29.

171. Jean B. Frey, *Corpus Inscriptionum Iudaicarum*, (Città del Vaticano, 1952), vol. 2, no. 1530.

172. Frey, *Corpus Inscriptionum Iudaicarum*, vol. 2, nos. 148, 149.

173. Frey, *Corpus Inscriptionum Iudaicarum*, vol. 2, no. 144, pp. 10-12.

174. BT *Ketubbot* 25a.

175. BT *Gittin* 88b.

176. Philo, *De Specialibus Legibus* 2.25.125.

177. Philo, *Quaestiones in Exodum* 1.7 on Exodus 12:5.

178. Philo, *Quaestiones in Genesin* 4.148 on Genesis 25:5-6.

179. Philo, *Hypothetica* 11.14-17.

180. On Jewish proselytism, see Louis H. Feldman, "Proselytism and Syncretism," in *The Diaspora in the Hellenistic-Roman World*, vol. of *World History of the Jewish People*, First Series, ed. Stern and Baras (Jerusalem: Am Oved, 1984), pp. 188-207, 340-345, 378-380 (in Hebrew), and "Jewish Proselytism," in *Eusebius, Judaism, and Christianity*, ed. Harold W. Attridge and Gohei Hata, forthcoming.

181. Philo, *De Vita Mosis* 2.5.27.

182. Philo, *De Virtutibus* 41.226.

183. Philo, *Legatio ad Gaium* 31.211.

184. *Apion* 2.210.

185. *Apion* 2.123.

186. *Apion* 2.258.

187. *Apion* 2.282.

188. For the many theories as to the interpretation of this verse, see Bernard J. Bamberger, *Proselytism in the Talmudic Period* (Cincinnati: Hebrew Union College, 1939), pp. 267-273.

189. For the evidence, see Jack Dean Kingsbury, "Matthew, the Gospel According to," in *Harper's Bible Dictionary*, ed. Paul J. Achtemeier (San Francisco: Harper & Row, 1985), p. 613.

190. *War* 7.45.

191. Horace, *Satires* 1.4.142-143.

192. Mentioned in Augustine, *City of God* 6.11.

193. Tacitus, *Histories* 5.5.1.

194. Juvenal, *Satires* 14.96-106.

195. Nahum Slouschz, *Hébraeo-Phéniciens et Judéo-Berbères: Introduction à l'histoire des juifs et du judaisme en Afrique* (Paris: Leroux, 1908) and his *Travels in North Africa* (Philadelphia: JPS, 1927).

196. BT *Menahot* 110a.

197. *War* 2.559-561.

198. See Lawrence H. Schiffman, "The Conversion of the Royal House of Adiabene in Josephus and Rabbinic Sources," in Feldman and Hata, *Josephus, Judaism* (see endnote 27), pp. 293-312. For a critical survey of the bibliography on the conversion, see Feldman, *Josephus and Modern Scholarship* (see endnote 30), pp. 730-732.

199. See esp., *Genesis Rabbah* on Genesis 46:10.

200. *Antiquities* 20.35.

201. See Jacob Neusner, "The Conversion of Adiabene to Judaism," *JBL* 83 (1964), pp. 60-66.

202. *Antiquities* 20.49-53.

203. Mishnah *Nazir* 3:6 and *Yoma* 3:10; BT *Sukkah* 2b.

204. *War* 2.520.

205. See Leon, *Jews of Ancient Rome* (see endnote 140), p. 15.

206. Valerius Maximus, *Facta et Dicta Memoribilia* 1.3.3.

207. *Antiquities* 18.81-84; cf. Tacitus, *Annals* 2.85; Suetonius, *Tiberius* 36; Dio Cassius, *Roman History* 57.18.5a.

208. Ernest L. Abel ("Were the Jews Banished from Rome in 19 A.D.?" *REJ* 127 [1968], pp. 383-386) argues that only the proselytes were driven out, since it would have been contrary to existing law, which Tiberius strictly obeyed, to banish any citizen without a trial. This seems likely since the Roman writer Tacitus, who was most hostile to the Jews, speaks of 4,200 Jewish freedmen being sent to Sardinia (*Annals* 2.85.4); and Suetonius, who is likewise hostile to them, is careful to mention the proselytes as included in the expulsion (*Tiberius* 36).

209. On the question of how such ideas might have been disseminated, see Louis H. Feldman, "Pro-Jewish Intimations in Anti-Jewish Remarks Cited in Josephus' *Against Apion*," *JQR* 78 (1987-1988), pp. 187-251.

210. Pseudo-Longinus, *On the Sublime* 9.9.

211. See Louis H. Feldman, "Jewish 'Sympathizers' in Classical Literature and Inscriptions," *TAPA* 81 (1950), pp. 200-208; "The Omnipresence of the God-Fearers," *BAR*, Sept./Oct. 1986, pp. 58-69.

212. Philo, *De Vita Mosis* 2.4.21-23.

213. *Apion* 2.282.

214. See Tcherikover, *Corpus Papyrorum Judaicarum* (see endnote 133), vol. 3, pp. 43-87.

215. Suetonius, *Tiberius* 32.2.

216. Petronius, fragment 37, Ernout.

217. Epictetus, mentioned in Arrian, *Dissertations* 2.19-21.

218. Published by Joyce Reynolds and Robert Tannenbaum, *Jews and God-Fearers at Aphrodisias: Greek Inscriptions with Commentary*, Cambridge Philological Society supp. 12 (Cambridge, MA: Cambridge Philological Society, 1987). See also, Louis H. Feldman, "Proselytes and 'Sympathizers' in the Light of the New In-

scriptions from Aphrodisias," *REJ* 148 (1989), pp. 265-305.

219. Robert S. MacLennan and A. Thomas Kraabel, "The God-Fearers—A Literary and Theological Invention," *BAR*, Sept./Oct. 1986, pp. 46-53.

220. JT *Megillah* 3.2.74a.

221. For other evidence of the existence of a class of God-fearers, see Feldman, "Omnipresence of the God-Fearers" (see endnote 211), pp. 58-69.

222. Juvenal, *Satires* 14.96-99.

223. See Leonard Greenspoon, "Mission to Alexandria: Truth and Legend About the Creation of the Septuagint, the First Bible Translation," *BR*, Aug. 1989, pp. 34-41.

224. Philo, *De Vita Mosis* 2.7.40-41.

225. Philo, *De Confusione Linguarum* 38.190. Occasionally, to be sure, Philo has etymologies of proper names which would seem to indicate a knowledge of Hebrew. But, as David Rokeah has demonstrated ("A New Onomasticon Fragment from Oxyrhynchus and Philo's Etymologies," *JTS* 19 [1968], pp. 70-82), Philo may well have derived such information from an *onomasticon* of Hebrew names similar to the one found at Oxyrhynchus.

226. Philo, *De Vita Mosis* 2.7.38.

227. Philo, *De Mutatione Nominum* 11.77-80; *Quaestiones in Genesin* 3.53.

228. See Alan Mendelson, *Secular Education in Philo of Alexandria* (Cincinnati: Hebrew Union College, 1982).

229. See Louis H. Feldman, "Philo's View on Music," *JJML* 9 (1986-1987), pp. 36-54.

230. Philo, *De Vita Mosis* 1.5.21-23.

231. Philo, *De Sacrificiis Abelis et Caini* 10.43-44; *De Congressu Quaerendae Eruditionis Gratia* 14.77-78.

232. Philo, *De Opificio Mundi* 25.77.

233. Philo, *De Cherubim* 24.80-81.

234. Philo, *Quod Omnis Probus Liber Sit* 5.26.

235. Philo, fragment, cited in Eusebius, *Praeparatio Evangelica* 8.14.58.

236. London Papyrus 1912, lines 92-95. See Louis H. Feldman, "The Orthodoxy of the Jews in Hellenistic Egypt," *JSS* 22 (1960), pp. 223-226.

237. BT *Avodah Zarah* 18b.

238. Philo, *De Ebrietate* 43.177.

239. Harry A. Wolfson, *Philo: Foundations of Religious Philosophy in Judaism, Christianity, and Islam* (Cambridge, MA: Harvard Univ. Press, 1947), vol. 2, pp. 439-460.

240. See Louis H. Feldman, *Studies in Judaica: Scholarship on Philo and Josephus (1937-*

1962) (New York: Yeshiva Univ., 1963), pp. 6-8, for a critical appraisal of Harry A. Wolfson's work and for references to major reviews of his work. On Philo's orthodoxy and orthopraxy, see Alan Mendelson, *Philo's Jewish Identity* (Atlanta: Scholars Press, 1988).

241. Philo, *Quis Rerum Divinarum Heres* 43.214.; *Quod Omnis Probus Liber Sit* 8.57.

242. Philo, *Quod Deterius Potiori Insidiari Soleat* 12.38-39.

243. Philo, *De Opificio Mundi* 44.129-130.

244. Philo, *De Abrahamo* 46.275.

245. Philo, *De Migratione Abrahami* 18.103.

246. Philo, *De Posteritate Caini* 18.63.

247. Philo, *De Confusione Linguarum* 11.41.

248. Philo, *De Fuga et Inventione* 20.112; *Quis Rerum Divinarum Heres* 20.188.

249. Philo, *De Specialibus Legibus* 1.59.319.

250. Philo, *De Cherubim* 14.49.

251. Philo, *De Cherubim* 14.49.

252. Philo, *De Migratione Abrahami* 7.35.

253. Philo, *De Opificio Mundi* 23.71.

254. Philo, *De Confusione Linguarum* 31.159.

255. Philo, *Quod Deterius Potiori Insidiari Soleat* 27.102.

256. Philo, *De Vita Mosis* 1.6.28.

257. Philo, *De Fuga et Inventione* 9.50.

258. Philo, *Quod Omnis Probus Liber Sit* 12.75-13.91; *Hypothetica* 11.1-18.

259. Philo, *De Vita Contemplativa* in its entirety.

T W O
The Life of Jesus

1. On the names of the Gospels, see E.P. Sanders and Margaret Davies, *Studying the Synoptic Gospels* (Philadelphia: Trinity Press International, 1989), pp. 5-16.

2. On the extra-canonical traditions, see Joachim Jeremias, *Unknown Sayings of Jesus*, Eng. transl. (London: SPCK, 1968); Christopher Tuckett, *Nag Hammadi Gospel Traditions: Synoptic Tradition in the Nag Hammadi Library* (Edinburgh: T & T Clark, 1986).

3. See W.D. Davies, *Invitation to the New Testament* (Garden City, NY: Doubleday, 1966), pp. 63-71.

4. There are numerous synopses available for study in both Greek and English. A good recent English synopsis is Robert Funk, *New Gospel Parallels: The Gospel of Mark*, 2 vols., rev. ed., Foundations and Facets Reference Series (Sonoma, CA: Polebridge Press, 1990).

5. See, for example, Jacob Neusner, *Rabbinic Traditions About the Pharisees Before 70*, 3 vols. (Leiden: Brill, 1971); *A History of Mishnaic Law*,

41 vols. (Leiden: Brill, 1974-1982).

6. For a list of secondary literature on criteria of authenticity, see E.P. Sanders, *Jesus and Judaism* (Philadelphia: Fortress, 1985), p. 357, n. 28.

7. Sanders, *Jesus and Judaism* (see endnote 6).

8. John's greater prominence is indicated in part by Jesus' appeal to his reputation in Mark 11:27-33 and parallels. Josephus also comments on John's great influence on the populace (*Antiquities* 18.116-119).

9. Apocrypha: Wisdom of Ben Sira [Sirach], or Ecclesiasticus, 36:11, cf. 48:10.

10. Dead Sea Scrolls: The War Scroll (1QM) 2.2f.; The Temple Scroll (11QTemple[a]) 18.14-16, 57.5f.

11. See Ben F. Meyer, *The Aims of Jesus* (Philadelphia: Trinity Press International; London: SCM, 1979).

12. *Antiquities* 18.117.

13. See Joachim Jeremias, *The Proclamation of Jesus*, Eng. transl. (London: SCM, 1971), pp. 108-113.

14. Albert Schweitzer, *The Quest of the Historical Jesus*, 3rd ed., Eng. transl. (New York, 1956), pp. 354-357.

15. Martin Hengel, *The Charismatic Leader and his Followers*, Eng. transl. (Edinburgh: T & T Clark; New York: Crossroad, 1981), pp. 50-63.

16. See most recently, E.P. Sanders, *Jewish Law from Jesus to the Mishnah* (Philadelphia: Trinity Press International, 1990), pp. 1-96.

17. David Daube, *The New Testament and Rabbinic Judaism* (London, 1956; repr. New York, 1973), pp. 55-62; W.D. Davies, *The Setting of the Sermon on the Mount* (Cambridge, UK, 1964), pp. 101-103.

18. Daube, *New Testament and Rabbinic Judaism* (see endnote 17), p. 60.

19. Letter of Aristeas 234.

20. Letter of Aristeas 170-171.

21. See Andre B. DuToit, "Hyperbolical Contrasts: A Neglected Aspect of Paul's Style," in *A South African Perspective on the New Testament*, ed. J.H. Petzer and P.J. Martin (Leiden: Brill, 1986), pp. 178-186.

22. Rudolf Bultmann, *The History of the Synoptic Tradition* (San Francisco: Harper & Row, 1963).

23. Geza Vermes, *Jesus the Jew: A Historian's Reading of the Gospels* (Philadelphia: Fortress, 1981); Hengel, *The Charismatic Leader* (see endnote 15); Ellis Rivkin, *What Crucified Jesus? The Political Execution of a Charismatic* (Nashville, TN: Abingdon, 1984); Sanders, *Jesus and Judaism* (see endnote 6), pp. 237-241.

24. On Jewish self-government and "the Sanhedrin," see E.P. Sanders, *Judaism: Practice and Belief, 63 BCE-66 CE* (Philadelphia: Trinity Press International, 1992), chap. 21; James McLaren, *Power and Politics in Palestine; The Jews and the Governing of their Land. 100 BC-AD 70* (Sheffield: SOTS, 1992).

25. *Antiquities* 17.217.

26. *War* 1.88; *Antiquities* 17.213-218; *War* 2.224-227; see also Matthew 26:5.

27. *Antiquities* 20.107.

28. *War* 6.300-301.

29. *War* 6.302-309.

30. In Macbeth, Banquo's ghost and the ghostly dagger, "a dagger of the mind"; in Hamlet, his father's ghost.

31. See, for example, Plutarch, *Brutus* 36.

32. 1 Kings 17:8-14; 2 Kings 4:18-36; Mark 5:21-43 (|| Matthew 9:18-26; Luke 8:40-56); Luke 7:11-17; Acts 9:36-43; John 11:5-44. See also Philostratus, *Life of Apollonius of Tyana* 4.45; Pliny, *Natural History* 26.13; Apuleius, *Florida* 19.

33. They had their own views of accuracy: see Sanders and M. Davies, *Studying the Synoptic Gospels* (see endnote 1), pp. 36-38.

T H R E E
After the Crucifixion—
Christianity Through Paul

1. Suetonius, *Claudius* 25.4.

2. This interpretation of the note in Suetonius has been disputed, but it remains the most plausible way of handling the evidence from both Roman and early Christian sources.

3. Tacitus, *Annals* 15.44.

4. Suetonius, *Nero* 16.

5. Sulpicius Severus, *Chronicle* 2.29.

6. Based on Robert Jewett, *A Chronology of Paul's Life* (Philadelphia: Fortress, 1979).

7. In Romans 15:28, Paul mentions his expectation of going beyond Rome to Spain, where the gospel has not yet been preached. There is no evidence that he ever reached this goal.

8. It is possible that Colossians, which uses language and expresses ideas not found in the other letters of Paul, was written in his name by one of Paul's disciples.

9. For a detailed reconstruction and content analysis of Q, see Howard Kee, *Jesus in History*, 2nd ed. (New York: Harcourt Brace Jovanovich, 1977), pp. 76-120.

10. The latter is the stance adopted by F.F. Bruce in his commentary on Acts (*The Acts of the Apostles* [Grand Rapids, MI: Eerdmans,

1972]). Useful surveys of scholarly studies on Acts include (from a conservative perspective): W.W. Gasque, *A History of the Criticism of the Acts of the Apostles* (Grand Rapids, MI: Eerdmans, 1975); and C.K. Barrett, *Luke the Historian in Recent Study* (London: Epworth, 1961). A defense of the historicity of Acts on a number of points is also offered by Martin Hengel in *Acts and the History of Earliest Christianity* (Philadelphia: Fortress, 1980). The detailed analyses of the historical evidence published a half century ago in five volumes by F.J. Foakes-Jackson and Kirsopp Lake, with Henry J. Cadbury (*The Beginnings of Christianity* [Macmillan, 1920; repr. Grand Rapids, MI: Baker 1966]), especially the two volumes edited by Cadbury (vol. 4, *Commentary*; vol. 5, *Additional Notes*), are still of great value in the examination of Acts against its literary and historical background.

11. See also Matthew 16:21, 17:23, 20:18-19 and Luke 9:22, 18:33.

12. See also Mark 13:26; Matthew 24:30-31; Luke 21:27.

13. Although the account of Jesus' last meal in John 13 does not include any of the details of the Eucharist, the language of giving thanks (*eucharistesas*) in John 6:11 shows that the cultic practice of the early Church lies behind his version of the feeding of the 5,000.

14. *Eccles. Hist.* 3.2. A full account of excavations at Pella in 1967 was published in Robert Huston Smith, *Pella of the Decapolis* (Wooster, OH: College of Wooster, 1973).

15. For details, see Eric Meyers and James Strange, *Archaeology, the Rabbis and Early Christianity* (Nashville, TN: Abingdon, 1981), pp. 81-87.

16. This is discussed in the introduction to my translation of the Testaments of the Twelve Patriarchs, in *The Old Testament Pseudepigrapha*, ed. James H. Charlesworth (Garden City, NY: Doubleday, 1983), vol. 1, pp. 779-780. Precisely the same Stoic concepts—natural law and conscience—appear in this document as in Paul's letters.

17. See Jacob Neusner, *From Politics to Piety: The Emergence of Pharisaic Judaism and Rabbinic Traditions about the Pharisees Before 70* (Englewood Cliffs, NJ: Prentice-Hall, 1973).

18. The Greek phrase *en emoi* could also mean "in me," which would imply an even more private encounter with the risen Christ than the usual translation, "to me."

19. The Greek term *paidagogos* refers to a servant assigned to rear children and keep them under control until they were able to assume

mature responsibilities.

20. The basic assessment of Acts as a historical source remains the older work of Cadbury in *The Beginnings of Christianity*, vols. 4 and 5 (see endnote 10). Recent studies include Hengel, *Acts and the History* (see endnote 10); Gerd Luedemann, *Earliest Christianity According to the Traditions in Acts: A Commentary* (London: SCM, 1989).

21. *Merkavah* (chariot) refers to the ancient picture of God as seated in a chariot-throne, combining imagery from the inner sanctuary of the Temple (1 Kings 7) and from Ezekiel's vision of the throne of God (Ezekiel 1).

22. *Agrammatos* means "unlettered," though it could mean merely "uneducated."

23. *Eccles. Hist.* 3.39.

24. My reconstruction of Q may be found in *Jesus in History* (see endnote 9). This has been used by Richard Edwards in his *Concordance of Q* (Missoula, MT: Scholars Press, 1975) and his *Theology of Q* (Philadelphia: Fortress, 1976) and by Norman Perrin in *The New Testament: An Introduction* (New York: Harcourt Brace Jovanovich, 1974), pp. 74-75.

25. In Paul's letters (Philemon 24), in the pseudo-Pauline material (Colossians 4:10; 2 Timothy 4:11) and in Acts (12:12,25, 15:37,39), he is referred to as associated with Paul as a co-worker. In 1 Peter 5:13 he is called "my son" by Peter.

26. See Vassilios Tzaferis, "A Pilgrimage to the Site of the Swine Miracle," *BAR*, Mar./Apr. 1989.

F O U R
Judaism From the Destruction of Jerusalem to the End of the Second Jewish Revolt: 70–135 C.E.

1. *Siddur Sim Shalom (A Prayer-book for Shabbat, Festivals and Weekdays)*, ed. J. Harlow (New York: Rabbinical Assembly, 1985), pp. 462-463.

2. *War* 7.1,1,1-2.

3. It is generally accepted today that the Qumran sect is to be identified with the Essenes described in detail by Josephus (*War* 2.8,2,120-161) and Philo (*Quod Omnis Probus Liber Sit* 75-91; *Hypothetica* 11,1-18). Previously, a number of scholars had questioned this identification and had suggested alternatively almost every sect known from Second Temple times.

4. *War* 7.6,6,216-218.

5. See Gedaliah Alon, *The Jews in Their Land in the Talmudic Age*, 2 vols. (Jerusalem: Magnes,

1980-1984), vol. 1, pp. 70-74; E. Mary Smallwood, *The Jews Under Roman Rule* (Leiden: Brill, 1976), pp. 339-345.

6. S.G.F. Brandon, *The Fall of Jerusalem and the Christian Church* (London: SPCK, 1968), pp. 167-184; S. Sowers, "The Circumstances and Recollection of the Pella-flight," *Theologische Zeitschrift* 26 (1970), pp. 305-320; J.J. Gunther, "The Fate of the Jerusalem Church," *Theologische Zeitschrift* 29 (1973), pp. 81-94; Raymond Pritz, *Nazarene Jewish Christianity* (Jerusalem: Magnes; Leiden: Brill, 1988), pp. 122-127.

7. The fall of Masada is now dated to 74 C.E. (instead of 73) by most scholars on the basis of epigraphic evidence stating that the Roman commander, Silva, arrived in Palestine a year later than previously assumed (see Werner Eck, *Senatoren von Vespasian bis Hadrian* [Munich: C.H. Beck, 1970], pp. 93-111).

8. *Eccles. Hist.* 3.12 and 19.

9. Tosefta *Sotah* 15:11.

10. For a handy summary of this spectrum of opinion, see George Nickelsburg, *Jewish Literature between the Bible and the Mishnah* (Philadelphia: Fortress, 1981), pp. 277-309.

11. It is widely assumed that 4 Ezra dates to the very end of the first century C.E. See Emil Schürer, *The History of the Jewish People in the Age of Jesus Christ (175 B.C.-A.D. 135)*, 3 vols., rev. and ed. Geza Vermes, Fergus Millar and Martin Goodman (Edinburgh: T & T Clark, 1973-1987), vol. 3, pp. 299-300.

12. It is generally assumed that the Fourth Sybil was written around the year 80 C.E., see Schürer, *History of the Jewish People* (see endnote 11), vol. 3, pp. 641-643. A sybil was a semimythical, semihistorical female figure from ancient Greek religion whose prophecies and oracles were dependent on divine inspiration. Jews as well as pagans wrote books under the Sybil pseudonym. See also *The Old Testament Pseudepigrapha: Apocalyptic Literature and Testaments*, 2 vols., ed. James H. Charlesworth (Garden City, NY: Doubleday, 1983), vol.1, pp. 381-389.

13. Schürer, *History of the Jewish People* (see endnote 11), vol. 3, pp.325-331.

14. See Dalia Trifon, "A Mishnah Fragment as Evidence of the Status of King Agrippa II," *Cathedra* 53 (1989), pp. 27-48 (in Hebrew).

15. A. Guttmann, *Rabbinic Judaism in the Making* (Detroit: Wayne State Univ., 1970), pp. 59-174, esp. pp. 102-104.

16. Robert Goldenberg, "The Broken Axis: Rabbinic Judaism and the Fall of Jerusalem," *JAAR* 45 (1977), pp. 869-882; Jacob Neusner,

"The Formation of Rabbinic Judaism: Yavneh (Jamnia) from A.D. 70 to 100," in *ANRW* 19/2 (1979), pp. 21-42; Peter Schäfer, "Die Flucht Joḥanan b. Zakkais aus Jerusalem und die Gründung des 'Lehrhauses' in Jabne," *ANRW* 19/2 (1979), pp. 43-101.

17. The periodization of these two stages is difficult to determine. It is generally considered to have taken place between 80 and 90 C.E.

18. JT *Shabbat* 16, 15d. The tradition of Yoḥanan's stay in the Galilee is revealing. He reportedly was asked but two questions during this time and supposedly reacted in the end with the exclamation, "Galilee, Galilee, you hate the Torah. In the end you will be handed over to land confiscators (*meˢsiqin*)." The authenticity of this reference, cited by a fourth-century Palestinian sage, has often been questioned. Nevertheless, it is difficult to imagine why such a comment would have been fabricated in the fourth century, at a time when the Galilee had become a center of rabbinic activity.

19. *Fathers According to Rabbi Nathan* A 14, B 28; BT *Sukkah* 28a; JT *Nedarim* 5, 39b.

20. Mishnah *Yadayim* 4:6; Tosefta *Parah* 3:8; BT *Bava Batra* 115b-116a; BT *Menahot* 65a-b.

21. *Midrash Tannaim*, 2 vols., ed. David Z. Hoffman (Berlin: H. Itzkowski, 1909), p. 58; *Fathers According to Rabbi Nathan* B 31.

22. *Mekhilta of Rabbi Ishmael*, Behodesh 11.

23. Mishnah *Sotah* 9:9; see also Tosefta *Sotah* 14:1-2.

24. *Fathers According to Rabbi Nathan* B 31.

25. Tosefta *Sotah* 15:12-14.

26. BT *Rosh Hashanah* 31b; BT *Sotah* 40a.

27. Mishnah *Rosh Hashanah* 4:1.

28. Mishnah *Rosh Hashanah* 4:3; Mishnah *Sukkah* 3:12.

29. Later this was interpreted to apply only to the month of Tishri.

30. Mishnah *Rosh Hashanah* 4:4.

31. BT *Rosh Hashanah* 31b; BT *Keritot* 9a; JT *Shekalim* 8, 4, 51b. This *takkanah* is problematic. The Tosefta (*Shekalim* 3:22) mentions it without attributing it to Yoḥanan, and it appears to have remained a matter of dispute among his students (*Sifre Zutta*, ed. Hayyim S. Horowitz [Leipzig: Gustav Fock, 1917], p. 283).

32. BT *Rosh Hashanah* 31b; BT *Beẓah* 5a-b. On the difficulty of attributing this *takkanah* to Yoḥanan, see the talmudic discussion itself, as well as Tosefta *Ma'aser Sheni* 5:15-16.

33. Mishnah *Avot* 1:2, following the interpretation of Judah Goldin, *Studies in Midrash and Related Literature* (Philadelphia: JPS, 1988), pp. 28-30.

34. *Fathers According to Rabbi Nathan* A 4.

35. Tosefta *Kelim–Bava Batra* 2:4.

36. *Sifre Numbers* 124.

37. Tosefta *Kelim–Bava Batra* 5:6; Tosefta *Kilayim* 1:3-4; Tosefta *Niddah* 4:3-4; Mishnah *Kelim* 5:4; Tosefta *Kelim–Bava Mezia* 11:2.

38. Tosefta *Sanhedrin* 2:13; BT *Shabbat* 11a.

39. Tosefta *Terumot* 2:13.

40. Tosefta *Berakhot* 4:15; Tosefta *Pesahim* 3:11 and parallels; Tosefta *Mikva'ot* 6:3.

41. Mishnah *Nega'im* 7:4; Tosefta *Demai* 5:24.

42. Mishnah *Gittin* 1:5; Tosefta *Shabbat* 13:2; Mishnah *Eruvin* 10:10; Tosefta *Mo'ed Katan* 2:15; Mishnah *Avodah Zarah* 3:4; BT *Avodah Zarah* 32a; Tosefta *Pesahim* 2:15-16; Tosefta *Terumot* 2:13.

43. BT *Niddah* 69b-71a.

44. BT *Rosh Hashanah* 26a; *Sifre Numbers* 4; Tosefta *Yevamot* 14:5; Mishnah *Yevamot* 16:7; *Genesis Rabbah* 33:5; BT *Avodah Zarah* 34a, 39a.

45. *Deuteronomy Rabbah* 2:24; Mishnah *Ma'aser Sheni* 5:9; Tosefta *Bezah* 2:12 and more. See Alon, *Jews in Their Land* (see endnote 5), vol. 1, pp. 124-131.

46. Tosefta *Sanhedrin* 8:1.

47. JT *Rosh Hashanah* 1,6, 57b; BT *Rosh Hashanah* 22a.

48. *Life* 38,189-194.

49. David Goodblatt, "The Jews of Palestine, 70-132 C.E.," in *Judea and Rome–The Jewish Revolts*, ed. Uriel Rappaport (Jerusalem: Am Oved, 1983), pp. 155-184 (in Hebrew).

50. Mishnah *Eduyyot* 7:7.

51. Further possible explanations as to the nature of the authority granted to Rabban Gamaliel include permission to go abroad and official appointment as Patriarch of the Jews.

52. Tosefta *Demai* 5:24.

53. Tosefta *Berakhot* 4:15.

54. *Sifre Numbers* 1:16; *Sifre Zutta* 18:7.

55. BT *Bava Mezia* 59b.

56. Mishnah *Rosh Hashanah* 2:8-9.

57. BT *Berakhot* 27b-28a; JT *Berakhot* 4,1, 7c-d. For an analysis of this tradition, see Robert Goldenberg, "The Deposition of Rabban Gamaliel II: An Examination of the Sources," *JJS* 23 (1972), pp. 167-190 (reprinted in *Persons and Institutions in Early Rabbinic Judaism*, ed. William S. Green [Missoula, MT: Scholars Press, 1977], pp. 9-47).

58. Lee I. Levine, "The Second Temple Synagogue: The Formative Years," in *The Synagogue in Late Antiquity*, ed. Levine (Philadelphia: ASOR, 1987), pp. 7-31.

59. Ismar Elbogen, *Prayer in Israel in Its Historical Development*, transl. and ed. Joshua Amir

and J. Heinemann (Tel Aviv: Dvir, 1972), pp. 185-195 (in Hebrew); Joseph Heinemann, *Prayer in the Talmud: Forms and Patterns* (Berlin: de Gruyter, 1977), pp. 15ff.; Naomi G. Cohen, "The Nature of Shim'on Hapekuli's Act," *Tarbiz* 52 (1983), pp. 547-555 (in Hebrew); Reuven Kimelman, "*Birkat Ha-Minim* and the Lack of Evidence for an Anti-Christian Jewish Prayer in Late Antiquity," in *Jewish and Christian Self-Definition*, vol. 2: *Aspects of Judaism in the Graeco-Roman Period*, ed. A.L. Baumgarten et al., pp. 226-244.

60. Roger T. Beckwith, "Formation of the Hebrew Bible," in *Mikra*, ed. Martin J. Mulder (Philadelphia: Fortress, 1988), pp. 58-61 and literature cited therein, esp. Sid Z. Leiman, *The Canonization of Hebrew Scripture: The Talmudic and Midrashic Evidence* (Hamden, UK: Archon, 1976) and "Inspiration and Canonicity: Reflections on the Formation of the Biblical Canon," in Baumgarten et al., *Jewish and Christian Self-Definition* (see endnote 59), vol. 2, pp. 56-63.

61. Shmuel Safrai, "Halakha," in *The Literature of the Sages*, 2 parts, ed. Safrai (Philadelphia: Fortress, 1987), part 1, pp. 185-200.

62. Sigmund Stein, "The Influence of Symposia Literature on the Pesach Haggada," *JJS* 8 (1957), pp. 13-44.

63. Schürer, *History of the Jewish People* (see endnote 11), vol. 1, pp. 534-557; *The Bar-Kokhva Revolt–A New Approach*, eds. Aharon Oppenheimer and Uriel Rappaport (Jerusalem: Yad Izhak Ben Zvi, 1984); Shimon Applebaum, "The Bar-Kokhba Rebellion," in Rappaport, *Judea and Rome* (see endnote 49), pp. 207-260; Smallwood, *Jews Under Roman Rule* (see endnote 5), pp. 428-466; Peter Schäfer, *Der Bar Kokhba-Aufstand: Studien zum zweiten jüdischen Krieg gegen Rom* (Tübingen: Mohr, 1981).

64. Benjamin Isaac and Aharon Oppenheimer, "The Revolt of Bar Kochba: Ideology and Modern Scholarship," *JJS* 36 (1985), pp. 33-60.

65. See for example, JT *Ta'anit* 4,8, 68d-69a.

66. Dio Cassius, *History of Rome* 69,14,1.

67. Aharon Oppenheimer, "The Messianism of Bar-Kokhba," in *Messianism and Eschatology*, ed. Zvi Baras (Jerusalem: Zalman Shazar Centre, 1983), pp. 153-165 (in Hebrew).

68. JT *Ta'anit* 4,8, 68d.

69. *Genesis Rabbah* 64:10.

70. Spartianus, *Vita Hadriani* 14:2, in *Scriptores Historiae Augustae*.

71. Dio Cassius, *History of Rome* 69,12.

72. *Eccles. Hist.* 4,6; Hugo Mantel, "The Causes of the Bar Kokba Revolt," *JQR* 58 (1968), pp. 274-296. See now Menachem Mor, *The Bar-*

Kochba Revolt: Its Extent and Effect (Jerusalem: Ben-Zvi Inst., 1991), pp. 41-59 (in Hebrew).

73. *Eccles. Hist.* 3,12; 19-20; 32.

74. Timothy D. Barnes, "Trajan and the Jews," *JJS* 40 (1989), pp. 145-162 and literature cited therein.

75. *Corpus Papyrorum Judaicarum*, 3 vols., ed. Victor Tcherikover and Alexander Fuks (Cambridge, MA: Harvard Univ. Press, 1964), vol.3, p. 258, no. 450.

76. Dio Cassius, *History of Rome* 68,32.

77. *Eccles. Hist.* 4,2.

78. *Eccles. Hist.* 4,2; Dio Cassius, *History of Rome* 68,32,1.

79. See, for example, *Supplementum Epigraphicum Graecum* (Leiden: Sijthoff, 1938), vol. 9, p. 252.

80. Smallwood, *Jews Under Roman Rule* (see endnote 5), pp. 412-415.

81. Smallwood, *Jews Under Roman Rule* (see endnote 5), pp. 415-421.

82. *Vita Hadriani* 5:2 (see endnote 70).

83. Mishnah *Sotah* 9:14; *Seder Olam*, ed. Adolphe Neubauer (Oxford: Clarendon, 1895), p. 66.

84. Israel Roll, "The Roman Road System in Judaea," in *The Jerusalem Cathedra*, 3 vols., ed. Lee I. Levine (Detroit: Wayne State Univ., 1983), vol. 1, pp. 136-161.

85. Saul Lieberman, "Persecution of the Religion of Israel," in *Jubilee Volume in Honor of Salo Baron* (Jerusalem: American Academy for Jewish Research, 1974), pp. 213-245 (in Hebrew); Moshe D. Herr, "Persecutions and Martyrdom in Hadrian's Days," *Scripta Hierosolymitana* 23 (1973), pp. 85-125.

F I V E

Christianity from the Destruction of Jerusalem to Constantine's Adoption of the New Religion: 70-312 C.E.

1. The first-century Jewish historian Josephus gives a graphic account of the event, *War* 6.4.5, 249-253.

2. The battle and its date are recorded by the Christian apologist Lactantius in *On the Deaths of Persecutors* 44 and by Eusebius, *Eccles. Hist.* 9.9.2-10, where the inscription on Constantine's statue is mentioned.

3. For general histories of the early Church, see Philip Carrington, *The Early Christian Church*, 2 vols. (Cambridge, UK: Cambridge Univ. Press, 1957); Jean Daniélou and Henri Marrou, *The Christian Centuries*, vol. 1: *First Six Hundred Years* (London: Darton, Longman &

Todd; New York: McGraw-Hill, 1964); Henry Chadwick, *The Early Church* (London: Penguin, 1967); Helmut Koester, *Introduction to the New Testament*, vol. 2: *History and Literature of Early Christianity* (Berlin: de Gruyter, 1982); W.H.C. Frend, *The Rise of Christianity* (Philadelphia: Fortress, 1984). A provocative study is Walter Bauer, *Orthodoxy and Heresy in Earliest Christianity* (rev. Georg Strecker; ed. Robert Kraft and Gerhard Krodel [Philadelphia: Fortress, 1971]); originally appeared as *Rechtgläubigkeit und Ketzerei im ältesten Christentum*, BHT 10 (Tübingen: Mohr [Siebeck], 1934). On this work, see Daniel J. Harrington, "The Reception of Walter Bauer's *Orthodoxy and Heresy in Earliest Christianity* During the Last Decade," in *The Light of All Nations: Essays on the Church in New Testament Research*, Good News Studies 3 (Wilmington, DE: Glazier, 1982), and Thomas A. Robinson, *The Bauer Thesis Examined: The Geography of Heresy in the Early Christian Church*, Studies in the Bible and Early Christianity 11 (Lewiston, NY: Edwin Mellen, 1988).

4. A comprehensive reference work is Johannes Quasten, *Patrology*, 3 vols. (Utrecht, Neth.: Spectrum, 1950-1960). Most of the literature is available in *The Ante-Nicene Fathers*, 10 vols., ed. Alexander Roberts and James Donalson (Edinburgh, 1885-1887; New York: Scribners, 1912-1927).

5. Much of the relevant data is collected in Graydon F. Snyder, *Ante Pacem: Archaeological Evidence of Church Life Before Constantine* (Macon, GA: Mercer Univ. Press, 1985). See also James Stevenson, *A New Eusebius: Documents Illustrative of the History of the Church to A.D. 337* (London: SPCK, 1957).

6. Yehudah Rapuano, "Did Philip Baptize the Eunuch at Ein Yael?" *BAR*, Nov./Dec. 1990, pp. 44-49. On the missionary efforts of the early Church, see E. Glenn Hinson, *The Evangelization of the Roman Empire* (Macon, GA: Mercer Univ. Press, 1981).

7. See *First Clement* 5.7.

8. See Adrian N. Sherwin-White, *The Letters of Pliny: A Historical and Social Commentary* (Oxford: Clarendon, 1966), for the texts and a commentary.

9. *Eccles. Hist.* 5.10.1-4; this fits what is known of the trade routes of the time.

10. For translations of the most important texts, often fragmentary, *New Testament Apocrypha*, 2 vols., ed. Edgar Hennecke and Wilhelm Schneemelcher; transl. R. McL. Wilson (Philadelphia: Westminster, 1963), vol. 2, pp. 167-570.

11. In general, see Martin Dibelius and Hans Conzelmann, *The Pastoral Epistles*, Hermeneia Commentaries (Philadelphia: Fortress, 1972).

12. Wayne Meeks (*The Moral World of the First Christians* [Philadelphia: Westminster, 1986]) usefully surveys the forms of ethical exhortation at work. Elizabeth Schüssler Fiorenza (*In Memory of Her: A Feminist Theological Reconstruction of Christian Origins* [New York: Crossroad, 1983]) treats perceptively the increasingly patriarchal character of Christianity in this period.

13. A Greek text of the *Didache* was discovered in 1875 in a library in Constantinople in a codex dating to 1057 C.E.

14. Another example of teaching on the "two ways" appears in the *Epistle of Barnabas* 18-20.

15. For the late first century, see Revelation 1:10; for the early second century, Ignatius, *Epistle to the Magnesians* 9 and *Epistle of Barnabas* 15.8. For the mid-second century data, cf. Justin Martyr, *1 Apology* 67.

16. For a full treatment of the text, see Harold W. Attridge, *The Epistle to the Hebrews*, Hermeneia Commentaries (Philadelphia: Fortress, 1989).

17. A recent analysis of *First Clement* is offered by Barbara Bowe, *A Church in Crisis: Ecclesiology and Paraenesis in Clement of Rome*, HDR 23 (Minneapolis: Fortress, 1988). On the issues of church order raised by the text, see John Fuellenbach, *Ecclesiastical Office and the Primacy of Rome*, Studies in Christian Antiquity 20 (Washington, DC: Catholic Univ. Press, 1980). Dates ranging from 70 to 140 have been proposed. See the discussion of the issue in Attridge, *Epistle to the Hebrews* (see endnote 16), pp. 6-8.

18. See *Eccles. Hist.* 3.4.9, 3.21.1, 5.6.2-3, citing Irenaeus, *Against Heresies* 3.3.3.

19. *First Clement* 42.

20. Of the critical problems of Ignatius' letters, see William R. Schoedel, *Ignatius of Antioch*, Hermeneia Commentaries (Philadelphia: Fortress, 1985). On the development of ecclesiastical office, see Hans von Campenhausen, *Ecclesiastical Authority and Spiritual Power in the Church of the First Three Centuries*, transl. J.A. Baker (Stanford, CA: Stanford Univ. Press, 1969), and Eric G. Jay, "From Presbyters-Bishops to Bishops and Presbyters," *SC* 1 (1983), pp. 125-162.

21. From Smyrna, modern Izmir, on the western shore of Asia Minor, Ignatius wrote to Ephesus, Magnesia and Tralles. From Troas, farther north on the coast, he wrote to Philadelphia and Smyrna, as well as a personal letter to Polycarp, bishop of Smyrna. Dates be-

tween 105 and 135 have been proposed for Ignatius' martyrdom. For a review of the issue, see William R. Schoedel, "Ignatius and the Reception of Matthew in Antioch," in *Social History of the Matthean Community*, ed. David L. Balch (Minneapolis: Fortress, 1991), pp. 129-177, esp. pp. 130-131.

22. Cf. Ignatius, *Magnesians* 10; *Philadelphians* 6.

23. Ignatius, *Trallians* 10; *Smyrneans* 2,5. It is possible that Ignatius is in fact dealing with two facets of a single problem, people who wanted to continue the observance of Jewish customs and who discounted the significance of Jesus' suffering humanity.

24. Cf., e.g., Ignatius, *Ephesians* 3-5; *Magnesians* 4, 6-7; *Trallians* 7; *Smyrneans* 8-9.

25. Ignatius, *Smyrneans* 8.2.

26. Justin Martyr, *First Apology* 65-67.

27. On the development of the liturgy, see Josef A. Jungmann, *The Early Liturgy: To the Time of Gregory the Great* (Notre Dame, IN: Univ. of Notre Dame Press, 1959).

28. *Eccles. Hist.* 4.11.7. For a recent discussion of his activities, see Gerd Luedemann, *Opposition to Paul in Jewish Christianity*, transl. M. Eugene Boring (Minneapolis: Fortress, 1989), pp. 155-168.

29. *Eccles. Hist.* 4.8.2.

30. The fragments are found *Eccles. Hist.* 2.22.4-18; 3.20.1-6; 3.32.3-8; 4.8.2; 4.22.4-9; reference to the succession of Christian leaders appears at *Eccles. Hist.* 4.22.3.

31. A defense of the Quartodeciman practice and its apostolic basis by Polycrates, bishop of Ephesus, survives in *Eccles. Hist.* 5.24.2-8.

32. See *Eccles. Hist.* 5.24.10-18.

33. For Victor and the response to his action, see *Eccles. Hist.* 5.24.9-10.

34. The fourth-century heresiologist Epiphanius (*Panarion* 48.1) gives a date of 157, but the date of Eusebius (*Eccles. Hist.* 5.4.3) is to be preferred. Cf., Hippolytus, *Refutation of All Heresies* 8.19.1-3.

35. According to an anti-Montanist named Apollonius, see *Eccles. Hist.* 5.18.2. For a collection of Montanist oracles, see Hennecke-Schneemelcher, *New Testament Apocrypha* (see endnote 10), vol. 2, pp. 685-689. Most recently see Ronald Heine, *The Montanist Oracles and Testimonia*, Patristic Monograph Series 14 (Macon, GA: Mercer Univ. Press, 1989).

36. *Eccles. Hist.* 5.16.1-17.4 preserves fragments of the major work of an anonymous writer as well as the work of Appollinarius opposing Montanism.

37. Note the letters preserved in *Eccles. Hist.*

5.19. The Roman bishop Eleutherus (c. 174-189) rejected Montanism in a written statement, to which Tertullian (*Against Praxeas* 1) refers.

38. See Gregory Dix, *The Treatise on the Apostolic Tradition of St. Hippolytus of Rome: Historical Introduction, Textual Materials and Translation* (London: SPCK; New York: Macmillan, 1937, repr., with corrections, preface and bibliography by Henry Chadwick, 1968); Bernard Botte, *Hippolyte de Rome, La Tradition Apostolique: Texte Latin, introduction, traduction et notes*, Sources chrétiennes 11 (Paris: Cerf, 1946). For English translation, see G.J. Cuming, *Hippolytus: A Text for Students*, Grove Liturgical Studies 8 (Nottingham, UK: Grove, 1976). For the ordination texts contained in this work and comparable liturgical sources, see Paul F. Bradshaw, *Ordination Rites of the Ancient Churches of East and West* (New York: Pueblo, 1990).

39. The *Didascalia* survives in its entirety in Syriac and in translations in Ethiopic and Arabic; portions were translated into Latin. The Greek original was incorporated in the fourth-century church order, the *Apostolic Constitutions*. See R.H. Connolly, *Didascalia apostolorum: The Syriac Version Translated and Accompanied by the Verona Latin fragments* (Oxford: Oxford Univ. Press, 1929).

40. Hippolytus' charges against Callistus are in *Refutation of All Heresies* 9.12.20-26.

41. On Roman Christianity and Hermas, see Carolyn Osiek, *Rich and Poor in the Shepherd of Hermas: An Exegetical-Social Investigation*, CBQ Monograph 15 (Washington, DC: CBA, 1983).

42. Tertullian, *On Modesty* 10.12.

43. Cyprian, *On the Lapsed*. See Peter Hinchliff, *Cyprian of Carthage and the Unity of the Christian Church* (London: Chapman, 1974).

44. Novatian had established a reputation as a theologian, particularly for his work *On the Trinity*. See Herbert Moore, *The Treatise of Novatian on the Trinity* (London: SPCK, 1919). On Modalism, see pp. 181 on the development of doctrine.

45. Eusebius (*Eccles. Hist.* 6.43.1-46.5) describes the controversy and the lively correspondence between Rome and various eastern bishops, although he calls the schismatic Roman Novatus.

46. A translation and useful commentary on Cyprian's extensive surviving correspondence is Graeme W. Clarke, *The Letters of St. Cyprian of Carthage*, 4 vols., Ancient Christian Writers 43-47 (New York: Newman, 1984-1989).

47. The attempt by John A.T. Robinson (*Redating the New Testament* [Philadelphia:

Westminster, 1976]) to date the Gospels much earlier has not won acceptance. Matthew 22:7 clearly alludes to the destruction of Jerusalem. Moreover, the cry attributed to the crowds at Matthew 27:25 is part of his attempt to explain the reason for the destruction of city and temple. Cf. also Matthew 23:26.

48. For these texts see William H. Brownlee, *The Midrash Pesher of Habakkuk*, SBL Monograph 24 (Missoula, MT: Scholars Press, 1979); Maurya P. Horgan, *Pesharim: Qumran Interpretations of Biblical Books*, CBQ Monograph 8 (Washington, DC: CBA, 1979).

49. Like Matthew, Luke was clearly written after the destruction of Jerusalem in 70, as indicated by the handling of the prophecy in Luke 21:20 as a reference to Jerusalem's fate.

50. On the literary qualities of Luke and Acts, see Charles H. Talbert, *Reading Luke: A Literary and Theological Commentary on the Third Gospel* (New York: Crossroad, 1982); Robert C. Tannehill, *The Narrative Unity of Luke-Acts*, 2 vols. (Philadelphia: Fortress, 1986-1989); David Aune, *The New Testament in Its Literary Environment* (Philadelphia: Westminster, 1987), pp. 77-157; Richard I. Pervo, *Profit with Delight: The Literary Genre of the Acts of the Apostles* (Philadelphia: Fortress, 1987).

51. For example, the Good Samaritan (Luke 10:30-37) and the Prodigal Son (Luke 15:11-32).

52. On the infancy narratives in general, see Raymond E. Brown, *The Birth of the Messiah* (Garden City, NY: Doubleday, 1977).

53. The historical reliability of Acts continues to be debated. For opposing views, see Martin Hengel, *Acts and the History of Earliest Christianity* (London: SCM, 1979), and Ernst Haenchen, *The Acts of the Apostles: A Commentary* (Philadelphia: Westminster, 1971). A judicious assessment is offered by Gerd Luedemann, *Early Christianity According to the Traditions in Acts* (Philadelphia: Fortress, 1987). The most recent critical commentary is Hans Conzelmann, *Acts of the Apostles*, Hermeneia Commentaries (Philadelphia: Fortress, 1987).

54. There has been considerable debate about Luke's attitudes toward the Jews. See Jacob Jervell, *Luke and the People of God* (Minneapolis: Augsburg, 1977); David Tiede, *Prophecy and History in Luke-Acts* (Philadelphia: Fortress, 1980); Donald Juel, *Luke-Acts: The Promise of History* (Atlanta: John Knox, 1983); Robert L. Brawley, *Luke-Acts and the Jews: Conflict, Apology, and Conciliation*, SBL Monograph 33 (Atlanta: Scholars Press, 1987); Jack T. Sanders, *The Jews in Luke-Acts* (Philadelphia: Fortress, 1987).

55. See, e.g., Acts 16:35-40 (officials at Philippi); Acts 18:12-15 (Gallio in Corinth); Acts 26:32 (Agrippa). Luke rationalizes contrary evidence. Thus, Felix left Paul in bondage merely to curry favor with the Jews (Acts 24:27).

56. On the critical problems of Colossians, see Eduard Lohse, *Colossians and Philemon*, Hermeneia Commentaries (Philadelphia: Fortress, 1971).

57. Numerous fine commentaries are available. See esp. Raymond E. Brown, *The Gospel According to John*, 2 vols., Anchor Bible 29, 29A (Garden City, NY: Doubleday, 1966-1970).

58. See, e.g., *Eccles. Hist.* 3.23.1-4; 3.28.6, citing second-century sources Irenaeus and Clement of Alexandria.

59. Clement of Alexandria, quoted in *Eccles. Hist.* 6.14.7.

60. Louis Martyn, *History and Theology in the Fourth Gospel*, 2nd ed. (Nashville, TN: Abingdon, 1979), has argued that the anti-Jewish polemic of the Fourth Gospel was occasioned by the *Birkat ha-Minim*, the blessing (in reality an imprecation) on heretics. For scepticism, see Reuven Kimelman, "*Birkat Ha-Minim* and the Lack of Evidence for an Anti-Christian Jewish Prayer in Late Antiquity," in *Jewish and Christian Self-Definition*, vol. 2: *Aspects of Judaism in the Graeco-Roman Period*, ed. A.L. Baumgarten et al. (Philadelphia: Fortress, 1981), pp. 226-244.

61. There is apparently an allusion to the tradition in Hebrews 11:37.

62. Ascension of Isaiah 3:21-31.

63. Ascension of Isaiah 3:23-24. A comprehensive thematic treatment of this sort of literature may be found in Jean Daniélou, *A History of Early Christian Doctrine before the Council of Nicaea*, vol. 1: *The Theology of Jewish Christianity* (London: Darton, Longman and Todd; Chicago: Regnery, 1964).

64. See *Antiquities* 20.9.1, 197-203.

65. For scepticism about the flight to Pella, recounted in *Eccles. Hist.* 3.5.3, see Gerd Luedemann, "The Successors of Pre-70 Jerusalem Christianity: A Critical Evaluation of the Pella-Tradition," in *Jewish and Christian Self-Definition*, vol. 1: *The Shaping of Christianity in the Second and Third Centuries*, ed. E.P. Sanders (Philadelphia: Fortress, 1980), pp. 161-173.

66. These works are part of the Nag Hammadi find, discussed below. Text and translation are in *Nag Hammadi Codices V, 2-5 and VI with Papyrus Berolinensis 8502, 1 and 4*, ed. Douglas M. Parrott, Nag Hammadi Studies 11 (Leiden: Brill, 1979), pp. 65-150.

67. For reports on the Nazoreans and Ebionites, see Irenaeus, *Against Heresies* 1.26.2; Hippolytus, *Refutation of All Heresies* 7.34; *Eccles. Hist.* 3.27.1-2; Epiphanius, *Panarion* 29-30. The latter is now available in Francis E. Williams, *The Panarion of Epiphanius of Salamis Book I (Sets 1-46)*, Nag Hammadi Studies 35 (Leiden: Brill, 1987).

68. The character and history of Jewish Christianity is much debated. Important discussions include: Hans Joachim Schoeps, *Jewish Christianity* (Philadelphia: Fortress, 1964); R.A. Pritz, *Nazarene Jewish Christianity: From the End of the New Testament Period Until Its Disappearance in the Fourth Century* (Jerusalem: Magnes; Leiden: Brill, 1988); Alan Segal, "Jewish Christianity," in *Eusebius, Judaism and Christianity*, ed. Harold W. Attridge and Gohei Hata (Detroit: Wayne State Univ. Press, 1992), pp. 326-354; and Luedemann, *Opposition to Paul in Jewish Christianity* (see endnote 28).

69. Many of the fragments of the *Book of Elchasai* are in Hippolytus, *Refutation of All Heresies* 9.13-17, 10.29.

70. The Elchasaites are mentioned in a sermon of Origen, preserved in *Eccles. Hist.* 6.38.1, as a recent phenomenon.

71. The circumstances of the discovery of the Cologne Mani Codex remain obscure. It was probably uncovered in Upper Egypt, perhaps around ancient Lycopolis, a Manichaean center, in the middle of this century, then acquired by the Cologne papyrus collection. For an account of the decipherment, see Albert Henrichs, "The Cologne Mani Codex Reconsidered," *Harvard Studies in Classical Philology* 83 (1979), pp. 339-367. The facsimile edition is Ludwig Koenen and Cornelia Römer, *Der Kölmner Mani-Kodex: Abbildungen und diplomatischer Text* (Bonn: Habelt, 1985). A translation is available in Ron Cameron and Arthur Dewey, *The Cologne Mani Codex (P. Colon. inv. nr. 4780) "Concerning the Origin of His Body,"* SBL Texts and Translations 15 (Missoula, MT: Scholars Press, 1979). On Manichaeism, see George Widengren, *Mani and Manichaeism* (New York: Holt, Rinehart & Winston, 1965).

72. *Eccles. Hist.* 7.31.2.

73. For the text and translation, see *Nag Hammadi Codex II,2-7, together with XIII.2*, Brit. Lib. Or. 4926(1), and P. Oxy. 1, 654, 655*, 2 vols., ed. Bentley Layton, Nag Hammadi Studies 20, 21 (Leiden: Brill, 1988-1989); vol. 1, pp. 37-93 (Coptic); vol. 1, pp. 95-128 (Greek fragments).

74. Various dates for the composition of the Gospel of Thomas have been proposed, from the mid-first to the late second century. For an early date, see Stevan L. Davies, *The Gospel of Thomas and Christian Wisdom* (New York: Seabury, 1983). Among those who argue for a late second-century date is Jacques-E. Ménard, *L'Evangile selon Thomas*, Nag Hammadi Studies 5 (Leiden: Brill, 1975). For a review of recent discussion, see the articles by Kenneth V. Neller, Klyne R. Snodgrass and Charles W. Hedrick in *SC* 7 (1989-1990), pp. 1-56, and the survey by Francis T. Fallon and Ron Cameron, "The Gospel of Thomas: A *Forschungsbericht* and Analysis," *ANRW* 2.25.5 (1988), pp. 4195-4251.

75. On the connection of the Gospel of Thomas and Edessa, see Helmut Koester, "GNOMAI DIAPHOROI: The Origin and Nature of Diversification in the History of Early Christianity," *HTR* 58 (1965), pp. 279-318, repr. in *Trajectories Through Early Christianity*, ed. Koester and James M. Robinson (Philadelphia: Fortress, 1971), pp. 114-157.

76. Gospel of Thomas, Saying 12.

77. In general see Attridge, *Epistle to the Hebrews* (see endnote 16).

78. An allusion to a current attempt to rebuild the Temple in Epistle of Barnabas 16:4 has sometimes been taken to indicate a date around the time of the revolt, but the reference is quite vague.

79. Eusebius (*Eccles. Hist.* 4.11.8) dates Justin's activity to the period of the popes Pius (c. 141-156) through Eleutherus (177-189). On Justin in general, see Leslie W. Barnard, *Justin Martyr: His Life and Thought* (Cambridge: Cambridge Univ. Press, 1967), and Eric F. Osborn, *Justin Martyr*, BHT 47 (Tübingen: Mohr [Siebeck], 1973).

80. See Justin Martyr, *Dialogue with Trypho* 2. His works are translated in Thomas B. Falls, *St. Justin Martyr, Fathers of the Church* (New York: Christian Heritage, 1949).

81. For discussion of this genre of controversy literature, see A. Lukyn Williams, *Adversus Judaeos: A Bird's-eye View of Christian Apology until the Renaissance* (Cambridge, UK: Cambridge Univ. Press, 1935); James Parkes, *The Conflict of the Church and the Synagogue: A Study in the Origins of Antisemitism*, repr. (New York: Athenaeum, 1979 [1934]); Rosemary Radford Ruether, *Faith and Fratricide: The Theological Roots of Anti-Semitism* (New York: Seabury, 1974).

82. See Origen, *Contra Celsum* 4.52.

83. For Melito's text, see Stuart G. Hall, *Melito of Sardis: On Pascha and Fragments*, Oxford Early Christian Texts (Oxford: Clarendon, 1979). On Melito and the Jews, see Robert

Wilken, "Melito, the Jewish Community at Sardis, and the Sacrifice of Isaac," *Theological Studies* 37 (1976), pp. 53-69.

84. For recent studies of the earliest stages of Christology, see James D.G. Dunn, *Christology in the Making: A New Testament Inquiry Into the Origins of the Doctrine of the Incarnation* (Philadelphia: Westminster, 1980); Marinus de Jonge, *Christology in Context: The Earliest Christian Response to Jesus* (Philadelphia: Westminster, 1988); Raymond E. Brown, "Christology," in *The New Jerome Biblical Commentary* (Englewood Cliffs, NJ: Prentice Hall, 1990), pp. 1354-1359; Larry W. Hurtado, *One God, One Lord: Early Christian Devotion and Ancient Jewish Monotheism* (Philadelphia: Fortress, 1988).

85. A comprehensive treatment of the brief letters is Raymond E. Brown, *The Epistles of John*, Anchor Bible 30 (Garden City, NY: Doubleday, 1982). For a briefer treatment of Johannine Christianity, see Brown, *Community of the Beloved Disciple* (New York: Paulist, 1979).

86. Justin Martyr, *Dialogue with Trypho* 35.5, 80.4; *First Apology* 26.5, 58.1-2.

87. Clement, *Stromateis* 3.12.1-25.4.

88. Irenaeus, *Against Heresies* 1.27.

89. Tertullian, *Against Marcion* and *Prescription of Heretics*.

90. For a discussion of the significance of Ephraem's *Prose Refutations*, see Han J.W. Drijvers, "Marcionism in Syria: Principles, Problems, Polemics," *SC* 6 (1987-1988), pp. 153-172; repr. in his *East of Antioch* (London: Variorum Reprints, 1984).

91. A brief, but useful assessment of the evidence is Gerhard May, "Marcion in Contemporary Views: Results and Open Questions," *SC* 6 (1987-1988), pp. 129-152.

92. A recent reassessment of Marcion's career, putting his activity earlier than maintained here, is R. Joseph Hoffmann, *On the Restitution of Christianity: An Essay on the Development of Radical Paulinist Theology in the Second Century* (Chico, CA: Scholars Press, 1984). According to Hoffmann, Luke-Acts and the Pastoral Epistles, among other products of the period, are a response to Marcion's radical Paulinism. Hoffmann restates his position in "How Then Know This Troublous Teacher? Further Reflections on Marcion and His Church," *SC* 6 (1987-1988), pp. 173-191.

93. Marcion's Bible is not extant and reconstructing it is a delicate task. A recent contribution is John J. Clabeaux, *A Lost Edition of the Letters of Paul: A Reassessment of the Text of the Pauline Corpus Attested by Marcion*, CBQ Monograph 21 (Washington, DC: CBA, 1989).

94. See Drijvers, "Marcionism in Syria" (see endnote 90), for a forceful statement of the importance of contemporary philosophy on Marcion's theology.

95. On the possible significance of Marcion in the development of the canon, see Hans von Campenhausen, *The Formation of the Christian Bible* (Philadelphia: Fortress, 1972). See also William R. Farmer and Denis M. Farkasfalvy, O. Cist., *The Formation of the New Testament Canon: An Ecumenical Approach*, ed. Harold W. Attridge (New York: Paulist, 1983).

96. A date after 172 is indicated by the reference to Montanism at the end of the Muratorian Canon. A much later date has been proposed by Albert C. Sundberg, "'Canon Muratori': A Fourth-Century List," *HTR* 66 (1973), pp. 1-41, but not all have been convinced. See Everett Ferguson, "Canon Muratori: Date and Provenance," *Studia Patristica* 18 (1982), pp. 677-683.

97. For the Infancy Gospel of Thomas and the Protoevangelium of James, see Hennecke-Schneemelcher, *New Testament Apocrypha* (see endnote 10), vol. 1, pp. 370-400.

98. The best overall survey is Kurt Rudolph, *Gnosis: The Nature and History of Gnosticism* (San Francisco: Harper & Row, 1983). See also Pheme Perkins, *The Gnostic Dialogue: The Early Church and the Crisis of Gnosticism* (New York: Paulist, 1980); Birger Pearson, *Gnosticism, Judaism, and Egyptian Christianity*, Studies in Antiquity and Christianity 5 (Minneapolis: Fortress, 1990). For examples of recent discussion, see Elaine Pagels, *The Gnostic Gospels* (New York: Random House, 1979); *The Rediscovery of Gnosticism*, ed. Bentley Layton, Proceedings of the International Conference on Gnosticism at Yale, March 28-31, 1978, Studies in the History of Religions—Supplements to *Numen*, 40, 41, 2 vols. (Leiden: Brill, 1980-1981); A.H.B. Logan and A.J.M. Wedderburn, *The New Testament and Gnosis: Essays in Honour of Robert McL. Wilson* (Edinburgh: T & T Clark, 1983); *Nag Hammadi, Gnosticism, and Early Christianity*, ed. Hedrick and Hodgson (Peabody, MA: Hendrickson, 1986); *Images of the Feminine in Gnosticism*, ed. Karen L. King, Studies in Antiquity and Christianity (Philadelphia: Fortress, 1988).

99. The position of the Church Fathers is still defended by some scholars, especially Simone Pétrement, *Le Dieu separé: les origines du gnosticisme* (Paris: Cerf, 1984).

100. See Justin Martyr, *First Apology* 26.2; Irenaeus, *Against Heresies* 1.23.1-4; *Eccles. Hist.* 2.13.1-15.1.

101. All of the texts are available in James M. Robinson, *The Nag Hammadi Library in English*, 2nd ed. (San Francisco: Harper & Row, 1988). For a selection of annotated texts and evidence from the Church Fathers, see Bentley Layton, *The Gnostic Scriptures* (New York: Doubleday, 1987).

102. Cf. Proverbs 8:22-31; Wisdom of Solomon 7:22-8:1.

103. Versions of this myth appear in texts such as *The Apocryphon of John*, *The Hypostasis of the Archons* and *The Origin of the World* from the Nag Hammadi library. The outlines of the myth are also found in the reports of heresiologists such as Irenaeus in the first book of *Against Heresies*.

104. For the possibility of such a process in the formation of Gnosticism, see Alan Segal, *Two Powers in Heaven: Rabbinic Reports about Christianity and Gnosticism* (Leiden: Brill, 1977).

105. The major testimonies are in Irenaeus, *Against Heresies* 1.25.1-6; Clement of Alexandria, *Stromateis* 3.2.5,2-9,3; 3.2.10,1. An extensive collection of evidence on the Carpocratians is in Morton Smith, *Clement of Alexandria and a Secret Gospel of Mark* (Cambridge, MA: Harvard Univ. Press, 1973).

106. For an assessment of the principal fragments, from Clement of Alexandria and Irenaeus, see Layton, *The Gnostic Scriptures* (see endnote 101), pp. 417-444. A different account of Basilides' teaching, possibly reflecting the views of followers, is found in Hippolytus, *Refutation of All Heresies* 7.20.1-27.13.

107. On Valentinus and contemporary philosophy, see G. Christopher Stead, "In Search of Valentinus," in Layton, *The Rediscovery of Gnosticism, I: The School of Valentinus* (see endnote 98), pp. 75-95; repr. in Stead, *Substance and Illusion in the Christian Fathers* (London: Variorum Reprints, 1985).

108. See *Eccles. Hist.* 4.11.1, "he flourished under Pius (c. 140-155) and remained until Anicetus (c. 155-166)."

109. Cf. Tertullian, *Against the Valentinians* 4.

110. See Layton, *The Gnostic Scriptures* (see endnote 101), pp. 229-248.

111. For a critical edition and commentary, see Harold W. Attridge and George W. MacRae, "The Gospel of Truth," in *Nag Hammadi Codex I (The Jung Codex)*, 2 vols., ed. Attridge, Nag Hammadi Studies 22-23 (Leiden: Brill, 1985), vol. 1 (text and translation), pp. 55-122; vol. 2 (notes), pp. 39-135.

112. For the letter to Flora, see Layton, *The Gnostic Scriptures* (see endnote 101), pp. 306-315.

113. Revisionist Valentinianism is found in another Nag Hammadi document, the *Tripartite Tractate*. The text and translation are in Harold W. Attridge and Elaine Pagels, "The Tripartite Tractate," in *Nag Hammadi Codex I* (see endnote 111), vol. 1, pp. 159-337, vol. 2, pp. 217-497. A later dating of the work, and a different assessment of its relationship with Origen, is offered by Einar Thomassen and Louis Painchaud, *Le Traité Tripartite (Nag Hammadi Codex I,5) texte établi, introduit et commenté*, Bibliothéque copte de Nag Hammadi, Section "Textes" 19 (Quebec: Presses de l'Univ. Laval, 1989).

114. The anonymous homily is often associated with either Corinth or Rome. Only the association with 1 Clement suggests such a localization. For the Alexandrian possibility, see Koester, *Introduction* (see endnote 3), vol. 2, pp. 233-236.

115. For reference to the work, see Justin Martyr, *First Apology* 1.26; cited in *Eccles. Hist.* 4.11.10.

116. On the debt to Philo among second-century theologians, see Henry Chadwick, "Philo and The Beginnings of Christian Philosophy," in *The Cambridge History of Later Greek and Early Medieval Philosophy*, ed. A.H. Armstrong (Cambridge, UK: Cambridge Univ. Press, 1967), pp. 137-192.

117. Cf. Justin Martyr, *Dialogue with Trypho* 61.2, for the notion, although not the technical Stoic terminology.

118. Justin Martyr, *First Apology* 46.2; *Second Apology* 13.3.

119. Text and translation are in Molly Whitaker, *Tatian, Oratio ad Graecos and Fragments*, Oxford Early Christian Texts (Oxford: Clarendon, 1982). For a discussion of the critical problems, see Robert M. Grant, *Greek Apologists of the Second Century* (Philadelphia: Westminster, 1988), pp. 112-132.

120. On the original language, see William L. Petersen, "New Evidence for the Question of the Original Language of the *Diatessaron*," in *Studien zum Text und zur Ethik des Neuen Testaments*, ed. W. Schrage, BZNW 47 (1986), pp. 325-343; on the *Diatessaron*'s later influence see Petersen's *The Diatessaron and Ephraem Syrus as Sources of Romanos the Melodist*, Corpus Scriptorum Christianorum Orientalium 475 (Louvain: Peeters, 1985).

121. The Greek fragment was edited by Carl H. Kraeling, *A Greek Fragment of Tatian's Diatessaron from Dura*, Studies and Documents 3 (London: Christophers, 1935). For the *Diatessaron*'s place in the history of the New

Testament text, see Bruce Metzger, *The Early Versions of the New Testament: Their Origin, Transmission, and Limitations* (Oxford: Clarendon, 1977), pp. 10-36.

122. Reports on Tatian are found in Irenaeus, *Against Heresies* 3.23.8, and *Eccles. Hist.* 4.29.3. The latter reports on the *Diatessaron* at 4.29.6.

123. Irenaeus (*Against Heresies* 1.28.1) and Eusebius (*Eccles. Hist.* 4.29.1-2) associate the movement with Marcion and suggest that Tatian introduced doctrinal innovations. The general phenomenon of sexual asceticism is ably explored by Peter Brown, *The Body and Society: Men, Women, and Sexual Renunciation in Early Christianity* (New York: Columbia Univ. Press, 1988).

124. Robinson, *The Nag Hammadi Library in English* (see endnote 101), p. 203.

125. On Syrian asceticism, see Arthur Vöbus, *Celibacy: A Requirement for Admission to Baptism in the Early Syrian Church* (Stockholm: Almqvist, 1954); and *History of Asceticism in the Syrian Orient*, CSCO 184 (Louvain: Secrétariat CSCO, 1958).

126. For a comprehensive review of the complex source-critical problems of the Pseudo-Clementine literature, see F. Stanley Jones, "The Pseudo-Clementines: A History of Research," *SC* 2 (1982), pp. 1-34, 63-96. Selections of the texts, governed by an older theory of its development, may be found in Hennecke-Schneemelcher, *New Testament Apocrypha* (see endnote 10), vol. 2, pp. 102-127, 532-570. For a recent study, see Luedemann, *Opposition to Paul* (see endnote 28), pp. 168-199.

127. *Pseudo-Clementine Homilies* 1.19.4.

128. *Pseudo-Clementine Homilies* 2.17.4.

129. *Eccles. Hist.* 5.5.8.

130. Eusebius (*Eccles. Hist.* 5.20.1-8, 5.23.3; 5.26) mentions various works. The *Demonstration of the Apostolic Teaching* survives in Armenian. See Joseph P. Smith, *St. Irenaeus, Proof of the Apostolic Preaching*, Ancient Christian Writers 16 (Westminster, MD: Newman, 1952).

131. Irenaeus, *Against the Heresies* 1.315-578.

132. He includes the Gospels, Pauline Epistles, Acts, Epistles of John and Revelation, and 1 Peter. Unlike the Muratorian Canon, he also includes the *Shepherd of Hermas*, but does not recognize the Epistle to the Hebrews. Until the fourth century, East and West differed over Hebrews and Revelation. The East favored Hebrews; the West Revelation. Both were finally included.

133. Irenaeus (*Against the Heresies* 3.11.8) links John with the lion, Luke with the calf, Matthew with the man and Mark with the eagle.

Later treatments regularly reverse the beasts of Mark and John.

134. Irenaeus, *Against the Heresies* 1.10.102, 3.3.1, 4.26.2.

135. The baptismal interrogation is attested for the early third century in Rome by Hippolytus, *Apostolic Tradition* 21-22. The practice was no doubt considerably older.

136. Irenaeus, *Against Heresies* 1.9.4. On the formation of creeds, see J.N.D. Kelly, *Early Christian Creeds* (New York: McKay, 1960).

137. Irenaeus, *Against the Heresies* 3.18.1, 5.14.2, 5.21.2. For a sensitive assessment of the theology of Irenaeus, see Rowan Greer, *Broken Lights and Mended Lives: Theology and Common Life in the Early Church* (University Park: Pennsylvania State Univ. Press, 1986).

138. Irenaeus, *Against the Heresies* 3.18.7.

139. Origen (*Contra Celsum* 8.12.14) indicates that Celsus had lodged such a charge.

140. *Eccles. Hist.* 5.28.10.

141. Hippolytus, *Refutation of All Heresies* 9.7.1-10.12, and his *Against Noetus.*

142. Hippolytus, *Refutation of All Heresies* 9.12.15-19; *Eccles. Hist.* 7.6.1, 7.26.1; Epiphanius, *Panarion* 72.1.

143. George W. Butterworth, *Clement of Alexandria, The Exhortation to the Greeks, the Rich Man's Salvation and the Fragment of an address entitled To the Newly Baptized* (Loeb).

144. See Simon P. Wood, C.P., *Clement of Alexandria, Christ the Educator*, Fathers of the Church 23 (New York: Fathers of the Church, 1954).

145. The work is incomplete. Book 7 promises a continuation, but Book 8 consists only of sketches. Book 7, on Clement's notion of a Christian Gnostic, was edited and translated by F.J.A. Hort and J.B. Mayor, *Clement of Alexandria, Miscellanies, Book VII. The Greek text with introduction, translation and notes* (London, New York: Macmillan, 1902). Selections from *Stromateis* 3 and 7, on marriage and spiritual perfection, are in Henry Chadwick, *Alexandrian Christianity*, Library of Christian Classics (London: SCM; Philadelphia: Westminster, 1954), pp. 15-165.

146. In general, see Timothy D. Barnes, *Tertullian: A Historical and Literary Study* (Oxford: Clarendon, 1971), valuable both for its critique of traditional views and for its constructive assessment of the man; for other texts and translations, see pp. 286-291. On Tertullian's rhetoric, see Robert D. Sider, *Ancient Rhetoric and the Art of Tertullian* (New York: Oxford Univ. Press, 1971).

147. For the former, see Tertullian, *Prescrip-*

tion of Heretics 13; for the latter, *Prescription of Heretics* 36.

148. An example of a Valentinian effort to reinterpret belief in the resurrection is found in a Nag Hammadi tractate, *On the Resurrection*.

149. The outlines of Origen's life are given in *Eccles. Hist.* 6. A useful introduction to Origen is Joseph W. Trigg, *Origen: The Bible and Philosophy in the Third-century Church* (Atlanta: John Knox, 1983). More technical is Henri Crouzel, *Origen: The Life and Thought of the First Great Theologian*, Eng. transl. (San Francisco: Harper & Row, 1989). For exploration of topics of current scholarly interest, see Charles Kannengiesser and William L. Petersen, *Origen of Alexandria: His World and His Legacy*, Christianity and Judaism in Antiquity 1 (Notre Dame, IN: Univ. of Notre Dame Press, 1988).

150. *Eccles. Hist.* 6.8.1-3.

151. Eusebius (*Eccles. Hist.* 6.21.3-4) discusses the visit to Julia Mammea, which took place in 232.

152. Henry Chadwick, *Origen: Contra Celsum, Translated with Introduction and Notes* (Cambridge, UK: Cambridge Univ. Press, 1965 [1953]). For a reconstruction of Celsus' work, see R. Joseph Hoffmann, *Celsus On the True Doctrine: A Discourse Against the Christians* (New York: Oxford Univ. Press, 1987).

153. For the commentary on John, see *The Ante-Nicene Fathers* (see endnote 4), vol. 9. The commentary on Romans survives only in fragments.

154. These works are available in Chadwick, *Alexandrian Christianity* (see endnote 145), pp. 171-429, and in Rowan A. Greer, *Origen, An Exhortation to Martyrdom, Prayer, First Principles: Book IV, Prologue to the Commentary on the Song of Songs, Homily XXVII on Numbers,* Classics of Western Spirituality (New York: Paulist, 1979).

155. George W. Butterworth, *Origen, On First Principles*, repr., with intro. by Henri de Lubac (New York: Harper & Row, 1966; repr., Gloucester, MA: Peter Smith, 1973 [1936]).

156. On Origen's interpretive methods, see Karen Jo Torjesen, *Hermeneutical Procedure and Theological Method in Origen's Exegesis* (Berlin: de Gruyter, 1986). For the influence of his interpretation on later authors, see Joseph W. Trigg, *Biblical Interpretation*, Message of the Fathers of the Church 9 (Wilmington, DE: Glazier, 1988).

157. Origen, *Homily on Jeremiah* 9.4; *On First Principles* 1.2.2.

158. See, e.g., the *Commentary on John* 10.37

(21), or *On Prayer* 15, where Origen insists that prayer is not directed to the Son, but to the Father.

159. For a general discussion of these theological developments, see Aloys Grillmeier, S.J., *Christ in the Christian Tradition*, vol. 1: *From the Apostolic Age to Chalcedon* (451), 2nd ed. (Atlanta: John Knox, 1975), and Jaroslav Pelikan, *The Christian Tradition: A History of the Development of Doctrine*, vol 1: *The Emergence of the Catholic Tradition* (100-600) (Chicago: Univ. of Chicago Press, 1971).

160. For translations, Robert T. Meyer, *St. Athanasius, The Life of Saint Antony*, Ancient Christian Writers (New York: Newman Press, 1950), and Robert C. Gregg, *Athanasius, The Life of Antony and the Letter to Marcellinus*, Classics of Western Spirituality (New York: Paulist, 1980).

161. For a review of the historical problems, see James H. Goehring, "The Origins of Monasticism," in Attridge and Hata, *Eusebius, Judaism and Christianity* (see endnote 68), pp. 235-255.

162. See Herbert Musurillo, S.J., *St. Methodius, The Symposium: A Treatise on Chastity*, Ancient Christian Writers 27 (New York: Newman, 1958).

163. For this work, see particularly Adela Yarbro Collins, *Crisis and Catharsis: The Power of the Apocalypse* (Philadelphia: Westminster, 1984), and Elizabeth Schüssler Fiorenza, *The Book of Revelation: Justice and Judgment* (Philadelphia: Fortress, 1985).

164. On Jewish apocalypticism, see esp. John J. Collins, *The Apocalyptic Imagination: An Introduction to the Jewish Matrix of Christianity* (New York: Crossroad, 1984).

165. For the texts and discussion of them, see Sherwin-White, *The Letters of Pliny* (see endnote 8).

166. Hadrian did so in a letter to a proconsul, Minucius Fundanus, preserved in Justin, *First Apology* 68, and *Eccles. Hist.* 4.9.1-3.

167. See, e.g., Tertullian, *Apology* 1.11-13.

168. For a general survey of persecution of Christians, see W.H.C. Frend, *Martyrdom and Persecution in the Early Church: A Study of a Conflict from the Maccabees to Donatus* (Oxford: Blackwell, 1965; repr., Grand Rapids: Baker, 1981).

169. On the apologetic movement in general, see most recently Grant, *Greek Apologists* (see endnote 119), with extensive bibliographies.

170. See *Eccles. Hist.* 4.3.2

171. On Quadratus and Aristides, see Grant, *Greek Apologists* (see endnote 119), pp. 35-39. The whole of Aristides' oration survives only

in Syriac, published by J.R. Harris, *The Apology of Aristides*, Texts and Studies 1.1 (Cambridge, UK: Cambridge Univ. Press, 1893). There are Greek fragments; see J. van Haelst, *Catalogue des papyrus littéraires juifs et chrétiens* (Paris: Sorbonne, 1976), nos. 623 and 624, and H.J.M. Milne, "A New Fragment of the Apology of Aristides," *JTS* 25 (1923-1924), pp. 73-77.

172. Eusebius (*Eccles. Hist.* 4.14.10-15.1) dates the event to 166-167, apparently in error. Robert M. Grant (*Augustus to Constantine* [San Francisco: HarperSanFrancisco, 1990], pp. 106-107) discusses the date, with reference to other treatments.

173. For the *Martyrdom of Polycarp*, see Lake, *The Apostolic Fathers*, vol. 2, pp. 309-345.

174. Eusebius (*Eccles. Hist.* 4.18.1-3) mentions two apologies and the manuscripts do contain two separate works, although the second is now usually viewed as an appendix to the first. On the date of Justin's apologies, see Grant, *Greek Apologists* (see endnote 119), p. 53.

175. For a survey of Greco-Roman attitudes, see Robert L. Wilken, *The Christians as the Romans Saw Them* (New Haven, CT: Yale Univ. Press, 1984).

176. Variations on these charges occur frequently. They appear, for instance, in connection with the martyrs of Lyons, according to Eusebius, citing a report by the churches of Lyons and Vienne sent to Christians in the provinces of Asia and Phrygia, *Eccles. Hist.* 5.1.1-63.

177. See Justin Martyr, *First Apology* 27.

178. On this traditional argument, see Arthur J. Droge, *Homer or Moses: Early Christian Interpretations of the History of Culture*, Hermeneutische Untersuchungen zur Theologie 26 (Tübingen: Mohr [Siebeck], 1988).

179. For a translation, see Stevenson, *A New Eusebius* (see endnote 5), pp. 28-30, and Herbert Musurillo, *The Acts of the Christian Martyrs* (Oxford: Clarendon, 1972), pp. 42-61.

180. Gaius, in an anti-Montanist writing, according to Eusebius (*Eccles. Hist.* 1.25.7).

181. The Vatican trophy competes with a site on the Via Appia that was venerated in the third century as the burial place of the apostles. For descriptions and bibliographies, see Snyder, *Ante Pacem* (see endnote 5), pp. 82-114. On the historical problems, see Henry Chadwick, "St. Peter and St. Paul in Rome: The Problem of the Memoria Apostolorum ad Catacumbas," *JTS* 8 (1957), pp. 31-52, repr. in his *History and Thought of the Early Church* (London: Variorum, 1982).

182. Lucian's account is found in his "Pass-ing of Peregrinus," in *Lucian*, Bk. 5, Loeb. Marcus Aurelius (*Meditations* 11.3) may have had the likes of Peregrinus in mind when he commented disdainfully on the stubbornness and histrionic display of Christian martyrs.

183. *Eccles. Hist.* 5.5.1-7. Apollinaris' claim that the legion was thereby named "thundering" is mistaken. The name *Fulminata* occurs at least a century earlier.

184. Recorded in *Eccles. Hist.* 4.26.12-14.

185. In *Eccles. Hist.* 4.26.7-11.

186. *Eccles. Hist.* 5.1.1-63.

187. For the account of the martyrdom, see Musurillo, *Acts of the Christian Martyrs* (see endnote 179), pp. 86-89. Tertullian (*Apology* 5.5-8) echoes the claim about bad emperors.

188. See Musurillo, *Acts of the Christian Martyrs* (see endnote 179), pp. 106-131.

189. *Eccles. Hist.* 6.34.1. For a defense of the historicity of the report, see Marta Sordi, *Christians and the Roman Empire* (Norman, OK: Univ. of Oklahoma Press; London, 1986), pp. 96-99.

190. For examples, see Stevenson, *A New Eusebius* (see endnote 5), p. 228.

191. *Eccles. Hist.* 7.13.1 preserves the text of Gallienus' letter to the Christian bishops.

192. For the general political situation and the occasion of the persecution, see Timothy D. Barnes, *Constantine and Eusebius* (Cambridge, MA: Harvard Univ. Press, 1981).

193. Diverse descriptions of the sign are found in Lactantius, *On the Deaths of Persecutors* 44.5, and Eusebius, *Life of Constantine* 1.26-31.

194. Two versions are extant, *Eccles. Hist.* 10.5.1-14, in Greek, and Lactantius, *On the Deaths of Persecutors* 48, in Latin.

195. For an insightful assessment of the debt of Eusebius to Origen see Charles Kannengiesser, "Eusebius of Caesarea, Origenist," in Attridge and Hata, *Eusebius, Judaism and Christianity* (see endnote 68), pp. 435-466.

196. On this massive undertaking, see Alden A. Mosshammer, *The Chronicle of Eusebius and Greek Chronographic Tradition* (Lewisburg, PA: Bucknell Univ. Press, 1979), and William Adler, "Eusebius' Chronicle and Its Legacy," in Attridge and Hata, *Eusebius, Judaism and Christianity* (see endnote 68), pp. 467-491.

197. Various hypotheses have been advanced for the process of composition of the work. See Barnes, *Constantine and Eusebius* (see endnote 192), pp. 126-147. On Eusebius and his work, see also Robert M. Grant, *Eusebius as Church Historian* (Oxford: Clarendon, 1980).

198. *Eccles. Hist.* 10.9.7-8; transl. from Lake, Oulton and Lawlor, *Eusebius, The Ecclesiastical History,* 2.479.

S I X
Judaism to the Mishnah: 135–220 C.E.

1. Edward Gibbon, *The Decline and Fall of the Roman Empire,* abridged, ed. D.M. Low (New York: Harcourt, Brace, 1960), "Prologue," chap. 3, p. 1.

2. *Eccles. Hist.* 4.6.2. The classic discussion is J. Rendel Harris, "Hadrian's Decree of Expulsion of the Jews from Jerusalem," *HTR* 19 (1926), pp. 199-206.

3. Michael Avi-Yonah, *The Jews of Palestine: A Political History from the Bar Kokhba War to the Arab Conquest* (Oxford: Blackwell, 1976), pp. 79-81; Joshua Schwartz, *Jewish Settlement in Judaea after the Bar Kochba War* (Jerusalem: Magnes, 1986), pp. 183-186 and 245-246 (in Hebrew).

4. This impression is not disputed by Schwartz, *Jewish Settlement* (see endnote 3). See the graph of the number of settlements in Avi-Yonah, *The Jews of Palestine* (see endnote 3), p. 20. See further Ze'ev Safrai, "The Bar-Kokhva Revolt and its Effect on Settlement," and Joshua Schwartz, "Judea in the Wake of the Bar-Kokhva Revolt," in *The Bar-Kokhva Revolt: A New Approach,* ed. Aharon Oppenheimer and Uriel Rappaport (Jerusalem: Yad Izhak ben Zvi, 1984), pp. 182-214 and 215-223 (in Hebrew).

5. Aharon Oppenheimer, "Jewish Lydda in the Roman Era," *HUCA* 59 (1988), pp. 115-136, esp. p. 130.

6. JT *Sanhedrin* 19a and BT *Berakhot* 63a-b. See Gedaliah Alon, *The Jews in Their Land in the Talmudic Age,* 2 vols. (Jerusalem: Magnes, 1980-1984; English ed.), vol. 2, pp. 670-672.

7. Emil Schürer, *The History of the Jewish People in the Age of Jesus Christ,* 4 vols., ed. Geza Vermes et al. (Edinburgh: T & T Clark, 1979), vol. 2, pp. 550-552.

8. BT *Sukkah* 52a.

9. See Joseph Heinemann, "The Messiah of Ephraim and the Premature Exodus of the Tribe of Ephraim," *HTR* 68 (1975), pp. 1-15.

10. Tosefta, *Avodah Zarah* 4(5).3-6; critical edition by M.S. Zuckermandel, p. 466.

11. Isaiah Gafni, "The Status of Eretz Israel in Reality and in Jewish Consciousness following the Bar-Kokhva Uprising," in Oppenheimer and Rappaport, *The Bar-Kokhva Revolt* (see endnote 4), pp. 224-232.

12. See Jonathan Goldstein's commentary on 2 Maccabees 6 and 7, Anchor Bible (Garden City, NY: Doubleday); *Die Entstehung der judischen Martyrologie,* ed. J.W. van Henten (Leiden: Brill, 1989).

13. *Apion* 1.42-45; cf. 1.191 (an excerpt from Hecateus or pseudo-Hecateus). See also 4 Maccabees.

14. Saul Lieberman, "The Persecution of the Religion of Israel," *Salo Baron Jubilee Volume,* 3 vols. (New York: American Academy for Jewish Research, 1974) vol. 3, pp. 213-245 (in Hebrew); Peter Schäfer, *Der Bar Kokhba Aufstand* (Tübingen: Mohr, 1981), chap. 7.

15. BT *Sanhedrin* 74a; Moshe D. Herr, "Persecutions and Martyrdom in Hadrian's Days," *Scripta Hierosolymitana* 23 (1973), pp. 85-125.

16. 1 Maccabees 1:15; Tosefta *Shabbat* 15:9, critical edition and commentary by Saul Lieberman, p. 71, and parallels.

17. Kaufmann Kohler, "Circumcision," *Jewish Encyclopedia* (1903), vol. 4, p. 93. See now Nissan Rubin, "On Drawing Down the Prepuce and Incision of the Foreskin (*Peri'ah*)," *Zion* 54 (1989), pp. 105-117.

18. Amnon Linder, *The Jews in Roman Imperial Legislation* (Detroit: Wayne State Univ., 1987), pp. 99-102, no. 1.

19. See Appian, in Menahem Stern, *Greek and Latin Authors on Jews and Judaism,* 3 vols. (Jerusalem: Israel Academy of Sciences, 1974-1984), vol. 2, pp. 179-181, no. 343.

20. Ammianus Marcellinus in Stern, *Greek and Latin Authors* (see endnote 19), vol. 2, pp. 605-607, no. 506.

21. Galen, in Stern, *Greek and Latin Authors* (see endnote 19), vol. 2, pp. 306-328, nos. 376-394; Celsus, ibid., vol. 2, pp. 224-305, no. 375.

22. Numenius of Apamea, in Stern, *Greek and Latin Authors* (see endnote 19), vol. 2, pp. 209-211, no. 363.

23. JT *Ma'aserot* 3:8 50d; BT *Bava Mezia* 83b-84a; *Pesikta de Rab Kahana,* critical edition by Mandelbaum, p. 195. The essential truthfulness of the story is not doubted by Avi-Yonah, *The Jews of Palestine* (see endnote 3), p. 71, or Alon, *The Jews in Their Land* (see endnote 6), pp. 540-541. Shamma Friedman has persuasively argued that the Babylonian version of the story is secondary to the Palestinian versions, but whether the Palestinian versions are "true" is still in doubt: Friedman, "On the historical aggada in the Babylonian Talmud," *Memorial Volume for Saul Lieberman* (Jerusalem: Lieberman Inst. of Talmudic Research, 1989), pp. 1-46, esp. pp. 4-14.

24. *Historia Augusta,* "Life of Septimius Severus," in Stern, *Greek and Latin Authors* (see

endnote 19), vol. 2, p. 625, no. 515.

25. For discussion, see Anthony R. Birley, *Septimius Severus the African Emperor*, 2nd ed. (New Haven, CT: Yale Univ. Press, 1988), p. 135 with n. 12; Stern's discussion of "Life of Septimius Severus" (see endnote 24), pp. 623-625. For the chronology (195 C.E.), I follow Birley.

26. Jean. B. Frey, *Corpus Inscriptionum Judaicarum*, 2 vols. (Rome: Pontificio Istituto di archeologia cristiana, 1936-1952), vol. 2, pp. 157-159, no. 972.

27. The passage from Jerome is quoted in Stern's commentary on the "Life of Septimius Severus" (see endnote 24), p. 624.

28. "Life of Septimius Severus" (see endnote 24), no. 514.

29. Linder, *The Jews in Roman Imperial Legislation* (see endnote 18), pp. 103-107, no. 2.

30. Gedaliah Alon, "The 'Strategoi' in the Palestinian Cities during the Roman Epoch," in *Jews, Judaism, and the Classical World* (Jerusalem: Magnes, 1977), pp. 458-475.

31. Jay Braverman, *Jerome's Commentary on Daniel* (Washington, DC: CBA, 1978), p. 120. The passage is also quoted by Stern in his commentary (see endnote 24). The identification of Severus with Septimius Severus and of Antoninus with Caracalla is beyond doubt; cf. Linder, *The Jews in Roman Imperial Legislation* (see endnote 18), pp. 103-107, no. 2, which also refers to Severus and Antoninus. Braverman's discussion (pp. 120-121, esp. p. 121, n. 5) is wrong. Jerome also quotes other Jews who argue that the verse refers to the emperor Julian.

32. Albert L. Baumgarten, "The Akiban Opposition," *HUCA* 50 (1979), pp. 179-197, and "Rabbi Judah I and his Opponents," *JSJ* 12 (1981), pp. 135-172.

33. David Weiss Halivni, "The Reception accorded to Rabbi Judah's Mishnah," in *Jewish and Christian Self-Definition*, vol. 2: *Aspects of Judaism in the Greco-Roman Period*, ed. A.L. Baumgarten et al. (Philadelphia: Fortress, 1981), pp. 204-212.

34. Alon, "Those Appointed for Money," in *Jews, Judaism* (see endnote 30), pp. 374-435.

35. These reasons are explored by Martin Goodman, "The Roman State and the Jewish Patriarch in the Third Century," in *Galilee in Late Antiquity*, ed. Lee I.A. Levine (forthcoming).

36. Harry J. Leon, *The Jews of Ancient Rome* (Philadelphia: JPS, 1960).

37. Eric M. Meyers and A. Thomas Kraabel, "Archaeology, Iconography, and Nonliterary Written Remains," in *Early Judaism and Its Mod-*

ern Interpreters, ed. Robert Kraft and George W. E. Nickelsburg (Atlanta: Scholars Press, 1986), pp. 175-210, esp. pp. 184-185.

38. Joyce Reynolds and Robert Tannenbaum, *Jews and God-Fearers at Aphrodisias* (Cambridge, UK: Cambridge Philological Soc., 1987). See also, Louis H. Feldman, "The Omnipresence of the God-Fearers," *BAR*, Sept./Oct. 1986, p. 58; Tannenbaum, "Jews and God-Fearers in the Holy City of Aphrodite," *BAR*, Sept./Oct. 1986; Robert S. MacLennan and Kraabel, "The God-Fearers—A Literary and Theological Invention," *BAR*, Sept./Oct. 1986.

39. Shaye J.D. Cohen, "Epigraphical Rabbis," *JQR* 72 (1981), pp. 1-17, esp. pp. 15-16. Tannenbaum, "Jews and God-Fearers" (see endnote 38), attempts to explain the Aphrodisias inscription in accordance with rabbinic norms, but the attempt is not successful.

40. Bernard J. Bamberger, *Proselytism in the Talmudic Period* (Cincinnati: Hebrew Union College, 1939; repr. New York: Ktav, 1968), pp. 238-243; Saul Lieberman, *Greek in Jewish Palestine* (New York: JTSem, 1942; repr. 1965), pp. 17-20.

41. Linder, *The Jews in Roman Imperial Legislation* (see endnote 18), pp. 402-411, no. 66.

42. See Jacob Neusner, *History of the Jews in Babylonia*, vol. 1 (Leiden: Brill, 1965).

43. J. Kaplan, "Excavations at Jaffa," *IEJ* 12 (1962), pp. 149-150.

44. For evidence and discussion, see Shaye J.D. Cohen, "The Place of the Rabbi in the Jewish Society of the Second Century," in Levine, *Galilee in Late Antiquity* (see endnote 35).

45. JT *Sotah* 7:1 21b.

46. Mishnah *Demai* 2:2-3. I do not accept the emendation suggested by Jacob N. Epstein (*Introduction to the Text of the Mishnah* [Jerusalem: Magnes, 1964], p. 1210) and accepted by Chaim Rabin (*Qumran Studies* [Oxford: Clarendon, 1957; repr. New York: Schocken, 1975], p. 12, n. 9).

47. On this transformation, see Alon, *Jews, Judaism* (see endnote 30), pp. 190-234, and Aharon Oppenheimer, *The Am Ha-Aretz* (Leiden, 1977), passim.

48. Tosefta *Berakhot* 6:18, ed. Lieberman, p. 38.

49. *Fathers according to Rabbi Nathan* A 21 (37b in Schechter's edition); compare the prayer of Nehunyah b. Haqqanah in Mishnah *Berakhot* 4:2 with the amplifications in the Talmudim.

50. The evidence for hatred between the rabbis and the *'amme ha'aretz* derives exclusively from the Babylonian Talmud (the major pas-

sage is BT *Pesahim* 49a-b) and seems not to reflect the social conditions of Palestine in the second and early third centuries. See Cohen, "The Place of the Rabbi" (see endnote 44). There was disdain but not hatred.

51. For their observance of the Sabbath and priestly offerings, see Tosefta *Demai* 5:2, ed. Saul Lieberman, p. 85. For their observance of the sabbatical year, see Tosefta *Eruvin* 5:10, ed. Lieberman, p. 113. In general, see Mishnah *Bekhorot* 4:10.

52. It used to be argued that the "monumental Galilean synagogues," the best known of which is at Capernaum, date from the second century C.E., but there is now growing consensus that they date from the late third century. See, for example, Lee I.A. Levine, *Ancient Synagogues Revealed* (Jerusalem: IES, 1981), pp. 45-62.

53. *Avot* 3:10.

54. Perhaps the most convenient collection of the material in English remains R. Travers Herford, *Christianity in Talmud and Midrash* (London: Williams and Norgate, 1903).

55. On apostates, see the brief discussion by Lawrence Schiffman, *Who Was a Jew?* (New York: Ktav, 1985), pp. 41-49. On the "way of outsiders," see Mishnah *Megillah* 4:8; on "way of the Amorite," Tosefta *Shabbat*, chap. 6.

56. A good place to begin work on this topic is Reuven Kimelman, "*Birkat Ha-Minim* and the Lack of Evidence for an Anti-Christian Jewish Prayer in Late Antiquity," in Baumgarten et al., *Jewish and Christian Self-Definition*, vol. 2 (see endnote 33), pp. 226-244. By the third century there is good evidence for real contact and discussion between rabbis and (Gentile) Christians, but that is outside the purview of this chapter.

57. For an excellent account of the patriarchate and its history, see Lee I. Levine, "The Jewish Patriarch (*Nasi*) in Third Century Palestine," *ANRW* 19,2 (1979), pp. 649-688.

58. Avi-Yonah, *The Jews of Palestine* (see endnote 3), pp. 39-42. Perhaps "Antoninus" had many identities, since rabbinic storytelling often combines several different historical personages to create a single archetype.

59. On Simonias, see JT *Yevamot* 12:7 13a = *Genesis Rabbah* 81:2, ed. Theodor-Albeck, p. 969; cf. JT *Hagigah* 1:7 76c and JT *Shevi'it* 6:1 36d. On Rabbi Romanus, see JT *Yevamot* 8:2 9b.

60. According to one tradition, Rabban Gamaliel removed from office the "head" of Gader (Gezer?), but the Talmudim also record a conflicting tradition and the entire matter is

very obscure. See JT *Rosh Hashanah* 1:6 57b = BT *Rosh Hashanah* 22a. In any case, Gamaliel is not said to have appointed anyone to a communal position.

61. Shaye J.D. Cohen, "Patriarchs and Scholarchs," in *PAAJR* 48 (1981), pp. 57-85 (with bibliography).

62. For evidence and details, see Cohen, "The Place of the Rabbi" (see endnote 44).

63. *Fathers according to Rabbi Nathan* A 6 and B 12-13, ed. Schechter, pp. 14b-17a, has a series of paradigmatic rags-to-riches stories meant to inspire students of Torah. They are not reliable "biographies."

64. Prejudice against goatherds and shepherds, goats and sheep: Mishnah *Demai* 2:3 (see endnote 46); Mishnah *Bava Kamma* 7:7; Tosefta *Bava Kamma* 8:10-15, Lieberman edition, pp. 38-40; Tosefta *Bava Mezia* 2:33, Lieberman edition, p. 72; Tosefta *Sanhedrin* 5:5, M.S. Zuckermandel edition, p. 423; Mishnah *Rosh Hashanah* 1:8. By the third century, rabbinic views had shifted; Rabbi Yoḥanan preferred sheep to land (BT *Hullin* 84a).

65. For evidence and discussion, see Cohen, "The Place of the Rabbi" (see endnote 44).

66. On tension between the well-to-do and the rabbis, and appointment to salaried posts, see Gedaliah Alon, "Ga'on, Ge'im," and "Those Appointed for Money," both in *Jews, Judaism* (see endnote 30); Lee I. Levine, *The Rabbinic Class of Roman Palestine* (Jerusalem: Yad Izhak ben Zvi, 1989; English ed.), pp. 167-176. On distribution of poor tithe, see JT *Pe'ah* 8:8 21a. On amoraic testimonies about organized charity, see Levine, *The Rabbinic Class*, pp. 162-167. In general, see Levine, *The Rabbinic Class*, pp. 139-151.

67. On Judah and the cities, see Adolph Büchler, "The Patriarch Rabbi Judah I and the Graeco-Roman Cities of Palestine," in *Studies in Jewish History*, ed. I. Brodie and J. Rabbinowitz (Oxford: Oxford Univ. Press, 1956), pp. 179-244, and Lee I. Levine, *Caesarea under Roman Rule* (Leiden: Brill, 1975), pp. 64-68. On urbanization see Levine, *The Rabbinic Class* (see endnote 66), pp. 25-33.

68. The two standard English translations are by Herbert Danby (Oxford: Oxford Univ. Press, 1933; frequently reprinted) and Neusner (New Haven: Yale Univ. Press, 1988).

69. See, e.g., Mishnah: *Shabbat* 7:1-2; *Kiddushin* 3:12; *Bava Kamma* 1:1; *Kelim* 1:5-9.

70. The Mishnah says virtually nothing about the rabbinate: how does one become a rabbi, what does it mean to be a rabbi, what is the authority of a rabbi, etc.?

71. Regular public prayer is discussed only briefly in tractates *Berakhot* and *Megillah*.

72. I fully agree with Jacob Neusner that the Mishnah is not a law book, but Neusner has not convinced me that it is a book of philosophy. Of course, the Mishnah has a philosophy, or a worldview, inherent in its rulings and its mode of discourse, just as all works of literature, or for that matter, all creations of the human intellect, have an inherent philosophy, but this fact does not mean that the Mishnah was intended by its creators to be a work of philosophy (unlike the treatises of Plato and Aristotle, which clearly were intended by their creators to be works of philosophy). Neusner first propounded his thesis in *Judaism: The Evidence of the Mishnah* (Chicago: Chicago Univ. Press, 1981), and has expanded on it in numerous recent publications. Although I do not accept Neusner's "philosophy" thesis, I have learned much from him as the following paragraphs show.

73. The evidence is assembled by Jacob N. Epstein, *Introduction to Tannaitic Literature* (Jerusalem: Magnes, 1957), p. 200.

74. Of course there may have been implicit rules which were known to the Mishnah's readers and therefore did not need to be spelled out. The Talmudim and later rabbinic commentators, who read the Mishnah as a law book, invested great energy in determining those rules.

75. David W. Halivni, *Midrash, Mishnah and Gemara* (Cambridge, MA: Harvard Univ. Press, 1986).

SEVEN

The World of the Talmud: From the Mishnah to the Arab Conquest

1. Population estimates for Palestine in late antiquity, as for much of the ancient world, are tenuous at best. The Jewish population of Roman Palestine has been estimated to have been as high as five to six million (cf. Jean Juster, *Les Juifs dans l'Empire Romain* [Paris: Librairie Paul Geuthner, 1914], vol. 1, pp. 209-212) and as little as half a millon (cf. C.C. McCown, "The Density of Population in Ancient Palestine," *JBL* 66 [1947], pp. 425-436). For another recent estimate, based on a calculation of maximum agricultural yields for the land, see Magen Broshi, "The Population of Western Palestine in the Roman-Byzantine Period," *BASOR* 236 (1979), pp. 1-10 (Broshi's notes include a useful bibliography of demographic studies of Roman Palestine). The closest to a scholarly consensus on the population of the area in the late third century is somewhere between 1.1 and 1.5 million, with approximately one-half to two-thirds million Jews (cf. *The History of Eretz Israel, The Roman Byzantine Period*, ed. Moshe D. Herr [Jerusalem: Keter, 1985], p. 109 [in Hebrew]); Herr claims that the early third century, under the Severans, is probably the last stage during which Jews represented an outright majority of the total population. (On population, see also endnotes 18, 36, 106 in chap. 1.)

2. See E. Mary Smallwood, *The Jews under Roman Rule* (Leiden: Brill, 1981), pp. 463-464.

3. See Michael Avi-Yonah, *The Jews under Roman and Byzantine Rule* (Jerusalem: Magnes, 1984), p. 75; Gedaliah Alon, *The Jews in Their Land in the Talmudic Age* (Jerusalem: Magnes, 1984), vol. 2, pp. 562-565, 742-746.

4. The concentration of Christians primarily in the *poleis* (Greek, "cities") of Roman Palestine is apparent from the list of bishops who participated in the Council of Nicaea; cf. Louis Félix Abel, *Geographie de la Palestine* (Paris: Librairie Lecoffre, 1938), vol. 2, p. 198. One interesting "controlled" method for measuring the growth of the Palestinian Christian community is through a comparison of Eusebius' *Onomasticon* in the original Greek with the Latin translation of Jerome completed a century later. Whereas Eusebius mentions only a few villages as populated primarily by Christians, the number rises dramatically in Jerome's rendition.

5. See Yaron Dan, "Eretz Israel in the 5th and 6th Centuries," in *Eretz Israel from the Destruction of the Second Temple to the Muslim Conquest*, ed. Zvi Baras et al. (Jerusalem: Yad Ben-Zvi, 1982), vol. 1, p. 265 (in Hebrew); Avi-Yonah, *Jews under Roman and Byzantine Rule* (see endnote 3), p. 241.

6. See Reuven Kimelman, "Birkat Ha-Minim and the Lack of Evidence for an Anti-Christian Jewish Prayer in Late Antiquity," in *Jewish and Christian Self-Definition*, vol. 2: *Aspects of Judaism in the Graeco-Roman Period*, ed. A.L. Baumgarten et al. (Philadelphia: Fortress, 1981), pp. 226-244.

7. BT *Sanhedrin* 97a.

8. *Antiquities* 18:310-379 (on Asineus and Anileus); 20:17-96 (on conversion of the royal family of Adiabene).

9. See Jacob Neusner's comments, "Jews and Judaism Under Iranian Rule: Bibliographical Reflections," *History of Religions* 8 (1968), p. 164, and in *Method and Meaning in Ancient Judaism* (Missoula, MT: Scholars Press, 1979), p. 6, and numerous other places; compare David M. Goodblatt, "Towards the Rehabilitation of

Talmudic History," in *History of Judaism: The Next Ten Years*, ed. Baruch Bokser (Chico, CA: Scholars Press, 1980), p. 32.

10. See Ramsay MacMullen, *Roman Government's Response to Crisis A.D. 235-337* (New Haven, CT: Yale Univ. Press, 1976).

11. See Smallwood, *Jews under Roman Rule* (see endnote 2), pp. 487-506; Alon, *Jews in Their Land* (see endnote 3), vol. 2, pp. 681-704.

12. BT *Gittin* 59a; BT *Sanhedrin* 36a; see Lee I. Levine, *The Rabbinic Class of Roman Palestine in Late Antiquity* (Jerusalem: Yad Ben-Zvi; New York: JTSem, 1989), pp. 33-38, and "The Period of Judah I," in Baras et al., *Eretz Israel from the Destruction* (see endnote 5), pp. 93-118.

13. Palestinian *aggadah* is replete with stories of patriarchs conducting correspondence with the emperors (e.g., *Genesis Rabbah* 75:5, p. 883 [on Judah I and Antoninus]), or even appearing before them in person (e.g., *Genesis Rabbah* 63:8, pp. 668-670 [on Judah III before Diocletian]).

14. See Lee I.A. Levine, "The Jewish Patriarch (Nasi) in Third Century Palestine," *ANRW* 2.19.2 (1979), pp. 649-688. A synagogue inscription from Stobi (Yugoslavia) dating from 280/81 attests to the position of the patriarch even in the internal affairs of this Diaspora community; cf. Levine, *The Rabbinic Class* (see endnote 12), p. 138, n. 29.

15. This diffusion of authority after the death of Judah I may also be reflected in the story of his last testament, BT *Ketubbot* 103b, wherein Judah divides his powers among three different individuals.

16. JT *Sanhedrin* 1:19a. Judah I apparently used his control over ordination to punish sages perceived to have misbehaved toward the patriarchate; cf. JT *Ta'anit* 4:68a; JT *Mo'ed Katan* 3:81c.

17. See Yehezkel Cohen, "The Time and Cause of the Transfer of the Patriarchate to Tiberias," *Zion* 39 (1974), pp. 114-122.

18. See Reuven Kimelman, "The Conflict between R. Yoḥanan and Resh Laqish on the Supremacy of the Patriarchate," *Proceedings of the 7th World Congress of Jewish Studies* (Jerusalem: Magnes, 1981), vol. 3, pp. 1-20. By the third century, the patriarchs apparently employed a private guard of Goths to be used against various opponents, including certain sages; cf. JT *Sanhedrin* 2:19d-20a (JT *Horayot* 3:47a).

19. See, for example, the cynical statements regarding "those who are appointed for money," JT *Bikkurim* 3:65d; cf. BT *Sanhedrin* 7b. See also Gedaliah Alon, "Those Appointed for Money," in *Jews, Judaism and the Classical World* (Jerusa-lem: Magnes, 1977), pp. 374ff.

20. *Genesis Rabbah* 78:11, p. 931 and 80:1, p. 950; JT *Sanhedrin* 9:20c-d.

21. See JT *Shevi'it* 5:36a (compare JT *Pe'ah* 1:15b). For a list of the various taxes, see Avi-Yonah, *Jews under Roman and Byzantine Rule* (see endnote 3), pp. 93-104. For similarities between Jews and other provincials, even to the extent of similar complaints about taxes, see Saul Lieberman, "Palestine in the Third and Fourth Centuries," *JQR* 36 (1945-1946), pp. 356-357.

22. *Genesis Rabbah* 24:1, p. 229; JT *Shevi'it* 9:38d; BT *Bava Batra* 8a. See also Daniel Sperber, *Roman Palestine 200-400: The Land* (Ramat-Gan, Israel: Bar-Ilan, 1978), pp. 102-118; on the pervasiveness of the Roman tax collector, unavoidable no matter where one goes, see also BT *Sanhedrin* 98b.

23. JT *Sanhedrin* 15:26b.

24. See Reuven Kimelman, *R. Yoḥanan of Tiberias: Aspects of the Social and Religious History of Third Century Palestine*, Ph.D. dissertation (Ann Arbor, MI: University Microfilms, 1980), and "Rabbi Yoḥanan and the Professionalization of the Rabbinate," *Annual of the Institute for Research in Jewish Law*, 9-10 (1982-1983), pp. 329-358.

25. See Levine, *The Rabbinic Class* (see endnote 12), p. 194; Aharon Oppenheimer, "Batei-Midrash in Eretz-Israel in the Early Amoraic Period," *Cathedra* 8 (1978), pp. 80-89 (in Hebrew); the only material evidence relating explicitly to a *beth midrash* is the basalt lintel found at Dabbura in the Golan (now in the Golan Museum), with the inscription: "This is the *beth-midrash* of Rabbi Eliezer Ha-Kappar," cf. Shlomit Nemlich and Ann Killebrew, "Rediscovering the Ancient Golan—The Golan Archaeological Museum," *BAR*, Nov./Dec. 1988. Certain halls or buildings adjacent to ancient synagogues may also have served as *batei midrash*, but this is frequently no more than speculation; for literature see Levine, *The Rabbinic Class* (see endnote 12), p. 29, n. 17.

26. The outstanding example of such a figure is Rabbi Abbahu of Caesarea, a late third-century sage who is referred to as "spokesman for his nation," cf. BT *Ketubbot* 17a; see also BT *Hagigah* 14a; JT *Avodah Zarah* 5:44d; cf. Lee I.A. Levine, "R. Abbahu of Caesarea," in *Christianity, Judaism amd Other Greco-Roman Cults, Studies for Morton Smith at Sixty*, ed. Jacob Neusner (Leiden: Brill, 1975), vol. 4, pp. 56-76.

27. See Samuel T. Lachs, "R. Abbahu and the Minnim," *JQR* 60 (1970), pp. 197-212. Levine

("R. Abbahu of Caesarea" [see endnote 26], p. 61) correctly notes, however, that the identification of R. Abbahu's intended target is not always clear, for Samaritans and Gnostics, and sometimes even pagans, are also frequently addressed.

28. JT *Ta'anit* 2:65b.

29. *Exodus Rabbah* 29:5.

30. BT *Avodah Zarah* 4a.

31. Much scholarship has been devoted to these comparative studies; cf., e.g., Ephraim E. Urbach, "The Repentance of the People of Nineveh and the Discussion between Jews and Christians," *Tarbiz* 20 (1950-1951), pp. 118-122, and "Rabbinic Exegesis and Origen's Commentaries on the Song of Songs," *Tarbiz* 30 (1960-1961), pp. 148-170; Reuven Kimelman, "Rabbi Yoḥanan and Origen on the Song of Songs: A Third Century Jewish-Christian Disputation," *HTR* 73 (1980), pp. 567-595.

32. JT *Shabbat* 6:7d.

33. *Genesis Rabbah* 14:2, p. 127; cf. Saul Lieberman, *Hellenism in Jewish Palestine* (New York: JTSem, 1950), pp. 76-77.

34. For a brief summary of the issue and citation to the major relevant scholarship, cf. Moshe D. Herr, "Hellenismos and the Jews in Eretz Israel," *Eshkolot*, n.s. 9-10 (1977-1978), pp. 20-27 (in Hebrew).

35. Saul Lieberman, *Greek in Jewish Palestine* (New York: JTSem, 1942); *Hellenism in Jewish Palestine* (see endnote 33); and "How Much Greek in Jewish Palestine," in *Biblical and Other Studies*, ed. A. Altman (Cambridge, MA: Harvard Univ. Press, 1963), pp. 123-141.

36. Cf. Henry A. Fischel, *Story and History: Observations on Greco-Roman Rhetoric and Pharisaism*, American Oriental Society, Middle-Western Branch, Semi-Centennial Volume, ed. Denis Sinor (Bloomington: Indiana Univ. Press, 1968), pp. 59-88.

37. *Sifre Deuteronomy* 343, pp. 394-395.

38. *Genesis Rabbah* 80:1, pp. 950-953; JT *Sanhedrin* 9:20c-d.

39. For the Greek synagogue inscriptions of Palestine, see most recently Leah Roth-Gerson, *The Greek Inscriptions from the Synagogues in Eretz-Israel* (Jerusalem: Yad Ben-Zvi, 1987) (in Hebrew). The Hebrew and Aramaic inscriptions of Palestinian synagogues were published by Joseph Naveh in *On Stone and Mosaic* (Jerusalem: IES, 1978). The linguistic differences between Galilean and Judean synagogues were noted by Shmuel Safrai, "The Synagogues South of Mt. Judah," *Immanuel* 3 (1973-1974), pp. 44-50.

40. For a possible explanation, see Herr,

"Hellenismos and the Jews" (see endnote 34), pp. 26-27.

41. For a summary of Diocletian's rule, cf. A.H.M. Jones, *The Later Roman Empire* (Oxford: Blackwell, 1964), vol. 1, pp. 37-76; on Diocletian and the Jews of Palestine, see Smallwood, *Jews under Roman Rule* (see endnote 2), pp. 533-538.

42. Diocletian passed through Palestine at least twice; he spent time in Tiberias in 286 (talmudic tradition places him in Paneas as well) and, following the winter of 296/97 and the suppression of a revolt in Alexandria, he again passed through the country to Antioch on his way to join Galerius for a counterattack against the Persians. On a possible third stay in Palestine, cf. Smallwood, *Jews under Roman Rule* (see endnote 2), p. 536, n. 40.

43. JT *Avodah Zarah* 5:44a. While this source exonerates Diocletian from anti-Jewish persecution, it specifically notes that the Samaritans were not exempted from forced participation in certain pagan rites. The rabbis point to Samaritan acquiescence to certain Roman demands, such as pouring libations on pagan sacrifices, as a justification for placing a distance between the Samaritans and the Jewish community "and therefore their wine was forbidden." For a discussion of the background and possible interpretations of this source, cf. Saul Lieberman, "The Martyrs of Caesarea," *Annuaire de l'Institut de Philologie et d'Histoire Orientales et Slavs* 7 (1939-1944), pp. 403-404.

44. See, for example, Eusebius' description of a martyr in Nicomedia, who "was . . . raised on high naked and had his whole body torn with scourges until he should give in . . . . But when he remained unmoved even under these sufferings, they proceeded to mix vinegar and salt together and pour them into the mangled parts of his body . . . and as he despised these pains also, a gridiron and fire were then produced, and the remnants of his body . . . were consumed by the fire, not all at once, in case he might find immediate release, but little by little . . . "; *Eccles. Hist.* 8.2 (quoted in Naphtali Lewis and Meyer Reinhold, *Roman Civilization*, Sourcebook 2: The Empire [New York: Columbia Univ. Press, 1955], pp. 599-600).

45. Lieberman, "Martyrs of Caesarea" (see endnote 43), p. 410.

46. Cf. Lieberman ("Palestine in the Third and Fourth Centuries" [see endnote 21], pp. 329ff.), who refutes the assumptions of Heinrich Graetz and others regarding the persecution of the Jews in the early stages of the Christian empire. Lieberman bases his argu-

ment primarily on the lack of any allusion to outright persecution in rabbinic literature; the same conclusion is arrived at by most scholars of Roman legislation in the fourth century; cf. Amnon Linder, *The Jews in Roman Imperial Legislation* (Detroit: Wayne State Univ. Press, 1987), pp. 67-74, and "The Roman Imperial Government and the Jews under Constantine," *Tarbiz* 44 (1974), pp. 95-143 (in Hebrew). See also Jeremy Cohen, "Roman Imperial Policy Towards the Jews from Constantine Until the End of the Palestinian Patriarchate (ca. 429)," *BS* 3/1 (1976), pp. 1-29.

47. Cf. James W. Parkes, *The Conflict of the Church and the Synagogue* (London: Soncino, 1934), pp. 174-175; Cohen, "Roman Imperial Policy" (see endnote 46), p. 3, n. 10.

48. Eusebius, *Life of Constantine* 3.18, PG 20, 1076. The Council of Nicaea determined that Easter would be the first Sunday following the full moon after the spring equinox; but not all Eastern churches agreed to sever the link between Easter and the Jewish Passover. For a summary of the entire issue, cf. Marcel Simon, *Verus Israel*, transl. H. McKeating (Oxford: Littman Library, Oxford Univ. Press, 1985), pp. 310-321; on Constantine's role in raising the issue of Easter at Nicaea, cf. Timothy D. Barnes, *Constantine and Eusebius* (Cambridge, MA: Harvard Univ. Press, 1981), p. 217; see also Lieberman, "Palestine in the Third and Fourth Centuries" (see endnote 21), p. 333.

49. Cf. Parkes, *Conflict of the Church* (see endnote 47), p. 176; Cohen, "Roman Imperial Policy" (see endnote 46), p. 4.

50. Linder, *Jews in Roman Imperial Legislation* (see endnote 46), pp. 67ff.

51. *Codex Theodosianus* 16.8.1 (October 18, 329); 16.8.5. All the relevant "Jewish" laws in the codex are quoted in the original and translated by Linder in *Jews in Roman Imperial Legislation* (see endnote note 46). For the fifth century: see *Codex Theodosianus* 16.8.26, pp. 124-132.

52. Cf. *Codex Theodosianus* 16.9.1; 16.9.2; 16.8.6. It is unclear whether Constantine or his successor Constantius was the originator of this law (see endnote 51), pp. 144-147.

53. Cf. Ephraim E. Urbach, "*Halakhot* Regarding Slavery as a Source for the Social History of the Second Temple and the Talmudic Period," *Zion* 25 (1960), pp. 175ff. (in Hebrew) (Eng. transl. in *Papers of the Institute of Jewish Studies* [Jerusalem: Magnes, 1964], vol. 1, pp. 1-95).

54. Cf. *Codex Theodosianus* 16.8.3 (December 11, 321) (see endnote 51). Until this time the Jews might have backed demands for ex-

emption from participation in the local councils by claiming that this would involve some contact with pagan activity; cf. Avi-Yonah, *Jews under Roman and Byzantine Rule* (see endnote 3), p. 163.

55. Cf. *Codex Theodosianus* 12.1.99; 16.8.13; 12.1.158 (see endnote 51), p. 121.

56. The doubts regarding historical evidence for this prohibition under Constantine stem from the fact that the law is found nowhere in Roman legal corpora, but rather is mentioned by various Christian authors, who obviously had an interest not only in establishing Jerusalem as a Christian city, but also in stressing the ongoing removal of the Jews from the city as part of the religious argument; cf. Avi-Yonah, *Jews under Roman and Byzantine Rule* (see endnote 3), pp. 163-165. On the prohibition from the days of Hadrian, see R. Harris, "Hadrian's Decree of Expulsion of the Jews from Jerusalem," *HTR* 19 (1926), pp. 199-206, but the historicity of that decree has also been doubted, see Linder, "The Roman Imperial Government" (see endnote 46), p. 136, n. 227, for a summary of the arguments against the existence of the prohibition.

57. This event would have served as the logical occasion for renewing the removal of Jews from Jerusalem, given the significance attached to the *encaenia* (consecration) of the Church of the Holy Sepulchre; cf. Joshua Schwarz, "The Encaenia of the Church of the Holy Sepulchre, The Temple of Solomon and the Jews," *Theologische Zeitschrift* 43 (1987), pp. 265-281.

58. Epiphanius, *Panarion*, 3.4-12; cf. Ze'ev Rubin, "*Joseph the Comes* and the Attempts to Convert the Galilee to Christianity in the Fourth Century C.E.," *Cathedra* 26 (1982), pp. 105-116 (in Hebrew).

59. Aurelius Victor, *De Caesaribus* 42.11.

60. Jerome, *Chronicon* a.355, PL 27, 686.

61. Socrates, *Ecclesiastical History* 2.33; Sozomen, *Ecclesiastical History* 4.7,5.

62. Cf. Benjamin Mazar, *Beit Shearim* (Jerusalem: IES, 1944), vol. 1, p. 26.

63. For a general survey on the sources for the Jewish revolt in the fourth century, see Barbara G. Nathanson, "The Fourth Century Jewish 'Revolt' During the Reign of Gallus" (unpublished dissertation, Duke 1981); see also, Peter Schäefer, "Der Aufstand gegen Gallus Caesar," in *Tradition and Re-Interpretation in Jewish and Early Christian Literature*, ed. J.W. Henten (Leiden: Brill, 1986), pp. 184ff.

64. For the influence of all these on Julian, see the literature cited by Menahem Stern, *Greek and Latin Authors on Jews and Judaism*, 3 vols.

(Jerusalem: Israel Academy for the Humanities and Sciences, 1980), vol. 2, p. 506, n. 2.

65. On this issue see David Rokeah, *Jews, Pagans and Christians in Conflict* (Jerusalem: Magnes; Leiden: Brill, 1982); Rokeah concludes that while "the Jews were no party to it [the pagan-Christian confrontation] . . . without the Jews' existence and independent attitude towards Christians and pagans alike, and without their holy scriptures and the writings of Hellenistic Jewry, the pagan-Christian polemic could not have taken the course and shape it did" (pp. 9-10).

66. Whether Julian had a knowledge of Judaism based only on the Bible is a point of contention among scholars; cf. Johanan H. Levy ("The Emperor Julian and the Building of the Temple," *Zion* 6 [1941], p. 3 [in Hebrew]; also in Levy's collected *Studies in Jewish Hellenism* [Jerusalem: Mosad Bialik, 1960]), who limits Julian's knowledge to the Bible, and Gedaliah Alon, *Studies in Jewish History* (Tel Aviv: Hakibutz Hameuchadl, 1958), vol. 2, p. 313-334 (in Hebrew).

67. The definitive study is Levy, *Studies in Jewish Hellenism* (see endnote 66); see also Mordechai Hak, "Is Julian's Proclamation a Forgery," *Yavne* 2 (1940), pp. 118-139 (in Hebrew).

68. *The Works of the Emperor Julian*, Loeb, transl. W.C. Wright, vol. 3, pp. 177-181; for one of the more recent and comprehensive commentaries on the letter, see Stern, *Greek and Latin Authors* (see endnote 64), vol. 2, pp. 559-568; see also Linder, *Jews in Roman Imperial Legislation* (see endnote 46), pp. 154-160.

69. *Against the Galileans*, in *Works of the Emperor Julian* (see endnote 68), pp. 313-427; for the sections relating directly to Jews in this work, see Stern, *Greek and Latin Authors* (see endnote 64), vol. 2, pp. 513-569.

70. Julian, *Against the Galileans* (see endnote 69) 191D-E and 224E, p. 385; Porphyry had already attacked the Christians on this issue, claiming that they "are very much mistaken when they believe that God is angered if someone else is called god and thereby acquires his appellation, whereas even rulers do not begrudge their subjects', or masters their slaves', having the same name; it is therefore forbidden as regards religion to suppose that God is more petty minded than men" (*Gegen die Christen*, ed. Adolf von Harnack [Berlin: Koenigliche Akademie der Wissenschaften, 1916], p. 93, no. 78; quoted by Rokeah, *Jews, Pagans and Christians* [see endnote 65], p. 128).

71. Julian, *Against the Galileans* (see endnote 69), 305D-306A, pp. 405-407.

72. Julian, *Against the Galileans* (see endnote 69), 306A-B, p. 407.

73. For Christian sources on this argument see Stern, *Greek and Latin Authors* (see endnote 64), vol. 2, p. 506, n. 3; the issue came up frequently in connection with the developing Christian theology around the notion of a "heavenly Jerusalem," cf. Joshua Prawer, "Christianity between Heavenly and Earthly Jerusalem" (in Hebrew), in *Jerusalem through the Ages*, The 25th Archaeological Convention (Jerusalem: IES, 1968), pp. 179-192; for talmudic references to the term "heavenly Jerusalem," see Ephraim E. Urbach, "Heavenly and Earthly Jerusalem," in *Jerusalem through the Ages*, pp. 156-171.

74. Sozomen, *Ecclesiastical History* 5.22.

75. Ammianus Marcellinus, *History* 23.1, Loeb, transl. John C. Rolfe, vol. 2, pp. 311f.

76. In particular the inscription from Isaiah 66:14, which is clearly part of a messianic context and which was found on a stone in the southern part of the Western Wall, beneath Robinson's Arch; cf. Benjamin Mazar, *The Mountain of the Lord* (New York: Doubleday, 1975).

77. Much has been written about the reasons for the apparent silence of the rabbis on the affair, signifying a possible reticence at backing a pagan attempt to restore Jerusalem not as part of a divine plan, but for his own political and religious reasons. Ephraim E. Urbach ("Cyrus and His Declaration in the Eyes of the Rabbis" *Molad* 19 [1961], p. 373 [in Hebrew]) points to Julian's obvious borrowing from Cyrus in his own letter to the Jews, but notes that the rabbis do not seem to be enamored of Cyrus either, aware of his motives in restoring the Jews to Jerusalem. Others have pointed to various messianic deliberations in rabbinic literature as being influenced by the events under Julian. See Michael Adler, "The Emperor Julian and the Jews," *JQR* o.s. 5 (1893), pp. 591-651; Wilhelm Bacher, "Statements of a Contemporary of the Emperor Julian on the Rebuilding of the Temple," *JQR* o.s. 10 (1898), pp. 168-172; see also Lieberman, "Martyrs of Caesarea" (see endnote 43), p. 412, and "Palestine in the Third and Fourth Centuries" (see endnote 21), p. 243.

One common view is that the rabbinic leadership of Palestine, headed by the patriarch from the house of David, was naturally wary of the resurgence of the priesthood and concomitant weakening of its own position should the Temple actually be restored, cf. Avi-Yonah, *Jews under Roman and Byzantine Rule* (see endnote 3), pp. 196-197. While doubts regarding Julian's promise may indeed have arisen at the time, I wonder how much we can really conclude from the "silence" of the sources. Not only must we be constantly aware of the ahistorical nature of the Palestinian Talmud and *midrashim*, but, as pointed out by various scholars, we would do well to note how little information on the second half of the fourth century made its way into the Palestinian Talmud (even if Julian's name is mentioned there).

78. *Codex Theodosianus* 7:8:2 (May 6, 368) (see endnote 51), pp. 161-164; this *hospitium*, known in rabbinic sources as *akhsania*, also interfered with certain Jewish legal steps taken for the purpose of creating a common domain on the Sabbath for all the residents of a courtyard. The issue is referred to in numerous talmudic texts, cf. Lieberman, "Palestine in the Third and Fourth Centuries" (see endnote 21), pp. 354-357.

79. *Codex Theodosianus* 16.8.13 (July 1, 397) (see endnote 51), alludes to earlier legislation, including that of Valens and Valentinian, which has not survived.

80. The nature of the correspondence between Libanius (a leading Greek rhetorician of the late fourth century, born and later taught at Antioch) and the patriarch of the period is evidence of the high regard in which the noted Greek rhetor of Antioch held the Jewish leader, cf. Stern, *Greek and Latin Authors* (see endnote 64), vol. 2, pp. 580-599. Another example of the power of the patriarchate is suggested in the letter of Jerome (letter 57, PL 22, col. 570), in which we learn that Hesychius, governor of Palestine, was executed for certain improper behavior toward the patriarch. As late as 415 Gamaliel VI was still in possession of the rank of honorary prefect, cf. *Codex Theodosianus* 16.8.22 (see endnote 51), p. 271.

81. See Avigdor Shinan, "Sermons, Targums, and the Reading from Scriptures in the Ancient Synagogue," in *The Synagogue in Late Antiquity*, ed. Lee I.A. Levine, (Philadelphia: ASOR, 1987), pp. 97-110. The synagogue also provided a framework for other communal services: The local school might be situated there, charity was pledged there, the site served as a local gathering place for any number of other purposes. An impressive bibliography on synagogues in the talmudic period exists; for the most recent list, cf. Menahem Mor and Uriel Rappaport, "Bibliography on Ancient Synagogues," in *Synagogues in Antiquity*, ed. A. Kasher et al. (Jerusalem: Yad Ben-Zvi, 1987), pp. 267-285.

82. John Chrysostom, *Homily Against the Jews*, PG 48, col. 847; cf. Wayne A. Meeks and Robert L. Wilken, *Jews and Christians in Antioch* (Missoula, MT: Scholars Press, 1978), p. 90.

83. John Chrysostom, *Homily Against the Jews* (see endnote 82), col. 851; Meeks and Wilken, *Jews and Christians* (see endnote 82), p. 96.

84. Ambrosius, *Epistle I* 40-41, PL 16, col. 1101; cf. Avi-Yonah, *Jews under Roman and Byzantine Rule* (see endnote 3), p. 212; Parkes, *Conflict of the Church* (see endnote 47), pp. 166-168.

85. *Codex Theodosianus* 16.8.9 (see endnote 51).

86. *Codex Theodosianus* 16.8.21 (August 6, 420) (see endnote 51).

87. *Codex Theodosianus* 16.8.25 (February 15, 423) (see endnote 51).

88. *Codex Theodosianus* 16.8.25 (February 15, 423) (see endnote 51).

89. Cf. Yoram Tsafrir, "The Byzantine Setting and Its Influence on Ancient Synagogues," in Levine, *The Synagogue in Late Antiquity* (see endnote 81), p. 152.

90. *Codex Theodosianus* 16.8.11 (see endnote 51).

91. *Codex Theodosianus* 16.8.14 (see endnote 51).

92. John Chrysostom, *Homily Against the Jews* (see endnote 82), cols. 835 and 911.

93. *Codex Theodosianus* 16.8.15 (see endnote 51).

94. *Codex Theodosianus* 16.8.22 (see endnote 51), pp. 267-272.

95. *Codex Theodosianus* 16.8.29 (see endote 51).

96. Cf. Linder, *Jews in Roman Imperial Legislation* (see endnote 46), p. 320; on the end of the patriarchate, see also Avi-Yonah, *Jews under Roman and Byzantine Rule* (see endnote 3), pp. 225-229.

97. See Yaron Dan, "Leadership of the Jewish Community in Eretz Israel in the Fifth and Sixth Centuries," in *Nation and History*, Papers Delivered at the Eighth World Congress of Jewish Studies, ed. Menahem Stern (Jerusalem, 1983), vol. 1, pp. 211-217 (in Hebrew); and "Eretz Israel in the Fifth and Sixth Centuries" (see endnote 5), vol. 1, pp. 273-275. Dan posits a reverse scenario as well, i.e., that a possible attempt by the Romans to abolish the patriarchate might have in fact served as catalyst for the 418 rebellion.

98. Cf. Dan, "Leadership of the Jewish Community" (see endnote 97), pp. 215-217.

99. For a historical overview of the period, cf. Avi-Yonah, *Jews under Roman and Byzantine*

Rule (see endnote 3), pp. 232-265; on the Byzantine administration of Palestine in the fifth and sixth centuries see Dan, "Leadership of the Jewish Community" (see endnote 97), pp. 275-299.

100. Cf. Naveh, *On Stone and Mosaic* (see endnote 39), p. 72-73 (Beth Alpha), p. 31-32 (Kfar Naburaya); Roth-Gerson, *Greek Inscriptions from the Synagogues* (see endnote 39), pp. 91f. (Gaza).

101. Cf. Michael Avi-Yonah, "The Economics of Byzantine Palestine," *IEJ* 8 (1958), pp. 39-51.

102. On pilgrimage to Palestine, cf. E.D. Hunt, *Holyland Pilgrimage in the Late Roman Empire, AD 312-460* (Oxford: Clarendon, 1984); John Wilkinson, *Jerusalem Pilgrims before the Crusades* (Jerusalem: Ariel, 1977); Jews in particular might serve as "tour guides" for Christian pilgrims, cf. Avi-Yonah, *Jews under Roman and Byzantine Rule* (see endnote 3), p. 222.

103. Eudocia remained for about one year, but subsequently left her husband and by 441/43 had returned to Palestine, where she remained until her death in 460.

104. Cf. Francois Nau, "Deux E'pisodes de l'histoire juive sous Theodose II (423 et 438)," *REJ* 83 (1927), pp. 184-202.

105. Cf. Francois Nau, "Résumé de Monographies Syriaques" *Revue de l'Orient chretien* 9 (1914), pp. 118f.

106. Cf. Avi-Yonah, *Jews under Roman and Byzantine Rule* (see endnote 3), pp. 251-253; *The Book of Himyarites*, ed. A. Moberg (Lund, Sweden: Gleerup, 1924), p. 7a (transl. on p. cv); see also Hayyim Z. Hirschberg, "Joseph, King of Himyar, and the Coming of Mar Zutra to Tiberias," in *All the Land of Naphtali*, 24th Archaeological Convention, October 1966, ed. Hirschberg, (Jerusalem: IES, 1967), pp. 139-146 (in Hebrew).

107. Ignazio Guidi, ed., "La lettera di Simeone vescovo di Beth Arsham," *Atti della R. Accademia de Lincei* 7 (1881), pp. 501ff.

108. Cf. Ephraim E. Urbach, "Mishmarot and Ma'amadot," *Tarbiz* 42 (1973), pp. 304-327 (in Hebrew).

109. Cf. Adolf Neubauer, *Medieaval Jewish Chronicles* (Oxford: Clarendon, 1895), vol. 2, p. 76.

110. Cf. Hayyim Z. Hirschberg, "Mar Zutra, Head of the Sanhedrin at Tiberias," in *All the Land of Naphtali* (see endnote 106), pp. 147-153; David A. Goodblatt, *Rabbinic Instruction in Sasanian Babylonia* (Leiden: Brill, 1975), p. 189.

111. Greek *Novellae* no. 146; the *Novellae* contained the new laws and/or constitutions pro-mulgated by Justinian after the publication of the *Codex* in 534.

112. *Novellae* no. 146 (see endnote 111).

113. Cf. Amnon Linder, *Jews in Roman Imperial Legislation* (see endnote 46), pp. 404, 409; Albert I. Baumgarten, "Justinian and the Jews," in *Rabbi Joseph H. Lookstein Memorial Volume*, ed. L. Landman (New York: Ktav, 1980), pp. 37-44.

114. This being the case, it is just as clear why the law goes on to threaten "the *Archipherekitae*, or possibly Presbyters or *Didaskeloi*"–for all three terms designate precisely those who preach. *Archipherekitae* is clearly a translation of *resh pirka*; *pirka* is a well-documented rabbinic term–mostly in BT but also found in JT–designating a popular type of sermon delivered in the synagogue. Thus the form *resh pirka* may be a secondary usage, designating some official or dignitary among the sages. (See most recently, Isaiah Gafni, *The Jews of Babylonia in the Talmudic Era* [Jerusalem: Merkaz Shazar, 1990], pp. 204-213 [in Hebrew].) The "preachers, elders and teachers" were, in the legislators' eyes and most probably following the lead of the Church, those spiritual leaders who "introduce ungodly nonsense."

115. While isolated rabbinic statements or portions of traditions may have been put in writing at an early stage, the point here is that these "hidden scrolls," as the rabbis referred to them, played no part in the process of formal academic study and teaching, but were used only privately by individual sages; cf. the classic chapter on this by Saul Lieberman ("The Publication of the Mishna") in *Hellenism in Jewish Palestine* (see endnote 33), pp. 83-99.

116. See the brief survey by Moshe D. Herr (*EJ*, vol. 9, col. 1510), who refers to these works as "classical amoraic *midrashim*."

117. One of the first and most important of these studies was conducted by Zacharias Frankel, *Mavo ha-Yerushalmi* (Breslau: 1870), pp. 18-40; see also Jacob N. Epstein, *Mevo'ot Le-Sifrut ha-Amora'im* (Jerusalem: Magnes-Dvir, 1962), p. 274. For a comprehensive bibliography on research of the Palestinian Talmud, see Baruch Bokser, "An Annotated Bibliographical Guide to the Study of the Palestinian Talmud," *ANRW* 2.19.2 (1979), pp. 139-256.

118. Cf. Epstein, *Mevo'ot Le-Sifrut ha-Amora'im* (see endnote 117), p. 274. For a recent note on the last stages of the amoraic period in Palestine, see Ya'akov Zussman, "Again on Yerushalmi Nezikin," in *Mehqerei Talmud*, ed. Zussman and D. Rosenthal (Jerusalem:

Magnes, 1990), p. 132-133 (in Hebrew). Zussman sets the final years of the Palestinian *amoraim* in the late 360s.

119. Cf. Jacob N. Epstein, *Mavo Le-Nusah ha-Mishnah*, 2nd ed. (Jerusalem: Magnes-Dvir, 1964), pp. 626ff. Numerous discrepancies between the two Talmudim can also be attributed to a variance in the text of the Mishnah used by the rabbis in the two lands, cf. Epstein, pp. 706ff.

120. "The days were most terrible, and from the time the new religion took over it was a period of distress for Israel . . . and who cannot understand that in such a difficult time there is no leisure to arrange one statement after another as is fitting . . . and let us not, therefore, be surprised if we sometimes do not find order in the Yerushalmi" (Frankel, *Mavo ha-Yerushalmi* [see endnote 117], p. 48). Some even suggested that the Palestinian Talmud underwent no redaction at all, but against this see Saul Lieberman, *The Talmud of Caesarea*, *Tarbiz* suppl., II, 4 (1931), p. 20f.

121. See, for example, Mishnah *Nedarim* 3:4.

122. But note the qualifying tone to this in Shmuel Shiloh, *Dinah De-Malkhuta Dina*, *The Law of the State Is Law* (Jerusalem: Jerusalem Academic Press, 1975), p. 23, n. 91 (in Hebrew).

123. The Palestinian Talmud has talmudic discourse for the Mishnaic orders: *Zera'im*, *Mo'ed*, *Nashim* and *Nezikin*, but not for *Kodashim* and *Tohorot*; whereas the Babylonian Talmud has no text for *Zera'im*, but has for most of *Kodashim*. On the question of the study of *Kodashim* in Palestine, see Epstein, *Mevo'ot Le-Sifrut ha-Amora'im* (see endnote 117), pp. 332-334. For a most comprehensive discussion on the question of *Sedarim*, for which we have no talmud, see Ya'akov Zussman, "Babylonian Sugyot to the Sedarim of Zera'im and Taharot," unpublished Ph.D. dissertation, Jerusalem 1969.

124. Lieberman, *The Talmud of Caesarea* (see endnote 120), but see Epstein, *Mevo'ot Le-Sifrut ha-Amora'im* (see endnote 117), pp. 283ff.

125. Cf. Moshe D. Herr, "On the Rabbinic Understanding of History," *Proceedings of the 6th World Congress of Jewish Studies* (Jerusalem: Magnes, 1977), pp. 129-142 (in Hebrew); Ephraim E. Urbach, "Halacha and History," in *Jews, Greeks and History, Essays in Honor of W.D. Davies*, ed. R. Hamerton-Kelley and R. Scroggs (Leiden: Brill, 1976), pp. 112-128. The phenomenon described here does not, however, totally preclude the possibility of arriving at "talmudic history," cf. Goodblatt, "Towards the Rehabili-

tation of Talmudic History" (see endnote 9), pp. 31-44.

126. *Sifre Deuteronomy* 49, p. 115.

127. Numerous midrashic statements allude to the growing public preference for *aggadah* over *halakhah* in sermons, cf. *Song of Songs Rabbah* 2.5; BT *Sotah* 40a; JT *Horayot* 3:48c.

128. For a survey of halakhic literature in Palestine following the redaction of the Palestinian Talmud, cf. Mordechai Margaliot, *Hilkhot Eretz Israel From the Geniza* (Jerusalem: Mossad Harav Kook, 1973), pp. 1-16.

129. Cf. Mordechai A. Friedman, "Marriage Laws Based on Ma'asim Livne Erez Yisra'el," *Tarbiz* 50 (1981), pp. 209-242, for one of the more recent articles on *sifre ha-ma'asim*, with most of the relevant bibliography. No historical study has yet been produced on *sifre ha-ma'asim*, save for an excellent M.A. thesis by Hillel Newman, "Ma'asim Livne Eretz Israel and Their Historical Background" (unpublished, Jerusalem, 1987).

130. *Seder Eliahu Rabbah* 20, p. 114.

131. *Lamentations Rabbah* 1.

132. BT *Yoma* 10a.

133. Cf. Zvi Baras, "The Persian Conquest and the End of Byzantine Rule," in Baras et al., *Eretz Israel from the Destruction* (see endnote 5), pp. 323-327 (in Hebrew).

134. Quoted in *Histoire d'Héraclius par l'évêque Sebeos*, ed. and transl. Frédéric Macler (Paris, 1904), p. 68.

135. Cf. Avi-Yonah, *Jews under Roman and Byzantine Rule* (see endnote 3), p. 260.

136. The best-known collection of these works is in Yehuda Even-Shmuel, ed., *Midrashei-Ge'ulah* (Jerusalem-Tel Aviv: Mossad Bialik, 1954); see, for example, *Seder Eliahu*, p. 42, where the angel Michael describes to Elijah the various kings due to appear before the advent of the Messiah; the names all correspond with the various names of the Persian and Byzantine kings of the time.

137. *Sefer Zerubavel*, *Midrashei Ge'ulah* (see endnote 136), p. 78.

138. Cf. *Histoire d'Héraclius* (see endnote 134), p. 71.

139. *Sefer Zerubavel* (see endnote 137), pp. 80-81.

140. Avi-Yonah, *Jews under Roman and Byzantine Rule* (see endnote 3), p. 270.

141. *Pesikta Rabbati*, ed. Meir Ish-Shalom (Vienna, 1880), p. 162; see Bernard Bamberger, "A Messianic Document of the Seventh Century," *HUCA* 15 (1940), pp. 425-431.

142. For a critical text of the poem with an introduction and commentary, see Yosef

Yahalom, "On the Validity of Literary Works as Historical Sources," *Cathedra* 11 (1979), pp. 125-133 (in Hebrew).

143. BT *Kiddushin* 72b.

144. See the material collected in *History of the Jewish People: The Restoration–The Persian Period*, ed. Hayim Tadmor (Jerusalem: Am-Oved, 1983) (in Hebrew); the most recent treatment of this is Gafni, *Jews of Babylonia* (see endnote 114), pp. 20-35, for the pre-Sassanian period.

145. *Antiquities* 11.133; 15.39; Philo, *Legatio ad Gaium* 216.

146. *War* 1.5.

147. For the story of Hananiah, nephew of Rabbi Joshua, who attempted to intercalate the calendar in Babylonia, see JT *Sanhedrin* 1:19a; BT *Berakhot* 63a-b.

148. The date itself is supplied by Rav Sherira Gaon in his well-known *Iggeret*, ed. Lewin, p. 78; for the veracity of this date, see Gafni, *Jews of Babylonia* (see endnote 114), pp. 255-257.

149. BT *Gittin* 6a; see H. Norman Strickman, "A Note on the Text of Babylonian Talmud Git. 6a," *JQR* 66 (1975-1976), pp. 173-175.

150. See endnote 109 for *Seder Olam Zuta*.

151. See the interesting story in BT *Bava Kamma* 117a; cf. Daniel Sperber, "On the Unfortunate Adventures of Rav Kahana," in *Irano-Judaica* 1, ed. Shaul Shaked (Jerusalem: Ben-Zvi Inst., 1982), pp. 83-100.

152. The definitive work on the history of the exilarchate is Moshe Beer, *The Babylonian Exilarchate in the Arsacid and Sassanian Periods* (Tel Aviv: Bar-Ilan/Dvir, 1970) (in Hebrew); see also Jacob Neusner, *A History of the Jews in Babylonia*, 5 vols. (Leiden: Brill, 1965-1970).

153. Cf. Goodblatt, *Rabbinic Instruction in Sasanian Babylonia* (see endnote 110); Gafni, *Jews of Babylonia* (see endnote 114), pp. 177-184.

154. Cf. Isaiah Gafni, " 'Staff and Legislator'– On New Types of Leadership in the Talmudic Era in Palestine and Babylonia," in *Priesthood and Monarchy*, ed. Gafni and G. Motzkin (Jerusalem: Merkaz Shazar, 1987), pp. 79-92.

155. BT *Yevamot* 63B.

156. See most recently Robert Brody, "Judaism in the Sasanian Empire: A Case Study in Religious Coexistence," in *Irano-Judaica* 2, ed. Shaul Shaked and A. Netzer (Jerusalem : Ben-Zvi Inst., 1990), pp. 52-62.

157. BT *Yoma* 10a.

158. William Wright, *The Homilies of Aphraates, The Persian Sage* (London: Williams and Norgate, 1869), vol. 1, p. 394.

159. BT *Kiddushin* 71a.

160. BT *Ketubbot* 110b.

161. Cf. Isaiah Gafni, "Expression and Types of 'Local Patriotism' among the Jews of Sasanian Babylonia," in *Irano-Judaica* 2 (see endnote 156), pp. 63-71.

E I G H T

The Religion of the Empire: Christianity from Constantine to the Arab Conquest

1. In April 311 Galerius issued an edict reversing the policy of persecution, but it did not end there. The persecutions of 311/12 claimed the lives of two famous bishops, Peter of Alexandria (November 311) and Lucian of Antioch (January 312); see Timothy D. Barnes, *Constantine and Eusebius* (Cambridge, MA: Harvard Univ. Press, 1981), p. 159.

2. See Timothy D. Barnes, "The Emperor Constantine's Good Friday Sermon," *JTS* 27 (1976), pp.414-22; *Constantine and Eusebius* (see endnote 1), pp. 73-76.

3. *To the Assembly of Saints* 26, in *LPNF*, 2nd series, vol. 1, *Eusebius* (New York: Christian Literature Co., 1890), p. 580, translation slightly altered.

4. Richard Krautheimer, *Three Christian Capitals: Topography and Politics* (Berkeley: Univ. of California Press, 1983), p. 41.

5. For this and the plan of the new Christian city, see Krautheimer, *Three Christian Capitals* (see endnote 4), pp. 45, 51-55. However, it is important to note that the city was not so Christian as Eusebius portrayed it; see p. 61.

6. Eusebius, *Life of Constantine* 4.60, in *LPNF*, vol. 1, p. 555.

7. For this and the following, see Dennis E. Groh, "Jews and Christians in Late Roman Palestine: Towards a New Chronology," *BA* 51 (1988), pp. 85-86.

8. Jeremy Cohen, "Roman Imperial Policy Toward the Jews From Constantine Until the End of the Palestinian Patriarchate (ca. 429 C.E.)," *BS* 3 (1976), p. 8; Robert L. Wilken, "The Jews and Christian Apologetics After Theodosius I *Cunctos Populos*," *HTR* 73 (1980), pp. 464-465.

9. Wilken, "The Jews and Christian Apologetics" (see endnote 8), p. 465.

10. Cohen, "Roman Imperial Policy" (see endnote 8), p. 6; Wilken, "The Jews and Christian Apologetics" (see endnote 8), p. 464.

11. *Codex Theodosianus* 16, 8.1 as translated in Cohen, "Roman Imperial Policy" (see endnote 8), p. 6.

12. Glenn F. Chesnut, *The First Christian Histories: Eusebius, Socrates, Sozomen, Theodoret,*

and Evagrius, 2nd ed. (Macon, GA: Mercer Univ. Press, 1986), pp. 134-136. Chesnut thinks the signs were apparent only by 335 C.E.; but Barnes, *Constantine and Eusebius* (see endnote 2), p. 162, thinks they were already apparent by 315 C.E.

13. *Codex Theodosianus* 16.10.10. See J. Stevenson, *Creeds, Councils, and Controversies: Documents Illustrative of the History of the Church A.D. 337-461* (New York: Seabury, 1966), p. 161. For subsequent edicts in the fifth and sixth century, see pp. 260, 261f., 263, 358. See also J.R. Planque et al., *The Church in the Christian Roman Empire,* vol. 1: *The Church and the Arian Crisis,* transl. Ernest C. Messenger (New York: Macmillan, 1953), pp.705-709.

14. Cf. N.Q. King, *The Emperor Theodosius and the Establishment of Christianity* (Philadelphia: Westminster, 1960), pp. 18, 30.

15. King, *Emperor Theodosius* (see endnote 14), p. 31.

16. King, *Emperor Theodosius* (see endnote 14), pp. 50-59.

17. Cf. Cohen, "Roman Imperial Policy" (see endnote 8), pp. 12-13.

18. See Peter Brown, "Aspects of the Christianization of the Roman Aristocracy," in *Religion and Society in the Age of St. Augustine* (New York: Harper & Row, 1972), pp. 161-182 (though Brown cautions us about overvaluing the importance of marriage and family in this process, p. 174).

19. Chesnut, *First Christian Histories* (see endnote 12), p. 122.

20. See Dennis E. Groh, "Grace and Backsliding in the Nicene Age: A Footnote on a Triumphalist Orthodoxy," *explor* 3 (1981), pp. 78-93.

21. Groh, "Jew and Christians" (see endnote 7), pp. 85-86.

22. See Libanius, *Funeral Oration Over Julian,* for the sad outcome of Julian's attempt to reestablish paganism and his tragic murder in the course of his campaign against the Persians.

23. For the most recent reconstruction of events, see R.P.C. Hanson, *The Search for the Christian Doctrine of God: The Arian Controversy 318-381* (Edinburgh: T & T Clark, 1988), pp. 133-135. Eusebius' letter, *Epistle ad Paulin.,* can be found in *Anthanasius' Werke,* fasc. 3, *Urkunden zur Geschichte des arianischen Streits: 318-328,* ed. Hans-Georg Optiz (Berlin: de Gruyter, 1935), Urk. 8.7.

24. He was, in fact, a distant relative of the future emperor Julian: Barnes, *Constantine and Eusebius* (see endnote 2), p. 70, n. 79.

25. Canon 15: see *The Trinitarian Controversy,*

ed. William G. Rusch, Sources of Early Christian Thought (Philadelphia: Fortress, 1980), p. 54.

26. Hanson, *Search for the Christian Doctrine* (see endnote 23), pp. 134-135.

27. Hanson, *Search for the Christian Doctrine* (see endnote 23), pp. 148-149.

28. The synodal letter of this council is available in Rusch, *Trinitarian Controversy* (see endnote 25), pp. 45-48.

29. The Creed of the Council of Nicaea is not the creed said in current churches. That Nicene Creed, produced by the Council of Constantinople in 381 C.E., was called "Nicene" because it claimed to encapsulate the faith which the Synod of Nicaea promulgated.

30. Alexander of Alexandria, *Epistle to Alexander of Thessalonica* 32-38, 47, in Rusch, *Trinitarian Controversy* (see endnote 25), pp. 39-40, 42.

31. Alexander, *Epistle to Alexander* 28 (see endnote 30), p. 38; Athanasius *De Decretis* 3.6, in Optiz, *Anthanasius' Werke* 6.4 (see endnote 23), p. 6.

32. For this view of Arianism, see Robert C. Gregg and Dennis E. Groh, "The Centrality of Soteriology in Early Arianism," *ATR* 59 (1977), pp. 260-278, and *Early Arianism–A View of Salvation* (Philadelphia: Fortress; London: SCM, 1981). For debates on this newer view of the controversy, see Groh, "New Directions in Arian Research," *ATR* 68 (1986), pp. 347-355. For a quite contrary view, see Rowan Williams, *Arius, Heresy and Tradition* (London: Darton, Longman & Todd, 1987).

33. The foregoing paragraph is from Groh, "Grace and Backsliding" (see endnote 20), p. 77. See also A.H.M. Jones, *The Roman Economy: Studies in Ancient Ecomonic and Administrative History,* ed. P.A. Brunt (Oxford: Blackwell, 1974), pp. 202-203 (for the solidus), p. 403 (on the bureaucratic freeze).

34. *The Creed of the Synod of Nicaea* (June 19, 325), in Rusch, *Trinitarian Controversy* (see endnote 25), p. 49.

35. Eusebius of Caesarea's *Letter to His Church,* in Rusch, *Trinitarian Controversy* (see endnote 25), p. 59.

36. Gregory of Nazianzus, *Oration XVIII* 17; quoted in H.M. Gwatkin, *Studies of Arianism,* 2nd ed. (Cambridge, UK: D. Bell, 1900), p. 46.

37. More recent research on Athanasius has tended to stress his tough-minded and even unfair political ploys (Hanson, *Search for the Christian Doctrine* [see endnote 23], pp. 240ff.) For Athanasius' literary quality, see Charles Kannengiesser, *Athanase d'Alexandrie: Evêque et*

écrivain (Paris: Beauchesne Editeur, 1983).

38. Hanson, *Search for the Christian Doctrine* (see endnote 23), pp. 268-273.

39. Three excellent (but quite different) books allow the reader to trace these debates: Manlio Simonetti, *La Crisi Ariana nel IV Secolo* (Rome: Institutum Patristicum "Augustinianum," 1975); Thomas A. Kopecek, *A History of Neo-Arianism*, 2 vols., Patristic Monograph Series 8 (Philadelphia: Philadelphia Patristic Foundation, 1979); Hanson, *Search for the Christian Doctrine* (see endnote 23).

40. Probably a citywide (hence pagan) reaction: J.W.C. Wand, *Doctors and Councils* (London: Faith Press, 1962), p. 25.

41. Hanson (*Search for the Christian Doctrine* [see endnote 23], pp. 678-679) also points out how independent of Athanasius was their theological tradition. I have followed Hanson in not giving the various parties names based on their favorite essence words for God and have avoided terms such as "Semi-Arian," in accordance with Hanson's warning about "labels" (p. 398).

42. Hanson, *Search for the Christian Doctrine* (see endnote 23), p. 731. Cf. Gregg and Groh, *Early Arianism* (see endnote 32), pp. 161-183, for this conflict of *will* and *nature* languages.

43. Hanson, *Search for the Christian Doctrine* (see endnote 23), p. 730ff.

44. Hanson, *Search for the Christian Doctrine* (see endnote 23), pp. 688, 698-699.

45. The Creed, said as the Nicene Creed in churches today (see endnote 29), was preserved in the statement of faith adopted by the Council of Chalcedon in 451 (see text below) and can be found in Richard A. Norris, Jr., *The Christological Controversy*, Sources of Christian Thought (Philadelphia: Fortress, 1980), p. 157. For the debates about whether this derives from the Council of Constantinople, see Hanson, *Search for the Christian Doctrine* (see endnote 23), pp. 812-815.

46. Cf. Dennis E. Groh, "Hans von Campenhausen on Canon, Positions and Problems," *Interpretation* 28 (1974), pp. 331-343.

47. Cf. Albert C. Sundberg, "Canon Muratori: A Fourth Century List," *HTR* 66 (1973), pp. 1-41, whose results have most recently been sustained by Geoffrey Hahneman, "More on Redating the Muratorian Fragment," in *Studia Patristica*, vol. 19, *Papers Presented to the Tenth International Conference on Patristic Studies Held in Oxford 1987* (Louvain: Peeters, 1989), pp. 364-365.

48. For this date and the process of canonization, see Albert C. Sundberg, "Canon of the NT," *Interpreter's Dictionary of the Bible, Suppl. Vol.* (Nashville, TN: Abingdon, 1976), pp. 136-140.

49. Sundberg, "Canon of the NT" (see endnote 48), p. 140.

50. Ramsay MacMullen, *Roman Social Relations 50 B.C.-284 A.D.* (New Haven, CT: Yale Univ. Press, 1974), p. 38.

51. For references, see Groh, "Jews and Christians" (see endnote 7), pp. 80-81, 89-92.

52. *Potentiores* appear in the Severan age at the latest, but the term becomes the preferred way of designating the wealthier class in the fourth century. See Jean Gagé, *Les classes sociales dans l'Empire romain* (Paris: Payot, 1964), p. 284; G. Cardascia, "L'Apparition dans le droit des classes d'"Honestiores' et 'Humiliores,' " *Revue historique de droit francais et étranger* 28 (1950), p. 309.

53. John Chrysostom, *Homily 87 (John 20:24-21:14)* in *Saint John Chrysostom, Commentary on St. John the Apostle and Evangelist: Homilies 48-88*, transl. Sister Thomas Aquinas Goggin, Fathers of the Church (New York: Fathers of the Church, 1960), pp. 467-468.

54. *Fthonos* and its compounds. Based on the Wisdom of Solomon 2:23-24, the text is often applied to the envy of the devil (cf. Athanasius, *Life of Antony* 5; *De Incarnations* 5). As a source of ecclesiastical discord, see *Ecclesiastical History* 7.1.7 and G.W.H. Lampe, *A Patristic Greek Lexicon* (Oxford: Clarendon, 1961), p.1474.

55. Peter Brown, *The Making of Late Antiquity* (Cambridge, MA: Harvard Univ. Press, 1978), p. 57. This behavior stands, as Brown points out, in stark contrast to the aristocratic commitment to a "parity model" of the earlier empire.

56. Cf. Russell Meiggs, *Roman Ostia*, 2nd ed. (Oxford: Clarendon, 1973), p. 259. Cf. John E. Stambaugh (*The Ancient Roman City* [Baltimore, MD: Johns Hopkins Univ. Press, 1988]), who calls Ostia in this period "an upper-class beach resort" (p. 274).

57. Yvon Thébert, "Private Life and Domestic Architecture in Roman Africa," in *A History of Private Life*, ed. Paul Veyne, vol. 1, *From Pagan Rome to Byzantium* (Cambridge, MA: Belknap, 1987), pp. 344-345.

58. Thébert, "Private Life and Domestic Architecture" (see endnote 57), p. 338. For a depiction and discussion of the House of Julius mosaic, see ibid., fig. 39, p. 396 and p. 375.

59. Thébert, "Private Life and Domestic Architecture" (see endnote 57), pp. 335, 337 (figs. 7-9), 341, 344-345.

60. See Mary G. Houston, *Ancient Greek, Roman, and Byzantine Costume and Decoration*, 2nd ed. (London: Adam & Charles Black, 1966), pp. 120ff. and endnote 61.

61. Quoted in Eunice Dauterman Maguire, Henry P. Maguire, and Maggie J. Duncan-Flowers, *Art and Holy Powers in the Early Christian House* (Urbana, IL: Univ. of Illinois Press, 1989), p. 31; cf. fig. 28, p. 30 for an example of this kind of tunic.

62. Maguire et al., *Art and Holy Powers* (see endnote 61), pp. 81-82.

63. Cf. John Hayes, *Late Roman Pottery* (London: British School at Rome, 1972): African Red Slip Ware, crosses and saints, p. 222, type E (11) and p. 227, Nos. 232-242; for Asia Minor wares, see Late Roman "C," pp. 363-368 (Groups II-III, Nos. 61-80, for crosses) and p. 262 (No. 58, for a priest). For the way both Jews and Christians were able to purchase small objects from the same workshops and employ similar artistic motifs, see now: Leonard Victor Rutgers, "Archaeological Evidence for the Interaction of Jews and Non-Jews in Late Antiquity," *AJA* 96 (1) (1992), pp. 104-109.

64. Cf. F. Van der Meer, *Augustine the Bishop: The Life and Work of a Father of the Church* (London: Sheed and Ward, 1961), pp. 389-390.

65. Peter Brown, "Late Antiquity," in Veyne, *A History of Private Life* (see endnote 57), p. 276.

66. Cf. Gagé, *Les classes sociales* (see endnote 52), p.283.

67. The *penes* and the *ptochos*: Evelyne Patlagean, *Pauvreté économique et pauvreté sociale à Byzance 4ᵉ-7ᵉ siècles* (Paris: Mouton & Ecole des Hautes Etudes en Sciences Sociales, 1977), pp. 25-29.

68. See Daniel Sperber, *Roman Palestine 200-400, The Land: Crisis and Change in Agrarian Society as Reflected in Rabbinic Sources* (Ramat-Gan, Israel: Bar-Ilan Univ., 1978), pp. 96-118.

69. Peter Brown, "The Holy Man in Late Antiquity," in *Society and the Holy in Late Antiquity* (Berkeley: Univ. of California Press, 1982), p. 115.

70. Sperber, *Roman Palestine 200-400* (see endnote 68).

71. MacMullen, *Roman Social Relations* (see endnote 50), p. 38.

72. Brown, *The Making of Late Antiquity* (see endnote 55), pp. 12, 56-57, 62-65.

73. Athanasius, *Life of Antony* 3.

74. E.A. Judge, *The Conversion of Rome: Ancient Sources of Modern Social Tension*, Macquarie Ancient History Association 1 (North Ryde, Australia: Macquarie Ancient History

Assoc., 1980), pp. 2-4.

75. Cf. Athanasius, *Life of Antony* 82-89. In Syria, the Holy Man tended to fill the time-honored place of the patron in village society; see Brown, "The Holy Man" (see endnote 69), pp. 120-128.

76. Palladius, *Historia Lausiaca* 38, quoted from Joseph Cullen Ayer, *A Source Book for Ancient Church History* (New York: Charles Scribner's Sons, 1913), p. 403.

77. *Longer Rule* (7th Rule), quoted in Owen Chadwick, *John Cassian*, 2nd ed. (Cambridge, UK: Cambridge Univ. Press, 1968), p. 60.

78. For the term, see Brown, *The Making of Late Antiquity* (see endnote 55), pp. 85-89.

79. Paulinus of Nola, *Epistle* 29.7, quoted in Elizabeth A. Clark, *Women in the Early Church*, Message of the Fathers of the Church 13 (Wilmington, DE: Michael Glazier, 1983), p. 217.

80. Cf. *The Sayings of the Desert Fathers: The Alphabetical Collection*, transl. Benedicta Ward (London: A.R. Mowbray, 1975), pp. 117-121, for Moses' *dicta*. For his history and life, see Frank M. Snowden, Jr., *Blacks in Antiquity: Ethiopians in the Greco-Roman Experience* (Cambridge, MA: Belknap, 1970), pp. 209-211; for a more negative assessment of attitudes of some early Christians to Moses' blackness, see now Peter Frost, "Attitudes Toward Blacks in the Early Christian Era," *SC* 8/1 (1991), pp. 5-6.

81. As, for example, in the end of a villa in Britain around 353-354 C.E.: see David S. Neal, *The Excavations of the Roman Villa in Gadebridge Park Hemel Hampstead 1963-8*, Society of Antiquaries of London (London: Thames and Hudson, 1974), p. 98.

82. John Percival, "The Villa in Italy and the Provinces," in *The Roman World*, ed. John Wacher (London: Routledge and Kegan Paul, 1987), pp. 540-541.

83. Cf. A.J. Parker, "Trade Within the Empire and Beyond the Frontiers," in Wacher, *The Roman World* (see endnote 82), p. 653.

84. J.H. Waszink, "Some Observations on the Appreciation of the 'Philosophy of the Barbarians' in Early Christian Literature," in *Melanges offerts à Mademoiselle Christine Mohrmann* (Utrecht-Anvers: Spectrum, 1963), pp. 41-56.

85. Cf. Lidia Storoni Mazzolani, *The Idea of the City in Roman Thought: From Walled City to Spiritual Commonwealth*, transl. S. O'Donnell (Bloomington: Indiana Univ. Press, 1970), pp. 26, 184.

86. E.A. Thompson, *The Visigoths in the Time of Ulfila* (Oxford: Clarendon, 1966), pp. 91, 98.

87. Socrates Scholasticus, *Ecclesiastical His-*

tory 7.10; Sozomen, *Ecclesiastical History* 9.9-10.

88. Stephen Johnson, *Later Roman Britain* (London: Granada, 1982), pp. 147-149, 162, 200. For Western Britain, the picture is one of gradual decline of the towns to the end of antiquity there, about 500 C.E. (p. 202).

89. The best biography of Augustine remains Peter Brown, *Augustine of Hippo. A Biography* (Berkeley: Univ. of California Press, 1967). For his religious development, see Dennis E. Groh, *Augustine: Religion of the Heart* (Nashville, TN: Graded Press, 1988).

90. *The Confessions of St. Augustine* 5.13, *Translated with an Introduction and Notes*, John K. Ryan (Garden City, NY: Image Books, 1960), p. 130.

91. On Augustine's developing notions of sexuality, see Peter Brown, *The Body and Society: Men, Women, and Sexual Renunciation in Early Christianity* (New York: Columbia Univ. Press, 1988), pp. 387-427.

92. F. Decret, *L'Afrique manichéenne, IVᵉ-Vᵉ siècles* (Paris, 1978), pp. 241-242.

93. See Alfred Warren Matthews, *The Development of St. Augustine From Neoplatonism to Christianity 386-391 A.D.* (Washington, DC: University Press of America, 1980).

94. See Brown, *Augustine of Hippo* (see endnote 89), pp. 146-157.

95. Augustine, *Confessions* 13.13.14 (see endnote 90), p. 343 alluding to 2 Corinthians 5:7.

96. Brown, *Augustine of Hippo* (see endnote 89), p. 234.

97. Brown, *Augustine of Hippo* (see endnote 89), p. 139.

98. See W.H.C. Frend, *The Donatist Church* (Oxford: Clarendon, 1985), pp. 15-24.

99. W.H.C. Frend, *The Rise of Christianity* (Philadelphia: Fortress, 1984), pp. 653-654.

100. Frend, *The Donatist Church* (see endnote 98), pp. xxii, 333-336. Jean-Paul Brisson (*Autonisme et Christianisme dans l'Afrique romaine de Septime Sévère à l'invasion vandale* [Paris: E. de Boccard, 1958]) downplayed the Berber backgrounds (see pp. 5, 28, 413-414) in favor of political, economic and theological/ecclesiastical factors, which Frend now accepts (*Donatist Church*, p. x).

101. Brown, *Augustine of Hippo* (see endnote 89), p. 226.

102. Frend, *Rise of Christianity* (see endnote 99), p. 672.

103. Frend, *Rise of Christianity* (see endnote 99), p. 672.

104. Cf. Ramsay MacMullen, *Christianizing the Roman Empire A.D. 100-400* (New Haven,

CT: Yale Univ. Press, 1984), p. 119.

105. Peter Brown, "Pelagius and his Supporters: Aims and Environment," in *Religion and Society* (see endnote 18), pp. 185-193.

106. Gerald Bonner, *St. Augustine of Hippo: Life and Controversies*, 2nd ed. (Norwich, UK: Canterbury Press, 1986), p. 320.

107. Joseph T. Lienhard, *Paulinus of Nola and Early Western Monasticism* (Cologne: Peter Hanstein Verlag, 1977), pp. 113-114.

108. Augustine, *Confessions* 10.29.40 and 10.37.60 (see endnote 90).

109. Cf. Brown, *Augustine of Hippo* (see endnote 89), pp. 351-352.

110. Cf. Brown, *The Body and Society* (see endnote 91), pp. 405-406; *Augustine and Sexuality*, Protocol of 46th Colloquy, Center for Hermeneutical Studies in Hellenistic and Modern Culture (Berkeley: Graduate Theological Union and Univ. of California, 1983), p. 7.

111. Augustine, *On the Merits* 2.26, 33.

112. Most recently and firmly by Elaine Pagels, *Adam, Eve, and the Serpent* (New York: Random House, 1988).

113. Cf. the Synod of Orange of 529 in J. Patout Burns, *Theological Anthropology*, Sources of Early Christian Thought (Philadelphia: Fortress, 1981), pp. 109-128.

114. Augustine, *City of God* 19.24, transl. Marcus Dodds (Edinburgh: T & T Clark, 1871), pp. 339-340.

115. Augustine, *City of God* 15.7; cf. 14.13 for *superbia* as the earthly city's chief sin.

116. Augustine, *City of God* 14.13.

117. Augustine, *City of God* 22.30, in *Saint Augustine: The City of God*, transl. Gerald C. Walsh (New York: Fathers of the Church, 1952), pp. 506-507.

118. Cf. Donald C. Earl, *The Moral and Political Tradition of Rome* (Ithaca, NY: Cornell Univ. Press, 1976 [1967]), pp. 122-132.

119. On envy, see endnote 54.

120. *The Rule of St. Benedict* 7, in *Western Asceticism*, Selected Translations with Introductions and Notes by Owen Chadwick, Library of Christian Classics 12 (Philadelphia: Westminster, 1958).

121. See Peter Brown, *The Cult of the Saints: Its Rise and Function in Latin Christianity* (Chicago: Univ. of Chicago Press; London: SCM, 1981), pp. 86-127.

122. Cf. Pope Leo I, *Sermo* 4.2-4.

123. Pope Gregory, *Dialogue* 3.24, in *Fathers of the Church*, transl. (New York: Fathers of the Church, 1959), p. 157.

124. The *Definition of Faith*, quoted from Norris, *The Christological Controversy* (see

endnote 45), p. 158.

125. See Judith Herrin, *The Formation of Christendom* (Princeton, NJ: Princeton Univ. Press, 1987), pp. 72-75 for the bishops role in the cities and p. 105 for the Roman Christian influence on the Franks.

126. *Vita S. Caesarii Arelatensis a discipulis scripta* 1.28-34, in *The Conversion of Western Europe 350-750*, ed. J.N. Hillgarth (Englewood Cliffs, NJ: Prentice-Hall, 1969), pp. 37-39.

127. See W.F. Volbach, *Early Christian Art* (London: Thames and Hudson, 1961), p. 336 and plate 131. Volbach's assertion that the building was an earlier pagan one must be corrected; it dates to 432-440 at the latest, see Richard Krautheimer, *Early Christian and Byzantine Architecture*, Pelican History of Art (Baltimore, MD: Penguin, 1965), p. 324, n. 46.

128. See D. Talbot Rice, *The Beginnings of Christian Art* (Nashville, TN: Abingdon, 1957), pp. 64-65.

129. For the passing of imperial conventions into the depictions of Christ, see Per Beskow, *Rex Gloriae*, transl. Eric J. Sharpe (Uppsala, Sweden: Almquist & Wiksells, 1962). Note the appearance of Roma on the pediment of the *Templum Urbis* depicted on the arch at Santa Maria Maggiore: Sabine G. MacCormack, *Art and Ceremonial in Late Antiquity* (Berkeley: Univ. of California Press, 1981), p. 366, n. 361.

130. Krautheimer, *Early Christian and Byzantine Architecture* (see endnote 127), pp. 137-138.

131. If anyone deserved her rest, it was Galla Placidia: see Stuart Irvin Oost, *Galla Placidia Augusta: A Biographical Essay* (Chicago: Univ. of Chicago Press, 1968).

132. Krautheimer, *Early Christian and Byzantine Architecture* (see endnote 127), p. 192.

133. See Thomas A. Kopecek, "Neo-Arian Religion: The Evidence of the *Apostolic Constitutions*," in *Arianism: Historical and Theological Reassessments*, ed. Robert C. Gregg (Philadelphia: Philadelphia Patristic Foundation, 1985), p. 174.

134. Guiseppe Bovini, *Ravenna Felix* (Ravenna, Italy: Edizione A. Longo, 1960), p. 31.

135. Bovini, *Ravenna Felix* (see endnote 134), pp. 35-40; note an earlier Arian hand still appears on the column of the representation of Theodoric's palace: see Alberto Busignani, *I Mosaici ravenati*, forma e colore (Firenza: Sadea editore, no date), pl. 26. For the significance of the Palatium mosaic, see MacCormack, *Art and Ceremonial* (see endnote 129), p. 237.

136. Busignani, *I Mosaici ravenati* (see endnote 135), pp. 31-32; MacCormack, *Art and Ceremonial* (see endnote 129), pp. 259-266, for the significance of the mosaics.

137. Cf. *Fragments* 74, 87, 93, 126, in Norris, *The Christological Controversy* (see endnote 45), pp. 109-111.

138. Frend, *Rise of Christianity* (see endnote 99), p. 635.

139. For the "schools" of Alexandria and Antioch, see R.V. Sellers, *Two Ancient Christologies* (London: SPCK, 1940).

140. J. Guillet, "Les Exégèses d'Alexandrie et d'Antioche. Conflit ou maltendue," *Recherches de science religieuse* 34 (1947), pp. 257-302. Despite its obvious methodological flaw of comparing Theodore of Mopsuestia to Origen, the comments on exegetical differences between the two schools are useful.

141. Herrin, *Formation of Christendom* (see endnote 125), pp. 119-120. For Theodore, see Richard A. Norris, Jr., *Manhood and Christ: A Study in the Christology of Theodore of Mopsuestia* (Oxford: Clarendon, 1963).

142. Socrates Scholasticus, *Ecclesiastical History* 7.34.

143. *Third Letter of Cyril to Nestorius*, quoted from Edward Rochie Hardy and Cyril C. Richardson, *Christology of the Later Fathers*, Library of Christian Classics 3 (Philadelphia: Westminster, 1954), p. 350.

144. Socrates Scholasticus, *Ecclesiastical History* 7.32.

145. For these, see R.V. Sellers, *The Council of Chalcedon. A Historical and Doctrinal Survey* (London: SPCK, 1961), pp. 3-129; Aloys Grillmeier, *Christ in Christian Tradition*, vol. 1: *From the Apostolic Age to Chalcedon (451)*, 2nd ed., transl. John Bowden (Atlanta: John Knox, 1975), pp. 520-539; Francis Young, *From Nicaea to Chalcedon* (Philadelphia: Fortress, 1983).

146. Sellers, *Council of Chalcedon* (see endnote 145), pp. 109-110.

147. Sellers, *Council of Chalcedon* (see endnote 145), p. 116.

148. For the text of Chalcedon on these points, see T. Herbert Bindley, *The Oecumenical Documents of the Faith*, 4th ed. (London: Methuen, 1950), p. 235. See also *Definition of Faith* (see endnote 124).

149. Frend, *Rise of Christianity* (see endnote 99), pp. 639, 772-773.

150. Sellers, *Council of Chalcedon* (see endnote 145), p. 125.

151. See W.H.C. Frend, *The Rise of the Monophysite Movement. Chapters in the History of the Church in the Fifth and Sixth Centuries* (Cambridge, UK: Cambridge Univ. Press,

1972).

152. See text above at endnote 141 for Justinian's attempts. For his attempts to "re-Chalcedonianize" the monasteries, see James E. Goehring, "Chalcedonian Power Politics and the Demise of Pachomian Monasticism," *Institute for Antiquity and Christianity. Occasional Papers* 15.

153. Frend, *Rise of the Monophysite Movement* (see endnote 151), pp. 292-293.

154. Aziz S. Atiya, *A History of Eastern Christianity* (London: Methuen, 1968), pp. 240-241.

155. Asher Ovadiah, *Corpus of the Byzantine Churches in the Holy Land*, Theophaneia 22 (Bonn: Peter Hanstein Verlag, 1970), p. 188. Eudocian churches include St. John the Baptist (Corpus No. 67, pp. 78-79), St. Stephen (Corpus No. 66, pp. 77-78), the church at Silwan (Corpus No. 78a, pp. 90-91). To the Silwan basilica should now be added the public building just above it on Mt. Zion from area H, City of David Excavations, only a corner of which has been excavated. My preliminary study of the section, plans and pottery from area H, filed as a preliminary report with Dr. Yigal Shiloh before his untimely death, confirms a date compatible with a Eudocian founding.

156. Cf. Robert L. Wilken, "The Restoration of Israel in Biblical Prophecy in the Early Byzantine Period," in *"To See Ourselves as Others See Us,"* ed. Jacob Neusner and Ernest S. Frerichs (Chico, CA: Scholars Press, 1985), pp. 460, 464, 464-465; and "Byzantine Palestine: A Christian Holy Land," *BA* 51 (1988), p. 217.

157. Cf. King, *Emperor Theodosius* (see endnote 14), p. 118; Cohen, "Roman Imperial Policy," (see endnote 8), pp. 1-29; Wilken, "Jews and Christian Apologetics," (see endnote 8), pp. 451-471.

158. King, *Emperor Theodosius* (see endnote 14), p. 177. Cf. S. Krauss, "The Jews in the Works of the Church Fathers," *JQR* 5 (1893), pp. 122-157; *JQR* 6 (1894), pp. 82-99.

159. See Gedaliah Alon, *The Jews in Their Land in the Talmudic Age (70-640 C.E.)*, transl. and ed. Gershon Levi (Cambridge, MA: Harvard Univ. Press, 1989), p. 740.

160. See Socrates Scholasticus, *Ecclesiastical History* 7.16, 17, 38, and 13, respectively.

161. For the Judaizers at Antioch, see Robert L. Wilken, *John Chrysostom and the Jews* (Berkeley: Univ. of California Press, 1983), pp. 67, 75.

162. *Adversus Judaeos Homily.* 1.6 (PG 48, 852) as cited by Wilken, *John Chrysostom and the Jews* (see endnote 161), p. 160.

163. For the frequency and nature of these references, see Robert L. Wilken, *Judaism and the Early Christian Mind: A Study of Cyril of Alexandria's Exegesis and Theology* (New Haven, CT: Yale Univ. Press, 1971), pp. 59-61.

164. Groh, "Jews and Christians" (see endnote 7).

165. Cf. Wilken, "Jews and Christian Apologetics" (see endnote 8), pp. 461-462; *Judaism and the Early Christian Mind* (see endnote 163), pp. 37, 53; *John Chrysostom and the Jews* (see endnote 161), p. 65.

166. On the lessened exegetical contact between contemporary Christians and Jews, see Judith R. Baskin, "Rabbinic Patristic Exegetical Contacts in Late Antiquity: A Bibliographical Reappraisal," in *Approaches to Ancient Judaism*, vol. 5: *Studies in Judaism in Its Graeco-Roman Context*, ed. William S. Green (Atlanta: Scholars Press, 1985), pp. 65-67; A.P. Hayman, "The Image of the Jew in the Syriac Anti-Jewish Polemical Literature," in Neusner and Frerichs, *"To See Ourselves as Others See Us"* (see endnote 156), p. 440.

167. Glanville Downey, "Caesarea and the Christian Church," in *The Joint Expedition to Caesarea Maritima*, vol. 1: *Studies in the History of Caesarea Maritima*, ed. Charles T. Fritsch (Missoula, MT: Scholars Press, 1975), p. 36.

168. Glanville Downey, *Gaza in the Early Sixth Century* (Norman: Univ. of Oklahoma Press, 1963), pp. 115-116.

169. Wilken, "Byzantine Palestine" (see endnote 156), pp. 216-217.

170. Joseph Shereshevski, "Urban Settlements in the Negev in the Byzantine Period," Ph.D. dissertation. Hebrew University of Jerusalem, 1986 (in Hebrew; English summary, pp. 1*-24*). A more popular view of such cities can be found in Abraham Negev, *Cities of the Desert* (Tel Aviv: E. Lewin-Epstein, 1966). For agricultural technology, see Philip Mayerson, "The Ancient Agricultural Regime of Nessana and the Central Negeb," in *Excavations at Nessana*, vol. 1, ed. H. Dunscomb Colt (London: British School of Archaeology in Jerusalem, 1962), pp. 211-269.

171. See Bellarmino Bagatti, *The Church From the Gentiles in Palestine. History and Archaeology* (Jerusalem: Franciscan Printing Press, 1971), pp. 71-72; Alon, *The Jews in Their Land* (see endnote 159), p. 753 for the text.

172. Eric M. Meyers, Ehud Netzer and Carol L. Meyers, "Sepphoris 'Ornament of All Galilee,'" *BA* 49 (1986), p.6.

173. Eric M. Meyers and James F. Strange, *Archaeology, The Rabbis, and Early Christianity* (Nashville, TN: Abingdon, 1981), pp. 128-137.

174. Alon, *The Jews in Their Land* (see

endnote 159), p. 756.

175. James F. Strange, "Diversity in Early Palestinian Christianity, Some Archaeological Evidences," *ATR* 65 (1983), p. 22.

176. Stanislao Loffreda, *The Sanctuaries of Tabgha,* transl. Claire Fennell (Jerusalem: Franciscan Printing Press, 1975); *Scavi di et-Tabgha,* Pubblicazioni dello Studium Biblicum Franciscanum, Collectio minor 7 (Jerusalem: Topographia dei PP. Francescani, 1970). For Kursi, see Dan Urman, "The Site of the Miracle of the Man with the Unclean Spirit," *Christian News from Israel* n.s. 22 (1971), pp. 72-76.

177. Krautheimer, *Early Christian and Byzantine Architecture* (see endnote 127), pp. 153-161, 180 (for St. Irene); William MacDonald, *Early Christian and Byzantine Architecture* (New York: George Braziller, 1971), pp. 34-36.

178. Ovadiah, *Corpus of the Byzantine Churches* (see endnote 155) (Corpus No. 78b), pp. 92-93.

179. Nahman Avigad, *Discovering Jerusalem* (Nashville, TN: Thomas Nelson, 1980), pp. 212-229.

180. Avigad, *Discovering Jerusalem* (see endnote 179), p. 245.

181. Ovadiah, *Corpus of the Byzantine Churches* (see endnote 155), Tables 1 and 7.

182. Pao Figueras, *Decorated Jewish Ossuaries* (Leiden: Brill, 1983), pp. 10-12. For a less clear contention that Jews ceased ossuary burial because of Christian imitation, see now Byron R. McCane, "Bones of Contention? Ossuaries and Reliquaries in Early Judaism and Christianity," *SC* 8/4 (1991), pp. 235-246.

183. See Groh, "Jews and Christians" (see endnote 7), pp. 84, 92.

184. Cf. N. Tzori, "Beth-Shean. City Area at the Foot of the Mound," *EAEHL,* vol. 1, p. 228.

185. Michael Avi-Yonah, *The Jews of Palestine: A Political History from the Bar Kokhba War to the Arab Conquest* (New York: Schocken, 1976), pp. 251, 254.

186. Avi-Yonah, *Jews of Palestine* (see endnote 185), pp. 261-270.

187. Herrin, *Formation of Christendom* (see endnote 125), pp. 194-195, 203-204; Avi-Yonah, *Jews of Palestine* (see endnote 185), p. 266 (for church destruction).

188. For the dates, see Avi-Yonah, *Jews of Palestine* (see endnote 185), pp. 272-275.

189. See Dennis E. Groh, "Judaism in Upper Galilee at the End of Antiquity: Excavations at Gush Halav and en-Nabratein," in *Studia Patristica XIX,* ed. E.A. Livingston (Louvain: Peeters, 1990), pp. 62-71; Zvi Uri Ma'oz and Ann Killebrew, "Ancient Qasrin: Synagogue and

Village," *BA* 51 (1988), pp. 10-11; Michael Piccirillo, "The Mosaics at Um er-Ras in Jordan," *BA* 51 (1988), p. 213.

190. Among the last popular forms are African Red Slip Ware, Forms 103-104, and Late Roman C (= now Phocaean Red Slip Ware), Form 10: see John Hayes, *Late Roman Pottery* (London: British School at Rome, 1972), pp. 157-167, 343-347; *A Supplement to Late Roman Pottery* (London: British School at Rome, 1980), LIX-LXI (for the name change of Late Roman C).

191. Cf. transitional coins, 650-700 C.E., found in the last floor of the synagogue at en-Nabratein: Eric M. Meyers et al., "Preliminary Report on the 1980 Excavations at en-Nabratein, Israel," *BASOR* 244 (1981), pp. 20-21. The Damascus mint was especially important for gold coins in the Omayyad Period: see Vassilios Tzaferis, *Excavations at Capernaum, vol. 1, 1978-1982* (Winona Lake, IN: Eisenbrauns, 1989), pp. 139, 142, 164.

192. The often repeated truism that Alexander the Great marks the reversal of trade patterns from East to West, has now been pushed back to the Persian period for its beginnings: cf. Ephraim Stern, *Material Culture of the Land of the Bible in the Persian Period 583-332 B.C.* (Warminster, UK: Aris & Phillips; Jerusalem: IES, 1982), p. 232.

N I N E

Christians and Jews in the First Six Centuries

1. Søren Kierkegaard, *Attack Upon "Christendom,"* transl. W. Lowrie (Princeton: Princeton Univ. Press, 1968), passim.

2. 1QpHab[akkuk] 7

3. *Pesikta* 39b.

4. 1QH[odayot] 8.16 (Thanksgiving Psalms).

5. *Antiquities* 13.13.5

6. *War* 1.4.6; *Antiquities* 13.14.2.

7. See *Antiquities* 20; also see Hegesippus, as quoted in *Ecclesiastical History* 2.23.

8. See the discussion and photograph in *Explorations* 5.1 (1991), p. 1.

9. See esp. Mishnah *Berakhot* 4:4; *Avot* 2:13.

10. *Antiquities* 18.63-64.

11. See esp. Murray Stein, "How Herod Moved Gigantic Blocks to Construct Temple Mount," *BAR,* May/June 1981, pp. 42-46.

12. Origen, *Exhortation to Martyrdom.*

13. See the bibliography, Greek text and English translation in *The Cologne Mani Codex,* ed. R. Cameron and A.J. Dewey, SBL Texts and Translations 15, Early Christian Literature Se-

ries 3 (Missoula, MT: Scholars Press, 1979).

14. John Chrysostom, *Homily Against the Jews* 48.844.

15. John Chrysostom, *Homily Against the Jews* 48.847.

16. Max I. Dimont, *Jews, God and History* (New York: Simon and Schuster, 1962), p. 154.

17. Melito, *Peri Pascha* (Concerning Passover [or Easter]) 96.

18. The earliest evidence of this fabricated account is in Origen's *Contra Celsum* (chap. 32), which dates from about 248. *Sefer Toledoth Yeshu* is a product of the early polemics that separated Jews and Christians. For Hebrew versions of the Toledoth Yeshu, see S. Krauss, *Das Leben Jesu nach Jüdischen Quellen* (Berlin, 1902); also see Krauss, "Une nouvelle recension hébraique du Toldot Yêsû," *Revue des Etudes Juives* n.s. 3 (1938), pp. 65-88; Krauss, "Jesus in Jewish Legend," *Jewish Encyclopedia* 7 (1907), pp. 170-173. A helpful work is M. Goldstein, *Jesus in the Jewish Tradition* (New York: Macmillan Co., 1950); see esp. "Toledoth Yeshu," pp. 147-166.

19. See the second-century tradition in Justin Martyr's *Dialogue with Trypho* 69; see BT *Sanhedrin* 43a.

20. Martyrdom of Isaiah 5; Psalms of Solomon 17:37; 4 Ezra 14:22.

21. Mishnah *Sotah* 9:6,15.

22. Dead Sea Scrolls, esp. 1QS, 1QSb, 1QH, CD, 4Q403-405.

23. James H. Charlesworth, *Jesus and the Dead Sea Scrolls*, Anchor Bible Reference Library (New York: Doubleday, 1992).

24. Tosefta, Sotah 13:2.

25. Tosefta, *Pesahim* 4:14.

26. Tosefta, *Sotah* 13:3; *Seder 'Olam Rabbah* 6.

Index

(Bold face numerals designate illustrations)